SIGNLL Conference on Computational Natural Language Learning 2018

Proceedings of the CoNLL 2018 Shared Task: Multilingual Parsing from Raw Text to Universal Dependencies

Brussels, Belgium
31 October - 1 November 2018

ISBN: 978-1-5108-7414-5

CoNLL 2018

**The SIGNLL Conference on
Computational Natural Language Learning**

**Proceedings of the CoNLL 2018 Shared Task:
Multilingual Parsing from Raw Text
to Universal Dependencies**

October 31 – November 1, 2018
Brussels, Belgium

Sponsors:

Google, Inc.

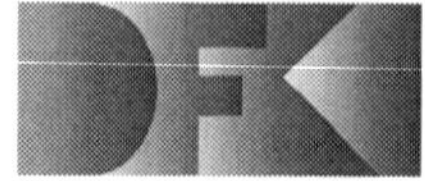
DFKI Berlin

CRACKER project

text & form

ÚFAL

Charles University

LINDAT/CLARIN

Czech Science Foundation
project No. 15-10472S

Introduction

This volume contains papers describing systems submitted to the *CoNLL 2018 Shared Task: Multilingual Parsing from Raw Text to Universal Dependencies,* and two overview papers: one summarizing the main task, its features, evaluation methodology for the main and additional metrics, and some interesting observations about the submitted systems and the task as a whole; the other overview paper discusses a complementary task focusing on *Extrinsic Parser Evaluation (EPE).*

This Shared Task (http://universaldependencies.org/conll18/) is an extension of the CoNLL 2017 Shared Task, with certain important differences. Like in the previous year, the data come from the Universal Dependencies project (http://universaldependencies.org), which provides annotated treebanks for a large number of languages using the same annotation scheme. The number of treebanks in the task (82) is similar to the previous year (81), but some treebanks from the 2017 task were not included in the present task, and some new treebanks were added instead. The datasets are samples from 57 different languages (all languages from the previous year, and eight new languages). In comparison to 2017, there were more low-resource languages with extremely little training data, calling for cross-lingual transfer techniques. Unlike 2017, none of the low-resource languages were "surprise languages".

Participants had to process all the test sets. The TIRA platform has been used for evaluation, as was the case already for the CoNLL 2015, 2016 and 2017 Shared Tasks, meaning that participants had to provide their code on a designated virtual machine to be run by the organizers to produce official results. However, test data have been published after the official evaluation period, and participants could run their systems at home to produce additional results they were allowed to include in the system description papers.

The systems were ranked according to three main evaluation metrics – LAS (Labeled Attachment Score), MLAS (Morphology-aware Labeled Attachment Score), and BLEX (BiLEXical Dependency Score). Like last year, participating systems minimally had to find labeled syntactic dependencies between words. In addition, this year's task featured new metrics that also scored a system's capacity to predict a morphological analysis of each word, including a part-of-speech tag, morphological features, and a lemma. Regardless of metric, the assumption was that the input should be raw text, with no gold-standard word or sentence segmentation, and no gold-standard morphological annotation. However, for teams who wanted to concentrate on one or more subtasks, segmentation and morphology predicted by a baseline system was made available.

The complementary EPE task seeks to provide better estimates of the relative utility of different parsers for a variety of downstream applications that depend centrally on the analysis of grammatical structure, viz. biomedical event extraction, negation resolution, and fine-grained opinion analysis. EPE 2018 was organized as an optional add-on exercise to the core task: the submitted systems were applied to extra texts, about 1.1 million tokens of English. It is interesting to see to what degree different intrinsic evaluation metrics from the core task correlate with end-to-end EPE results, and comparison to earlier EPE campaigns—with other types of dependency representations and additional sources of training data—further helps to put the core task into perspective.

A total of 25 systems ran successfully and have been ranked (http://universaldependencies.org/conll18/results.html); 17 teams submitted parser outputs for the EPE test set. While there are clear overall winners in each of the evaluation metrics, we would like to thank all participants for working hard on their submissions and adapting their systems not only to the datasets available, but also to the evaluation platform. We would like to thank all of them for their effort, since it is the participants who are the core of any shared task's success.

We would like to thank the CoNLL organizers for their support and the reviewers for helping to improve the submitted system papers. Special thanks go to Martin Potthast of the TIRA platform for handling such a large number of systems, running often for several hours each, and for being very responsive and helpful to us and all system participants, round the clock during the evaluation phase and beyond. We also thank to the 200+ people working on the Universal Dependencies project during the past four years, without whom there would be no data.

Daniel Zeman, Jan Hajič, Martin Popel, Milan Straka, Joakim Nivre, Filip Ginter and Slav Petrov, the organizers of the CoNLL 2018 Shared Task: Multilingual Parsing from Raw Text to Universal Dependencies
Stephan Oepen, main organizer of the EPE 2018 task

Prague, September 2018

Chairs:

Daniel Zeman, Charles University, Prague
Jan Hajič, Charles University, Prague

Support Team:

Joakim Nivre, Uppsala University
Filip Ginter, University of Turku
Slav Petrov, Google
Milan Straka, Charles University, Prague
Martin Popel, Charles University, Prague

TIRA support:

Martin Potthast, Leipzig University

Data Providers:

We are immensely grateful to the maintainers and contributors of the Universal Dependencies
treebanks used in this shared task.

Extrinsic Evaluation Liaisons:

Jari Björne, University of Turku
Murhaf Fares, University of Oslo
Stephan Oepen, University of Oslo

Table of Contents

CoNLL 2018 Shared Task: Multilingual Parsing
from Raw Text to Universal Dependencies

Daniel Zeman[1], Jan Hajič[1], Martin Popel[1], Martin Potthast[2],
Milan Straka[1], Filip Ginter[3], Joakim Nivre[4], and Slav Petrov[5]

[1]Charles University, Faculty of Mathematics and Physics
[2]Universität Leipzig, [3]University of Turku
[4]Uppsala University, [5]Google AI Language

```
{zeman|hajic|popel|straka}@ufal.mff.cuni.cz,
martin.potthast@uni-leipzig.de, figint@utu.fi,
joakim.nivre@lingfil.uu.se, slav@google.com
```


Abstract

Every year, the Conference on Computational Natural Language Learning (CoNLL) features a shared task, in which participants train and test their learning systems on the same data sets. In 2018, one of two tasks was devoted to learning dependency parsers for a large number of languages, in a real-world setting without any gold-standard annotation on the input. All test sets followed the unified annotation scheme of Universal Dependencies (Nivre et al., 2016). This shared task constitutes a 2nd edition—the first one took place in 2017 (Zeman et al., 2017); the main metric from 2017 was kept, allowing for easy comparison, and two new main metrics were introduced. New datasets added to the Universal Dependencies collection between mid-2017 and the spring of 2018 contributed to the increased difficulty of the task this year. In this overview paper, we define the task and the updated evaluation methodology, describe data preparation, report and analyze the main results, and provide a brief categorization of the different approaches of the participating systems.

1 Introduction

The 2017 CoNLL shared task on universal dependency parsing (Zeman et al., 2017) picked up the thread from the influential shared tasks in 2006 and 2007 (Buchholz and Marsi, 2006; Nivre et al., 2007) and evolved it in two ways: (1) the parsing process started from raw text rather than gold standard tokenization and part-of-speech tagging, and (2) the syntactic representations were consistent across languages thanks to the Universal Dependencies framework (Nivre et al., 2016). The 2018 CoNLL shared task on universal dependency parsing starts from the same premises but adds a focus on morphological analysis as well as data from new languages.

Like last year, participating systems minimally had to find labeled syntactic dependencies between words, i.e., a syntactic head for each word, and a label classifying the type of the dependency relation. In addition, this year's task featured new metrics that also scored a system's capacity to predict a morphological analysis of each word, including a part-of-speech tag, morphological features, and a lemma. Regardless of metric, the assumption was that the input should be raw text, with no gold-standard word or sentence segmentation, and no gold-standard morphological annotation. However, for teams who wanted to concentrate on one or more subtasks, segmentation and morphology predicted by the baseline UDPipe system (Straka et al., 2016) was made available just like last year.

There are eight new languages this year: Afrikaans, Armenian, Breton, Faroese, Naija, Old French, Serbian, and Thai; see Section 2 for more details. The two new evaluation metrics are described in Section 3.

Proceedings of the CoNLL 2018 Shared Task: Multilingual Parsing from Raw Text to Universal Dependencies, pages 1–21
Brussels, Belgium, October 31 – November 1, 2018. ©2018 Association for Computational Linguistics
https://doi.org/10.18653/v1/K18-2001

2 Data

In general, we wanted the participating systems to be able to use any data that is available free of charge for research and educational purposes (so that follow-up research is not obstructed). We deliberately did not place upper bounds on data sizes (in contrast to e.g. Nivre et al. (2007)), despite the fact that processing large amounts of data may be difficult for some teams. Our primary objective was to determine the capability of current parsers provided with large amounts of freely available data.

In practice, the task was formally closed, i.e., we listed the approved data resources so that all participants were aware of their options. However, the selection was rather broad, ranging from Wikipedia dumps over the OPUS parallel corpora (Tiedemann, 2012) to morphological transducers. Some of the resources were proposed by the participating teams.

We provided dependency-annotated training and test data, and also large quantities of crawled raw texts. Other language resources are available from third-party servers and we only referred to the respective download sites.

2.1 Training Data: UD 2.2

Training and development data came from the Universal Dependencies (UD) 2.2 collection (Nivre et al., 2018). This year, the official UD release immediately followed the test phase of the shared task. The training and development data were available to the participating teams as a prerelease; these treebanks were then released exactly in the state in which they appeared in the task.[1] The participants were instructed to only use the UD data from the package released for the shared task. In theory, they could locate the (yet unreleased) test data in the development repositories on GitHub, but they were trusted that they would not attempt to do so.

82 UD treebanks in 57 languages were included in the shared task;[2] however, nine of the smaller treebanks consisted solely of test data, with no data at all or just a few sentences available for training. 16 languages had two or more treebanks

from different sources, often also from different domains.[3] See Table 1 for an overview.

61 treebanks contain designated development data. Participants were asked not to use it for training proper but only for evaluation, development, tuning hyperparameters, doing error analysis etc. Seven treebanks have reasonably-sized training data but no development data; only two of them, Irish and North Sámi, are the sole treebanks of their respective languages. For those treebanks cross-validation had to be used during development, but the entire dataset could be used for training once hyperparameters were determined. Five treebanks consist of extra test sets: they have no training or development data of their own, but large training data exist in other treebanks of the same languages (Czech-PUD, English-PUD, Finnish-PUD, Japanese-Modern and Swedish-PUD, respectively). The remaining nine treebanks are low-resource languages. Their "training data" was either a tiny sample of a few dozen sentences (Armenian, Buryat, Kazakh, Kurmanji, Upper Sorbian), or there was no training data at all (Breton, Faroese, Naija, Thai). Unlike in the 2017 task, these languages were not "surprise languages", that is, the participants knew well in advance what languages to expect. The last two languages are particularly difficult: Naija is a pidgin spoken in Nigeria; while it can be expected to bear some similarity to English, its spelling is significantly different from standard English, and no resources were available to learn it. Even harder was Thai with a writing system that does not separate words by spaces; the Facebook word vectors were probably the only resource among the approved additional data where participants could learn something about words in Thai (Rosa and Mareček, 2018; Smith et al., 2018). It was also possible to exploit the fact that there is a 1-1 sentence mapping between the Thai test set and the other four PUD test sets.[4]

Participants received the training and development data with gold-standard tokenization, sentence segmentation, POS tags and dependency re-

---

[1] UD 2.2 also contains other treebanks that were not included in the task for various reasons, and that may have been further developed even during the duration of the task.

[2] Compare with the 81 treebanks and 49 languages in the 2017 task.

[3] We distinguish treebanks of the same language by their short names or acronyms. Hence, the two treebanks of Ancient Greek are identified as Perseus and PROIEL, the three treebanks of Latin are ITTB, Perseus and PROIEL, etc.

[4] While the test datasets were not available to the teams when they developed their systems, the documentation of the treebanks was supplied together with the training data, hence the teams could learn that the PUD treebanks were parallel.

Language	Tbk Code	2017	TrWrds
Afrikaans	af_afribooms	NA	34 K
Ancient Greek	grc_perseus	grc	160 K
Ancient Greek	grc_proiel	grc_proiel	187 K
Arabic	ar_padt	ar	224 K
Armenian	hy_armtdp	NA	1 K
Basque	eu_bdt	eu	73 K
Breton	br_keb	NA	0 K
Bulgarian	bg_btb	bg	124 K
Buryat	bxr_bdt	bxr	0 K
Catalan	ca_ancora	ca	418 K
Chinese	zh_gsd	zh	97 K
Croatian	hr_set	hr	154 K
Czech	cs_cac	cs_cac	473 K
Czech	cs_fictree	NA	134 K
Czech	cs_pdt	cs	1,173 K
Czech	cs_pud	cs_pud	0 K
Danish	da_ddt	da	80 K
Dutch	nl_alpino	nl	186 K
Dutch	nl_lassysmall	nl_lassysmall	75 K
English	en_ewt	en	205 K
English	en_gum	NA	54 K
English	en_lines	en_lines	50 K
English	en_pud	en_pud	0 K
Estonian	et_edt	et	288 K
Faroese	fo_oft	NA	0 K
Finnish	fi_ftb	fi_ftb	128 K
Finnish	fi_pud	fi_pud	0 K
Finnish	fi_tdt	fi	163 K
French	fr_gsd	fr	357 K
French	fr_sequoia	fr_sequoia	51 K
French	fr_spoken	NA	15 K
Galician	gl_ctg	gl	79 K
Galician	gl_treegal	gl_treegal	15 K
German	de_gsd	de	264 K
Gothic	got_proiel	got	35 K
Greek	el_gdt	el	42 K
Hebrew	he_htb	he	138 K
Hindi	hi_hdtb	hi	281 K
Hungarian	hu_szeged	hu	20 K
Indonesian	id_gsd	id	98 K
Irish	ga_idt	ga	14 K

Language	Tbk Code	2017	TrWrds
Italian	it_isdt	it	276 K
Italian	it_postwita	NA	99 K
Japanese	ja_gsd	ja	162 K
Japanese	ja_modern	NA	0 K
Kazakh	kk_ktb	kk	1 K
Korean	ko_gsd	ko	57 K
Korean	ko_kaist	NA	296 K
Kurmanji	kmr_mg	kmr	0 K
Latin	la_ittb	la_ittb	270 K
Latin	la_perseus	la	18 K
Latin	la_proiel	la_proiel	172 K
Latvian	lv_lvtb	lv	81 K
Naija	pcm_nsc	NA	0 K
North Sámi	sme_giella	sme	17 K
Norwegian	no_bokmaal	no_bokmaal	244 K
Norwegian	no_nynorsk	no_nynorsk	245 K
Norwegian	no_nynorsklia	NA	4 K
Old Church Slavonic	cu_proiel	cu	37 K
Old French	fro_srcmf	NA	136 K
Persian	fa_seraji	fa	121 K
Polish	pl_lfg	NA	105 K
Polish	pl_sz	pl	63 K
Portuguese	pt_bosque	pt	207 K
Romanian	ro_rrt	ro	185 K
Russian	ru_syntagrus	ru_syntagrus	872 K
Russian	ru_taiga	NA	10 K
Serbian	sr_set	NA	66 K
Slovak	sk_snk	sk	81 K
Slovenian	sl_ssj	sl	113 K
Slovenian	sl_sst	sl_sst	19 K
Spanish	es_ancora	es_ancora	445 K
Swedish	sv_lines	sv_lines	48 K
Swedish	sv_pud	sv_pud	0 K
Swedish	sv_talbanken	sv	67 K
Thai	th_pud	NA	0 K
Turkish	tr_imst	tr	38 K
Ukrainian	uk_iu	uk	75 K
Upper Sorbian	hsb_ufal	hsb	0 K
Urdu	ur_udtb	ur	109 K
Uyghur	ug_udt	ug	19 K
Vietnamese	vi_vtb	vi	20 K

Table 1: Overview of the 82 test treebanks. **TbkCode** = Treebank identifier, consisting of the ISO 639 language code followed by a treebank-specific code. **2017** = Code of the corresponding treebank in the 2017 task if applicable ("NA" otherwise). **TrWrds** = Size of training data, rounded to the nearest thousand words.

lations; and for most languages also lemmas and morphological features.

Cross-domain and cross-language training was allowed and encouraged. Participants were free to train models on any combination of the training treebanks and apply it to any test set.

2.2 Supporting Data

To enable the induction of custom embeddings and the use of semi-supervised methods in general, the participants were provided with supporting resources primarily consisting of large text corpora for many languages in the task, as well as embeddings pre-trained on these corpora. In total, 5.9 M sentences and 90 G words in 45 languages are available in CoNLL-U format (Ginter et al., 2017); the per-language sizes of the corpus are listed in Table 2.

See Zeman et al. (2017) for more details on how the raw texts and embeddings were processed. Note that the resource was originally prepared for the 2017 task and it was not extended to include the eight new languages; however, some of the new languages are covered by the word vectors provided by Facebook (Bojanowski et al., 2016) and approved for the shared task.

Language	Words
English (en)	9,441 M
German (de)	6,003 M
Portuguese (pt)	5,900 M
Spanish (es)	5,721 M
French (fr)	5,242 M
Polish (pl)	5,208 M
Indonesian (id)	5,205 M
Japanese (ja)	5,179 M
Italian (it)	5,136 M
Vietnamese (vi)	4,066 M
Turkish (tr)	3,477 M
Russian (ru)	3,201 M
Swedish (sv)	2,932 M
Dutch (nl)	2,914 M
Romanian (ro)	2,776 M
Czech (cs)	2,005 M
Hungarian (hu)	1,624 M
Danish (da)	1,564 M
Chinese (zh)	1,530 M
Norwegian-Bokmål (no)	1,305 M
Persian (fa)	1,120 M
Finnish (fi)	1,008 M
Arabic (ar)	963 M
Catalan (ca)	860 M
Slovak (sk)	811 M
Greek (el)	731 M
Hebrew (he)	615 M
Croatian (hr)	583 M
Ukrainian (uk)	538 M
Korean (ko)	527 M
Slovenian (sl)	522 M
Bulgarian (bg)	370 M
Estonian (et)	328 M
Latvian (lv)	276 M
Galician (gl)	262 M
Latin (la)	244 M
Basque (eu)	155 M
Hindi (hi)	91 M
Norwegian-Nynorsk (no)	76 M
Kazakh (kk)	54 M
Urdu (ur)	46 M
Irish (ga)	24 M
Ancient Greek (grc)	7 M
Uyghur (ug)	3 M
Kurdish (kmr)	3 M
Upper Sorbian (hsb)	2 M
Buryat (bxr)	413 K
North Sámi (sme)	331 K
Old Church Slavonic (cu)	28 K
Total	90,669 M

Table 2: Supporting data overview: Number of words (M = million; K = thousand) for each language.

2.3 Test Data: UD 2.2

Each of the 82 treebanks mentioned in Section 2.1 has a test set. Test sets from two different treebanks of one language were evaluated separately as if they were different languages. Every test set contains at least 10,000 words (including punctuation marks). UD 2.2 treebanks that were smaller than 10,000 words were excluded from the shared task. There was no upper limit on the test data; the largest treebank had a test set comprising 170K words. The test sets were officially released as a part of UD 2.2 immediately after the shared task.[5]

3 Evaluation Metrics

There are three main evaluation scores, dubbed **LAS**, **MLAS** and **BLEX.** All three metrics reflect word segmentation and relations between content words. LAS is identical to the main metric of the 2017 task, allowing for easy comparison; the other two metrics include part-of-speech tags, morphological features and lemmas. Participants who wanted to decrease task complexity could concentrate on improvements in just one metric; however, all systems were evaluated with all three metrics, and participants were strongly encouraged to output all relevant annotation, even if they just copy values predicted by the baseline model.

When parsers are applied to raw text, the metric must be adjusted to the possibility that the number of nodes in gold-standard annotation and in the system output vary. Therefore, the evaluation starts with aligning system nodes and gold nodes. A dependency relation cannot be counted as correct if one of the nodes could not be aligned to a gold node. See Section 3.4 and onward for more details on alignment.

The evaluation software is a Python script that computes the three main metrics and a number of additional statistics. It is freely available for download from the shared task website.[6]

3.1 LAS: Labeled Attachment Score

The standard evaluation metric of dependency parsing is the *labeled attachment score* (LAS), i.e., the percentage of nodes with correctly assigned reference to the parent node, including the label (type) of the relation. For scoring purposes, only

[5] http://hdl.handle.net/11234/1-2837
[6] http://universaldependencies.org/conll18/conll18_ud_eval.py

Content	nsubj, obj, iobj, csubj, ccomp, xcomp, obl, vocative, expl, dislocated, advcl, advmod, discourse, nmod, appos, nummod, acl, amod, conj, fixed, flat, compound, list, parataxis, orphan, goeswith, reparandum, root, dep
Function	aux, cop, mark, det, clf, case, cc
Ignored	punct

Table 3: Universal dependency relations considered as pertaining to content words and function words, respectively, in MLAS. Content word relations are evaluated directly; words attached via functional relations are treated as features of their parent nodes.

Features	PronType, NumType, Poss, Reflex, Foreign, Abbr, Gender, Animacy, Number, Case, Definite, Degree, VerbForm, Mood, Tense, Aspect, Voice, Evident, Polarity, Person, Polite

Table 4: Universal features whose values are evaluated in MLAS. Any other features are ignored.

universal dependency labels were taken into account, which means that language-specific subtypes such as `expl:pv` (pronoun of a pronominal verb), a subtype of the universal relation `expl` (expletive), were truncated to `expl` both in the gold standard and in the system output before comparing them.

In the end-to-end evaluation of our task, LAS is re-defined as the harmonic mean (F_1) of precision P and recall R, where

$$P = \frac{\#correctRelations}{\#systemNodes} \tag{1}$$

$$R = \frac{\#correctRelations}{\#goldNodes} \tag{2}$$

$$LAS = \frac{2PR}{P + R} \tag{3}$$

Note that attachment of all nodes including punctuation is evaluated. LAS is computed separately for each of the 82 test files and a macro-average of all these scores is used to rank the systems.

3.2 MLAS: Morphology-Aware Labeled Attachment Score

MLAS aims at cross-linguistic comparability of the scores. It is an extension of CLAS (Nivre and Fang, 2017), which was tested experimentally in the 2017 task. CLAS focuses on dependencies between content words and disregards attachment of function words; in MLAS, function words are not ignored, but they are treated as features of content words. In addition, part-of-speech tags and morphological features are evaluated, too.

The idea behind MLAS is that function words often correspond to morphological features in other languages. Furthermore, languages with many function words (e.g., English) have longer sentences than morphologically rich languages (e.g., Finnish), hence a single error in Finnish costs the parser significantly more than an error in English according to LAS.

The core part is identical to LAS (Section 3.1): for aligned system and gold nodes, their respective parent nodes are considered; if the system parent is not aligned with the gold parent, or if the universal relation label differs, the word is not counted as correctly attached. Unlike LAS, certain types of relations (Table 3) are not evaluated directly. Words attached via such relations (in either system or gold data) are not counted as independent words. Instead, they are treated as features of the content words they belong to. Therefore, a system-produced word counts as correct if it is aligned and attached correctly, its universal POS tag and selected morphological features (Table 4) are correct, all its function words are attached correctly, and their POS tags and features are also correct. Punctuation nodes are neither content nor function words; their attachment is ignored in MLAS.

3.3 BLEX: Bilexical Dependency Score

BLEX is similar to MLAS in that it focuses on relations between content words. Instead of morphological features, it incorporates lemmatization in the evaluation. It is thus closer to semantic content and evaluates two aspects of UD annotation that are important for language understanding: dependencies and lexemes. The inclusion of this metric should motivate the competing teams to model lemmas, the last important piece of annotation that is not captured by the other metrics. A system that scores high in all three metrics will thus be a general-purpose language-analysis tool that tackles segmentation, morphology and surface syntax.

Computation of BLEX is analogous to LAS and MLAS. Precision and recall of correct attachments is calculated, attachment of function words and punctuation is ignored (Table 3). An attachment is correct if the parent and child nodes are aligned to the corresponding nodes in gold standard, if the universal dependency label is correct, and if the lemma of the child node is correct.

A few UD treebanks lack lemmatization (or, as in Uyghur, have lemmas only for some words and not for others). A system may still be able to predict the lemmas if it learns them in other treebanks. Such system should not be penalized just because no gold standard is available; therefore, if the gold lemma is a single underscore character ("_"), any system-produced lemma is considered correct.

3.4 Token Alignment

UD defines two levels of token/word segmentation. The lower level corresponds to what is usually understood as tokenization. However, unlike some popular tokenization schemes, it does not include any normalization of the non-whitespace characters. We can safely assume that any two tokenizations of a text differ only in whitespace while the remaining characters are identical. There is thus a 1-1 mapping between gold and system non-whitespace characters, and two tokens are aligned if all their characters match.

3.5 Syntactic Word Alignment

The higher segmentation level is based on the notion of *syntactic word*. Some languages contain *multi-word tokens* (MWT) that are regarded as contractions of multiple syntactic words. For example, the German token *zum* is a contraction of the preposition *zu* "to" and the article *dem* "the".

Syntactic words constitute independent nodes in dependency trees. As shown by the example, it is not required that the MWT is a pure concatenation of the participating words; the simple token alignment thus does not work when MWTs are involved. Fortunately, the CoNLL-U file format used in UD clearly marks all MWTs so we can detect them both in system output and in gold data. Whenever one or more MWTs have overlapping spans of surface character offsets, the longest common subsequence algorithm is used to align syntactic words within these spans.

3.6 Sentence Segmentation

Words are aligned and dependencies are evaluated in the entire file without considering sentence segmentation. Still, the accuracy of sentence boundaries has an indirect impact on attachment scores: any missing or extra sentence boundary necessarily makes one or more dependency relations incorrect.

3.7 Invalid Output

If a system fails to produce one of the 82 files or if the file is not valid CoNLL-U format, the score of that file (counting towards the system's macro-average) is zero.

Formal validity is defined more leniently than for UD-released treebanks. For example, a non-existent dependency type does not render the whole file invalid, it only costs the system one incorrect relation. However, cycles and multi-root sentences are disallowed. A file is also invalid if there are character mismatches that could make the token-alignment algorithm fail.

3.8 Extrinsic Parser Evaluation

The metrics described above are all *intrinsic* measures: they evaluate the grammatical analysis task per se, with the hope that better scores correspond to output that is more useful for downstream NLP applications. Nevertheless, such correlations are not automatically granted. We thus seek to complement our task with an *extrinsic* evaluation, where the output of parsing systems is exploited by applications like biological event extraction, opinion analysis and negation scope resolution.

This optional track involves English only. It is organized in collaboration with the EPE initiative;[7] for details see Fares et al. (2018).

4 TIRA: The System Submission Platform

Similarly to our 2017 task and to some other recent CoNLL shared tasks, we employed the cloud-

---

[7] http://epe.nlpl.eu/

based evaluation platform TIRA (Potthast et al., 2014),[8] which implements the *evaluation as a service* paradigm (Hanbury et al., 2015). Instead of processing test data on their own hardware and submitting the outputs, participants submit working software. Naturally, software submissions bring about additional overhead for both organizers and participants, whereas the goal of an evaluation platform like TIRA is to reduce this overhead to a bearable level.

4.1 Blind Evaluation

Traditionally, evaluations in shared tasks are half-blind (the test data are shared with participants while the ground truth is withheld). TIRA enables fully blind evaluation, where the software is locked in a datalock together with the test data, its output is recorded but all communication channels to the outside are closed or tightly moderated. The participants do not even see the input to their software. This feature of TIRA was not too important in the present task, as UD data is not secret, and the participants were simply trusted that they would not exploit any knowledge of the test data they might have access to.

However, closing down all communication channels also has its downsides, since participants cannot check their running software; before the system run completes, even the task moderator does not see whether the system is really producing output and not just sitting in an endless loop. In order to alleviate this extra burden, we made two modifications compared to the previous year: 1. Participants were explicitly advised to invoke shorter runs that process only a subset of the test files. The organizers would then stitch the partial runs into one set of results. 2. Participants were able to see their scores on the test set rounded to the nearest multiple of 5%. This way they could spot anomalies possibly caused by ill-selected models. The exact scores remained hidden because we did not want the participants to fine-tune their systems against the test data.

4.2 Replicability

It is desirable that published experiments can be re-run yielding the same results, and that the algorithms can be tested on alternative test data in the future. Ensuring both requires that a to-be-evaluated software is preserved in working con-dition for as long as possible. TIRA supplies participants with a virtual machine, offering a range of commonly used operating systems. Once deployed and tested, the virtual machines are archived to preserve the software within.

In addition, some participants agreed to share their code so that we decided to collect the respective projects in an open source repository hosted on GitHub.[9]

5 Baseline System

We prepared a set of baseline models using UD-Pipe 1.2 (Straka and Straková, 2017).

The baseline models were released together with the UD 2.2 training data. For each of the 73 treebanks with non-empty training data we trained one UDPipe model, utilizing training data for training and development data for hyperparameter tuning. If a treebank had no development data, we cut 10% of the training sentences and considered it as development data for the purpose of tuning hyperparameters of the baseline model (employing only the remainder of the original training data for the actual training in that case).

In addition to the treebank-specific models, we also trained a "mixed model" on samples from all treebanks. Specifically, we utilized the first 200 training sentences of each treebank (or less in case of small treebanks) as training data, and at most 20 sentences from each treebank's development set as development data.

The baseline models, together with all information needed to replicate them (hyperparameters, the modified train-dev split where applicable, and pre-computed word embeddings for the parser) are available from `http://hdl.handle.net/11234/1-2859`.

Additionally, the released archive also contains the training and development data with predicted morphology. Morphology in development data was predicted using the baseline models, morphology in training data via "jack-knifing" (split the training set into 10 parts, train a model on 9 parts, use it to predict morphology in the tenth part, repeat for all 10 target parts). The same hyperparameters were used as those used to train the baseline model on the entire training set.

The UDPipe baseline models are able to reconstruct nearly all annotation from CoNLL-U files – they can generate segmentation, tokenization,

---

Treebank without training data	Substitution model
Breton KEB	mixed model
Czech PUD	Czech PDT
English PUD	English EWT
Faroese OFT	mixed model
Finnish PUD	Finnish TDT
Japanese Modern	Japanese GSD
Naija NSC	mixed model
Swedish PUD	Swedish Talbanken
Thai PUD	mixed model

Table 5: Substitution models of the baseline systems for treebanks without training data.

multi-word token splitting, morphological annotation (lemmas, UPOS, XPOS and FEATS) and dependency trees. Participants were free to use any part of the model in their systems – for all test sets, we provided UDPipe processed variants in addition to raw text inputs.

Baseline UDPipe Shared Task System The shared task baseline system employs the UDPipe 1.2 baseline models. For the nine treebanks without their own training data, a substitution model according to Table 5 was used.

6 Results

6.1 Official Parsing Results

Table 6 gives the main ranking of participating systems by the LAS F_1 score macro-averaged over all 82 test files. The table also shows the performance of the baseline UDPipe system; 17 of the 25 systems managed to outperform it. The baseline is comparatively weaker than in the 2017 task (only 12 out of 32 systems beat the baseline there). The ranking of the baseline system by MLAS is similar (Table 7) but in BLEX, the baseline jumps to rank 13 (Table 8). Besides the simple explanation that UDPipe 1.2 is good at lemmatization, we could also hypothesize that some teams put less effort in building lemmatization models (see also the last column in Table 10).

Each ranking has a different winning system, although the other two winners are typically closely following. The same 8–10 systems occupy best positions in all three tables, though with variable mutual ranking. Some teams seem to have deliberately neglected some of the evaluated attributes: Uppsala is rank 7 in LAS and MLAS, but 24 in

Team	LAS
1. HIT-SCIR (Che et al.)	75.84
2. TurkuNLP (Kanerva et al.)	73.28
3. UDPipe Future (Straka)	73.11
LATTICE (Lim et al.)	73.02
ICS PAS (Rybak and Wróblewska)	73.02
6. CEA LIST (Duthoo and Mesnard)	72.56
7. Uppsala (Smith et al.)	72.37
Stanford (Qi et al.)	72.29
9. AntNLP (Ji et al.)	70.90
NLP-Cube (Boroş et al.)	70.82
11. ParisNLP (Jawahar et al.)	70.64
12. SLT-Interactions (Bhat et al.)	69.98
13. IBM NY (Wan et al.)	69.11
14. UniMelb (Nguyen and Verspoor)	68.66
15. LeisureX (Li et al.)	68.31
16. KParse (Kırnap et al.)	66.58
17. Fudan (Chen et al.)	66.34
18. BASELINE UDPipe 1.2	65.80
19. Phoenix (Wu et al.)	65.61
20. CUNI x-ling (Rosa and Mareček)	64.87
21. BOUN (Özateş et al.)	63.54
22. ONLP lab (Seker et al.)	58.35
23. iParse (no paper)	55.83
24. HUJI (Hershcovich et al.)	53.69
25. ArmParser (Arakelyan et al.)	47.02
26. SParse (Önder et al.)	1.95

Table 6: Ranking of the participating systems by the labeled attachment F_1-score (**LAS**), macro-averaged over 82 test sets. Pairs of systems with significantly ($p < 0.05$) different LAS are separated by a line. Citations refer to the corresponding system-description papers in this volume.

BLEX; IBM NY is rank 13 in LAS but 24 in MLAS and 23 in BLEX.

While the LAS scores on individual treebanks are comparable to the 2017 task, the macro average is not, because the set of treebanks is different, and the impact of low-resource languages seems to be higher in the present task.

We used bootstrap resampling to compute 95% confidence intervals: they are in the range ± 0.11 to ± 0.16 (% LAS/MLAS/BLEX) for all systems except SParse (where it is ± 0.00).

Team	MLAS
1. UDPipe Future (Praha)	61.25
2. TurkuNLP (Turku)	60.99
Stanford (Stanford)	60.92
4. ICS PAS (Warszawa)	60.25
5. CEA LIST (Paris)	59.92
6. HIT-SCIR (Harbin)	59.78
7. Uppsala (Uppsala)	59.20
8. NLP-Cube (Bucureşti)	57.32
9. LATTICE (Paris)	57.01
10. AntNLP (Shanghai)	55.92
11. ParisNLP (Paris)	55.74
12. SLT-Interactions (Bengaluru)	54.52
13. LeisureX (Shanghai)	53.70
UniMelb (Melbourne)	53.62
15. KParse (İstanbul)	53.25
16. Fudan (Shanghai)	52.69
17. BASELINE UDPipe 1.2	52.42
Phoenix (Shanghai)	52.26
19. BOUN (İstanbul)	50.40
CUNI x-ling (Praha)	50.35
21. ONLP lab (Ra'anana)	46.09
22. iParse (Pittsburgh)	45.65
23. HUJI (Yerushalayim)	44.60
24. IBM NY (Yorktown Heights)	40.61
25. ArmParser (Yerevan)	36.28
26. SParse (İstanbul)	1.68

Table 7: Ranking of the participating systems by **MLAS,** macro-averaged over 82 test sets. Pairs of systems with significantly ($p < 0.05$) different MLAS are separated by a line.

Team	BLEX
1. TurkuNLP (Turku)	66.09
2. HIT-SCIR (Harbin)	65.33
3. UDPipe Future (Praha)	64.49
ICS PAS (Warszawa)	64.44
5. Stanford (Stanford)	64.04
6. LATTICE (Paris)	62.39
CEA LIST (Paris)	62.23
8. AntNLP (Shanghai)	60.91
9. ParisNLP (Paris)	60.70
10. SLT-Interactions (Bengaluru)	59.68
11. UniMelb (Melbourne)	58.67
12. LeisureX (Shanghai)	58.42
13. BASELINE UDPipe 1.2	55.80
Phoenix (Shanghai)	55.71
15. NLP-Cube (Bucureşti)	55.52
16. KParse (İstanbul)	55.26
17. CUNI x-ling (Praha)	54.07
Fudan (Shanghai)	54.03
19. BOUN (İstanbul)	53.45
20. iParse (Pittsburgh)	48.71
21. HUJI (Yerushalayim)	48.05
22. ArmParser (Yerevan)	39.18
23. IBM NY (Yorktown Heights)	32.55
24. Uppsala (Uppsala)	32.09
25. ONLP lab (Ra'anana)	28.29
26. SParse (İstanbul)	1.71

Table 8: Ranking of the participating systems by **BLEX,** macro-averaged over 82 test sets. Pairs of systems with significantly ($p < 0.05$) different BLEX are separated by a line.

We used paired bootstrap resampling to compute whether the difference between two neighboring systems is significant ($p < 0.05$).[10]

6.2 Secondary Metrics

In addition to the main LAS ranking, we evaluated the systems along multiple other axes, which may shed more light on their strengths and weaknesses. This section provides an overview of selected secondary metrics for systems matching or surpassing the baseline; a large number of additional results are available at the shared task website.[11]

The website also features a LAS ranking of unofficial system runs, i.e. those that were not marked by their teams as primary runs, or were even run after the official evaluation phase closed and test data were unblinded. The difference from the official results is much less dramatic than in 2017, with the exception of the team SParse, who managed to fix their software and produce more valid output files.

As an experiment, we also applied the 2017 system submissions to the 2018 test data. This allows us to test how many systems can actually be used to produce new data without a glitch, as well as to see to what extent the results change over one year and two releases of UD. Here it should be noted that not all of the 2018 task languages and treebanks were present in the 2017 task, therefore causing many systems fail due to an unknown language or treebank code. The full results of this

---

[10]Using Udapi (Popel et al., 2017) eval.Conll18, marked by the presence or absence of horizontal lines in Tables 6–8.

[11]http://universaldependencies.org/conll18/results.html

Team	Toks	Wrds	Sents
1. Uppsala	97.60	98.18	83.80
2. HIT-SCIR	**98.42**	98.12	**83.87**
3. CEA LIST	98.16	97.78	82.79
4. CUNI x-ling	98.09	97.74	**82.80**
5. TurkuNLP	97.83	97.42	**83.03**
6. SLT-Interactions	97.51	97.09	83.01
7. UDPipe Future	97.46	97.04	**83.64**
8. Phoenix	97.46	97.03	82.91
9. BASELINE UDPipe	97.39	96.97	**83.01**
ParisNLP	97.39	96.97	83.01
AntNLP	97.39	96.97	83.01
UniMelb	97.39	96.97	83.01
BOUN	97.39	96.97	83.01
ICS PAS	97.39	96.97	83.01
LATTICE	97.39	96.97	83.01
LeisureX	97.39	96.97	83.01
KParse	97.39	96.97	83.01
18. Fudan	97.38	96.96	82.85
19. IBM NY	97.30	96.92	**83.51**
20. ONLP lab	97.28	96.86	83.00
21. NLP-Cube	**97.36**	96.80	82.55
22. Stanford	96.19	95.99	76.55
23. HUJI	94.95	94.61	**80.84**
24. ArmParser	79.75	79.41	13.33
25. iParse	78.45	78.11	**68.37**
26. SParse	2.32	2.32	2.34

Table 9: Tokenization, word segmentation and sentence segmentation (ordered by word F_1 scores; out-of-order scores in the other two columns are bold).

Team	UPOS	Feats	Lemm
1. Uppsala	90.91	87.59	58.50
2. HIT-SCIR	90.19	84.24	**88.82**
3. CEA LIST	89.97	**86.83**	**88.90**
4. TurkuNLP	89.81	86.70	**91.24**
5. LATTICE	89.53	83.74	87.84
6. UDPipe Future	89.37	**86.67**	**89.32**
7. Stanford	89.01	85.47	88.32
8. ICS PAS	88.70	85.14	87.99
9. CUNI x-ling	88.68	84.56	**88.96**
10. NLP-Cube	88.50	**85.08**	81.21
11. SLT-Interactions	88.12	83.72	**87.51**
12. IBM NY	88.02	59.11	59.51
13. UniMelb	87.90	**83.74**	87.84
14. KParse	87.62	**84.32**	86.26
15. Phoenix	87.49	83.87	**87.69**
16. ParisNLP	87.35	83.74	**87.84**
17. BASELINE UDPipe	87.32	83.74	87.84
AntNLP	87.32	83.74	87.84
19. ONLP lab	87.25	83.67	57.10
20. Fudan	87.25	83.47	**85.91**
21. BOUN	87.19	**83.73**	**87.68**
22. LeisureX	87.15	83.46	**87.77**
23. HUJI	85.06	81.51	85.61
24. ArmParser	72.99	69.91	72.22
25. iParse	71.38	68.64	71.68
26. SParse	2.25	2.29	2.28

Table 10: Universal POS tags, features and lemmas (ordered by UPOS F_1 scores; out-of-order scores in the other two columns are bold).

experiment are available on the shared task website.[12]

Table 9 evaluates detection of tokens, syntactic words and sentences. About a third of the systems trusted the baseline segmentation; this is less than in 2017. For most languages and in aggregate, the segmentation scores are very high and their impact on parsing scores is not easy to prove; but it likely played a role in languages where segmentation is hard. For example, HIT-SCIR's word segmentation in Vietnamese surpasses the second system by a margin of 6 percent points; likewise, the system's advantage in LAS and MLAS (but not in BLEX!) amounts to 7–8 points. Similarly, Uppsala and ParisNLP achieved good segmenta-

tion scores (better than their respective macro-averages) on Arabic. They were able to translate it into better LAS, but not MLAS and BLEX, where there were too many other chances to make an error.

The complexity of the new metrics, especially MLAS, is further underlined by Table 10: Uppsala is the clear winner in both UPOS tags and morphological features, but 6 other teams had better dependency relations and better MLAS. Note that as with segmentation, morphology predicted by the baseline system was available, though only a few systems seem to have used it without attempting to improve it.

6.3 Partial Results

Table 11 gives the three main scores averaged over the 61 "big" treebanks (training data larger than

[12] http://universaldependencies.org/conll18/results-2017-systems.html

Team	LAS	MLAS	BLEX
1. HIT-SCIR	84.37	70.12	75.05
2. Stanford	83.03	**72.67**	**75.46**
3. TurkuNLP	81.85	71.27	**75.83**
4. UDPipe Future	81.83	**71.71**	74.67
5. ICS PAS	81.72	70.30	74.42
6. CEA LIST	81.66	**70.89**	72.32
7. LATTICE	80.97	66.27	71.50
8. NLP-Cube	80.48	**67.79**	64.76
9. ParisNLP	80.29	65.88	**70.95**
10. Uppsala	80.25	**68.81**	36.02
11. SLT-Interactions	79.67	64.95	**69.77**
12. AntNLP	79.61	**65.43**	70.34
13. LeisureX	77.98	63.79	68.55
14. UniMelb	77.69	63.17	68.25
15. IBM NY	77.55	47.34	36.68
16. Fudan	75.42	**62.28**	**62.90**
17. KParse	74.84	**62.40**	**63.84**
18. BASELINE UDPipe	74.14	61.27	**64.67**
19. Phoenix	73.93	61.12	64.47
20. BOUN	72.85	60.00	62.99
21. CUNI x-ling	71.54	58.33	61.63
22. ONLP lab	67.08	55.20	33.08
23. iParse	66.55	**55.37**	**58.80**
24. HUJI	62.07	53.20	56.90
25. ArmParser	58.14	45.87	49.25
26. SParse	2.63	2.26	2.30

Table 11: Average LAS on the 61 "big" treebanks (ordered by LAS F_1 scores; out-of-order scores in the other two columns are bold).

Team	LAS	MLAS	BLEX
1. CUNI x-ling	27.89	6.13	13.98
2. Uppsala	25.87	5.16	9.03
3. CEA LIST	23.90	3.75	**10.99**
4. HIT-SCIR	23.88	2.88	10.50
5. LATTICE	23.39	**4.38**	10.01
6. TurkuNLP	22.91	3.59	**11.40**
7. IBM NY	21.88	2.62	7.17
8. UDPipe Future	21.75	**2.82**	**8.80**
9. ICS PAS	19.26	1.89	6.17
10. AntNLP	18.59	**3.43**	**8.61**
11. KParse	17.84	3.32	6.58
12. SLT-Interactions	17.47	1.79	**6.95**
13. Stanford	17.45	**2.76**	**7.63**
14. BASELINE UDPipe	17.17	**3.44**	7.63
UniMelb	17.17	3.44	7.63
16. LeisureX	17.16	3.43	7.63
17. Phoenix	16.99	3.02	**8.00**
18. NLP-Cube	16.85	**3.39**	7.05
19. ParisNLP	16.52	2.53	6.75
20. ONLP lab	15.98	**3.58**	4.96
21. Fudan	15.45	2.98	**6.61**
22. BOUN	14.78	2.59	6.43
23. HUJI	8.53	0.92	2.77
24. ArmParser	7.47	**1.86**	**3.54**
25. iParse	2.82	0.23	0.97
26. SParse	0.00	0.00	0.00

Table 12: Average LAS, MLAS and BLEX on the 9 low-resource languages: Armenian (hy), Breton (br), Buryat (bxr), Faroese (fo), Kazakh (kk), Kurmanji (kmr), Naija (pcm), Thai (th) and Upper Sorbian (hsb) (ordered by LAS F_1 scores; out-of-order scores in the other two columns are bold).

test data, development data available). Higher scores reflect the fact that models for these test sets are easier to learn: enough data is available, no cross-lingual or cross-domain learning is necessary (the extra test sets are not included here). Regarding ranking, the Stanford system makes a remarkable jump when it does not have to carry the load of underresourced languages: from rank 8 to 2 in LAS, from 3 to 1 in MLAS and from 5 to 2 in BLEX.

Table 12 gives the LAS F_1 score on the nine low-resource languages only. Here we have a true specialist: The team CUNI x-ling lives up to its name and wins in all three scores, although in the overall ranking they fall even slightly behind the baseline. On the other hand, the scores are extremely low and the outputs are hardly useful for any downstream application. Especially morphol-

ogy is almost impossible to learn from foreign languages, hence the much lower values of MLAS and BLEX. BLEX is a bit better than MLAS, which could be explained by cases where a word form is identical to its lemma. However, there are significant language-by-language differences; the best LAS on Faroese and Upper Sorbian surpassing 45%. This probably owes to the presence of many Germanic and Slavic treebanks in training data, including some of the largest datasets in UD. Three languages, Buryat, Kurmanji and Upper Sorbian, were introduced in the 2017 task as

Team	LAS	MLAS	BLEX
1. HIT-SCIR	69.53	45.94	53.30
2. LATTICE	68.12	45.03	51.71
3. ICS PAS	66.90	**49.24**	**54.89**
4. TurkuNLP	64.48	47.63	53.54
5. UDPipe Future	64.21	47.53	49.53
6. AntNLP	63.73	42.24	48.31
7. Uppsala	63.60	**46.00**	29.25
8. ParisNLP	60.84	40.71	**46.08**
9. CEA LIST	57.34	39.97	43.39
10. KParse	57.32	39.20	**43.61**
11. NLP-Cube	56.78	37.13	38.30
12. SLT-Interactions	56.74	35.73	**42.90**
13. IBM NY	56.13	26.51	25.23
14. UniMelb	56.12	**36.09**	**42.09**
15. BASELINE UDPipe	55.01	**38.80**	41.06
LeisureX	55.01	38.80	41.06
17. Phoenix	54.63	38.38	40.72
Fudan	54.63	38.15	40.07
19. CUNI x-ling	54.33	38.10	**40.70**
20. BOUN	50.18	34.29	36.75
21. Stanford	48.56	**34.86**	**38.55**
22. ONLP lab	47.49	32.74	22.39
23. iParse	38.79	28.03	**29.62**
24. HUJI	36.74	24.47	27.70
25. ArmParser	34.54	22.94	25.26
26. SParse	0.00	0.00	0.00

Table 13: Average attachment score on the 7 small treebanks: Galician TreeGal, Irish, Latin Perseus, North Sámi, Norwegian Nynorsk LIA, Russian Taiga and Slovenian SST (ordered by LAS F_1 scores; out-of-order scores in the other two columns are bold).

Team	LAS	MLAS	BLEX
1. HIT-SCIR	74.20	55.52	62.34
2. Stanford	73.14	**58.75**	61.96
3. LATTICE	72.34	55.60	60.42
4. Uppsala	72.27	**57.80**	29.73
5. ICS PAS	72.18	**58.07**	**60.97**
6. TurkuNLP	71.78	57.54	**63.25**
7. UDPipe Future	71.57	**57.93**	61.52
8. CEA LIST	70.45	54.99	57.83
9. NLP-Cube	69.83	**55.01**	54.15
10. IBM NY	69.40	46.59	38.12
11. AntNLP	68.87	**53.47**	**57.71**
12. UniMelb	68.72	52.05	56.77
13. Phoenix	66.97	**52.26**	55.69
14. BASELINE UDPipe	66.63	51.75	54.87
15. KParse	66.55	51.29	54.45
16. SLT-Interactions	64.73	48.47	**54.90**
17. CUNI x-ling	64.70	**49.71**	52.72
18. ParisNLP	64.09	48.79	**53.16**
19. Fudan	63.54	45.54	50.73
20. LeisureX	61.05	41.95	50.60
21. BOUN	56.46	41.91	45.12
22. HUJI	56.35	**46.52**	**50.10**
23. iParse	44.20	33.43	38.18
24. ONLP lab	43.33	30.20	20.08
25. ArmParser	0.00	0.00	0.00
SParse	0.00	0.00	0.00

Table 14: Average attachment score on the 5 additional test sets for high-resource languages: Czech PUD, English PUD, Finnish PUD, Japanese Modern and Swedish PUD (ordered by LAS F_1 scores; out-of-order scores in the other two columns are bold).

surprise languages and had higher scores there.[13] This is because in 2017, the segmentation, POS tags and morphology UDPipe models were trained on the test data, applied to it via cross-validation, and made available to the systems. Such an approach makes the conditions unrealistic, therefore it was not repeated this year. Consequently, parsing these languages is now much harder.

In contrast, the results on the 7 treebanks with "small" training data and no development data (Table 13) are higher on average, but again the variance is significant. The smallest treebank

in the group, Norwegian Nynorsk LIA, has only 3583 training words. There are two larger Norwegian treebanks that could be used as additional training sources. However, the LIA treebank consists of spoken dialects and is probably quite dissimilar to the other treebanks. The same can be said about Slovenian SST and the other Slovenian treebank; SST is the most difficult dataset in the group, despite of having almost 20K of its own training words. Other treebanks, like Russian Taiga and Galician TreeGal, have much better scores (74% LAS, about 61% MLAS and 64% BLEX). There are also two treebanks that are the sole representatives of their languages: Irish and North Sámi. Their best LAS is around 70%: com-

---

parable to Nynorsk LIA but much better than SST. ICS PAS is the most successful system in the domain of small treebanks, especially when judged by MLAS and BLEX.

Table 14 gives the average LAS on the 5 extra test sets (no own training data, but other treebanks of the same language exist). Four of them come from the Parallel UD (PUD) collection introduced in the 2017 task (Zeman et al., 2017). The fifth, Japanese Modern, turned out to be one of the toughest test sets in this shared task. There is another Japanese treebank, GSD, with over 160K training tokens, but the Modern dataset seems almost inapproachable with models trained on GSD. A closer inspection reveals why: despite its name, it is actually a corpus of historical Japanese, although from the relatively recent Meiji and Taishō periods (1868–1926). An average sentence in GSD is about $1.3\times$ longer than in Modern. GSD has significantly more tokens tagged as auxiliaries, but more importantly, the top ten AUX lemmas in the two treebanks are completely disjoint sets. Some other words are out-of-vocabulary because their preferred spelling changed. For instance, the demonstrative pronoun *sore* is written using hiragana in GSD, but a kanji character is used in Modern. Striking differences can be observed also in dependency relations: in GSD, 3.7% relations are nsubj (subject), and 1.2% are cop (copula). In Modern, there is just 0.13% of subjects, and not a single occurrence of a copula.

See Tables 15, 16 and 17 for a ranking of all test sets by the best scores achieved on them by any parser. Note that this cannot be directly interpreted as a ranking of languages by their parsing difficulty: many treebanks have high ranks simply because the corresponding training data is large. Table 18 compares average LAS and MLAS for each treebank.

Finally, Tables 19 and 20 show the treebanks where word and sentence segmentation was extremely difficult (judged by the average parser score). Not surprisingly, word segmentation is difficult for the low-resource languages and for languages like Chinese, Vietnamese, Japanese and Thai, where spaces do not separate words. Notably the Japanese GSD set is not as difficult, but whoever trusted it, crashed on the "Modern" set. Sentence segmentation was particularly hard for treebanks without punctuation, i.e., most of the classical languages and spoken data.

Treebank	LAS	Best system	Avg	StDev
1. pl_lfg	94.86	HIT-SCIR	85.89	± 6.97
2. ru_syntagrus	92.48	HIT-SCIR	79.68	± 9.09
3. hi_hdtb	92.41	HIT-SCIR	**85.16**	± 5.32
4. pl_sz	92.23	HIT-SCIR	81.47	± 7.27
5. cs_fictree	92.02	HIT-SCIR	**82.10**	± 7.26
6. it_isdt	92.00	HIT-SCIR	**87.61**	± 4.12
7. cs_pdt	91.68	HIT-SCIR	82.18	± 6.91
8. ca_ancora	91.61	HIT-SCIR	**83.61**	± 6.01
9. cs_cac	91.61	HIT-SCIR	82.69	± 6.93
10. sl_ssj	91.47	HIT-SCIR	75.00	± 9.13
11. no_bokmaal	91.23	HIT-SCIR	**79.80**	± 7.29
12. bg_btb	91.22	HIT-SCIR	**82.52**	± 5.88
13. no_nynorsk	90.99	HIT-SCIR	78.55	± 7.88
14. es_ancora	90.93	HIT-SCIR	**82.84**	± 6.17
15. fi_pud	90.23	HIT-SCIR	68.87	±15.61
16. fr_sequoia	89.89	LATTICE	**80.55**	± 5.91
17. el_gdt	89.65	HIT-SCIR	**80.65**	± 6.05
18. nl_alpino	89.56	HIT-SCIR	77.76	± 7.42
19. sk_snk	88.85	HIT-SCIR	76.53	± 7.24
20. fi_tdt	88.73	HIT-SCIR	73.55	± 9.39
21. sr_set	88.66	Stanford	**79.84**	± 6.57
22. sv_talbanken	88.63	HIT-SCIR	77.71	± 6.50
23. fi_ftb	88.53	HIT-SCIR	76.89	± 7.60
24. uk_iu	88.43	HIT-SCIR	72.47	± 8.25
25. fa_seraji	88.11	HIT-SCIR	**78.71**	± 6.04
26. en_pud	87.89	LATTICE	74.51	± 8.28
27. pt_bosque	87.81	Stanford	**80.49**	± 5.46
28. hr_set	87.36	HIT-SCIR	78.37	± 6.42
29. fro_srcmf	87.12	UDPipe Future	74.38	±16.74
30. la_ittb	87.08	HIT-SCIR	**77.00**	± 7.42
31. ko_kaist	86.91	HIT-SCIR	**77.10**	± 8.72
32. fr_gsd	86.89	HIT-SCIR	**79.43**	± 5.47
33. ro_rrt	86.87	HIT-SCIR	75.77	± 7.66
34. nl_lassysmall	86.84	HIT-SCIR	75.08	± 6.59
35. da_ddt	86.28	HIT-SCIR	75.02	± 6.47
36. cs_pud	86.13	HIT-SCIR	73.24	± 9.97
37. af_afribooms	85.47	HIT-SCIR	**76.61**	± 6.17
38. et_edt	85.35	HIT-SCIR	72.08	± 8.71
39. ko_gsd	85.14	HIT-SCIR	71.88	±10.53
40. en_gum	85.05	LATTICE	**74.20**	± 6.27
41. en_ewt	84.57	HIT-SCIR	**75.99**	± 5.40
42. eu_bdt	84.22	HIT-SCIR	72.08	± 8.83
43. sv_lines	84.08	HIT-SCIR	**73.76**	± 5.98
44. lv_lvtb	83.97	HIT-SCIR	67.76	± 9.01
45. ur_udtb	83.39	HIT-SCIR	**75.89**	± 4.69
46. ja_gsd	83.11	HIT-SCIR	73.68	± 4.55
47. gl_ctg	82.76	Stanford	72.46	± 7.13
48. hu_szeged	82.66	HIT-SCIR	67.05	± 8.63
49. en_lines	81.97	HIT-SCIR	**72.28**	± 5.59
50. de_gsd	80.36	HIT-SCIR	70.13	± 7.14
51. sv_pud	80.35	HIT-SCIR	67.02	± 9.23
52. id_gsd	80.05	HIT-SCIR	**73.05**	± 4.69
53. it_postwita	79.39	HIT-SCIR	64.95	± 6.88
54. grc_perseus	79.39	HIT-SCIR	59.01	±15.56
55. grc_proiel	79.25	HIT-SCIR	**65.02**	±14.58
56. ar_padt	77.06	Stanford	64.07	± 6.41
57. zh_gsd	76.77	HIT-SCIR	60.32	± 6.14
58. he_htb	76.09	Stanford	58.73	± 5.29
59. fr_spoken	75.78	HIT-SCIR	**64.66**	± 5.35
60. cu_proiel	75.73	Stanford	62.64	± 6.98
61. gl_treegal	74.25	UDPipe Future	**64.65**	± 5.61
62. ru_taiga	74.24	ICS PAS	56.27	± 9.16
63. la_proiel	73.61	HIT-SCIR	**61.25**	± 6.87
64. la_perseus	72.63	HIT-SCIR	46.91	±11.12
65. ga_idt	70.88	TurkuNLP	**58.37**	± 7.05
66. no_nynorsklia	70.34	HIT-SCIR	50.33	± 9.28
67. sme_giella	69.87	LATTICE	**51.10**	±14.32
68. got_proiel	69.55	Stanford	**60.55**	± 4.93
69. ug_udt	67.05	HIT-SCIR	54.27	± 6.90
70. tr_imst	66.44	HIT-SCIR	**55.61**	± 6.49
71. sl_sst	61.39	HIT-SCIR	47.07	± 5.84
72. vi_vtb	55.22	HIT-SCIR	40.40	± 4.43
73. fo_oft	49.43	CUNI x-ling	27.87	± 9.75
74. hsb_ufal	46.42	SLT-Interactions	26.48	± 8.90
75. br_keb	38.64	CEA LIST	13.27	± 8.77
76. hy_armtdp	37.01	LATTICE	**22.39**	± 7.91
77. kk_ktb	31.93	Uppsala	19.11	± 6.34
78. kmr_mg	30.41	IBM NY	**20.27**	± 6.14
79. pcm_nsc	30.07	CUNI x-ling	13.19	± 5.76
80. ja_modern	28.33	Stanford	**18.92**	± 5.14
81. bxr_bdt	19.53	AntNLP	11.45	± 4.28
82. th_pud	13.70	CUNI x-ling	1.38	± 2.83

Table 15: Treebank ranking by best parser LAS (Avg=average LAS over all systems, out-of-order scores in bold).

	Treebank	MLAS	Best system	Avg	StDev
1.	pl_lfg	86.93	UDPipe Future	73.73	± 7.29
2.	ru_syntagrus	86.76	UDPipe Future	71.63	± 9.36
3.	cs_pdt	85.10	UDPipe Future	**73.61**	± 6.32
4.	cs_fictree	84.23	ICS PAS	69.91	± 7.77
5.	ca_ancora	84.07	UDPipe Future	**74.62**	± 7.69
6.	es_ancora	83.93	Stanford	74.61	± 7.43
7.	it_isdt	83.89	Stanford	**77.14**	± 8.89
8.	fi_pud	83.78	Stanford	62.38	±14.83
9.	no_bokmaal	83.68	UDPipe Future	**70.75**	± 8.92
10.	cs_cac	83.42	UDPipe Future	**71.39**	± 6.89
11.	bg_btb	83.12	UDPipe Future	**73.18**	± 7.15
12.	fr_sequoia	82.55	Stanford	70.42	± 9.04
13.	sl_ssj	82.38	Stanford	62.41	± 9.18
14.	no_nynorsk	81.86	UDPipe Future	**68.62**	± 9.45
15.	ko_kaist	81.29	HIT-SCIR	**70.18**	± 9.36
16.	ko_gsd	80.85	HIT-SCIR	63.73	±16.02
17.	fi_tdt	80.84	Stanford	65.27	± 9.22
18.	fa_seraji	80.83	UDPipe Future	**71.23**	± 7.77
19.	pl_sz	80.77	Stanford	64.80	± 8.49
20.	fro_srcmf	80.28	UDPipe Future	65.19	±16.58
21.	la_ittb	79.84	ICS PAS	67.77	± 8.37
22.	fi_ftb	79.65	TurkuNLP	66.11	± 8.86
23.	sv_talbanken	79.32	Stanford	**68.05**	± 8.49
24.	ro_rrt	78.68	TurkuNLP	67.43	± 7.24
25.	el_gdt	78.66	Stanford	64.29	± 8.28
26.	fr_gsd	78.44	Stanford	**69.33**	± 8.59
27.	hi_hdtb	78.30	UDPipe Future	68.48	± 5.88
28.	sr_set	77.73	UDPipe Future	67.33	± 5.96
29.	da_ddt	77.31	Stanford	65.00	± 6.89
30.	et_edt	76.97	TurkuNLP	63.59	± 8.34
31.	nl_alpino	76.52	Stanford	62.82	± 9.81
32.	en_ewt	76.33	Stanford	**66.84**	± 5.86
33.	pt_bosque	75.94	Stanford	66.22	± 6.76
34.	cs_pud	75.81	UDPipe Future	60.47	±11.36
35.	af_afribooms	75.67	UDPipe Future	**63.76**	± 7.06
36.	sk_snk	75.01	Stanford	56.82	± 8.32
37.	en_pud	74.86	Stanford	**63.05**	± 7.89
38.	nl_lassysmall	74.11	Stanford	61.95	± 9.12
39.	hr_set	73.44	Stanford	60.08	± 7.07
40.	en_gum	73.24	ICS PAS	**61.72**	± 7.69
41.	ja_gsd	72.62	HIT-SCIR	59.52	± 6.20
42.	uk_iu	72.27	UDPipe Future	55.45	± 8.08
43.	en_lines	72.25	ICS PAS	**62.35**	± 8.04
44.	eu_bdt	71.73	UDPipe Future	58.49	± 8.62
45.	gl_ctg	70.92	Stanford	57.92	±14.10
46.	ar_padt	68.54	Stanford	53.28	± 6.12
47.	it_postwita	68.50	Stanford	51.72	± 8.80
48.	id_gsd	68.36	Stanford	**61.03**	± 6.49
49.	lv_lvtb	67.89	Stanford	53.31	± 7.96
50.	hu_szeged	67.13	UDPipe Future	53.08	± 8.01
51.	zh_gsd	66.62	HIT-SCIR	50.42	± 5.87
52.	sv_lines	66.58	Stanford	**57.40**	± 7.43
53.	fr_spoken	64.67	HIT-SCIR	53.17	± 5.61
54.	he_htb	63.38	Stanford	45.22	± 4.94
55.	cu_proiel	63.31	Stanford	**50.28**	± 6.69
56.	ru_taiga	61.59	ICS PAS	37.16	± 7.53
57.	gl_treegal	60.63	UDPipe Future	**47.35**	± 5.93
58.	grc_proiel	60.27	Stanford	**47.62**	±11.82
59.	la_proiel	59.36	Stanford	**47.79**	± 6.90
60.	de_gsd	58.04	TurkuNLP	39.13	±10.35
61.	ur_udtb	57.98	TurkuNLP	**49.64**	± 4.21
62.	no_nynorsklia	57.51	ICS PAS	37.08	± 7.78
63.	sme_giella	57.47	TurkuNLP	**38.29**	±12.37
64.	got_proiel	56.45	UDPipe Future	**46.18**	± 5.36
65.	tr_imst	55.73	Stanford	45.26	± 6.15
66.	grc_perseus	54.98	HIT-SCIR	35.65	±12.31
67.	sv_pud	51.74	TurkuNLP	**39.41**	± 7.78
68.	la_perseus	49.77	ICS PAS	28.67	± 8.06
69.	vi_vtb	47.61	HIT-SCIR	**32.45**	± 7.28
70.	sl_sst	45.93	ICS PAS	**33.12**	± 5.33
71.	ga_idt	45.79	TurkuNLP	**33.70**	± 5.18
72.	ug_udt	45.78	UDPipe Future	**35.08**	± 5.96
73.	br_keb	13.91	Uppsala	1.52	± 3.34
74.	hy_armtdp	13.36	CUNI x-ling	**5.94**	± 2.92
75.	ja_modern	11.82	Uppsala	**6.45**	± 2.59
76.	hsb_ufal	9.09	LATTICE	4.66	± 2.37
77.	kk_ktb	8.93	CUNI x-ling	**5.04**	± 2.34
78.	kmr_mg	7.98	IBM NY	4.01	± 1.96
79.	th_pud	6.29	CUNI x-ling	0.42	± 1.27
80.	pcm_nsc	5.30	KParse	**3.00**	± 1.30
81.	bxr_bdt	2.98	AntNLP	1.33	± 0.72
82.	fo_oft	1.07	CUNI x-ling	0.37	± 0.21

Table 16: Treebank ranking by best parser MLAS.

	Treebank	BLEX	Best system	Avg	StDev
1.	pl_lfg	90.42	TurkuNLP	72.81	±16.96
2.	ru_syntagrus	88.65	TurkuNLP	68.57	±18.07
3.	cs_pdt	87.91	HIT-SCIR	**74.41**	±14.88
4.	cs_fictree	87.81	ICS PAS	71.10	±16.26
5.	cs_cac	86.79	TurkuNLP	**71.61**	±18.18
6.	hi_hdtb	86.74	HIT-SCIR	**75.80**	± 9.28
7.	pl_sz	86.29	TurkuNLP	67.33	±17.15
8.	no_bokmaal	85.82	UDPipe Future	**69.52**	±13.54
9.	ca_ancora	85.47	UDPipe Future	**72.60**	±12.31
10.	es_ancora	84.92	HIT-SCIR	72.10	±12.71
11.	it_isdt	84.76	ICS PAS	**75.42**	±10.72
12.	fr_sequoia	84.67	ICS PAS	70.63	±11.66
13.	no_nynorsk	84.44	TurkuNLP	67.43	±14.10
14.	la_ittb	84.37	TurkuNLP	**68.10**	±17.85
15.	bg_btb	84.31	TurkuNLP	**68.13**	±15.02
16.	fro_srcmf	84.11	UDPipe Future	**70.46**	±16.40
17.	sr_set	83.28	TurkuNLP	65.62	±17.61
18.	sl_ssj	83.23	Stanford	62.54	±17.20
19.	fi_ftb	82.44	TurkuNLP	59.66	±16.50
20.	fi_pud	82.44	TurkuNLP	52.25	±18.50
21.	sv_talbanken	81.44	TurkuNLP	**66.45**	±13.18
22.	fi_tdt	81.24	TurkuNLP	54.70	±17.25
23.	fr_gsd	81.18	HIT-SCIR	**69.61**	±10.58
24.	ro_rrt	80.97	TurkuNLP	63.53	±15.84
25.	sk_snk	80.74	TurkuNLP	58.35	±15.07
26.	pt_bosque	80.62	TurkuNLP	**68.71**	±11.27
27.	en_pud	80.53	LATTICE	64.73	±10.88
28.	cs_pud	80.53	ICS PAS	64.62	±16.03
29.	hr_set	80.50	TurkuNLP	**64.64**	±17.13
30.	fa_seraji	80.44	Stanford	**68.38**	± 7.39
31.	el_gdt	80.09	TurkuNLP	63.26	±15.60
32.	ko_kaist	79.55	TurkuNLP	57.32	±20.78
33.	et_edt	79.37	TurkuNLP	57.06	±16.14
34.	nl_alpino	79.15	HIT-SCIR	**64.29**	±10.83
35.	en_ewt	78.44	HIT-SCIR	**67.53**	± 8.47
36.	uk_iu	78.38	TurkuNLP	57.78	±15.95
37.	eu_bdt	78.15	TurkuNLP	**60.52**	±15.24
38.	da_ddt	78.07	TurkuNLP	**63.16**	±11.41
39.	sv_lines	77.01	ICS PAS	63.13	±11.72
40.	id_gsd	76.56	Stanford	62.52	± 7.89
41.	nl_lassysmall	76.54	HIT-SCIR	60.92	±11.93
42.	af_afribooms	76.44	TurkuNLP	**63.87**	± 9.62
43.	ko_gsd	76.31	TurkuNLP	54.13	±17.78
44.	en_lines	75.29	HIT-SCIR	**62.29**	± 9.27
45.	gl_ctg	75.14	Stanford	60.86	±10.82
46.	ur_udtb	73.79	TurkuNLP	**62.93**	± 6.42
47.	ja_gsd	73.79	HIT-SCIR	60.87	± 6.04
48.	en_gum	73.57	ICS PAS	**61.02**	± 8.59
49.	hu_szeged	73.17	TurkuNLP	55.42	±10.95
50.	zh_gsd	72.97	HIT-SCIR	**55.66**	± 6.26
51.	lv_lvtb	72.40	TurkuNLP	53.42	±14.56
52.	de_gsd	71.40	HIT-SCIR	**54.86**	±14.99
53.	cu_proiel	71.31	Stanford	51.27	±15.35
54.	ar_padt	70.06	Stanford	49.13	±18.98
55.	it_postwita	69.34	HIT-SCIR	**50.97**	± 8.76
56.	grc_proiel	69.03	TurkuNLP	48.58	±19.91
57.	la_proiel	67.60	TurkuNLP	**51.03**	±14.56
58.	sv_pud	66.12	TurkuNLP	50.20	±11.30
59.	fr_spoken	65.63	HIT-SCIR	**52.57**	± 7.29
60.	he_htb	65.04	Stanford	47.22	± 6.60
61.	ru_taiga	64.36	ICS PAS	39.32	±10.49
62.	gl_treegal	64.29	UDPipe Future	**49.38**	± 8.18
63.	got_proiel	63.98	Stanford	48.79	±13.77
64.	no_nynorsklia	60.98	ICS PAS	41.20	± 8.64
65.	tr_imst	60.13	TurkuNLP	**45.39**	±10.38
66.	sme_giella	60.10	TurkuNLP	35.76	±12.68
67.	grc_perseus	58.68	TurkuNLP	**36.48**	±16.03
68.	ug_udt	55.42	HIT-SCIR	**41.64**	± 8.09
69.	ga_idt	55.18	TurkuNLP	37.83	± 7.61
70.	la_perseus	52.75	ICS PAS	30.16	±11.05
71.	sl_sst	50.94	ICS PAS	**37.20**	± 6.87
72.	vi_vtb	44.02	Stanford	35.50	± 3.74
73.	pcm_nsc	26.04	CUNI x-ling	12.07	± 5.63
74.	hsb_ufal	21.09	LATTICE	11.26	± 4.97
75.	br_keb	20.70	TurkuNLP	4.19	± 4.93
76.	hy_armtdp	19.04	CUNI x-ling	**10.68**	± 4.37
77.	fo_oft	14.40	CUNI x-ling	7.32	± 3.33
78.	ja_modern	13.79	Stanford	**7.70**	± 2.86
79.	kmr_mg	13.66	LATTICE	**8.44**	± 3.11
80.	kk_ktb	11.33	CUNI x-ling	6.75	± 2.95
81.	th_pud	10.77	CUNI x-ling	0.91	± 2.11
82.	bxr_bdt	6.65	AntNLP	**3.39**	± 1.61

Table 17: Treebank ranking by best parser BLEX.

Treebank	LAS	MLAS	Diff	Language
1. de_gsd	70.13	39.13	31.01	German
2. sv_pud	67.02	39.41	27.61	Swedish
3. fo_oft	27.87	0.37	27.50	Faroese
4. ur_udtb	75.89	49.64	26.25	Urdu
5. ga_idt	58.37	33.70	24.66	Irish
6. grc_perseus	59.01	35.65	23.36	Ancient Greek
7. hsb_ufal	26.48	4.66	21.82	Upper Sorbian
8. sk_snk	76.53	56.82	19.71	Slovak
9. ug_udt	54.27	35.08	19.20	Uyghur
10. ru_taiga	56.27	37.16	19.12	Russian
11. hr_set	78.37	60.08	18.29	Croatian
12. la_perseus	46.91	28.67	18.24	Latin
13. grc_proiel	65.02	47.62	17.40	Ancient Greek
14. gl_treegal	64.65	47.35	17.30	Galician
15. uk_iu	72.47	55.45	17.01	Ukrainian
16. hi_hdtb	85.16	68.48	16.68	Hindi
17. pl_sz	81.47	64.80	16.67	Polish
18. hy_armtdp	22.39	5.94	16.45	Armenian
19. el_gdt	80.65	64.29	16.36	Greek
20. sv_lines	73.76	57.40	16.36	Swedish
21. kmr_mg	20.27	4.01	16.26	Kurmanji
22. nl_alpino	77.76	62.82	14.95	Dutch
23. gl_ctg	72.46	57.92	14.55	Galician
24. lv_lvtb	67.76	53.31	14.45	Latvian
25. got_proiel	60.55	46.18	14.37	Gothic
26. pt_bosque	80.49	66.22	14.27	Portuguese
27. ja_gsd	73.68	59.52	14.16	Japanese
28. kk_ktb	19.11	5.04	14.07	Kazakh
29. hu_szeged	67.05	53.08	13.96	Hungarian
30. sl_sst	47.07	33.12	13.95	Slovenian
31. eu_bdt	72.08	58.49	13.59	Basque
32. he_htb	58.73	45.22	13.51	Hebrew
33. la_proiel	61.25	47.79	13.46	Latin
34. no_nynorsklia	50.33	37.08	13.25	Norwegian
35. it_postwita	64.95	51.72	13.22	Italian
36. nl_lassysmall	75.08	61.95	13.14	Dutch
37. af_afribooms	76.61	63.76	12.84	Afrikaans
38. sme_giella	51.10	38.29	12.82	North Sámi
39. cs_pud	73.24	60.47	12.77	Czech
40. sl_ssj	75.00	62.41	12.59	Slovenian
41. sr_set	79.84	67.33	12.50	Serbian
42. en_gum	74.20	61.72	12.48	English
43. ja_modern	18.92	6.45	12.47	Japanese
44. cu_proiel	62.64	50.28	12.36	Old Church Slavonic
45. cs_fictree	82.10	69.91	12.19	Czech
46. pl_lfg	85.89	73.73	12.17	Polish
47. id_gsd	73.05	61.03	12.02	Indonesian
48. br_keb	13.27	1.52	11.75	Breton
49. fr_spoken	64.66	53.17	11.49	French
50. en_pud	74.51	63.05	11.46	English
51. cs_cac	82.69	71.39	11.29	Czech
52. ar_padt	64.07	53.28	10.79	Arabic
53. fi_ftb	76.89	66.11	10.78	Finnish
54. it_isdt	87.61	77.14	10.47	Italian
55. tr_imst	55.61	45.26	10.34	Turkish
56. pcm_nsc	13.19	3.00	10.19	Naija
57. fr_sequoia	80.55	70.42	10.13	French
58. bxr_bdt	11.45	1.33	10.12	Buryat
59. fr_gsd	79.43	69.33	10.10	French
60. da_ddt	75.02	65.00	10.02	Danish
61. no_nynorsk	78.55	68.62	9.93	Norwegian
62. en_lines	72.28	62.35	9.93	English
63. zh_gsd	60.32	50.42	9.90	Chinese
64. sv_talbanken	77.71	68.05	9.66	Swedish
65. bg_btb	82.52	73.18	9.34	Bulgarian
66. la_ittb	77.00	67.77	9.23	Latin
67. fro_srcmf	74.38	65.19	9.18	Old French
68. en_ewt	75.99	66.84	9.15	English
69. no_bokmaal	79.80	70.75	9.05	Norwegian
70. ca_ancora	83.61	74.62	8.99	Catalan
71. cs_pdt	82.18	73.61	8.57	Czech
72. et_edt	72.08	63.59	8.50	Estonian
73. ro_rrt	75.77	67.43	8.33	Romanian
74. fi_tdt	73.55	65.27	8.28	Finnish
75. es_ancora	82.84	74.61	8.23	Spanish
76. ko_gsd	71.88	63.73	8.15	Korean
77. ru_syntagrus	79.68	71.63	8.05	Russian
78. vi_vtb	40.40	32.45	7.95	Vietnamese
79. fa_seraji	78.71	71.23	7.48	Persian
80. ko_kaist	77.10	70.18	6.92	Korean
81. fi_pud	68.87	62.38	6.49	Finnish
82. th_pud	1.38	0.42	0.96	Thai

Table 18: Treebank ranking by difference between average parser LAS and MLAS.

Treebank	Best	Best system	Avg	StDev
70. bxr_bdt	99.24	IBM NY	88.64	± 8.09
71. fi_pud	99.69	Uppsala	88.13	±10.81
72. zh_gsd	96.71	HIT-SCIR	86.91	± 3.83
73. fo_oft	99.47	CUNI x-ling	86.76	±10.68
74. ar_padt	96.81	Stanford	86.62	± 7.00
75. kmr_mg	96.97	Uppsala	86.61	± 7.16
76. kk_ktb	97.40	Uppsala	85.55	± 7.45
77. br_keb	92.45	TurkuNLP	83.76	± 7.37
78. he_htb	93.98	Stanford	82.45	± 3.80
79. vi_vtb	93.46	HIT-SCIR	81.71	± 3.73
80. pcm_nsc	99.71	CEA LIST	79.94	±10.69
81. ja_modern	75.69	HIT-SCIR	59.40	± 7.70
82. th_pud	69.93	Uppsala	17.16	±20.57

Table 19: Treebanks with most difficult word segmentation (by average parser F_1).

Treebank	Best	Best system	Avg	StDev
73. grc_proiel	51.84	HIT-SCIR	42.46	± 7.33
74. cu_proiel	48.67	Stanford	35.54	± 4.02
75. la_proiel	39.61	Stanford	33.40	± 5.39
76. got_proiel	38.23	Stanford	27.22	± 4.47
77. it_postwita	65.90	Stanford	25.25	±14.30
78. sl_sst	24.43	NLP-Cube	20.92	± 4.70
79. fr_spoken	24.17	Stanford	20.43	± 2.89
80. th_pud	12.37	TurkuNLP	1.75	± 3.68
81. pcm_nsc	0.93	Stanford	0.06	± 0.19
82. ja_modern	0.23	Stanford	0.01	± 0.04

Table 20: Treebanks with most difficult sentence segmentation (by average parser F_1).

7 Analysis of Submitted Systems

Table 21 gives an overview of 24 of the systems evaluated in the shared task. The overview is based on a post-evaluation questionnaire to which 24 of 25 teams responded. Systems are ordered alphabetically by name and their LAS rank is indicated in the second column.

Looking first at word and sentence segmentation, we see that, while a clear majority of systems (19/24) rely on the baseline system for segmentation, slightly more than half (13/24) have developed their own segmenter, or tuned the baseline segmenter, for at least a subset of languages. This is a development from 2017, where only 7 out of 29 systems used anything other than the baseline segmenter.

When it comes to morphological analysis, including universal POS tags, features and lemmas, all systems this year include some such component, and only 6 systems rely entirely on the base-

System	R	Segment	Morph	Syntax	WEmb	Additional Data	MultiLing
AntNLP	9	Base	Base	Single-G	FB	None	Own$_S$
ArmParser	25	Base	Own	Single	FB	None	None
BOUN	21	Base	Base	Single-T	Base	None	None
CEA LIST	6	Base	B$_L$/Own	Single-G/T	B/FB	OPUS/Wikt	Own$_L$
CUNI x-ling	20	B/Own	B/Own	Single/Ens	FB/None	O/UM/WALS/Wiki	Own$_{L,S}$
Fudan	17	Base	Base	Ensemble	None	None	Own$_{L,S}$
HIT-SCIR	1	B/Own	Base	Ensemble	B/FB/Crawl	None	Own$_{L,S}$
HUJI	24	Base	Base	Single-T	FB	None	Own$_L$
IBM NY	13	B/Own	B/Joint	Ensemble-T	B/FB	Wiki	Own$_{L,S}$
ICS PAS	3	Base	Own	Single-G	FB/None	None	None
KParse	16	B/Own	Own	Single	Other	None	Own$_L$
LATTICE	3	Base	Own$_U$	Single-G/Ens	B/FB/Crawl	OPUS/Wiki	Own$_{L,S}$
LeisureX	15	Base	Own	Single	Base	None	Own$_L$
NLP-Cube	9	Own	Own	Single	FB	None	Own$_L$
ONLP lab	22	Base	Base	Single-T	None	UML	None
ParisNLP	11	B/Own	B/Own	Single-G	FB	UML	Own$_L$
Phoenix	19	Own	Own$_U$	Single	Train	None	Own$_L$
SLT-Interactions	12	B/Own	Own	Single	Crawl	None	Own$_L$
SParse	26	B/Own	Own	Single-G	Crawl	None	Own$_L$
Stanford	7	Own	Own	Single-G	B/FB	None	None
TurkuNLP	2	B/Own	Own	Single-G	B/FB	OPUS/Aper	Own$_L$
UDPipe Future	3	Own	Joint	Single-G	B/FB	None	None
UniMelb	14	Base	Joint	Single	Base	None	Base
Uppsala	7	Own	Own$_{U,F}$	Single-T	B/FB/Wiki	OPUS/Wiki/Aper	Own$_{L,S}$

Table 21: Classification of participating systems. **R** = LAS ranking. **Segment** = word/sentence segmentation. **Morph** = morphological analysis, including universal POS tags [U], features [F] and lemmas [L], with subscripts for subsets [Joint = morphological component trained jointly with syntactic parser]. **Syntax** = syntactic parsing [Single = single parser; Ensemble (or Ens) = parser ensemble; G = graph-based; T = transition-based]. **WEmb** = pre-trained word embeddings [FB = Facebook; Crawl = trained on web crawl data provided by the organizers; Wiki = trained on Wikipedia data; Train = trained on treebank training data]. **Additional Data** = data used in addition to treebank training sets [OPUS (or O) = OPUS, Aper = Apertium morphological analysers, Wikt = Wiktionary, Wiki = Wikipedia, UM = UniMorph, UML = Universal Morphological Lattices, WALS = World Atlas of Language Structures]. **MultiLing** = multilingal models used for low-resource (L) or small (S) languages. In all columns, Base (or B) refers to the Baseline UDPipe system or the baseline word embeddings provided by the organizers, while None means that there is no corresponding component in the system.

line UDPipe system. This is again quite different from 2017, where more than half the systems either just relied on the baseline tagger (13 systems) or did not predict any morphology at all (3 systems). We take this to be primarily a reflection of the fact that two out of three official metrics included (some) morphological analysis this year, although 3 systems did not predict the lemmas required for the BLEX metric (and 2 systems only predicted universal POS tags, no features). As far as we can tell from the questionnaire responses,

only 3 systems used a model where morphology and syntax were predicted jointly.[14]

For syntactic parsing, most teams (19) use a single parsing model, while 5 teams, including the winning HIT-SCIR system, build ensemble models, either for all languages or a subset of them. When it comes to the type of parsing model, we observe that graph-based models are more popular than transition-based models this year, while the opposite was true in 2017. We hypothesize that

---

[14]The ONLP lab system also has a joint model but in the end used the baseline morphology as it gave better results.

this is due to the superior performance of the Stanford graph-based parser in last year's shared task, and many of the high-performing systems this year either incorporate that parser or a reimplementation of it.[15]

The majority of parsers make use of pre-trained word embeddings. Most popular are the Facebook embeddings, which are used by 17 systems, followed by the baseline embeddings provided by the organizers (11), and embeddings trained on web crawl data (4).[16] When it comes to additional data, over and above the treebank training sets and pre-trained word embeddings, the most striking observation is that a majority of systems (16) did not use any at all. Those that did primarily used OPUS (5), Wikipedia dumps (3), Apertium morphological analyzers (2), and Universal Morphological Lattices (2). The CUNI x-ling system, which focused on low-resource languages, also exploited UniMorph and WALS (in addition to OPUS and Wikipedia).

Finally, we note that a majority of systems make use of models trained on multiple languages to improve parsing for languages with little or no training data. According to the questionnaire responses, 15 systems use multilingual models for the languages classified as "low-resource", while 7 systems use them for the languages classified as "small".[17] Only one system relied on the baseline delexicalized parser trained on data from all languages.

8 Conclusion

The CoNLL 2018 Shared Task on UD parsing, the second in the series, was novel in several respects. Besides using cross-linguistically consistent linguistic representations, emphasizing end-to-end processing of text, and in using a multiply parallel test set, as in 2017, it was unusual also in featuring an unprecedented number of languages and treebanks and in integrating cross-lingual learning for resource-poor languages. Compared to the first edition of the task in 2017, this year several languages were provided with little-to-no resources, whereas in 2017, predicted morphology trained on

the language in question was available for all of the languages. The most extreme example of these is Thai, where the only accessible resource was the Facebook Research Thai embeddings model and the OPUS parallel corpora. This year's task also introduced two additional metrics that take into account morphology and lemmatization. This encouraged the development of truly end-to-end full parsers, producing complete parses including morphological features and lemmas in addition to the syntactic tree. This also aimed to improve the utility of the systems developed in the shared task for later downstream applications. For most UD languages, these parsers represent a new state of the art for end-to-end dependency parsing.

The analysis of the shared task results has so far only scratched the surface, and we refer to the system description papers for more in-depth analysis of individual systems and their performance. For many previous CoNLL shared tasks, the task itself has only been the starting point of a long and fruitful research strand, enabled by the resources created for the task. We hope and believe that the 2017 and 2018 UD parsing tasks will join this tradition.

Acknowledgments

We are grateful to all the contributors to Universal Dependencies; without their effort a task like this simply wouldn't be possible.

The work described herein, including data preparation for the *CoNLL 2018 UD Shared Task*, has been supported by the following grants and projects: "CRACKER," H2020 Project No. 645357 of the European Commission; "MANYLA," Grant No. GA15-10472S of the Grant Agency of the Czech Republic; FIN-CLARIN; and the LINDAT/CLARIN research infrastructure project funded by the Ministry of Education, Youth and Sports of the Czech Republic, Project. No. LM2015071. The data for the *CoNLL 2018 UD Shared Task* are available also via the LINDAT/CLARIN repository.

---

[15]This is true of at least 3 of the 5 best performing systems.

[16]The baseline embeddings were the same as in 2017 and therefore did not cover new languages, which may partly explain the greater popularity of the Facebook embeddings this year.

[17]We know that some teams used them also for clusters involving high-resource languages, but we have no detailed statistics on this usage.

References

Gor Arakelyan, Karen Hambardzumyan, and Hrant Khachatrian. 2018. Towards JointUD: Part-of-speech tagging and lemmatization using recurrent neural networks. In *Proceedings of the CoNLL 2018 Shared Task: Multilingual Parsing from Raw Text to*

Universal Dependencies. Association for Computational Linguistics.

Riyaz Ahmad Bhat, Irshad Ahmad Bhat, and Srinivas Bangalore. 2018. The SLT-Interactions parsing system at the CoNLL 2018 shared task. In *Proceedings of the CoNLL 2018 Shared Task: Multilingual Parsing from Raw Text to Universal Dependencies*. Association for Computational Linguistics.

Piotr Bojanowski, Edouard Grave, Armand Joulin, and Tomas Mikolov. 2016. Enriching word vectors with subword information *arXiv preprint arXiv:1607.04606*.

Tiberiu Boroș, Stefan Daniel Dumitrescu, and Ruxandra Burtica. 2018. NLP-Cube: End-to-end raw text processing with neural networks. In *Proceedings of the CoNLL 2018 Shared Task: Multilingual Parsing from Raw Text to Universal Dependencies*. Association for Computational Linguistics.

Sabine Buchholz and Erwin Marsi. 2006. CoNLL-X shared task on multilingual dependency parsing. In *Proceedings of the 10th Conference on Computational Natural Language Learning (CoNLL-X)*. Association for Computational Linguistics, pages 149–164. http://anthology.aclweb.org/W/W06/W06-29.pdf#page=165.

Wanxiang Che, Yijia Liu, Yuxuan Wang, Bo Zheng, and Ting Liu. 2018. Towards better UD parsing: Deep contextualized word embeddings, ensemble, and treebank concatenation. In *Proceedings of the CoNLL 2018 Shared Task: Multilingual Parsing from Raw Text to Universal Dependencies*. Association for Computational Linguistics.

Danlu Chen, Mengxiao Lin, Zhifeng Hu, and Xipeng Qiu. 2018. A simple yet effective joint training method for cross-lingual universal dependency parsing. In *Proceedings of the CoNLL 2018 Shared Task: Multilingual Parsing from Raw Text to Universal Dependencies*. Association for Computational Linguistics.

Elie Duthoo and Olivier Mesnard. 2018. CEA LIST : Processing low-resource languages for CoNLL 2018. In *Proceedings of the CoNLL 2018 Shared Task: Multilingual Parsing from Raw Text to Universal Dependencies*. Association for Computational Linguistics.

Murhaf Fares, Stephan Oepen, Lilja Øvrelid, Jari Björne, and Richard Johansson. 2018. The 2018 shared task on extrinsic parser evaluation: On the downstream utility of English universal dependency parsers. In *Proceedings of the CoNLL 2018 Shared Task: Multilingual Parsing from Raw Text to Universal Dependencies*. Association for Computational Linguistics, Brussels, Belgium.

Filip Ginter, Jan Hajič, Juhani Luotolahti, Milan Straka, and Daniel Zeman. 2017. CoNLL 2017 shared task - automatically annotated raw texts and word embeddings. LINDAT/CLARIN digital library at the Institute of Formal and Applied Linguistics, Charles University. http://hdl.handle.net/11234/1-1989.

Allan Hanbury, Henning Müller, Krisztian Balog, Torben Brodt, Gordon V. Cormack, Ivan Eggel, Tim Gollub, Frank Hopfgartner, Jayashree Kalpathy-Cramer, Noriko Kando, Anastasia Krithara, Jimmy Lin, Simon Mercer, and Martin Potthast. 2015. Evaluation-as-a-Service: Overview and Outlook. *ArXiv e-prints* http://arxiv.org/abs/1512.07454.

Daniel Hershcovich, Omri Abend, and Ari Rappoport. 2018. Universal dependency parsing with a general transition-based DAG parser. In *Proceedings of the CoNLL 2018 Shared Task: Multilingual Parsing from Raw Text to Universal Dependencies*. Association for Computational Linguistics.

Ganesh Jawahar, Benjamin Muller, Amal Fethi, Louis Martin, Éric de La Clergerie, Benoît Sagot, and Djamé Seddah. 2018. ELMoLex: Connecting ELMo and lexicon features for dependency parsing. In *Proceedings of the CoNLL 2018 Shared Task: Multilingual Parsing from Raw Text to Universal Dependencies*. Association for Computational Linguistics.

Tao Ji, Yufang Liu, Yijun Wang, Yuanbin Wu, and Man Lan. 2018. AntNLP at CoNLL 2018 shared task: A graph-based parser for universal dependency parsing. In *Proceedings of the CoNLL 2018 Shared Task: Multilingual Parsing from Raw Text to Universal Dependencies*. Association for Computational Linguistics.

Jenna Kanerva, Filip Ginter, Niko Miekka, Akseli Leino, and Tapio Salakoski. 2018. Turku neural parser pipeline: An end-to-end system for the CoNLL 2018 shared task. In *Proceedings of the CoNLL 2018 Shared Task: Multilingual Parsing from Raw Text to Universal Dependencies*. Association for Computational Linguistics.

Ömer Kırnap, Erenay Dayanık, and Deniz Yuret. 2018. Tree-stack LSTM in transition based dependency parsing. In *Proceedings of the CoNLL 2018 Shared Task: Multilingual Parsing from Raw Text to Universal Dependencies*. Association for Computational Linguistics.

Zuchao Li, Shexia He, Zhuosheng Zhang, and Hai Zhao. 2018. Joint learning of pos and dependencies for multilingual universal dependency parsing. In *Proceedings of the CoNLL 2018 Shared Task: Multilingual Parsing from Raw Text to Universal Dependencies*. Association for Computational Linguistics.

KyungTae Lim, Cheoneum Park, Changki Lee, and Thierry Poibeau. 2018. SEx BiST: A multi-source trainable parser with deep contextualized lexical representations. In *Proceedings of the CoNLL 2018 Shared Task: Multilingual Parsing from Raw Text to Universal Dependencies*. Association for Computational Linguistics.

Dat Quoc Nguyen and Karin Verspoor. 2018. An improved neural network model for joint pos tagging and dependency parsing. In *Proceedings of the CoNLL 2018 Shared Task: Multilingual Parsing from Raw Text to Universal Dependencies*. Association for Computational Linguistics.

Joakim Nivre, Mitchell Abrams, Željko Agić, Lars Ahrenberg, Lene Antonsen, Maria Jesus Aranzabe, Gashaw Arutie, Masayuki Asahara, Luma Ateyah, Mohammed Attia, Aitziber Atutxa, Liesbeth Augustinus, Elena Badmaeva, Miguel Ballesteros, Esha Banerjee, Sebastian Bank, Verginica Barbu Mititelu, John Bauer, Sandra Bellato, Kepa Bengoetxea, Riyaz Ahmad Bhat, Erica Biagetti, Eckhard Bick, Rogier Blokland, Victoria Bobicev, Carl Börstell, Cristina Bosco, Gosse Bouma, Sam Bowman, Adriane Boyd, Aljoscha Burchardt, Marie Candito, Bernard Caron, Gauthier Caron, Gülşen Cebiroğlu Eryiğit, Giuseppe G. A. Celano, Savas Cetin, Fabricio Chalub, Jinho Choi, Yongseok Cho, Jayeol Chun, Silvie Cinková, Aurélie Collomb, Çağrı Çöltekin, Miriam Connor, Marine Courtin, Elizabeth Davidson, Marie-Catherine de Marneffe, Valeria de Paiva, Arantza Diaz de Ilarraza, Carly Dickerson, Peter Dirix, Kaja Dobrovoljc, Timothy Dozat, Kira Droganova, Puneet Dwivedi, Marhaba Eli, Ali Elkahky, Binyam Ephrem, Tomaž Erjavec, Aline Etienne, Richárd Farkas, Hector Fernandez Alcalde, Jennifer Foster, Cláudia Freitas, Katarína Gajdošová, Daniel Galbraith, Marcos Garcia, Moa Gärdenfors, Kim Gerdes, Filip Ginter, Iakes Goenaga, Koldo Gojenola, Memduh Gökırmak, Yoav Goldberg, Xavier Gómez Guinovart, Berta Gónzales Saavedra, Matias Grioni, Normunds Grūzītis, Bruno Guillaume, Céline Guillot-Barbance, Nizar Habash, Jan Hajič, Jan Hajič jr., Linh Hà Mỹ, Na-Rae Han, Kim Harris, Dag Haug, Barbora Hladká, Jaroslava Hlaváčová, Florinel Hociung, Petter Hohle, Jena Hwang, Radu Ion, Elena Irimia, Tomáš Jelínek, Anders Johannsen, Fredrik Jørgensen, Hüner Kaşıkara, Sylvain Kahane, Hiroshi Kanayama, Jenna Kanerva, Tolga Kayadelen, Václava Kettnerová, Jesse Kirchner, Natalia Kotsyba, Simon Krek, Sookyoung Kwak, Veronika Laippala, Lorenzo Lambertino, Tatiana Lando, Septina Dian Larasati, Alexei Lavrentiev, John Lee, Phương Lê Hồng, Alessandro Lenci, Saran Lertpradit, Herman Leung, Cheuk Ying Li, Josie Li, Keying Li, KyungTae Lim, Nikola Ljubešić, Olga Loginova, Olga Lyashevskaya, Teresa Lynn, Vivien Macketanz, Aibek Makazhanov, Michael Mandl, Christopher Manning, Ruli Manurung, Cătălina Mărănduc, David Mareček, Katrin Marheinecke, Héctor Martínez Alonso, André Martins, Jan Mašek, Yuji Matsumoto, Ryan McDonald, Gustavo Mendonça, Niko Miekka, Anna Missilä, Cătălin Mititelu, Yusuke Miyao, Simonetta Montemagni, Amir More, Laura Moreno Romero, Shinsuke Mori, Bjartur Mortensen, Bohdan Moskalevskyi, Kadri Muischnek, Yugo Murawaki, Kaili Müürisep, Pinkey Nainwani, Juan Ignacio Navarro Horñiacek, Anna Nedoluzhko, Gunta Nešpore-Bērzkalne, Lương Nguyễn Thị, Huyền Nguyễn Thị Minh, Vitaly Nikolaev, Rattima Nitisaroj, Hanna Nurmi, Stina Ojala, Adédayọ̀ Olúòkun, Mai Omura, Petya Osenova, Robert Östling, Lilja Øvrelid, Niko Partanen, Elena Pascual, Marco Passarotti, Agnieszka Patejuk, Siyao Peng, Cenel-Augusto Perez, Guy Perrier, Slav Petrov, Jussi Piitulainen, Emily Pitler, Barbara Plank, Thierry Poibeau, Martin Popel, Lauma Pretkalniņa, Sophie Prévost, Prokopis Prokopidis, Adam Przepiórkowski, Tiina Puolakainen, Sampo Pyysalo, Andriela Rääbis, Alexandre Rademaker, Loganathan Ramasamy, Taraka Rama, Carlos Ramisch, Vinit Ravishankar, Livy Real, Siva Reddy, Georg Rehm, Michael Rießler, Larissa Rinaldi, Laura Rituma, Luisa Rocha, Mykhailo Romanenko, Rudolf Rosa, Davide Rovati, Valentin Roșca, Olga Rudina, Shoval Sadde, Shadi Saleh, Tanja Samardžić, Stephanie Samson, Manuela Sanguinetti, Baiba Saulīte, Yanin Sawanakunanon, Nathan Schneider, Sebastian Schuster, Djamé Seddah, Wolfgang Seeker, Mojgan Seraji, Mo Shen, Atsuko Shimada, Muh Shohibussirri, Dmitry Sichinava, Natalia Silveira, Maria Simi, Radu Simionescu, Katalin Simkó, Mária Šimková, Kiril Simov, Aaron Smith, Isabela Soares-Bastos, Antonio Stella, Milan Straka, Jana Strnadová, Alane Suhr, Umut Sulubacak, Zsolt Szántó, Dima Taji, Yuta Takahashi, Takaaki Tanaka, Isabelle Tellier, Trond Trosterud, Anna Trukhina, Reut Tsarfaty, Francis Tyers, Sumire Uematsu, Zdeňka Urešová, Larraitz Uria, Hans Uszkoreit, Sowmya Vajjala, Daniel van Niekerk, Gertjan van Noord, Viktor Varga, Veronika Vincze, Lars Wallin, Jonathan North Washington, Seyi Williams, Mats Wirén, Tsegay Woldemariam, Tak-sum Wong, Chunxiao Yan, Marat M. Yavrumyan, Zhuoran Yu, Zdeněk Žabokrtský, Amir Zeldes, Daniel Zeman, Manying Zhang, and Hanzhi Zhu. 2018. Universal dependencies 2.2. LINDAT/CLARIN digital library at the Institute of Formal and Applied Linguistics (ÚFAL), Faculty of Mathematics and Physics, Charles University. http://hdl.handle.net/11234/1-2837.

Joakim Nivre, Marie-Catherine de Marneffe, Filip Ginter, Yoav Goldberg, Jan Hajič, Christopher Manning, Ryan McDonald, Slav Petrov, Sampo Pyysalo, Natalia Silveira, Reut Tsarfaty, and Daniel Zeman. 2016. Universal Dependencies v1: A multilingual treebank collection. In *Proceedings of the 10th International Conference on Language Resources and Evaluation (LREC 2016)*. European Language Resources Association, Portorož, Slovenia, pages 1659–1666. http://www.lrec-conf.org/proceedings/lrec2016/summaries/348.html.

Joakim Nivre and Chiao-Ting Fang. 2017. Universal dependency evaluation. In *Proceedings of the NoDaLiDa 2017 Workshop on Universal Dependencies (UDW 2017)*. pages 86–95.

Joakim Nivre, Johan Hall, Sandra Kübler, Ryan McDonald, Jens Nilsson, Sebastian Riedel, and Deniz Yuret. 2007. The CoNLL 2007 shared task on dependency parsing. In *Proceedings of the CoNLL Shared Task Session of EMNLP-CoNLL 2007*. Association for Computational Linguistics, pages 915–932. http://www.aclweb.org/anthology/D/D07/D07-1.pdf#page=949.

Berkay Furkan Önder, Can Gümeli, and Deniz Yuret. 2018. SParse: Koç University graph-based parsing system for the CoNLL 2018 shared task. In *Proceedings of the CoNLL 2018 Shared Task: Multilingual Parsing from Raw Text to Universal Dependencies*. Association for Computational Linguistics.

Şaziye Betül Özateş, Arzucan Özgür, Tunga Güngör, and Balkız Öztürk. 2018. A morphology-based representation model for LSTM-based dependency parsing of agglutinative languages. In *Proceedings of the CoNLL 2018 Shared Task: Multilingual Parsing from Raw Text to Universal Dependencies*. Association for Computational Linguistics.

Martin Popel, Zdeněk Žabokrtský, and Martin Vojtek. 2017. Udapi: Universal API for universal dependencies. In *NoDaLiDa 2017 Workshop on Universal Dependencies*. Göteborgs universitet, Göteborg, Sweden, pages 96–101. http://aclweb.org/anthology/W/W17/W17-0412.pdf.

Martin Potthast, Tim Gollub, Francisco Rangel, Paolo Rosso, Efstathios Stamatatos, and Benno Stein. 2014. Improving the reproducibility of PAN's shared tasks: Plagiarism detection, author identification, and author profiling. In Evangelos Kanoulas, Mihai Lupu, Paul Clough, Mark Sanderson, Mark Hall, Allan Hanbury, and Elaine Toms, editors, *Information Access Evaluation meets Multilinguality, Multimodality, and Visualization. 5th International Conference of the CLEF Initiative (CLEF 14)*. Springer, Berlin Heidelberg New York, pages 268–299. https://doi.org/10.1007/978-3-319-11382-1_22.

Peng Qi, Timothy Dozat, Yuhao Zhang, and Christopher D. Manning. 2018. Universal dependency parsing from scratch. In *Proceedings of the CoNLL 2018 Shared Task: Multilingual Parsing from Raw Text to Universal Dependencies*. Association for Computational Linguistics.

Rudolf Rosa and David Mareček. 2018. CUNI x-ling: Parsing under-resourced languages in CoNLL 2018 UD shared task. In *Proceedings of the CoNLL 2018 Shared Task: Multilingual Parsing from Raw Text to Universal Dependencies*. Association for Computational Linguistics.

Piotr Rybak and Alina Wróblewska. 2018. Semi-supervised neural system for tagging, parsing and lematization. In *Proceedings of the CoNLL 2018 Shared Task: Multilingual Parsing from Raw Text to Universal Dependencies*. Association for Computational Linguistics.

Amit Seker, Amir More, and Reut Tsarfaty. 2018. Universal morpho-syntactic parsing and the contribution of lexica: Analyzing the ONLP submission to the CoNLL 2018 shared task. In *Proceedings of the CoNLL 2018 Shared Task: Multilingual Parsing from Raw Text to Universal Dependencies*. Association for Computational Linguistics.

Aaron Smith, Bernd Bohnet, Miryam de Lhoneux, Joakim Nivre, Yan Shao, and Sara Stymne. 2018. 82 treebanks, 34 models: Universal dependency parsing with multi-treebank models. In *Proceedings of the CoNLL 2018 Shared Task: Multilingual Parsing from Raw Text to Universal Dependencies*. Association for Computational Linguistics.

Milan Straka. 2018. UDPipe 2.0 prototype at CoNLL 2018 UD shared task. In *Proceedings of the CoNLL 2018 Shared Task: Multilingual Parsing from Raw Text to Universal Dependencies*. Association for Computational Linguistics.

Milan Straka, Jan Hajič, and Jana Straková. 2016. UDPipe: trainable pipeline for processing CoNLL-U files performing tokenization, morphological analysis, POS tagging and parsing. In *Proceedings of the 10th International Conference on Language Resources and Evaluation (LREC 2016)*. European Language Resources Association, Portorož, Slovenia.

Milan Straka and Jana Straková. 2017. Tokenizing, POS tagging, lemmatizing and parsing UD 2.0 with UDPipe. In *Proceedings of the CoNLL 2017 Shared Task: Multilingual Parsing from Raw Text to Universal Dependencies*. Association for Computational Linguistics.

Jörg Tiedemann. 2012. Parallel data, tools and interfaces in OPUS. In Nicoletta Calzolari (Conference Chair), Khalid Choukri, Thierry Declerck, Mehmet Ugur Dogan, Bente Maegaard, Joseph Mariani, Jan Odijk, and Stelios Piperidis, editors, *Proceedings of the Eight International Conference on Language Resources and Evaluation (LREC'12)*. European Language Resources Association (ELRA), Istanbul, Turkey.

Hui Wan, Tahira Naseem, Young-Suk Lee, Vittorio Castelli, and Miguel Ballesteros. 2018. IBM Research at the CoNLL 2018 shared task on multilingual parsing. In *Proceedings of the CoNLL 2018 Shared Task: Multilingual Parsing from Raw Text to Universal Dependencies*. Association for Computational Linguistics.

Yingting Wu, Hai Zhao, and Jia-Jun Tong. 2018. Multilingual universal dependency parsing from raw text with low-resource language enhancement. In *Proceedings of the CoNLL 2018 Shared Task: Multilingual Parsing from Raw Text to Universal Dependencies*. Association for Computational Linguistics.

Daniel Zeman, Martin Popel, Milan Straka, Jan Hajič, Joakim Nivre, Filip Ginter, Juhani Luotolahti, Sampo Pyysalo, Slav Petrov, Martin Potthast, Francis Tyers, Elena Badmaeva, Memduh Gökırmak, Anna Nedoluzhko, Silvie Cinková, Jan Hajič jr., Jaroslava Hlaváčová, Václava Kettnerová, Zdeňka Urešová, Jenna Kanerva, Stina Ojala, Anna Missilä, Christopher Manning, Sebastian Schuster, Siva Reddy, Dima Taji, Nizar Habash, Herman Leung, Marie-Catherine de Marneffe, Manuela Sanguinetti, Maria Simi, Hiroshi Kanayama, Valeria de Paiva, Kira Droganova, Héctor Martínez Alonso, Çağrı Çöltekin, Umut Sulubacak, Hans Uszkoreit, Vivien Macketanz, Aljoscha Burchardt, Kim Harris, Katrin Marheinecke, Georg Rehm, Tolga Kayadelen, Mohammed Attia, Ali Elkahky, Zhuoran Yu, Emily Pitler, Saran Lertpradit, Michael Mandl, Jesse Kirchner, Hector Fernandez Alcalde, Jana Strnadova, Esha Banerjee, Ruli Manurung, Antonio Stella, Atsuko Shimada, Sookyoung Kwak, Gustavo Mendonça, Tatiana Lando, Rattima Nitisaroj, and Josie Li. 2017. Conll 2017 shared task: Multilingual parsing from raw text to universal dependencies. In *Proceedings of the CoNLL 2017 Shared Task: Multilingual Parsing from Raw Text to Universal Dependencies*. Association for Computational Linguistics, Vancouver, Canada, pages 1–19. http://www.aclweb.org/anthology/K17-3001.

The 2018 Shared Task on Extrinsic Parser Evaluation:
On the Downstream Utility of English Universal Dependency Parsers

Murhaf Fares♣ Stephan Oepen♣, Lilja Øvrelid♣, Jari Björne♠, Richard Johansson♡

♣ University of Oslo, Department of Informatics
♠ University of Turku, Department of Future Technologies
♡ Chalmers Technical University and University of Gothenburg, Department of Computer Science and Engineering

`epe-organizers@nlpl.eu`

Abstract

We summarize empirical results and tentative conclusions from the Second Extrinsic Parser Evaluation Initiative (EPE 2018). We review the basic task setup, downstream applications involved, and end-to-end results for seventeen participating parsers. Based on both quantitative and qualitative analysis, we correlate intrinsic evaluation results at different layers of morphsyntactic analysis with observed downstream behavior.

1 Background and Motivation

The Second Extrinsic Parser Evaluation Initiative (EPE 2018) was organized as an optional track of the 2018 Shared Task on Multilingual Parsing from Raw Text to Universal Dependencies (Zeman et al., 2018) at the Conference on Computational Natural Language Learning (CoNLL 2018). In the following, we distinguish the tracks as the EPE vs. the 'core' UD parsing tasks, respectively. One focus of the UD parsing task in 2018 was on different intrinsic evaluation metrics, such that the connection to the EPE framework provides new opportunities for correlating *intrinsic* metrics with *downstream* utility to three relevant applications, viz. biological event extraction, fine-grained opinion analysis, and negation resolution. Unlike the strongly multilingual core task, the EPE framework for the time being is limited to English.

A previous instance of the EPE initiative (see § 2 below) embraced diversity and accepted submissions of parser outputs that varied along several dimensions, including different types of syntactic or semantic dependency representations, variable parser training data in type and volume, and of course diverse approaches to input segmentation and parsing. In contrast, the association of

EPE 2018 with the UD parsing task 'fixes' two of these dimensions: All submitted systems output basic Universal Dependency (UD; McDonald et al., 2013; Nivre et al., 2016) trees (following the conventions of UD version 2.x) and parser training data was limited to the English UD treebanks provided for the core task.

2 History: The EPE 2017 Infrastructure

What we somewhat interchangeably refer to as the EPE framework or the EPE infrastructure was originally assembled in mid-2017, to enable the First Shared Task on Extrinsic Parser Evaluation (EPE 2017; Oepen et al., 2017), which was organized as a joint event by the Fourth International Conference on Dependency Linguistics (DepLing 2017) and the 15th International Conference on Parsing Technologies (IWPT 2017). The framework is characterized by a collection of 'downstream' natural language 'understanding' applications that are assumed to depend on the analysis of grammatical structure. For each downstream application, there are commonly used reference data sets (often from past shared tasks) and evaluation metrics. In the EPE context, state-of-the-art systems for these applications have been generalized to accept as inputs a broad variety of syntactico-semantic dependency representations (i.e. parser outputs submitted for extrinsic evaluation) and to automatically retrain (and tune, to some degree) for each specific parser. The following paragraphs briefly summarize each of the downstream systems and main results from the EPE 2017 competition.

Dependency Representations For compatibility with different linguistic schools in syntacticosemantic analysis, the EPE framework assumes a comparatively broad definition of suitable interface

Proceedings of the CoNLL 2018 Shared Task: Multilingual Parsing from Raw Text to Universal Dependencies, pages 22–33
Brussels, Belgium, October 31 – November 1, 2018. ©2018 Association for Computational Linguistics
https://doi.org/10.18653/v1/K18-2002

representations to grammatical analysis (Oepen et al., 2017; p. 6):

> The term (bi-lexical) dependency representation in the context of EPE 2017 is interpreted as a graph whose nodes are anchored in surface lexical units, and whose edges represent labeled directed relations between two nodes. Each node corresponds to a sub-string of the underlying linguistic signal (input string), identified by character stand-off pointers. Node labels can comprise a non-recursive attribute–value matrix (or 'feature structure'), for example to encode lemma and part of speech information. Each graph can optionally designate one or more 'top' nodes, broadly interpreted as the root-level head or highest-scoping predicate (Kuhlmann and Oepen, 2016).

In principle, this notion of dependency representations is broad in that it allows nodes that do not correspond to (full) surface tokens, partial or full overlap of nodes, as well as graphs that transcend fully connected rooted trees. Participating teams in the original EPE 2017 initiative did in fact take advantage of all these degrees of freedom, whereas in connection to the 2018 UD parsing task such variation is excluded by design.

Biological Event Extraction   The Turku Event Extraction System (TEES) (Björne, 2014) is a program developed for the automated extraction of *events*, complex relations used to define the semantic structure of a sentence. These events differ from pairwise binary relations in that they have a defined trigger node, usually a verb, they can have multiple arguments, and other events can be used as event arguments, forming complex nested relations. Events can be seen as graphs, where named entities and triggers are the *nodes* and the arguments linking these are the *edges*. In this graph model, an event is implicitly defined as a trigger node and its set of outgoing edges.

The TEES system approaches event extraction as a task of graph generation, modelling it as a pipeline of consecutive, atomic classification tasks. The first step is *entity detection* where each token in the sentence is predicted as an entity node or as negative. In the second step of *edge detection*, argument edges are predicted for all valid, directed pairs of nodes. In the third, *unmerging* step, overlapping events are 'pulled apart' by duplicating trigger nodes. In the optional fourth step of *modifier detection*, binary modifiers (such as speculation or negation) can be predicted for the detected events. All of the classification steps in the TEES system rely on rich feature representations generated to a large degree from syntactic dependency parses. All classification tasks are implemented using the $SVM^{multiclass}$ classifier (Joachims, 1999).

TEES has been developed using corpora from the Biomedical Natural Language Processing (BioNLP) domain, in particular the event corpora from the BioNLP Shared Tasks. These tasks define their own annotation schemes and provide standardized evaluation services. In the context of the EPE challenge we use the BioNLP 2009 GENIA corpus and its associated evaluation program to measure the impact of different parses on event extraction performance (Kim et al., 2009). The metric used for comparing the EPE submissions is the primary 'approximate span and recursive mode' metric of the original Shared Task, a micro-averaged F_1 score for the nine event classes of the corpus.

The specialized domain language presents unique challenges for parsers not specifically optimized for this domain, so using this data set to evaluate open-domain parses may result in overall lower performance than with parsers specifically trained on e.g. the GENIA treebank (Tateisi et al., 2005). When using the EPE parse data, TEES features encompass the type and direction for the dependencies combined wit the text span and a single part of speech for the tokens; lemmas are not used.

Negation Resolution   The EPE negation resolution system is called Sherlock (Lapponi et al., 2012, 2017) and implements the perspective on negation defined by Morante and Daelemans (2012) through the creation of the Conan Doyle Negation Corpus for the Shared Task of the 2012 Joint Conference on Lexical and Computational Semantics (*SEM 2012). Negation instances are annotated as tri-partite structures: Negation *cues* can be full tokens (e.g. *not*), multi-word expressions (*by no means*), or sub-tokens (*un* in *unfortunate*); for each cue, its *scope* is defined as the possibly discontinuous sequence of (sub-)tokens affected by the negation. Additionally, a subset of in-scope tokens can be marked as negated *events* or *states*, provided that the sentence is factual and the events in question did not take place. In the EPE context, gold-standard negation cues are provided, because this sub-task has been found relatively insensitive to grammatical structure (Velldal et al., 2012).

Sherlock approaches negation resolution as a sequence labeling problem, using a Conditional Random Field (CRF) classifier (Lavergne et al., 2010). The token-wise negation annotations contain multiple layers of information. Tokens may or may not be negation cues and they can be either in or out of scope for a specific cue; in-scope tokens may or may not be negated events. Moreover, multiple negation instances may be (partially or fully) overlapping. Before presenting the CRF with the annotations, Sherlock 'flattens' all negation instances in a sentence, assigning a six-valued extended 'begin–inside–outside' labeling scheme. After classification, hierarchical (overlapping) negation structures are reconstructed using a set of post-processing heuristics.

The features of the classifier include different combinations of token-level observations, such as surface forms, part-of-speech tags, lemmas, and dependency labels. In addition, we extract both token and dependency distance to the nearest cue, together with the full shortest dependency path. Standard evaluation measures from the original shared task include scope tokens (ST), scope match (SM), event tokens (ET), and full negation (FN) F_1 scores. ST and ET are token-level scores for in-scope and negated event tokens, respectively, where a true positive is a correctly retrieved token of the relevant class (Morante and Blanco, 2012). FN is the strictest of these measures and the primary negation metric used in the EPE context—counting as true positives only perfectly retrieved full scopes, including an exact match on negated events.

Opinion Analysis The system by Johansson and Moschitti (2013) marks up expressions of opinion and emotion in a pipeline comprised of three separate classification steps, combined with end-to-end reranking; it was previously generalized and adapted for the EPE framework by Johansson (2017). The system is based on the annotation model and the annotated corpus developed in the MPQA project (Wiebe et al., 2005). The main component in this annotation scheme is the *opinion expression*; examples include case such as *dislike*, *praise*, *horrible*, or *one of a kind*. Each expression is associated with an *opinion holder*: an entity that expresses the opinion or experiences the emotion. Furthermore, every non-objective opinion expression is assigned a *polarity*: positive, negative, or neutral.

The opinion expression and polarity classifiers rely near-exclusively on token-level information, viz. n-grams comprising surface forms, lemmas,

and PoS tags. Conversely, the opinion holder extraction and reranking modules make central use of structural information, i.e. paths and topological properties in one or more syntactico-semantic dependency graph(s).

In the EPE context, we evaluated how well the participating systems extract the three types of structures mentioned above: expressions, holders, and polarities. In each case, soft-boundary precision and recall measures were computed (Johansson and Moschitti, 2013; Johansson, 2017). Furthermore, for the detailed analysis we evaluated the opinion holder extractor separately, using gold-standard opinion expressions. We refer to this task as *in-vitro holder extraction*, and this score is used for the overall ranking of submissions when averaging F_1 scores across the three EPE downstream applications. The reason for highlighting this score is that it is the one most strongly affected by the design of the dependency representation.

Participating Teams Nine teams participated in EPE 2017, in the order of overall rank: Stanford–Paris (Schuster et al., 2017), Szeged (Szántó and Farkas, 2017), Paris–Stanford (Schuster et al., 2017), Universitat Pompeu Fabra (Mille et al., 2017), East China Normal University (Ji et al., 2017), Peking (Chen et al., 2017), Prague (Straka et al., 2017), and the University of Washington (Peng et al., 2017). These teams submitted 49 distinct runs that encompassed many different families of dependency representations, various approaches to preprocessing and parsing, and variable types and volumes of training data. The dependency representations employed by the participants varied from more syntactically oriented schemes—e.g. Stanford Basic (de Marneffe et al., 2006), CoNLL 2008–style (Surdeanu et al., 2008), and UD—to more semantically oriented representations, such as the Deep Syntactic Structures of Ballesteros et al. (2015), DELPH-IN MRS Dependencies (DM; Ivanova et al., 2012), or Enju Predicate–Argument Structures (PAS; Miyao, 2006). The teams also employed wildly variable volumes of training data, ranging from around 200,000 tokens (the English UD treebanks) to 1,7 million tokens (combining the venerable Wall Street Journal, Brown, and GENIA treebanks).

Results The team with the overall best result was the Stanford–Paris system with an overall score of 60.51, followed by the Szeged (58.57) and Paris–

Stanford (56.81) teams. The Stanford–Paris system obtained the best results for event extraction (when using the Stanford Basic representation), as well as for negation resolution (with enhanced Universal Dependencies). The Szeged system was the top performer in the opinion analysis subtask and employed the 'classic' CoNLL 2008 representation. The results further showed that a larger training set had a positive impact on results for the Stanford–Paris and Prague teams, who systematically varied the amount of training data in their experimental runs. In general however, it proved difficult to compare results across different teams due to the fact that these varied along multiple dimensions: the parser (and its output quality), the representation, input preprocessing, and the volume and type of training data. In this respect, EPE 2018 controls for several of these factors (dependency representation and amount of training data) and thus enables a more straightforward comparison across teams and analysis of the relationship between intrinsic and extrinsic parser performance.

3 Refinements: Towards EPE 2018

To integrate the EPE infrastructure with the 2018 UD parsing task, a number of extensions and revisions have been realized. These included provisioning the EPE data and a basic validation tool for parser outputs on the TIRA platform (Potthast et al., 2014) as well as technical improvements in two of the downstream systems (the opinion analysis system remains unchanged from EPE 2017). In the following paragraphs, we survey some of these adaptations for the EPE 2018 setup and comment on how these revisions limit comparability to end-to-end results from the 2017 campaign.

Document Collections The EPE parser inputs are comprised of training, development, and evaluation data for the three downstream applications, in total some 1900 documents, or around 850,000 tokens of running text. Reading and parsing thousands of small files (for the opinion analysis and event extraction tasks) proved to be a bottleneck for several systems in the EPE 2017 shared task, as parsers had to reload for each input file. For the convenience of 2018 participants, we have 'packed' the original large collections of small documents into three large files—one for each downstream application. The packing scheme inserts special 'delimiter paragraphs' at document boundaries, using the following general format:

Document 0020030 ends.

To not interfere with the grammatical analysis of immediate context, each delimiter is preceded and followed by three consecutive newlines—seeking to ensure that it is treated as a four-token utterance of its own in sentence splitting and tokenization.

When preparing submitted parser outputs for end-to-end evaluation, the delimiters allowed reconstructing the original document collections and data splits for each of the three EPE data sets. Overall, we did not observe unwanted side effects of the delimiters; there are, however, a few instances where the delimiter string itself can be tokenized (and sometimes sentence-split) in unexpected ways, including by the CoNLL 2018 baseline parser, such as splitting the numerical identifier into two tokens and breaking up the delimiter string as two sentences. The EPE 2018 unpacker robustly handles such cases, effectively ignoring sentence and token boundaries in scanning parser outputs for delimiter strings, and we have no reason to believe that the delimiters have negatively affected the parsing systems of participants.

Biological Event Extraction The TEES system used in the EPE 2018 task is largely unchanged from the 2017 version. However, the training and evaluation setup has been revised in order to achieve optimal performance when evaluating the submitted parses.

The BioNLP 2009 Shared Task, which serves as the EPE event extraction application, consists of three subtasks (Kim et al., 2009). Subtask 1 is the core task which defines a number of event types to extract. Subtask 2 extends the first with the addition of non-protein entities and secondary event arguments. Subtask 3 adds speculation and negation modifiers in the form of binary attributes to be predicted for each event. Thus, subtasks 1 and 2 define the event graph, and subtask 1 annotations can be seen as subgraphs of subtask 2.

In earlier versions of the TEES system, subtask evaluation was linked to subtask training, so that when the system was trained using subtask 1 annotations it was also evaluated for the same subtask. However, TEES generally achieves better performance on subtask 1 when trained on subtask 2 (or 3) annotations. We speculate this might be caused by the machine learning system trying to predict at least some edges for the 'gaps' left by not including subtask 2 annotations.

In the version of TEES updated for EPE 2018,

evaluation has been decoupled from training data selection, so it is now possible to evaluate the system for the primary subtask 1 while still training on the full subtask 2 graphs. The end result is higher (and hopefully more stable) performance when evaluating the submitted parses, but unfortunately the EPE 2018 event extraction downstream task results are therefore not fully comparable with the 2017 ones.

Negation Resolution   The Sherlock system used in the EPE 2018 task differs from the one used in EPE 2017 in two ways. First, we fixed a bug in the 2017 system related to a limited, but important, 'leak' of gold-standard annotations into system predictions. This leak was a side effect of the (legitimate) use of gold-standard information for negation cues, where the presence of multi-word cues (such as *neither ... nor* or *by no means*) could lead to the injection of gold-standard scope and event annotations in post-processing after classification, effectively overwriting actual system predictions under certain conditions.

The second difference between the 2017 and 2018 versions of Sherlock pertains to automated hyper-parameter tuning. The two main components in the Sherlock pipeline are two CRF classifiers, one for scope and one for event tokens. Sherlock in 2017 used the default hyper-parameters in the Wapiti implementation, i.e. unlike the other two EPE downstream systems it lacked the ability to automatically tune for each specific set of parser outputs. In EPE 2018, we introduced a comprehensive hyper-parameter grid search over the development set to identify the best-performing values for each system individually. Specifically, we optimized the L1 and L2 regularization hyper-parameters as well as the stopping threshold in Wapiti for both the scope and negated event classifiers. Briefly, the grid search starts with training Sherlock using all possible combinations of a broad range of candidate values along these six dimensions, leading to a total of some 6400 configurations trained using different hyper-parameter settings. These systems are then sorted in two consecutive steps that reflect the pipelined architecture of Sherlock: First, we rank the configurations based on their scope resolution scores on the development set and choose the best-performing hyper-parameters for the scope classifier among the n systems whose score falls within an experimentally defined range below the top-ranking system. Then, we re-rank this subset

of n systems based on their full negation score on the development set and again select the best-performing hyper-parameters from among an experimentally defined range below the the best system. To mitigate the risk of overfitting, in both stages, the choice of the best-performing hyper-parameters is based a simple 'voting' scheme, picking hyper-parameter values that are most common in the top n configurations. This tuning process was applied separately to all parser outputs submitted to EPE 2018.

Overall, the corrected version of Sherlock combined with automated hyper-parameter tuning leads to a more robust and systematic evaluation on the downstream application of negation resolution. While this also means that the EPE 2018 results on negation resolution are not strictly compatible to the earlier 2017 campaign, it appears that the two Sherlock revisions offset each other at least when averaging over all submissions: the bug fix caused a drop in full negation scores of close to two F_1 points, but hyper-parameter tuning regained that performance loss to an accuracy of one decimal point (on average).

4   Task Overview

To minimize technical barriers to entry, the EPE parser inputs were installed on the TIRA platform alongside the data sets for the core UD parsing task, using the exact same general formats. The EPE document collections were provided as either 'raw', running text, or in pre-segmented form, with sentence and token boundaries predicted by the UDPipe baseline system of the core task. Parser outputs were collected in CoNLL-U format (again, for parallelism with the core task) and were then transferred from TIRA to the cluster that actually runs the EPE infrastructure. Here, all submissions were 'unpacked' (see § 3 above) and converted to the general EPE dependency graph format. Further details on the task schedule, technical infrastructure, submitted parser outputs, and end-to-end results are available from the task web site:

`http://epe.nlpl.eu`

Participating Teams   Sixteen teams participated in the EPE 2018 campaign, in addition to the baseline parser provided by the core UD parsing task; we refer to the summary paper for the core task for a high-level characterization of participating

Team	Words		Sentences		Lemmas		UPOS		XPOS		LAS		MLAS		BLEX		Intrinsic
	$\langle\rangle$	#	$\langle\rangle$	#	$\langle\rangle$	#	$\langle\rangle$	#	$\langle\rangle$	#	$\langle\rangle$	#	$\langle\rangle$	#	$\langle\rangle$	#	#
AntNLP	99.62	3	84.44	6	95.39	5	93.93	10	92.86	5	81.93	5	70.61	8	73.38	7	8
ArmParser	99.58	14	18.71	16	89.93	13	90.30	16	57.42	13	60.52	16	44.89	16	52.17	13	16
Baseline	99.62	3	84.44	6	95.39	5	93.93	10	92.86	5	76.33	13	65.86	13	67.43	11	11
IBM-NY	99.44	16	84.44	6	75.24	16	93.37	15	22.51	15	77.72	12	46.68	15	47.83	15	15
ICS-PAS	99.62	3	84.44	6	96.13	3	95.50	5	92.86	5	83.00	2	73.45	1	75.63	2	3
LATTICE-18	99.62	3	84.44	6	95.39	5	96.41	1	92.86	5	84.67	1	72.93	3	76.57	1	2
NLP-Cube	99.64	1	85.49	2	93.61	12	95.37	7	94.535	3	81.67	6	71.02	7	70.77	8	7
ONLP-lab	99.62	3	84.44	6	76.61	14	93.93	10	0.0525	16	65.92	15	57.01	14	46.32	16	13
ParisNLP-18	99.62	3	84.44	6	95.39	5	93.93	10	92.86	5	78.70	11	67.31	10	70.59	10	10
Phoenix	99.46	15	84.69	5	95.15	11	93.90	14	92.825	12	76.28	14	66.47	12	67.41	12	14
SLT-Interactions	99.62	3	84.44	6	95.39	5	95.86	2	92.86	5	81.51	8	69.91	9	73.44	6	5
SParse	0.00	17	0.00	17	0.00	17	0.00	17	0.00	17	0.00	17	0.00	17	0.00	17	17
Stanford-18	99.64	2	87.77	1	95.96	4	95.82	4	95.13	2	82.06	4	73.04	2	74.99	4	1
TurkuNLP-18	99.62	3	84.44	6	96.50	1	94.91	8	94.3	4	82.44	3	72.52	5	75.26	3	4
UDPipe-Future	99.59	13	84.81	4	96.43	2	95.86	3	95.195	1	81.64	7	72.56	4	74.81	5	6
Uppsala-18	99.62	12	85.44	3	75.40	15	95.41	6	22.52	14	81.37	9	71.34	6	50.46	14	12
UniMelb	99.62	3	84.44	6	95.39	5	94.68	9	92.86	5	79.19	10	66.95	11	70.77	9	9

Table 1: Summary of a selection of intrinsic evaluation scores from the core UD parsing task on English treebanks only. Columns labeled $\langle\rangle$ and # indicate the macro-averaged F_1 of each metric over the four English treebanks and the corresponding ranking of each team, respectively. The metrics are, from left to right: word and sentence segmentation; lemmatization; coarse and fine-grained parts of speech (UPOS and XPOS, respectively); labeled attachment score (LAS); morphology-aware labeled attachment score (MLAS); bi-lexical dependency score (BLEX); and finally an aggregate 'intrinsic' score, reflecting the average of ranks of each team. Teams shown in bold are included in the correlation analysis to intrinsic measures in § 5.

approaches and bibliographic references to individual system descriptions (Zeman et al., 2018). The names of all participants are shown in Table 1. Most teams submitted only one run with the exception of NLP-Cube (three runs) and SParse (four); in these cases, all runs have been scored, but only the most recent submission was considered for the final evaluation and comparison with intrinsic measures.

We conducted a post-submission survey among participants, to gauge the comparability of the parsing systems submitted to the core UD parsing task vs. those used for parsing the EPE data, e.g. software versions, training regimes, or other configuration options.[1] Twelve teams responded to the survey, and hence the following details only apply to those who responded. Almost all participants used (parts of) the English training data provided by the UD parsing shared task (which is the only training data allowed in EPE 2018), except for the UniMelb team who accidentally used their own UD conversions of the WSJ and GENIA treebanks. Therefore, UniMelb was excluded from the competition, but we report their scores as an additional point of comparison. Of all the systems that used 'legitimate'

training data, only LATTICE used different training data for their EPE submission than in their core task system. Two of the survey respondents—NLP-Cube and SParse—indicated that they had made changes to their systems that render the EPE and core task results incomparable. The four teams that did not respond to the survey and the four teams for which the survey revealed limited comparability to core task results (i.e. UniMelb, LATTICE, NLP-Cube, and SParse; shown in italics in Tables 1 and 2) were not considered in our quantitative correlation analysis between intrinsic and extrinsic metrics (see § 5 below). Finally, only four of the survey respondents (NLP-Cube, Phoenix, UDPipe-Future, and Uppsala-18) indicated that their parsers had used raw texts as inputs, i.e. applied their own sentence and token segmentation. The other eight respondents, in contrast, had availed themselves of the pre-segmented inputs provided as an alternative form of the EPE parser inputs.

Intrinsic Metrics In our view, one of the most intriguing opportunities of aligning EPE 2018 with the core UD parsing task lies in the comparison of intrinsic and extrinsic evaluation results. In other words, we seek to shed light on the degrees to which observations made in intrinsic evaluation allow one to predict downstream success for a specific application, as well as on which (intrinsically measurable) layers of grammatical analysis most directly impact end-to-end performance. For these

---

[1]To not interfere with the busy final weeks of the core task, the EPE submission deadline was two weeks later. Hence, we could not technically enforce that the exact same software configurations were used in both component tasks, and in fact at least two teams had to resort to revising their parsers in order to complete processing of the comparatively large EPE input files.

reasons, we extracted a comprehensive array of intrinsic evaluation results for parsers represented in EPE 2018 from the in-depth result summary for the core UD parsing task.[2]

Table 1 summarizes our selection of intrinsic observations, where the first six metrics seek to isolate performance at all relevant layers of grammatical analysis, viz. word and sentence segmentation, lexical analysis (lemmatization and tagging), and syntactic structure (labeled attachment scores, or LAS). The table further includes the other two official metrics of the core task, which by design blend together some of these layers, i.e. morphology-aware labeled attachment score and bi-lexical dependency score, which evaluate LAS plus tagging and morphological features[3] and LAS plus lemmatization, respectively.

In all cases, the results in Table 1 reflect (macro-averaged) performance over the English UD treebanks only. Several of the best-performing systems across all languages of the core task also submitted to EPE 2018, including ICS-PAS, LATTICE, Stanford, TurkuNLP-18, and UDPipe-Future. These systems also populate the top ranks in the aggregate English-only intrinsic evaluation, even though there is some 'jitter' in their relative ranks across individual metrics. In a few cases, the results in Table 1 actually reveal system idiosyncrasies: IBM-NY and Uppsala-18 do not predict XPOS values, whereas the XPOS field in the ONLP-lab parser outputs merely contains a copy of the coarse-grained UPOS predictions. The nine parsers that started from pre-segmented EPE documents all tie for third and sixth rank in sentence splitting and tokenization, respectively.

5   Official Results

End-to-end extrinsic evaluation results for the EPE 2018 campaign are summarized in Table 2.[4] For each of the three downstream applications, the table shows precision, recall, and F_1 scores on the corresponding EPE evaluation set. Additionally, we indicate for each application whether coarse- or fine-grained parts of speech were used (see below)

and provide an aggregate ranking of participating teams based on macro-averaged F_1 scores.

The parser that gives rise to overall best downstream results across the three EPE applications is UDPipe-Future, even though it is not the top performer for any of the individual applications. Differences in average scores for the best-performing systems are small, however, with less than 0.4 F_1 points between the first and the fifth overall rank. Many of the best-performing systems when judged in terms of extrinsic results correspond to what one might have predicted from our summary of English-only intrinsic results (see § 4 above): in addition to UDPipe-Future, also SLT-Interactions, Stanford, and TurkuNLP-18 are in the intersection of the top-five intrinsic and extrinsic ranks. The system that ranks second in the extrinsic perspective (NLP-Cube), on the other hand, indicated in our participant survey that they had made changes to the parser inbetween their submissions to the core vs. the EPE tasks.

If one ranks systems individually for each downstream application and compares across each row, the majority of teams appear to obtain broadly comparable rankings on different applications. Nevertheless, there are a few notable exceptions. ArmParser achieves the best results on negation resolution but otherwise ranks in the bottom segment on event extraction and opinion analysis. Manual inspection of the parser outputs submitted reveals that ArmParser zealously over-segments (as is also evident in its low intrinsic score on sentence splitting in Table 1): it breaks the 1089 sentences of the gold-standard negation evaluation data into a little more than two thousand isolated token sequences. While the EPE infrastructure deals robustly with segmentation mismatches, this discrepancy uncovers a technical issue in our way of interfacing to the original *SEM 2012 scorer: the 'annotation projection' described by Lapponi et al. (2017) will present the scorer with shortened and, hence, simplified gold standards to compare to. In other words, the high negation scores for ArmParser indicate an unwarranted reward for its dealing in artificially short 'sentences'.

Another stark asymmetry in per-application ranks pertains to TurkuNLP-18, which shows top results on negation resolution and opinion analysis but ranks in the bottom quarter on the event extraction application (which happens to be developed at the same site). While the unexpectedly

---

[2]Intrinsic results were automatically scraped from the official http://universaldependencies.org/conll18/results.html page.

[3]None of the current EPE downstream systems actually considers morphological features, although the EPE interface format does in principle provide for their representation.

[4]A multitude of additional scores, including against the development sections for each downstream application, are available from the task web site at http://epe.nlpl.eu.

Team	Event Extraction				Negation Resolution				Opinion Analysis				$\langle\rangle$	#
	PoS	P	R	F_1	PoS	P	R	F_1	PoS	P	R	F_1		
AntNLP	U	54.00	44.97	49.07	X	100	39.54	56.67	X	64.37	55.76	59.76	55.17	10
ArmParser	U	53.76	39.28	45.39	X	99.12	42.75	**59.74**	X	60.13	51.65	55.57	53.57	15
Baseline	U	39.63	53.43	45.51	X	100	40.30	57.45	X	61.67	55.95	58.67	53.88	13
IBM-NY	U	53.08	43.81	48.00	U	100	39.16	56.28	U	62.03	56.03	58.88	54.39	12
ICS-PAS	U	56.41	43.97	49.42	X	100	39.54	56.67	X	63.73	57.67	60.55	55.55	6
LATTICE-18	X	58.93	43.12	**49.80**	X	100	39.16	56.28	X	63.91	56.88	60.19	55.42	9
NLP-Cube	U	56.54	42.65	48.62	X	100	40.15	57.30	X	64.95	59.24	61.96	55.96	3
ONLP-lab	U	54.08	41.67	47.07	U	100	36.88	53.89	U	62.94	56.37	59.47	53.48	16
ParisNLP-18	X	55.66	43.56	48.87	X	100	40.68	57.83	X	63.01	56.78	59.73	55.48	8
Phoenix	U	47.23	40.98	43.88	X	100	41.06	58.22	X	63.16	55.87	59.29	53.80	14
SLT-Interactions	X	56.32	43.97	49.38	X	100	41.06	58.22	U	65.47	56.56	60.69	56.10	2
SParse	X	50.62	41.04	45.33	X	100	40.30	57.45	X	63.44	57.94	60.57	54.45	11
Stanford-18	U	59.26	41.14	48.56	X	100	41.29	58.45	X	63.33	57.68	60.37	55.80	5
TurkuNLP-18	U	52.64	42.05	46.75	X	100	42.59	**59.74**	X	64.23	58.26	61.10	55.86	4
UDPipe-Future	U	53.97	45.98	49.66	X	100	41.29	58.45	X	63.47	57.72	60.46	56.19	1
Uppsala-18	U	58.04	43.43	49.68	U	100	36.74	53.74	U	64.67	61.68	**63.14**	55.52	7
UniMelb	X	58.52	49.43	53.59	X	100	41.83	58.99	X	66.67	62.88	64.72	59.10	

Table 2: Summary of EPE 2018 results. The columns show, from left to right: team name, PoS tags used (UPOS or XPOS), precision, recall, and F_1 across the three downstream applications, average F_1 across applications, and finally the overall rank of each team. The best F_1 score for each downstream task is indicated in bold. The UniMelb submission is considered outside the competition due to the use of additional training data; teams shown in bold are included in the correlation analysis to intrinsic measures in § 5.

low performance in the combination of the Turku parser with the Turku event extraction system reassuringly indicates that there was no collusion in Finland, we have so far been unable to form a hypothesis about what might be the cause for this performance discrepancy. Conversely, Uppsala-18 is among the top performers for event extraction and opinion analysis but obtains the lowest F_1 results on negation resolution in the EPE 2018 field. The Uppsala parser is one of the few that does not predict fine-grained parts of speech, which the Sherlock negation system appears to strongly prefer over the far more coarse-grained UPOS tags (see below). We conjecture that the lack of XPOS predictions in the Uppsala-18 parser outputs is at least an important factor in the uncharacteristically poor negation results for this system.

UPOS vs. XPOS   Recall that the EPE 2018 infrastructure automatically retrains and tunes each downstream system for each system submission. An additional aspect in which the downstream systems could be optimized towards a particular parser is, of course, feature engineering and selection. For full generality and applicability across different types of syntactico-semantic dependency representations, the current EPE applications restrict themselves to a range of broad token-level and structural features that do not invoke individual linguistic configurations (e.g. indicators of passive voice)— including conjunctions of individual features that

have been clearly observed to be beneficial (see § 2 above and references there). All three downstream systems employ 'vintage' classifiers (CRFs and SVMs) for which regularization techniques and best practices are well established, such that one can hope for a certain degree of feature selection during training.

Reflecting availability of two distinct assignments of parts of speech in all but a few of the EPE 2018 submissions, we conducted one round of feature adaptation in the downstream systems, viz. determining whether to use the coarse-grained, universal UPOS or the finer-grained, English-specific XPOS values for each combination of parser outputs and downstream system. This selection was based on optimizing the primary metric for each application on the development data, and the results are indicated in the three PoS columns in Table 2.

XPOS appears to work better in general, possibly reflecting that it makes available additional distinctions, including some inflectional morphology.[5] There are a few notable exceptions to this generalization, however, and they appear application-dependent to some degree. In particular the event extraction system often obtains better results when using UPOS, whereas for negation resolution

---

[5] Reflecting the above design constraints and desire for cross-framework applicability, the EPE downstream systems do not currently consider the morphological features that are increasingly an integral part of the Universal Dependencies framework.

XPOS (where available) universally yields higher end-to-end scores, and UPOS is only used with the three systems that do not predict fine-grained tags. Almost the same holds for the opinion analysis application, with the one exception of the SLT-Interactions submission, whose UPOS predictions actually yield better results (though the actual differences are small). Based on these observations, one might expect Uppsala-18 (which only predicts UPOS) to be at a disadvantage for opinion analysis too, but other factors in this combination appear more important (as Uppsala-18 actually obtains the best overall opinion results).

Correlation Analysis To obtain a better understanding of the relationships between intrinsic and extrinsic perspectives on parser performance, we perform a quantitative correlation analysis over pairs of evaluation metrics. We compute a rank correlation matrix of intrinsic and extrinsic measures, limited to the sub-set of nine systems which are known to be fully comparable across intrinsic and extrinsic evaluation, i.e. where there were no substantive changes to the parsers following the completion of the core UD parsing task. We further limit our analysis to the intrinsic evaluation metrics pertaining to English (see Table 1), combined with the downstream per-application F_1 scores and an average rank score called *extrinsic* in the following, which aggregates the average rank of each system across the three downstream applications. Figure 1 shows a heatmap of Spearman's rank correlation coefficients (ρ) for all pairs of intrinsic and extrinsic metrics.

In general, we observe high degrees of correlation among intrinsic measures, albeit less so for the segmentation metrics, in particular sentence segmentation.[6] We find the strongest correlations between the intrinsic average and the BLEX measure (0.98), XPOS and lemmas (0.96), BLEX and lemmas (0.93), and UPOS and MLAS (0.92). Further, BLEX correlates stronger with the average intrinsic metric than LAS and MLAS, so if one were to search for a single, indicative intrinsic measure, BLEX might offer a combined indicator across analysis layers. We note that the correlation scores pertaining to XPOS must be interpreted with some care, given that two of the systems involved (IBM-

---

[6]Only one third of the systems considered in the correlation matrix actually apply their own sentence splitting and tokenization (see § 4 above). Accordingly, the corresponding metrics are bound to exhibit far less interesting variation in the correlation analysis.

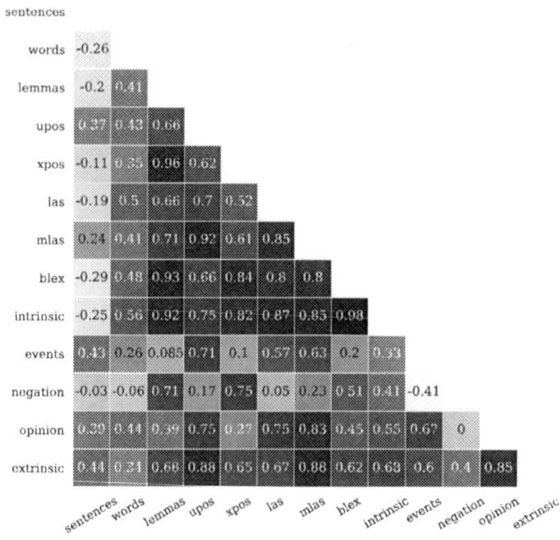

Figure 1: Correlation matrix of intrinsic and extrinsic metrics.

NY and Uppsala-18) do not predict XPOS, so that their ranks according to this metric will not correspond to their performance on other metrics.

If we examine the correlation between intrinsic and extrinsic metrics, we also observe some strong correlations—which is of course a very welcome observation. In particular, we find a strong correlation between the average extrinsic metric and the intrinsic UPOS and MLAS metrics (0.88). The correlation with UPOS is perhaps somewhat surprising as UPOS is not used by the majority of systems. Still, it appears that the ability to correctly predict universal PoS tags provides a useful indicator of downstream parser performance. We further observe strong to moderate correlations between the individual intrinsic metrics and the overall extrinsic average.

When examining per-application correlations to intrinsic performance we find that each of the individual downstream metrics shows a correlation with the intrinsic average, but for all three less so than the extrinsic average. While seemingly counter-intuitive, maybe, we interpret this as indicative of a certain degree of complementarity among the three downstream applications. Taken together, they lead to better correspondences with intrinsic metrics, an observation which holds also true for several of the individual intrinsic metrics, viz. UPOS, MLAS, and BLEX. This is in accordance with the observation in the results overview above: there is no parser to suit all needs, such that in principle at least it would make sense to pick a different parser for each of the three downstream applications.

Downstream results obtained by the different parsers for the event extraction application, correlate most strongly with the UPOS metric (0.71), followed by LAS (0.63) and MLAS (0.57). This fits well with the observation that most of the top-scoring systems in the event task actually make use of UPOS (see above). The event extraction application does not use lemmas among its features, hence it shows no observable correlation to this particular intrinsic metric. For the negation application, on the other hand, the strongest correlation is with the XPOS metric (0.75), followed by lemmas (0.71) and BLEX (0.51). XPOS seems to be the favoured PoS choice for this task (see Table 2), so this again is in line with the most effective type of PoS for the majority of systems.

When it comes to the opinion analysis application, its rankings correlate most strongly with the intrinsic ranking of parsers by MLAS (0.83), followed by LAS and UPOS (both 0.75). It thus seems that this application depends more strongly on a syntactic or structural metric such as MLAS, in comparison to the other downstream applications. We also find that the opinion scores somewhat surprisingly correlate more with UPOS (0.75) than XPOS (0.27), which does not obviously follow from the best-performing choice of tag set. We leave further investigation of the relative importance of PoS tagging to the EPE opinion analysis system to future work (see § 6 below).

Comparison to 2017 Owing to the updates in downstream systems summarized in § 3 above, the end-to-end scores in Table 2 are not strictly comparable to results from the EPE 2017 campaign (Oepen et al., 2017). Nevertheless, we believe that a 'ballpark' comparison can be informative.[7] The best-performing parser in 2017 enabled end-to-end scores of 50.23, 66.16, and 65.14 F_1 points on event extraction, negation resolution, and opinion analysis, respectively. This was the Stanford–Paris submission (run #06), outputting enhanced UD graphs and trained on about 1.7 million tokens of annotated text from the Brown, WSJ, and GE-

NIA corpora (Schuster et al., 2017). In contrast, the overall best parser in the EPE 2018 field delivers F_1 results of 49.66, 58.45, and 56.19 (UDPipe-Future). Taking into account that event scores in 2017 may have been slightly under-estimated, negation scores moderately inflated, and opinion scores fully comparable—it seems fair to say that the 'pure' English UD parsers from the EPE 2018 campaign do not facilitate the same high levels of downstream performance. In the 2017 campaign, end-to-end results for the event extraction application were very competitive, and those for negation resolution advanced the state of the art. This is not the case in the 2018 field, which we tentatively attribute to the limited volume of English training data, the strict 'treeness' assumptions in most current dependency parsers, and quite possibly the inability of the EPE downstream applications to take advantage of the UD morphological features.

6 Reflections and Outlook

In our view, the considerable effort for both participants and organizers of running an additional track at the 2018 CoNLL Shared Task on Universal Dependency Parsing is rewarded through (a) a valuable, complementary perspective on the contrastive evaluation of different parsing systems, as well as through (b) a window of comparison to the state of the art in three representative language 'understanding' applications. From a sufficiently high level of abstraction, we see many reassuring correspondences between intrinsic parser evaluation and actual downstream utility. At the same time, we find that not even a comprehensive 'battery' of layered intrinsic metrics can fully inform the relative comparison of different parsers with regard to their contributions to downstream performance.

In hindsight, we would have liked to obtain an even tigher experimental setup, without any remaining uncertainty about comparability of participating systems across the two tracks. If we were to run another EPE campaign (unlikely as that may feel just now), the EPE data bundles should also include relevant test data for intrinsic evaluation. In more immediate follow-up work, we plan to re-compute and publish end-to-end results for the submissions from the EPE 2017 campaign, for full comparability, as well as further investigate the relative contributions of individual analysis layers to the various downstream applications through additional control experiments and ablation studies.

---

[7] In addition to the parameters suggested for such comparison in § 3 above, we find this belief supported by alignment of results for the one system that participated in both EPE campaigns in very similar configurations: the Prague submission (run #00) in 2017 (Straka et al., 2017) corresponds closely to the 2018 UDPipe baseline. F_1 results for the three downstream applications in 2017 were 43.58, 58.83, and 59.79—compared to 2018 scores of 45.51, 57.45, and 58.67.

Acknowledgments

This work was in large parts conducted while the second and third authors were fellows in residence of the Center for Advanced Studies (CAS) at the Norwegian Academy of Science and Letters. The EPE 2018 campaign was in part funded by the Nordic e-Infrastructure Collaboration (NeIC) through their support to the Nordic Language Processing Laboratory (NLPL; `http://www.nlpl.eu`). We are grateful to our NLPL and CAS colleagues and to the Nordic tax payers. Dan Zeman, Martin Potthast, Jan Hajič, and Milan Straka have been exceptionally helpful on behalf of the organizing team for the core UD parsing task. We gratefully acknowledge the support by Sophia Ananiadou and Matthew Shardlow with our using the BioNLP 2009 evaluation data. We thank Joakim Nivre and Erik Velldal for their contributions to the overall task design and result analysis.

References

Miguel Ballesteros, Bernd Bohnet, Simon Mille, and Leo Wanner. 2015. Data-driven deep-syntactic dependency parsing. *Natural Language Engineering* 22:1–36.

Jari Björne. 2014. *Biomedical Event Extraction with Machine Learning*. Ph.D. thesis, University of Turku, Turku, Finland.

Yufei Chen, Junjie Cao, Weiwei Sun, and Xiaojun Wan. 2017. Peking at EPE 2017: A comparison of tree approximation, transition-based, and maximum subgraph models for semantic dependency analysis. In *Proceedings of the 2017 Shared Task on Extrinsic Parser Evaluation at the Fourth International Conference on Dependency Linguistics and the 15th International Conference on Parsing Technologies*. Pisa, Italy, page 60–64.

Marie-Catherine de Marneffe, Bill MacCartney, and Christopher D. Manning. 2006. Generating typed dependency parses from phrase structure parses. In *Proceedings of the 5th International Conference on Language Resources and Evaluation*. Genoa, Italy, page 449–454.

Angelina Ivanova, Stephan Oepen, Lilja Øvrelid, and Dan Flickinger. 2012. Who did what to whom? A contrastive study of syntacto-semantic dependencies. In *Proceedings of the 6th Linguistic Annotation Workshop*. Jeju, Republic of Korea, page 2–11.

Tao Ji, Yuekun Yao, Qi Zheng, Yuanbin Wu, and Man Lan. 2017. ECNU at EPE 2017: Universal dependencies representations parser. In *Proceedings of the 2017 Shared Task on Extrinsic Parser Evaluation at the Fourth International Conference on Dependency*

Linguistics and the 15th International Conference on Parsing Technologies. Pisa, Italy, page 40–46.

Thorsten Joachims. 1999. Making large-scale SVM learning practical. In Bernhard Schölkopf, Christopher J. C. Burges, and Alexander J. Smola, editors, *Advances in Kernel Methods. Support Vector Learning*, MIT Press, Cambridge, MA, USA, page 41–56.

Richard Johansson. 2017. EPE 2017: The Trento–Gothenburg opinion extraction system. In *Proceedings of the 2017 Shared Task on Extrinsic Parser Evaluation at the Fourth International Conference on Dependency Linguistics and the 15th International Conference on Parsing Technologies*. Pisa, Italy, page 31–39.

Richard Johansson and Alessandro Moschitti. 2013. Relational features in fine-grained opinion analysis. *Computational Linguistics* 39(3):473–509.

Jin-Dong Kim, Tomoko Ohta, Sampo Pyysalo, Yoshinobu Kano, and Jun'ichi Tsujii. 2009. Overview of BioNLP'09 Shared Task on event extraction. In *Proceedings of the Workshop on Current Trends in Biomedical Natural Language Processing. Shared Task*. Boulder, CO, USA, page 1–9.

Marco Kuhlmann and Stephan Oepen. 2016. Towards a catalogue of linguistic graph banks. *Computational Linguistics* 42(4):819–827.

Emanuele Lapponi, Stephan Oepen, and Lilja Øvrelid. 2017. EPE 2017: The Sherlock negation resolution downstream application. In *Proceedings of the 2017 Shared Task on Extrinsic Parser Evaluation at the Fourth International Conference on Dependency Linguistics and the 15th International Conference on Parsing Technologies*. Pisa, Italy, page 25–30.

Emanuele Lapponi, Erik Velldal, Lilja Øvrelid, and Jonathon Read. 2012. UiO2. Sequence-labeling negation using dependency features. In *Proceedings of the 1st Joint Conference on Lexical and Computational Semantics*. Montréal, Canada, page 319–327.

Thomas Lavergne, Olivier Cappé, and François Yvon. 2010. Practical very large scale CRFs. In *Proceedings of the 48th Meeting of the Association for Computational Linguistics*. Uppsala, Sweden, page 504–513.

Ryan McDonald, Joakim Nivre, Yvonne Quirmbach-Brundage, Yoav Goldberg, Dipanjan Das, Kuzman Ganchev, Keith Hall, Slav Petrov, Hao Zhang, and Oscar Täckström. 2013. Universal dependency annotation for multilingual parsing. In *Proceedings of the 51th Meeting of the Association for Computational Linguistics*. Sofia, Bulgaria, page 92–97.

Simon Mille, Roberto Carlini, Ivan Latorre, and Leo Wanner. 2017. UPF at EPE 2017: Transduction-based deep analysis. In *Proceedings of the 2017 Shared Task on Extrinsic Parser Evaluation at the Fourth International Conference on Dependency*

Linguistics and the 15th International Conference on Parsing Technologies. Pisa, Italy, page 76 – 84.

Yusuke Miyao. 2006. *From Linguistic Theory to Syntactic Analysis. Corpus-Oriented Grammar Development and Feature Forest Model.* Doctoral dissertation, University of Tokyo, Tokyo, Japan.

Roser Morante and Eduardo Blanco. 2012. *SEM 2012 Shared Task. Resolving the scope and focus of negation. In *Proceedings of the 1st Joint Conference on Lexical and Computational Semantics*. Montréal, Canada, page 265 – 274.

Roser Morante and Walter Daelemans. 2012. ConanDoyle-neg. Annotation of negation in Conan Doyle stories. In *Proceedings of the 8th International Conference on Language Resources and Evaluation*. Istanbul, Turkey, page 1563 – 1568.

Joakim Nivre, Marie-Catherine de Marneffe, Filip Ginter, Yoav Goldberg, Jan Hajič, Christopher D. Manning, Ryan McDonald, Slav Petrov, Sampo Pyysalo, Natalia Silveira, Reut Tsarfaty, and Daniel Zeman. 2016. Universal Dependencies v1. A multilingual treebank collection. In *Proceedings of the 10th International Conference on Language Resources and Evaluation*. Portorož, Slovenia, page 1659 – 1666.

Stephan Oepen, Lilja Øvrelid, Jari Björne, Richard Johansson, Emanuele Lapponi, Filip Ginter, and Erik Velldal. 2017. The 2017 Shared Task on Extrinsic Parser Evaluation. Towards a reusable community infrastructure. In *Proceedings of the 2017 Shared Task on Extrinsic Parser Evaluation at the Fourth International Conference on Dependency Linguistics and the 15th International Conference on Parsing Technologies*. Pisa, Italy, page 1 – 16.

Hao Peng, Sam Thomson, and Noah A. Smith. 2017. Deep multitask learning for semantic dependency parsing. In *Proceedings of the 55th Meeting of the Association for Computational Linguistics*. Vancouver, Canada, page 2037 – 2048.

Martin Potthast, Tim Gollub, Francisco Rangel, Paolo Rosso, Efstathios Stamatatos, and Benno Stein. 2014. Improving the reproducibility of PAN's shared tasks. Plagiarism detection, author identification, and author profiling. In Evangelos Kanoulas, Mihai Lupu, Paul Clough, Mark Sanderson, Mark Hall, Allan Hanbury, and Elaine Toms, editors, *Information Access Evaluation meets Multilinguality, Multimodality, and Visualization. 5th International Conference of the CLEF Initiative*. Springer, Berlin, Germany, page 268 – 299.

Sebastian Schuster, Eric De La Clergerie, Marie Candito, Benoît Sagot, Christopher D. Manning, and Djamé Seddah. 2017. Paris and Stanford at EPE 2017: Downstream evaluation of graph-based dependency representations. In *Proceedings of the 2017 Shared Task on Extrinsic Parser Evaluation at the Fourth International Conference on Dependency Linguistics and the 15th International Conference on Parsing Technologies*. Pisa, Italy, page 47 – 59.

Milan Straka, Jana Straková, and Jan Hajič. 2017. Prague at EPE 2017: The UDPipe system. In *Proceedings of the 2017 Shared Task on Extrinsic Parser Evaluation at the Fourth International Conference on Dependency Linguistics and the 15th International Conference on Parsing Technologies*. Pisa, Italy, page 65 – 74.

Mihai Surdeanu, Richard Johansson, Adam Meyers, Lluís Màrquez, and Joakim Nivre. 2008. The CoNLL 2008 Shared Task on Joint Parsing of Syntactic and Semantic Dependencies. In *Proceedings of the 12th Conference on Natural Language Learning*. Manchester, UK, page 159 – 177.

Zsolt Szántó and Richárd Farkas. 2017. Szeged at EPE 2017: First experiments in a generalized syntactic parsing framework. In *Proceedings of the 2017 Shared Task on Extrinsic Parser Evaluation at the Fourth International Conference on Dependency Linguistics and the 15th International Conference on Parsing Technologies*. Pisa, Italy, page 75 – 79.

Yuka Tateisi, Akane Yakushiji, Tomoko Ohta, and Jun'ichi Tsujii. 2005. Syntax annotation for the GENIA corpus. In *Proceedings of the 2nd International Joint Conference on Natural Language Processing. Companion Volume*. Jeju, Korea.

Erik Velldal, Lilja Øvrelid, Jonathon Read, and Stephan Oepen. 2012. Speculation and negation: Rules, rankers, and the role of syntax. *Computational Linguistics* 38(2):369 – 410.

Janyce Wiebe, Theresa Wilson, and Claire Cardie. 2005. Annotating expressions of opinions and emotions in language. *Language Resources and Evaluation* 39(2-3):165 – 210.

Daniel Zeman, Jan Hajič, Martin Popel, Martin Potthast, Milan Straka, Filip Ginter, Joakim Nivre, and Slav Petrov. 2018. CoNLL 2018 Shared Task. Multilingual Parsing from Raw Text to Universal Dependencies. In *Proceedings of the CoNLL 2018 Shared Task: Multilingual Parsing from Raw Text to Universal Dependencies*. Brussels, Belgium, page 1 – 20.

CEA LIST : Processing low-resource languages for CoNLL 2018 Shared Task

Elie Duthoo   **Olivier Mesnard**
CEA, LIST, Laboratory of Vision and Content Engineering
elie.duthoo@protonmail.com
olivier.mesnard@cea.fr

Abstract

In this paper, we describe the first CEA LIST participation at the CoNLL 2018 shared task. The submitted system is based on the state of the art parser from CoNLL 2017, that has been improved by the addition of morphological features predictions and the integration of additional resources to provide accurate models for low-resource languages. Our approach ranked 5th of 27 participants in MLAS for building morphology aware dependency trees, 2nd for morphological features only, and 3rd for tagging (UPOS) and parsing (LAS) low-resource languages.

1 Introduction

The CoNLL 2018 Shared Task (Zeman et al., 2018) is dedicated to developing dependency parsers on many languages, including low-resource languages. Our system uses the Stanford team parser[1] (Dozat et al., 2017) which was at the state of the art during the CoNLL 2017 shared task. We will refer to it as "stf parser" in this article. We also used UDPipe (Straka et al., 2016) for tokenization, sentence segmentation, word alignment, lemmas and XPOS tags. Our main purpose is not to propose a new parser system, our approach is mainly focused on the adaptation of existing systems to low-resources languages.

However, we also propose some improvements of the stf parser on multiple levels: (1) the training time is shorter and the models are more accurate for features and XPOS tags predictions (even if we didn't use the predicted XPOS tags in the final submission) (2) we studied the hyper-parameters in order to find the best configuration (3) we im-

plemented an optimal tree construction instead of a greedy one, based on Stanford team recommendations in their 2017 paper.

We spent five man-month to provide these results, with two additional man-month dedicated to Breton corpus.

For low-resource languages, we based our approach on the following available data : OPUS corpus, Wikipedia data (Wiktionary) and word embeddings.

2 Architecture

Our architecture mainly reused the proposed architecture of the 2017 state of the art system. Here is a brief reminder to explain what we used and how we used it. The model uses character embeddings, pre-trained word embeddings and post-trained word embeddings.

- Firstly, the raw text is processed by UDPipe.
- Then the stf tagger annotates the data with UPOS, XPOS and Features tags. Both the tagger and the parser use bi-LSTM layers on word embeddings. The tagger and the parser are separately trained models even if the models structures are really close.
- Finally, for each word, the parser concatenates one word level embedding (which is the sum of chars + pre-trained + trained embeddings) with one POS tag level embedding (UPOS + XPOS + features). POS tag embeddings are also learned during the training. We didn't use lemmas. The stf parser is graph-based.

We only used XPOS tags where they were contributing to the UPOS, XPOS, features trio. We evaluated this contribution by comparing the number of unique XPOS tags per corpus to the number of unique features. Some XPOS tags contains multiple tag information (which is almost always

---

[1] https://github.com/tdozat/Parser-v2

Proceedings of the CoNLL 2018 Shared Task: Multilingual Parsing from Raw Text to Universal Dependencies, pages 34–44
Brussels, Belgium, October 31 – November 1, 2018. ©2018 Association for Computational Linguistics
https://doi.org/10.18653/v1/K18-2003

the case for the features) and could thus contribute more to the word embedding. For almost all languages, the parser is based on three bi-LSTM layers (300neurons/layer) and the tagger on two bi-LSTM layers(200neurons/layer). The tagger ends with a 120 neurons lReLU layer. The parser ends with a 500 neurons lReLU layer for learning arc probabilities, and a 170 neurons lReLU layer for predicting the labels of the dependencies. For languages with less than 1500 sentences, we used a parser composed of only one bi-LSTM layer and smaller lReLU layers.

We only kept the best system evaluated on dev data for each language on each of the last two steps. Our measure for the tagger was the combination of UPOS and Features annotations (like Alltags without XPOS), if UDPipe was better than stf, we used UDPipe. Our measure for the parser was the LAS. For the evaluation, the predicted XPOS tags were removed from the parsed file and changed to the UDPipe ones, however the predicted XPOS were used by the parser when they were predicted by the tagger. We didn't evaluate the XPOS tags as we needed to sort the sub-XPOS tags (these sub-POS tags are sorted in alphabetical order for features which is really more convenient). The problem was only that we had to sort the sub-XPOS tags in order to have a score on them, but sorting them is not required to have them used in the parser.

A table has been produced to summarize the configuration (cf table 1).

3 Enhancements

3.1 Features

The initial architecture provided by Stanford team was restricted to predicting UPOS tags only, or UPOS tags and XPOS tags. We added a third type of tagger to predict UPOS tags, XPOS tags and morphological features at the same time.

As we said earlier, the tagger takes into account characters by using a LSTM on each character and using a linear attention layer on the LSTM outputs, so we did expect great results on features. However, POS tags are heterogeneously formatted: the UPOS tag represents only one information, but a feature tag generally contains many sub-tags, and XPOS tags may also contain sub-tags depending on the treebank. The original architecture didn't tackle this problem and was processing all tags as if they were unary tags.

It means, for example, that for Latin-ITTB, the tagger ended with a lReLU layer that was choosing the best class between 3129 classes.

We added a lReLU layer for each sub-class at the end of the network so that the backpropagation only backpropagates error on a subclass level, thus being more accurate when building character embeddings. This architecture was extended to XPOS tags, as they may also contains subclasses. Finally the score that was used to stop the training and keep the best model was the "UPOS and Features" score, counting a word ok only if it had the exact UPOS tag and the exact features tags.

To sum up, for each sub-category (for example, the tense of a verb), a different lReLU layer determines if the word corresponds to one of the sub-category possible values (*none*, *present*, *future*, *past*..).

3.2 Hyperparameters

In order to understand the impact of the parameters on the architecture, we performed some random search optimization on hyperparameters, for a subset of languages (Russian, Hebrew, French, Uyghur, Vietnamese, Ancient Greek and Bulgarian) that we considered representative. We studied the following parameters: dropout on word embeddings, dropout on character embeddings, word embeddings merging strategy (whether to sum or concatenate the word embedding coming from characters and the pre/post trained word embeddings), case sensitivity, number of bi-LSTM layers, number of neurons for bi-LSTM, lReLU layers sizes, lReLU layers dropout, and some optimizer parameters like the learning rate.

- **number of bi-LSTM** The number of bi-LSTM layers deeply affects the score probably because of the vanishing gradient problem. Best scores were achieved for one to three bi-LSTM. With four layers, some models fail to converge and with five layers, no converging model is found.
- **dropout** For dropout on character embeddings, we found that is wasn't useful (initial value was 0.5 (50%) but optimal value was between 0 and 0.1). Other dropout did not have a clear influence.
- **learning rate** The learning rate was tuned based on the model (tagger / parser) as the optimal value wasn't the same depending on the task and

Lang	Tokenizer	Tagger	XPOS	Parser	Smaller neural network
af-afribooms	baseline	stf	used	stf	yes
br-keb	nl-alpino	stf	unused	stf	no
bxr-bdt	baseline	udp	unused	udp	no
en-lines	baseline	stf	used	stf	no
fo-oft	da-ddt	stf	unused	stf	no
fr-spoken	baseline	stf	unused	stf	yes
ga-idt	baseline	udp	unused	udp	yes
gl-ctg	baseline	stf	used	stf	no
gl-treegal	baseline	udp	unused	udp	no
hsb-ufal	baseline	udp	unused	udp	no
hu-szeged	baseline	stf	unused	stf	yes
hy-armtdp	baseline	udp	unused	stf	yes
kk-ktb	baseline	udp	unused	udp	no
kmr-mg	baseline	udp	unused	udp	no
ko-gsd	baseline	stf	used	stf	no
ko-kaist	baseline	stf	used	stf	no
la-ittb	baseline	stf	used	stf	no
la-perseus	baseline	udp	unused	udp	no
nl-alpino	baseline	stf	used	stf	no
nl-lassysmall	baseline	stf	used	stf	no
no-nynorsklia	baseline	udp	unused	no-nynorsk	no
pcm-nsc	en-lines	stf	unused	stf	no
ru-taiga	baseline	udp	unused	ru-syntagrus	no
sl-sst	baseline	udp	unused	udp	no
sme-giella	baseline	udp	unused	udp	no
th-pud	own	stf	used	stf	no
vi-vtb	baseline	stf	used	stf	yes
zh-gsd	baseline	stf	used	stf	no
all others	baseline	stf	unused	stf	no

Other models used

cs-pud & cs-pdt, sv-pud & sv-lines, fi-pud & fi-tdt, ja-modern & ja-gsd (udp), en-pud & en-gum

| pcm-nsc | en-lines (stf without post-trained embeddings) |

Table 1: Summary table of specific configurations per languages. udp = UDPipe architecture

both tasks didn't have the same optimal architecture.

- **other parameters** Other parameters did not have a clear empirical influence on the score, such as the number of neurons on each layer (from 50 to 500) and other parameters of the optimizer.

3.3 Stopping criteria

Depending on the model (tagger/parser), the stopping criteria was based on UPOSandFeats score or LAS. The first thing we did with the parser was to improve the training time. The previous algorithm stopped the training only if the model didn't improve at all for 5000 iterations (which could correspond to 2 hours on our environment), or after a maximum number of iterations. This means that the training would go on even for an improvement of 0.01% each hour. In practice, with this config-

uration, the longest model took 24 hours to train. We added two stopping criteria:

- The first is the time, the training time shouldn't exceed 2 hours. The training time depends on the architecture so we chose the value depending on our experiments

- The second is the average progression of the system per hour during the last 20 validations (we set one validation each 120 iteration). If the system was under 0.1% per hour, we stopped the training.

With these criteria, almost all models are converging really fast (in 30 minutes they were already close by 1% to their best score).

3.4 Optimal directed spanning tree

The graph-based model parser predicts a probability of parent for each word of the sentence. The default algorithm in the stf parser is greedy but the Stanford team recommended to implement an optimal algorithm to provide non-projective dependency trees as a lot of treebanks contains at least one non-projective tree.

In fact, 99% of all trees are projectives (non-weighted average across all proportions in all treebanks). But building the optimal non-projective spanning tree based on probabilities should also help in building projective trees (as projective trees are a subset of non-projective trees), and some treebanks contain a lot more of non-projective trees (10% for Ancient Greek Perseus).

We implemented the Chu-Liu-Edmonds algorithm (Edmonds, 1967) and evaluated the result. We didn't notice a great improvement (less than 0.1%), we suppose that the probabilities were high enough so that a greedy algorithm doesn't have troubles predicting the optimal tree by always choosing the highest probability.

Empirically, the stf parser does build more nonprojective trees than in the training set, one could consider implementing the Eisner algorithm (Eisner, 1996) and make a compromise between Edmonds and Eisner algorithms based on the probabilities in each tree and on the non-projective proportion wished.

3.5 Including an embedding from the tagger in the parser

In the stf parser, the tagger and the parser are separated. The parser builds its own UPOS tag embeddings but do not take into account the probabilities of each tag proposed by the tagger. The fact that one word has one tag instead of another could be subjective in some circumstances and as the tagger doesn't get 100% in UPOS tag prediction, the parser should get the information that the tag it is reading is just a choice over many others, based on probabilities.

For some languages like French, the tagger could confuse verbs and auxiliaries. For these tags, the probability could be something like 70% verb and 30% auxiliary, and the tagger will label the word as a "verb". Making a mistake on which word is a verb and which one is an auxiliary affects the dependency tree. We therefore extracted these probabilities from the tagger to introduce them in the parser.

This experiment didn't show a clear improvement in the results. We think that the parser has trouble learning from these probabilities because they are almost always at one (the tagger rarely makes mistakes). Maybe one could improve the system by

not adding the probabilities directly but the output of the layer before the softmax. This improvement was not included in the final submission.

4 Cross-lingual transfer for low-resource languages

The rest of our work was focused on cross-lingual transfer methods and data mining to address the problem of low-resource languages. The main idea of our models is to build an artificial treebank on which we could learn a tagger / parser. As exposed by (Tiedemann and Agić, 2016), many techniques may be used to build artificial treebanks. They identified mainly 1) model transfer (for example, building a delexicalized parser from a rich-resource language and using it directly on a target language corpus annotated beforehand with POS tags), 2) direct annotation projection (relying on word alignments of a bitext to project POS annotation), 3) treebank translation and 4) cross-lingual word embeddings. The use of partial annotations with dictionary may complete these four techniques. We relied on quality of available data to choose the best suited technique. Our analysis started on all low-resource languages but we applied our process to only 3 languages: Breton, Faroese and Thai because of the lack of valuable data for others[2]. Extending the capacities of our models is certainly doable but a lot of regularization on data should be done. We present a summary of our choices in table 2.

4.1 Breton

Breton treebank has been built with direct annotation projection (Tiedemann and Agić, 2016). There were neither training nor evaluation treebank for Breton. Breton is member of Celtic language family but no large treebank exists in this family (Irish_IDT is a 1020 only sentences corpus). We decided to use the most valuable and available resources for Breton: Wiktionary, word embeddings from Facebook[3], combined as in Wisniewski et al. (2014) with cross-lingual projection from a larger parallel corpus to build our own artificial learning corpus.

We selected OfisPublik from OPUS (Tiedemann, 2009) site as parallel corpus for cross lingual

---

[2]We also had results on Upper Sorbian but failed to submit the model.

[3]https://git.io/fbjDv

Role	Breton	Thai	Faroese
Tokenization	model transfer	dictionary	model transfer
POS	annotation projection+Wiktionary	annotation projection+Wiktionary	model transfer (*)
Dependencies	annotation projection	model transfer (*)	model transfer (*)

Table 2: choices made to build our artificial treebanks for low-resource languages (*) with cross-lingual embeddings

transfer. This corpus is composed of more than 60.000 sentences dumped from a bilingual institutional site about Breton language[4].

We proceeded as follow:

Statistics on parse tree: We computed some statistics on Irish treebank: the counts of occurrences of all types of arc, indexed by triples (head UPOS, dependency UPOS, arc label) to setup a prior distribution probability.

Lexicon: We built a lexicon of form-category from the most recent brwiktionary dump (20/05/2018). We obtain 26650 entries with mostly one category. When there are more than one category, we preserved the order, assessing that the most frequent category is the first mentioned in Wiktionary. Using links to other Wiktionaries we manually translated the 53 categories into UPOS tag.

Parallel corpus: We filtered the parallel corpus and excluded some sentences: those with less than 3 words (br or fr), those with more than 30 words (br or fr) and those whose ratio of size of original sentence upon translated sentence is not in the range [1/3,3].

Tokenization: We used UDPipe with Dutch model to tokenize the Breton side of the parallel corpus. We chose Dutch because it preserves "c'h" sequence of character which is the transcript of a very frequent consonant in Breton.

Word Alignment: We built a word alignment of the tokenized parallel corpus with efmaral[5]. We used forward and reverse alignment and combined them with *atools* from fastalign[6] with *grow-diag-final-and* mode.

Annotation: We used UDPipe to annotate the French side corpus with baseline UDPipe model for French.

POS tagging: We have performed UPOS annotation within four steps.

1. Use our lexicon to annotate supposedly non ambiguous tokens with word type: when the form of a token has an entry with only one category, the value is used as UPOS.
2. Use our lexicon to annotate ambiguous tokens with hypotheses of word type : when a form has an entry with more than one category, the set of values is associated to the token within the *upos_lexicon* attribute.
3. Used bre2fre alignment to collect hypotheses of token type: when a token is in the bre2fre mapping, we collect the UPOS of all tokens in French side within the *upos_alignment* attribute
4. Intersect *upos_alignment* and *upos_lexicon* to select most likely UPOS.

At the end of the process, sentences without complete POS tagging are discarded.

Lemma: We have not built any specific solution for lemmatisation and we reproduce the form as value for lemma.

Features: We have projected features from the French side. Because there is no features in our lexicon, features comes only from cross-lingual projection. At the end of first pass we collect all features annotation and we add this data to our lexicon. Then, we use this enhanced lexicon as source to annotate tokens with features when this information exists in the lexicon.

Head and label: We walk through French dependency tree starting from root node, and use alignment fre2bre to project dependency annotation (arc and label) when structures of French and Breton seem to be the same. We initialize a stack with the pair (root of French tree, root of Breton tree), the second member is chosen as the word aligned with root of French tree.

As long as the stack is not empty:

- pop a pair (*fre_head*, *bre_head*)
- get *fre_child*ren from *fre_head* and get UPOS from each *fre_child*
- for each *bre_node* in fre2bre alignment of each *fre_child*
- if many conditions are met (there is only one *bre_node* aligned with *fre_child*, *fre_child* and *bre_node* have same POS, there is only one word aligned with *fre_head*) we simply project head

[4]http://www.fr.brezhoneg.bzh
[5]https://github.com/robertostling/efmaral
[6]https://github.com/clab/fast_align

and label, i.e. head of *bre_node* is *bre_head*, label is label of arc (*fre_child*, *fre_head*).

- when such conditions are not met, we create hypothesis of dependency with most likely pair of nodes: *bre_node* with *bre_head* but also with all siblings of *bre_node*. We use statistics to associate a probability to each of these hypotheses.
- add to stack (*fre_child*, *bre_node*)

Finally, we build the parse tree with Chu-Edmonds algorithm from the set of hypotheses.

Learning and prediction: We use this artificial treebank to learn the UDPipe tagger and the stf parser. We use the UDPipe tokenizer with Dutch model to preprocess the raw test text.

Evaluation: Because no evaluation data exists, we relied on another language pair (French-German) to experiment the cross-lingual projection process. We build a lexicon from dewiktionary with a mapping from Wiktionary tags to UPOS tags. We select the 15.000 most frequent forms in German based on word embeddings order. We use PUD_French and PUD_German treebanks as parallel corpus. We get a F1 measure of 72% on UPOS on and 28% on LAS which let us hope similar results with French-Breton pair. These figures are not far from our official results 75% in UPOS and 38% in LAS.

4.2 Faroese, Thai, and all other low-resource languages

We started by exploring all the data we had available for the shared task: Wikipedia, word embeddings and parallel corpus, to build a low-resource language strategy.

We used cross-lingual word representations for building lexicalized taggers and parsers through model transfer and annotation projection for tag disambiguation.

4.2.1 Tokenizing Thai

The Thai language agglutinates a lot of words so it can't be tokenized with spaces. Dictionary Based Longest Matching yielded good enough results (Haruechaiyasak et al., 2008), so we built a dictionary for Thai based on all words from the embeddings and the Wiktionary. Then we tokenized the opus Thai corpus with dictionary, and learned an UDPipe model on it to facilitate the integration of the model in the final submission.

However, we didn't know how to define the end of each sentence in Thai, knowing that UDPipe won't define an end based on words or on sentences lengths. We tried to build our own tokenizer based on word embeddings, sentence lengths, word lengths and eventually a dictionary to improve the "only character embedding based" model. Even if we lacked the time to finalize this contribution, we did manage to reach a f1 score close to UDPipe with random forest classifier on English LinES corpus (-0.2% tokens, -5% sentences). The tokenization score for Thai is 64.17%.

4.2.2 Building word alignment on sentences and a bilingual dictionary with OPUS

We used efmaral (Östling and Tiedemann, 2016) to get word alignment on OPUS. As we needed to be extremely confident on the built alignments, the null-prior parameter was set to 0.95 (it doesn't stop the word aligner from making mistakes on some words).

The dictionary was built based on aligned words.

4.2.3 Tagging Thai

Three sources of information are available for tagging without annotated data:

- OPUS : tagging a rich-resource language and transferring tags to the low-resource language
- Embeddings alignment : aligning embeddings from one embedding cloud to another. Then using the source tagger on the aligned embeddings
- Data mining : parsing the Wiktionary to find the possible tags of each word

We can combine these methods to do disambiguation. The Thai language was tagged by using the same method as Breton. We extracted a list of each possible tags (UPOS) from the Wiktionary. Then we used annotated parallel corpus from Korean to disambiguate Thai tags. We weren't aware of a close enough language to Thai so we were only able to transfer from a distant language.

4.2.4 Embeddings alignment : tagging and parsing Faroese

For Faroese, the Wiktionary data didn't seem to be workable (no UPOS tag / not enough words) and no OPUS data were available. We thus used the only available source of informations : embeddings. We built a supervised cross-lingual embedding mapper that could work in an unsupervised way by using similar tokens between languages (when languages are close enough). The mapper is not limited by the number of word or the size of the embedding contrary to MUSE (Lample et al., 2017). We found out that the HIT team had a similar approach in 2015 (Guo et al., 2015).

The Faroese language is close to three other languages : Danish, Norwegian and Swedish. The strategy was to build a bilingual tagger and a bilingual lexicalized parser for Swedish-Norwegian, evaluate our approach on Danish and export it on Faroese. All embeddings (Swedish, Danish and Faroese) were aligned in the Norwegian embedding cloud. The architecture used was the Stanford one, we only used gold and aligned embeddings (pretrained) and character embeddings (no post-trained embeddings as they are highly language dependent and based on word's form and not word's embedding position in the cloud).

The algorithm of the mapper is described in Algorithm 1: it uses the built bilingual dictionary (1,n) to (1,n) and all tokens of common form in embeddings as input, as well as the embeddings of the two languages.

Then, each embedding of the source language is aligned with the embeddings of the target language. The general case is the 1 to n relation, for which the source token is assigned an average of each of the n tokens in the target language. So if we have a 1 to 1 relation, the source token embedding is equal to the target token embedding. The dictionary was filtered by removing entries with cardinality above 4.

For words that are not in the dictionary, we use the n-closest embeddings in the source cloud which are in the dictionary. Each of these tokens has an alignment in the target cloud, so we do a weighted average of their aligned embeddings in the target cloud based on their distance in the source cloud to find the embedding of the token which is not in the dictionary.

This approach could be enhanced by taking into account the direction to go from each of the word in the source cloud to the target cloud, and averaging these informations to locate the unknown point in the target cloud (algorithm 1).

At this point we have cross-lingual embeddings. Building a bilingual corpus should help to reduce the bias of a monolingual model as well as learning with both original (Norwegian) and potentially biased aligned (Swedish) embeddings. We built a corpus based on UD ones (Nivre et al., 2017), merging the same number of sentences from Norwegian and Swedish into one file.We then trained a

Data: Source embeddings;
target embeddings;
dictionaries (opus + similar words)
Result: source aligned with target
init: define n closest words parameter;
for *each source embedding s of token ts* **do**
    let e be the embedding of ts in target;
    if *ts in dictionary* **then**
        ss = target words for ts in dic;
        es = embeddings of ss;
        e = avg(es);
    else
        cs = closest n word embeddings to s
          which are in dic;
        es = embeddings of the n closest word
          in target;
        e = weighted_avg(es, dist(cs,s));

Algorithm 1: Close-points embedding alignment algorithm; the n parameter was set to 5

bilingual tagger and parser on this corpus without post-trained embeddings and evaluated it (cf table 3). SVNO : Swedish+Norwegian. DA : Danish. FO : Faroese.

We then used this bilingual model on Faroese Wikipedia sentences to have a treebank, annotating it by using aligned Faroese embeddings, and we trained a Faroese model on this treebank with original embeddings, hoping it could fix some inconsistencies coming from the alignment as the final model will use regularizations on original Facebook embeddings. In the end, we have a Faroese tagger and a Faroese parser.

4.2.5 Other languages

The method described in the previous section has been tested on other languages but did not produce results significantly better than the baseline. Not counting Thai, Faroese and Breton, there are 6 low-resource languages:

- For Buryat and Kurmanji we didn't find a close enough language to do unsupervised embedding alignment as no parallel corpus / Wiktionary were available.
- For Kazakh, we tried to build a Turkish-Russian model, ending with around 50% in UPOS.
- For Armenian, we tried a Persian-Greek model but we had troubles handling the character embeddings (Armenian characters aren't the same), ending with 23% in UPOS (and if you

Scores	SVNO score	No-transfer score
UPOS SV	93%	96%
UPOS DA	74%	97%
Feats SV	85%	92%
Feats DA	50%	97%
LAS SV	74%	83%
LAS DA	48%	84%
LAS SVNO	85%	
UPOS FO	64%	
Feats FO	34%	
LAS FO	47%	

Table 3: SVNO models results, compared to stf model trained on monolingual gold data.

don't include character embeddings, you can't distinguish some proper noun from numbers).

- For Naija, no data (OPUS/embedding/Wiktionary) was found, so we used English models.
- Finally for Upper Sorbian we had better results with a Polish-Czech model, ending with 75% UPOS and 37% LAS (evaluated on the 23 available sentences as we don't need training sentences), but we lacked of time to upload the model and finalize our contribution to the task.

We tried to use embeddings alignment from MUSE on Upper Sorbian, but it didn't provide results as there wasn't enough Upper Sorbian embeddings.

5 Training

For the final submission, we trained around 190 models (including bilingual ones) which took 3 days on 3 GPU NVIDIA 1080 Ti. We did this full training 4 times, each time changing a parameter: whether to include language specific dependency annotation in the training, case-sensitive parser or to change the tokenization used (reference tokenization or UDPipe tokenization as validation set). The submitted result was the best model out of the four runs.

6 Results

We'll only detail some results. A summary table for low-resource languages we worked on has been produced (cf table 4).

We got some good ranks on the total average, but these scores were deeply affected by our rank in low-resource languages. For example, getting +64 points in Thai (with just a dictionary approach based on known words) is the same as getting 0.8 points on each other treebanks which is far more harder.

Still, we ranked 2nd in morphological features, showing that the stf architecture was able to handle morphological informations.

We ranked 2nd in tokenization (low-resource and global) because of our work on the Thai language (the 5 teams that got more than the baseline in Thai ended up in the top 5 on the global tokenization score). However our score for Thai tokenization (64%) is far more bellow other scores for tokenizing Thai in literature, based on other corpus which weren't available for this shared task.

We also ranked 3rd in UPOS (low-resource and global). We think that learning morphological features during the training help a model to get better results in UPOS as it could use the embeddings learned with morphological features to predict UPOS tags as well.

For big treebanks, we ranked 5th in UPOS probably because we took the SOTA and improved it. We also stand below TurkuNLP for morphological features on big treebanks (93.68% for 93.82%), they also used the biLSTM architecture but they inferred tags without sub-categories.

Finally we ranked 5th in MLAS which seems to be the more representative score overall as it evaluates morphology and dependency as a whole, and it doesn't give much importance to low-resource languages because a cumulative low score in UPOS and LAS results in a close to 0 MLAS.

A summary table can be found at the end of the article.

7 Conclusion

Our multilingual model seems to produce great results by enabling the production of a lexicalized parser for low-resource languages. This could

Lang	Tokens			UPOS			LAS		
	Base	Our	Best	Base	Our	Best	Base	Our	Best
Thai	8.56	64.17	69.93	5.86	31.46	39.42	0.70	0.47	13.70
Faroese	99.51	99.03	99.51	44.66	63.53	65.54	25.19	47.17	49.43
Breton	92.26	92.50	94.49	30.74	75.39	85.01	10.25	**38.64**	38.64

Table 4: Summary score table for 3 low-resource languages

open the road to an universal parser (as long as we have embeddings and a dictionary for a language) with improved performance over the mixed model provided for the shared task.

However, multiple steps are required in order to achieve a unique model. First, one should merge the tagger and the parser into one unique model, by learning the parser with representation learned by the tagger, and by eventually allowing the tagger to complete POS tags based on dependency learned embeddings.

Our transfer methods should be evaluated more carefully. Because we didn't have much time, we didn't find a way to evaluate our embeddings mapper in an other way than through the UPOS and dependency scores of our bilingual models.

Multiple strategies are still available from our work: how to select the best languages for transfer? How much languages should be used? How does these parameters change from one low-resource language to another ? etc.

Finally, to build an universal parser, we should distinguish multiple embeddings. The post-trained embeddings should be divided in two categories, the universal post-trained embeddings which changes the pretrained embeddings values based on their position into the embeddings cloud; and the language specific post-trained embeddings which should be based on the form and the language of the token. Including pretrained character embeddings and post-trained character embeddings could also help for languages with specific characters, for which we could at least map punctuations and numbers characters for tagging.

References

Timothy Dozat, Peng Qi, and Christoper Manning. 2017. Stanford's graph-based neural dependency parser at the conll 2017 shared task pages 20–30.

Jack Edmonds. 1967. Optimum branching. In *Journal of Research of the national Bureau of Standards B71(4)*. pages 233–240.

Jason Eisner. 1996. Three new probabilistic models for dependency parsing: An exploration. In *Proceedings of the 16th International Conference on Computational Linguistics*. http://aclweb.org/anthology/C96-1058.

Jiang Guo, Wanxiang Che, David Yarowsky, Haifeng Wang, and Ting Liu. 2015. Cross-lingual dependency parsing based on distributed representations. In *Proceedings of the 53rd Annual Meeting of the Association for Computational Linguistics and the 7th International Joint Conference on Natural Language Processing (Volume 1: Long Papers)*. Association for Computational Linguistics, pages 1234–1244. https://doi.org/10.3115/v1/P15-1119.

Choochart Haruechaiyasak, Sarawoot Kongyoung, and Matthew Dailey. 2008. A comparative study on thai word segmentation approaches 1:125 – 128.

Guillaume Lample, Alexis Conneau, Ludovic Denoyer, and Marc'Aurelio Ranzato. 2017. Unsupervised machine translation using monolingual corpora only. *arXiv preprint arXiv:1711.00043* .

Joakim Nivre et al. 2017. Universal Dependencies 2.0. LINDAT/CLARIN digital library at the Institute of Formal and Applied Linguistics, Charles University, Prague, http://hdl.handle.net/11234/1-1983. http://hdl.handle.net/11234/1-1983.

Robert Östling and Jörg Tiedemann. 2016. Efficient word alignment with Markov Chain Monte Carlo. *Prague Bulletin of Mathematical Linguistics* 106:125–146. http://ufal.mff.cuni.cz/pbml/106/art-ostling-tiedemann.pdf.

Milan Straka, Jan Hajič, and Jana Straková. 2016. UDPipe: trainable pipeline for processing CoNLL-U files performing tokenization, morphological analysis, POS tagging and parsing. In *Proceedings of the 10th International Conference on Language Resources and Evaluation (LREC 2016)*. European Language Resources Association, Portoro, Slovenia.

Jörg Tiedemann. 2009. News from OPUS - A collection of multilingual parallel corpora with tools and interfaces. In N. Nicolov, K. Bontcheva, G. Angelova, and R. Mitkov, editors, *Recent Advances in Natural Language Processing*, John Benjamins, Amsterdam/Philadelphia, Borovets, Bulgaria, volume V, pages 237–248.

Jörg Tiedemann and Zeljko Agić. 2016. Synthetic tree-
banking for cross-lingual dependency parsing. *Journal of Artificial Intelligence Research* 55:209–248.

Guillaume Wisniewski, Nicolas Pcheux, Souhir
Gahbiche-braham, François Yvon, and Université Paris Sud. 2014. Cross-lingual part-of-speech
tagging through ambiguous learning. In *In Proceedings of the 2014 Conference on Empirical Methods
in Natural Language Processing*. pages 1779–1785.

Daniel Zeman, Jan Hajič, Martin Popel, Martin Potthast, Milan Straka, Filip Ginter, Joakim Nivre, and
Slav Petrov. 2018. CoNLL 2018 Shared Task: Multilingual Parsing from Raw Text to Universal Dependencies. In *Proceedings of the CoNLL 2018
Shared Task: Multilingual Parsing from Raw Text to
Universal Dependencies*. Association for Computational Linguistics, Brussels, Belgium, pages 1–20.

	tokens	upos	ufeats	las	mlas
af_afribooms	99.75 (5)	97.24 (7)	96.91 (3)	84.16 (7)	73.15 (4)
ar_padt	99.98 (2)	90.35 (7)	86.93 (6)	71.84 (8)	62.17 (5)
bg_btb	99.92 (4)	98.72 (4)	97.38 (4)	89.59 (5)	82.55 (3)
br_keb	92.5 (2)	75.39 (2)	43.55 (3)	38.64 (1)	4.15 (3)
bxr_bdt	97.07 (4)	41.66 (8)	38.34 (3)	12.61 (11)	2.09 (5)
ca_ancora	99.97 (5)	98.49 (7)	97.75 (7)	90.22 (6)	82.09 (6)
cs_cac	99.97 (7)	98.83 (9)	93.8 (6)	89.55 (10)	79.92 (6)
cs_fictree	99.97 (6)	98.4 (6)	95.57 (4)	91.22 (4)	81.87 (3)
cs_pdt	99.93 (5)	98.44 (12)	92.75 (8)	89.06 (11)	78.63 (10)
cs_pud	99.28 (4)	96.86 (4)	90.43 (7)	84.89 (3)	71.65 (7)
cu_proiel	100 (1)	96.09 (3)	89.98 (1)	73.13 (5)	61.79 (4)
da_ddt	99.87 (4)	97.38 (4)	96.7 (5)	83.69 (3)	75.27 (4)
de_gsd	99.58 (4)	93.42 (10)	89.3 (4)	78.19 (4)	56.18 (4)
el_gdt	99.86 (4)	97.64 (4)	94.56 (2)	88.18 (6)	76.44 (3)
en_ewt	99.03 (5)	95.01 (7)	95.55 (6)	82.88 (4)	74.46 (4)
en_gum	99.75 (3)	95.07 (7)	95.97 (4)	81.47 (6)	70.59 (5)
en_lines	99.95 (3)	96.47 (8)	96.49 (5)	78.61 (7)	70.05 (8)
en_pud	98.79 (24)	93.28 (24)	95.27 (3)	79.84 (15)	69.97 (13)
es_ancora	99.97 (4)	98.61 (7)	98.08 (4)	89.58 (5)	82.33 (5)
et_edt	99.91 (5)	97 (5)	95.19 (4)	83.52 (4)	75.87 (4)
eu_bdt	99.96 (6)	95.97 (5)	92.19 (3)	83.13 (2)	71.7 (2)
fa_seraji	100 (2)	97.05 (6)	97.13 (3)	86.18 (2)	80.38 (5)
fi_ftb	100 (2)	95.83 (6)	96.23 (4)	87.14 (3)	79.09 (2)
fi_pud	99.63 (4)	97.32 (5)	96.29 (6)	88.59 (5)	82.42 (3)
fi_tdt	99.69 (4)	96.53 (7)	94.78 (6)	85.99 (4)	78.59 (5)
fo_oft	99.03 (23)	63.53 (2)	33.52 (5)	47.17 (2)	0.8 (2)
fr_gsd	99.66 (7)	96.1 (9)	95.85 (4)	85.03 (8)	76.41 (8)
fr_sequoia	99.79 (5)	97.4 (9)	96.77 (6)	87.66 (7)	80.2 (4)
fr_spoken	100 (2)	95.91 (6)	100 (2)	69.83 (9)	57.88 (8)
fro_srcmf	100 (2)	95.87 (3)	97.59 (2)	86.78 (3)	79.62 (2)
ga_idt	99.3 (5)	89.21 (9)	78.79 (5)	62.93 (14)	37.66 (8)
gl_ctg	99.84 (4)	96.98 (3)	99.01 (4)	81.6 (5)	69.28 (5)
gl_treegal	99.69 (2)	91.09 (10)	89.59 (5)	66.16 (12)	49.13 (11)
got_proiel	100 (2)	95.71 (3)	88.87 (3)	68.32 (4)	54.8 (3)
grc_perseus	99.96 (5)	91.94 (5)	89.71 (6)	73.41 (4)	52.14 (5)
grc_proiel	100 (2)	96.87 (7)	91.33 (4)	75.02 (6)	58.36 (6)
he_htb	99.98 (2)	82.6 (4)	80.82 (4)	63.66 (6)	51.3 (5)
hi_hdtb	100 (2)	97.38 (7)	93.56 (4)	91.72 (3)	77.59 (4)
hr_set	99.92 (4)	97.8 (7)	89.81 (7)	86.18 (5)	70.11 (6)
hsb_ufal	98.6 (3)	65.75 (6)	49.8 (2)	23.64 (16)	3.55 (14)
hu_szeged	99.81 (3)	95.4 (3)	92.75 (1)	76.96 (6)	65.68 (4)
hy_armtdp	97.21 (4)	65.4 (8)	57.07 (2)	28.41 (7)	7.58 (7)
id_gsd	100 (2)	93.94 (1)	95.35 (6)	78.84 (3)	67.81 (3)
it_isdt	99.75 (5)	97.91 (6)	97.61 (3)	90.01 (7)	82.44 (5)
it_postwita	99.73 (3)	95.9 (4)	96 (3)	71.77 (11)	59.12 (7)
ja_gsd	90.46 (6)	88.9 (6)	90.45 (6)	74.55 (8)	61.74 (9)
ja_modern	65.98 (5)	48.44 (8)	64.11 (9)	22.71 (9)	8.1 (9)
kk_ktb	93.11 (6)	48.94 (11)	46.86 (4)	24.21 (4)	7.62 (5)
kmr_mg	94.33 (4)	59.31 (6)	48.39 (2)	23.92 (9)	5.47 (7)
ko_gsd	99.81 (6)	96.12 (4)	99.62 (5)	83.61 (3)	79.21 (3)
ko_kaist	100 (2)	95.37 (4)	100 (2)	86.41 (3)	80.48 (3)
la_ittb	99.94 (5)	97.82 (13)	95.93 (4)	85.17 (7)	77.97 (5)
la_perseus	100 (2)	83.34 (11)	72.07 (8)	47.61 (12)	30.16 (11)
la_proiel	99.99 (5)	96.69 (3)	90.7 (4)	71.07 (4)	58.79 (3)
lv_lvtb	99.4 (6)	95.17 (2)	91.29 (3)	80.29 (5)	67.27 (2)
nl_alpino	99.83 (5)	95.84 (7)	95.66 (7)	85.79 (7)	73.38 (6)
nl_lassysmall	99.82 (6)	95.93 (7)	95.59 (5)	82.17 (7)	70.9 (5)
no_bokmaal	99.78 (6)	97.85 (6)	96.19 (5)	89.73 (4)	81.96 (5)
no_nynorsk	99.93 (5)	97.72 (4)	96.3 (4)	88.97 (5)	80.55 (5)
no_nynorsklia	99.99 (2)	85.15 (12)	86.54 (6)	56.87 (10)	41.73 (9)
pcm_nsc	99.71 (1)	57.21 (2)	43.09 (2)	16.06 (9)	2.35 (20)
pl_lfg	99.86 (7)	98.54 (4)	94.67 (6)	94.62 (3)	86.26 (4)
pl_sz	99.99 (3)	98.05 (4)	92.24 (4)	91.31 (4)	80.44 (4)
pt_bosque	99.71 (2)	96.61 (3)	95.85 (2)	87.72 (2)	75.72 (2)
ro_rrt	99.67 (6)	97.47 (5)	96.75 (6)	85.9 (4)	77.7 (4)
ru_syntagrus	99.6 (7)	98.2 (9)	95.69 (6)	89.96 (11)	83.27 (6)
ru_taiga	98.14 (2)	86.53 (11)	76.01 (7)	63.85 (7)	40.9 (8)
sk_snk	100 (2)	96.61 (4)	90.89 (2)	86.38 (4)	73.44 (2)
sl_ssj	98.29 (6)	96.85 (5)	93.11 (4)	86.72 (6)	78.65 (2)
sl_sst	100 (2)	88.5 (12)	80.15 (7)	46.95 (13)	34.19 (12)
sme_giella	99.84 (3)	87.69 (7)	82.41 (5)	56.98 (14)	46.05 (10)
sr_set	99.97 (2)	98.04 (3)	93.63 (5)	87.92 (5)	76.95 (4)
sv_lines	99.96 (3)	96.74 (2)	89.18 (5)	81.46 (4)	65.84 (5)
sv_pud	98.52 (6)	92.98 (9)	73.32 (21)	76.23 (11)	42.8 (13)
sv_talbanken	99.78 (7)	97.5 (3)	96.48 (5)	85.69 (6)	78.19 (5)
th_pud	64.17 (2)	31.46 (3)	60.22 (2)	0.47 (17)	0.16 (5)
tr_imst	99.86 (3)	93.42 (5)	91.94 (1)	63.78 (4)	55 (3)
ug_udt	99.22 (7)	89.43 (1)	87.07 (2)	62.75 (8)	43.82 (4)
uk_iu	99.67 (5)	97.03 (5)	90.71 (3)	83.64 (6)	71.12 (4)
ur_udtb	100 (2)	94.12 (4)	83.53 (3)	81.89 (4)	56.85 (3)
vi_vtb	84.26 (7)	77.38 (6)	83.99 (6)	44.35 (6)	37.98 (5)
zh_gsd	89.55 (7)	85.06 (9)	88.57 (8)	65.34 (9)	55.2 (8)

Table 5: Summary table for main scores. Green: top 1, yellow: top 3, orange: top 5

Semi-Supervised Neural System for Tagging, Parsing and Lemmatization

Piotr Rybak
Institute of Computer Science,
Polish Academy of Sciences
`piotr.cezary.rybak@gmail.com`

Alina Wróblewska
Institute of Computer Science,
Polish Academy of Sciences
`alina@ipipan.waw.pl`

Abstract

This paper describes the ICS PAS system which took part in CoNLL 2018 shared task on Multilingual Parsing from Raw Text to Universal Dependencies. The system consists of jointly trained tagger, lemmatizer, and dependency parser which are based on features extracted by a biLSTM network. The system uses both fully connected and dilated convolutional neural architectures. The novelty of our approach is the use of an additional loss function, which reduces the number of cycles in the predicted dependency graphs, and the use of self-training to increase the system performance. The proposed system, i.e. ICS PAS (Warszawa), ranked 3th/4th in the official evaluation[1] obtaining the following overall results: 73.02 (LAS), 60.25 (MLAS) and 64.44 (BLEX).

1 Introduction

Most of contemporary NLP systems for machine translation, question answering, sentiment analysis, etc. operate on preprocessed texts, i.e. texts with tokenised, part-of-speech tagged, and possibly syntactically parsed sentences. Therefore, the development of high-quality pipelines of NLP tools or entire systems for language preprocessing is still an important issue. The vast majority of language preprocessing frameworks take advantage of the statistical methods, especially the supervised or semi-supervised statistical methods. Based on training data, language preprocessing tools learn to analyse sentences and to predict morphosyntactic annotations of these sentences.

The supervised methods require gold-standard training data whose creation is a time-consuming and expensive process. Nevertheless, the morphosyntactically annotated data sets are publicly available for many languages, in particular within Universal Dependencies initiative (UD, Nivre et al., 2016). The initiators of UD aim at developing a cross-linguistically consistent annotation schema and at building a large multilingual collection of sentences annotated according to this schema with the universal part-of-speech tags and the universal dependency trees.

UD treebanks are nowadays used for multilingual system development (Nivre et al., 2018). The history of developing multilingual systems dates back to 2006 and 2007, when two shared tasks on multilingual dependency parsing were organised at the Conference on Computational Natural Language Learning (CoNLL, Buchholz and Marsi, 2006; Nivre et al., 2007). After 10 years, the shared task was organised again in 2017 (Zeman et al., 2017), and currently there is its fourth edition (Zeman et al., 2018).

In this paper we describe our solution submitted to the CoNLL 2018 Universal Dependency shared task. The system and the trained models for participating treebanks are publicly available.[2] Our system takes a tokenised sentence as input. The sentence tokenisation is predicted by the baseline model (Straka and Straková, 2017).

Each word is represented both as an external word embedding and as a character-based word embedding estimated by a dilated convolutional neural network encoder (CNN, Yu and Koltun, 2016). The concatenation of these embeddings is fed to a bidirectional long short-term memory network (biLSTM, Graves and Schmidhuber, 2005; Hochreiter and Schmidhuber, 1997) which ex-

---

[1]`http://universaldependencies.org/conll18/results.html`

[2]`https://github.com/360er0/COMBO`

Proceedings of the CoNLL 2018 Shared Task: Multilingual Parsing from Raw Text to Universal Dependencies, pages 45–54
Brussels, Belgium, October 31 – November 1, 2018. ©2018 Association for Computational Linguistics
`https://doi.org/10.18653/v1/K18-2004`

tracts the final features (see Section 2.1). The tagger takes extracted features and predicts universal part-of-speech tags, language-specific tags and morphological features using three separate fully connected neural networks with one hidden layer (see Section 2.2). The lemmatizer uses a dilated CNN to predict lemmas based on characters of corresponding words and features previously extracted by a biLSTM encoder (see Section 2.3). As a scoring function, the graph-based dependency parser uses simple dot product of the vector representations of a dependent and its governor. These representations are output by two single fully connected layers which take feature vectors extracted by a biLSTM encoder as input. A novel loss function penalizes cycles, in order to reduce their number in the predicted dependency graphs (see Section 2.4.2). Chu-Liu-Edmonds algorithm (Chu and Liu, 1965; Edmonds, 1967) constructs the final dependency tree. The dependency labels are predicted with a fully connected neural network based on the dependent and its governor embeddings as well (see Section 2.4 for more details on the parser's architecture). The system architecture is schematised in Figure 1.

The whole system is end-to-end trained, separately for each treebank provided for the purposes of the shared task. The technical details of the implemented system are given in Section 3. Additionally, for 20 selected treebanks self-training is used to increase the performance of the models (see Section 3.4). The proposed technique of self-training has an impact on the quality of tagging, lemmatisation and parsing (see Section 4.3). The article ends with the presentation of the results achieved by our system (see Section 4) and some conclusions (see Section 5).

2 Architecture Overview

2.1 Feature Extraction

The system accepts an input in the form of tokenised sentences that can be annotated with additional morphosyntactic information: lemmas, part-of-speech tags, and morphological features. However, as the goal of the shared task is to predict not only dependency trees but also parts of speech, lemmas and morphological features,[3] we decide to use words as the only input.

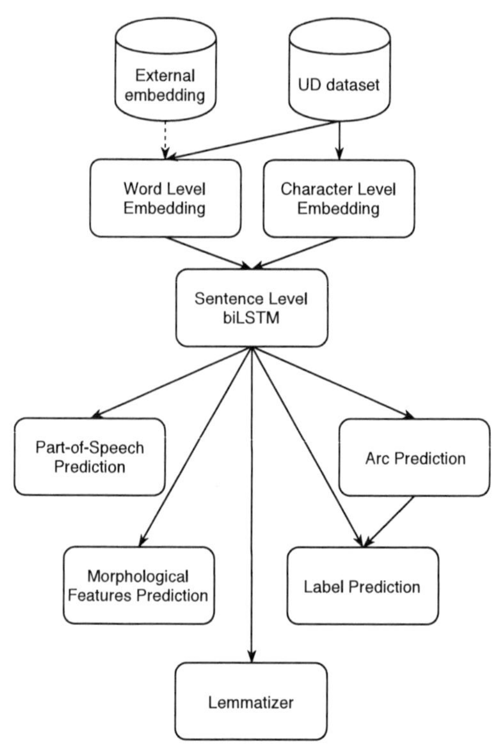

Figure 1: The schema of the system architecture.

2.1.1 Word Level Embedding

Each input word is represented as a vector using the external pre-trained embedding. Words not present in the external embedding are replaced with the "unknown" word and represented as a random vector drawn from the normal distribution with the mean and the variance calculated based on other word embedding vectors. Both the external embedding itself and the vector representing "unknown" word are fixed during the training, but they are transformed by a single fully connected layer. This transformation serves similar purpose as a trainable embedding, but helps with generalization, since it will also transform vectors for words available in the external embedding, but not in the training set.

2.1.2 Character Level Embedding

Additionally, each word is represented as the character-based word embedding extracted with a dilated convolutional neural network (CNN). We decide to use the dilated CNN instead of commonly used biLSTM encoder to speed up the training of the system.

---

[3]Not all treebanks are annotated with lemmas and morphological features.

First, each word is transformed to a sequence of the trainable character embeddings. Moreover, the special symbols "beginning-of-word" and "end-of-word" are added to the sequence to represent the beginning and the end of the word. Then the dilated CNN encoder is used. Since the encoder also outputs a sequence, we use the global max-pooling operation to obtain the final word embedding. This procedure is reasonable for estimating embeddings of out-of-vocabulary words, especially in languages with rich morphology.

2.1.3 Sentence Level biLSTM

Both word representations are concatenated together and fed into the sentence level biLSTM network. The network learns contexts for each word and extracts the final features for each of these words.

2.2 Tagger

2.2.1 Part-of-Speech Tags

The tagger is implemented as a fully connected network with one hidden layer and soft-max activation function. The tagger takes the features extracted by the biLSTM as input and predicts a universal part-of-speech tag and a language-specific tag for each word.

2.2.2 Morphological Features

Similar approach is used to predict morphological features. Each morphological feature is represented as an attribute-value pair (e.g. Number=Sing) and each word is annotated with a set of appropriate attribute-value pairs in training data. We therefore decide to treat the problem of morphological features prediction as several classification problems (see Figure 2).

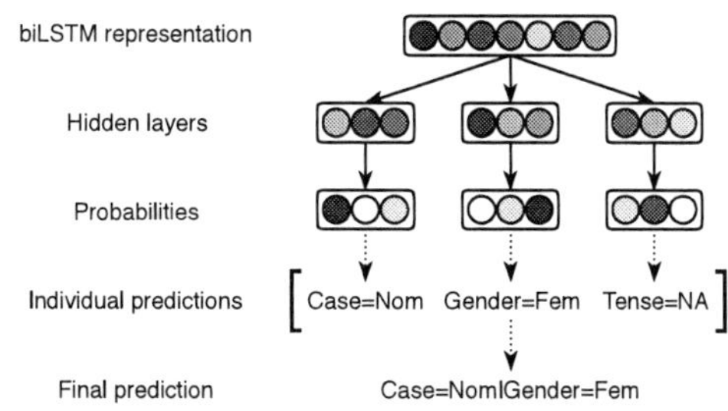

Figure 2: The morphological features prediction.

For each attribute its value is predicted with a fully connected network with one hidden layer and soft-max activation function. Various words are defined by the sets of various morphological features. Since for each word only some attributes are present in the set of morphological features, the possible values are extended with "not applicable" label. It allows the model to learn that an attribute is not present in the set of morphological features of a particular word.

2.3 Lemmatizer

Lemmatizer takes two different inputs. First, features extracted by the biLSTM encoder are used, however their dimensionality is reduced with a single fully connected layer. Next, the word, for which we want to predict a lemma, is converted to a sequence of characters. The special symbols "beginning-of-word" and "end-of-word" are added to the sequence to represent the beginning and the end of the word. Each character in the sequence is represented as a trainable embedding vector. The final input to the lemmatizer is a sequence of character embeddings concatenated with the reduced version of features extracted by the biLSTM encoder. Note that each character embedding is concatenated with exactly the same extracted feature vector.

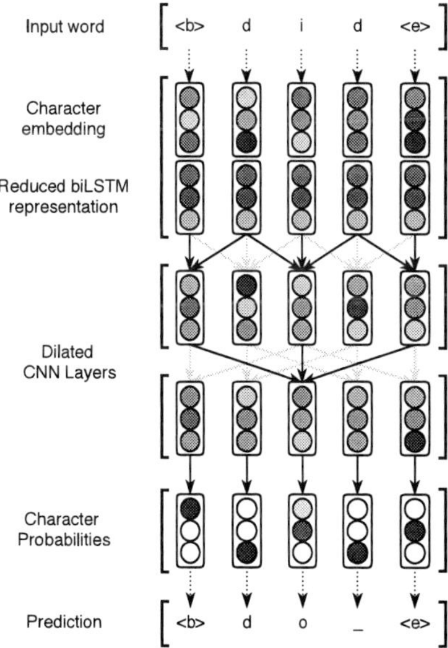

Figure 3: The lemmas prediction.

Then the dilated convolutional neural network followed by soft-max function converts given input to the sequence of probabilities of one-hot encoded characters of the predicted lemma (see Figure 3).

2.4 Parser

2.4.1 Arc Prediction

Two single fully connected layers transform features extracted by the biLSTM encoder into head and dependent vector representations. A fully connected dependency graph is defined with an adjacency matrix. The columns of the matrix correspond to heads represented with heads' vector representations and the rows correspond to dependents represented with dependents' vector representations. The elements of the adjacency matrix, in turn, are dot products of all pairs of the head and dependent vector representations. Soft-max function is then applied to each row of the matrix to predict the adjacent head-dependent pairs (see Figure 4).

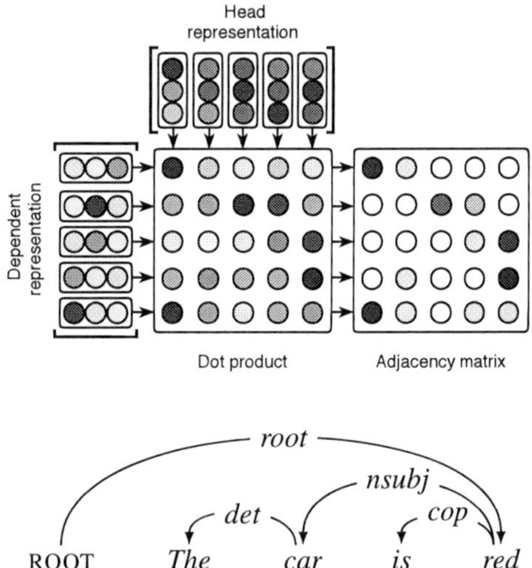

Figure 4: The adjacency matrix and the extracted dependency tree of the sentence *The car is red*.

2.4.2 Loss Function

In order to force the network to predict the correct head for each dependent and thus a correct dependency tree, the cross-entropy loss function is used for each row in the adjacency matrix. Note however that such formulation of the problem can lead the network to predict an adjacency matrix with cycles.

We aim to get an adjacency matrix for which a simple greedy algorithm would suffice to construct the correct tree. Therefore, we propose an additional 'cycle-penalty' loss function which reduces the number of cycles in the predicted adjacency matrix:

$$\text{loss}(A) = \sum_{k=1}^{K} \text{tr}(A^k)$$

The non-zero trace of A^k indicates that there are the paths of the length k in the graph represented by the adjacency matrix A (Norman, 1965). Therefore, by minimizing the sum of the traces of the subsequent powers of A we reduce the number of cycles in the predicted graph. In an ideal scenario K should be equal to the length of the sentence, but in practice even $K = 3$ helps to reduce the number of cycles. The final loss used to train the arc prediction model is a sum of cross-entropy loss and 'cycle-penalty' loss.

If the smoothed adjacent matrix still contains cycles, Chu-Liu-Edmonds algorithm (Chu and Liu, 1965; Edmonds, 1967) is applied to extract the properly built dependency tree in the final step of the prediction procedure.

2.4.3 Label Prediction

In order to predict the label for each arc of the predicted dependency tree, the vector representations of the arc's head and its dependent are calculated. These representations do not correspond to those used during the arc prediction, but they are obtained in a similar way. The estimated vector of the dependent is concatenated with the weighted average of its predicted head vector. The weights correspond to probabilities of a word being the dependent's head predicted by the arc model described in the previous section. It is not possible to take just the vector of a single predicted head, because it would prevent the model to be trained together with the rest of the system, as argmax operation is not differentiable. The concatenated vector representations are then fed to a single fully connected layer with soft-max activation function.

3 Implementation Details

3.1 Network Hyperparameters

Word Embedding We use 300-dimensional fastText word embeddings (Grave et al., 2018),[4]

---

[4]https://github.com/facebookresearch/
fastText/blob/master/docs/crawl-vectors.
md

which are then converted to 100-dimensional vectors by a single fully connected layer. The embedding is not available for some languages, i.e. for Old Church Slavonic ('cu_proiel'), Old French ('fro_srcmf'), Gothic ('got_proiel'), Kurmanji ('kmr_mg'), North Sámi ('sme_giella') or it seems incorrect, i.e. in Slovak ('sk_snk'). Therefore, we estimate the embedding for these languages during the training of the whole system.

Character Embedding The character level embedding is calculated with three convolutional layers with 512, 128 and 64 filters with dilation rates equal to 1, 2 and 4. All of the filters have the kernel of size 3. The input character embedding has the size of 64.

Final Word Embedding The final word embedding is the concatenation of the 100-dimensional word embedding and the 64-dimensional character-based word embedding. It has thus 164 dimensions.

Feature Extraction Two biLSTM layers with 512 hidden units are used to extract the final features.

Tagger The tagger uses a fully connected network with the hidden layer of the size 64. The model to predict morphological features uses the hidden layer of 128 neurons.

Lemmatizer The lemmatizer uses three convolutional layers with 256 filters and dilation rates equal to 1, 2 and 4. All of the filters have the kernel of size 3. Then the final convolutional layer with the kernel size equal to 1 is used to predict lemmas. The input characters, represented as the embeddings with 256 dimensions, are concatenated with the features extracted with the biLSTM encoder and reduced to 32 dimensions with a single fully connected layer.

Parser The arc model uses heads' and dependents' vector representations with 512 dimensions. The labelling model uses 128-dimensional vectors.

All fully connected layers use *tanh* activation function and all convolutional layers use rectified linear unit (ReLU, Nair and Hinton, 2010).

3.2 Regularization

We apply both Gaussian Dropout (with the dropout rate of 0.25) and Gaussian Noise (with the standard deviation on 0.2) to the final word embedding[5] and after processing each biLSTM layer. All fully connected layers use the standard dropout (Srivastava et al., 2014) with the dropout rate of 0.25. The biLSTM layers use both the standard and recurrent dropout with the rate of 0.25. Moreover, the biLSTM and convolutional layers use L2 regularization with the rate of 1×10^{-6} and the trainable embeddings use L2 regularization with the rate of 1×10^{-5}.

3.3 Training

We use cross-entropy loss for all parts of the system. The loss for the arc prediction model is a sum of cross-entropy loss and novel loss (see Section 2.4.2). The final loss is the weighted sum of losses with the following weights for each task:

- 0.05 for part-of-speech tagging,

- 0.2 for morphological features prediction,

- 0.05 for lemmatization,

- 0.2 for arc prediction,

- 0.8 for label prediction.

The whole system is optimized with ADAM (Kingma and Ba, 2014) with the learning rate equal to 0.002 and $\beta_1 = \beta_2 = 0.9$. Typically, the batch size of approximately 2500 words is used, however for a few of the smallest treebanks the batch size is reduced to 1000 or even 75 words. Each batch consists of sentences with a similar length, but the ordering of batches is randomized within each epoch. Each observation (i.e. sentence) is weighted with the log of the sentence length that forces the model to focus on longer (and usually more difficult) sentences. The model is trained for maximum of 400 epochs and the learning rate is reduced twice by the factor of two when the validation score reaches plateau. For languages with multiple treebanks, first a general model is trained on all sentences from these treebanks and then the model is fine-tuned for each treebank.

3.4 Self-training

For 20 arbitrarily selected treebanks, mostly the smallest ones, self-training method (Triguero et al., 2015) is used to increase the performance of

____
[5] https://keras.io/layers/noise/

the system. First the model is trained in a standard way, as described in the previous sections. Then the 'semi-supervised' training set is built. It contains sentences with the total of approximately 25M words taken from raw data[6] provided by CoNLL 2018 organizers. For Uyghur language only 3M words are available. The provided data sets come either from Wikipedia or Commom Crawl. Where it is possible we choose the sentences from Common Crawl, due to longer (on average) sentence sizes. The pre-trained model is then used to predict dependency trees, lemmas and part-of-speech tags for all sentences in the 'semi-supervised' training set. Finally, the new model is trained on this 'semi-supervised' training set for only one epoch and fine-tuned on the gold-standard training data, using the standard training procedure.

3.5 Languages with No Resources

Our solution for processing treebanks with no training data is very simple. We choose another language for which training data is available and train the model on this data. The estimated model is used for predictions in the language with no training data. We use the following treebank pairs:

- 'br_keb' (Breton)[7] – 'ga_idt' (Irish),

- 'fo_oft' (Faroese) – 'no_nynorsk' (Norwegian),

- 'pcm_nsc' (Naija) – 'en_ewt' (English),

- 'th_pud' (Thai) – 'vi_vtb' (Vietnamese).

The parallel UD treebanks for Czech, English, Finish, and Swedish, and the treebank for modern Japanese are processed with the models estimated on other treebanks for the respective languages:

- 'cs_pud' – 'cs_pdt' (Czech),

- 'en_pud' – 'en_ewt' (English),

- 'fi_pud' – 'fi_tdt' (Finish),

- 'sv_pud' – 'sv_talbanken' (Swedish),

- 'ja_modern' – 'ja_gsd' (Japanese).

4 Results

4.1 Overview

In the official evaluation[8] (Zeman et al., 2018) our system ranks 3th/4th for all three main metrics (ex aequo with LATTICE and UDPipe Future for LAS). It performs particularly well on small treebanks with no development data, but a reasonable size of the training set. For example, the system ranks 1st in terms of all three measures on Russian 'ru_taiga' treebank, 1st (MLAS and BLEX) and 2nd (LAS) on Latin 'la_perseus' treebank and spoken Slovenian 'sl_sst' treebank, and 1st (MLAS and BLEX) and 3rd (LAS) on spoken Norwegian 'no_nynorsklia' treebank. It is worth noting that overall MLAS and BLEX scores obtained by our system trained on small treebanks are currently the state of the art (see Table 1). With respect to LAS score, our system ranks 3rd.

Category	LAS	MLAS	BLEX
All	73.02	60.25	64.44
Big	81.72	70.30	74.42
PUD	72.18	58.07	60.97
Small	66.90	**49.24**	**54.89**
Low-resource	19.26	1.89	6.17

Table 1: Official results of our system in CoNLL shared task. State-of-the-art results are in bold.

Regarding to processing big treebanks, our system performs very well on Czech 'cs_fictree' treebank and English 'en_gum' treebank (1st place in MLAS and BLEX, and 2nd place in LAS), and Latin 'la_ittb' treebank (1st place in MLAS and BLEX, and 3rd place in LAS). It is very important to note that most of the mentioned languages, i.e. Russian, Latin, Slovenian, Norwegian, and Czech, are Indo-European languages (fusional). Furthermore, for other fusional languages, e.g. Galician, Ancient Greek, Polish, Ukrainian, Dutch, Swedish, French, Italian, Spanish, Basque, our system provides quite satisfying results as well. It follows that our system is especially appropriate for processing fusional languages.

Our last observation concerns the usefulness of external word embeddings for NLP system with a neural architecture. The languages without external word embeddings (see Section 3.1) are pro-

---

[6]https://lindat.mff.cuni.cz/repository/xmlui/handle/11234/1-1989

[7]The first language in each row has no training data and is parsed with the model estimated for the second language in the pair.

[8]http://universaldependencies.org/conll18/results.html

cessed by our system significantly below its overall performance. Hence, the external word embeddings are crucial for a neural NLP system.

4.2 Impact of Loss Function

For 15 arbitrarily selected treebanks we train the models without the additional loss function and we compare UAS scores of these models with UAS scores obtained by the models estimated with the additional loss function (with $K = 3$, see Section 2.4.2). Moreover for each treebank we calculate what would be the fraction of trees with cycles if we use the greedy algorithm to construct the predicted trees.

Note that the following results cannot be directly compared to the official test results. First we report the scores on the validation set. Second we use the gold-standard segmentation instead of the segmentation predicted by the baseline model.

Treebank	UAS		% Cycles	
	without	with	without	with
ar_padt	86.23	86.39	7.70	4.51
bg_btb	92.32	92.45	1.26	1.52
cu_proiel	86.94	86.49	4.19	3.91
da_ddt	86.61	86.24	5.14	4.61
de_gsd	87.74	87.64	3.50	2.63
es_ancora	92.39	92.49	3.08	3.39
fa_seraji	90.30	90.44	5.18	4.51
got_proiel	83.88	83.57	5.48	4.57
hr_set	90.34	90.50	6.71	4.95
hu_szeged	81.99	82.48	11.34	9.75
id_gsd	84.33	84.47	6.98	6.98
lv_lvtb	85.69	85.58	6.28	4.66
pt_bosque	92.65	92.63	1.25	1.43
ro_rrt	91.04	90.89	2.39	2.53
vi_vtb	68.92	69.02	15.00	12.63
Average	86.76	86.75	5.70	4.84

Table 2: Comparison of the models trained with and without the additional loss function.

The additional loss only slightly decreases UAS (see the second and the third column in Table 2). However, it also has only a small impact on the cycles reduction (see the fourth and the fifth column in Table 2). If there is a lot of cycles in the graphs predicted without the additional loss, e.g. 7.7% cycles in 'ar_padt' (Arabic), the number of cycles is significantly reduced with the addi-

tional loss function, i.e. the reduction by 3.2 p.p. If the rate of cycles is lower, e.g. 4.19% in 'cu_proiel' (Old Church Slavonic), fewer cycles are corrected, i.e. the reduction by 0.28 p.p. Finally, there are four treebanks – 'bg_btb' (Bulgarian), 'es_ancora' (Spanish), 'pt_bosque' (Portuguese), and 'ro_rrt' (Romanian), for which the additional loss function slightly increases the number of cycles.

4.3 Impact of Self-training

We test the impact of self-training method on the performance of the system trained on 20 selected treebanks. Again the models are tested on the validation set with the gold-standard segmentation.

Comparing the results of the models estimated on training data with the results of the models estimated with the self-training method (see Table 3), we notice that self-training significantly increases the performance of the system. There is an increase for all metrics for all treebanks except for 'zh_gsd' (Chinese). On average there is an increase of 1.2 p.p. for LAS, 2.9 p.p. for MLAS and 1.7 p.p. for BLEX.

5 Conclusion

We described the ICS PAS system which took part in CoNLL 2018 shared task. Our goal was to build one system for preprocessing natural languages, i.e. for part-of-speech tagging, lemmatisation and dependency parsing. The three system's modules – tagger, lemmatizer and parser – are jointly trained. The proposed neural system ranks 3th/4th in the official evaluation of the shared task. It is worth nothing that the system is especially useful for estimating the models on relative sparse data (small treebanks), as it overcame other systems in terms of MLAS and BLEX. Furthermore, our system is especially appropriate for processing Indo-European fusional languages.

The self-training procedure significantly increases the performance of the system. The proposed loss function, in turn, has only a slight impact on the cycles reduction and UAS scores. The external word embeddings are crucial for our neural-based system.

Treebank	LAS		MLAS		BLEX	
	std	self	std	self	std	self
bg_btb	88.84	89.23	79.39	80.12	78.89	79.21
da_ddt	83.24	84.89	72.40	75.76	76.73	78.93
el_gdt	87.89	89.19	73.55	76.98	74.06	77.30
eu_bdt	81.58	82.85	65.94	68.15	76.29	77.49
fa_seraji	86.91	87.22	80.19	81.18	80.86	81.36
ga_idt	N/A	N/A	N/A	N/A	N/A	N/A
he_htb	84.39	85.60	71.31	73.63	73.87	75.34
hr_set	86.06	86.22	71.17	71.61	79.01	79.38
hu_szeged	77.39	80.55	60.77	67.28	70.55	74.41
id_gsd	77.62	77.97	64.27	66.22	74.03	74.62
kk_ktb	N/A	N/A	N/A	N/A	N/A	N/A
lv_lvtb	80.52	82.67	65.53	69.11	71.71	74.19
ro_rrt	85.88	86.68	76.49	77.57	79.47	80.39
sk_snk	83.44	85.52	56.05	66.69	72.77	77.13
tr_imst	64.07	64.95	49.26	51.97	57.15	58.87
ug_udt	63.89	65.50	38.21	41.83	51.48	53.89
uk_iu	85.83	87.91	68.35	73.69	78.35	81.65
ur_udtb	80.91	81.34	52.92	53.48	71.09	71.72
vi_vtb	58.82	60.52	49.29	51.87	54.85	56.93
zh_gsd	77.09	76.71	65.17	64.88	69.68	68.93
Average	79.69	80.86	64.46	67.33	71.71	73.43

Table 3: Comparison of the standard (std) and self-training (self) models on the validation set using the gold-standard segmentation. Note that 'kk_ktb' (Kazakh) and 'ga_idt' (modern Irish) treebanks do not have validation sets, so we are unable to report any results.

Acknowledgements

The research presented in this paper was founded by SONATA 8 grant no 2014/15/D/HS2/03486 from the National Science Centre Poland and by the Polish Ministry of Science and Higher Education as part of the investment in the CLARIN-PL research infrastructure.

References

Sabine Buchholz and Erwin Marsi. 2006. CoNLL-X shared task on Multilingual Dependency Parsing. In *Proceedings of the Tenth Conference on Computational Natural Language Learning*. pages 149–164.

Yoeng Jin Chu and Tseng Hong Liu. 1965. On the Shortest Arborescence of a Directed Graph. *Science Sinica* 14:1396–1400.

Jack Edmonds. 1967. Optimum Branchings. *Journal of Research of the National Bureau of Standards* 71B(4):233–240.

Edouard Grave, Piotr Bojanowski, Prakhar Gupta, Armand Joulin, and Tomas Mikolov. 2018. Learning word vectors for 157 languages. In *Proceedings of the International Conference on Language Resources and Evaluation (LREC 2018)*.

Alex Graves and Jürgen Schmidhuber. 2005. Framewise Phoneme Classification with Bidirectional LSTM and Other Neural Network Architectures. *Neural Networks* 18(5):602–610.

Sepp Hochreiter and Jürgen Schmidhuber. 1997. Long short-term memory. *Neural Computation* 9(8):1735–1780.

Diederik P. Kingma and Jimmy Ba. 2014. Adam: A Method for Stochastic Optimization. *CoRR* abs/1412.6980. http://arxiv.org/abs/1412.6980.

Vinod Nair and Geoffrey E. Hinton. 2010. Rectified Linear Units Improve Restricted Boltzmann Machines. In *Proceedings of ICML'10*, pages 807–814.

Joakim Nivre, Mitchell Abrams, Željko Agić, Lars Ahrenberg, Lene Antonsen, Maria Jesus Aranzabe, Gashaw Arutie, Masayuki Asahara, Luma Ateyah,

Mohammed Attia, Aitziber Atutxa, Liesbeth Augustinus, Elena Badmaeva, Miguel Ballesteros, Esha Banerjee, Sebastian Bank, Verginica Barbu Mititelu, John Bauer, Sandra Bellato, Kepa Bengoetxea, Riyaz Ahmad Bhat, Erica Biagetti, Eckhard Bick, Rogier Blokland, Victoria Bobicev, Carl Börstell, Cristina Bosco, Gosse Bouma, Sam Bowman, Adriane Boyd, Aljoscha Burchardt, Marie Candito, Bernard Caron, Gauthier Caron, Gülşen Cebiroğlu Eryiğit, Giuseppe G. A. Celano, Savas Cetin, Fabricio Chalub, Jinho Choi, Yongseok Cho, Jayeol Chun, Silvie Cinková, Aurélie Collomb, Çağrı Çöltekin, Miriam Connor, Marine Courtin, Elizabeth Davidson, Marie-Catherine de Marneffe, Valeria de Paiva, Arantza Diaz de Ilarraza, Carly Dickerson, Peter Dirix, Kaja Dobrovoljc, Timothy Dozat, Kira Droganova, Puneet Dwivedi, Marhaba Eli, Ali Elkahky, Binyam Ephrem, Tomaž Erjavec, Aline Etienne, Richárd Farkas, Hector Fernandez Alcalde, Jennifer Foster, Cláudia Freitas, Katarína Gajdošová, Daniel Galbraith, Marcos Garcia, Moa Gärdenfors, Kim Gerdes, Filip Ginter, Iakes Goenaga, Koldo Gojenola, Memduh Gökırmak, Yoav Goldberg, Xavier Gómez Guinovart, Berta Gonzáles Saavedra, Matias Grioni, Normunds Grūzītis, Bruno Guillaume, Céline Guillot-Barbance, Nizar Habash, Jan Hajič, Jan Hajič jr., Linh Hà Mỹ, Na-Rae Han, Kim Harris, Dag Haug, Barbora Hladká, Jaroslava Hlaváčová, Florinel Hociung, Petter Hohle, Jena Hwang, Radu Ion, Elena Irimia, Tomáš Jelínek, Anders Johannsen, Fredrik Jørgensen, Hüner Kaşıkara, Sylvain Kahane, Hiroshi Kanayama, Jenna Kanerva, Tolga Kayadelen, Václava Kettnerová, Jesse Kirchner, Natalia Kotsyba, Simon Krek, Sookyoung Kwak, Veronika Laippala, Lorenzo Lambertino, Tatiana Lando, Septina Dian Larasati, Alexei Lavrentiev, John Lee, Phuong Lê Hông, Alessandro Lenci, Saran Lertpradit, Herman Leung, Cheuk Ying Li, Josie Li, Keying Li, KyungTae Lim, Nikola Ljubešić, Olga Loginova, Olga Lyashevskaya, Teresa Lynn, Vivien Macketanz, Aibek Makazhanov, Michael Mandl, Christopher Manning, Ruli Manurung, Cătălina Mărănduc, David Mareček, Katrin Marheinecke, Héctor Martínez Alonso, André Martins, Jan Mašek, Yuji Matsumoto, Ryan McDonald, Gustavo Mendonça, Niko Miekka, Anna Missilä, Cătălin Mititelu, Yusuke Miyao, Simonetta Montemagni, Amir More, Laura Moreno Romero, Shinsuke Mori, Bjartur Mortensen, Bohdan Moskalevskyi, Kadri Muischnek, Yugo Murawaki, Kaili Müürisep, Pinkey Nainwani, Juan Ignacio Navarro Horñiacek, Anna Nedoluzhko, Gunta Nešpore-Bērzkalne, Luong Nguyên Thị, Huyên Nguyên Thị Minh, Vitaly Nikolaev, Rattima Nitisaroj, Hanna Nurmi, Stina Ojala, Adédayò Olúòkun, Mai Omura, Petya Osenova, Robert Östling, Lilja Øvrelid, Niko Partanen, Elena Pascual, Marco Passarotti, Agnieszka Patejuk, Siyao Peng, Cenel-Augusto Perez, Guy Perrier, Slav Petrov, Jussi Piitulainen, Emily Pitler, Barbara Plank, Thierry Poibeau, Martin Popel, Lauma Pretkalniņa, Sophie Prévost, Prokopis Prokopidis, Adam Przepiórkowski, Tiina Puolakainen, Sampo Pyysalo, Andriela Rääbis, Alexandre Rademaker, Loganathan Ramasamy, Taraka Rama, Carlos Ramisch, Vinit Ravishankar, Livy Real, Siva Reddy, Georg Rehm, Michael Rießler, Larissa Rinaldi, Laura Rituma, Luisa Rocha, Mykhailo Romanenko, Rudolf Rosa, Davide Rovati, Valentin Roşca, Olga Rudina, Shoval Sadde, Shadi Saleh, Tanja Samardžić, Stephanie Samson, Manuela Sanguinetti, Baiba Saulīte, Yanin Sawanakunanon, Nathan Schneider, Sebastian Schuster, Djamé Seddah, Wolfgang Seeker, Mojgan Seraji, Mo Shen, Atsuko Shimada, Muh Shohibussirri, Dmitry Sichinava, Natalia Silveira, Maria Simi, Radu Simionescu, Katalin Simkó, Mária Šimková, Kiril Simov, Aaron Smith, Isabela Soares-Bastos, Antonio Stella, Milan Straka, Jana Strnadová, Alane Suhr, Umut Sulubacak, Zsolt Szántó, Dima Taji, Yuta Takahashi, Takaaki Tanaka, Isabelle Tellier, Trond Trosterud, Anna Trukhina, Reut Tsarfaty, Francis Tyers, Sumire Uematsu, Zdeňka Urešová, Larraitz Uria, Hans Uszkoreit, Sowmya Vajjala, Daniel van Niekerk, Gertjan van Noord, Viktor Varga, Veronika Vincze, Lars Wallin, Jonathan North Washington, Seyi Williams, Mats Wirén, Tsegay Woldemariam, Taksum Wong, Chunxiao Yan, Marat M. Yavrumyan, Zhuoran Yu, Zdeněk Žabokrtský, Amir Zeldes, Daniel Zeman, Manying Zhang, and Hanzhi Zhu. 2018. Universal Dependencies 2.2. LINDAT/CLARIN digital library at the Institute of Formal and Applied Linguistics (ÚFAL), Faculty of Mathematics and Physics, Charles University. http://hdl.handle.net/11234/1-2837.

Joakim Nivre, Marie-Catherine de Marneffe, Filip Ginter, Yoav Goldberg, Jan Hajič, Christopher D. Manning, Ryan T. McDonald, Slav Petrov, Sampo Pyysalo, Natalia Silveira, Reut Tsarfaty, and Daniel Zeman. 2016. Universal Dependencies v1: A Multilingual Treebank Collection. In *Proceedings of the Tenth International Conference on Language Resources and Evaluation LREC 2016*. pages 1659–1666.

Joakim Nivre, Johan Hall, Sandra Kübler, Ryan McDonald, Jens Nilsson, Sebastian Riedel, and Deniz Yuret. 2007. The CoNLL 2007 Shared Task on Dependency Parsing. In *Proceedings of the CoNLL Shared Task Session of EMNLP-CoNLL 2007*. pages 915–932.

R. L. Norman. 1965. A matrix method for location of cycles of a directed graph. *AIChE Journal* 11(3):450–452. https://doi.org/10.1002/aic.690110316.

Nitish Srivastava, Geoffrey Hinton, Alex Krizhevsky, Ilya Sutskever, and Ruslan Salakhutdinov. 2014. Dropout: A simple way to prevent neural networks from overfitting. *Journal of Machine Learning Research* 15:1929–1958. http://jmlr.org/papers/v15/srivastava14a.html.

Milan Straka and Jana Straková. 2017. Tokenizing, POS Tagging, Lemmatizing and Parsing UD 2.0

with UDPipe. In *Proceedings of the CoNLL 2017 Shared Task: Multilingual Parsing from Raw Text to Universal Dependencies*. Association for Computational Linguistics, Vancouver, Canada, pages 88–99. http://www.aclweb.org/anthology/K/K17/K17-3009.pdf.

Isaac Triguero, Salvador García, and Francisco Herrera. 2015. Self-labeled techniques for semi-supervised learning: taxonomy, software and empirical study. *Knowledge and Information Systems* 42:245–284. https://doi.org/https://doi.org/10.1007/s10115-013-0706-y.

Fisher Yu and Vladlen Koltun. 2016. Multi-Scale Context Aggregation by Dilated Convolutions. *CoRR* abs/1511.07122. http://arxiv.org/abs/1511.07122.

Daniel Zeman, Jan Hajič, Martin Popel, Martin Potthast, Milan Straka, Filip Ginter, Joakim Nivre, and Slav Petrov. 2018. CoNLL 2018 Shared Task: Multilingual Parsing from Raw Text to Universal Dependencies. In *Proceedings of the CoNLL 2018 Shared Task: Multilingual Parsing from Raw Text to Universal Dependencies*. Association for Computational Linguistics, Brussels, Belgium, pages 1–20.

Daniel Zeman, Martin Popel, Milan Straka, Jan Hajič, Joakim Nivre, Filip Ginter, Juhani Luotolahti, Sampo Pyysalo, Slav Petrov, Martin Potthast, Francis Tyers, Elena Badmaeva, Memduh Gökırmak, Anna Nedoluzhko, Silvie Cinková, Jan Hajič jr., Jaroslava Hlaváčová, Václava Kettnerová, Zdenka Urešová, Jenna Kanerva, Stina Ojala, Anna Missilä, Christopher D. Manning, Sebastian Schuster, Siva Reddy, Dima Taji, Nizar Habash, Herman Leung, Marie-Catherine de Marneffe, Manuela Sanguinetti, Maria Simi, Hiroshi Kanayama, Valeria dePaiva, Kira Droganova, Héctor Martínez Alonso, Çağrı Çöltekin, Umut Sulubacak, Hans Uszkoreit, Vivien Macketanz, Aljoscha Burchardt, Kim Harris, Katrin Marheinecke, Georg Rehm, Tolga Kayadelen, Mohammed Attia, Ali Elkahky, Zhuoran Yu, Emily Pitler, Saran Lertpradit, Michael Mandl, Jesse Kirchner, Hector Fernandez Alcalde, Jana Strnadová, Esha Banerjee, Ruli Manurung, Antonio Stella, Atsuko Shimada, Sookyoung Kwak, Gustavo Mendonça, Tatiana Lando, Rattima Nitisaroj, and Josie Li. 2017. CoNLL 2017 Shared Task: Multilingual Parsing from Raw Text to Universal Dependencies. In *Proceedings of the CoNLL 2017 Shared Task: Multilingual Parsing from Raw Text to Universal Dependencies*. Association for Computational Linguistics, pages 1–19. http://www.aclweb.org/anthology/K/K17/K17-3001.pdf.

Towards Better UD Parsing: Deep Contextualized Word Embeddings, Ensemble, and Treebank Concatenaton

Wanxiang Che, Yijia Liu, Yuxuan Wang, Bo Zheng, Ting Liu
Research Center for Social Computing and Information Retrieval
Harbin Institute of Technology, China
{car,yjliu,yxwang,bzheng,tliu}@ir.hit.edu.cn

Abstract

This paper describes our system (HIT-SCIR) submitted to the CoNLL 2018 shared task on Multilingual Parsing from Raw Text to Universal Dependencies. We base our submission on Stanford's winning system for the CoNLL 2017 shared task and make two effective extensions: 1) incorporating deep contextualized word embeddings into both the part of speech tagger and dependency parser; 2) ensembling parsers trained with different initialization. We also explore different ways of concatenating treebanks for further improvements. Experimental results on the development data show the effectiveness of our methods. In the final evaluation, our system was ranked first according to LAS (75.84%) and outperformed the other systems by a large margin.

1   Introduction

In this paper, we describe our system (HIT-SCIR) submitted to CoNLL 2018 shared task on Multilingual Parsing from Raw Text to Universal Dependencies (Zeman et al., 2018). We base our system on Stanford's winning system (Dozat et al., 2017, §2) for the CoNLL 2017 shared task (Zeman et al., 2017).

Dozat and Manning (2016) and its extension (Dozat et al., 2017) have shown very competitive performance in both the shared task (Dozat et al., 2017) and previous parsing works (Ma and Hovy, 2017; Shi et al., 2017a; Liu et al., 2018b; Ma et al., 2018). A natural question that arises is how can we further improve their part of speech (POS) tagger and dependency parser via a simple yet effective technique. In our system, we make two noteworthy extensions to their tagger and parser:

- Incorporating the deep contextualized word embeddings (Peters et al., 2018, ELMo: Embeddings from Language Models) into the word representaton (§3);

- Ensembling parsers trained with different initialization (§4).

For some languages in the shared task, multiple treebanks of different domains are provided. Treebanks which are of the same language families are provided as well. Letting these treebanks help each other has been shown an effective way to improve parsing performance in both the cross-lingual-cross-domain parsing community and last year's shared tasks (Ammar et al., 2016; Guo et al., 2015; Che et al., 2017; Shi et al., 2017b; Björkelund et al., 2017). In our system, we apply the simple concatenation to the treebanks that are potentially helpful to each other and explore different ways of concatenation to improve the parser's performance (§5).

In dealing with the small treebanks and treebanks from low-resource languages (§6), we adopt the word embedding transfer idea in the cross-lingual dependency parsing (Guo et al., 2015) and use the bilingual word vectors transformation technique (Smith et al., 2017)[1] to map *fast-text*[2] word embeddings (Bojanowski et al., 2016) of the source rich-resource language and target low-resource language into the same space. The transferred parser trained on the source language is used for the target low-resource language.

We conduct experiments on the development data to study the effects of ELMo, parser ensemble, and treebank concatenation. Experimental results show that these techniques substantially im-

---

[1] https://github.com/Babylonpartners/fastText_multilingual
[2] https://github.com/facebookresearch/fastText

Proceedings of the CoNLL 2018 Shared Task: Multilingual Parsing from Raw Text to Universal Dependencies, pages 55–64
Brussels, Belgium, October 31 – November 1, 2018. ©2018 Association for Computational Linguistics
https://doi.org/10.18653/v1/K18-2005

prove the parsing performance. Using these techniques, our system achieved an averaged LAS of 75.84 on the official test set and was ranked the first according to LAS (Zeman et al., 2018). This result significantly outperforms the others by a large margin.[3]

We release our pre-trained ELMo for many languages at `https://github.com/HIT-SCIR/ELMoForManyLangs`.

2 Deep Biaffine Parser

We based our system on the tagger and parser of Dozat et al. (2017). The core idea of the tagger and parser is using an LSTM network to produce the vector representation for each word and then predict POS tags and dependency relations using the representation. For the tagger whose input is the word alone, this representation is calculated as

$$\mathbf{h}_i = \text{BiLSTM}(\mathbf{h}_0, (\mathbf{v}_1^{(word)}, ..., \mathbf{v}_n^{(word)}))_i$$

where $\mathbf{v}_i^{(word)}$ is the word embeddings. After getting $\mathbf{h}_i$, the scores of tags are calculated as

$$\mathbf{h}_i^{(pos)} = \text{MLP}^{(pos)}(\mathbf{h}_i)$$
$$\mathbf{s}_i^{(pos)} = W \cdot \mathbf{h}_i^{(pos)} + \mathbf{b}^{(pos)}$$
$$y_i^{(pos)} = \underset{j}{\text{argmax}}\, s_{i,j}^{(pos)}$$

where each element in $\mathbf{s}_i^{(pos)}$ represents the possibility that i-th word is assigned with corresponding tag.

For the parser whose inputs are the word and POS tag, such representation is calculated as

$$\mathbf{x}_i = \mathbf{v}_i^{(word)} \oplus \mathbf{v}_i^{(tag)}$$
$$\mathbf{h}_i = \text{BiLSTM}(\mathbf{h}_0, (\mathbf{x}_1, ..., \mathbf{x}_n))_i$$

And a pair of representations are fed into a biaffine classifier to predict the possibility that there is a dependency arc between these two words. The scores over all head words are calculated as

$$\mathbf{s}_i^{(arc)} = H^{(arc\text{-}head)} W^{(arc)} \mathbf{h}_i^{(arc\text{-}dep)}$$
$$+ H^{(arc\text{-}head)} \mathbf{b}^{(arc)}$$
$$y^{(arc)} = \underset{j}{\text{argmax}}\, s_{i,j}^{(arc)}$$

where $\mathbf{h}_i^{(arc\text{-}dep)}$ is computed by feeding $\mathbf{h}_i$ into an MLP and $H^{(arc\text{-}head)}$ is the stack of $\mathbf{h}_i^{(arc\text{-}head)}$

---

[3] `http://universaldependencies.org/conll18/results.html`

which is calculated in the same way as $\mathbf{h}_i^{(arc\text{-}dep)}$ but using another MLP. After getting the head $y^{(arc)}$ word, its relation with i-th word is decided by calculating

$$\mathbf{s}_i^{(rel)} = \mathbf{h}_{y^{(arc)}}^{T(rel\text{-}head)} \mathbf{U}^{(rel)} \mathbf{h}_i^{(rel\text{-}dep)}$$
$$+ W^{(rel)}(\mathbf{h}_i^{(rel\text{-}dep)} \oplus \mathbf{h}_{y^{(arc)}}^{T(rel\text{-}head)})$$
$$+ \mathbf{b}^{(rel)},$$
$$y^{(rel)} = \underset{j}{\text{argmax}}\, s_{i,j}^{(rel)}$$

where $\mathbf{h}^{(rel\text{-}head)}$ and $\mathbf{h}^{(rel\text{-}dep)}$ are calculated in the same way as $\mathbf{h}_i^{(arc\text{-}dep)}$ and $\mathbf{h}_i^{(arc\text{-}head)}$.

This decoding process can lead to cycles in the result. Dozat et al. (2017) employed an iterative fixing methods on the cycles. We encourage the reader of this paper to refer to their paper for more details on training and decoding.

For both the biaffine tagger and parser, the word embedding $\mathbf{v}_i^{(word)}$ is obtained by summing a fine-tuned token embedding $\mathbf{w}_i$, a fixed word2vec embedding $\mathbf{p}_i$, and an LSTM-encoded character representation $\hat{\mathbf{v}}_i$ as

$$\mathbf{v}_i^{(word)} = \mathbf{w}_i + \mathbf{p}_i + \hat{\mathbf{v}}_i.$$

3 Deep Contextualized Word Embeddings

Deep contextualized word embeddings (Peters et al., 2018, ELMo) has shown to be very effective on a range of syntactic and semantic tasks and it's straightforward to obtain ELMo by using an LSTM network to encode words in a sentence and training the LSTM network with language modeling objective on large-scale raw text. More specifically, the $\mathbf{ELMo}_i$ is computed by first computing the hidden representation $\mathbf{h}_i^{(LM)}$ as

$$\mathbf{h}_i^{(LM)} = \text{BiLSTM}^{(LM)}(\mathbf{h}_0^{(LM)}, (\tilde{\mathbf{v}}_1, ..., \tilde{\mathbf{v}}_n))_i$$

where $\tilde{\mathbf{v}}_i$ is the output of a CNN over characters, then attentively summing and scaling different layers of $\mathbf{h}_{i,j}^{(LM)}$ with s_j and γ as

$$\mathbf{ELMo}_i = \gamma \sum_{j=0}^{L} s_j \mathbf{h}_{i,j}^{(LM)},$$

where L is the number of layers and $\mathbf{h}_{i,0}^{(LM)}$ is identical to $\tilde{\mathbf{v}}_i$. In our system, we follow Peters et al. (2018) and use a two-layer bidirectional LSTM as our BiLSTM$^{(LM)}$.

56

In this paper, we study the usage of ELMo for improving both the tagger and parser and make several simplifications. Different from Peters et al. (2018), we treat the output of ELMo as a fixed representation and do not tune its parameters during tagger and parser training. Thus, we cancel the layer-wise attention scores s_j and the scaling factor γ, which means

$$\mathbf{ELMo}_i = \sum_{j=0}^{2} \mathbf{h}_{i,j}^{(LM)}.$$

In our preliminary experiments, using $\mathbf{h}_{i,0}^{(LM)}$ for $\mathbf{ELMo}_i$ yields better performance on some treebanks. In our final submission, we decide using either $\sum_{j=0}^{2} \mathbf{h}_{i,j}^{(LM)}$ or $\mathbf{h}_{i,0}^{(LM)}$ based on their development.

After getting $\mathbf{ELMo}_i$, we project it to the same dimension as $\mathbf{v}_i^{(word)}$ and use it as an additional word embedding. The calculation of $\mathbf{v}_i^{(word)}$ becomes

$$\mathbf{v}_i^{(word)} = \mathbf{w}_i + \mathbf{p}_i + \hat{\mathbf{v}}_i + W^{(ELMo)} \cdot \mathbf{ELMo}_i$$

for both the tagger and parser. We need to note that training the tagger and parser includes $W^{(ELMo)}$. To avoid overfitting, we impose a dropout function on projected vector $W^{(ELMo)} \cdot \mathbf{ELMo}_i$ during training.

4 Parser Ensemble

According to Reimers and Gurevych (2017), neural network training can be sensitive to initialization and Liu et al. (2018a) shows that ensemble neural network trained with different initialization leads to performance improvements. We follow their works and train three parsers with different initialization, then ensemble these parsers by averaging their softmaxed output scores as

$$\mathbf{s}_i^{(rel)} = \frac{1}{3} \sum_{m=1}^{3} \mathrm{softmax}(\mathbf{s}_i^{(m,rel)}).$$

5 Treebank Concatenation

For 15 out of the 58 languages in the shared task, multiple treebanks from different domains are provided. There are also treebanks that come from the same language family. Taking the advantages of the relation between treebanks has been shown a promising direction in both the research community (Ammar et al., 2016; Guo et al., 2015, 2016a)

and in the CoNLL 2017 shared task (Che et al., 2017; Björkelund et al., 2017; Shi et al., 2017b). In our system, we adopt the treebank concatenation technique as Ammar et al. (2016) with one exception: only a group of treebanks from the same language (*cross-domain concatenation*) or a pair of treebanks that are typologically or geographically correlated (*cross-lingual concatenation*) is concatenated.

In our system, we tried cross-domain concatenation on *nl, sv, ko, it, en, fr, gl, la, ru*, and *sl*.[4] We also tried cross-lingual concatenation on *ug-tr, uk-ru, ga-en*, and *sme-fi* following Che et al. (2017). However, due to the variance in vocabulary, grammatical genre, and even annotation, treebank concatenation does not guarantee to improve the model's performance. We decide the usage of concatenation by examining their development set performance. For some small treebanks which do not have development set, whether using treebank concatenation is decided through 5-fold cross validation.[5] We show the experimental results of treebank concatenation in Section 9.3.

6 Low Resources Languages

In the shared task, 5 languages are presented with training set of less than 50 sentences. 4 languages do not even have any training data. It's difficult to train reasonable parser on these low-resource languages. We deal with these treebanks by adopting the word embedding transfer idea of Guo et al. (2015). We transfer the word embeddings of the rich-resource language to the space of low-resource language using the bilingual word vectors transformation technique (Smith et al., 2017) and trained a parser using the source treebank with only pretrained word embeddings on the transformed space as $\mathbf{v}_i^{(word)} = \mathbf{p}_i$. The transformation matrix is automatically learned on the *fasttext* word embeddings using the same tokens shared by two languages (like punctuation).

Table 1 shows our source languages for the target low-resource languages. For a treebank with a few training data, its source language is decided by testing the source parser's performance on the

---

[4]We opt out *cs, fi*, and *pl* because all the treebanks of these languages are relatively large – they have more than 10K training sentences.

[5]We use *udpipe* for this part of experiments because we consider the effect of treebank concatenation as being irrelevant to the parser architecture and *udpipe* has the speed advantage in both training and testing.

target	br	fo	th	hy	kk	bxr	kmr	hsb
source	ga	no	zh	et	tr	hi	fa	pl

Table 1: Cross-lingual transfer settings for low-resource target languages.

training data.[6] For a treebank without any training data, we choose the source language according to their language family.[7]

Naija presents an exception for our method since it does not have *fasttext* word embeddings and embedding transformation is infeasible. Since it's a dialect of English, we use the full pipeline of *en_ewt* for *pcm_nsc* instead.

7 Preprocessing

Besides improving the tagger and parser, we also consider the preprocessing as an important factor to the final performance and improve it by using the state-of-the-art system for sentence segmentation, or developing our own word segmentor for languages whose tokenizations are non-trival.

7.1 Sentence Segmentation

For some treebanks, sentence segmentation can be problematic since there is no explicitly sentence delimiters. de Lhoneux et al. (2017) and Shao (2017) presented a joint tokenization and sentence segmentation model (denoted as *Uppsala segmentor*)[8] that outperformed the baseline model in last year's shared task (Zeman et al., 2017). We select a set of treebanks whose *udpipe* sentence segmentation F-scores are lower than 95 on the development set and use Uppsala segmentor instead.[9] Using the Uppsala segmentor leads to a development improvement of 7.67 F-score in these treebanks over *udpipe* baseline and it was ranked the first according to sentence segmentation in the final evaluation.

7.2 Tokenization for Chinese, Japanese, and Vietnamese

Tokenization is non-trivial for languages which do not have explicit word boundary markers, like Chinese, Japanese, and Vietnamese. We develop our own tokenizer (denoted as *SCIR tokenizer*) for these three languages. Following Che et al. (2017) and Zheng et al. (2017), we model the tokenization as labeling the word boundary tag[10] on characters and use features derived from large-scale unlabeled data to further improve the performance.[11] In addition to the pointwise mutual information (PMI), we also incorporate the character ELMo into our tokenizer. Embeddings of these features are concatenated along with a bigram character embeddings as input. These techniques lead to the best tokenization performance on all the related treebanks and the average improvement over *udpipe* baseline is 7.5 in tokenization F-score.[12]

7.3 Preprocessing for Thai

Thai language presents a unique challenge in the preprocessing. Our survey on the Thai Wikipedia indicates that there is no explicit sentence delimiter and obtaining Thai words requires tokenization. To remedy this, we use the whitespace as sentence delimiter and use the lexicon-based word segmentation – forward maximum matching algorithm for Thai tokenization. Our lexicon is derived from the *fasttext* word embeddings by preserving the top 10% frequent words.

7.4 Lemmatization and Morphology Tagging

We did not make an effort on lemmatization and morphology tagging, but only use the baseline model. This lags our performance in the MLAS and BLEX evaluation, in which we were ranked 6th and 2nd correspondingly. However, since our method, especially incorporating ELMo, is not limited to particular task, we expect it to improve both the lemmatization and morphology tagging and achieve better MLAS and BLEX scores.

8 Implementation Details

Pretrained Word Embeddings. We use the 100-dimensional pretrained word embeddings released by the shared task for the large languages. For the small treebanks and treebanks for low-resource languages where cross-lingual transfer is required, we use the 300-dimensional *fasttext* word embeddings. Old French treebank

---

[6] We use *udpipe* for this test. When training the parser, the small set of target training data is also used.

[7] Thai does not have a treebank in the same family. We choose Chinese as source language because of geographical closeness and both these two languages are SVO in typology.

[8] https://github.com/yanshao9798/segmenter/

[9] We use Uppsala segmentor for *it_postwita*, *got_proiel*, *la_poroiel*, *cu_proiel*, *grc_proiel*, *sl_ssj*, *nl_lassysmall*, *fi_tdt*, *pt_bosque*, *da_ddt*, *id_gsd*, *el_gdt*, and *et_edt*.

[10] We use the BIES scheme.

[11] For Vietnamese where whitespaces occur both inter- and intra-words, we treat the whitespace-separated token as a character.

[12] on *ja_gsd*, *ja_modern*, *vi_vtb*, and *zh_gsd*.

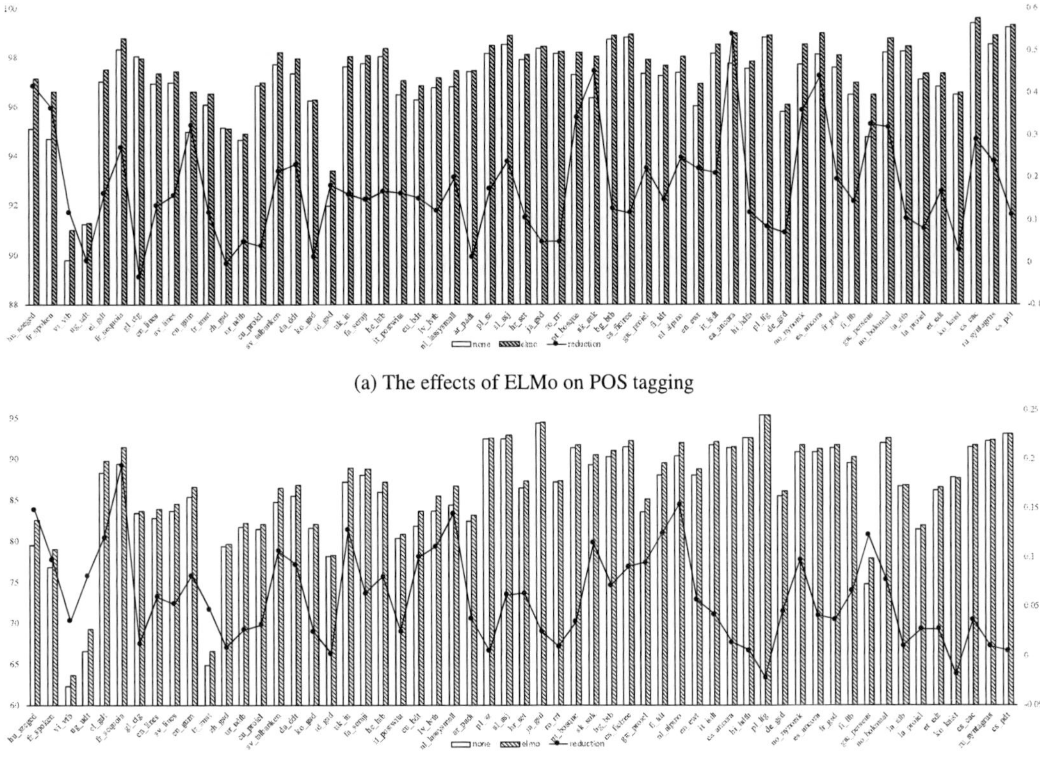

(a) The effects of ELMo on POS tagging

(b) The effects of ELMo on dependency parsing

Figure 1: The effects of ELMo. Treebanks are sorted from the smallest to the largest.

(*fro_srcmf*) presents the only exceptions and we use the French embeddings instead. For all the embeddings, we only use 10% of the most frequent words.

ELMo. We use the same hyperparameter settings as Peters et al. (2018) for BiLSTM$^{(LM)}$ and the character CNN. We train their parameters as training a bidirectional language model on a set of 20-million-words data randomly sampled from the raw text released by the shared task for each language. Similar to Peters et al. (2018), we use the *sample softmax* technique to make training on large vocabulary feasible (Jean et al., 2015). However, we use a window of 8192 words surrounding the target word as negative samples and it shows better performance in our preliminary experiments. The training of ELMo on one language takes roughly 3 days on an NVIDIA P100 GPU.

Biaffine Parser. We use the same hyperparameter settings as Dozat et al. (2017). When trained with ELMo, we use a dropout of 33% on the projected vectors.

SCIR Tokenizer. We use a 50-dimensional character bigram embeddings. For the character ELMo whose input is a character, the language model predict next character in the same way as the word ELMo. The final model is an ensemble of five single tokenizers.

Uppsala Segmentor. We use the default settings for the Uppsala segmentor and the final model is an ensemble of three single segmentors.

9 Results

9.1 Effects of ELMo

We study the effect of ELMo on the large treebanks and report the results of a single tagger and parser with and without ELMo. Figure 1a shows the tagging results on the development set and Figure 1b shows the parsing results. Using ELMo in the tagger leads to a macro-averaged improvement of 0.56% in UPOS and the macro-averaged error reduction is 17.83%. Using ELMo in the parser leads to a macro-averaged improvement of 0.84% in LAS and the macro-averaged error reduction is 7.88%.

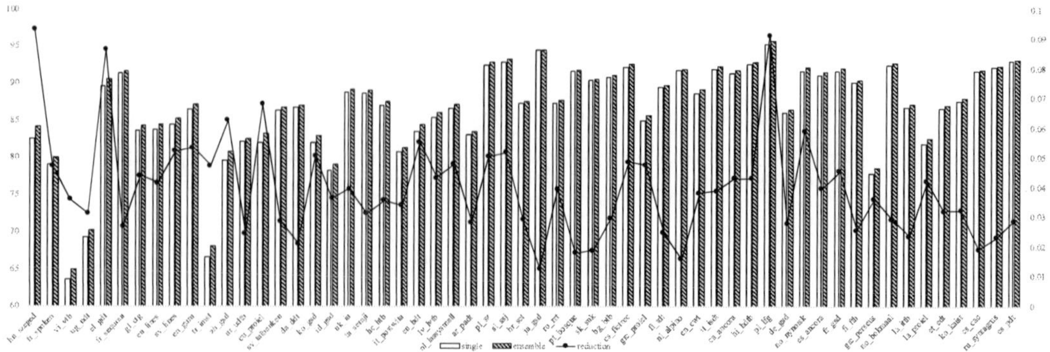

Figure 2: The effects of ensemble on dependency parsing. Treebanks are sorted according to the number of training sentences from left to right.

	nl	apino	lassysmall		*sv*	lines	talbanken		*ko*	gsd	kaist		*it*	isdt	postwita
# train	12.2	5.8		# train	2.7	4.3		# train	4.4	23.0		# train	13.1	5.4
single	91.87	86.82		single	84.64	86.39		single	82.05	**87.83**		single	**92.01**	80.79
concat.	**92.08**	**89.34**		concat.	**85.76**	**86.77**		concat.	**83.73**	87.61		concat.	91.80	**82.54**

	en	ewt	gum	lines		*fr*	gsd	sequoia	spoken
# train	12.5	2.9	2.7		# train	14.6	2.2	1.2
single	**88.75**	**86.52**	83.86		single	**91.64**	**91.44**	79.06
concat.	88.74	85.65	**85.30**		concat.	91.44	90.51	**81.99**

Table 2: The developement performance with cross-domain concatenation for languages which has multiple treebanks. *single* means training the parser on it own treebank without concatenation. *# train* shows the number of training sentences in the treebank measured in thousand.

ELMo improves the tagging performance almost on every treebank, except for *zh_gsd* and *gl_ctg*. Similar trends are witnessed in the parsing experiments with *ko_kaist* and *pl_lfg* being the only treebanks where ELMo slightly worsens the performance.

We also study the relative improvements in dependence on the size of the treebank. The line in Figure 1a and Figure 1b shows the error reduction from using ELMo on each treebank. However, no clear relation is revealed between the treebank size and the gains using ELMo.

9.2 Effects of Ensemble

We also test the effect of ensemble and show the results in Figure 2. Parser ensemble leads to an averaged improvement of 0.55% in LAS and the averaged error reduction is 4.0%. These results indicate that ensemble is an effective way to improve the parsing performance. The relationship between gains using ensemble and treebank size is also studied in this figure and the trend is that small treebank benefit more from the ensemble. We address this to the fact that the ensemble im-

proves the model's generalization ability in which the parser trained on small treebank is weak due to overfitting.

9.3 Effects of Treebank Concatenation

As mentioned in Section 5, we study the effects of both the *cross-domain concatenation* and *cross-lingual concatenation*.

Cross-Domain Concatenation. For the treebanks which have development set, the development performances are shown in Table 2. Numbers of sentences in the training set are also shown in this table. The general trend is that for the treebank with small training set, cross-domain concatenation achieves better performance. While for those with large training set, concatenation does not improve the performance or even worsen the results.

For the small treebanks which do not have development set, the 5 fold cross validation results are shown in Table 3 in which concatenation improves most of the treebanks except for *gl_treegal*.

gl	treegal		*la*	perseus		*no*	nynorsklia		*ru*	taiga		*sl*	sst
# train	0.6		# train	1.3		# train	0.3		# train	0.9		# train	2.1
treegal	**66.71**		perseus	44.05		nynorsklia	51.05		taiga	54.70		sst	55.15
+ctg	56.73		+proiel	**50.78**		+nynorsk	**58.49**		+syntagrus	**60.75**		+ssj	**59.52**

Table 3: The 5-fold cross validation results for the cross-domain concatenation of treebank which does not have development set.

	ug_udt			uk_iu			ga_idt			sme_giella
ug_udt	**69.27**		uk_iu	88.84		ga_idt	**62.84**	sme_giella	**66.33**
+tr_imst	19.27		+ru_syntagus	**90.74**		+en_ewt	51.00		+fi_ftb	59.86

Table 4: Cross-lingual concatenation results. The results for *ug_udt* and *uk_iu* are obtained on the development set. The results for *ga_idt* and *sme_giella* are obtained with *udpipe* by 5-fold cross validation.

	Δ-sent.	udpipe	uppsala
fi_tdt	+0.69	88.13	**88.67**
et_edt	+1.22	86.33	**86.36**
nl_lassysmall	+1.39	88.08	**88.60**
da_ddt	+1.56	86.21	**86.51**
el_gdt	+1.57	**90.08**	89.96
cu_proiel	+1.72	72.79	**74.04**
pt_bosque	+1.83	**90.73**	90.20
id_gsd	+2.46	74.14	**78.83**
la_proiel	+4.82	73.21	**74.22**
got_proiel	+5.36	67.55	**68.40**
grc_proiel	+5.86	79.67	**80.72**
sl_ssj	+18.81	88.43	**92.27**
it_postwita	+30.40	74.91	**79.26**
	Δ-word	udpipe	scir
ja_gsd	+4.07	80.53	**85.23**
zh_gsd	+7.16	66.16	**75.78**
vi_vtb	+9.02	48.58	**57.53**

Table 5: The effects of improved preprocessing on the parsing performance. The first block shows the effects of sentence segmentation improvement. Δ-sent. means the sentence segmentation F-score difference between Uppsala segmentor and *udpipe*. The second block shows the effects of word segmentation improvement. Δ-word means the word segmentation in F-score difference between SCIR tokenizer and *udpipe*.

Cross-Lingual Concatenation. The experimental results of cross-lingual concatenation are shown in Table 4. Unfortunately, concatenating treebanks from different languages only achieves improved performance on *uk_iu*. This results also indicate that in cross lingual parsing, sophisticated methods like word embeddings transfer (Guo et al., 2015, 2016b) and treebank transfer (Guo et al., 2016a) are still necessary.

9.4 Effects of Better Preprocessing

We also study how preprocessing contributes to the final parsing performance. The experimental results on the development set are shown in Table 5. From this table, the performance of word segmentation is almost linearly correlated with the final performance. Similar trends on sentence segmentation performance are witnessed but *el_gdt* and *pt_bosque* presents some exceptions where better preprocess leads drop in the final parsing performance.

9.5 Parsing Strategies and Test Set Evaluation

Using the development set and cross validation, we choose the best model and data combination and the choices are shown in Table 6 along with the test evaluation. From this table, we can see that our system gains more improvements when both ELMo and parser ensemble are used. For some treebanks, concatenation also contributes to the improvements. Parsing Japanese, Vietnamese, and Chinese clearly benefits from better word segmentation. Since most of the participant teams use single parser for their system, we also remove the parser ensemble and do a post-contest evaluation. The results are also shown in this table. Our system without ensemble achieves an macro-averaged LAS of 75.26, which unofficially ranks the first according to LAS in the shared task.

We report the time and memory consumption. A full run over the 82 test sets on the TIRA virtual machine (Potthast et al., 2014) takes about 40 hours and consumes about 4G RAM memory.

10 Conclusion

Our system submitted to the CoNLL 2018 shared task made several improvements on last year's winning system from Dozat et al. (2017), including incorporating deep contextualized word embeddings, parser ensemble, and treebank concatenation. Experimental results on the development set show the effectiveness of our methods. Using these techniques, our system achieved an averaged LAS of 75.84% and obtained the first place in LAS in the final evaluation.

11 Credits

There are a few references we would like to give proper credit, especially to data providers: the core Universal Dependencies paper from LREC 2016 (Nivre et al., 2016), the UD version 2.2 datasets (Nivre et al., 2018), the baseline *udpipe* model released by Straka et al. (2016), the deep contextualized word embeddings code released by Peters et al. (2018), the biaffine tagger and parser released by Dozat et al. (2017), the joint sentence segmentor and tokenizer released by de Lhoneux et al. (2017), and the evaluation platform TIRA (Potthast et al., 2014).

Acknowledgments

We thank the reviewers for their insightful comments, and the HIT-SCIR colleagues for the coordination on the machine usage. This work was supported by the National Key Basic Research Program of China via grant 2014CB340503 and the National Natural Science Foundation of China (NSFC) via grant 61300113 and 61632011.

References

Waleed Ammar, George Mulcaire, Miguel Ballesteros, Chris Dyer, and Noah Smith. 2016. Many languages, one parser. *TACL* 4.

Anders Björkelund, Agnieszka Falenska, Xiang Yu, and Jonas Kuhn. 2017. Ims at the conll 2017 ud shared task: Crfs and perceptrons meet neural networks. In *Proc. of the CoNLL 2017 Shared Task: Multilingual Parsing from Raw Text to Universal Dependencies*. http://www.aclweb.org/anthology/K17-3004.

Piotr Bojanowski, Edouard Grave, Armand Joulin, and Tomas Mikolov. 2016. Enriching word vectors with subword information. *CoRR* abs/1607.04606. http://arxiv.org/abs/1607.04606.

Wanxiang Che, Jiang Guo, Yuxuan Wang, Bo Zheng, Huaipeng Zhao, Yang Liu, Dechuan Teng, and Ting Liu. 2017. The hit-scir system for end-to-end parsing of universal dependencies. In *Proc. of the CoNLL 2017 Shared Task: Multilingual Parsing from Raw Text to Universal Dependencies*. http://www.aclweb.org/anthology/K17-3005.

Miryam de Lhoneux, Yan Shao, Ali Basirat, Eliyahu Kiperwasser, Sara Stymne, Yoav Goldberg, and

Joakim Nivre. 2017. From raw text to universal dependencies - look, no tags! In *Proc. of the CoNLL 2017 Shared Task: Multilingual Parsing from Raw Text to Universal Dependencies*. http://www.aclweb.org/anthology/K17-3022.

Timothy Dozat and Christopher D. Manning. 2016. Deep biaffine attention for neural dependency parsing. *CoRR* abs/1611.01734.

Timothy Dozat, Peng Qi, and Christopher D. Manning. 2017. Stanford's graph-based neural dependency parser at the conll 2017 shared task. In *Proc. of CoNLL 2017 Shared Task: Multilingual Parsing from Raw Text to Universal Dependencies*.

Jiang Guo, Wanxiang Che, Haifeng Wang, and Ting Liu. 2016a. A universal framework for inductive transfer parsing across multi-typed treebanks. In *Proc. of Coling*. http://www.aclweb.org/anthology/C16-1002.

Jiang Guo, Wanxiang Che, David Yarowsky, Haifeng Wang, and Ting Liu. 2015. Cross-lingual dependency parsing based on distributed representations. In *Proc. of ACL*.

Jiang Guo, Wanxiang Che, David Yarowsky, Haifeng Wang, and Ting Liu. 2016b. A representation learning framework for multi-source transfer parsing. In *AAAI*. pages 2734–2740.

Sébastien Jean, Kyunghyun Cho, Roland Memisevic, and Yoshua Bengio. 2015. On using very large target vocabulary for neural machine translation. In *Proc. of ACL*. http://www.aclweb.org/anthology/P15-1001.

Yijia Liu, Wanxiang Che, Huaipeng Zhao, Bing Qin, and Ting Liu. 2018a. Distilling knowledge for search-based structured prediction. *CoRR* abs/1805.11224. http://arxiv.org/abs/1805.11224.

Yijia Liu, Yi Zhu, Wanxiang Che, Bing Qin, Nathan Schneider, and Noah A. Smith. 2018b. Parsing tweets into universal dependencies. In *Proc. of NAACL*. http://aclweb.org/anthology/N18-1088.

Xuezhe Ma and Eduard Hovy. 2017. Neural probabilistic model for non-projective mst parsing. In *Proc. of IJCNLP*. http://www.aclweb.org/anthology/I17-1007.

Xuezhe Ma, Zecong Hu, Jingzhou Liu, Nanyun Peng, Graham Neubig, and Eduard H. Hovy. 2018. Stack-pointer networks for dependency parsing. *CoRR* abs/1805.01087. http://arxiv.org/abs/1805.01087.

Joakim Nivre, Marie-Catherine de Marneffe, Filip Ginter, Yoav Goldberg, Jan Hajič, Christopher Manning, Ryan McDonald, Slav Petrov, Sampo Pyysalo, Natalia Silveira, Reut Tsarfaty, and Daniel Zeman. 2016. Universal Dependencies v1: A multilingual treebank collection. In *Proc. of LREC-2016*.

Joakim Nivre et al. 2018. Universal Dependencies 2.2. LINDAT/CLARIN digital library at the Institute of Formal and Applied Linguistics, Charles University, Prague, http://hdl.handle.net/11234/SUPPLYTHENEWPERMANENTIDHERE!

Matthew Peters, Mark Neumann, Mohit Iyyer, Matt Gardner, Christopher Clark, Kenton Lee, and Luke Zettlemoyer. 2018. Deep contextualized word representations. In *Proc. of NAACL.* http://aclweb.org/anthology/N18-1202.

Martin Potthast, Tim Gollub, Francisco Rangel, Paolo Rosso, Efstathios Stamatatos, and Benno Stein. 2014. Improving the reproducibility of PAN's shared tasks: Plagiarism detection, author identification, and author profiling. In Evangelos Kanoulas, Mihai Lupu, Paul Clough, Mark Sanderson, Mark Hall, Allan Hanbury, and Elaine Toms, editors, *Information Access Evaluation meets Multilinguality, Multimodality, and Visualization. 5th International Conference of the CLEF Initiative (CLEF 14).* Springer, Berlin Heidelberg New York, pages 268–299. https://doi.org/10.1007/978-3-319-11382-1_22.

Nils Reimers and Iryna Gurevych. 2017. Reporting score distributions makes a difference: Performance study of lstm-networks for sequence tagging. In *Proc. of EMNLP.*

Yan Shao. 2017. Cross-lingual word segmentation and morpheme segmentation as sequence labelling. *CoRR* abs/1709.03756. http://arxiv.org/abs/1709.03756.

Tianze Shi, Liang Huang, and Lillian Lee. 2017a. Fast(er) exact decoding and global training for transition-based dependency parsing via a minimal feature set. In *Proc. of EMNLP.* https://www.aclweb.org/anthology/D17-1002.

Tianze Shi, Felix G. Wu, Xilun Chen, and Yao Cheng. 2017b. Combining global models for parsing universal dependencies. In *Proc. of the CoNLL 2017 Shared Task: Multilingual Parsing from Raw Text to Universal Dependencies.* http://www.aclweb.org/anthology/K17-3003.

Samuel L. Smith, David H. P. Turban, Steven Hamblin, and Nils Y. Hammerla. 2017. Offline bilingual word vectors, orthogonal transformations and the inverted softmax. *CoRR* abs/1702.03859. http://arxiv.org/abs/1702.03859.

Milan Straka, Jan Hajič, and Jana Straková. 2016. UD-Pipe: trainable pipeline for processing CoNLL-U files performing tokenization, morphological analysis, POS tagging and parsing. In *Proc. of LREC-2016.*

Daniel Zeman, Jan Hajič, Martin Popel, Martin Potthast, Milan Straka, Filip Ginter, Joakim Nivre, and Slav Petrov. 2018. CoNLL 2018 Shared Task: Multilingual Parsing from Raw Text to Universal Dependencies. In *Proc. of the CoNLL 2018 Shared Task: Multilingual Parsing from Raw Text to Universal Dependencies.*

Daniel Zeman, Martin Popel, Milan Straka, Jan Hajič, Joakim Nivre, Filip Ginter, Juhani Luotolahti, Sampo Pyysalo, Slav Petrov, Martin Potthast, Francis Tyers, Elena Badmaeva, Memduh Gökırmak, Anna Nedoluzhko, Silvie Cinková, Jan Hajič jr., Jaroslava Hlaváčová, Václava Kettnerová, Zdeňka Urešová, Jenna Kanerva, Stina Ojala, Anna Missilä, Christopher Manning, Sebastian Schuster, Siva Reddy, Dima Taji, Nizar Habash, Herman Leung, Marie-Catherine de Marneffe, Manuela Sanguinetti, Maria Simi, Hiroshi Kanayama, Valeria de Paiva, Kira Droganova, Héctor Martínez Alonso, Çağrı Çöltekin, Umut Sulubacak, Hans Uszkoreit, Vivien Macketanz, Aljoscha Burchardt, Kim Harris, Katrin Marheinecke, Georg Rehm, Tolga Kayadelen, Mohammed Attia, Ali Elkahky, Zhuoran Yu, Emily Pitler, Saran Lertpradit, Michael Mandl, Jesse Kirchner, Hector Fernandez Alcalde, Jana Strnadova, Esha Banerjee, Ruli Manurung, Antonio Stella, Atsuko Shimada, Sookyoung Kwak, Gustavo Mendonça, Tatiana Lando, Rattima Nitisaroj, and Josie Li. 2017. CoNLL 2017 Shared Task: Multilingual Parsing from Raw Text to Universal Dependencies.

Bo Zheng, Wanxiang Che, Jiang Guo, and Ting Liu. 2017. Enhancing lstm-based word segmentation using unlabeled data. In *Chinese Computational Linguistics and Natural Language Processing Based on Naturally Annotated Big Data.*

ltcode	sent+tokenize	tagger	parser	LAS	w/o ens.	ref. LAS
af_afribooms	udpipe: self	biaffine (none): self	biaffine (none)*3: self	85.47 (1)	84.41 (5)	85.45
ar_padt	udpipe: self	biaffine ($h_{0,1,2}$): self	biaffine ($h_{0,1,2}$)*3: self	73.63 (2)	73.34 (3)	77.06
bg_btb	udpipe: self	biaffine (h_0): self	biaffine (h_0)*3: self	91.22 (1)	90.89 (1)	90.41
br_keb	udpipe: self	biaffine_trans: self+ga_idt	biaffine_trans*3: self+ga_idt	8.54 (21)	7.82 (21)	38.64
bxr_bdt	udpipe: self	biaffine_trans: self+hi_hdtb	biaffine_trans*3: self+hi_hdtb	15.44 (6)	15.69 (6)	19.53
ca_ancora	udpipe: self	biaffine (h_0): self	biaffine ($h_{0,1,2}$)*3: self	91.61 (1)	91.29 (1)	90.82
cs_cac	udpipe: self	biaffine (h_0): self	biaffine (h_0)*3: self	91.61 (1)	91.33 (1)	91.00
cs_fictree	udpipe: self	biaffine ($h_{0,1,2}$): self	biaffine ($h_{0,1,2}$)*3: self	92.02 (1)	91.39 (3)	91.83
cs_pdt	udpipe: self	biaffine (h_0): self	biaffine ($h_{0,1,2}$)*3: self	91.68 (1)	91.45 (1)	90.57
cs_pud	udpipe: cs_pdt	biaffine (h_0): cs_pdt	biaffine ($h_{0,1,2}$)*3: cs_pdt	86.13 (1)	85.89 (1)	85.35
cu_proiel	uppsala: self	biaffine ($h_{0,1,2}$): self	biaffine ($h_{0,1,2}$)*3: self	74.29 (3)	73.29 (4)	75.73
da_ddt	uppsala: self	biaffine (h_0): self	biaffine ($h_{0,1,2}$)*3: self	86.28 (1)	85.54 (1)	84.88
de_gsd	udpipe: self	biaffine (h_0): self	biaffine ($h_{0,1,2}$)*3: self	80.36 (1)	79.81 (1)	79.03
el_gdt	uppsala: self	biaffine (h_0): self	biaffine ($h_{0,1,2}$)*3: self	89.65 (1)	88.88 (3)	89.59
en_ewt	udpipe: self	biaffine (h_0): self	biaffine ($h_{0,1,2}$)*3: self	84.57 (1)	83.88 (2)	84.02
en_gum	udpipe: self	biaffine (h_0): self	biaffine ($h_{0,1,2}$)*3: self	84.42 (2)	83.57 (2)	85.05
en_lines	udpipe: self	biaffine ($h_{0,1,2}$): self	biaffine (h_0)*3: self+en_ewt+en_gum	81.97 (1)	81.67 (1)	81.44
en_pud	udpipe: en_ewt	biaffine (h_0): en_ewt	biaffine ($h_{0,1,2}$)*3: en_ewt	87.73 (2)	87.26 (2)	87.89
es_ancora	udpipe: self	biaffine (h_0): self	biaffine ($h_{0,1,2}$)*3: self	90.93 (1)	90.62 (1)	90.47
et_edt	uppsala: self	biaffine (h_0): self	biaffine ($h_{0,1,2}$)*3: self	85.35 (1)	84.74 (1)	84.15
eu_bdt	udpipe: self	biaffine ($h_{0,1,2}$): self	biaffine (h_0)*3: self	84.22 (1)	83.42 (1)	83.13
fa_seraji	udpipe: self	biaffine ($h_{0,1,2}$): self	biaffine ($h_{0,1,2}$)*3: self	88.11 (1)	87.60 (1)	86.18
fi_ftb	udpipe: self	biaffine ($h_{0,1,2}$): self	biaffine (h_0)*3: self	88.53 (1)	88.00 (1)	87.86
fi_pud	udpipe: fi_tdt	biaffine (h_0): fi_tdt	biaffine (h_0)*3: fi_tdt	90.23 (1)	89.58 (1)	89.37
fi_tdt	uppsala: self	biaffine (h_0): self	biaffine (h_0)*3: self	88.73 (1)	88.68 (1)	87.64
fo_oft	udpipe: no_bokmaal	biaffine_trans: no_bokmaal	biaffine_trans*3: no_bokmaal	44.05 (4)	44.17 (4)	49.43
fr_gsd	udpipe: self	biaffine (h_0): self	biaffine ($h_{0,1,2}$)*3: self	86.89 (1)	86.81 (1)	86.46
fr_sequoia	udpipe: self	biaffine ($h_{0,1,2}$): self	biaffine ($h_{0,1,2}$)*3: self	89.65 (2)	89.12 (2)	89.89
fr_spoken	udpipe: self	biaffine (h_0): self	biaffine ($h_{0,1,2}$)*3: self+fr_gsd+fr_sequoia	75.78 (1)	75.09 (1)	74.31
fro_srcmf	udpipe: self	biaffine (none): self	biaffine (none)*3: self	87.07 (2)	86.53 (3)	87.12
ga_idt	udpipe: self	biaffine (none): self	biaffine (none)*3: self	68.57 (5)	66.80 (7)	70.88
gl_ctg	udpipe: self	biaffine (none): self	biaffine (none)*3: self	82.35 (2)	81.80 (3)	82.76
gl_treegal	udpipe: self	biaffine (none): self	biaffine (none)*3: self	72.88 (4)	71.27 (8)	74.25
got_proiel	uppsala: self	biaffine (none): self	biaffine (none)*3: self	69.26 (3)	67.61 (5)	69.55
grc_perseus	udpipe: self	biaffine ($h_{0,1,2}$): self	biaffine ($h_{0,1,2}$)*3: self	79.39 (1)	78.53 (1)	74.29
grc_proiel	uppsala: self	biaffine (h_0): self	biaffine ($h_{0,1,2}$)*3: self	79.25 (1)	78.35 (1)	76.76
he_htb	udpipe: self	biaffine (h_0): self	biaffine (h_0)*3: self	67.05 (3)	66.67 (3)	76.09
hi_hdtb	udpipe: self	biaffine ($h_{0,1,2}$): self	biaffine (h_0)*3: self	92.41 (1)	92.13 (1)	91.75
hr_set	udpipe: self	biaffine (h_0): self	biaffine ($h_{0,1,2}$)*3: self	87.36 (1)	86.82 (1)	86.76
hsb_ufal	udpipe: self	biaffine_trans: self+pl_lfg	biaffine_trans*3: self+pl_lfg	37.68 (4)	35.42 (4)	46.42
hu_szeged	udpipe: self	biaffine (h_0): self	biaffine (h_0)*3: self	82.66 (1)	80.96 (1)	79.47
hy_armtdp	udpipe: self	biaffine_trans: self+et_edt	biaffine_trans*3: self+et_edt	33.90 (3)	30.87 (3)	37.01
id_gsd	uppsala: self	biaffine ($h_{0,1,2}$): self	biaffine ($h_{0,1,2}$)*3: self	80.05 (1)	79.19 (1)	79.13
it_isdt	udpipe: self	biaffine (h_0): self	biaffine ($h_{0,1,2}$)*3: self	92.00 (1)	91.71 (1)	91.47
it_postwita	uppsala: self	biaffine ($h_{0,1,2}$): self	biaffine ($h_{0,1,2}$)*3: self+it_isdt	79.39 (1)	78.69 (1)	78.62
ja_gsd	udpipe+scir: self	biaffine (h_0): self	biaffine (h_0)*3: self	83.11 (1)	82.70 (1)	79.97
ja_modern	udpipe+scir: ja_gsd	biaffine (h_0): self	biaffine (h_0)*3: ja_gsd	26.58 (4)	25.16 (4)	28.33
kk_ktb	udpipe: self	biaffine_trans: self+tr_imst	biaffine_trans*3: self+tr_imst	23.92 (10)	23.18 (13)	31.93
kmr_mg	udpipe: self	biaffine_trans: self+fa_seraji	biaffine_trans*3: self+fa_seraji	26.26 (5)	24.58 (6)	30.41
ko_gsd	udpipe: self	biaffine (h_0): self	biaffine ($h_{0,1,2}$)*3: self	85.14 (1)	84.76 (1)	84.31
ko_kaist	udpipe: self	biaffine (h_0): self	biaffine ($h_{0,1,2}$)*3: self	86.91 (1)	86.61 (2)	86.84
la_ittb	udpipe: self	biaffine ($h_{0,1,2}$): self	biaffine ($h_{0,1,2}$)*3: self	87.08 (1)	86.50 (2)	86.54
la_perseus	udpipe: self	biaffine (h_0): self+la_proiel	biaffine ($h_{0,1,2}$)*3: self+la_proiel	72.63 (1)	72.67 (1)	68.07
la_proiel	uppsala: self	biaffine (h_0): self	biaffine ($h_{0,1,2}$)*3: self	73.61 (1)	72.42 (1)	71.76
lv_lvtb	udpipe: self	biaffine (h_0): self	biaffine (h_0)*3: self	83.97 (1)	83.04 (1)	81.85
nl_alpino	udpipe: self	biaffine (h_0): self	biaffine ($h_{0,1,2}$)*3: self+nl_lassysmall	89.56 (1)	89.31 (1)	87.49
nl_lassysmall	uppsala: self	biaffine ($h_{0,1,2}$): self	biaffine ($h_{0,1,2}$)*3: self+nl_alpino	86.84 (1)	86.57 (1)	84.27
no_bokmaal	udpipe: self	biaffine ($h_{0,1,2}$): self	biaffine ($h_{0,1,2}$)*3: self	91.23 (1)	90.89 (1)	90.37
no_nynorsk	udpipe: self	biaffine (h_0): self	biaffine ($h_{0,1,2}$)*3: self	90.99 (1)	90.62 (1)	89.46
no_nynorsklia	udpipe: self	biaffine (h_0): self+no_nynorsk	biaffine ($h_{0,1,2}$)*3: self+no_nynorsk	70.34 (1)	69.06 (1)	68.71
pcm_nsc	udpipe: en_ewt	biaffine (h_0): en_ewt	biaffine ($h_{0,1,2}$)*3: en_ewt	24.48 (2)	25.16 (2)	30.07
pl_lfg	udpipe: self	biaffine (h_0): self	biaffine ($h_{0,1,2}$)*3: self	94.86 (1)	94.63 (1)	94.62
pl_sz	udpipe: self	biaffine (h_0): self	biaffine ($h_{0,1,2}$)*3: self	92.23 (1)	91.67 (1)	91.59
pt_bosque	uppsala: self	biaffine ($h_{0,1,2}$): self	biaffine ($h_{0,1,2}$)*3: self	87.61 (3)	87.32 (5)	87.81
ro_rrt	udpipe: self	biaffine (h_0): self	biaffine ($h_{0,1,2}$)*3: self	86.87 (1)	86.07 (3)	86.33
ru_syntagrus	udpipe: self	biaffine ($h_{0,1,2}$): self	biaffine (h_0)*3: self	92.48 (1)	92.26 (1)	91.72
ru_taiga	udpipe: self	biaffine ($h_{0,1,2}$): self+ru_syntagrus	biaffine ($h_{0,1,2}$)*3: self+ru_syntagrus	71.81 (3)	71.62 (3)	74.24
sk_snk	udpipe: self	biaffine ($h_{0,1,2}$): self	biaffine ($h_{0,1,2}$)*3: self	88.85 (1)	88.29 (1)	87.59
sl_ssj	uppsala: self	biaffine (h_0): self	biaffine ($h_{0,1,2}$)*3: self	91.47 (1)	91.08 (2)	91.26
sl_sst	udpipe: self	biaffine (h_0): self	biaffine ($h_{0,1,2}$)*3: self+sl_ssj	61.39 (1)	59.90 (1)	58.12
sme_giella	udpipe: self	biaffine (none): self	biaffine ($h_{0,1,2}$)*3: self	69.06 (3)	67.43 (5)	69.87
sr_set	udpipe: self	biaffine (none): self	biaffine ($h_{0,1,2}$)*3: self	88.33 (3)	87.78 (5)	88.66
sv_lines	udpipe: self	biaffine (h_0): self	biaffine (h_0)*3: self+sv_talbanken	84.08 (1)	83.64 (1)	81.97
sv_pud	udpipe: sv_lines	biaffine (h_0): sv_lines	biaffine (h_0)*3: sv_lines+sv_talbanken	80.35 (1)	79.78 (1)	79.71
sv_talbanken	udpipe: self	biaffine ($h_{0,1,2}$): self	biaffine (h_0)*3: self+sv_lines	88.63 (1)	88.26 (1)	86.45
th_pud	thai	biaffine_trans: zh_gsd	biaffine_trans*3: zh_gsd	0.64 (14)	0.61 (15)	13.70
tr_imst	udpipe: self	biaffine (h_0): self	biaffine ($h_{0,1,2}$)*3: self	66.44 (1)	64.91 (1)	64.79
ug_udt	udpipe: self	biaffine (h_0): self	biaffine (h_0)*3: self	67.05 (1)	66.20 (1)	65.23
uk_iu	udpipe: self	biaffine (h_0): self	biaffine (h_0)*3: self+ru_syntagrus	88.43 (1)	87.79 (1)	85.16
ur_udtb	udpipe: self	biaffine (h_0): self	biaffine (h_0)*3: self	83.39 (1)	82.17 (1)	82.15
vi_vtb	udpipe+scir: self	biaffine ($h_{0,1,2}$): self	biaffine (h_0)*3: self	55.22 (1)	53.92 (1)	47.41
zh_gsd	udpipe+scir: self	biaffine (none): self	biaffine ($h_{0,1,2}$)*3: self	76.77 (1)	75.55 (1)	71.04
average				75.84 (1)	75.26 (1)	

Table 6: The strategies used in the final submission. The *toolkit* and *model* are separated by colon. (*uppsala*: the Uppsala segmentor; *scir*: our segmentor; *biaffine*: the biaffine tagger and parser; *biaffine_trans*: our transfer parser for low-resource languages.) h_0 and $h_{0,1,2}$ denotes the ELMo used to train the model. h_0 means using $\mathbf{h}_{i,0}^{(LM)}$ and $h_{0,1,2}$ means using $\sum_{j=0}^{2} \mathbf{h}_{i,j}^{(LM)}$. *self* denotes that the model is trained with the treebank itself. If the model field is not filled with *self*, the model is trained with treebank concatenation. The *ref.* column shows the top performing system if we are not top, or the second-best performing system on LAS. We also show the results without parser ensemble and our unofficial ranks of this system.

Joint Learning of POS and Dependencies for Multilingual Universal Dependency Parsing

Zuchao Li[1,2,*]**, Shexia He**[1,2,*]**, Zhuosheng Zhang**[1,2]**, Hai Zhao**[1,2,†]

[1]Department of Computer Science and Engineering, Shanghai Jiao Tong University
[2]Key Laboratory of Shanghai Education Commission for Intelligent Interaction
and Cognitive Engineering, Shanghai Jiao Tong University, Shanghai, China
{charlee,heshexia,zhangzs}@sjtu.edu.cn, zhaohai@cs.sjtu.edu.cn

Abstract

This paper describes the system of team *LeisureX* in the *CoNLL 2018 Shared Task: Multilingual Parsing from Raw Text to Universal Dependencies*. Our system predicts the part-of-speech tag and dependency tree jointly. For the basic tasks, including tokenization, lemmatization and morphology prediction, we employ the official baseline model (UDPipe). To train the low-resource languages, we adopt a sampling method based on other rich-resource languages. Our system achieves a macro-average of 68.31% LAS F1 score, with an improvement of 2.51% compared with the UDPipe.

1 Introduction

The goal of Universal Dependencies (UD) (Nivre et al., 2016; Zeman et al., 2017) is to develop multilingual treebank, whose annotations of morphology and syntax are cross-linguistically consistent. In this paper, we describe our system for the CoNLL 2018 Shared Task: Multilingual Parsing from Raw Text to Universal Dependencies (Zeman et al., 2018), and we focus only on the subtasks of part-of-speech (POS) tagging and dependency parsing. For the intermediate steps, including tokenization, lemmatization and morphology prediction, we tackle them by the official baseline model (UDPipe)[1].

Dependency parsing that aims to predict the existence and type of linguistic dependency relations between words, is a fundamental part in natural language processing (NLP) tasks (Li et al., 2018c; He et al., 2018). Many referential natural language processing studies (Zhang et al., 2018; Bai and Zhao, 2018; Cai et al., 2018; Li et al., 2018b; Wang et al., 2018; Qin et al., 2017) can also contribute to the universal dependency parsing system. Universal dependency parsing focuses on learning syntactic dependency structure over many typologically different languages, even low-resource languages in a real-world setting. Within the dependency parsing literature, there are two dominant techniques, graph-based (McDonald et al., 2005; Ma and Zhao, 2012; Kiperwasser and Goldberg, 2016; Dozat and Manning, 2017) and transition-based parsing (Nivre, 2003; Dyer et al., 2015; Zhang et al., 2017). Graph-based dependency parsers enjoy the advantage of the global search which learns the scoring functions for all possible parsing trees to find the globally highest scoring one while transition-based dependency parsers build dependency trees from left to right incrementally, which makes the series of multiple choice decisions locally.

In our system, we adopt the transition-based dependency parsing in view of its relatively lower time complexity. Our system implements universal dependency parsing based on the stack-pointer networks (STACKPTR) parser introduced by (Ma et al., 2018). Furthermore, previous work (Straka et al., 2016; Nguyen et al., 2017) showed that POS tags are helpful to dependency parsing. In particular, (Nguyen et al., 2017) pointed out that parsing performance could be improved by the merit of accurate POS tags and the context of syntactic parse tree could help resolve POS ambiguities. Therefore, we seek to jointly learn POS tagging and dependency parsing.

---

* These authors made equal contribution.[†] Corresponding author. This paper was partially supported by National Key Research and Development Program of China (No. 2017YFB0304100), National Natural Science Foundation of China (No. 61672343 and No. 61733011), Key Project of National Society Science Foundation of China (No. 15-ZDA041), The Art and Science Interdisciplinary Funds of Shanghai Jiao Tong University (No. 14JCRZ04).

[1]https://ufal.mff.cuni.cz/udpipe/

Proceedings of the CoNLL 2018 Shared Task: Multilingual Parsing from Raw Text to Universal Dependencies, pages 65–73
Brussels, Belgium, October 31 – November 1, 2018. ©2018 Association for Computational Linguistics
https://doi.org/10.18653/v1/K18-2006

As Long short-term memory (LSTM) networks (Hochreiter and Schmidhuber, 1997) have shown significant representational effectiveness to a wide range of NLP tasks, we leverage bidirectional LSTMs (BiLSTM) to learn shared representations for both POS tagging and dependency parsing. In addition, to train the low-resource languages, we adopt a sampling method based on other rich-resource languages.

In terms of all the above model improvement, compared to the UDPipe baseline, our system achieves a macro-average of 68.31% LAS F1 score, with an improvement of 2.51% in this task.

2   Our Model

In this section, we describe our joint model[2] for POS tagging and dependency parsing in the CoNLL 2018 Shared Task, which is built on the STACKPTR parser introduced by (Ma et al., 2018). Our model is mainly composed of three components, the representation (Section 2.1), POS tagger (Section 2.2) and dependency parser (Section 2.3). Figure 1 illustrates the overall model.

2.1   Representation

Representation is a key component in various NLP models, and good representations should ideally model both complex characteristics and linguistic contexts. In our system, we follow the bi-directional LSTM-CNN architecture (BiLSTM-CNNs) (Chiu and Nichols, 2016; Ma and Hovy, 2016), where CNNs encode word information into character-level representation and BiLSTM models context information of each word.

Character Level Representation   Though word embedding is popular in many existing parsers, they are not ideal for languages with high out-of-vocabulary (OOV) ratios. Hence, our system introduces the character-level (Li et al., 2018a) representation to address the challenge. Formally, given a word $w = \{BOW, c_1, c_2, ..., c_n, EOW\}$, where two special BOW (begin-of-word) and EOW (end-of-word) tags indicate the begin and end positions respectively, we use the CNN to extract character-level representation as follows:

$$e^c = MaxPool(Conv(w))$$

---

[2]Our code will be available here: `https://github.com/bcmi220/joint_stackptr`.

where the CNN is similar to the one in (Chiu and Nichols, 2016), but we use only characters as the inputs to CNN, without character type features.

Word Level Representation   Word embedding is a standard component of most state-of-the-art NLP architectures. Due to their ability to capture syntactic and semantic information of words from large scale unlabeled texts, we pre-train the word embeddings from the given training dataset by word2vec (Mikolov et al., 2013) toolkit. For low-resource languages without available training data, we sample the training dataset from similar languages to generate a mixed dataset.

2.2   POS Tagger

To enrich morphological information, we also incorporate UPOS tag embeddings into the representation. Therefore, we jointly predict the UPOS tag in our system. The architecture for the POS tagger in our model is almost identical to that of the parser (Dozat et al., 2017). The tagger uses a BiLSTM over the concatenation of word embeddings and character embeddings:

$$s_i^{pos} = BiLSTM^{pos}(e_i^w \odot e_i^c)$$

Then we calculate the probability of tag for each type using affine classifiers as follows:

$$h_i^{pos} = MLP^{pos}(s_i^{pos})$$
$$r_i^{pos} = W^{pos} h_i^{pos} + b^{pos}$$
$$y_i^{pos} = arg\max(r_i)$$

The tag classifier is trained jointly using cross-entropy losses that are summed together with the dependency parser loss during optimization.

Context-sensitive Representation   In order to integrate contextual information, we concatenate the character embedding e_c, pre-trained word embedding e_w and UPOS tag embedding e_{pos}, then feed them into the BiLSTM. We take the bidirectional vectors at the final layer as the context-sensitive representation:

$$\overrightarrow{s_i} = LSTM_{forward}(e_i^w \odot e_i^c \odot e_i^{pos})$$
$$\overleftarrow{s_i} = LSTM_{backward}(e_i^w \odot e_i^c \odot e_i^{pos})$$
$$s_i = \overrightarrow{s_i} \odot \overleftarrow{s_i}$$

Notably, we use the UPOS tag from the output of our POS tagging model.

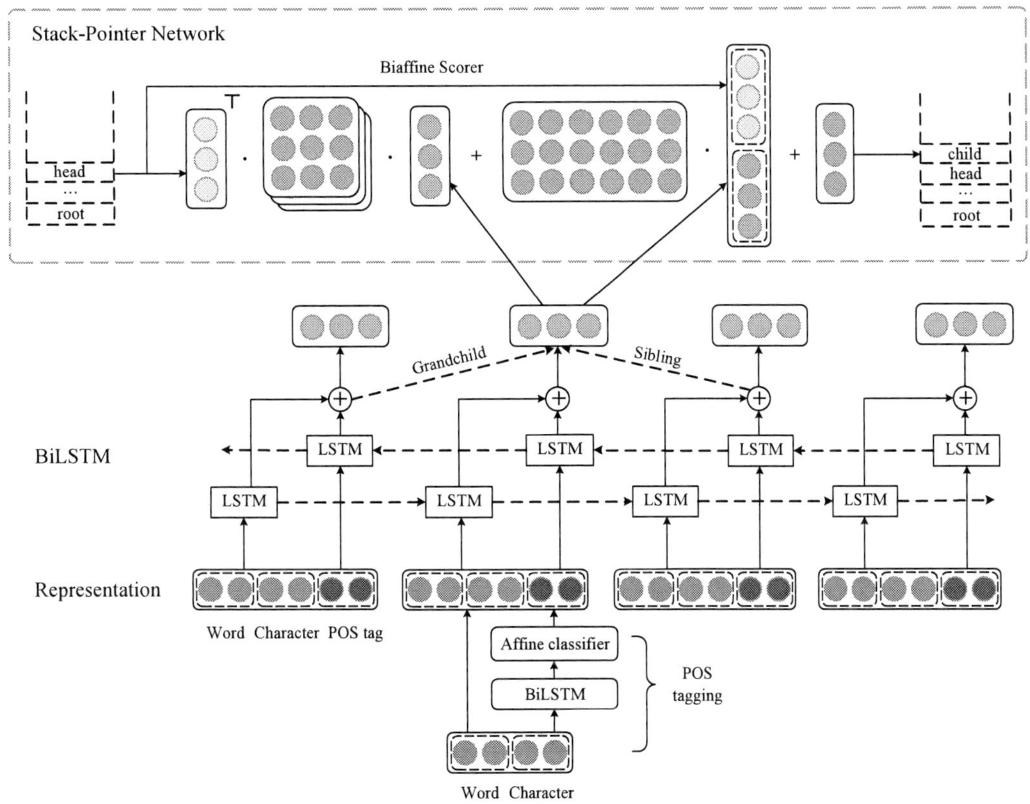

Figure 1: The joint model for POS tagging and dependency parsing.

2.3 Dependency Parsing

The universal dependency parsing component of our system is built on the current state-of-the-art approach STACKPTR, which combines pointer networks (Vinyals et al., 2015) with an internal stack for tracking the status of depth-first search. It benefits from the global information of the sentence and all previously derived subtree structures, and removes the left-to-right restriction in classical transition-based parsers.

The STACKPTR parser mainly consists of two parts: encoder and decoder. The encoder based on BiLSTM-CNNs architecture takes the sequence of tokens and their POS tags as input, then encodes it into encoder hidden state s_i. The internal stack σ is initialized with dummy *ROOT*. For decoder (a uni-directional RNN), it receives the input from last step and outputs decoder hidden state h_t. The pointer neural network takes the top element w_h in the stack σ at each timestep t as current head to select a specific child w_c with biaffine attention

mechanism (Dozat and Manning, 2017) for attention score function in all possible head-dependent pairs. Then the child w_c will be pushed onto the stack σ for next step when $c \neq h$, otherwise it indicates that all children of the current head h have been selected, therefore the head w_h will be popped out of the stack σ. The attention scoring function used is given as follows and the pointer neural network uses a^t as pointer to select the child element:

$$e_i^t = h_t^T \mathbf{W} s_i + \mathbf{U}^T h_t + \mathbf{V}^T s_i + \mathbf{b}$$
$$a^t = softmax(e^t)$$

More specifically, the decoder maintains a list of available words in test phase. For each head h at each decoding step, the selected child will be removed from the list to make sure that it cannot be selected as a child of other head words.

Given a dependency tree, there may be multiple children for a specific head. This results in more than one valid selection for each time step, which might confuse the decoder. To address this problem, the parser introduces an inside-outside order to utilize second-order sibling information, which has been proven to be an important feature for parsing process (McDonald and Pereira, 2006; Koo and Collins, 2010). To utilize the second-order information, the parser replaces the input of decoder from s_i as follows:

$$\beta_i = s_s \circ s_h \circ s_i$$

where s and h indicate the sibling and head index of node i, $\circ$ is the element-wise sum operation to ensure no additional model parameters.

2.4 Loss Function

The training objective of pur system is to learn the probability of UPOS tags $P_{\theta^{pos}}(y_{pos}|x)$ and the dependency trees $P_{\theta^{dep}}(y_{dep}|x, y'_{pos})$. Given a sentence x, the probabilities are factorized as:

$$P_{\theta^{pos}}(y_{pos}|x) = \sum_{i=1}^{k} P_{\theta^{pos}}(p_i|x)$$

$$y'_{pos} = \arg \max_{y_{pos} \in Y_{pos}} \left(P_{\theta^{pos}}(y_{pos}|x)\right)$$

$$P_{\theta^{dep}}(y_{dep}|x, y'_{pos}) = \sum_{i=1}^{k} P_{\theta^{dep}}(p_i|p_{<i}, x, y'_{pos})$$

$$= \prod_{i=1}^{k} \prod_{j=1}^{l_i} P_{\theta^{dep}}(c_{i,j}|c_{i,<j}, p_{<i}, x, y'_{pos})$$

where θ^{pos} and θ^{dep} represent the model parameters respectively. $p_{<i}$ denotes the preceding dependency paths that have already been generated. $c_{i,j}$ represents the j_{th} word in p_i and $c_{i,j}$ denotes all the proceeding words on the path p_i.

Therefore, the whole loss is the sum of three objectives:

$$Loss = Loss_{pos} + Loss_{arc} + Loss_{label}$$

where the $Loss_{pos}$, $Loss_{arc}$ and $Loss_{label}$ are the conditional likelhood of their corresponding target, using the cross-entropy loss. Specifically, we train a dependency label classifier following Dozat and Manning (2017), which takes the dependency head-child pair as input features.

3 System Implements

Our system focuses on three targets: the UPOS tag, dependency arc and dependency relation. Therefore, we rely on the UDPipe model (Straka

Treebank	Sampling
Breton KEB	English, Irish
Czech PUD	Czech PDT
English PUD	English EWT
Faroese OFT	Norwegian, English, Danish, Swedish, German, Dutch
Finnish PUD	Finnish TDT
Japanese Modern	Japanese GSD
Naija NSC	English
Swedish PUD	Swedish Talbanken
Thai PUD	English, Chinese, Hindi, Vietnamese

Table 1: Language substitution for treebanks without training data

et al., 2016) to provide a pipeline from raw text to basic dependency structures, including a tokenizer, tagger and the dependency predictor.

For treebanks with non-empty training dataset (including treebanks whose training set is very small), we utilize the baseline model UDPipe trained on corresponding treebank, which has been provided by the organizer. For the remaining nine treebanks without training data, we construct the train dataset by sampling from the other training datasets according to the language similarity inspired by (Zhao et al., 2009, 2010; Wang et al., 2015, 2016), as detailed in Table 1.

Our system adopts the hyper-parameter configuration in (Ma et al., 2018), with a few exceptions. We initialize word vectors with 50-dimensional pretrained word embeddings, 100-dimensional tag embeddings and 512-dimensional recurrent states (in each direction). Our system drops embeddings and hidden states independently with 33% probability. We optimize with Adam (Kingma and Ba, 2015), setting the learning rate to $1e^{-3}$ and $\beta_1 = \beta_2 = 0.9$. Moreover, we train models for up to 100 epochs with batch size 32 on 3 NVIDIA GeForce GTX 1080Ti GPUs with 200 to 500 sentences per second and occupying 2 to 3 GB graphic memory each model. A full run over the test datasets on the TIRA virtual machine (Potthast et al., 2014) takes about 12 hours.

4 Results

Table 2 reports the official evaluation results of our system in several metrics of treebanks from the CoNLL 2018 shared task (?). For dependency parsing, our model outperforms the baseline

Results	Ours	Baseline	Best
LAS	68.31	65.80	75.84
MLAS	53.70	52.42	61.25
BLEX	58.42	55.80	66.09
UAS	74.03	71.64	80.51
CLAS	63.85	60.77	72.36
UPOS	87.15	87.32	90.91
XPOS	83.91	85.00	86.67
Morphological features	83.46	83.74	87.59
Morphological tags	76.68	77.62	80.30
Lemmas	87.77	87.84	91.24
Sentence segmentation	83.01	83.01	83.87
Word segmentation	96.97	96.97	98.18
Tokenization	97.39	97.39	98.42

Table 2: Results on all treebanks.

Results	Ours	Baseline	Best
LAS	77.98	74.14	84.37
MLAS	63.79	61.27	72.67
BLEX	68.55	64.67	75.83
UAS	82.27	78.78	87.61
CLAS	73.59	69.13	81.29
UPOS	93.71	93.71	96.23
XPOS	91.81	91.81	95.16
Morphological features	90.85	90.85	94.14
Morphological tags	87.56	87.56	91.50
Lemmas	93.34	93.34	96.08
Sentence segmentation	86.09	86.09	89.52
Word segmentation	98.81	98.81	99.21
Tokenization	99.24	99.24	99.51

Table 3: Results on big treebank only.

with absolute gains (1.28-3.08%) on average LAS, UAS, MLAS and CLAS. These results show that our joint model could improve the performance of universal dependency parsing. Surprisingly, in the case of POS tagging, our joint model obtains lower averaged accuracy in both UPOS and XPOS. The possible reason for performance degradation may be that we select all hyper-parameters based on English and do not tune them individually.

Furthermore, we also compare the performance of our system with the baseline and the best scorer on big treebanks (Table 3), PUD treebanks (Table 4), low-resource languages (Table 5), respectively.

Since our model applies the baseline model for tokenization and segmentation, we show all results of focused metrics on each treebank in Table 6. In addition, we compare our model with the best and the average results of top ten models on each treebank, using LAS F1 for the evaluation metric, as shown in Figure 2.

5 Conclusion

In this paper, we describe our system in the CoNLL 2018 shared task on UD parsing. Our system uses a transition-based neural network architecture for dependency parsing, which predicts the UPOS tag and dependencies jointly. Combining pointer networks with an internal stack to track the status of the top-down, depth-first search in the parsing decoding procedure, the STACKPTR parser is able to capture information from the whole sentence and all the previously derived subtrees, removing the left-to-right restriction in classical transition-based parsers, while maintaining

Results	Ours	Baseline	Best
LAS	61.05	66.63	74.20
MLAS	41.95	51.75	58.75
BLEX	50.60	54.87	63.25
UAS	67.88	71.22	78.42
CLAS	57.34	61.29	69.86
UPOS	82.45	85.23	87.51
XPOS	35.66	54.27	55.98
Morphological features	78.89	83.41	87.05
Morphological tags	34.68	50.32	51.90
Lemmas	82.24	83.37	85.76
Sentence segmentation	75.53	75.53	76.04
Word segmentation	92.61	92.61	94.57
Tokenization	92.61	92.61	94.57

Table 4: Results on PUD treebank only.

Results	Ours	Baseline	Best
LAS	17.16	17.17	27.89
MLAS	3.43	3.44	6.13
BLEX	7.63	7.63	13.98
UAS	30.07	30.08	39.23
CLAS	13.42	13.42	22.18
UPOS	45.17	45.20	61.07
XPOS	54.68	54.23	54.73
Morphological features	38.03	38.03	48.95
Morphological tags	25.86	25.72	25.91
Lemmas	54.25	54.25	64.42
Sentence segmentation	65.99	65.99	67.50
Word segmentation	84.95	84.95	93.38
Tokenization	85.76	85.76	93.34

Table 5: Results on low-resource languages only.

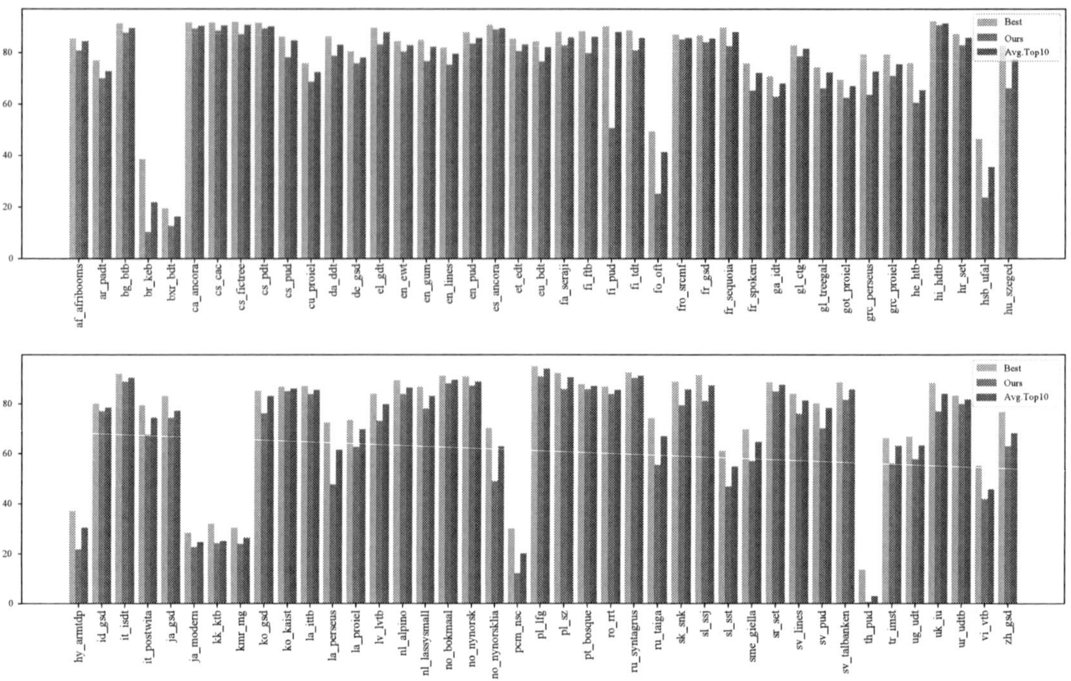

Figure 2: LAS F1 score per treebank. For comparison, we include the best official result and the average of the top ten results on each treebank.

linear parsing steps. Furthermore, our model is single instead of ensemble, and it does not utilize lemmas or morphological features. Results show that our system achieves 68.31% in macro-averaged LAS F1-score on the official blind test. Further improvements could be obtained by multilingual embeddings and adopting ensemble methods.

References

Hongxiao Bai and Hai Zhao. 2018. Deep enhanced representation for implicit discourse relation recognition. In *Proceedings of the 27th International Conference on Computational Linguistics*. pages 571–583.

Jiaxun Cai, Shexia He, Zuchao Li, and Hai Zhao. 2018. A full end-to-end semantic role labeler, syntactic-agnostic over syntactic-aware? In *Proceedings of the 27th International Conference on Computational Linguistics*. pages 2753–2765.

Jason PC Chiu and Eric Nichols. 2016. Named entity recognition with bidirectional LSTM-CNNs. *Transactions of the Association for Computational Linguistics* 4:357–370.

Timothy Dozat and Christopher D Manning. 2017. Deep biaffine attention for neural dependency parsing. *ICLR* .

Timothy Dozat, Peng Qi, and Christopher D Manning. 2017. Stanford's graph-based neural dependency parser at the conll 2017 shared task. *Proceedings of the CoNLL 2017 Shared Task: Multilingual Parsing from Raw Text to Universal Dependencies* pages 20–30.

Chris Dyer, Miguel Ballesteros, Wang Ling, Austin Matthews, and Noah A. Smith. 2015. Transition-based dependency parsing with stack long short-term memory pages 334–343.

Shexia He, Zuchao Li, Hai Zhao, and Hongxiao Bai. 2018. Syntax for semantic role labeling, to be, or not to be. In *Proceedings of the 56th Annual Meeting of the Association for Computational Linguistics (Volume 1: Long Papers)*. pages 2061–2071.

Sepp Hochreiter and Jrgen Schmidhuber. 1997. Long short-term memory. *Neural Computation* 9(8):1735–1780.

Diederik P Kingma and Jimmy Ba. 2015. Adam: A method for stochastic optimization. In *ICLR*.

Eliyahu Kiperwasser and Yoav Goldberg. 2016. Simple and accurate dependency parsing using bidirectional LSTM feature representations. *Transactions of the Association for Computational Linguistics* 4:313–327.

	UPOS	UAS	LAS	MLAS		UPOS	UAS	LAS	MLAS
af_afribooms	95.12	84.64	80.75	66.96	ar_padt	89.34	74.45	70.11	57.21
bg_btb	97.72	91.24	87.69	77.56	br_keb	30.74	27.80	10.25	0.37
bxr_bdt	41.66	29.20	12.61	2.09	ca_ancora	98.00	91.87	89.38	80.87
cs_cac	98.32	91.07	88.46	74.28	cs_fictree	97.28	91.07	87.12	71.98
cs_pdt	98.21	91.59	89.37	78.20	cs_pud	94.67	84.09	78.17	59.57
cu_proiel	93.70	75.18	68.68	55.36	da_ddt	95.44	82.21	78.74	67.34
de_gsd	91.58	80.31	75.73	36.39	el_gdt	95.63	86.64	83.17	65.02
en_ewt	93.62	83.32	80.46	70.58	en_gum	93.24	81.09	76.68	63.05
en_lines	94.71	80.71	75.26	65.04	en_pud	94.15	86.77	83.49	70.23
es_ancora	98.14	91.35	89.09	81.01	et_edt	95.50	84.18	80.59	70.39
eu_bdt	92.34	81.06	76.49	60.75	fa_seraji	96.01	86.76	82.78	75.38
fi_ftb	92.28	84.23	79.83	66.53	fi_pud	84.86	62.87	50.67	36.39
fi_tdt	94.37	84.72	80.88	70.42	fo_oft	44.66	42.64	25.19	0.36
fro_srcmf	94.30	90.32	85.15	75.66	fr_gsd	95.75	87.25	84.08	74.58
fr_sequoia	95.84	85.16	82.50	71.23	fr_spoken	92.94	71.81	65.30	52.73
ga_idt	89.21	72.66	62.93	37.66	gl_ctg	96.26	81.60	78.60	65.00
gl_treegal	91.09	71.61	66.16	49.13	got_proiel	94.31	69.71	62.62	48.19
grc_perseus	82.37	70.08	63.68	33.28	grc_proiel	95.87	75.19	71.05	52.44
he_htb	80.87	64.90	60.53	46.03	hi_hdtb	95.75	94.18	90.83	72.03
hr_set	96.33	88.39	83.06	60.93	hsb_ufal	65.75	35.02	23.64	3.55
hu_szeged	90.59	73.91	66.23	50.36	hy_armtdp	65.40	36.81	21.79	6.84
id_gsd	92.99	83.49	77.12	64.70	it_isdt	97.05	91.01	88.91	79.66
it_postwita	93.94	72.74	67.48	54.38	ja_gsd	87.85	76.14	74.43	60.32
ja_modern	48.44	29.36	22.71	8.10	kk_ktb	48.94	39.45	24.21	7.62
kmr_mg	59.31	32.86	23.92	5.47	ko_gsd	93.44	80.91	76.27	68.93
ko_kaist	93.32	87.43	85.11	76.91	la_ittb	97.21	86.64	83.96	73.55
la_perseus	83.34	58.45	47.61	30.16	la_proiel	94.84	68.02	62.62	49.11
lv_lvtb	91.70	78.74	73.13	55.05	nl_alpino	94.04	87.76	83.91	68.47
nl_lassysmall	94.06	82.34	78.13	64.55	no_bokmaal	96.51	90.30	88.11	78.94
no_nynorsk	96.07	89.67	87.26	76.85	no_nynorsklia	85.15	57.92	48.95	37.60
pcm_nsc	44.44	26.11	12.18	4.60	pl_lfg	96.77	93.67	90.94	74.89
pl_sz	95.50	89.64	85.83	64.03	pt_bosque	95.99	88.48	85.80	70.70
ro_rrt	96.62	89.06	83.94	74.60	ru_syntagrus	97.84	92.09	90.28	80.63
ru_taiga	86.53	63.58	55.51	36.79	sk_snk	93.15	83.42	79.43	55.02
sl_ssj	94.46	84.01	81.18	65.00	sl_sst	88.50	54.16	46.95	34.19
sme_giella	87.69	63.80	56.98	46.05	sr_set	96.84	89.50	84.90	70.68
sv_lines	93.97	81.32	76.04	59.25	sv_pud	90.12	76.30	70.19	35.44
sv_talbanken	95.36	85.27	81.57	71.64	th_pud	5.65	0.71	0.62	0.01
tr_imst	91.64	64.02	56.07	44.49	ug_udt	87.48	71.29	57.89	37.46
uk_iu	94.80	81.43	77.01	56.96	ur_udtb	92.13	86.14	79.99	51.65
vi_vtb	75.29	47.32	41.77	34.18	zh_gsd	83.47	66.45	63.05	51.64

Table 6: Performances of focused metrics on each treebank.

Terry Koo and Michael Collins. 2010. Efficient third-order dependency parsers. In *Proceedings of the 48th Annual Meeting of the Association for Computational Linguistics*. Association for Computational Linguistics, pages 1–11.

Haonan Li, Zhisong Zhang, Yuqi Ju, and Hai Zhao. 2018a. Neural character-level dependency parsing for Chinese. In *The Thirty-Second AAAI Conference on Artificial Intelligence (AAAI-18)*.

Zuchao Li, Jiaxun Cai, Shexia He, and Hai Zhao. 2018b. Seq2seq dependency parsing. In *Proceedings of the 27th International Conference on Computational Linguistics*. pages 3203–3214.

Zuchao Li, Shexia He, Jiaxun Cai, Zhuosheng Zhang, Hai Zhao, Gongshen Liu, Linlin Li, and Luo Si. 2018c. A unified syntax-aware framework for semantic role labeling. In *Proceedings of the 2018 Conference on Empirical Methods in Natural Language Processing*.

Xuezhe Ma and Eduard Hovy. 2016. End-to-end sequence labeling via bi-directional LSTM-CNNs-CRF. In *Proceedings of the 54th Annual Meeting of the Association for Computational Linguistics (Volume 1: Long Papers)*. volume 1, pages 1064–1074.

Xuezhe Ma, Zecong Hu, Jingzhou Liu, Nanyun Peng, Graham Neubig, and Eduard Hovy. 2018. Stack-pointer networks for dependency parsing. In *Proceedings of the 56th Annual Meeting of the Association for Computational Linguistics (Volume 1: Long Papers)*. pages 1403–1414.

Xuezhe Ma and Hai Zhao. 2012. Fourth-order dependency parsing. In *24th International Conference on Computational Linguistics*. page 785.

Ryan McDonald, Koby Crammer, and Fernando Pereira. 2005. Online large-margin training of dependency parsers. In *Proceedings of the 43rd annual meeting on association for computational linguistics*. Association for Computational Linguistics, pages 91–98.

Ryan McDonald and Fernando Pereira. 2006. Online learning of approximate dependency parsing algorithms. In *11th Conference of the European Chapter of the Association for Computational Linguistics*.

Tomas Mikolov, Kai Chen, Greg Corrado, and Jeffrey Dean. 2013. Efficient estimation of word representations in vector space. In *ICLR Workshop*.

Dat Quoc Nguyen, Mark Dras, and Mark Johnson. 2017. A novel neural network model for joint pos tagging and graph-based dependency parsing. In *Proceedings of the CoNLL 2017 Shared Task: Multilingual Parsing from Raw Text to Universal Dependencies*. Vancouver, Canada, pages 134–142.

Joakim Nivre. 2003. An efficient algorithm for projective dependency parsing. In *Proceedings of the 8th International Workshop on Parsing Technologies (IWPT)*. Citeseer, pages 149–160.

Joakim Nivre, Marie-Catherine de Marneffe, Filip Ginter, Yoav Goldberg, Jan Hajič, Christopher Manning, Ryan McDonald, Slav Petrov, Sampo Pyysalo, Natalia Silveira, Reut Tsarfaty, and Daniel Zeman. 2016. Universal Dependencies v1: A multilingual treebank collection. In *Proceedings of the 10th International Conference on Language Resources and Evaluation (LREC 2016)*. Portoro, Slovenia, pages 1659–1666.

Martin Potthast, Tim Gollub, Francisco Rangel, Paolo Rosso, Efstathios Stamatatos, and Benno Stein. 2014. Improving the reproducibility of PAN's shared tasks: Plagiarism detection, author identification, and author profiling. In Evangelos Kanoulas, Mihai Lupu, Paul Clough, Mark Sanderson, Mark Hall, Allan Hanbury, and Elaine Toms, editors, *Information Access Evaluation meets Multilinguality, Multimodality, and Visualization. 5th International Conference of the CLEF Initiative (CLEF 14)*. Berlin Heidelberg New York, pages 268–299.

Lianhui Qin, Zhisong Zhang, Hai Zhao, Zhiting Hu, and Eric Xing. 2017. Adversarial connective-exploiting networks for implicit discourse relation classification. In *Proceedings of the 55th Annual Meeting of the Association for Computational Linguistics (Volume 1: Long Papers)*. volume 1, pages 1006–1017.

Milan Straka, Jan Hajič, and Jana Straková. 2016. UD-Pipe: trainable pipeline for processing CoNLL-U files performing tokenization, morphological analysis, POS tagging and parsing. In *Proceedings of the 10th International Conference on Language Resources and Evaluation (LREC 2016)*. Portoro, Slovenia.

Oriol Vinyals, Meire Fortunato, and Navdeep Jaitly. 2015. Pointer networks. In *Advances in Neural Information Processing Systems*. pages 2692–2700.

Rui Wang, Masao Utiyama, Isao Goto, Eiichiro Sumita, Hai Zhao, and Bao-Liang Lu. 2016. Converting continuous-space language models into n-gram language models with efficient bilingual pruning for statistical machine translation. *ACM Transactions on Asian and Low-Resource Language Information Processing* 15(3):11.

Rui Wang, Hai Zhao, Bao-Liang Lu, Masao Utiyama, and Eiichiro Sumita. 2015. Bilingual continuous-space language model growing for statistical machine translation. *IEEE/ACM Transactions on Audio, Speech, and Language Processing* 23(7):1209–1220.

Rui Wang, Hai Zhao, Sabine Ploux, Bao-Liang Lu, Masao Utiyama, and Eiichiro Sumita. 2018. Graph-based bilingual word embedding for statistical machine translation. *ACM Transactions on Asian and Low-Resource Language Information Processing (TALLIP)* 17(4):31.

Daniel Zeman, Jan Hajič, Martin Popel, Martin Potthast, Milan Straka, Filip Ginter, Joakim Nivre, and

Slav Petrov. 2018. CoNLL 2018 Shared Task: Multilingual Parsing from Raw Text to Universal Dependencies. In *Proceedings of the CoNLL 2018 Shared Task: Multilingual Parsing from Raw Text to Universal Dependencies*. Association for Computational Linguistics, Brussels, Belgium, pages 1–20.

Daniel Zeman, Martin Popel, Milan Straka, Jan Hajič, Joakim Nivre, Filip Ginter, Juhani Luotolahti, Sampo Pyysalo, Slav Petrov, Martin Potthast, Francis Tyers, Elena Badmaeva, Memduh Gökırmak, Anna Nedoluzhko, Silvie Cinková, Jan Hajič jr., Jaroslava Hlaváčová, Václava Kettnerová, Zdeňka Urešová, Jenna Kanerva, Stina Ojala, Anna Missilä, Christopher Manning, Sebastian Schuster, Siva Reddy, Dima Taji, Nizar Habash, Herman Leung, Marie-Catherine de Marneffe, Manuela Sanguinetti, Maria Simi, Hiroshi Kanayama, Valeria de Paiva, Kira Droganova, Héctor Martínez Alonso, Çağrı Çöltekin, Umut Sulubacak, Hans Uszkoreit, Vivien Macketanz, Aljoscha Burchardt, Kim Harris, Katrin Marheinecke, Georg Rehm, Tolga Kayadelen, Mohammed Attia, Ali Elkahky, Zhuoran Yu, Emily Pitler, Saran Lertpradit, Michael Mandl, Jesse Kirchner, Hector Fernandez Alcalde, Jana Strnadova, Esha Banerjee, Ruli Manurung, Antonio Stella, Atsuko Shimada, Sookyoung Kwak, Gustavo Mendonça, Tatiana Lando, Rattima Nitisaroj, and Josie Li. 2017. CoNLL 2017 Shared Task: Multilingual Parsing from Raw Text to Universal Dependencies. In *Proceedings of the CoNLL 2017 Shared Task: Multilingual Parsing from Raw Text to Universal Dependencies*. Vancouver, Canada, pages 1–19.

Zhirui Zhang, Shujie Liu, Mu Li, Ming Zhou, and Enhong Chen. 2017. Stack-based multi-layer attention for transition-based dependency parsing. In *Proceedings of the 2017 Conference on Empirical Methods in Natural Language Processing*. Copenhagen, Denmark, pages 1677–1682.

Zhuosheng Zhang, Yafang Huang, and Hai Zhao. 2018. Subword-augmented embedding for cloze reading comprehension. In *Proceedings of the 27th International Conference on Computational Linguistics*. pages 1802–1814.

Hai Zhao, Yan Song, and Chunyu Kit. 2010. How large a corpus do we need: Statistical method versus rule-based method. *Training (M)* 8(2.71):0–83.

Hai Zhao, Yan Song, Chunyu Kit, and Guodong Zhou. 2009. Cross language dependency parsing using a bilingual lexicon. In *Proceedings of the Joint Conference of the 47th Annual Meeting of the ACL and the 4th International Joint Conference on Natural Language Processing of the AFNLP: Volume 1-Volume 1*. Association for Computational Linguistics, pages 55–63.

Multilingual Universal Dependency Parsing from Raw Text with Low-resource Language Enhancement

Yingting Wu[1,2], **Hai Zhao**[1,2,]*, **Jia-Jun Tong**[1,2]

[1]Department of Computer Science and Engineering, Shanghai Jiao Tong University
[2]Key Laboratory of Shanghai Education Commission for Intelligent Interaction
and Cognitive Engineering, Shanghai Jiao Tong University, Shanghai, 200240, China
`wuyingting@sjtu.edu.cn`, `zhaohai@cs.sjtu.edu.cn`, `tong2j1994@gmail.com`

Abstract

This paper describes the system of our team Phoenix for participating *CoNLL 2018 Shared Task: Multilingual Parsing from Raw Text to Universal Dependencies*. Given the annotated gold standard data in CoNLL-U format, we train the tokenizer, tagger and parser separately for each treebank based on an open source pipeline tool UDPipe. Our system reads the plain texts for input, performs the pre-processing steps (tokenization, lemmas, morphology) and finally outputs the syntactic dependencies. For the low-resource languages with no training data, we use cross-lingual techniques to build models with some close languages instead. In the official evaluation, our system achieves the macro-averaged scores of 65.61%, 52.26%, 55.71% for LAS, MLAS and BLEX respectively.

1 Introduction

Universal Dependencies (UD) (Nivre et al., 2016) is a framework that provides cross-linguistically consistent grammatical annotations for various languages, which enables comparative evaluations for some cross-lingual learning tasks. As a follow up of *CoNLL 2017 UD Shared Task* (Zeman et al., 2017), the goal of *CoNLL 2018 UD Shared Task* (Zeman et al., 2018) is to develop multilingual dependency parsers from raw text for many typologically different languages with training data from UD project. The task comprises 82 test sets from 57 languages. However, there are a category of low-resource languages that have little or no training data, which requires cross-lingual techniques (Zeman and Resnik, 2008; Tiedemann, 2015) with the help of the data from other languages.

In this paper, we present the system of our team Phoenix for multilingual universal dependency parsing from raw text. The targeted task is a challenging one in terms of deep learning based natural language processing (Wu and Zhao, 2018; Bai and Zhao, 2018; Cai et al., 2018; Li et al., 2018; Zhang et al., 2018; Zhang and Zhao, 2018; He et al., 2018; Wang et al., 2017; Qin et al., 2017). We adopt the trainable open source tool UDPipe 1.2 (Straka et al., 2016; Straka and Straková, 2017) to train the dependency parser for each test set with UD version 2.2 (Nivre et al., 2018) treebanks as training data. There are three main components of our model to perform, tokenization, Part-of-Speech (POS) tagging and dependency parsing. When evaluated on the web interface of TIRA (Potthast et al., 2014) platform, the system reads the raw text for input and chooses the corresponding model for a particular test set with a model selector. After the tokenization and tagging on the raw text, the system finally outputs the syntactic dependencies in the CoNLL-U format. To deal with the low-resource languages which have no training data, some cross-lingual techniques are applied by training with other related or close languages. Our official submission obtains macro-averaged scores of 65.61%, 52.26%, 55.71% for LAS, MLAS and BLEX on all treebanks.

The rest of this paper is organized as follows. Section 2 introduces the architecture overview of our system. Section 3 gives the implementation details and the specific strategies applied for the low-resource languages. Finally, we report and an-

---

* Corresponding author. This paper was partially supported by National Key Research and Development Program of China (No. 2017YFB0304100), National Natural Science Foundation of China (No. 61672343 and No. 61733011), Key Project of National Society Science Foundation of China (No. 15-ZDA041), The Art and Science Interdisciplinary Funds of Shanghai Jiao Tong University (No. 14JCRZ04).

Proceedings of the CoNLL 2018 Shared Task: Multilingual Parsing from Raw Text to Universal Dependencies, pages 74–80
Brussels, Belgium, October 31 – November 1, 2018. ©2018 Association for Computational Linguistics
https://doi.org/10.18653/v1/K18-2007

alyze the official results with the three main evaluation metrics in Section 4.

2 System Overview

Figure 1 illustrates the overall architecture of our system for training and predicting. In the training procedure, the system takes as input the treebanks (training set) of CoNLL-U format and trains a model for each of them. Every model has three components, tokenizer, tagger and parser. As we train the parser, pretrained word embeddings for word forms in the word2vec format are applied. In the predicting procedure, the system takes as input the raw text (test set) and selects a model according to the language code and treebank code. With the selected model, the system outputs the syntactic head and the type of the dependency relation for each word.

2.1 Training Data

Our models are trained by using only UD 2.2 treebanks provided by the *CoNLL 2018 UD Shared Task* without any other additional data. There are 82 test sets from 57 languages, and 61 of the 82 treebanks are large enough to provide training and development sets. However, the other 21 treebanks lack of development data and some of them even have no training data. Among these low-resource treebanks, 7 have training data with still reasonable size; 5 are extra test sets in languages where another large treebank exists; 9 are low-resource languages with no training data available (Breton, Faroese, Naija, Thai) or the training set being just a tiny sample (Armenian, Buryat, Kazakh, Kurmanji, Upper Sorbian). For the treebanks that still have training data but without development data, we split the last 10% of the training data as the development set to tune model hyperparameters even if the training set is very small. To deal with those having no training data, we train the parsers with the treebanks of the same languages or related languages. The details will be given in Section 3.4.

2.2 Word Embedding

We adopt pretrained embeddings for word forms with the provided training data by word2vec (Mikolov et al., 2013). The parameter settings of word2vec are shown in Table 1. We use the skip-gram model to train the word vectors with a dimension of 50. The context window is set

to 10 words and the word will be dropped if its frequency is less than twice. After converting CoNLL-U to the horizontal format (replacing spaces within word forms with a Unicode character), we train the word embeddings of each treebank on the UD data for 15 iterations.

Parameters	Value
algorithm	skip-gram
size	50
window	10
min-count	2
iterations	15

Table 1: Parameters for training word embeddings.

2.3 Model Selector

Since we train models individually for every languages and treebanks, a model selector is needed to decide which model to use when predicting. The model selector in our system simply reads the json file in the test file folder and assigns the corresponding trained model for each test set according to the language code and treebank code.

3 Model Description

3.1 Tokenizer

In our system pipeline, the first step is the sentence segmentation and tokenization which is performed jointly in UDPipe. A single-layer bidirectional GRU network is used to train the tokenizer which predicts for each character whether it is the last one in a sentence or the last one in a token. In UD treebanks, the text is structured on several levels: document, paragraph, sentence and token. A MISC feature SpaceAfter=No is defined to denote that a given token is not followed by a space. Thus, the tokenizer is trained according to the SpaceAfter=No features in the CoNLL-U files.

The parameters used for training the tokenizer are listed in Table 2. The segmenter and tokenizer network employs character embeddings and is trained using dropout both before and after the recurrent units. The GRU dimension, dropout probability and learning rate are tuned on the development set. All the tokenizers are trained for 100 epochs. Other parameters like tokenize_url and allow_spaces are set as default.

75

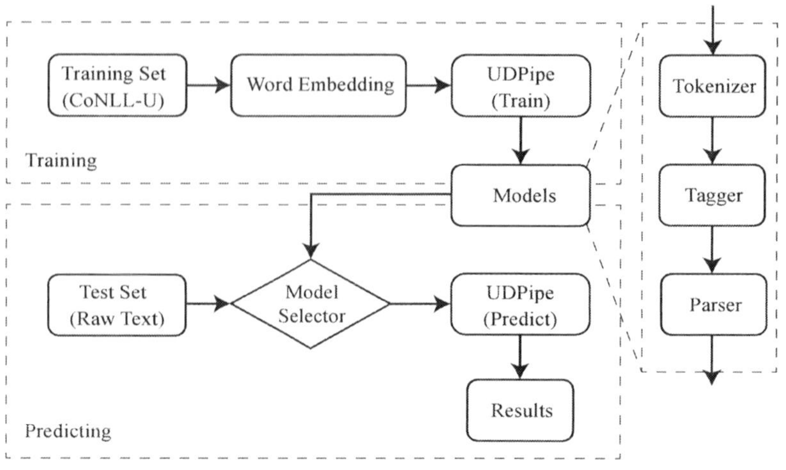

Figure 1: System architecture

Parameters	Value
tokenize_url	1
allow_spaces	1
batch size	50,100
dimension	24, 64
dropout	0.1, 0.2, 0.3
early_stop	1
epochs	100
learning_rate	0.002, 0.005, 0.01

Table 2: Parameters for training the tokenizers.

Parameters	Value
models	2
templates_1	tagger
guesser_suffix_rules_1	4, 6, 8, 10, 12
guesser_enrich_dictionary_1	4, 5, 6
guesser_prefixes_max_1	0, 4
templates_2	lemmatizer
guesser_suffix_rules_2	4, 6, 8
guesser_enrich_dictionary_2	4, 5, 6
guesser_prefixes_max_2	0, 4
iterations	20
early_stopping	1

Table 3: Parameters for training the taggers.

3.2 Tagger

The second step in our system pipeline is to generate some POS tags and other morphological features for the tokenized data, which will be utilized as the input for the final dependency parser. We adopt the built-in tagger in UDPipe, which is based on an open source morphological analysis tool MorphoDita (Straková et al., 2014). In this step, the tagger will produce the following outputs:

Lemma: Lemma or stem of word form.

UPOS: Universal POS tag.

XPOS: Language-specific POS tag.

FEATS: List of morphological features from the universal feature inventory or from a defined language-specific extension.

We use two MorphoDita models to produce different features, whose effectiveness has been verified in (Straka et al., 2016). The first model called *tagger* generates the UPOS, XPOS and FEATS tags while the second one called *lemmatizer* performs lemmatization.

The tagger consists of a guesser and an averaged perceptron. The guesser generates several triplets (UPOS, XPOS, FEATS) for each word according to its last four characters. The averaged perceptron with a fixed set of features disambiguates the generated tags (Straka et al., 2016; Straková et al., 2014).

The structure of the lemmatizer is similar to the tagger. A guesser produces (lemma rule, UPOS) tuples and an averaged perceptron performs disambiguation. The lemmatizer generates a lemma from a word by stripping some affix and adding new affix according to the last four characters of a word and its prefix.

The training parameters of the two models for different treebanks are provided in Table 3.

Parameters	Value
embedding_form	50
embedding_upostag	20
embedding_feats	20
embedding_deprel	20
hidden_layer	200
batch_size	10
iterations	30
l2	0.3, 0.5
learning_rate	0.01, 0.02
learning_rate_final	0.001
structured_interval	0, 8, 10
transition_oracle	static, dynamic, static_lazy
transition_system	projective, link2, swap
use_gold_tags	1

Table 4: Parameters for training the parsers.

3.3 Parser

The final parsing step is performed using Parsito (Straka et al., 2015), which is a transition-based parser with a neural-network classifier. The parser supports several transition systems including a projective arc-standard system (Nivre, 2008), a partially non-projective link2 system (Gómez-Rodríguez et al., 2014) and a fully non-projective swap system (Nivre, 2009). Meanwhile, the transition oracles can be configured into static oracles, dynamic oracle for the arc-standard system (Goldberg et al., 2014) or a search-based oracle (Straka et al., 2015).

We use the golden Lemmas, UPOS, XPOS and FEATS tags for both the training and development data when training the parser. The parser employs FORM embeddings of dimension 50, and UPOS, FEATS, DEPREL embeddings of dimension 20. The FORM embeddings are pretrained with word2vec using the training data, and the other embeddings are initialized randomly. All the embeddings are updated for each iteration during training. The hidden layer size is set to 200 and the batch size is limited to 30. All the parsing models are trained for 10 iterations. The training parameters for different datasets are reported in Table 4. The optimal parameters are chosen to maximize the accuracy on the development set.

3.4 Low-resource Treebanks

In the UD 2.2 datasets provided by the shared task, there are low-resource treebanks with little or even no training data. As we have stated before, in this work, we mainly focus on the strategy to deal with the treebanks without any training data in this section.

For the ones with other treebanks in the same languages, we trained models both on the mixture of all those treebanks and on the largest treebank as the official baseline did. For those without other treebanks in the same language, the direct solution is to use other related treebanks as training data. Hence, we take advantage of the cross-lingual knowledge and train the mixture models with the treebanks of similar or related languages. Specifically, we manually selected treebanks with similar languages as the ingredients of a mixture dataset according to many factors such as grammar, morphology and vocabulary. The training and development sets of the selected treebanks are merged together on which we train and evaluate the results. The no-training-data treebanks and their corresponding training sets are shown in Table 5.

4 Results

The final results are evaluated blindly on TIRA platform. There are three main scoring metrics, LAS, MLAS and BLEX. Our system ranks 19 in LAS, 17 in MLAS and 13 in BLEX on the main metric ranking board. The main evaluation scores of our system on all treebanks, big treebanks, PUD treebanks, small treebanks and low-resource languages are shown in Table 6. Overall, our system gives a similar performance to the BASELINE UDPipe 1.2 system, which is not surprising as we closely followed the hyper-parameter settings and data splitting of the baseline system on big and small treebanks.

As described in Section 3.4, we select training sets differently for the low-resource treebanks including PUD treebanks and other treebanks without training data. Table 7 shows the results comparison with the baseline system on those treebanks. Our system shows a consistent improvement over the baseline model for all the three metrics on PUD treebanks, which suggests that enlarging training data with different types of treebanks of the same language indeed helps building a better model. Our system shows a slight ad-

Low-resource Treebanks	Training Treebanks
Czech PUD	Czech PDT / Czech (PDT, CAC, FicTree)
English PUD	English EWT / English (EWT, GUM, LinES)
Finnish PUD	Finnish TDT / Finnish (TDT, FTB)
Japanese Modern	Japanese GSD
Swedish PUD	Swedish Talbanken / Swedish (Talbanken, LinES)
Breton KEB	Irish (IDT), Latin (ITTB, Persus, PROIEL), Old French (SRCMF), French (GSD, Sequoia, Spoken)
Faroese OFT	Danish (DDT), Norwegian (Bokmaal, Nynorsk, NynorskLIA)
Naija NSC	English (EWT, GUM, LinES), Portuguese (Bosque)
Thai PUD	Hindi (HDTB), Vietnamese (VTB), Chinese (GSD), English (EWT, GUM, LinES)

Table 5: The training data for the low-resource treebanks.

Target Treebanks	LAS	MLAS	BLEX
Big treebanks	73.93	61.12	64.47
PUD treebanks	66.97	52.26	55.69
Small treebanks	54.63	38.38	40.72
Low-resource	16.99	3.02	8.00
All treebanks	65.61	52.26	55.71

Table 6: Evaluation scores of our system on different types of treebanks.

Metrics	PUD Treebanks		Low-resource	
	Ours	Base	Ours	Base
LAS	**66.97**	66.63	16.99	17.17
MLAS	**52.26**	51.75	3.02	3.44
BLEX	**55.69**	54.87	**8.00**	7.63

Table 7: Comparison of our system (Ours) and baseline system (Base) on PUD treebanks and low-resource languages.

Target Treebanks	Selected Model	LAS	Rank
cs_pud	cs_pdt	80.34	16
en_pud	en_all	79.69	16
fi_pud	fi_tdt	80.19	14
ja_modern	ja_gsd	22.90	6
sv_pud	sv_all	71.75	15
Macro-average		66.97	13

Table 8: LAS F1 scores and rankings of our system on PUD treebanks.

vantage over baseline on low-resource treebanks in BLEX, which indicates that low-resource languages can be trained with similar languages.

Target Treebanks	LAS	Rank
bxr_bdt	9.04	20
hsb_ufal	23.43	21
hy_armtdp	23.37	14
kk_ktb	23.00	14
kmr_mg	19.08	19
br_keb	8.88	20
fo_oft	29.13	12
pcm_nsc	16.25	8
th_pud	0.75	5
Macro-average	16.99	17

Table 9: LAS F1 scores and rankings of our system on low-resource languages.

Table 8 shows the results on each PUD treebanks and our selected model for testing. The models with suffix '_all' represent those trained with all treebanks of the same language. During the test phase, we evaluated both models trained with all treebanks of the same language and with the largest treebank of that language, and compared the rounded results to decide which one to take for our final system. The model trained by mixed English and Swedish treebanks with all data of the same languages shows better performance than those of the single largest treebank. However, the models trained by the largest Czech and Finnish treebanks get a higher score. We conjecture that more training data may provide more information for the modeling while too large training sets will also bring noise for a specific domain.

Metrics	F1 Score	Rank
UAS	71.27	19
CLAS	60.62	19
UPOS	87.49	15
XPOS	84.83	13
Morphological features	83.87	11
All morphological tags	77.47	10
Lemmas	87.69	14
Sentence segmentation	82.91	17
Word segmentation	97.03	8
Tokenization	97.46	7

Table 10: Other metrics and rankings of our system.

Table 9 shows the LAS F1 scores and rankings of each low-resource language. Note that our system has a good performance on pcm_nsc and th_pud treebanks when most teams get an unsatisfying result. It also proves that our data selection method is effective for improving the model performance to some extent. Table 10 shows the F1 scores and our system rankings on other metrics. In particular, our system ranks first in the Sentence Segmentation F1 score of PUD treebanks.

5 Conclusion

In this paper, we describe our system to *CoNLL 2018 UD Shared Task*. In our system, we focus on the accuracy improvement of the low resource treebanks against the baseline. The results of the official blind test show that our system achieves 65.61%, 52.26%, 55.71% in macro-averaged LAS, MLAS and BLEX.

References

Hongxiao Bai and Hai Zhao. 2018. Deep enhanced representation for implicit discourse relation recognition. In *Proceedings of the 27th International Conference on Computational Linguistics*. Association for Computational Linguistics, pages 571–583. http://aclweb.org/anthology/C18-1048.

Jiaxun Cai, Shexia He, Zuchao Li, and Hai Zhao. 2018. A full end-to-end semantic role labeler, syntactic-agnostic over syntactic-aware? In *Proceedings of the 27th International Conference on Computational Linguistics*. Association for Computational Linguistics, pages 2753–2765. http://aclweb.org/anthology/C18-1233.

Yoav Goldberg, Francesco Sartorio, and Giorgio Satta. 2014. A tabular method for dynamic oracles in transition-based parsing. *Transactions of the association for Computational Linguistics* 2:119–130.

Carlos Gómez-Rodríguez, Francesco Sartorio, and Giorgio Satta. 2014. A polynomial-time dynamic oracle for non-projective dependency parsing. In *Proceedings of the 2014 Conference on Empirical Methods in Natural Language Processing*. Association for Computational Linguistics, Doha, Qatar, pages 917–927. http://www.aclweb.org/anthology/D14-1099.

Shexia He, Zuchao Li, Hai Zhao, and Hongxiao Bai. 2018. Syntax for semantic role labeling, to be, or not to be. In *Proceedings of the 56th Annual Meeting of the Association for Computational Linguistics (Volume 1: Long Papers)*. Association for Computational Linguistics, pages 2061–2071. http://aclweb.org/anthology/P18-1192.

Zuchao Li, Jiaxun Cai, Shexia He, and Hai Zhao. 2018. Seq2seq dependency parsing. In *Proceedings of the 27th International Conference on Computational Linguistics*. Association for Computational Linguistics, pages 3203–3214. http://aclweb.org/anthology/C18-1271.

Tomas Mikolov, Ilya Sutskever, Kai Chen, Greg S Corrado, and Jeff Dean. 2013. Distributed representations of words and phrases and their compositionality. In *Advances in neural information processing systems*. pages 3111–3119.

Joakim Nivre. 2008. Algorithms for deterministic incremental dependency parsing. *Computational Linguistics* 34(4):513–553.

Joakim Nivre. 2009. Non-projective dependency parsing in expected linear time. In *Proceedings of the Joint Conference of the 47th Annual Meeting of the ACL and the 4th International Joint Conference on Natural Language Processing of the AFNLP*. Association for Computational Linguistics, Suntec, Singapore, pages 351–359. http://www.aclweb.org/anthology/P/P09/P09-1040.

Joakim Nivre, Marie-Catherine de Marneffe, Filip Ginter, Yoav Goldberg, Jan Hajič, Christopher Manning, Ryan McDonald, Slav Petrov, Sampo Pyysalo, Natalia Silveira, Reut Tsarfaty, and Daniel Zeman. 2016. Universal Dependencies v1: A multilingual treebank collection. In *Proceedings of the 10th International Conference on Language Resources and Evaluation*. European Language Resources Association, Portoro, Slovenia, pages 1659–1666.

Joakim Nivre et al. 2018. Universal Dependencies 2.2. LINDAT/CLARIN digital library at the Institute of Formal and Applied Linguistics, Charles University, Prague. http://hdl.handle.net/11234/1-2837.

Martin Potthast, Tim Gollub, Francisco Rangel, Paolo Rosso, Efstathios Stamatatos, and Benno Stein. 2014. Improving the reproducibility of PAN's shared tasks: Plagiarism detection, author identification, and author profiling. In Evangelos Kanoulas, Mihai Lupu, Paul Clough, Mark Sanderson, Mark Hall, Allan Hanbury, and Elaine Toms, editors, *Information Access Evaluation meets Multilinguality, Multimodality, and Visualization. 5th International Conference of the CLEF Initiative*. Springer, Berlin Heidelberg New York, pages 268–299. https://doi.org/10.1007/978-3-319-11382-1_22.

Lianhui Qin, Zhisong Zhang, Hai Zhao, Zhiting Hu, and Eric Xing. 2017. Adversarial connective-exploiting networks for implicit discourse relation classification. In *Proceedings of the 55th Annual Meeting of the Association for Computational Linguistics (Volume 1: Long Papers)*. Association for Computational Linguistics, pages 1006–1017. https://doi.org/10.18653/v1/P17-1093.

Milan Straka, Jan Hajič, and Jana Straková. 2016. UD-Pipe: trainable pipeline for processing CoNLL-U files performing tokenization, morphological analysis, POS tagging and parsing. In *Proceedings of the 10th International Conference on Language Resources and Evaluation*. European Language Resources Association, Portoro, Slovenia.

Milan Straka, Jan Hajič, Jana Straková, and Jan Hajič jr. 2015. Parsing universal dependency treebanks using neural networks and search-based oracle. In *Proceedings of 14th International Workshop on Treebanks and Linguistic Theories*.

Milan Straka and Jana Straková. 2017. Tokenizing, pos tagging, lemmatizing and parsing ud 2.0 with udpipe. In *Proceedings of the CoNLL 2017 Shared Task: Multilingual Parsing from Raw Text to Universal Dependencies*. Association for Computational Linguistics, pages 88–99. https://doi.org/10.18653/v1/K17-3009.

Jana Straková, Milan Straka, and Jan Hajič. 2014. Open-Source Tools for Morphology, Lemmatization, POS Tagging and Named Entity Recognition. In *Proceedings of 52nd Annual Meeting of the Association for Computational Linguistics: System Demonstrations*. Association for Computational Linguistics, Baltimore, Maryland, pages 13–18. http://www.aclweb.org/anthology/P/P14/P14-5003.pdf.

Jörg Tiedemann. 2015. Cross-lingual dependency parsing with universal dependencies and predicted pos labels. In *Proceedings of the 3rd International Conference on Dependency Linguistics*. pages 340–349.

Hao Wang, Hai Zhao, and Zhisong Zhang. 2017. A transition-based system for universal dependency parsing. In *Proceedings of the CoNLL 2017 Shared Task: Multilingual Parsing from Raw Text to Universal Dependencies*. Association for Computational Linguistics, pages 191–197. https://doi.org/10.18653/v1/K17-3020.

Yingting Wu and Hai Zhao. 2018. Finding better subword segmentation for neural machine translation. In *Proceedings of the 17th China National Conference on Computational Linguistics*.

Daniel Zeman, Jan Hajič, Martin Popel, Martin Potthast, Milan Straka, Filip Ginter, Joakim Nivre, and Slav Petrov. 2018. CoNLL 2018 Shared Task: Multilingual Parsing from Raw Text to Universal Dependencies. In *Proceedings of the CoNLL 2018 Shared Task: Multilingual Parsing from Raw Text to Universal Dependencies*. Association for Computational Linguistics, Brussels, Belgium, pages 1–20.

Daniel Zeman, Martin Popel, Milan Straka, Jan Hajic, Joakim Nivre, Filip Ginter, Juhani Luotolahti, Sampo Pyysalo, Slav Petrov, Martin Potthast, Francis Tyers, Elena Badmaeva, Memduh Gokirmak, Anna Nedoluzhko, Silvie Cinkova, Jan Hajic jr., Jaroslava Hlavacova, Václava Kettnerová, Zdenka Uresova, Jenna Kanerva, Stina Ojala, Anna Missilä, Christopher D. Manning, Sebastian Schuster, Siva Reddy, Dima Taji, Nizar Habash, Herman Leung, Marie-Catherine de Marneffe, Manuela Sanguinetti, Maria Simi, Hiroshi Kanayama, Valeria de Paiva, Kira Droganova, Héctor Martínez Alonso, Çağr Çöltekin, Umut Sulubacak, Hans Uszkoreit, Vivien Macketanz, Aljoscha Burchardt, Kim Harris, Katrin Marheinecke, Georg Rehm, Tolga Kayadelen, Mohammed Attia, Ali Elkahky, Zhuoran Yu, Emily Pitler, Saran Lertpradit, Michael Mandl, Jesse Kirchner, Hector Fernandez Alcalde, Jana Strnadová, Esha Banerjee, Ruli Manurung, Antonio Stella, Atsuko Shimada, Sookyoung Kwak, Gustavo Mendonca, Tatiana Lando, Rattima Nitisaroj, and Josie Li. 2017. CoNLL 2017 shared task: Multilingual parsing from raw text to universal dependencies. In *Proceedings of the CoNLL 2017 Shared Task: Multilingual Parsing from Raw Text to Universal Dependencies*. Association for Computational Linguistics, Vancouver, Canada, pages 1–19. http://www.aclweb.org/anthology/K17-3001.

Daniel Zeman and Philip Resnik. 2008. Cross-language parser adaptation between related languages. In *Proceedings of the 3rd International Joint Conference on Natural Language Processing Workshop on NLP for Less Privileged Languages*.

Zhuosheng Zhang, Jiangtong Li, Pengfei Zhu, Hai Zhao, and Gongshen Liu. 2018. Modeling multi-turn conversation with deep utterance aggregation. In *Proceedings of the 27th International Conference on Computational Linguistics*. Association for Computational Linguistics, pages 3740–3752. http://aclweb.org/anthology/C18-1317.

Zhuosheng Zhang and Hai Zhao. 2018. One-shot learning for question-answering in gaokao history challenge. In *Proceedings of the 27th International Conference on Computational Linguistics*. Association for Computational Linguistics, pages 449–461. http://aclweb.org/anthology/C18-1038.

An improved neural network model for joint POS tagging and dependency parsing

Dat Quoc Nguyen and **Karin Verspoor**
School of Computing and Information Systems
The University of Melbourne, Australia
{dqnguyen, karin.verspoor}@unimelb.edu.au

Abstract

We propose a novel neural network model for joint part-of-speech (POS) tagging and dependency parsing. Our model extends the well-known BIST graph-based dependency parser (Kiperwasser and Goldberg, 2016) by incorporating a BiLSTM-based tagging component to produce automatically predicted POS tags for the parser. On the benchmark English Penn treebank, our model obtains strong UAS and LAS scores at 94.51% and 92.87%, respectively, producing 1.5+% absolute improvements to the BIST graph-based parser, and also obtaining a state-of-the-art POS tagging accuracy at 97.97%. Furthermore, experimental results on parsing 61 "big" Universal Dependencies treebanks from raw texts show that our model outperforms the baseline UDPipe (Straka and Straková, 2017) with 0.8% higher average POS tagging score and 3.6% higher average LAS score. In addition, with our model, we also obtain state-of-the-art downstream task scores for biomedical event extraction and opinion analysis applications.

Our code is available together with all pre-trained models at: https://github.com/datquocnguyen/jPTDP.

1 Introduction

Dependency parsing – a key research topic in natural language processing (NLP) in the last decade (Buchholz and Marsi, 2006; Nivre et al., 2007a; Kübler et al., 2009) – has also been demonstrated to be extremely useful in many applications such as relation extraction (Culotta and Sorensen, 2004; Bunescu and Mooney, 2005), semantic parsing (Reddy et al., 2016) and machine translation (Galley and Manning, 2009). In general, dependency parsing models can be categorized as graph-based (McDonald et al., 2005) and transition-based (Yamada and Matsumoto, 2003; Nivre, 2003). Most traditional graph- or transition-based models define a set of core and combined features (McDonald and Pereira, 2006; Nivre et al., 2007b; Bohnet, 2010; Zhang and Nivre, 2011), while recent state-of-the-art models propose neural network architectures to handle feature-engineering (Dyer et al., 2015; Kiperwasser and Goldberg, 2016; Dozat and Manning, 2017; Ma and Hovy, 2017).

Most traditional and neural network-based parsing models use automatically predicted POS tags as essential features. However, POS taggers are not perfect, resulting in error propagation problems. Some work has attempted to avoid using POS tags for dependency parsing (Dyer et al., 2015; Ballesteros et al., 2015; de Lhoneux et al., 2017), however, to achieve the strongest parsing scores these methods still require automatically assigned POS tags. Alternatively, joint POS tagging and dependency parsing has also attracted a lot of attention in NLP community as it could help improve both tagging and parsing results over independent modeling (Li et al., 2011; Hatori et al., 2011; Lee et al., 2011; Bohnet and Nivre, 2012; Zhang et al., 2015; Zhang and Weiss, 2016; Yang et al., 2018).

In this paper, we present a novel neural network-based model for jointly learning POS tagging and dependency paring. Our joint model extends the well-known BIST graph-based dependency parser (Kiperwasser and Goldberg, 2016) with an additional lower-level BiLSTM-based tagging component. In particular, this tagging component generates predicted POS tags for the parser component. Evaluated on the benchmark English Penn treebank test Section 23, our model pro-

Proceedings of the CoNLL 2018 Shared Task: Multilingual Parsing from Raw Text to Universal Dependencies, pages 81–91
Brussels, Belgium, October 31 – November 1, 2018. ©2018 Association for Computational Linguistics
https://doi.org/10.18653/v1/K18-2008

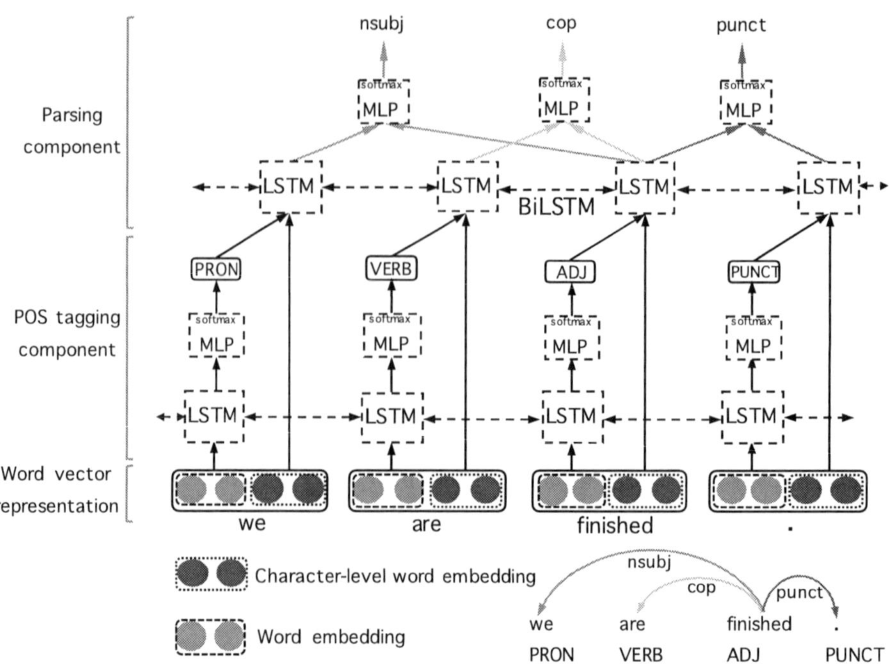

Figure 1: Illustration of our new model for joint POS tagging and graph-based dependency parsing.

duces a 1.5+% absolute improvement over the BIST graph-based parser with a strong UAS score of 94.51% and LAS score of 92.87%; and also obtaining a state-of-the-art POS tagging accuracy of 97.97%. In addition, multilingual parsing experiments from raw texts on 61 "big" Universal Dependencies treebanks (Zeman et al., 2018) show that our model outperforms the baseline UDPipe (Straka and Straková, 2017) with 0.8% higher average POS tagging score, 3.1% higher UAS and 3.6% higher LAS. Furthermore, experimental results on downstream task applications (Fares et al., 2018) show that our joint model helps produce state-of-the-art scores for biomedical event extraction and opinion analysis.

2 Our joint model

This section presents our model for joint POS tagging and graph-based dependency parsing. Figure 1 illustrates the architecture of our joint model which can be viewed as a two-component mixture of a tagging component and a parsing component. Given word tokens in an input sentence, the tagging component uses a BiLSTM to learn "latent" feature vectors representing these word tokens. Then the tagging component feeds these feature vectors into a multilayer perceptron with one

hidden layer (MLP) to predict POS tags. The parsing component then uses another BiLSTM to learn another set of latent feature representations, based on both the input word tokens and the predicted POS tags. These latent feature representations are fed into a MLP to decode dependency arcs and another MLP to label the predicted dependency arcs.

2.1 Word vector representation

Given an input sentence s consisting of n word tokens $w_1, w_2, ..., w_n$, we represent each ith word w_i in s by a vector $\mathbf{e}_i$. We obtain $\mathbf{e}_i$ by concatenating word embedding $\mathbf{e}_{w_i}^{(w)}$ and character-level word embedding $\mathbf{e}_{w_i}^{(c)}$:

$$\mathbf{e}_i = \mathbf{e}_{w_i}^{(w)} \circ \mathbf{e}_{w_i}^{(c)} \tag{1}$$

Here, each word type w in the training data is represented by a real-valued word embedding $\mathbf{e}_w^{(w)}$. Given the word type w consisting of k characters $w = c_1 c_2 ... c_k$ where each jth character in w is represented by a character embedding $\mathbf{c}_j$, we use a sequence BiLSTM (BiLSTM$_{seq}$) to learn its character-level vector representation (Ballesteros et al., 2015; Plank et al., 2016). The input to BiLSTM$_{seq}$ is the sequence of k character embeddings $\mathbf{c}_{1:k}$, and the output is a concatenation of outputs of a forward LSTM (LSTM$_f$) reading the input in its regular order and a reverse LSTM (LSTM_r) reading the input in reverse:

$$\mathbf{e}_w^{(c)} = \text{BiLSTM}_{\text{seq}}(\mathbf{c}_{1:k}) = \text{LSTM}_f(\mathbf{c}_{1:k}) \circ \text{LSTM}_r(\mathbf{c}_{k:1})$$

2.2 Tagging component

We feed the sequence of vectors $\mathbf{e}_{1:n}$ with an additional context position index i into another BiLSTM ($\text{BiLSTM}_{\text{pos}}$), resulting in latent feature vectors $\boldsymbol{v}_i^{(\text{pos})}$ each representing the ith word w_i in s:

$$\boldsymbol{v}_i^{(\text{pos})} = \text{BiLSTM}_{\text{pos}}(\mathbf{e}_{1:n}, i) \tag{2}$$

We use a MLP with softmax output (MLP_{pos}) on top of the $\text{BiLSTM}_{\text{pos}}$ to predict POS tag of each word in s. The number of nodes in the output layer of this MLP_{pos} is the number of POS tags. Given $\boldsymbol{v}_i^{(\text{pos})}$, we compute an output vector as:

$$\boldsymbol{\vartheta}_i = \text{MLP}_{\text{pos}}(\boldsymbol{v}_i^{(\text{pos})}) \tag{3}$$

Based on output vectors $\boldsymbol{\vartheta}_i$, we then compute the cross-entropy objective loss $\mathcal{L}_{\textbf{POS}}(\hat{\mathbf{t}}, \mathbf{t})$, in which $\hat{\mathbf{t}}$ and $\mathbf{t}$ are the sequence of predicted POS tags and sequence of gold POS tags of words in the input sentence s, respectively (Goldberg, 2016). Our tagging component thus can be viewed as a simplified version of the POS tagging model proposed by Plank et al. (2016), without their additional auxiliary loss for rare words.

2.3 Parsing component

Assume that $p_1, p_2, ..., p_n$ are the predicted POS tags produced by the tagging component for the input words. We represent each ith predicted POS tag by a vector embedding $\mathbf{e}_{p_i}^{(\text{P})}$. We then create a sequence of vectors $\boldsymbol{x}_{1:n}$ in which each $\boldsymbol{x}_i$ is produced by concatenating the POS tag embedding $\mathbf{e}_{p_i}^{(\text{P})}$ and the word vector representation $\mathbf{e}_i$:

$$\mathbf{x}_i = \mathbf{e}_{p_i}^{(\text{P})} \circ \mathbf{e}_i = \mathbf{e}_{p_i}^{(\text{P})} \circ \mathbf{e}_{w_i}^{(\text{w})} \circ \mathbf{e}_{w_i}^{(\text{C})} \tag{4}$$

We feed the sequence of vectors $\mathbf{x}_{1:n}$ with an additional index i into a BiLSTM ($\text{BiLSTM}_{\text{dep}}$), resulting in latent feature vectors $\boldsymbol{v}_i$ as follows:

$$\boldsymbol{v}_i = \text{BiLSTM}_{\text{dep}}(\mathbf{x}_{1:n}, i) \tag{5}$$

Based on latent feature vectors $\boldsymbol{v}_i$, we follow a common arc-factored parsing approach to decode dependency arcs (McDonald et al., 2005). In particular, a dependency tree can be formalized as a directed graph. An arc-factored parsing approach learns the scores of the arcs in the graph (Kübler

et al., 2009). Here, we score an arc by using a MLP with a one-node output layer (MLP_{arc}) on top of the $\text{BiLSTM}_{\text{dep}}$:

$$\text{score}_{\text{arc}}(i, j) \tag{6}$$
$$= \text{MLP}_{\text{arc}}\big(\boldsymbol{v}_i \circ \boldsymbol{v}_j \circ (\boldsymbol{v}_i * \boldsymbol{v}_j) \circ |\boldsymbol{v}_i - \boldsymbol{v}_j|\big)$$

where $(\boldsymbol{v}_i * \boldsymbol{v}_j)$ and $|\boldsymbol{v}_i - \boldsymbol{v}_j|$ denote the element-wise product and the absolute element-wise difference, respectively; and $\boldsymbol{v}_i$ and $\boldsymbol{v}_j$ are correspondingly the latent feature vectors associating to the ith and j^{th} words in s, computed by Equation 5.

Given the arc scores, we use the Eisner (1996)'s decoding algorithm to find the highest scoring projective parse tree:

$$\text{score}(s) = \underset{\hat{y} \in \mathcal{Y}(s)}{\text{argmax}} \sum_{(h,m) \in \hat{y}} \text{score}_{\text{arc}}(h, m) \tag{7}$$

where $\mathcal{Y}(s)$ is the set of all possible dependency trees for the input sentence s while $\text{score}_{\text{arc}}(h, m)$ measures the score of the arc between the head h^{th} word and the modifier m^{th} word in s.

Following Kiperwasser and Goldberg (2016), we compute a margin-based hinge loss $\mathcal{L}_{\textbf{ARC}}$ with loss-augmented inference to maximize the margin between the gold unlabeled parse tree and the highest scoring incorrect tree.

For predicting dependency relation type of a head-modifier arc, we use another MLP with softmax output (MLP_{rel}) on top of the $\text{BiLSTM}_{\text{dep}}$. Here, the number of the nodes in the output layer of this MLP_{rel} is the number of dependency relation types. Given an arc (h, m), we compute an output vector as:

$$\mathbf{v}_{(h,m)} \tag{8}$$
$$= \text{MLP}_{\text{rel}}\big(\boldsymbol{v}_h \circ \boldsymbol{v}_m \circ (\boldsymbol{v}_h * \boldsymbol{v}_m) \circ |\boldsymbol{v}_h - \boldsymbol{v}_m|\big)$$

Based on output vectors $\mathbf{v}_{(h,m)}$, we also compute another cross-entropy objective loss $\mathcal{L}_{\textbf{REL}}$ for relation type prediction, using only the gold labeled parse tree.

Our parsing component can be viewed as an extension of the BIST graph-based dependency model (Kiperwasser and Goldberg, 2016), where we additionally incorporate the character-level vector representations of words.

2.4 Joint model training

The training objective loss of our joint model is the sum of the POS tagging loss $\mathcal{L}_{\text{POS}}$, the structure loss $\mathcal{L}_{\text{ARC}}$ and the relation labeling loss $\mathcal{L}_{\text{REL}}$:

$$\mathcal{L} = \mathcal{L}_{\text{POS}} + \mathcal{L}_{\text{ARC}} + \mathcal{L}_{\text{REL}} \tag{9}$$

The model parameters, including word embeddings, character embeddings, POS embeddings, three one-hidden-layer MLPs and three BiLSTMs, are learned to minimize the sum $\mathcal{L}$ of the losses.

Most neural network-based joint models for POS tagging and dependency parsing are transition-based approaches (Alberti et al., 2015; Zhang and Weiss, 2016; Yang et al., 2018), while our model is a graph-based method. In addition, the joint model JMT (Hashimoto et al., 2017) defines its dependency parsing task as a head selection task which produces a probability distribution over possible heads for each word (Zhang et al., 2017).

Our model is the successor of the joint model jPTDP v1.0 (Nguyen et al., 2017) which is also a graph-based method. However, unlike our model, jPTDP v1.0 uses a BiLSTM to learn "shared" latent feature vectors which are then used for both POS tagging and dependency parsing tasks, rather than using two separate layers. As mentioned in Section 4, our model generally outperforms jPTDP v1.0 with 2.5+% LAS improvements on universal dependencies (UD) treebanks.

2.5 Implementation details

Our model is released as jPTDP v2.0, available at `https://github.com/datquocnguyen/jPTDP`. Our jPTDP v2.0 is implemented using DYNET v2.0 (Neubig et al., 2017) with a fixed random seed.[1] Word embeddings are initialized either randomly or by pre-trained word vectors, while character and POS tag embeddings are randomly initialized. For learning character-level word embeddings, we use one-layer $\text{BiLSTM}_{\text{seq}}$, and set the size of LSTM hidden states to be equal to the vector size of character embeddings.

We apply dropout (Srivastava et al., 2014) with a 67% keep probability to the inputs of BiLSTMs and MLPs. Following Iyyer et al. (2015) and Kiperwasser and Goldberg (2016), we also apply *word dropout* to learn an embedding for unknown words: we replace each word token w appearing $\#(w)$ times in the training set with a special "unk" symbol with probability $\text{p}_{unk}(w) = \frac{0.25}{0.25+\#(w)}$. This procedure only involves the word embedding part in the input word vector representation.

We optimize the objective loss using Adam (Kingma and Ba, 2014) with an initial learning rate at 0.001 and no mini-batches. For training,

we run for 30 epochs, and restart the Adam optimizer and anneal its initial learning rate at a proportion of 0.5 every 10 epochs. We evaluate the *mixed accuracy* of correctly assigning POS tag together with dependency arc and relation type on the development set after each training epoch. We choose the model with the highest mixed accuracy on the development set, which is then applied to the test set for the evaluation phase.

For all experiments presented in this paper, we use 100-dimensional word embeddings, 50-dimensional character embeddings and 100-dimensional POS tag embeddings. We also fix the number of hidden nodes in MLPs at 100. Due to limited computational resource, for experiments presented in Section 3, we perform a minimal grid search of hyper-parameters to select the number of $\text{BiLSTM}_{\text{pos}}$ and $\text{BiLSTM}_{\text{dep}}$ layers from $\{1, 2\}$ and the size of LSTM hidden states in each layer from $\{128, 256\}$. For experiments presented in sections 4 and 5, we fix the number of BiLSTM layers at 2 and the size of hidden states at 128.

3 Experiments on English Penn treebank

Experimental setup: We evaluate our model using the English WSJ Penn treebank (Marcus et al., 1993). We follow a standard data split to use sections 02-21 for training, Section 22 for development and Section 23 for test (Chen and Manning, 2014), employing the Stanford conversion toolkit v3.3.0 to generate dependency trees with Stanford basic dependencies (de Marneffe and Manning, 2008).

Word embeddings are initialized by 100-dimensional GloVe word vectors pre-trained on Wikipedia and Gigaword (Pennington et al., 2014).[2] As mentioned in Section 2.5, we perform a minimal grid search of hyper-parameters and find that the highest mixed accuracy on the development set is obtained when using 2 BiLSTM layers and 256-dimensional LSTM hidden states (in Table 1, we present scores obtained on the development set when using 2 BiLSTM layers).

Main results: Table 2 compares our UAS and LAS scores on the test set with previous published results in terms of the dependency annotations.[3]

---

[1] `https://github.com/clab/dynet`

[2] `https://nlp.stanford.edu/projects/glove`

[3] Choe and Charniak (2016) reported the highest UAS score at 95.9% and LAS score at 94.1% to date on the test set, using the Stanford conversion toolkit v3.3.0 to convert the output constituent trees into dependency representations.

#states	With punctuations			Without pun.	
	POS	UAS	LAS	UAS	LAS
128	**97.64**	93.68	92.11	94.42	92.61
256	97.63	**93.89**	**92.33**	**94.63**	**92.82**
Chen and Manning (2014)				92.0	89.7
Dyer et al. (2015)				93.2	90.9
BIST-graph [K&G16]				93.3	91.0
Zhang et al. (2017)				94.30	91.95
Ma and Hovy (2017)				94.77	92.66
Dozat and Manning (2017)				**95.24**	**93.37**

Table 1: Results on the development set. **#states** and "**Without pun.**" denote the size of LSTM hidden states and the scores computed without punctuations, respectively. "POS" indicates the POS tagging accuracy. [K&G16] denotes results reported in Kiperwasser and Goldberg (2016).

Model	POS	UAS	LAS
Chen and Manning (2014)	97.3	91.8	89.6
Dyer et al. (2015)	97.3	93.1	90.9
Weiss et al. (2015)	97.44	93.99	92.05
BIST-graph [K&G16]	97.3	93.1	91.0
BIST-transition [K&G16]	97.3	93.9	91.9
Kuncoro et al. (2016)	97.3	94.26	92.06
Andor et al. (2016)	97.44	94.61	92.79
Zhang et al. (2017)	97.3	94.10	91.90
Ma and Hovy (2017)	97.3	94.88	92.98
Dozat and Manning (2017)	97.3	**95.44**	**93.76**
Dozat and Manning (2017) [•]	97.3	95.66	94.03
Bohnet and Nivre (2012) [⋆]	97.42	93.67	92.68
Alberti et al. (2015)	97.44	94.23	92.36
Zhang and Weiss (2016)	_	93.43	91.41
Hashimoto et al. (2017)	_	**94.67**	**92.90**
Yang et al. (2018)	97.54	94.18	92.26
Our model	**97.97**	94.51	92.87

Table 2: Results on the test set. POS tagging accuracies are computed on all tokens. UAS and LAS are computed without punctuations. [•]: the treebank was converted with the Stanford conversion toolkit v3.5.0. [⋆]: the treebank was converted with the head rules of Yamada and Matsumoto (2003). For both [•] and [⋆], obtained parsing scores are just for reference, not for comparison.

The first 11 rows present scores of dependency parsers in which POS tags were predicted by using an external POS tagger such as the Stanford tagger (Toutanova et al., 2003). The last 6 rows present scores for joint models. Clearly, our model produces very competitive parsing results. In particular, our model obtains a UAS score at 94.51% and a LAS score at 92.87% which are about 1.4% and 1.9% absolute higher than UAS and LAS scores of the BIST graph-based model (Kiperwasser and Goldberg, 2016), respectively. Our model also does better than the previous transition-based joint models in Alberti et al. (2015), Zhang and Weiss (2016) and Yang et al. (2018), while obtaining similar UAS and LAS scores to the joint model JMT proposed by Hashimoto et al. (2017).

We achieve 0.9% lower parsing scores than the state-of-the-art dependency parser of Dozat and Manning (2017). While also a BiLSTM- and graph-based model, it uses a more sophisticated attention mechanism "*biaffine*" for better decoding dependency arcs and relation types. In future work, we will extend our model with the *biaffine* attention mechanism to investigate the benefit for our model. Other differences are that they use a higher dimensional representation than ours, but rely on predicted POS tags.

We also obtain a state-of-the-art POS tagging accuracy at 97.97% on the test Section 23, which is about 0.4+% higher than those by Bohnet and Nivre (2012), Alberti et al. (2015) and Yang et al. (2018). Other previous joint models did not mention their specific POS tagging accuracies.[4]

4 UniMelb in the CoNLL 2018 shared task on UD parsing

Our UniMelb team participated with jPTDP v2.0 in the CoNLL 2018 shared task on parsing 82 treebank test sets (in 57 languages) from raw text to universal dependencies (Zeman et al., 2018). The 82 treebanks are taken from UD v2.2 (Nivre et al., 2018), where 61/82 test sets are for "big" UD treebanks for which both training and development data sets are available and 5/82 test sets are extra "parallel" test sets in languages where another big treebank exists. In addition, 7/82 test sets are for "small" UD treebanks for which development data is not available. The remaining 9/82 sets are in low-resource languages without training data or with a few gold-annotation sample sentences.

For the 7 small treebanks without development data available, we split training data into two parts with a ratio 9:1, and then use the larger part for training and the smaller part for development. For each big or small treebank, we train a joint model for *universal* POS tagging and dependency parsing, using a fixed random seed and a fixed set

---

[4]Hashimoto et al. (2017) showed that JMT obtains a POS tagging accuracy of 97.55% on WSJ sections 22-24.

System	All (82)	Big (61)	PUD (5)	Small (7)	Low (9)
UPOS UDPipe 1.2	87.32	93.71	85.23	**87.36**	45.20
UniMelb	**87.90**	**94.50**	**85.33**	87.12	45.20
goldseg.	-	95.63	90.21	87.64	-
UAS UDPipe 1.2	71.64	78.78	71.22	63.17	30.08
UniMelb	**74.16**	**81.83**	**73.17**	**64.71**	30.08
goldseg.	-	85.01	81.81	67.46	-
LAS UDPipe 1.2	65.80	74.14	66.63	55.01	17.17
UniMelb	**68.65**	**77.69**	**68.72**	**56.12**	17.17
goldseg.	-	80.68	75.03	58.65	-

Table 3: Official macro-average F1 scores computed on all tokens for UniMelb and the baseline UDPipe 1.2 in the CoNLL 2018 shared task on UD parsing from raw texts (Zeman et al., 2018). "UPOS" denotes the universal POS tagging score. "All", "Big", "PUD", "Small" and "Low" refer to the macro-average scores over all 81, 61 big treebank, 5 parallel, 7 small treebank and 9 low-resource treebank test sets, respectively. "goldseg." denotes the scores of our jPTDP v2.0 model regarding gold segmentation, detailed in Table 4.

of hyper-parameters as mentioned in Section 2.5.[5] We evaluate the mixed accuracy on the development set after each training epoch, and select the model with the highest mixed accuracy.

For parsing from raw text to universal dependencies, we employ CoNLL-U test files preprocessed by the baseline UDPipe 1.2 (Straka and Straková, 2017). Here, we utilize the tokenization, word and sentence segmentation predicted by UDPipe 1.2. For 68 big and small treebank test files, we use the corresponding trained joint models. We use the joint models trained for *cs_pdt*, *en_ewt*, *fi_tdt*, *ja_gsd* and *sv_talbanken* to process 5 parallel test files *cs_pud*, *en_pud*, *fi_pud*, *ja_modern* and *sv_pud*, respectively. Since we do not focus on low-resource languages, we employ the baseline UDPipe 1.2 to process 9 low-resource treebank test files. The final test runs are carried out on the TIRA platform (Potthast et al., 2014).

Table 3 presents our results in the CoNLL 2018 shared task on multilingual parsing from raw texts to universal dependencies (Zeman et al., 2018). Over all 82 test sets, we outperform the baseline UDPipe 1.2 with 0.6% absolute higher average UPOS F1 score and 2.5+% higher average UAS

and LAS F1 scores. In particular, for the "big" category consisting of 61 treebank test sets, we obtain 0.8% higher UPOS and 3.1% higher UAS and 3.6% higher LAS than UDPipe 1.2.

Our (UniMelb) official LAS-based rank is at 14th place while the baseline UDPipe 1.2 is at 18th place over total 26 participating systems.[6] However, it is difficult to make a clear comparison between our jPTDP v2.0 and the parsing models used in other top systems. Several better participating systems simply reuse the state-of-the-art *biaffine* dependency parser (Dozat and Manning, 2017; Dozat et al., 2017), constructing ensemble models or developing treebank concatenation strategies to obtain larger training data, which is likely to produce better scores than ours (Zeman et al., 2018).

Recall that the shared task focuses on parsing from raw texts. Most higher-ranking systems aim to improve the pre-processing steps of tokenization[7], word[8] and sentence[9] segmentation, resulting in significant improvements in final parsing scores. For example, in the CoNLL 2017 shared task on UD parsing (Zeman et al., 2017), UDPipe 1.2 obtained 0.1+% higher average tokenization and word segmentation scores and 0.2% higher average sentence segmentation score than UDPipe 1.1, resulting in 1+% improvement in the final average LAS F1 score while both UDPipe 1.2 and UDPipe 1.1 shared exactly the same remaining components. Utilizing better pre-processors, as used in other participating systems, should likewise improve our final parsing scores.

In Table 3, we also present our average UPOS, UAS and LAS accuracies with respect to (w.r.t.) gold-standard tokenization, word and sentence segmentation. For more details and future comparison, Table 4 presents the UPOS, UAS and LAS scores w.r.t. gold-standard segmentation, obtained by jPTDP v2.0 on each UD v2.2–CoNLL 2018 shared task test set. Compared to the scores presented in Table 3 in Nguyen et al. (2017) on overlapped treebanks, our model jPTDP v2.0 generally produces 2.5+% improvements in UAS and LAS scores to jPTDP v1.0 (Nguyen et al., 2017).

---

[5]We initialize word embeddings by 100-dimensional pre-trained vectors from Ginter et al. (2017). For a language where pre-trained word vectors are not available in Ginter et al. (2017), word embeddings are randomly initialized.

[6]`http://universaldependencies.org/conll18/results.html`

[7]`http://universaldependencies.org/conll18/results-tokens.html`

[8]`http://universaldependencies.org/conll18/results-words.html`

[9]`http://universaldependencies.org/conll18/results-sentences.html`

Treebank	Code	UPOS	UAS	LAS	Treebank	Code	UPOS	UAS	LAS
Afrikaans-AfriBooms	af_afribooms	95.73	82.57	78.89	Italian-ISDT	it_isdt	98.01	92.33	90.20
Ancient_Greek-PROIEL	grc_proiel	96.05	77.57	72.84	Italian-PoSTWITA	it_postwita	95.41	84.20	79.11
Ancient_Greek-Perseus	grc_perseus	88.95	65.09	58.35	Japanese-GSD	ja_gsd	97.27	94.21	92.02
Arabic-PADT	ar_padt	96.33	86.08	80.97	Japanese-Modern [p]	ja_modern	70.53	66.88	49.51
Basque-BDT	eu_bdt	93.62	79.86	75.07	Korean-GSD	ko_gsd	93.35	81.32	76.58
Bulgarian-BTB	bg_btb	98.07	91.47	87.69	Korean-Kaist	ko_kaist	93.53	83.59	80.74
Catalan-AnCora	ca_ancora	98.46	90.78	88.40	Latin-ITTB	la_ittb	98.12	82.99	79.96
Chinese-GSD	zh_gsd	93.26	82.50	77.51	Latin-PROIEL	la_proiel	95.54	74.95	69.76
Croatian-SET	hr_set	97.42	88.74	83.62	Latin-Perseus [s]	la_perseus	82.36	57.21	46.28
Czech-CAC	cs_cac	98.87	89.85	87.13	Latvian-LVTB	lv_lvtb	93.53	81.06	76.13
Czech-FicTree	cs_fictree	97.98	88.94	85.64	North_Sami-Giella [s]	sme_giella	87.48	65.79	58.09
Czech-PDT	cs_pdt	98.74	89.64	87.04	Norwegian-Bokmaal	no_bokmaal	97.73	89.83	87.57
Czech-PUD [p]	cs_pud	96.71	87.62	82.28	Norwegian-Nynorsk	no_nynorsk	97.33	89.73	87.29
Danish-DDT	da_ddt	96.18	82.17	78.88	Norwegian-NynorskLIA [s]	no_nynorsklia	85.22	64.14	54.31
Dutch-Alpino	nl_alpino	95.62	86.34	82.37	Old_Church_Slavonic-PROIEL	cu_proiel	93.69	80.59	73.93
Dutch-LassySmall	nl_lassysmall	95.21	86.46	82.14	Old_French-SRCMF	fro_srcmf	95.12	86.65	81.15
English-EWT	en_ewt	95.48	87.55	84.71	Persian-Seraji	fa_seraji	96.66	88.07	84.07
English-GUM	en_gum	94.10	84.88	80.45	Polish-LFG	pl_lfg	98.22	95.29	93.10
English-LinES	en_lines	95.55	80.34	75.40	Polish-SZ	pl_sz	97.05	90.98	87.66
English-PUD [p]	en_pud	95.25	87.49	84.25	Portuguese-Bosque	pt_bosque	96.76	88.67	85.71
Estonian-EDT	et_edt	96.87	85.45	82.13	Romanian-RRT	ro_rrt	97.43	88.74	83.54
Finnish-FTB	fi_ftb	94.53	86.10	82.45	Russian-SynTagRus	ru_syntagrus	98.51	91.00	88.91
Finnish-PUD [p]	fi_pud	96.44	87.54	84.60	Russian-Taiga [s]	ru_taiga	85.49	65.52	56.33
Finnish-TDT	fi_tdt	96.12	86.07	82.92	Serbian-SET	sr_set	97.40	89.32	85.03
French-GSD	fr_gsd	97.11	89.45	86.43	Slovak-SNK	sk_snk	95.18	85.88	81.89
French-Sequoia	fr_sequoia	97.92	89.71	87.43	Slovenian-SSJ	sl_ssj	97.79	88.26	86.10
French-Spoken	fr_spoken	94.25	79.80	73.45	Slovenian-SST	sl_sst [s]	89.50	66.14	58.13
Galician-CTG	gl_ctg	97.12	85.09	81.93	Spanish-AnCora	es_ancora	98.57	90.30	87.98
Galician-TreeGal [s]	gl_treegal	93.66	77.71	71.63	Swedish-LinES	sv_lines	95.51	83.60	78.97
German-GSD	de_gsd	94.07	81.45	76.68	Swedish-PUD [p]	sv_pud	92.10	79.53	74.53
Gothic-PROIEL	got_proiel	93.45	79.80	71.85	Swedish-Talbanken	sv_talbanken	96.55	86.53	83.01
Greek-GDT	el_gdt	96.59	87.52	84.64	Turkish-IMST	tr_imst	92.93	70.53	62.55
Hebrew-HTB	he_htb	96.24	87.65	82.64	Ukrainian-IU	uk_iu	95.24	83.47	79.38
Hindi-HDTB	hi_hdtb	96.94	93.25	89.83	Urdu-UDTB	ur_udtb	93.35	86.74	80.44
Hungarian-Szeged	hu_szeged	92.07	76.18	69.75	Uyghur-UDT	ug_udt	87.63	76.14	63.37
Indonesian-GSD	id_gsd	93.29	84.64	77.71	Vietnamese-VTB	vi_vtb	87.63	67.72	58.27
Irish-IDT [s]	ga_idt	89.74	75.72	65.78		**Average**	94.49	83.11	78.18

Table 4: UPOS, UAS and LAS scores computed on all tokens of our jPTDP v2.0 model regarding gold-standard segmentation on 73 CoNLL-2018 shared task test sets "Big", "PUD" and "Small" – UD v2.2 (Nivre et al., 2018). **[p]** and **[s]** denote the "PUD" extra parallel and small test sets, respectively. For each treebank, a joint model is trained using a fixed set of hyper-parameters as mentioned in Section 2.5.

5   UniMelb in the EPE 2018 campaign

Our UniMelb team also participated with jPTDP v2.0 in the 2018 Extrinsic Parser Evaluation (EPE) campaign (Fares et al., 2018).[10] The EPE 2018 campaign runs in collaboration with the CoNLL 2018 shared task, which aims to evaluate dependency parsers by comparing their performance on three downstream tasks: biomedical event extraction (Björne et al., 2017), negation resolution (Lapponi et al., 2017) and opinion analysis (Johansson, 2017). Here, participants only need to provide parsing outputs of English raw texts used in these downstream tasks; the campaign organizers then compute end-to-end downstream task scores. General background can be also found in the first EPE edition 2017 (Oepen et al., 2017).

Unlike EPE 2017, the EPE 2018 campaign limited the training data to the English UD treebanks only. We unfortunately were unaware of this restriction during development of our model. Thus, we trained a jPTDP v2.0 model on dependency trees generated with the Stanford basic dependencies on a combination of the WSJ treebank, sections 02-21, and the training split of the GENIA treebank (Tateisi et al., 2005). We used the fixed set of hyper-parameters as used for the CoNLL 2018 shared task as mentioned in Section 2.5.[11] We then submitted the parsing outputs by run-

---

[10]http://epe.nlpl.eu

[11]Word embeddings are initialized by the 100-dimensional pre-trained GloVe word vectors.

Task	Development set				Evaluation set			
	Pre.	Rec.	F1	SP17	Pre.	Rec.	F1	SP17
Event extraction	57.87	51.20	**54.33**$_1$	52.67$_{54.59}$	58.52	49.43	**53.59**$_1$	50.29$_{50.23}$
Negation resolution	100.0	44.51	61.60$_3$	**64.85**$_{65.37}$	100.0	41.83	58.99$_3$	**65.13**$_{66.16}$
Opinion analysis	69.12	64.65	**66.81**$_1$	66.63$_{68.53}$	66.67	62.88	**64.72**$_1$	63.72$_{65.14}$
Average	–	–	60.91$_1$	**61.38**$_{62.83}$	–	–	59.10$_1$	**59.71**$_{60.51}$

Table 5: Downstream task scores Precision (Prec.), Recall (Rec.) and F1 for our UniMelb team. The *subscript* in the F1 column denotes the unofficial rank of UniMelb over 17 participating teams at EPE 2018 (Fares et al., 2018). "SP17" denotes the F1 scores obtained by the EPE 2017 system Stanford-Paris (Schuster et al., 2017) with respect to (w.r.t.) the Stanford basic dependencies. The *subscript* in the SP17 column denotes the F1 scores obtained by Stanford-Paris w.r.t. the UD-v1-enhanced type of dependency representations, in which the average F1 score at 60.51 is the highest one at EPE 2017.

ning our trained model on the pre-processed to-kenized and sentence-segmented data provided by the campaign on the TIRA platform.

Table 5 presents the results we obtained for three downstream tasks at EPE 2018 (Fares et al., 2018). Since we employed external training data, our obtained scores are not officially ranked. In total 17 participating teams, we obtained the highest average F1 score over the three downstream tasks (i.e., we ranked first, unofficially). In particular, we achieved the highest F1 scores for both biomedical event extraction and opinion analysis. Our results may be high because the training data we used is larger than the English UD treebanks used by other teams.

Table 5 also presents scores from the Stanford-Paris team (Schuster et al., 2017)—the first-ranked team at EPE 2017 (Oepen et al., 2017). Both EPE 2017 and 2018 campaigns use the same downstream task setups, therefore the downstream task scores are directly comparable. Note that Stanford-Paris employed the state-of-the-art *bi-affine* dependency parser (Dozat et al., 2017) with larger training data. In particular, Stanford-Paris not only used the WSJ sections 02-21 and the training split of the GENIA treebank (as we did), but also included the Brown corpus. The downstream application of negation resolution requires parsing of fiction, which is one the genres included in the Brown corpus. Hence it is reasonable that the Stanford-Paris team produced better negation resolution scores than we did.

However, in terms of the Stanford basic dependencies, while we employ a less accurate parsing model with smaller training data, we obtain higher downstream task scores for event extraction and opinion analysis than the Stanford-Paris

team. Consequently, better intrinsic parsing performance does not always imply better extrinsic downstream application performance. Similar observations on the biomedical event extraction and opinion analysis tasks can also be found in Nguyen and Verspoor (2018) and Gómez-Rodríguez et al. (2017), respectively. Further investigations of this pattern requires much deeper understanding of the architecture of the downstream task systems, which is left for future work.

6 Conclusion

In this paper, we have presented a novel neural network model for joint POS tagging and graph-based dependency parsing. On the benchmark English WSJ Penn treebank, our model obtains strong parsing scores UAS at 94.51% and LAS at 92.87%, and a state-of-the-art POS tagging accuracy at 97.97%.

We also participated with our joint model in the CoNLL 2018 shared task on multilingual parsing from raw texts to universal dependencies, and obtained very competitive results. Specifically, using the same CoNLL-U files pre-processed by UDPipe (Straka and Straková, 2017), our model produced 0.8% higher POS tagging, 3.1% higher UAS and 3.6% higher LAS scores on average than UDPipe on 61 big UD treebank test sets. Furthermore, our model also helps obtain state-of-the-art downstream task scores for the biomedical event extraction and opinion analysis applications.

We believe our joint model can serve as a new strong baseline for both intrinsic POS tagging and dependency parsing tasks as well as for extrinsic downstream applications. Our code and pre-trained models are available at: `https://github.com/datquocnguyen/jPTDP`.

Acknowledgments

This work was supported by the ARC Discovery Project DP150101550 and ARC Linkage Project LP160101469.

References

Chris Alberti, David Weiss, Greg Coppola, and Slav Petrov. 2015. Improved Transition-Based Parsing and Tagging with Neural Networks. In *Proceedings of EMNLP*. pages 1354–1359.

Daniel Andor, Chris Alberti, David Weiss, Aliaksei Severyn, Alessandro Presta, Kuzman Ganchev, Slav Petrov, and Michael Collins. 2016. Globally Normalized Transition-Based Neural Networks. In *Proceedings of ACL*. pages 2442–2452.

Miguel Ballesteros, Chris Dyer, and Noah A. Smith. 2015. Improved Transition-based Parsing by Modeling Characters instead of Words with LSTMs. In *Proceedings of EMNLP*. pages 349–359.

Jari Björne, Filip Ginter, and Tapio Salakoski. 2017. EPE 2017: The Biomedical event extraction downstream application. In *Proceedings of the EPE 2017 Shared Task*. pages 17–24.

Bernd Bohnet. 2010. Very high accuracy and fast dependency parsing is not a contradiction. In *Proceedings of COLING*. pages 89–97.

Bernd Bohnet and Joakim Nivre. 2012. A Transition-Based System for Joint Part-of-Speech Tagging and Labeled Non-Projective Dependency Parsing. In *Proceedings of EMNLP-CoNLL*. pages 1455–1465.

Sabine Buchholz and Erwin Marsi. 2006. CoNLL-X shared task on multilingual dependency parsing. In *Proceedings of CoNLL*. pages 149–164.

Razvan Bunescu and Raymond Mooney. 2005. A Shortest Path Dependency Kernel for Relation Extraction. In *Proceedings of HLT/EMNLP*. pages 724–731.

Danqi Chen and Christopher Manning. 2014. A fast and accurate dependency parser using neural networks. In *Proceedings of EMNLP*. pages 740–750.

Do Kook Choe and Eugene Charniak. 2016. Parsing as Language Modeling. In *Proceedings of EMNLP*. pages 2331–2336.

Aron Culotta and Jeffrey Sorensen. 2004. Dependency Tree Kernels for Relation Extraction. In *Proceedings of ACL*. pages 423–429.

Miryam de Lhoneux, Yan Shao, Ali Basirat, Eliyahu Kiperwasser, Sara Stymne, Yoav Goldberg, and Joakim Nivre. 2017. From Raw Text to Universal Dependencies - Look, No Tags! In *Proceedings of the CoNLL 2017 Shared Task*. pages 207–217.

Marie-Catherine de Marneffe and Christopher D. Manning. 2008. The Stanford Typed Dependencies Representation. In *Proceedings of the Workshop on Cross-Framework and Cross-Domain Parser Evaluation*. pages 1–8.

Timothy Dozat and Christopher D. Manning. 2017. Deep Biaffine Attention for Neural Dependency Parsing. In *Proceedings of ICLR*.

Timothy Dozat, Peng Qi, and Christopher D. Manning. 2017. Stanford's Graph-based Neural Dependency Parser at the CoNLL 2017 Shared Task. In *Proceedings of the CoNLL 2017 Shared Task*. pages 20–30.

Chris Dyer, Miguel Ballesteros, Wang Ling, Austin Matthews, and Noah A. Smith. 2015. Transition-Based Dependency Parsing with Stack Long Short-Term Memory. In *Proceedings of ACL-IJCNLP*. pages 334–343.

Jason M. Eisner. 1996. Three New Probabilistic Models for Dependency Parsing: An Exploration. In *Proceedings of COLING*. pages 340–345.

Murhaf Fares, Stephan Oepen, Lilja vrelid, Jari Björne, and Richard Johansson. 2018. The 2018 Shared Task on Extrinsic Parser Evaluation. On the downstream utility of English universal dependency parsers. In *Proceedings of the CoNLL 2018 Shared Task*. page to appear.

Michel Galley and Christopher D. Manning. 2009. Quadratic-Time Dependency Parsing for Machine Translation. In *Proceedings of ACL-IJCNLP*. pages 773–781.

Filip Ginter, Jan Hajič, Juhani Luotolahti, Milan Straka, and Daniel Zeman. 2017. CoNLL 2017 Shared Task - Automatically Annotated Raw Texts and Word Embeddings. http://hdl.handle.net/11234/1-1989.

Yoav Goldberg. 2016. A Primer on Neural Network Models for Natural Language Processing. *Journal of Artificial Intelligence Research* 57:345–420.

Carlos Gómez-Rodríguez, Iago Alonso-Alonso, and David Vilares. 2017. How important is syntactic parsing accuracy? an empirical evaluation on rule-based sentiment analysis. *Artificial Intelligence Review* .

Kazuma Hashimoto, caiming xiong, Yoshimasa Tsuruoka, and Richard Socher. 2017. A Joint Many-Task Model: Growing a Neural Network for Multiple NLP Tasks. In *Proceedings of EMNLP*. pages 1923–1933.

Jun Hatori, Takuya Matsuzaki, Yusuke Miyao, and Jun'ichi Tsujii. 2011. Incremental Joint POS Tagging and Dependency Parsing in Chinese. In *Proceedings of IJCNLP*. pages 1216–1224.

Mohit Iyyer, Varun Manjunatha, Jordan Boyd-Graber, and Hal Daumé III. 2015. Deep Unordered Composition Rivals Syntactic Methods for Text Classification. In *Proceedings of ACL-IJCNLP*. pages 1681–1691.

Richard Johansson. 2017. EPE 2017: The Trento–Gothenburg opinion extraction system. In *Proceedings of the EPE 2017 Shared Task*. pages 31–39.

Diederik P. Kingma and Jimmy Ba. 2014. Adam: A Method for Stochastic Optimization. *CoRR* abs/1412.6980.

Eliyahu Kiperwasser and Yoav Goldberg. 2016. Simple and Accurate Dependency Parsing Using Bidirectional LSTM Feature Representations. *Transactions of ACL* 4:313–327.

Sandra Kübler, Ryan McDonald, and Joakim Nivre. 2009. *Dependency Parsing*. Synthesis Lectures on Human Language Technologies, Morgan & cLaypool publishers.

Adhiguna Kuncoro, Miguel Ballesteros, Lingpeng Kong, Chris Dyer, and Noah A. Smith. 2016. Distilling an Ensemble of Greedy Dependency Parsers into One MST Parser. In *Proceedings of EMNLP*. pages 1744–1753.

Emanuele Lapponi, Stephan Oepen, and Lilja Øvrelid. 2017. EPE 2017: The Sherlock negation resolution downstream application. In *Proceedings of the EPE 2017 Shared Task*. pages 25–30.

John Lee, Jason Naradowsky, and David A. Smith. 2011. A Discriminative Model for Joint Morphological Disambiguation and Dependency Parsing. In *Proceedings of ACL-HLT*. pages 885–894.

Zhenghua Li, Min Zhang, Wanxiang Che, Ting Liu, Wenliang Chen, and Haizhou Li. 2011. Joint Models for Chinese POS Tagging and Dependency Parsing. In *Proceedings of EMNLP*. pages 1180–1191.

Xuezhe Ma and Eduard Hovy. 2017. Neural Probabilistic Model for Non-projective MST Parsing. In *Proceedings of IJCNLP*. pages 59–69.

Mitchell P. Marcus, Beatrice Santorini, and Mary Ann Marcinkiewicz. 1993. Building a Large Annotated Corpus of English: The Penn Treebank. *Computational Linguistics* 19(2):313–330.

Ryan McDonald, Koby Crammer, and Fernando Pereira. 2005. Online large-margin training of dependency parsers. In *Proceedings of ACL*. pages 91–98.

Ryan McDonald and Fernando Pereira. 2006. Online Learning of Approximate Dependency Parsing Algorithms. In *Proceedings of EACL*. pages 81–88.

Graham Neubig, Chris Dyer, Yoav Goldberg, Austin Matthews, Waleed Ammar, Antonios Anastasopoulos, Miguel Ballesteros, David Chiang, Daniel Clothiaux, Trevor Cohn, Kevin Duh, Manaal Faruqui, Cynthia Gan, Dan Garrette, Yangfeng Ji, Lingpeng Kong, Adhiguna Kuncoro, Gaurav Kumar, Chaitanya Malaviya, Paul Michel, Yusuke Oda, Matthew Richardson, Naomi Saphra, Swabha Swayamdipta, and Pengcheng Yin. 2017. DyNet: The Dynamic Neural Network Toolkit. *arXiv preprint arXiv:1701.03980* .

Dat Quoc Nguyen, Mark Dras, and Mark Johnson. 2017. A Novel Neural Network Model for Joint POS Tagging and Graph-based Dependency Parsing. In *Proceedings of the CoNLL 2017 Shared Task*. pages 134–142.

Dat Quoc Nguyen and Karin Verspoor. 2018. From POS tagging to dependency parsing for biomedical event extraction. *arXiv preprint arXiv:1808.03731* .

Joakim Nivre. 2003. An efficient algorithm for projective dependency parsing. In *Proceedings of IWPT*.

Joakim Nivre, Mitchell Abrams, et al. 2018. Universal Dependencies 2.2. http://hdl.handle.net/11234/1-2837.

Joakim Nivre, Johan Hall, Sandra Kübler, Ryan McDonald, Jens Nilsson, Sebastian Riedel, and Deniz Yuret. 2007a. The CoNLL 2007 Shared Task on Dependency Parsing. In *Proceedings of the CoNLL Shared Task Session of EMNLP-CoNLL 2007*.

Joakim Nivre, Johan Hall, Jens Nilsson, Atanas Chanev, Gülsen Eryigit, Sandra Kübler, Svetoslav Marinov, and Erwin Marsi. 2007b. MaltParser: A language-independent system for data-driven dependency parsing. *Natural Language Engineering* 13(2):95–135.

Stephan Oepen, Lilja Øvrelid, Jari Björne, Richard Johansson, Emanuele Lapponi, Filip Ginter, and Erik Velldal. 2017. The 2017 Shared Task on Extrinsic Parser Evaluation. Towards a reusable community infrastructure. In *Proceedings of the EPE 2017 Shared Task*. pages 1–16.

Jeffrey Pennington, Richard Socher, and Christopher Manning. 2014. Glove: Global Vectors for Word Representation. In *Proceedings of EMNLP*. pages 1532–1543.

Barbara Plank, Anders Søgaard, and Yoav Goldberg. 2016. Multilingual Part-of-Speech Tagging with Bidirectional Long Short-Term Memory Models and Auxiliary Loss. In *Proceedings of ACL*. pages 412–418.

Martin Potthast, Tim Gollub, Francisco Rangel, Paolo Rosso, Efstathios Stamatatos, and Benno Stein. 2014. Improving the Reproducibility of PAN's Shared Tasks: Plagiarism Detection, Author Identification, and Author Profiling. In *Proceedings of CLEF Initiative*. pages 268–299.

Siva Reddy, Oscar Täckström, Michael Collins, Tom Kwiatkowski, Dipanjan Das, Mark Steedman, and Mirella Lapata. 2016. Transforming Dependency Structures to Logical Forms for Semantic Parsing. *Transactions of ACL* 4:127–141.

Sebastian Schuster, Eric De La Clergerie, Marie Candito, Benoit Sagot, Christopher D. Manning, and Djamé Seddah. 2017. Paris and Stanford at EPE 2017: Downstream Evaluation of Graph-based Dependency Representations. In *Proceedings of the EPE 2017 Shared Task*. pages 47–59.

Nitish Srivastava, Geoffrey Hinton, Alex Krizhevsky, Ilya Sutskever, and Ruslan Salakhutdinov. 2014. Dropout: A Simple Way to Prevent Neural Networks from Overfitting. *Journal of Machine Learning Research* 15:1929–1958.

Milan Straka and Jana Straková. 2017. Tokenizing, POS Tagging, Lemmatizing and Parsing UD 2.0 with UDPipe. In *Proceedings of the CoNLL 2017 Shared Task*. pages 88–99.

Yuka Tateisi, Akane Yakushiji, Tomoko Ohta, and Jun'ichi Tsujii. 2005. Syntax Annotation for the GENIA Corpus. In *Proceedings of IJCNLP: Companion Volume*. pages 220–225.

Kristina Toutanova, Dan Klein, Christopher D. Manning, and Yoram Singer. 2003. Feature-Rich Part-of-Speech Tagging with a Cyclic Dependency Network. In *Proceedings of NAACL-HLT*.

David Weiss, Chris Alberti, Michael Collins, and Slav Petrov. 2015. Structured training for neural network transition-based parsing. In *Proceedings of ACL-IJCNLP*. pages 323–333.

Hiroyasu Yamada and Yuji Matsumoto. 2003. Statistical dependency analysis with support vector machines. In *Proceedings IWPT*. pages 195–206.

Liner Yang, Meishan Zhang, Yang Liu, Maosong Sun, Nan Yu, and Guohong Fu. 2018. Joint POS Tagging and Dependence Parsing With Transition-Based Neural Networks. *IEEE/ACM Trans. Audio, Speech & Language Processing* 26(8):1352–1358.

Daniel Zeman, Jan Hajič, Martin Popel, Martin Potthast, Milan Straka, Filip Ginter, Joakim Nivre, and Slav Petrov. 2018. CoNLL 2018 Shared Task: Multilingual Parsing from Raw Text to Universal Dependencies. In *Proceedings of the CoNLL 2018 Shared Task*. pages 1–20.

Daniel Zeman, Martin Popel, Milan Straka, Jan Hajic, Joakim Nivre, et al. 2017. CoNLL 2017 Shared Task: Multilingual Parsing from Raw Text to Universal Dependencies. In *Proceedings of the CoNLL 2017 Shared Task*. pages 1–19.

Xingxing Zhang, Jianpeng Cheng, and Mirella Lapata. 2017. Dependency Parsing as Head Selection. In *Proceedings of EACL*. pages 665–676.

Yuan Zhang, Chengtao Li, Regina Barzilay, and Kareem Darwish. 2015. Randomized greedy inference for joint segmentation, pos tagging and dependency parsing. In *Proceedings of NAACL-HLT*. pages 42–52.

Yuan Zhang and David Weiss. 2016. Stack-propagation: Improved Representation Learning for Syntax. In *Proceedings of ACL*. pages 1557–1566.

Yue Zhang and Joakim Nivre. 2011. Transition-based dependency parsing with rich non-local features. In *Proceedings ACL-HLT*. pages 188–193.

IBM Research at the CoNLL 2018 Shared Task on Multilingual Parsing

Hui Wan   Tahira Naseem   Young-Suk Lee   Vittorio Castelli   Miguel Ballesteros
IBM Research AI
1101 Kitchawan Rd, Yorktown Heights, NY 10598, USA
`hwan,tnaseem,ysuklee,vittorio@us.ibm.com`
`miguel.ballesteros@ibm.com`

Abstract

This paper presents the IBM Research AI submission to the CoNLL 2018 Shared Task on Parsing Universal Dependencies. Our system implements a new joint transition-based parser, based on the Stack-LSTM framework and the Arc-Standard algorithm, that handles tokenization, part-of-speech tagging, morphological tagging and dependency parsing in one single model. By leveraging a combination of character-based modeling of words and recursive composition of partially built linguistic structures we qualified 13th overall and 7th in low resource. We also present a new sentence segmentation neural architecture based on Stack-LSTMs that was the 4th best overall.

1   Introduction

The CoNLL 2018 Shared Task on Parsing Universal dependencies consists of parsing raw text from different sources and domains into Universal Dependencies (Nivre et al., 2016, 2017a) for more than 60 languages and domains.[1] The task includes extremely low resource languages, like Kurmanji or Buriat, and high-resource languages like English or Spanish. The competition therefore invites to learn how to make parsers for low-resource language better by exploiting resources available for the high-resource languages. The task also includes languages from almost all language families, including Creole languages like Nigerian Pidgin[2] and completely different scripts (i.e. Chinese, Latin alphabet, Cyrillic alphabet, or Arabic). For further description of the task, data, framework and evaluation please refer to (Nivre et al., 2018, 2017b; Zeman et al., 2018; Potthast et al., 2014; Nivre and Fang, 2017).

In this paper we describe the IBM Research AI submission to the Shared Task on Parsing Universal Dependencies. Our starting point is the Stack-LSTM[3] parser (Dyer et al., 2015; Ballesteros et al., 2017) with character-based word representations (Ballesteros et al., 2015), which we extend to handle tokenization, POS tagging and morphological tagging. Additionally, we apply the ideas presented by Ammar et al. (2016) to all low resource languages since they benefited from high-resource languages in the same family. Finally, we also present two different ensemble algorithms that boosted our results (see Section 2.4).

Participants are requested to obtain parses from raw texts. This means that, sentence segmentation, tokenization, POS tagging and morphological tagging need to be done besides parsing. Participants can choose to use the baseline pipeline (UDPipe 1.2 (Straka et al., 2016)) for those steps besides parsing, or create their own implementation. We choose to use our own implementation for most of the languages. However, in a few treebanks with very hard tokenization, like Chinese and Japanese, we rely on UDPipe 1.2 and a run of our base parser (section 2.1), since this produces better results.

For the rest of languages, we produce parses from raw text that may be in documents (and thus we need to find the sentence markers within those documents); for some of the treebanks we adapted Ballesteros and Wanner (2016) punctuation prediction system (which is also based in the Stack-LSTM framework) to predict sentence markers. Given that the text to be segmented into sentences

---

[1] This is the second run of the task, please refer to (Zeman et al., 2017) for the 2017 Shared Task.

[2] `https://en.wikipedia.org/wiki/Nigerian_Pidgin`

[3] We use the dynamic neural network library Dynet - `http://dynet.io/` - (Neubig et al., 2017) to implement our parser.

92

Proceedings of the CoNLL 2018 Shared Task: Multilingual Parsing from Raw Text to Universal Dependencies, pages 92–102
Brussels, Belgium, October 31 – November 1, 2018. ©2018 Association for Computational Linguistics
https://doi.org/10.18653/v1/K18-2009

can be of a significant length, we implemented a sliding-window extension of the punctuation prediction system where the Stack-LSTM is reinitialized and primed when the window is advanced (see Section 3 for details).

Our system ranked 13th overall, 7th for low resource languages and 4th in sentence segmentation. It was also the best qualifying system in low resource language, Kurmanji, evidencing the effectiveness of our adaptation of Ammar et al. (2016) approach (see Section 2.3).

2 Our Parser

In this Section we present our base parser (see Section 2.1), our joint architecture (see Section 2.2) and our cross-lingual approach (see Section 2.3).

2.1 Stack-LSTM Parser

Our base model is the Stack-LSTM parser (Dyer et al., 2015; Ballesteros et al., 2017) with character-based word representations (Ballesteros et al., 2015). This parser implements the Arc-Standard with SWAP parsing algorithm (Nivre, 2004, 2009) and it uses Stack-LSTMs to model three data structures: a buffer B initialized with the sequence of words to be parsed, a stack S containing partially built parses, and a list A of actions previously taken by the parser. This parser expects tokenized input and a unique POS tag associated with every token.

We use Ballesteros et al. (2015) version of the parser which means that we compute character-based word vectors using bidirectional LSTMs (Graves and Schmidhuber, 2005); but, in addition, we also add pretrained word embeddings for all languages. The intention is to improve in morphologically rich languages and compensate for the rest of languages in which modeling characters is not that important.

2.2 Joint tokenization, tagging and dependency parsing

Inspired by joint models like the ones by Bohnet et al. (2013), Zhang and Clark (2008), Rasooli and Tetreault (2013); Alberti et al. (2015); Swayamdipta et al. (2016), among others, we extend the transition-based parser presented in 2.1 with extra actions that handle tokenization, UPOS tagging and morphological tagging.

Actions: Actions RIGHT-ARC(r) , LEFT-ARC(r) and SWAP remain unchanged, where r represents the label assigned to the arc. The following actions are modified or added for the joint transition-based system.

1. SHIFT is extended to SHIFT(p, f) in which p is the UPOS tag assigned to the token being shifted, f is the Morphological tag. This is the same as in (Bohnet et al., 2013).

2. A new action TOKENIZE(i) is added to handle tokenization within the sentence. TOKENIZE(i) tokenizes the string at the top of the buffer at offset i. The resulted two tokens are put at the top of the buffer. When a string needs to be tokenized into more than two tokens, a series of TOKENIZE and SHIFT actions will do the work.

3. A new action SPLIT is added to handle splitting of a string which is more complicated than inserting whitespace, for example, the word "des" in French is splitted into "de" and "les", as shown in Figure 2. SPLIT splits the top of the buffer token into a list of new tokens. The resulted tokens are then put at the top of the buffer.

4. A new action MERGE is added to handle the "compound" form of token that appears sometimes in training data. For example, in the French treebank, "200 000" (with a whitespace) is often treated as one token. In our parser, this is obtained by applying MERGE when "200" is at the top of stack, and "000" is at the top of buffer.

Figure 1 describes 1) parser transitions applied to the stack and buffer and 2) the resulting stack and buffer states. Figure 2 gives an example of transition sequence in our joint system.

Modules: Our joint system extends the transition-based parser in Section 2.1 with extra modules to handle tokenization, UPOS and morphological tagging. The final loss function is the sum of the loss functions from the parser itself and these extra modules. Due to time limitation we did not introduce weights in the sum.

1. Tokenization module. When a string appears at buffer top, for each offset inside the string, predict whether to tokenize here. If tokenization happens at some offset i, apply TOKENIZE(i) and transit to next state accordingly. If no tokenization happens, predict an

Stack$_t$	Buffer$_t$	Action	Stack$_{t+1}$	Buffer$_{t+1}$	Dependency
$S, (\mathbf{u}, u), (\mathbf{v}, v)$	B	RIGHT-ARC(r)	$S, (g_r(\mathbf{u}, \mathbf{v}), u)$	B	$u \xrightarrow{r} v$
$S, (\mathbf{u}, u), (\mathbf{v}, v)$	B	LEFT-ARC(r)	$S, (g_r(\mathbf{v}, \mathbf{u}), v)$	B	$u \xleftarrow{r} v$
$S, (\mathbf{u}, u), (\mathbf{v}, v)$	$(\mathbf{w}, w), B$	SWAP	$S, (\mathbf{v}, v)$	$(\mathbf{u}, u), (\mathbf{w}, w), B$	—
S	$(\mathbf{u}, u), B$	SHIFT(p, f)	$S, (\mathbf{u}, u)$	B	—
S	$(\mathbf{w}, w), B$	TOKENIZE(i)	S	$(\mathbf{w_1}, w_1), (\mathbf{w_2}, w_2), B$	—
S	$(\mathbf{w}, w), B$	SPLIT($w_1, ..., w_n$)	S	$(\mathbf{w_1}, w_1), ..., (\mathbf{w_n}, w_n), B$	—
$S, (\mathbf{u}, u)$	$(\mathbf{v}, v), B$	MERGE	S	$(g(\mathbf{u}, \mathbf{v}), \text{``}u\,v\text{''}), B$	—

Figure 1: Parser transitions indicating the action applied to the stack and buffer and the resulting state. Bold symbols indicate (learned) embeddings of words and relations, script symbols indicate the corresponding words and relations. g_r and g are compositions of embeddings. w_1 and w_2 are obtained by tokenizing w at offset i. "$u\,v$" is the "compound" form of word.

Transition	Stack	Buffer	Dependency	Tags
	[]	[Le-1, canton-2, des-3, Ulis-4, compte-5, 25-6, 785-7, habitants.-8]		
SHIFT(Le, DET)	[Le-1]	[canton-2, des-3, Ulis-4, compte-5, 25-6, 785-7, habitants.-8]		(Le, DET)
SHIFT(canton, NOUN)	[Le-1, canton-2]	[des-3, Ulis-4, compte-5, 25-6, 785-7, habitants.-8]		(canton, NOUN)
SPLIT(des, de les)	[Le-1, canton-2]	[de-3, les-4, Ulis-5, compte-6, 25-7, 785-8, habitants.-9]		
LEFTARC(det)	[canton-2]	[de-3, les-4, Ulis-5, compte-6, 25-7, 785-8, habitants.-9]	Le $\xleftarrow{det}$ canton	
SHIFT(de, ADP)	[canton-2, de-3]	[les-4, Ulis-5, compte-6, 25-7, 785-8, habitants.-9]		(de, ADP)
SHIFT(les, DET)	[canton-2, de-3, les-4]	[Ulis-5, compte-6, 25-7, 785-8, habitants.-9]		(les, DET)
SHIFT(Ulis, PROPN)	[canton-2, de-3, les-4, Ulis-5]	[compte-6, 25-7, 785-8, habitants.-9]		(Ulis, PROPN)
LEFTARC(det)	[canton-2, de-3, Ulis-5]	[compte-6, 25-7, 785-8, habitants.-9]	les $\xleftarrow{det}$ Ulis	
LEFTARC(case)	[canton-2, Ulis-5]	[compte-6, 25-7, 785-8, habitants.-9]	de $\xleftarrow{case}$ Ulis	
RIGHTARC(nmod)	[canton-2]	[compte-6, 25-7, 785-8, habitants.-9]	canton $\xrightarrow{nmod}$ Ulis	
SHIFT(compte, VERB)	[canton-2, compte-6]	[25-7, 785-8, habitants.-9]		(compte, VERB)
LEFTARC(nsubj)	[compte-6]	[25-7, 785-8, habitants.-9]	canton $\xleftarrow{nsubj}$ compte	
SHIFT(25, NUM)	[compte-6, 25-7]	[785-8, habitants.-9]		(25, NUM)
MERGE	[compte-6]	[25 785-7, habitants.-8]		
SHIFT(25 785, NUM)	[compte-6, 25 785-7]	[habitants.-8]		(25 785, NUM)
TOKENIZE(offset=9)	[compte-6, 25 785-7]	[habitants-8, .-9]		
SHIFT(habitants, NOUN)	[compte-6, 25 785-7, habitants-8]	[.-9]		(habitants, NOUN)
LEFTARC(nummod)	[compte-6, habitants-8]	[.-9]	compte $\xleftarrow{nummod}$ 25 785	
RIGHTARC(obj)	[compte-6]	[.-9]	compte $\xrightarrow{obj}$ habitants	
SHIFT(., PUNCT)	[compte-6, .-9]	[ ]		(., PUNCT)
RIGHTARC(punct)	[compte-6]	[ ]	compte $\xrightarrow{punct}$.	

Figure 2: Transition sequence for "*Le canton des Ulis compte 25 785 habitants.*" with the joint model in Section 2.2. "habitants.-8" means that "habitants." is the 8th token in the current token stream. Morphological tags are omitted in this figure.

action from the set of other (applicable) actions, and transit accordingly.

2. Tagging module. If SHIFT is predicted as the next action, a sub-routine will call classifiers to predict POS and morph-features. The joint system could also predict lemma, but experiment results lead to the decision of not predicting lemma.

3. Split module. If SPLIT is predicted as the next action, a sub-routine will call classifiers to predict the output of SPLIT.

Word embeddings: Parser state representation is composed by three Stack-LSTM's: stack, buffer, actions, as in (Ballesteros et al., 2017). To represent each word in the stack and the buffer, we use character-based word embeddings together with pretrained embeddings and word embeddings trained in the system. The character-based word embeddings are illustrated in Figure 3. For tokenization module, we deployed a character-based embeddings to represent not only the string to tokenize, but also the offset, as illustrated in Figure 4.

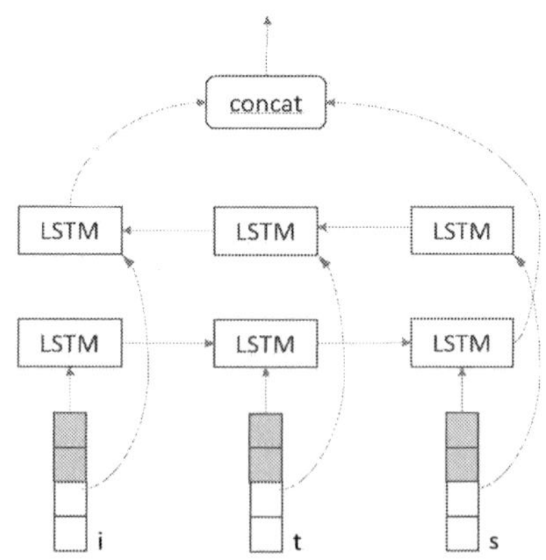

Figure 3: Character-based embeddings from bi-LSTMs to represent the token "its".

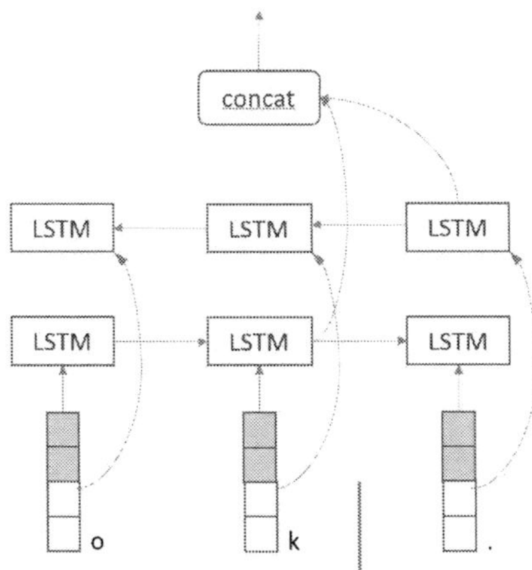

Figure 4: Character-based embeddings from bi-LSTMs to represent the string "ok." and the offset 2 in consideration.

2.3 Cross-Lingual Parser

We adapted cross-lingual architecture of Ammar et al. (2016) (also based in the Stack-LSTM parser) in our joint model presented in Section 2.2 to handle low-resource and zero-shot languages. This architecture enables effective training of the Stack-LSTM parser on multilingual training data. Words in each language are represented by multilingual word embeddings to allow cross-lingual sharing; whereas language specific characteristics are captured by means of language embeddings. Ammar et al. (2016) experiment with a) pre-specified language embeddings based on linguistic features and b) language embeddings learned jointly with the other parameters. The former requires external linguistic knowledge and the latter can be trained only when all languages in the set have enough annotated training data. We take a third approach – we pretrain language embeddings on raw text (explained in next section) and then keep them fixed during parser training. In our implementation, pretrained language embeddings are concatenated with word representation and with parser state.

We use cross-lingual version of our parser for all zero-shot languages (these are: Breton, Naija, Faroese and Thai), most low resource languages (these are: Buryat, Kurmanji, Kazakh, Sorbian Upper, Armenian, Irish, Vietnamese, Northern Sami and Uyghur), and some other languages in which we observed strong improvements on development data when parsing with a cross-lingual model trained in the same language family (these are: Ancient Greek – grc_proiel and grc_perseus, Swedish – sv_pud, Norwegian

| | Nearest Neighbors | | |
	Character	Word	Sub-Word
German	Dutch	Swedish	Afrikaans
Portuguese	Galician	Galician	Galician
Ukrainian	Bulgarian	Bulgarian	Russian
Hindi	Hebrew	Urdu	Urdu
Kazakh	Ukrainian	Buryat	Buryat
Kurmanji	Turkish	Urdu	Naija
Persian	Arabic	Uyghur	Uyghur

Table 1: Nearest neighbors of a variety of languages based on language vectors learned via models of varying granularities: Characters, Words and Sub-Word units (BPEs)

Nynorsk – no_nynorsklia).

In zero-shot setup, we observed that language embeddings in fact hurt parser performance[4]. This is consistent with the findings of Ammar et al. (2016) for a similar setup as noted in footnote 30. In such cases, we trained multilingual parser without language embeddings, relying only on multilingual word embeddings.

Language embeddings: Ammar et al. (2016) architecture utilizes language embeddings that capture language nuances and allow generalization. We adapt the method of Östling and Tiedemann (2017) to pretrain language embeddings. This method is essentially a character-level language model, where a 2-layered LSTM predicts next character at each time step given previous character inputs. A language vector is concatenated to each input as well as the hidden layer before final softmax. The model is trained on a raw corpus containing texts from different languages. Language vectors are shared within the same language.

The model of Östling and Tiedemann (2017) operates at the level of characters; They restrict their experiments to the languages that are written in Latin, Cyrillic or Greek scripts. However, the shared task data spanned a variety of languages with scripts not included in this set. Moreover, there are languages in the shared task that are closely related yet written in different scripts – examples include Hindi-Urdu and Hebrew-Arabic pairs. In preliminary experiments, we found that the language vectors learned via the character-based model, fail to capture language similarities when the script is different. We therefore employ three variations of Östling and Tiedemann (2017) model that differ in granularity of input

---

[4]We performed this experiment in an off-line, artificiality created zero-shot setup.

units: we use 1) characters, 2) words and 3) sub-word units (Byte Pair Encodings, BPEs, Sennrich et al. (2015)) as inputs. Table 1 shows the nearest neighbors of a variety of languages based on the language vectors from each model. Notice that the nearest neighbor of Hindi is Urdu only when model operates on word and sub-word levels. The vectors learned from the three versions are concatenated to form final language embeddings.

This method requires a multilingual corpus for training. We take the first 20K tokens from each training corpus – for the corpora that had fewer tokens, additional raw text is taken from OPUS resources. For BPE inputs, we limit the size of BPE vocabulary to 100,000 symbols.

Multilingual word embeddings: The cross-lingual parser of Ammar et al. (2016) requires word vectors for each language to be in the same universal space. To this end, we use alignment matrices provided by Smith et al. (2017) for Bojanowski et al. (2017) word embeddings. However, for several low-resource languages, pre-computed alignment matrices were not available. These include Naija, Faroese, Kurmanji, Northern Sami, Uyghur, Buryat and Irish. For these languages, to map monolingual embeddings to multilingual space, we seed the mapping algorithm of Smith et al. (2017) with freely available dictionaries[5] combined with shared vocabulary with one of the already mapped languages.

2.4 Sentence-based Ensemble and MST Ensemble

2.4.1 Graph-based ensemble

We adapt Sagae and Lavie (2006) ensemble method to our Stack-LSTM only models (see Section 2.1) to obtain the final parses of Chinese, Japanese, Hebrew, Hungarian, Turkish and Czech. Kuncoro et al. (2016) already tried an ensemble of several Stack-LSTM parser models achieving state-of-the-art in English, German and Chinese, which motivated us to improve the results of our greedy decoding method.[6]

---

[5]Bilingual dictionaries used for multilingual mapping of word embeddings,
https://people.uta.fi/ km56049/same/svocab.html
https://github.com/apertium/apertium-kmr-eng
https://github.com/apertium/apertium-fao-nor

[6]Kuncoro et al. (2016) developed ensemble distillation into a single model which we did not attempt to try for the Shared Task but we leave for future developments.

2.4.2 Model Rescoring: Sentence Level Ensemble

For all of the languages and treebank combinations except for Chinese, Japanese, Hebrew, Hungarian, Turkish and Czech, we apply a sentence-level ensemble technique to obtain the final parses.

We train 10-20 parsing models per language-treebank (see Section 4.2). For an input sentence, with each model we generate a parsing output and a parsing score by adding up the scores of all the actions along the transition sequence (see Figure 1) . Then for each input sentence, we choose the parsing output with the highest model score. The joint model handles tokenization before considering other parsing actions, and makes tokenization decision on every offset; this means that we need to include the normalized score for each tokenization decision. The score assigned to tokenizing a string S at offset n is $(\sum_{i=1...n-1} Score_{keep}(S, i) + Score_{tok}(S, n))/n$, and the score assigned to keeping S as a whole is $(\sum_{i=1...len(S)} Score_{keep}(S, i))/len(S)$.

This simple technique worked fairly well, leading to significant LAS F1 improvement compared with the single model output. From 77.53 LAS in average on single model output of 58 treebanks dev set, 10-model ensemble improves LAS to 78.75 and 20-model ensemble improves LAS to 79.79. Due to time limitation, we only ran a 20-model sentence-level ensemble on 15 treebanks (ar_padt, ca_ancora, cs_fictree, cu_proiel, da_ddt, el_gdt, en_ewt, fr_sequoia, fro_srcmf, gl_ctg, hi_hdtb, ko_gsd, ko_kaist, pl_sz, pt_bosque) while in the rest we ran a 10-model ensemble.

In multi-lingual setting, we ran 5-model ensemble in most cases except grc_proiel, grc_perseus and sv_lines where 10-models ensembles were used for decoding and no_nynorsklia where a single model was used for decoding.

3 Sentence Segmentation

For sentence segmentation we adapted the punctuation prediction system by Ballesteros and Wanner (2016). This model is derived from the Stack-LSTM parser introduced in Section 2.1 and it uses the same architecture (including a stack, a buffer and a stack containing the transitions already taken) but it is restricted to two distinct transitions, either SHIFT or BREAK (which adds a sentence marker between two tokens). The system is therefore context dependent and it makes decisions about sentence boundaries regardless of punctuation symbols or other typical indicative markers.[7]

We only applied our sentence segmentation system for the datasets in which we surpassed the development sets baseline numbers provided by the organizers of the Shared Task by a significant margin, these are: bg_btb, es_ancora, et_edt, fa_seraji, id_gsd, it_postwita, la_proiel, and ro_rrt.

Handling document segmentation: In 58 of the 73 datasets with training data, the train.txt file contains less than 10 paragraphs, and 53 of these contain no paragraph breaks. Thus, if we assumed (incorrectly) that paragraph breaks occur at sentence boundaries and naïvely used paragraphs as training units for the sentence break detector, we would face a huge computational hurdle: we would accumulate the loss over hundreds of thousands of words before computing backpropagation. We addressed this issue by adopting a sliding window approach. The data is segmented into windows containing W words with an overlap of O words. Each window is treated as a training unit, where the loss is computed, the optimizer is invoked and the stack LSTM state is reset. The main challenge of a sliding window approach is to compensate for edge effects: a trivial implementation would ignore the right and left context, which results in diminished ability of detecting sentence breaks near the beginning and the end of the window. Since we desire to keep W to a manageable size, we cannot ignore edge effects. We use two different approaches to provide left and right context to the stack LSTM. The right context is provided by the last O words of the window (with the obvious exception of the last window). Thus, the sentence segmentation algorithm predicts sentence breaks for the first $W - O$ words. To provide left context, we snapshot the stack and action buffer after the last prediction in the window, we slide the window to the right by $W - O$ words, we reset the LSTM state, and we prime the input buffer with the L words to the left of the new window, the action buffer with the most recent L actions, and the stack with the L topmost entries from the snapshot. We explored using different parameter for the window overlap and the size of the left context, and concluded that asymmetric ap-

proaches did not provide an advantage over selecting $L = O$. The parameters for the system used for the evaluation are $W = 100$, $L = O = 30$.

4 Models

4.1 Stack-LSTM

For 6 treebanks (cs_pdt, he_htb, ja_gsd, hu_szeged, tr_imst, zh_gsd), we trained 20 baseline Stack-LSTM models for parsing (utilizing UDPipe pre-processing for sentence segmentation, tokenization and UPOS tagging) per treebank. And the 20 parsing model outputs are rescored with graph-based ensemble (see Section 2.4.2). Independent LSTM models are trained on each treebank for labeling.

All models for the 6 treebanks are trained with dimension 200. Except for ja_gsd and zh_gsd, the models are trained with character embeddings.

We utilized diverse set of word embeddings for Stack-LSTM and graph-based models: cs_pdt, he_htb and tr_imst (CoNLL2017 embedding with dimension 100), ja_gsd (in-house cross-lingual embeddings with dimension 300), hu_szeged and zh_gsd (Facebook embeddings with dimension 300).

4.2 Joint Models

We set input and hidden-layer dimension to 100 and action vector dimension to 20. CoNLL 2017 pretrained embeddings (dimension 100) were used wherever available. We used Facebook embeddings (dimension 300) for af_afribooms, got_proiel and sr_set.

For en_pud and fi_pud where no training and dev set is available, the models trained from the biggest treebank in the same language (en_ewt and fi_tdt) are used to parse the testset. ru_syntagrus model is used to parse ru_taiga testset because of higher score. For gl_treegal and la_perseus where no development data is available, 1/10 of training data is set aside as development set.

We use sentence-based ensemble (see Section 2.4.2) for all models since the parser presented in Section 2.2 may produce a different number of tokens in the output due to tokenization.

4.3 Cross Lingual

Cross-lingual models are trained with input and hidden layers of dimension 100 each, and action vectors of dimension 20. Pretrained multilingual

---

[7]We again used character-based word representations (Ballesteros et al., 2015) and pretrained word embeddings in the same way as the system described in Section 2.1.

Target Treebank	Set of Training Treebanks
pcm_nsc	en_ewt, pt_bosque
fo_oft	no_bokmaal, no_nynorsk, sv_lines, sv_talbanken, da_ddt, sme_giella
br_keb	af_afribooms, en_ewt, nl_alpino, de_gsd, got_proiel, ga_idt
th_pud	id_gsd, vi_vtb
kmr_mg	hi_hdtb, ur_udtb, fa_seraji, kmr_mg
vi_vtb	id_gsd, vi_vtb, hu_szeged
bxr_bdt	ug_udt, bxr_bdt, fa_seraji, tr_imst
ug_udt	ug_udt, bxr_bdt, fa_seraji, tr_imst
kk_ktb	uk_iu, bg_bdt, sk_snk, sl_ssj, sl_sst, hr_set, cs_fictree, pl_lfg, lv_lvtb, cu_proiel, bxr_bdt, hsb_ufal, kk_ktb
hsb_ufal	uk_iu, bg_bdt, sk_snk, sl_ssj, sl_sst, hr_set, cs_fictree, pl_lfg, lv_lvtb, cu_proiel, bxr_bdt, hsb_ufal, kk_ktb
sme_giella	no_bokmaal, no_nynorsk, sv_lines, sv_talbanken, da_ddt, sme_giella
ga_idt	af_afribooms, en_ewt, nl_alpino, de_gsd, got_proiel, ga_idt
hy_armtdp	grc_perseus, grc_proiel, el_gdt, hy_armtdp
grc_perseus	grc_perseus, grc_proiel, el_gdt, hy_armtdp
grc_proiel	grc_perseus, grc_proiel, el_gdt, hy_armtdp
sv_pud	no_bokmaal, no_nynorsk, sv_lines, sv_talbanken, da_ddt, sme_giella
no_nyrosklia	no_bokmaal, no_nynorsk, sv_lines, sv_talbanken, da_ddt, sme_giella
sl_sst	uk_iu, bg_bdt, sk_snk, sl_ssj, sl_sst, hr_set, cs_fictree, pl_lfg, lv_lvtb, cu_proiel, bxr_bdt, hsb_ufal, kk_ktb

Table 2: For each target treebank (left column), the parser was trained on a set of related languages' treebanks (right column). Top section contains zero-shot languages (no training data at all), middle section lists low resource languages (with small amounts of training data) and the bottom section lists the test treebanks for which little or no in-domain training data was provided but a different training treebank of the same language was available.

word embeddings are of dimension 300 and pre-trained language embeddings are of dimension 192 (concatenation of three 64 length vectors).

For each target language, cross-lingual parser is trained on a set of treebanks from related languages. Table 2 details the sets of source treebanks used to train the parser for each target treebank. In the case of low resource languages, training algorithm is modified to sample from each language equally often. This is to ensure that the parser is still getting most of its signal from the language of interest. In all cross-lingual experiments, sentence level ensemble (see Section 2.4.2) is used.

4.4 Segmentation

Sentence segmentation models have hidden layer dimension equal to 100. It relies on the fast-Text embeddings (Bojanowski et al., 2017), which have dimension equal to 300. The sliding window width is of 100 words, and the overlap between adjacent windows is 30 words.

5 Results

Table 4 presents the average F1 LAS results grouped by treebank size and type of our system compared to the baseline UDPipe 1.2 (Straka and Straková, 2017). Table 3 presents the F1 LAS results for all languages compared to the baseline UDPipe 1.2. Our system substantially surpassed the baseline but it is far from the best system of the task in most cases. Some exceptions are the

low resource languages like kmr_mg in which our system is the best, bxr_bdt in which it is the second best and hsb_ufal in which it is the 3rd best; probably due to our cross-lingual approach (see Section 2.3). In ko_gsd and ko_kaist our scores are 17.61 and 13.56 higher than the baseline UDPipe 1.2 as a result of character-based embeddings (similar result as (Ballesteros et al., 2015)), but still far from the best system.

It is worth noting that, on most treebanks our system used joint model to do tokenization in one pass together with parsing, and we trained with no more than UD-2.2 training data. Our overall tokenization score is 97.30, very close (-0.09) to the baseline UDPipe 1.2, our tokenization score on big treebanks is 99.24, the same as the baseline.

For sentence segmentation, as explained in Section 3, we only used our system for the treebanks in which it performed better than the baseline in the development set. We ranked 4th, 0.5 above the baseline and 0.36 below the top-ranking system. Table 5 shows the results of our system for the 8 treebanks for which we submitted a run with our own sentence segmenter. For the other treebanks we used the baseline UDPipe 1.2. We remark that for la_projel, where no punctuation marks are available, our system outperformed UDPipe Future by 3.79 and UDPipe 1.2 by 3.99. Finally, for it_postwita, a dataset where the punctuation is as indicative of sentence breaks and other character patterns, our system outperformed UDPipe future

Treebank	Baseline	Ours	Treebank	Baseline	Ours
af_afribooms	77.88%	80.53% (13)	ar_padt	66.41%	69.13% (15)
bg_btb	84.91%	86.83% (15)	br_keb	10.25%	9.45% (18)
bxr_bdt	12.61%	19.22% (2)	ca_ancora	85.61%	87.60% (16)
cs_cac	83.72%	87.08% (15)	cs_fictree	82.49%	85.83% (15)
cs_pdt	83.94%	87.08% (14)	cs_pud	80.08%	83.00% (12)
cu_proiel	65.46%	69.65% (10)	da_ddt	75.43%	77.87% (15)
de_gsd	70.85%	73.91% (16)	el_gdt	82.11%	84.37% (13)
en_ewt	77.56%	78.37% (16)	en_gum	74.20%	76.11% (17)
en_lines	73.10%	74.31% (16)	en_pud	79.56%	81.13% (13)
es_ancora	84.43%	86.90% (16)	et_edt	75.02%	79.89% (15)
eu_bdt	70.13%	75.09% (15)	fa_seraji	79.10%	82.71% (15)
fi_ftb	75.64%	81.33% (13)	fi_pud	80.15%	83.49% (12)
fi_tdt	76.45%	79.79% (15)	fo_oft	25.19%	38.84% (7)
fr_gsd	81.05%	84.32% (13)	fro_srcmf	79.27%	83.49% (11)
fr_sequoia	81.12%	82.79% (15)	fr_spoken	65.56%	65.34% (17)
ga_idt	62.93%	61.45% (19)	gl_ctg	76.10%	76.81% (17)
gl_treegal	66.16%	62.44% (12)	got_proiel	62.16%	63.52% (11)
grc_perseus	57.75%	66.23% (11)	grc_proiel	67.57%	71.77% (13)
he_htb	57.86%	60.17% (15)	hi_hdtb	87.15%	89.72% (14)
hr_set	78.61%	82.64% (15)	hsb_ufal	23.64%	42.33% (3)
hu_szeged	66.76%	67.25% (16)	hy_armtdp	21.79%	19.25% (20)
id_gsd	74.37%	77.03% (15)	it_isdt	86.26%	87.14% (18)
it_postwita	66.81%	73.85% (5)	ja_gsd	72.32%	73.29% (15)
ja_modern	22.71%	22.74% (7)	kk_ktb	24.21%	23.72% (12)
kmr_mg	23.92%	30.41% (1)	ko_gsd	61.40%	79.01% (13)
ko_kaist	70.25%	83.81% (15)	la_ittb	75.95%	82.43% (15)
la_perseus	47.61%	43.40% (19)	la_proiel	59.66%	64.69% (14)
lv_lvtb	69.43%	73.17% (14)	nl_alpino	77.60%	81.43% (15)
nl_lassysmall	74.56%	76.49% (17)	no_bokmaal	83.47%	86.64% (16)
no_nynorsk	82.13%	85.31% (16)	no_nynorsklia	48.95%	58.28% (8)
pcm_nsc	12.18%	13.03% (12)	pl_lfg	87.53%	90.42% (15)
pl_sz	81.90%	82.81% (17)	pt_bosque	82.07%	84.12% (16)
ro_rrt	80.27%	82.87% (14)	ru_syntagrus	84.59%	87.79% (15)
ru_taiga	55.51%	63.00% (9)	sk_snk	75.41%	77.91% (16)
sl_ssj	77.33%	82.22% (13)	sl_sst	46.95%	48.36% (11)
sme_giella	56.98%	55.97% (18)	sr_set	82.07%	83.84% (16)
sv_lines	74.06%	75.90% (16)	sv_pud	70.63%	76.65% (9)
sv_talbanken	77.91%	80.63% (16)	th_pud	0.70%	0.67% (12)
tr_imst	54.04%	57.19% (16)	ug_udt	56.26%	60.25% (14)
uk_iu	74.91%	77.74% (14)	ur_udtb	77.29%	79.80% (15)
vi_vtb	39.63%	43.48% (7)	zh_gsd	57.91%	60.63% (16)

Table 3: Final F1 LAS results of our system compared with the baseline. We show our ranking for the particular treebank between parenthesis next to our score.

by 29.84 and UDPipe 1.2 by 36.99.

The 2018 edition of the Extrinsic Parser Evaluation Initiative (EPE 2018) (Fares et al., 2018) runs in collaboration with the 2018 Shared Task on Multilingual Parsing. Parsers are evaluated against the three EPE downstream systems: biological event extraction, fine-grained opinion analysis, and negation resolution. This provides opportunities for correlating intrinsic metrics with downstream effects on the three relevant applications. Our system qualified 12th overall, being 10th in event extraction, 13th in negation resolution and 14th in opinion analysis.

Treebank	Baseline	Ours
All	65.80%	69.11% (13)
Big treebanks	74.14%	77.55% (15)
PUD treebanks	66.63%	69.40% (10)
Small treebanks	55.01%	56.13% (18)
Low resource	17.17%	21.88% (7)

Table 4: Average F1 LAS results (grouped by treebank size and type) of our system compared with the baseline. We show our ranking in the same category between parenthesis next to our score.

Treebank	Baseline	Ours (Rank)
bg_btb	92.85	92.24 (24)
es_ancora	98.26	97.89 (24)
et_edt	90.02	91.29 (6)
fa_seraji	98.74	98.09(24)
id_gsd	92.00	92.03 (6)
it_postwita	21.80	58.79 (2)
la_proiel	35.16	39.15 (2)
ro_rrt	93.72	94.40 (5)

Table 5: Sentence segmentation F1 and rank, compared to baseline. We only include the results in which our system surpassed the baseline in the development set.

6 Conclusion

We presented the IBM Research submission to the CoNLL 2018 Shared Task on Universal Dependency Parsing. We presented a new transition-based algorithm for joint (1) tokenization, (2) tagging and (3) parsing that extends the arc-standard algorithm with new transitions. In addition, we also used the same Stack-LSTM framework for sentence segmentation achieving good results.

Acknowledgments

We thank Radu Florian, Todd Ward and Salim Roukos for useful discussions.

References

Chris Alberti, David Weiss, Greg Coppola, and Slav Petrov. 2015. Improved transition-based parsing and tagging with neural networks. In *Proceedings of the 2015 Conference on Empirical Methods in Natural Language Processing, EMNLP 2015, Lisbon, Portugal, September 17-21, 2015*, pages 1354–1359.

Waleed Ammar, George Mulcaire, Miguel Ballesteros, Chris Dyer, and Noah Smith. 2016. Many languages, one parser. *Transactions of the Association for Computational Linguistics*, 4:431–444.

Miguel Ballesteros, Chris Dyer, Yoav Goldberg, and Noah A. Smith. 2017. Greedy transition-based dependency parsing with stack lstms. *Computational Linguistics*, 43(2):311–347.

Miguel Ballesteros, Chris Dyer, and Noah A. Smith. 2015. Improved transition-based parsing by modeling characters instead of words with LSTMs. In *Proceedings of the Conference on Empirical Methods in Natural Language Processing (EMNLP)*, pages 349–359.

Miguel Ballesteros and Leo Wanner. 2016. A neural network architecture for multilingual punctuation generation. In *Proceedings of the 2016 Conference on Empirical Methods in Natural Language Processing*, pages 1048–1053. Association for Computational Linguistics.

Bernd Bohnet, Joakim Nivre, Igor Boguslavsky, Richárd Farkas, Filip Ginter, and Jan Hajič. 2013. Joint morphological and syntactic analysis for richly inflected languages. *Transactions of the Association for Computational Linguistics*, 1:415–428.

Piotr Bojanowski, Edouard Grave, Armand Joulin, and Tomas Mikolov. 2017. Enriching word vectors with subword information. *Transactions of the Association for Computational Linguistics*, 5:135–146.

Chris Dyer, Miguel Ballesteros, Wang Ling, Austin Matthews, and Noah A. Smith. 2015. Transition-based dependency parsing with stack long short-term memory. In *Proceedings of the 53rd Annual Meeting of the Association for Computational Linguistics (ACL)*, pages 334–343.

Murhaf Fares, Stephan Oepen, Lilja Øvrelid, Jari Björne, and Richard Johansson. 2018. The 2018 Shared Task on Extrinsic Parser Evaluation. On the downstream utility of English Universal Dependency parsers. In *Proceedings of the 22nd Conference on Natural Language Learning*, Brussels, Belgia.

Alex Graves and Jürgen Schmidhuber. 2005. Framewise phoneme classification with bidirectional LSTM and other neural network architectures. *Neural Networks*, 18(5-6):602–610.

Adhiguna Kuncoro, Miguel Ballesteros, Lingpeng Kong, Chris Dyer, and Noah A. Smith. 2016. Distilling an ensemble of greedy dependency parsers into one mst parser. In *Proceedings of the 2016 Conference on Empirical Methods in Natural Language Processing*, pages 1744–1753. Association for Computational Linguistics.

Graham Neubig, Chris Dyer, Yoav Goldberg, Austin Matthews, Waleed Ammar, Antonios Anastasopoulos, Miguel Ballesteros, David Chiang, Daniel Clothiaux, Trevor Cohn, Kevin Duh, Manaal Faruqui, Cynthia Gan, Dan Garrette, Yangfeng Ji, Lingpeng Kong, Adhiguna Kuncoro, Gaurav Kumar, Chaitanya Malaviya, Paul Michel, Yusuke Oda, Matthew Richardson, Naomi Saphra, Swabha Swayamdipta, and Pengcheng Yin. 2017. DyNet: The dynamic neural network toolkit. *arXiv preprint arXiv:1701.03980*.

Joakim Nivre. 2004. Inductive dependency parsing. Technical Report 04070, Växjö University, School of Mathematics and Systems Engineering.

Joakim Nivre. 2009. Non-projective dependency parsing in expected linear time. In *Proceedings of the Joint Conference of the 47th Annual Meeting of the ACL and the 4th International Joint Conference on Natural Language Processing of the AFNLP (ACL-IJCNLP)*, pages 351–359.

Joakim Nivre, Željko Agić, Lars Ahrenberg, Lene Antonsen, Maria Jesus Aranzabe, Masayuki Asahara, Luma Ateyah, Mohammed Attia, Aitziber Atutxa, Liesbeth Augustinus, Elena Badmaeva, Miguel Ballesteros, Esha Banerjee, Sebastian Bank, Verginica Barbu Mititelu, John Bauer, Kepa Bengoetxea, Riyaz Ahmad Bhat, Eckhard Bick, Victoria Bobicev, Carl Börstell, Cristina Bosco, Gosse Bouma, Sam Bowman, Aljoscha Burchardt, Marie Candito, Gauthier Caron, Gülşen Cebiroğlu Eryiğit, Giuseppe G. A. Celano, Savas Cetin, Fabricio Chalub, Jinho Choi, Silvie Cinková, Çağrı Çöltekin, Miriam Connor, Elizabeth Davidson, Marie-Catherine de Marneffe, Valeria de Paiva, Arantza Diaz de Ilarraza, Peter Dirix, Kaja Dobrovoljc, Timothy Dozat, Kira Droganova, Puneet Dwivedi, Marhaba Eli, Ali Elkahky, Tomaž Erjavec, Richárd Farkas, Hector Fernandez Alcalde, Jennifer Foster, Cláudia Freitas, Katarína Gajdošová, Daniel Galbraith, Marcos Garcia, Moa Gärdenfors, Kim Gerdes, Filip Ginter, Iakes Goenaga, Koldo Gojenola, Memduh Gökırmak, Yoav Goldberg, Xavier Gómez Guinovart, Berta Gonzáles Saavedra, Matias Grioni, Normunds Grūzītis, Bruno Guillaume, Nizar Habash, Jan Hajič, Jan Hajič jr., Linh Hà Mỹ, Kim Harris, Dag Haug, Barbora Hladká, Jaroslava Hlaváčová, Florinel Hociung, Petter Hohle, Radu Ion, Elena Irimia, Tomáš Jelínek, Anders Johannsen, Fredrik Jørgensen, Hüner Kaşıkara, Hiroshi Kanayama, Jenna Kanerva, Tolga Kayadelen, Václava Kettnerová, Jesse Kirchner, Natalia Kotsyba, Simon Krek, Veronika Laippala, Lorenzo Lambertino, Tatiana Lando, John Lee, Phương Lê Hồng, Alessandro Lenci, Saran Lertpradit, Herman Leung, Cheuk Ying Li, Josie Li, Keying Li, Nikola Ljubešić, Olga Loginova, Olga Lyashevskaya, Teresa Lynn, Vivien Macketanz, Aibek Makazhanov, Michael Mandl, Christopher Manning, Cătălina Mărănduc, David Mareček, Katrin Marheinecke, Héctor Martínez Alonso, André Martins, Jan Mašek, Yuji Matsumoto, Ryan McDonald, Gustavo Mendonça, Niko Miekka, Anna Missilä, Cătălin Mititelu, Yusuke Miyao, Simonetta Montemagni, Amir More, Laura Moreno Romero, Shinsuke Mori, Bohdan Moskalevskyi, Kadri Muischnek, Kaili Müürisep, Pinkey Nainwani, Anna Nedoluzhko, Gunta Nešpore-Bērzkalne, Lương Nguyễn Thị, Huyền Nguyễn Thị Minh, Vitaly Nikolaev, Hanna Nurmi, Stina Ojala, Petya Osenova, Robert Östling, Lilja Øvrelid, Elena Pascual, Marco Passarotti, Cenel-Augusto Perez, Guy Perrier, Slav Petrov, Jussi Piitulainen, Emily Pitler, Barbara Plank, Martin Popel, Lauma Pretkalniņa, Prokopis Prokopidis, Tiina Puolakainen, Sampo Pyysalo, Alexandre Rademaker, Loganathan Ramasamy, Taraka Rama, Vinit Ravishankar, Livy Real, Siva Reddy, Georg Rehm, Larissa Rinaldi, Laura Rituma, Mykhailo Romanenko, Rudolf Rosa, Davide Rovati, Benoît Sagot, Shadi Saleh, Tanja Samardžić, Manuela Sanguinetti, Baiba Saulīte, Sebastian Schuster, Djamé Seddah, Wolfgang Seeker, Mojgan Seraji, Mo Shen, Atsuko Shimada, Dmitry Sichinava, Natalia Silveira, Maria Simi, Radu Simionescu, Katalin Simkó, Mária Šimková, Kiril Simov, Aaron Smith, Antonio Stella, Milan Straka, Jana Strnadová, Alane Suhr, Umut Sulubacak, Zsolt Szántó, Dima Taji, Takaaki Tanaka, Trond Trosterud, Anna Trukhina, Reut Tsarfaty, Francis Tyers, Sumire Uematsu, Zdeňka Urešová, Larraitz Uria, Hans Uszkoreit, Sowmya Vajjala, Daniel van Niekerk, Gertjan van Noord, Viktor Varga, Eric Villemonte de la Clergerie, Veronika Vincze, Lars Wallin, Jonathan North Washington, Mats Wirén, Tak-sum Wong, Zhuoran Yu, Zdeněk Žabokrtský, Amir Zeldes, Daniel Zeman, and Hanzhi Zhu. 2017a. Universal dependencies 2.1. LINDAT/CLARIN digital library at the Institute of Formal and Applied Linguistics (ÚFAL), Faculty of Mathematics and Physics, Charles University.

Joakim Nivre and Chiao-Ting Fang. 2017. Universal dependency evaluation. In *Proceedings of the NoDaLiDa 2017 Workshop on Universal Dependencies (UDW 2017)*, pages 86–95.

Joakim Nivre, Marie-Catherine de Marneffe, Filip Ginter, Yoav Goldberg, Jan Hajič, Christopher D. Manning, Ryan McDonald, Slav Petrov, Sampo Pyysalo, Natalia Silveira, Reut Tsarfaty, and Dan Zeman. 2016. Universal Dependencies v1: A multilingual treebank collection. In *Proceedings of the 10th International Conference on Language Resources and Evaluation (LREC)*.

Joakim Nivre et al. 2017b. Universal Dependencies 2.0 – CoNLL 2017 shared task development and test data. LINDAT/CLARIN digital library at the Institute of Formal and Applied Linguistics, Charles University, Prague, http://hdl.handle.net/11234/1-2184.

Joakim Nivre et al. 2018. Universal Dependencies 2.2. LINDAT/CLARIN digital library at the Institute of Formal and Applied Linguistics, Charles University, Prague, http://hdl.handle.net/11234/.

Robert Östling and Jörg Tiedemann. 2017. Continuous multilinguality with language vectors. In *Proceedings of the 15th Conference of the European Chapter of the Association for Computational Linguistics: Volume 2, Short Papers*, pages 644–649. Association for Computational Linguistics.

Martin Potthast, Tim Gollub, Francisco Rangel, Paolo Rosso, Efstathios Stamatatos, and Benno Stein. 2014. Improving the reproducibility of PAN's shared tasks: Plagiarism detection, author identification, and author profiling. In *Information Access Evaluation meets Multilinguality, Multimodality, and Visualization. 5th International Conference of the CLEF Initiative (CLEF 14)*, pages 268–299, Berlin Heidelberg New York. Springer.

Mohammad Sadegh Rasooli and Joel Tetreault. 2013. Joint parsing and disfluency detection in linear time. In *Proceedings of the 2013 Conference on Empirical Methods in Natural Language Processing*, pages 124–129, Seattle, Washington, USA. Association for Computational Linguistics.

Kenji Sagae and Alon Lavie. 2006. Parser combination by reparsing. In *Proceedings of the Human Language Technology Conference of the NAACL, Companion Volume: Short Papers*, pages 129–132.

Rico Sennrich, Barry Haddow, and Alexandra Birch. 2015. Neural machine translation of rare words with subword units. *arXiv preprint arXiv:1508.07909*.

Samuel L. Smith, David H. P. Turban, Steven Hamblin, and Nils Y. Hammerla. 2017. Offline bilingual word vectors, orthogonal transformations and the inverted softmax. *CoRR*, abs/1702.03859.

Milan Straka, Jan Hajič, and Jana Straková. 2016. UD-Pipe: trainable pipeline for processing CoNLL-U files performing tokenization, morphological analysis, POS tagging and parsing. In *Proceedings of the 10th International Conference on Language Resources and Evaluation (LREC 2016)*, Portorož, Slovenia. European Language Resources Association.

Milan Straka and Jana Straková. 2017. Tokenizing, pos tagging, lemmatizing and parsing ud 2.0 with ud-pipe. In *Proceedings of the CoNLL 2017 Shared Task: Multilingual Parsing from Raw Text to Universal Dependencies*, pages 88–99. Association for Computational Linguistics.

Swabha Swayamdipta, Miguel Ballesteros, Chris Dyer, and Noah A. Smith. 2016. Greedy, joint syntactic-semantic parsing with stack lstms. *CoRR*, abs/1606.08954.

Daniel Zeman, Filip Ginter, Jan Hajič, Joakim Nivre, Martin Popel, Milan Straka, and et al. 2017. CoNLL 2017 Shared Task: Multilingual Parsing from Raw Text to Universal Dependencies. In *Proceedings of the CoNLL 2017 Shared Task: Multilingual Parsing from Raw Text to Universal Dependencies*, pages 1–20. Association for Computational Linguistics.

Daniel Zeman, Jan Hajič, Martin Popel, Martin Potthast, Milan Straka, Filip Ginter, Joakim Nivre, and Slav Petrov. 2018. CoNLL 2018 Shared Task: Multilingual Parsing from Raw Text to Universal Dependencies. In *Proceedings of the CoNLL 2018 Shared Task: Multilingual Parsing from Raw Text to Universal Dependencies*, pages 1–20, Brussels, Belgium. Association for Computational Linguistics.

Yue Zhang and Stephen Clark. 2008. Joint word segmentation and POS tagging using a single perceptron. In *Proceedings of the 46th Annual Meeting of the Association for Computational Linguistics (ACL)*, pages 888–896.

Universal Dependency Parsing with a
General Transition-Based DAG Parser

Daniel Hershcovich[1,2]   **Omri Abend**[2]   **Ari Rappoport**[2]

[1]The Edmond and Lily Safra Center for Brain Sciences
[2]School of Computer Science and Engineering
Hebrew University of Jerusalem
`{danielh,oabend,arir}@cs.huji.ac.il`

Abstract

This paper presents our experiments with applying TUPA to the CoNLL 2018 UD shared task. TUPA is a general neural transition-based DAG parser, which we use to present the first experiments on recovering enhanced dependencies as part of the general parsing task. TUPA was designed for parsing UCCA, a cross-linguistic semantic annotation scheme, exhibiting reentrancy, discontinuity and non-terminal nodes. By converting UD trees and graphs to a UCCA-like DAG format, we train TUPA almost without modification on the UD parsing task. The generic nature of our approach lends itself naturally to multitask learning. Our code is available at `https://github.com/CoNLL-UD-2018/HUJI`.

1 Introduction

In this paper, we present the HUJI submission to the CoNLL 2018 shared task on Universal Dependency parsing (Zeman et al., 2018). We focus only on parsing, using the baseline system, UDPipe 1.2 (Straka et al., 2016; Straka and Straková, 2017) for tokenization, sentence splitting, part-of-speech tagging and morphological tagging.

Our system is based on TUPA (Hershcovich et al., 2017, 2018, see §3), a transition-based UCCA parser. UCCA (Universal Conceptual Cognitive Annotation; Abend and Rappoport, 2013) is a cross-linguistic semantic annotation scheme, representing events, participants, attributes and relations in a directed acyclic graph (DAG) structure. UCCA allows reentrancy to support argument sharing, discontinuity (corresponding to non-projectivity in dependency formalisms) and non-terminal nodes (as opposed to dependencies,

which are bi-lexical). To parse Universal Dependencies (Nivre et al., 2016) using TUPA, we employ a bidirectional conversion protocol to represent UD trees and graphs in a UCCA-like unified DAG format (§2).

Enhanced dependencies. Our method treats *enhanced dependencies*[1] as part of the dependency graph, providing the first approach, to our knowledge, for supervised learning of enhanced UD parsing. Due to the scarcity of enhanced dependencies in UD treebanks, previous approaches (Schuster and Manning, 2016; Reddy et al., 2017) have attempted to recover them using language-specific rules. Our approach attempts to learn them from data: while only a few UD treebanks contain any enhanced dependencies, similar structures are an integral part of UCCA and its annotated corpora (realized as reentrancy by remote edges; see §2), and TUPA supports them as a standard feature.

As their annotation in UD is not yet widespread and standardized, enhanced dependencies are *not included* in the evaluation metrics for UD parsing, and so TUPA's ability to parse them is not reflected in the official shared task scores. However, we believe these enhancements, representing case information, elided predicates, and shared arguments due to conjunction, control, raising and relative clauses, provide richer information to downstream semantic applications, making UD better suited for text understanding. We propose an evaluation metric specific to enhanced dependencies, *enhanced LAS* (§5.1), and use it to evaluate our method.

---

[1]`http://universaldependencies.org/u/overview/enhanced-syntax.html`

Proceedings of the CoNLL 2018 Shared Task: Multilingual Parsing from Raw Text to Universal Dependencies, pages 103–112
Brussels, Belgium, October 31 – November 1, 2018. ©2018 Association for Computational Linguistics
https://doi.org/10.18653/v1/K18-2010

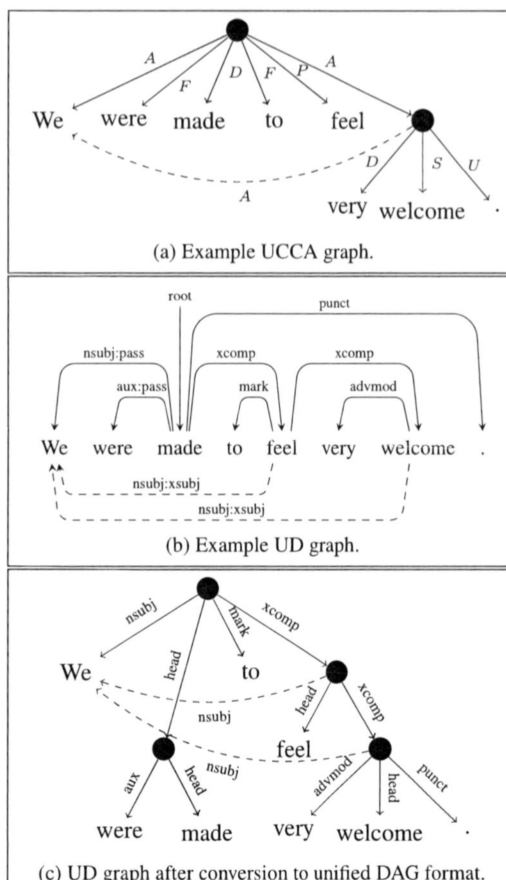

(a) Example UCCA graph.

(b) Example UD graph.

(c) UD graph after conversion to unified DAG format.

Figure 1: (a) Example UCCA annotation for the sentence "We were made to feel very welcome.", containing a control verb, *made*. The dashed *A* edge is a *remote edge*. (b) Bilexical graph annotating the same sentence in UD (`reviews-077034-0002` from `UD_English-EWT`). Enhanced dependencies appear below the sentence. (c) The same UD graph, after conversion to the unified DAG format. Intermediate non-terminals and *head* edges are introduced, to get a UCCA-like structure.

2 Unified DAG Format

To apply TUPA to UD parsing, we convert UD trees and graphs into a unified DAG format (Hershcovich et al., 2018). The format consists of a rooted DAG, where the tokens are the terminal nodes.[2] Edges are labeled (but not nodes), and are divided into *primary* and *remote* edges, where the primary edges form a tree (all nodes have at most one primary parent, and the root has none). Remote edges (denoted as dashed edges in Figure 1)

enable reentrancy, and thus form a DAG together with primary edges. Figure 1 shows an example UCCA graph, and a UD graph (containing two enhanced dependencies) before and after conversion. Both annotate the same sentence from the English Web Treebank (Silveira et al., 2014)[3].

Conversion protocol. To convert UD into the unified DAG format, we add a pre-terminal for each token, and attach the pre-terminals according to the original dependency edges: traversing the tree from the root down, for each head token we create a non-terminal parent with the edge label *head*, and add the node's dependents as children of the created non-terminal node (see Figure 1c). This creates a constituency-like structure, which is supported by TUPA's transition set (see §3.1).

Although the enhanced dependency graph is not necessarily a supergraph of the basic dependency tree, the graph we convert to the unified DAG format is their union: any enhanced dependnecies that are distinct from the basic dependency of a node (by having a different head or universal dependency relation) are converted to *remote edges* in the unified DAG format.

To convert graphs in the unified DAG format back into dependency graphs, we collapse all *head* edges, determining for each terminal what is the highest non-terminal headed by it, and then attaching the terminals to each other according to the edges among their headed non-terminals.

Input format. Enhanced dependencies are encoded in the 9th column of the CoNLL-U format, by an additional head index, followed by a colon and dependency relation. Multiple enhanced dependencies for the same node are separated by pipes. Figure 2 demonstrates this format. Note that if the basic dependency is repeated in the enhanced graph (`3:nsubj:pass` in the example), we do not treat it as an enhanced dependency, so that the converted graph will only contain each edge once. In addition to the UD relations defined in the basic representations, enhanced dependencies may contain the relation `ref`, used for relative clauses. In addition, they may contain more specific relation subtypes, and optionally also case information.

Language-specific extensions and case information. Dependencies may contain language-

---

[2]Our conversion code supports full conversion between UCCA and UD, among other representation schemes, and is publicly available at `http://github.com/danielhers/semstr/tree/master/semstr/conversion`.

[3]`https://catalog.ldc.upenn.edu/LDC2012T13`

```
1 We we PRON PRP Case=Nom|Number=Plur|Person=1|PronType=Prs 3 nsubj:pass 3:nsubj:pass|5:nsubj:xsubj|7:nsubj:xsubj _
```

Figure 2: Example line from CoNLL-U file with two enhanced dependencies: `5:nsubj:xsubj` and `7:nsubj:xsubj`.

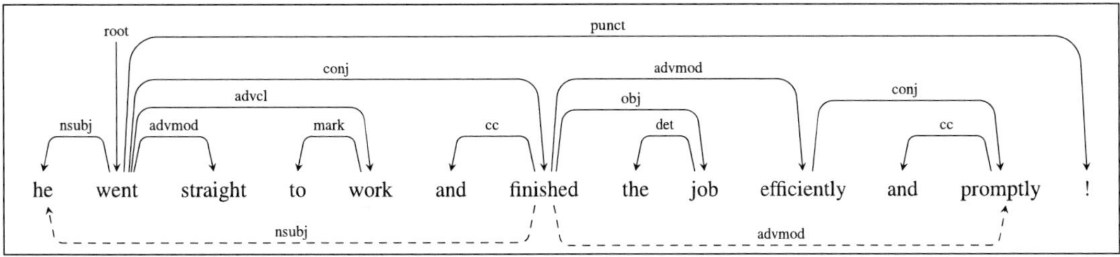

Figure 3: UD graph from `reviews-341397-0003` (`UD_English-EWT`), containing conjoined predicates and arguments.

specific relation subtypes, encoded as a suffix separated from the universal relation by a colon. These extensions are ignored by the parsing evaluation metrics, so for example, the subtyped relation `nsubj:pass` (Figure 1b) is considered the same as the universal relation `nsubj` for evaluation purposes. In the enhanced dependencies, these suffixes may also contain case information, which may be represented by the lemma of an adposition. For example, the "peace" → "earth" dependency in Figure 4 is augmented as `nmod:on` in the enhanced graph (not shown in the figure because it shares the universal relation with the basic dependency).

In the conversion process, we strip any language-specific extensions from both basic and enhanced dependencies, leaving only the universal relations. Consequently, case information that might be encoded in the enhanced dependencies is lost, and we do not handle it in our current system.

Ellipsis and null nodes. In addition to enhanced dependencies, the enhanced UD representation adds null nodes to represented elided predicates. These, too, are ignored in the standard evaluation. An example is shown in Figure 4, where an elided "wish" is represented by the node E9.1. The elided predicate's dependents are attached to its argument "peace" in the basic representation, and the argument itself is attached as an `orphan`. In the enhanced representation, all arguments are attached to the null node as if the elided predicate was present.

While UCCA supports empty nodes without surface realization in the form of *implicit units*, previous work on UCCA parsing has removed these from the graphs. We do the same for UD parsing, dropping null nodes and their associated

dependencies upon conversion to the unified DAG format. We leave parsing elided predicates for future work.

Propagation of conjuncts. Enhanced dependencies contain dependencies between conjoined predicates and their arguments, and between predicates and their conjoined arguments or modifiers. While these relations can often be inferred from the basic dependencies, in many cases they require semantic knowledge to parse correctly. For example, in Figure 3, the enhanced dependencies represent the shared subject ("he") among the conjoined predicates ("went" and "finished"), and the conjoined modifiers ("efficiently" and "promptly") for the second predicate ("finished"). However, there are no enhanced dependencies between the first predicate and the second predicate's modifiers (e.g. "went" → "efficiently"), as semantically only the subject is shared and not the modifiers.

Relative clauses. Finally, enhanced graphs attach predicates of relative clauses directly to the antecedent modified by the relative clause, adding a `ref` dependency between the antecedent and the relative pronoun. An example is shown in Figure 5a. While these graphs may contain cycles ("robe" ↔ "made" in the example), they are removed upon conversion to the unified DAG format by the introduction of non-terminal nodes (see Figure 5b).

3 General Transition-based DAG Parser

We now turn to describing TUPA (Hershcovich et al., 2017, 2018), a general transition-based parser (Nivre, 2003). TUPA uses an extended set of transitions and features that supports reentrancies, discontinuities and non-terminal nodes. The parser state is composed of a buffer B of tokens

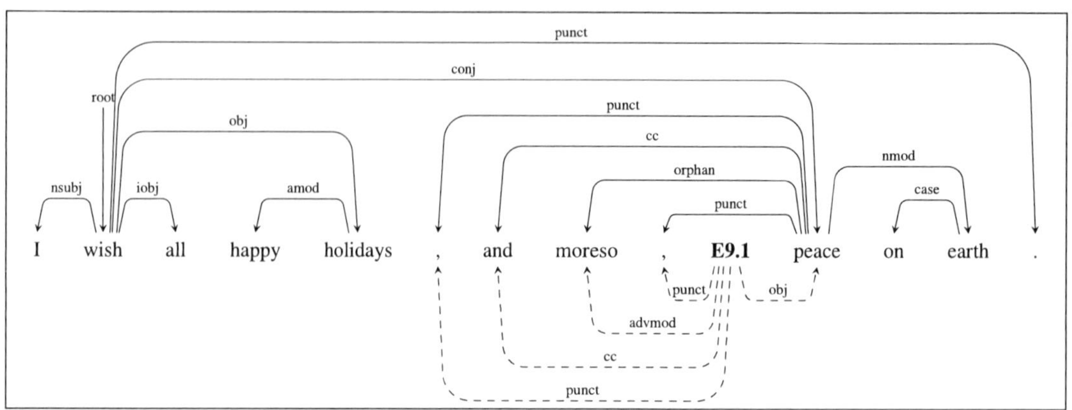

Figure 4: `newsgroup-groups.google.com_GuildWars_086f0f64ab633ab3_ENG_20041111_173500-0051` (UD_English-EWT), containing a null node (**E9.1**) and case information (nmod:on).

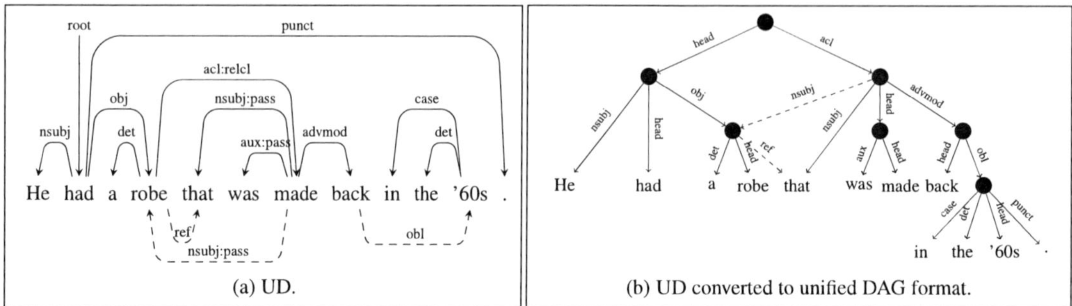

(a) UD.

(b) UD converted to unified DAG format.

Figure 5: (a) `reviews-255261-0007` (UD_English-EWT), containing a relative clause, and (b) the same graph after conversion to the unified DAG format. The cycle is removed due to the non-terminal nodes introduced in the conversion.

and nodes to be processed, a stack S of nodes currently being processed, and a graph $G = (V, E, \ell)$ of constructed nodes and edges, where V is the set of *nodes*, E is the set of *edges*, and $\ell : E \to L$ is the *label* function, L being the set of possible labels. Some states are marked as *terminal*, meaning that G is the final output. A classifier is used at each step to select the next transition based on features encoding the parser's current state. During training, an oracle creates training instances for the classifier, based on gold-standard annotations.

3.1 Transition Set

Given a sequence of tokens $w_1, \ldots, w_n$, we predict a rooted graph G whose terminals are the tokens. Parsing starts with the root node on the stack, and the input tokens in the buffer.

The TUPA transition set, shown in Figure 6, includes the standard SHIFT and REDUCE operations, NODE$_X$ for creating a new non-terminal node and an X-labeled edge, LEFT-EDGE$_X$ and RIGHT-EDGE$_X$ to create a new primary X-labeled edge, LEFT-REMOTE$_X$ and RIGHT-REMOTE$_X$ to create a new remote X-labeled edge, SWAP to handle discontinuous nodes, and FINISH to mark the state as terminal.

The REMOTE$_X$ transitions are not required for parsing trees, but as we treat the problem as general DAG parsing due to the inclusion of enhanced dependencies, we include these transitions.

3.2 Transition Classifier

To predict the next transition at each step, TUPA uses a BiLSTM with feature embeddings as inputs, followed by an MLP and a softmax layer for classification. The model is illustrated in Figure 7. Inference is performed greedily, and training is done with an oracle that yields the set of all optimal transitions at a given state (those that lead to a state from which the gold graph is still reachable). Out of this set, the actual transition performed in training is the one with the highest score given by the classifier, which is trained to maximize the sum of log-likelihoods of all optimal transitions at each step.

106

Before Transition				Transition	After Transition					Condition
Stack	Buffer	Nodes	Edges		Stack	Buffer	Nodes	Edges	Terminal?	
S	$x \mid B$	V	E	SHIFT	$S \mid x$	B	V	E	−	
$S \mid x$	B	V	E	REDUCE	S	B	V	E	−	
$S \mid x$	B	V	E	NODE$_X$	$S \mid x$	$y \mid B$	$V \cup \{y\}$	$E \cup \{(y,x)_X\}$	−	$x \neq \text{root}$
$S \mid y,x$	B	V	E	LEFT-EDGE$_X$	$S \mid y,x$	B	V	$E \cup \{(x,y)_X\}$	−	$\begin{cases} x \notin w_{1:n}, \\ y \neq \text{root}, \\ y \not\rightsquigarrow_G x \end{cases}$
$S \mid x,y$	B	V	E	RIGHT-EDGE$_X$	$S \mid x,y$	B	V	$E \cup \{(x,y)_X\}$	−	
$S \mid y,x$	B	V	E	LEFT-REMOTE$_X$	$S \mid y,x$	B	V	$E \cup \{(x,y)_X^*\}$	−	
$S \mid x,y$	B	V	E	RIGHT-REMOTE$_X$	$S \mid x,y$	B	V	$E \cup \{(x,y)_X^*\}$	−	
$S \mid x,y$	B	V	E	SWAP	$S \mid y$	$x \mid B$	V	E	−	$\mathrm{i}(x) < \mathrm{i}(y)$
[root]	$\emptyset$	V	E	FINISH	$\emptyset$	$\emptyset$	V	E	+	

Figure 6: The transition set of TUPA. We write the stack with its top to the right and the buffer with its head to the left. $(\cdot,\cdot)_X$ denotes a primary X-labeled edge, and $(\cdot,\cdot)_X^*$ a remote X-labeled edge. $\mathrm{i}(x)$ is the swap index (see §3.3). In addition to the specified conditions, the prospective child in an EDGE transition must not already have a primary parent.

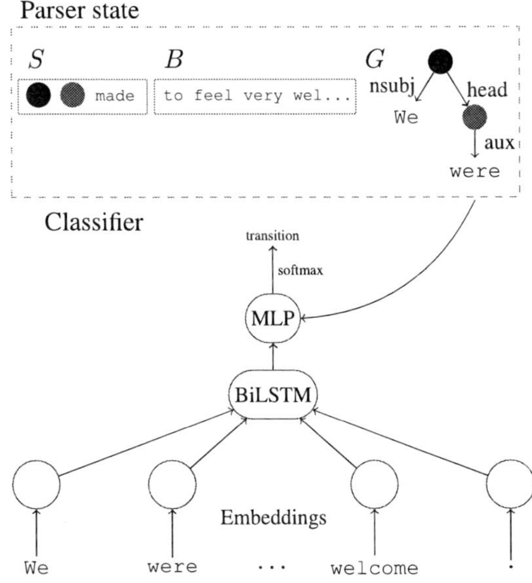

Figure 7: Illustration of the TUPA model, adapted from Hershcovich et al. (2018). Top: parser state (stack, buffer and intermediate graph). Bottom: BiLTSM architecture. Vector representation for the input tokens is computed by two layers of bidirectional LSTMs. The vectors for specific tokens are concatenated with embedding and numeric features from the parser state (for existing edge labels, number of children, etc.), and fed into the MLP for selecting the next transition.

Features. We use vector embeddings representing the words, lemmas, coarse (universal) POS tags and fine-grained POS tags, provided by UDPipe 1.2 during test. For training, we use the gold-annotated lemmas and POS tags. In addition, we use one-character prefix, three-character suffix, shape (capturing orthographic features, e.g., "Xxxx") and named entity type, provided by spaCy;[4] punctuation and gap type features (Maier and Lichte, 2016), and previously predicted edge labels and parser actions. These embeddings are

initialized randomly, except for the word embeddings, which are initialized with the 250K most frequent word vectors from fastText for each language (Bojanowski et al., 2017),[5] pre-trained over Wikipedia and updated during training. We do not use word embeddings for languages without pre-trained fastText vectors (Ancient Greek, North Sami and Old French).

To the feature embeddings, we concatenate numeric features representing the node height, number of (remote) parents and children, and the ratio between the number of terminals to total number of nodes in the graph G.

Table 1 lists all feature used for the classifier. Numeric features are taken as they are, whereas categorical features are mapped to real-valued embedding vectors. For each non-terminal node, we select a *head terminal* for feature extraction, by traversing down the graph according to a priority order on edge labels (otherwise selecting the leftmost child). The priority order is:

```
parataxis, conj, advcl, xcomp
```

3.3 Constraints

During training and parsing, we apply constraints on the parser state to limit the possible transitions to valid ones.

A generic constraint implemented in TUPA is that stack nodes that have been swapped should not be swapped again (Hershcovich et al., 2018). To implement this constraint, we define a *swap index* for each node, assigned when the node is created. At initialization, only the root node and terminals exist. We assign the root a swap index of 0, and for each terminal, its position in the text (starting at 1). Whenever a node is created as a result

---

Nodes	
s_0	`wmtuepT#^$xhqyPCIEMN`
s_1	`wmtueT#^$xhyN`
s_2	`wmtueT#^$xhy`
s_3	`wmtueT#^$xhyN`
b_0	`wmtuT#^$hPCIEMN`
b_1, b_2, b_3	`wmtuT#^$`
$s_0l, s_0r, s_1l, s_1r,$	`wme#^$`
$s_0ll, s_0lr, s_0rl, s_0rr,$	
$s_1ll, s_1lr, s_1rl, s_1rr$	
$s_0L, s_0R, s_1L,$	`wme#^$`
s_1R, b_0L, b_0R	
Edges	
$s_0 \rightarrow s_1, s_0 \rightarrow b_0,$	`x`
$s_1 \rightarrow s_0, b_0 \rightarrow s_0$	
$s_0 \rightarrow b_0, b_0 \rightarrow s_0$	`e`
Past actions	
a_0, a_1	`eA`
Global	`node ratio`

Table 1: Transition classifier features.
s_i: stack node i from the top. b_i: buffer node i.
xl, xr (xL, xR): x's leftmost and rightmost children (parents). `w`: head terminal text. `m`: lemma. `u`: coarse (universal) POS tag. `t`: fine-grained POS tag. `h`: node's height. `e`: label of its first incoming edge. `p`: any separator punctuation between s_0 and s_1. `q`: count of any separator punctuation between s_0 and s_1. `x`: numeric value of gap type (Maier and Lichte, 2016). `y`: sum of gap lengths. `P`, `C`, `I`, `E`, and `M`: number of parents, children, implicit children, remote children, and remote parents. `N`: numeric value of the head terminal's named entity IOB indicator. `T`: named entity type. `#`: word shape (capturing orthographic features, e.g. "Xxxx" or "dd"). `^`: one-character prefix. `$`: three-character suffix.
$x \rightarrow y$ refers to the existing edge from x to y. `x` is an indicator feature, taking the value of 1 if the edge exists or 0 otherwise, `e` refers to the edge label, and a_i to the transition taken $i + 1$ steps ago.
`A` refers to the action type (e.g. SHIFT/RIGHT-EDGE/NODE), and `e` to the edge label created by the action.
`node ratio` is the ratio between non-terminals and terminals (Hershcovich et al., 2017).

of a NODE transition, its swap index is the arithmetic mean of the swap indices of the stack top and buffer head.

In addition, we enforce UD-specific constraints, resulting from the nature of the converted DAG format: every non-terminal node must have a single outgoing `head` edge: once it has one, it may not get another, and until it does, the node may not be reduced.

4 Training details

The model is implemented using DyNet v2.0.3 (Neubig et al., 2017).[6] Unless otherwise noted, we use the default values provided by the package. We use the same hyperparameters as used in previous experiments on UCCA parsing (Hershcovich et al., 2018), without any hyperparameter

tuning on UD treebanks.

Hyperparameter	Value
Pre-trained word dim.	300
Lemma dim.	200
Coarse (universal) POS tag dim.	20
Fine-grained POS tag dim.	20
Named entity dim.	3
Punctuation dim.	1
Shape dim.	3
Prefix dim.	2
Suffix dim.	3
Action dim.	3
Edge label dim.	20
MLP layers	2
MLP dimensions	50
BiLSTM layers	2
BiLSTM dimensions	500

Table 2: Hyperparameter settings.

4.1 Hyperparameters

We use dropout (Srivastava et al., 2014) between MLP layers, and recurrent dropout (Gal and Ghahramani, 2016) between BiLSTM layers, both with $p = 0.4$. We also use word, lemma, coarse- and fine-grained POS tag dropout with $\alpha = 0.2$ (Kiperwasser and Goldberg, 2016): in training, the embedding for a feature value w is replaced with a zero vector with a probability of $\frac{\alpha}{\#(w)+\alpha}$, where $\#(w)$ is the number of occurrences of w observed. In addition, we use *node dropout* (Hershcovich et al., 2018): with a probability of 0.1 at each step, all features associated with a single node in the parser state are replaced with zero vectors. For optimization we use a minibatch size of 100, decaying all weights by 10^{-5} at each update, and train with stochastic gradient descent for 50 epochs with a learning rate of 0.1, followed by AMSGrad (Sashank J. Reddi, 2018) for 250 epochs with $\alpha = 0.001$, $\beta_1 = 0.9$ and $\beta_2 = 0.999$. We found this training strategy better than using only one of the optimization methods, similar to findings by Keskar and Socher (2017). We select the epoch with the best LAS-F1 on the development set. Other hyperparameter settings are listed in Table 2.

4.2 Small Treebanks

For corpora with less than 100 training sentences, we use 750 epochs of AMSGrad instead of 250.

---

[6]`http://dynet.io`

For corpora with no development set, we use 10-fold cross-validation on the training set, each time splitting it to 80% training, 10% development and 10% validation. We perform the normal training procedure on the training and development subsets, and then select the model from the fold with the best LAS-F1 on the corresponding validation set.

4.3 Multilingual Model

For the purpose of parsing languages with no training data, we use a delexicalized multilingual model, trained on the shuffled training sets from all corpora, with no word, lemma, fine-grained tag, prefix and suffix features. We train this model for two epochs using stochastic gradient descent with a learning rate of 0.1 (we only trained this many epochs due to time constraints).

4.4 Out-of-domain Evaluation

For test treebanks without corresponding training data, but with training data in the same language, during testing we use the model trained on the largest training treebank in the same language.

5 Results

Official evaluation was done on the TIRA online platform (Potthast et al., 2014). Our system (named "HUJI") ranked 24th in the LAS-F1 ranking (with an average of 53.69 over all test treebanks), 23rd by MLAS (average of 44.6) and 21st by BLEX (average of 48.05). Since our system only performs dependency parsing and not other pipeline tasks, we henceforth focus on LAS-F1 (Nivre and Fang, 2017) for evaluation.

After the official evaluation period ended, we discovered several bugs in the conversion between the CoNLL-U format and the unified DAG format, which is used by TUPA for training and is output by it (see §2). We did not re-train TUPA on the training treebanks after fixing these bugs, but we did re-evaluate the already trained models on all test treebanks, and used the fixed code for converting their output to CoNLL-U. This yielded an unofficial average test LAS-F1 of 58.48, an improvement of 4.79 points over the official average score. In particular, for two test sets, `ar_padt` and `gl_ctg`, TUPA got a zero score in the official evaluation due to a bug with the treatment of multi-token words. These went up to 61.9 and 71.42, respectively. We also evaluated the trained

	TUPA (official)	TUPA (unofficial)	UDPipe (baseline)
All treebanks	53.69	58.48	65.80
Big treebanks	62.07	67.36	74.14
PUD treebanks	56.35	56.82	66.63
Small treebanks	36.74	41.19	55.01
Low-resource	8.53	12.68	17.17

Table 3: Aggregated test LAS-F1 scores for our system (TUPA) and the baseline system (UDPipe 1.2).

TUPA models on all available development treebanks after fixing the bugs.

Table 3 presents the averaged scores on the shared task test sets, and Figure 8 the (official and unofficial) LAS-F1 scores obtained by TUPA on each of the test and development treebanks.

5.1 Evaluation on Enhanced Dependencies

Since the official evaluation ignores enhanced dependencies, we evaluate them separately using a modified version of the shared task evaluation script[7]. We calculate the *enhanced LAS*, identical to the standard LAS except that the set of dependencies in both gold and predicted graphs are the enhanced dependencies instead of the basic dependencies: ignoring null nodes and any enhanced dependency sharing a head with a basic one, we align the words in the gold graph and the system's graph as in the standard LAS, and define

$$P = \frac{\#\text{correct}}{\#\text{system}}, R = \frac{\#\text{correct}}{\#\text{gold}}, F1 = 2 \cdot \frac{P \cdot R}{P + R}.$$

Table 4 lists the enhanced LAS precision, recall and F1 score on the test treebanks with any enhanced dependencies, as well as the percentage of enhanced dependencies in each test treebank, calculated as $100 \cdot \frac{\#\text{enhanced}}{\#\text{enhanced} + \#\text{words}}$.

Just as remote edges in UCCA parsing are more challenging than primary edges (Hershcovich et al., 2017), parsing enhanced dependencies is a harder task than standard UD parsing, as the scores demonstrate. However, TUPA learns them successfully, getting as much as 56.55 enhanced LAS-F1 (on the Polish LFG test set).

5.2 Ablation Experiments

The TUPA transition classifier for some of the languages uses named entity features calculated

---

[7]`https://github.com/CoNLL-UD-2018/`
`HUJI/blob/master/tupa/scripts/conll18_`
`ud_eval.py`

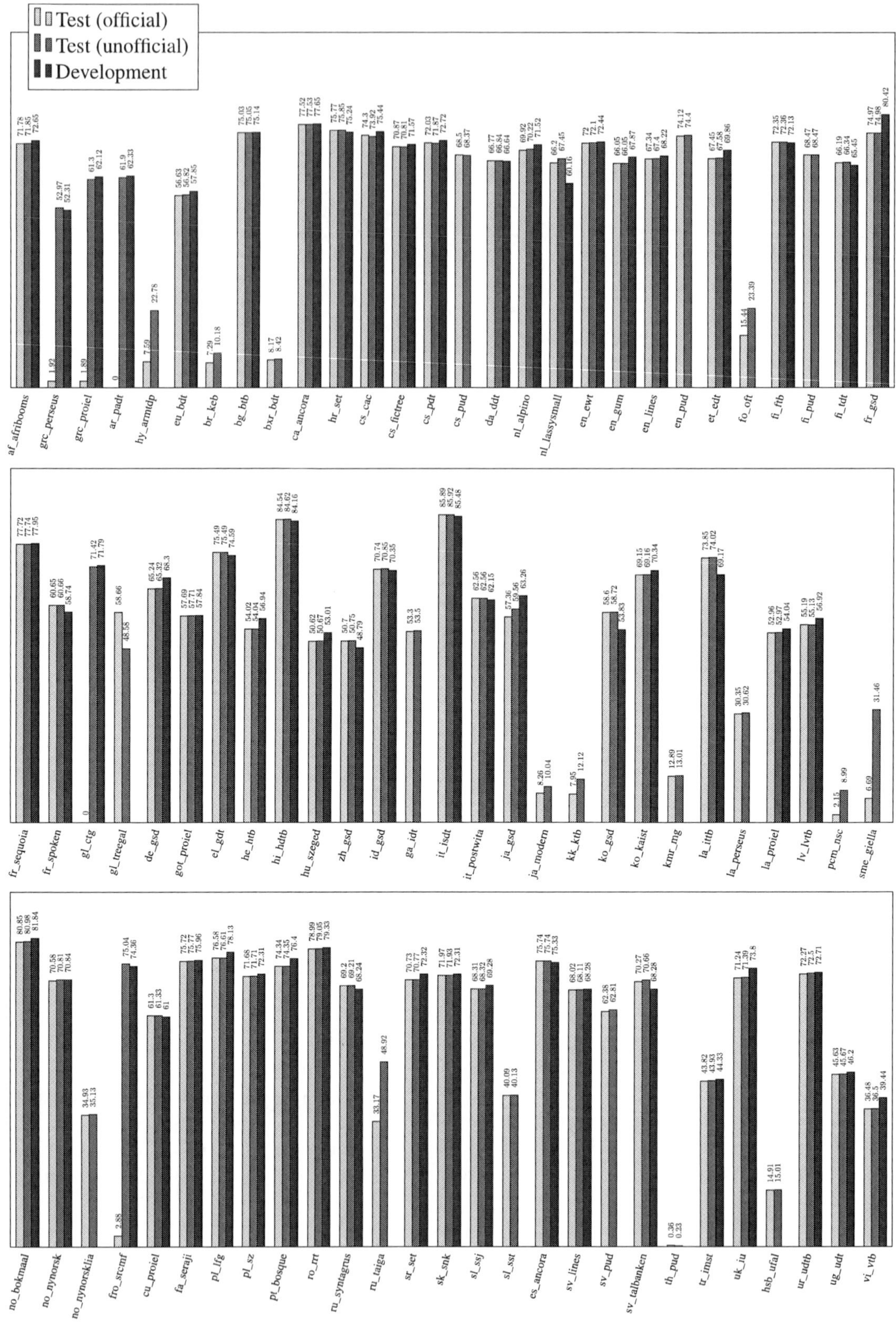

Figure 8: TUPA's LAS-F1 per treebank: official and unofficial test scores, and development scores (where available).

Treebank	Enhanced LAS			% Enhanced
	P	**R**	**F1**	hanced
ar_padt	28.51	16.24	20.69	5.30
cs_cac	54.94	35.69	43.27	7.57
cs_fictree	48.78	18.53	26.85	4.30
cs_pdt	49.46	26.47	34.48	4.61
nl_alpino	56.04	50.81	53.30	4.80
nl_lassysmall	49.71	51.30	50.49	4.13
en_ewt	57.36	52.05	54.58	4.36
en_pud	58.99	50.00	54.13	5.14
fi_tdt	40.20	31.37	35.24	7.34
lv_lvtb	31.76	18.70	23.54	4.12
pl_lfg	59.19	54.13	56.55	2.61
sk_snk	37.28	21.61	27.36	3.91
sv_pud	45.40	39.58	42.29	6.36
sv_talbanken	50.15	43.20	46.42	6.89

Table 4: TUPA's enhanced LAS precision, recall and F1 per test treebank with any enhanced dependencies, and percentage of enhanced dependencies in test treebank.

by spaCy.[8] For German, Spanish, Portuguese, French, Italian, Dutch and Russian, the spaCy named entity recognizer was trained on Wikipedia (Nothman et al., 2013). However, the English model was trained on OntoNotes[9], which is in fact not among the additional resources allowed by the shared task organizers. To get a fair evaluation and to quantify the contribution of the NER features, we re-trained TUPA on the English EWT (`en_ewt`) training set with the same hyperparameters as in our submitted model, just without these features. As Table 5 shows, removing the NER features (−NER) only slightly hurts the performance, by 0.28 LAS-F1 points on the test treebank, and 0.63 on the development treebank.

As further ablation experiments, we tried removing POS features, pre-trained word embeddings, and remote edges (the latter enabling TUPA to parse enhanced dependencies). Removing the POS features does hurt performance to a larger degree, by 2.87 LAS-F1 points on the test set, while removing the pre-trained word embeddings even slightly improves the performance. Removing remote edges and transitions from TUPA causes a very small decrease in LAS-F1, and of course enhanced dependencies can then no longer be produced at all.

---

[8] https://spacy.io/api/annotation
[9] https://catalog.ldc.upenn.edu/LDC2013T19

Model	LAS-F1		Enhanced LAS-F1	
	Test	**Dev**	**Test**	**Dev**
Original	72.10	72.44	54.58	57.13
−NER	71.82	71.81	55.31	54.65
−POS	69.23	69.54	53.78	49.12
−Embed.	72.33	72.55	56.26	54.54
−Remote	72.08	72.32	0.00	0.00

Table 5: Ablation LAS-F1 and Enhanced LAS-F1 on the English EWT development and test set. NER: named entity features. POS: part-of-speech tag features (both universal and fine-grained). Embed.: external pre-trained word embeddings (fastText). Remote: remote edges and transitions in TUPA.

6 Conclusion

We have presented the HUJI submission to the CoNLL 2018 shared task on parsing Universal Dependencies, based on TUPA, a general transition-based DAG parser. Using a simple conversion protocol to convert UD into a unified DAG format, training TUPA as-is on the UD treebanks yields results close to the UDPipe baseline for most treebanks in the standard evaluation. While other systems ignore enhanced dependencies, TUPA learns to produce them too as part of the general dependency parsing process. We believe that with hyperparameter tuning and more careful handling of cross-lingual and cross-domain parsing, TUPA can be competitive on the standard metrics too.

Furthermore, the generic nature of our parser, which supports many representation schemes, as well as domains and languages, will allow improving performance by multitask learning (cf. Hershcovich et al., 2018), which we plan to explore in future work.

Acknowledgments

This work was supported by the Israel Science Foundation (grant no. 929/17) and by the HUJI Cyber Security Research Center in conjunction with the Israel National Cyber Bureau in the Prime Minister's Office.

References

Omri Abend and Ari Rappoport. 2013. Universal Conceptual Cognitive Annotation (UCCA). In *Proc. of ACL*, pages 228–238.

Piotr Bojanowski, Edouard Grave, Armand Joulin, and Tomas Mikolov. 2017. Enriching word vectors with subword information. *TACL*, 5:135–146.

Yarin Gal and Zoubin Ghahramani. 2016. A Theoretically Grounded Application of Dropout in Recurrent Neural Networks. In D D Lee, M Sugiyama, U V Luxburg, I Guyon, and R Garnett, editors, *Advances in Neural Information Processing Systems 29*, pages 1019–1027. Curran Associates, Inc.

Daniel Hershcovich, Omri Abend, and Ari Rappoport. 2017. A transition-based directed acyclic graph parser for UCCA. In *Proc. of ACL*, pages 1127–1138.

Daniel Hershcovich, Omri Abend, and Ari Rappoport. 2018. Multitask parsing across semantic representations. In *Proc. of ACL*, pages 373–385.

Nitish Shirish Keskar and Richard Socher. 2017. Improving generalization performance by switching from Adam to SGD. *CoRR*, abs/1712.07628.

Eliyahu Kiperwasser and Yoav Goldberg. 2016. Simple and accurate dependency parsing using bidirectional LSTM feature representations. *TACL*, 4:313–327.

Wolfgang Maier and Timm Lichte. 2016. Discontinuous parsing with continuous trees. In *Proc. of Workshop on Discontinuous Structures in NLP*, pages 47–57.

Graham Neubig, Chris Dyer, Yoav Goldberg, Austin Matthews, Waleed Ammar, Antonios Anastasopoulos, Miguel Ballesteros, David Chiang, Daniel Clothiaux, Trevor Cohn, Kevin Duh, Manaal Faruqui, Cynthia Gan, Dan Garrette, Yangfeng Ji, Lingpeng Kong, Adhiguna Kuncoro, Gaurav Kumar, Chaitanya Malaviya, Paul Michel, Yusuke Oda, Matthew Richardson, Naomi Saphra, Swabha Swayamdipta, and Pengcheng Yin. 2017. DyNet: The dynamic neural network toolkit. *CoRR*, abs/1701.03980.

Joakim Nivre. 2003. An efficient algorithm for projective dependency parsing. In *Proc. of IWPT*, pages 149–160.

Joakim Nivre and Chiao-Ting Fang. 2017. Universal dependency evaluation. In *Proceedings of the NoDaLiDa 2017 Workshop on Universal Dependencies (UDW 2017)*, pages 86–95.

Joakim Nivre, Marie-Catherine de Marneffe, Filip Ginter, Yoav Goldberg, Jan Hajic, Christopher D. Manning, Ryan McDonald, Slav Petrov, Sampo Pyysalo, Natalia Silveira, Reut Tsarfaty, and Daniel Zeman. 2016. Universal dependencies v1: A multilingual treebank collection. In *Proc. of LREC*.

Joel Nothman, Nicky Ringland, Will Radford, Tara Murphy, and James R Curran. 2013. Learning multilingual named entity recognition from wikipedia. *Artificial Intelligence*, 194:151–175.

Martin Potthast, Tim Gollub, Francisco Rangel, Paolo Rosso, Efstathios Stamatatos, and Benno Stein. 2014. Improving the reproducibility of PAN's shared tasks: Plagiarism detection, author identification, and author profiling. In *Information Access Evaluation meets Multilinguality, Multimodality, and Visualization. 5th International Conference of the CLEF Initiative (CLEF 14)*, pages 268–299, Berlin Heidelberg New York. Springer.

Siva Reddy, Oscar Täckström, Slav Petrov, Mark Steedman, and Mirella Lapata. 2017. Universal semantic parsing. pages 89–101.

Sanjiv Kumar Sashank J. Reddi, Satyen Kale. 2018. On the convergence of Adam and beyond. *ICLR*.

Sebastian Schuster and Christopher D. Manning. 2016. Enhanced English Universal Dependencies: An improved representation for natural language understanding tasks. In *Proc. of LREC*. ELRA.

Natalia Silveira, Timothy Dozat, Marie-Catherine de Marneffe, Samuel Bowman, Miriam Connor, John Bauer, and Chris Manning. 2014. A gold standard dependency corpus for English. In *Proc. of LREC*.

Nitish Srivastava, Geoffrey Hinton, Alex Krizhevsky, Ilya Sutskever, and Ruslan Salakhutdinov. 2014. Dropout: A simple way to prevent neural networks from overfitting. *Journal of Machine Learning Research*, 15:1929–1958.

Milan Straka, Jan Hajič, and Jana Straková. 2016. UDPipe: trainable pipeline for processing CoNLL-U files performing tokenization, morphological analysis, POS tagging and parsing. In *Proceedings of the 10th International Conference on Language Resources and Evaluation (LREC 2016)*, Portoro, Slovenia. European Language Resources Association.

Milan Straka and Jana Straková. 2017. Tokenizing, pos tagging, lemmatizing and parsing ud 2.0 with udpipe. In *Proceedings of the CoNLL 2017 Shared Task: Multilingual Parsing from Raw Text to Universal Dependencies*, pages 88–99, Vancouver, Canada. Association for Computational Linguistics.

Daniel Zeman, Jan Hajič, Martin Popel, Martin Potthast, Milan Straka, Filip Ginter, Joakim Nivre, and Slav Petrov. 2018. CoNLL 2018 Shared Task: Multilingual Parsing from Raw Text to Universal Dependencies. In *Proceedings of the CoNLL 2018 Shared Task: Multilingual Parsing from Raw Text to Universal Dependencies*, pages 1–20, Brussels, Belgium. Association for Computational Linguistics.

82 Treebanks, 34 Models: Universal Dependency Parsing with Multi-Treebank Models

Aaron Smith[*]   Bernd Bohnet[†]   Miryam de Lhoneux[*]

Joakim Nivre[*]   Yan Shao[*]   Sara Stymne[*]

[*]Department of Linguistics and Philology
Uppsala University
Uppsala, Sweden

[†]Google Research
London, UK

Abstract

We present the Uppsala system for the CoNLL 2018 Shared Task on universal dependency parsing. Our system is a pipeline consisting of three components: the first performs joint word and sentence segmentation; the second predicts part-of-speech tags and morphological features; the third predicts dependency trees from words and tags. Instead of training a single parsing model for each treebank, we trained models with multiple treebanks for one language or closely related languages, greatly reducing the number of models. On the official test run, we ranked 7th of 27 teams for the LAS and MLAS metrics. Our system obtained the best scores overall for word segmentation, universal POS tagging, and morphological features.

1   Introduction

The CoNLL 2018 Shared Task on Multilingual Parsing from Raw Text to Universal Dependencies (Zeman et al., 2018) requires participants to build systems that take as input raw text, without any linguistic annotation, and output full labelled dependency trees for 82 test treebanks covering 46 different languages. Besides the labeled attachment score (LAS) used to evaluate systems in the 2017 edition of the Shared Task (Zeman et al., 2017), this year's task introduces two new metrics: morphology-aware labeled attachment score (MLAS) and bi-lexical dependency score (BLEX). The Uppsala system focuses exclusively on LAS and MLAS, and consists of a three-step pipeline. The first step is a model for joint sentence and word segmentation which uses the BiRNN-CRF framework of Shao et al. (2017, 2018) to predict sentence and word boundaries in the raw input and

simultaneously marks multiword tokens that need non-segmental analysis. The second component is a part-of-speech (POS) tagger based on Bohnet et al. (2018), which employs a sentence-based character model and also predicts morphological features. The final stage is a greedy transition-based dependency parser that takes segmented words and their predicted POS tags as input and produces full dependency trees. While the segmenter and tagger models are trained on a single treebank, the parser uses multi-treebank learning to boost performance and reduce the number of models.

After evaluation on the official test sets (Nivre et al., 2018), which was run on the TIRA server (Potthast et al., 2014), the Uppsala system ranked 7th of 27 systems with respect to LAS, with a macro-average F1 of 72.37, and 7th of 27 systems with respect to MLAS, with a macro-average F1 of 59.20. It also reached the highest average score for word segmentation (98.18), universal POS (UPOS) tagging (90.91), and morphological features (87.59).

Corrigendum: After the test phase was over, we discovered that we had used a non-permitted resource when developing the UPOS tagger for Thai PUD (see Section 4). Setting our LAS, MLAS and UPOS scores to 0.00 for Thai PUD gives the corrected scores: LAS 72.31, MLAS 59.17, UPOS 90.50. This does not affect the ranking for any of the three scores, as confirmed by the shared task organizers.

2   Resources

All three components of our system were trained principally on the training sets of Universal Dependencies v2.2 released to coincide with the shared task (Nivre et al., 2018). The tagger and parser also make use of the pre-trained word em-

113

Proceedings of the CoNLL 2018 Shared Task: Multilingual Parsing from Raw Text to Universal Dependencies, pages 113–123
Brussels, Belgium, October 31 – November 1, 2018. ©2018 Association for Computational Linguistics
https://doi.org/10.18653/v1/K18-2011

beddings provided by the organisers, as well as Facebook word embeddings (Bojanowski et al., 2017), and both word and character embeddings trained on Wikipedia text[1] with word2vec (Mikolov et al., 2013). For languages with no training data, we also used external resources in the form of Wikipedia text, parallel data from OPUS (Tiedemann, 2012), the Moses statistical machine translation system (Koehn et al., 2007), and the Apertium morphological transducer for Breton.[2]

3 Sentence and Word Segmentation

We employ the model of Shao et al. (2018) for joint sentence segmentation and word segmentation. Given the input character sequence, we model the prediction of word boundary tags as a sequence labelling problem using a BiRNN-CRF framework (Huang et al., 2015; Shao et al., 2017). This is complemented with an attention-based LSTM model (Bahdanau et al., 2014) for transducing non-segmental multiword tokens. To enable joint sentence segmentation, we add extra boundary tags as in de Lhoneux et al. (2017a).

We use the default parameter settings introduced by Shao et al. (2018) and train a segmentation model for all treebanks with at least 50 sentences of training data. For treebanks with less or no training data (except Thai discussed below), we substitute a model for another treebank/language:

- For Japanese Modern, Czech PUD, English PUD and Swedish PUD, we use the model trained on the largest treebank from the same language (Japanese GSD, Czech PDT, English EWT and Swedish Talbanken).

- For Finnish PUD, we use Finnish TDT rather than the slightly larger Finnish FTB, because the latter does not contain raw text suitable for training a segmenter.

- For Naija NSC, we use English EWT.

- For other test sets with little or no training data, we select models based on the size of the intersection of the character sets measured on Wikipedia data (see Table 2 for details).[3]

Thai Segmentation of Thai was a particularly difficult case: Thai uses a unique script, with no spaces between words, and there was no training data available. Spaces in Thai text can function as sentence boundaries, but are also used equivalently to commas in English. For Thai sentence segmentation, we exploited the fact that four other datasets are parallel, i.e., there is a one-to-one correspondence between sentences in Thai and in Czech PUD, English PUD, Finnish PUD and Swedish PUD.[4] First, we split the Thai text by white space and treat the obtained character strings as potential sentences or sub-sentences. We then align them to the segmented sentences of the four parallel datasets using the Gale-Church algorithm (Gale and Church, 1993). Finally, we compare the sentence boundaries obtained from different parallel datasets and adopt the ones that are shared within at least three parallel datasets.

For word segmentation, we use a trie-based segmenter with a word list derived from the Facebook word embeddings.[5] The segmenter retrieves words by greedy forward maximum matching (Wong and Chan, 1996). This method requires no training but gave us the highest word segmentation score of 69.93% for Thai, compared to the baseline score of 8.56%.

4 Tagging and Morphological Analysis

We use two separate instantiations of the tagger[6] described in Bohnet et al. (2018) to predict UPOS tags and morphological features, respectively. The tagger uses a Meta-BiLSTM over the output of a sentence-based character model and a word model. There are two features that mainly distinguishes the tagger from previous work. The character BiLSTMs use the full context of the sentence in contrast to most other taggers which use words only as context for the character model. This character model is combined with the word model in the Meta-BiLSTM relatively late, after two layers of BiLSTMs.

For both the word and character models, we use two layers of BiLSTMs with 300 LSTM cells per layer. We employ batches with 8000 words and 20000 characters. We keep all other hyperparameters as defined in Bohnet et al. (2018). From the training schema described in the above

---

[1] https://dumps.wikimedia.org/backup-index-bydb.html

[2] https://github.com/apertium/apertium-bre

[3] North Sami Giella was included in this group by mistake, as we underestimated the size of the treebank.

[4] This information was available in the README files distributed with the training data and available to all participants.

[5] github.com/facebookresearch/fastText

[6] https://github.com/google/meta_tagger

paper, we deviate slightly in that we perform early stopping on the word, character and meta-model independently. We apply early stopping due to the performance of the development set (or training set when no development set is available) and stop when no improvement occurs in 1000 training steps. We use the same settings for UPOS tagging and morphological features.

To deal with languages that have little or no training data, we adopt three different strategies:

- For the PUD treebanks (except Thai), Japanese Modern and Naija NSC, we use the same model substitutions as for segmentation (see Table 2).

- For Faroese we used the model for Norwegian Nynorsk, as we believe this to be the most closely related language.

- For treebanks with small training sets we use only the provided training sets for training. Since these treebanks do not have development sets, we use the training sets for early stopping as well.

- For Breton and Thai, which have no training sets and no suitable substitution models, we use a bootstrapping approach to train taggers as described below.

Bootstrapping We first annotate an unlabeled corpus using an external morphological analyzer. We then create a (fuzzy and context-independent) mapping from the morphological analysis to universal POS tags and features, which allows us to relabel the annotated corpus and train taggers using the same settings as for other languages. For Breton, we annotated about 60,000 sentences from Breton OfisPublik, which is part of OPUS,[7] using the Apertium morphological analyzer. The Apertium tags could be mapped to universal POS tags and a few morphological features like person, number and gender. For Thai, we annotated about 33,000 sentences from Wikipedia using PyThaiNLP[8] and mapped only to UPOS tags (no features). Unfortunately, we realized only after the test phase that PyThaiNLP was not a permitted resource, which invalidates our UPOS tagging scores for Thai, as well as the LAS and MLAS scores which depend on the tagger. Note, however, that the score for morphological features

is not affected, as we did not predict features at all for Thai. The same goes for sentence and word segmentation, which do not depend on the tagger.

Lemmas Due to time constraints we chose not to focus on the BLEX metric in this shared task. In order to avoid zero scores, however, we simply copied a lowercased version of the raw token into the lemma column.

5 Dependency Parsing

We use a greedy transition-based parser (Nivre, 2008) based on the framework of Kiperwasser and Goldberg (2016b) where BiLSTMs (Hochreiter and Schmidhuber, 1997; Graves, 2008) learn representations of tokens in context, and are trained together with a multi-layer perceptron that predicts transitions and arc labels based on a few BiLSTM vectors. Our parser is extended with a SWAP transition to allow the construction of non-projective dependency trees (Nivre, 2009). We also introduce a static-dynamic oracle to allow the parser to learn from non-optimal configurations at training time in order to recover better from mistakes at test time (de Lhoneux et al., 2017b).

In our parser, the vector representation x_i of a word type w_i before it is passed to the BiLSTM feature extractors is given by:

$$x_i = e(w_i) \circ e(p_i) \circ \text{BiLSTM}(ch_{1:m}).$$

Here, $e(w_i)$ represents the word embedding and $e(p_i)$ the POS tag embedding (Chen and Manning, 2014); these are concatenated to a character-based vector, obtained by running a BiLSTM over the characters $ch_{1:m}$ of w_i.

With the aim of training multi-treebank models, we additionally created a variant of the parser which adds a treebank embedding $e(tb_i)$ to input vectors in a spirit similar to the language embeddings of Ammar et al. (2016) and de Lhoneux et al. (2017a):

$$x_i = e(w_i) \circ e(p_i) \circ \text{BiLSTM}(ch_{1:m}) \circ e(tb_i).$$

We have previously shown that treebank embeddings provide an effective way to combine multiple monolingual heterogeneous treebanks (Stymne et al., 2018) and applied them to low-resource languages (de Lhoneux et al., 2017a). In this shared task, the treebank embedding model was used both monolingually, to combine several treebanks for a single language, and multilingually, mainly for closely related languages, both

---

[7] https://opus.nlpl.eu/OfisPublik.php
[8] https://github.com/PyThaiNLP/pythainlp/wiki/PyThaiNLP-1.4

for languages with no or small treebanks, and for languages with medium and large treebanks, as described in Section 6.

During training, a word embedding for each word type in the training data is initialized using the pre-trained embeddings provided by the organizers where available. For the remaining languages, we use different strategies:

- For Afrikaans, Armenian, Buryat, Gothic, Kurmanji, North Sami, Serbian and Upper Sorbian, we carry out our own pre-training on the Wikipedia dumps of these languages, tokenising them with the baseline UDPipe models and running the implementation of word2vec in the Gensim Python library[9] with 30 iterations and a minimum count of 1.

- For Breton and Thai, we use specially-trained multilingual embeddings (see Section 6).

- For Naija and Old French, we substitute English and French embeddings, respectively.

- For Faroese, we do not use pre-trained embeddings. While it is possible to train such embeddings on Wikipedia data, as there is no UD training data for Faroese we choose instead to rely on its similarity to other Scandinavian languages (see Section 6).

Word types in the training data that are not found amongst the pre-trained embeddings are initialized randomly using Glorot initialization (Glorot and Bengio, 2010), as are all POS tag and treebank embeddings. Character vectors are also initialized randomly, except for Chinese, Japanese and Korean, in which case we pre-train character vectors using word2vec on the Wikipedia dumps of these languages. At test time, we first look for out-of-vocabulary (OOV) words and characters (i.e., those that are not found in the treebank training data) amongst the pre-trained embeddings and otherwise assign them a trained OOV vector.[10] A variant of word dropout is applied to the word embeddings, as described in Kiperwasser and Goldberg (2016a), and we apply dropout also to the character vectors.

We use the extended feature set of Kiperwasser and Goldberg (2016b) (top 3 items on the stack together with their rightmost and leftmost depen-

---

Character embedding dimension	500
Character BiLSTM layers	1
Character BiLSTM output dimension	200
Word embedding dimension	100
POS embedding dimension	20
Treebank embedding dimension	12
Word BiLSTM layers	2
Word BiLSTM hidden/output dimension	250
Hidden units in MLP	100
Word dropout	0.33
α (for OOV vector training)	0.25
Character dropout	0.33
p_{agg} (for exploration training)	0.1

Table 1: Hyper-parameter values for parsing.

dents plus first item on the buffer with its leftmost dependent). We train all models for 30 epochs with hyper-parameter settings shown in Table 1. Note our unusually large character embedding sizes; we have previously found these to be effective, especially for morphologically rich languages (Smith et al., 2018). Our code is publicly available. We release the version used here as UUParser 2.3.[11]

Using Morphological Features Having a strong morphological analyzer, we were interested in finding out whether or not we can improve parsing accuracy using predicted morphological information. We conducted several experiments on the development sets for a subset of treebanks. However, no experiment gave us any improvement in terms of LAS and we decided not to use this technique for the shared task.

What we tried was to create an embedding representing either the full set of morphological features or a subset of potentially useful features, for example case (which has been shown to be useful for parsing by Kapociute-Dzikiene et al. (2013) and Eryigit et al. (2008)), verb form and a few others. That embedding was concatenated to the word embedding at the input of the BiLSTM. We varied the embedding size (10, 20, 30, 40), tried different subsets of morphological features, and tried with and without using dropout on that embedding. We also tried creating an embedding of a concatenation of the universal POS tag and the Case feature and replace the POS embedding with this one. We are currently unsure why none of these experiments were successful and plan to investigate this

---

[9]https://radimrehurek.com/gensim/

[10]An alternative strategy is to have the parser store embeddings for all words that appear in either the training data or pre-trained embeddings, but this uses far more memory.

[11]https://github.com/UppsalaNLP/uuparser

in the future. It would be interesting to find out whether or not this information is captured somewhere else. A way to test this would be to use diagnostic classifiers on vector representations, as is done for example in Hupkes et al. (2018) or in Adi et al. (2017).

6 Multi-Treebank Models

One of our main goals was to leverage information across treebanks to improve performance and reduce the number of parsing models. We use two different types of models:

1. Single models, where we train one model per treebank (17 models applied to 18 treebanks, including special models for Breton KEB and Thai PUD).

2. Multi-treebank models

   - Monolingual models, based on multiple treebanks for one language (4 models, trained on 10 treebanks, applied to 11 treebanks).
   - Multilingual models, based on treebanks from several (mostly) closely related languages (12 models, trained on 48 treebanks, applied to 52 treebanks; plus a special model for Naija NSC).

When a multi-treebank model is applied to a test set from a treebank with training data, we naturally use the treebank embedding of that treebank also for the test sentences. However, when parsing a test set with no corresponding training data, we have to use one of the other treebank embeddings. In the following, we refer to the treebank selected for this purpose as the *proxy* treebank (or simply *proxy*).

In order to keep the training times and language balance in each model reasonable, we cap the number of sentences used from each treebank to 15,000, with a new random sample selected at each epoch. This only affects a small number of treebanks, since most training sets are smaller than 15,000 sentences. For all our multi-treebank models, we apply the treebank embeddings described in Section 5. Where two or more treebanks in a multilingual model come from the same language, we use separate treebank embeddings for each of them. We have previously shown that multi-treebank models can boost LAS in many cases, especially for small treebanks, when applied monolingually (Stymne et al., 2018), and applied it to low-resource languages (de Lhoneux et al., 2017a). In this paper, we add POS tags and pre-trained embeddings to that framework, and extend it to also cover multilingual parsing for languages with varying amounts of training data.

Treebanks sharing a single model are grouped together in Table 2. To decide which languages to combine in our multilingual models, we use two sources: knowledge about language families and language relatedness, and clusterings of treebank embeddings from training our parser with all available languages. We created clusterings by training single parser models with treebank embeddings for all treebanks with training data, capping the maximum number of sentences per treebank to 800. We then used Ward's method to perform a hierarchical cluster analysis.

We found that the most stable clusters were for closely related languages. There was also a tendency for treebanks containing old languages (i.e., Ancient Greek, Gothic, Latin and Old Church Slavonic) to cluster together. One reason for these languages parsing well together could be that several of the 7 treebanks come from the same annotation projects, four from PROIEL, and two from Perseus, containing consistently annotated and at least partially parallel data, e.g., from the Bible.

For the multi-treebank models, we performed preliminary experiments on development data investigating the effect of different groupings of languages. The main tendency we found was that it was better to use smaller groups of closely related languages rather than larger groups of slightly less related languages. For example, using multilingual models only for Galician-Portuguese and Spanish-Catalan was better than combining all Romance languages in a larger model, and combining Dutch-German-Afrikaans was better than also including English.

A case where we use less related languages is for languages with very little training data (31 sentences or less), believing that it may be beneficial in this special case. We implemented this for Buryat, Uyghur and Kazakh, which are trained with Turkish, and Kurmanji, which is trained with Persian, even though these languages are not so closely related. For Armenian, which has only 50 training sentences, we could not find a close enough language, and instead train a single model on the available data. For the four languages that are not in a multilingual cluster but have more than one available treebank, we use monolingual multi-treebank models (English, French, Italian and Korean).

For the nine treebanks that have no training data we use different strategies:

- For Japanese Modern, we apply the mono-treebank Japanese GSD model.

- For the four PUD treebanks, we apply the multi-treebank models trained using the other treebanks from that language, with the largest available treebank as proxy (except for Finnish, where we prefer Finnish TDT over FTB; cf. Section 3 and Stymne et al. (2018)).

- For Faroese, we apply the model for the Scandinavian languages, which are closely related, with Norwegian Nynorsk as proxy (cf. Section 4). In addition, we map the Faroese characters {Íýúð}, which do not occur in the other Scandinavian languages, to {Iyud}.

- For Naija, an English-based creole, whose treebank according to the README file contains spoken language data, we train a special multilingual model on English EWT and the three small spoken treebanks for French, Norwegian, and Slovenian, and usd English EWT as proxy.[12]

- For Thai and Breton, we create multilingual models trained with word and POS embeddings only (i.e., no character models or treebank embeddings) on Chinese and Irish, respectively. These models make use of multilingual word embeddings provided with Facebook's MUSE multilingual embeddings,[13] as described in more detail below.

For all multi-treebank models, we choose the model from the epoch that has the best mean LAS score among the treebanks that have available development data. This means that treebanks without development data rely on a model that is good for other languages in the group. In the cases of the mono-treebank Armenian and Irish models, where there is no development data, we choose the

model from the final training epoch. This also applies to the Breton model trained on Irish data.

Thai–Chinese For the Thai model trained on Chinese, we were able to map Facebook's monolingual embeddings for each language to English using MUSE, thus creating multilingual Thai-Chinese embeddings. We then trained a monolingual parser model using the mapped Chinese embeddings to initialize all word embeddings, and ensuring that these were not updated during training (unlike in the standard parser setup described in Section 5). At test time, we look up all OOV word types, which are the great majority, in the mapped Thai embeddings first, otherwise assign them to a learned OOV vector. Note that in this case, we had to increase the word embedding dimension in our parser to 300 to accomodate the larger Facebook embeddings.

Breton–Irish For Breton and Irish, the Facebook software does not come with the necessary resources to map these languages into English. Here we instead created a small dictionary by using all available parallel data from OPUS (Ubuntu, KDE and Gnome, a total of 350K text snippets), and training a statistical machine translation model using Moses (Koehn et al., 2007). From the lexical word-to-word correspondences created, we kept all cases where the translation probabilities in both directions were at least 0.4 and the words were not identical (in order to exclude a lot of English noise in the data), resulting in a word list of 6027 words. We then trained monolingual embeddings for Breton using word2vec on Wikipedia data, and mapped them directly to Irish using MUSE. A parser model was then trained, similarly to the Thai-Chinese case, using Irish embeddings as initialization, turning off updates to the word embeddings, and applying the mapped Breton embeddings at test time.

7 Results and Discussion

Table 2 shows selected test results for the Uppsala system, including the two main metrics LAS and MLAS (plus a mono-treebank baseline for LAS),[14] the sentence and word segmentation accuracy, and the accuracy of UPOS tagging and morphological features (UFEATS). To make the table more readable, we have added a simple color

---

[12]We had found this combination to be useful in preliminary experiments where we tried to parse French Spoken without any French training data.

[13]https://github.com/facebookresearch/MUSE

[14]Since our system does not predict lemmas, the third main metric BLEX is not very meaningful.

LANGUAGE	TREEBANK	LAS		MLAS	SENTS	WORDS	UPOS	UFEATS	SEGMENTATION	TAGGING	PARSING
ARABIC	PADT	73.54	73.54	61.04	68.06	96.19	90.70	88.25			
ARMENIAN	ARMTDP	23.90	23.90	6.97	57.44	93.20	75.39	54.45			
BASQUE	BDT	78.12	78.12	67.67	100.00	100.00	96.05	92.50			
BULGARIAN	BTB	88.69	88.69	81.20	95.58	99.92	98.85	97.51			
BRETON	KEB	33.62	33.62	13.91	91.43	90.97	85.01	70.26	FRENCH GSD	SPECIAL*	
CHINESE	GSD	69.17	69.17	59.53	99.10	93.52	89.15	92.35			
GREEK	GDT	86.39	86.39	72.29	91.92	99.69	97.26	93.65			
HEBREW	HTB	67.72	67.72	44.19	100.00	90.98	80.26	79.49			
HUNGARIAN	SZEGED	73.97	73.97	56.22	94.57	99.78	94.60	86.87			
INDONESIAN	GSD	78.15	78.15	67.90	93.47	99.99	93.70	95.83			
IRISH	IDT	68.14	68.14	41.72	94.90	99.60	91.55	81.78			
JAPANESE	GSD	79.97	79.97	65.47	94.92	93.32	91.73	91.66			
JAPANESE	MODERN	28.27	28.27	11.82	0.00	72.76	54.60	71.06	JAPANESE GSD		
LATVIAN	LVTB	76.97	76.97	63.90	96.97	99.67	94.95	91.73			
OLD FRENCH	SRCMF	78.71	78.71	69.82	59.15	100.00	95.48	97.26			
ROMANIAN	RRT	84.33	84.33	76.00	95.81	99.74	97.46	97.25			
THAI	PUD	4.86	4.86	2.22	11.69	69.93	33.75	65.72	SPECIAL*		
VIETNAMESE	VTB	46.15	46.15	40.03	88.69	86.71	78.89	86.43			
AFRIKAANS	AFRIBOOMS	79.47	78.89	66.35	99.65	99.37	96.28	95.39			
DUTCH	ALPINO	83.58	81.73	71.11	89.04	99.62	95.78	95.89			
	LASSYSMALL	82.25	79.59	70.88	73.62	99.87	96.18	95.85			
GERMAN	GSD	75.48	75.15	53.67	79.36	99.37	94.02	88.13			
ANCIENT GREEK	PERSEUS	65.17	62.95	44.31	98.93	99.97	92.40	90.12			
	PROIEL	72.24	71.58	54.98	51.17	99.99	97.05	91.04			
GOTHIC	PROIEL	63.40	60.58	49.79	31.97	100.00	93.43	88.60			
LATIN	ITTB	83.00	82.55	75.38	94.54	99.99	98.34	96.78			
	PERSEUS	58.32	49.86	37.57	98.41	100.00	88.73	78.86			
	PROIEL	64.10	63.85	51.45	37.64	100.00	96.21	91.46			
OLD CHURCH SLAVONIC	PROIEL	70.44	70.31	58.31	44.56	99.99	95.76	88.91			
BURYAT	BDT	17.96	8.45	1.26	93.18	99.04	50.83	40.63	RUSSIAN SYNTAGRUS		
KAZAKH	KTB	31.93	23.85	8.62	94.21	97.40	61.72	48.45	RUSSIAN SYNTAGRUS		
TURKISH	IMST	61.34	61.77	51.23	96.63	97.80	93.72	90.42			
UYGHUR	UDT	62.94	62.38	42.54	83.47	99.69	89.19	87.00			
CATALAN	ANCORA	88.94	88.68	81.39	99.35	99.79	98.38	97.90			
SPANISH	ANCORA	88.79	88.65	81.75	97.97	99.92	98.69	98.23			
CROATIAN	SET	84.62	84.13	70.53	96.97	99.93	97.93	91.70			
SERBIAN	SET	86.99	85.14	75.54	93.07	99.94	97.61	93.70			
SLOVENIAN	SSJ	87.18	87.28	77.81	93.23	99.62	97.99	94.73			
	SST	56.06	53.27	41.22	23.98	100.00	93.18	84.75			
CZECH	CAC	89.49	88.94	82.25	100.00	99.94	99.17	95.84			
	FICTREE	89.76	87.78	80.63	98.72	99.85	98.42	95.52			
	PDT	88.15	88.09	82.39	92.29	99.96	99.07	96.89			
	PUD	84.36	83.35	74.46	96.29	99.62	97.02	93.66	CZECH PDT		
POLISH	LFG	93.14	92.85	84.09	99.74	99.91	98.57	94.68			
	SZ	89.80	88.48	77.28	98.91	99.94	97.95	91.82			
SLOVAK	SNK	86.34	83.80	71.15	88.11	99.98	96.57	89.51			
UPPER SORBIAN	UFAL	28.85	2.70	3.43	73.40	95.15	58.91	42.10	SPANISH ANCORA		
DANISH	DDT	80.08	79.68	71.19	90.10	99.85	97.14	97.03			
FAROESE	OFT	41.69	39.94	0.70	95.32	99.25	65.54	34.56	DANISH DDT		NORWEGIAN NYNORSK
NORWEGIAN	BOKMAAL	88.30	87.68	81.68	95.13	99.84	98.04	97.18			
	NYNORSK	87.40	86.23	79.42	92.09	99.94	97.57	96.88			
	NYNORSKLIA	59.66	55.51	45.51	99.86	99.99	90.02	89.62			
SWEDISH	LINES	80.53	78.33	65.38	85.17	99.99	96.64	89.54			
	PUD	78.15	75.52	49.73	91.57	98.78	93.12	78.53	SWEDISH TALBANKEN		
	TALBANKEN	84.26	83.29	76.74	96.45	99.96	97.45	96.82			
ENGLISH	EWT	81.47	81.18	72.98	75.41	99.10	95.28	96.02			
	GUM	81.28	79.23	69.62	81.16	99.71	94.67	95.80			
	LINES	78.64	76.28	70.18	88.18	99.96	96.47	96.52			
	PUD	84.09	83.67	72.49	97.02	99.69	95.23	95.16	ENGLISH EWT		
ESTONIAN	EDT	81.09	81.47	74.11	92.16	99.96	97.16	95.80			
FINNISH	FTB	84.19	83.12	76.40	87.91	99.98	96.30	96.73			
	PUD	86.48	86.48	80.52	92.95	99.69	97.59	96.84	FINNISH TDT		
	TDT	84.33	84.24	77.50	91.12	99.78	97.06	95.58			
NORTH SAAMI	GIELLA	64.85	64.14	51.67	98.27	99.32	90.44	85.03	GERMAN GSD		
FRENCH	GSD	85.61	85.16	76.79	95.40	99.30	96.86	96.26			
	SEQUOIA	87.39	86.26	79.97	87.33	99.44	97.92	97.47			
	SPOKEN	71.26	69.44	60.12	23.54	100.00	95.51	100.00			
GALICIAN	CTG	78.41	78.27	65.52	96.46	98.01	95.80	97.78			
	TREEGAL	72.67	70.16	58.22	82.97	97.90	93.25	92.15			
PORTUGUESE	BOSQUE	84.41	84.27	71.76	90.89	99.00	95.90	95.41			
HINDI	HDTB	89.37	89.23	74.62	99.02	100.00	97.44	93.55			
URDU	UDTB	80.40	79.85	52.15	98.60	100.00	93.66	80.78			
ITALIAN	ISDT	89.43	89.37	81.17	99.38	99.55	97.79	97.36			
	POSTWITA	76.75	76.46	66.46	54.00	99.04	95.61	95.63			
KOREAN	GSD	81.92	81.12	77.25	92.78	99.87	95.61	99.63			
	KAIST	84.98	84.74	78.90	100.00	100.00	95.21	100.00			
KURMANJI	MG	29.54	7.61	5.77	90.85	96.97	61.33	48.26	SPANISH ANCORA		
PERSIAN	SERAJI	83.39	83.22	76.97	99.50	99.60	96.79	97.02			
NAIJA	NSC	20.44	19.44	3.55	0.00	98.53	57.19	36.09	ENGLISH EWT		SPECIAL*
RUSSIAN	SYNTAGRUS	89.00	89.39	81.01	98.79	99.61	98.59	94.89			
	TAIGA	65.49	59.32	46.07	66.40	97.81	89.32	82.15			
UKRAINIAN	IU	82.70	81.41	59.15	93.42	99.76	96.89	81.95			
ALL	OFFICIAL	72.37	70.71	59.20	83.80	98.18	90.91	87.59			
ALL	CORRECTED	72.31	70.65	59.17	83.80	98.18	90.50	87.59			
BIG		80.25	79.61	68.81	87.23	99.10	95.59	93.65			
PUD		72.27	71.46	57.80	75.57	94.11	87.51	87.05			
SMALL		63.60	60.06	46.00	80.68	99.23	90.93	84.91			
LOW-RESOURCE	OFFICIAL	25.87	18.26	5.16	67.50	93.38	61.07	48.95			
LOW-RESOURCE	CORRECTED	25.33	17.72	4.91	67.50	93.38	57.32	48.95			

Table 2: Results for LAS (+ mono-treebank baseline), MLAS, sentence and word segmentation, UPOS tagging and morphological features (UFEATS). Treebanks sharing a parsing model grouped together; substitute and proxy treebanks for segmentation, tagging, parsing far right (SPECIAL models detailed in the text). Confidence intervals for coloring: $< \mu - \sigma <$ | $< \mu - \mathrm{SE} < \mu < \mu + \mathrm{SE} <$ | $< \mu + \sigma <$ | .

coding. Scores that are significantly higher/lower than the mean score of the 21 systems that successfully parsed all test sets are marked with two shades of green/red. The lighter shade marks differences that are outside the interval defined by the standard error of the mean ($\mu \pm \text{SE}$, $\text{SE} = \sigma/\sqrt{N}$) but within one standard deviation (std dev) from the mean. The darker shade marks differences that are more than one std dev above/below the mean ($\mu \pm \sigma$). Finally, scores that are no longer valid because of the Thai UPOS tagger are crossed out in yellow cells, and corrected scores are added where relevant.

Looking first at the LAS scores, we see that our results are significantly above the mean for all aggregate sets of treebanks (ALL, BIG, PUD, SMALL, LOW-RESOURCE) with an especially strong result for the low-resource group (even after setting the Thai score to 0.00). If we look at specific languages, we do particularly well on low-resource languages like Breton, Buryat, Kazakh and Kurmanji, but also on languages like Arabic, Hebrew, Japanese and Chinese, where we benefit from having better word segmentation than most other systems. Our results are significantly worse than the mean only for Afrikaans AfriBooms, Old French SRCMF, Galician CTG, Latin PROIEL, and Portuguese Bosque. For Galician and Portuguese, this may be the effect of lower word segmentation and tagging accuracy.

To find out whether our multi-treebank and multi-lingual models were in fact beneficial for parsing accuracy, we ran a post-evaluation experiment with one model per test set, each trained only on a single treebank. We refer to this as the mono-treebank baseline, and the LAS scores can be found in the second (uncolored) LAS column in Table 2. The results show that merging treebanks and languages did in fact improve parsing accuracy in a remarkably consistent fashion. For the 64 test sets that were parsed with a multi-treebank model, only four had a (marginally) higher score with the mono-treebank baseline model: Estonian EDT, Russian SynTagRus, Slovenian SSJ, and Turkish IMST. Looking at the aggregate sets, we see that, as expected, the pooling of resources helps most for LOW-RESOURCE (25.33 vs. 17.72) and SMALL (63.60 vs. 60.06), but even for BIG there is some improvement (80.21 vs. 79.61). We find these results very encouraging, as they indicate that our treebank embedding method is a reli-

able method for pooling training data both within and across languages. It is also worth noting that this method is easy to use and does not require extra external resources used in most work on multilingual parsing, like multilingual word embeddings (Ammar et al., 2016) or linguistic re-write rules (Aufrant et al., 2016) to achieve good results.

Turning to the MLAS scores, we see a very similar picture, but our results are relatively speaking stronger also for PUD and SMALL. There are a few striking reversals, where we do significantly better than the mean for LAS but significantly worse for MLAS, including Buryat BDT, Hebrew HTB and Ukrainian IU. Buryat and Ukrainian are languages for which we use a multilingual model for parsing, but not for UPOS tagging and morphological features, so it may be due to sparse data for tags and morphology, since these languages have very little training data. This is supported by the observation that low-resource languages in general have a larger drop from LAS to MLAS than other languages.

For sentence segmentation, the Uppsala system achieved the second best scores overall, and results are significantly above the mean for all aggregates except SMALL, which perhaps indicates a sensitivity to data sparseness for the data-driven joint sentence and word segmenter (we see the same pattern for word segmentation). However, there is a much larger variance in the results than for the parsing scores, with altogether 23 treebanks having scores significantly below the mean.

For word segmentation, we obtained the best results overall, strongly outperforming the mean for all groups except SMALL. We know from previous work (Shao et al., 2018) that our word segmenter performs well on more challenging languages like Arabic, Hebrew, Japanese, and Chinese (although we were beaten by the Stanford team for the former two and by the HIT-SCIR team for the latter two). By contrast, it sometimes falls below the mean for the easier languages, but typically only by a very small fraction (for example 99.99 vs. 100.00 for 3 treebanks). Finally, it is worth noting that the maximum-matching segmenter developed specifically for Thai achieved a score of 69.93, which was more than 5 points better than any other system.

Our results for UPOS tagging indicate that this may be the strongest component of the system, although it is clearly helped by getting its input from a highly accurate word segmenter. The Uppsala system ranks first overall with scores more than one std dev above the mean for all aggregates. There is also much less variance than in the segmentation results, and scores are significantly below the mean only for five treebanks: Galician CTG, Gothic PROIEL, Hebrew HTB, Upper Sorbian UFAL, and Portuguese Bosque. For Galician and Upper Sorbian, the result can at least partly be explained by a lower-than-average word segmentation accuracy.

The results for morphological features are similar to the ones for UPOS tagging, with the best overall score but with less substantial improvements over the mean. The four treebanks where scores are significantly below the mean are all languages with little or no training data: Upper Sorbian UFAL, Hungarian Szeged, Naija NSC and Ukrainian IU.

All in all, the 2018 edition of the Uppsala parser can be characterized as a system that is strong on segmentation (especially word segmentation) and prediction of UPOS tags and morphological features, and where the dependency parsing component performs well in low-resource scenarios thanks to the use of multi-treebank models, both within and across languages. For what it is worth, we also seem to have the highest ranking single-parser transition-based system in a task that is otherwise dominated by graph-based models, in particular variants of the winning Stanford system from 2017 (Dozat et al., 2017).

8   Extrinsic Parser Evaluation

In addition to the official shared task evaluation, we also participated in the 2018 edition of the Extrinsic Parser Evaluation Initiative (EPE) (Fares et al., 2018), where parsers developed for the CoNLL 2018 shared task were evaluated with respect to their contribution to three downstream systems: biological event extraction, fine-grained opinion analysis, and negation resolution. The downstream systems are available for English only, and we participated with our English model trained on English EWT, English LinES and English GUM, using English EWT as the proxy.

In the extrinsic evaluation, the Uppsala system ranked second for event extraction, first for opinion analysis, and 16th (out of 16 systems) for negation resolution. Our results for the first two tasks are better than expected, given that our system ranks in the middle with respect to intrinsic evaluation on English (9th for LAS, 6th for UPOS). By contrast, our performance is very low on the negation resolution task, which we suspect is due to the fact that our system only predicts universal part-of-speech tags (UPOS) and not the language specific PTB tags (XPOS), since the three systems that only predict UPOS are all ranked at the bottom of the list.

9   Conclusion

We have described the Uppsala submission to the CoNLL 2018 shared task, consisting of a segmenter that jointly extracts words and sentences from a raw text, a tagger that provides UPOS tags and morphological features, and a parser that builds a dependency tree given the words and tags of each sentence. For the parser we applied multi-treebank models both monolingually and multilingually, resulting in only 34 models for 82 treebanks as well as significant improvements in parsing accuracy especially for low-resource languages. We ranked 7th for the official LAS and MLAS scores, and first for the unofficial scores on word segmentation, UPOS tagging and morphological features.

Acknowledgments

We are grateful to the shared task organizers and to Dan Zeman and Martin Potthast in particular, and we acknowledge the computational resources provided by CSC in Helsinki and Sigma2 in Oslo through NeIC-NLPL (www.nlpl.eu). Aaron Smith was supported by the Swedish Research Council.

References

Yossi Adi, Einat Kermany, Yonatan Belinkov, Ofer Lavi, and Yoav Goldberg. 2017.   Fine-grained Analysis of Sentence Embeddings Using Auxiliary Prediction Tasks. In *International Conference on Learning Representations*.

Waleed Ammar, George Mulcaire, Miguel Ballesteros, Chris Dyer, and Noah Smith. 2016.   Many Languages, One Parser. *Transactions of the Association for Computational Linguistics* 4:431–444.

Lauriane Aufrant, Guillaume Wisniewski, and François Yvon. 2016.   Zero-resource Dependency Parsing: Boosting Delexicalized Cross-lingual Transfer with Linguistic Knowledge. In *Proceedings of the 26th International Conference on Computational Linguistics (COLING)*. pages 119–130.

Dzmitry Bahdanau, Kyunghyun Cho, and Yoshua Bengio. 2014. Neural Machine Translation by Jointly Learning to Align and Translate. *arXiv preprint arXiv:1409.0473* .

Bernd Bohnet, Ryan McDonald, Goncalo Simoes, Daniel Andor, Emily Pitler, and Joshua Maynez. 2018. Morphosyntactic Tagging with a Meta-BiLSTM Model over Context Sensitive Token Encodings. In *Proceedings of the 56th Annual Meeting of the Association for Computational Linguistics (ACL)*.

Piotr Bojanowski, Edouard Grave, Armand Joulin, and Tomas Mikolov. 2017. Enriching Word Vectors with Subword Information. *Transactions of the Association for Computational Lingustics* 5:135–146.

Danqi Chen and Christopher Manning. 2014. A Fast and Accurate Dependency Parser using Neural Networks. In *Proceedings of the Conference on Empirical Methods in Natural Language Processing (EMNLP)*. pages 740–750.

Miryam de Lhoneux, Yan Shao, Ali Basirat, Eliyahu Kiperwasser, Sara Stymne, Yoav Goldberg, and Joakim Nivre. 2017a. From Raw Text to Universal Dependencies – Look, No Tags! In *Proceedings of the CoNLL 2017 Shared Task: Multilingual Parsing from Raw Text to Universal Dependencies*.

Miryam de Lhoneux, Sara Stymne, and Joakim Nivre. 2017b. Arc-Hybrid Non-Projective Dependency Parsing with a Static-Dynamic Oracle. In *Proceedings of the 15th International Conference on Parsing Technologies*. pages 99–104.

Timothy Dozat, Peng Qi, and Christopher D. Manning. 2017. Stanford's Graph-based Neural Dependency Parser at the CoNLL 2017 Shared Task. In *Proceedings of the CoNLL 2017 Shared Task: Multilingual Parsing from Raw Text to Universal Dependencies*. pages 20–30.

Gülsen Eryigit, Joakim Nivre, and Kemal Oflazer. 2008. Dependency Parsing of Turkish. *Computational Linguistics* 34.

Murhaf Fares, Stephan Oepen, Lilja Øvrelid, Jari Björne, and Richard Johansson. 2018. The 2018 Shared Task on Extrinsic Parser Evaluation. On the downstream utility of English universal dependency parsers. In *Proceedings of the 22nd Conference on Computational Natural Language Learning (CoNLL)*.

William A Gale and Kenneth W Church. 1993. A program for aligning sentences in bilingual corpora. *Computational linguistics* 19(1):75–102.

Xavier Glorot and Yoshua Bengio. 2010. Understanding the difficulty of training deep feedforward neural networks. In *Aistats*. pages 249–256.

Alex Graves. 2008. *Supervised Sequence Labelling with Recurrent Neural Networks*. Ph.D. thesis, Technical University Munich.

Sepp Hochreiter and Jürgen Schmidhuber. 1997. Long short-term memory. *Neural Computation* 9(8):1735–1780.

Zhiheng Huang, Wei Xu, and Kai Yu. 2015. Bidirectional LSTM-CRF models for sequence tagging. *arXiv preprint arXiv:1508.01991* .

Dieuwke Hupkes, Sara Veldhoen, and Willem Zuidema. 2018. Visualisation and 'Diagnostic Classifiers' Reveal how Recurrent and Recursive Neural Networks Process Hierarchical Structure. *Journal of Artificial Intelligence Research* 61:907–926.

Jurgita Kapociute-Dzikiene, Joakim Nivre, and Algis Krupavicius. 2013. Lithuanian dependency parsing with rich morphological features. In *Proceedings of the fourth workshop on statistical parsing of morphologically-rich languages*. pages 12–21.

Eliyahu Kiperwasser and Yoav Goldberg. 2016a. Easy-First Dependency Parsing with Hierarchical Tree LSTMs. *Transactions of the Association for Computational Linguistics* 4:445–461.

Eliyahu Kiperwasser and Yoav Goldberg. 2016b. Simple and Accurate Dependency Parsing Using Bidirectional LSTM Feature Representations. *Transactions of the Association for Computational Linguistics* 4:313–327.

Philipp Koehn, Hieu Hoang, Alexandra Birch, Chris Callison-Burch, Marcello Federico, Nicola Bertoldi, Brooke Cowan, Wade Shen, Christine Moran, Richard Zens, Chris Dyer, Ondrej Bojar, Alexandra Constantin, and Evan Herbst. 2007. Moses: Open source toolkit for statistical machine translation. In *Proceedings of the 45th Annual Meeting of the ACL, Demo and Poster Sessions*. Prague, Czech Republic, pages 177–180.

Tomas Mikolov, Ilya Sutskever, Kai Chen, Greg S Corrado, and Jeff Dean. 2013. Distributed Representations of Words and Phrases and their Compositionality. In *Advances in Neural Information Processing Systems*. pages 3111–3119.

Joakim Nivre. 2008. Algorithms for Deterministic Incremental Dependency Parsing. *Computational Linguistics* 34(4):513–553.

Joakim Nivre. 2009. Non-Projective Dependency Parsing in Expected Linear Time. In *Proceedings of the Joint Conference of the 47th Annual Meeting of the ACL and the 4th International Joint Conference on Natural Language Processing of the AFNLP (ACL-IJCNLP)*. pages 351–359.

Joakim Nivre, Mitchell Abrams, Željko Agić, et al. 2018. Universal Dependencies 2.2. LINDAT/CLARIN digital library at the Institute of Formal and Applied Linguistics (ÚFAL), Faculty of Mathematics and Physics, Charles University. http://hdl.handle.net/11234/1-2837.

Martin Potthast, Tim Gollub, Francisco Rangel, Paolo Rosso, Efstathios Stamatatos, and Benno Stein. 2014. Improving the Reproducibility of PAN's Shared Tasks: Plagiarism Detection, Author Identification, and Author Profiling. In Evangelos Kanoulas, Mihai Lupu, Paul Clough, Mark Sanderson, Mark Hall, Allan Hanbury, and Elaine Toms, editors, *Information Access Evaluation. Multilinguality, Multimodality, and Visualization. 5th International Conference of the CLEF Initiative (CLEF 14)*. pages 268–299.

Yan Shao, Christian Hardmeier, and Joakim Nivre. 2018. Universal Word Segmentation: Implementation and Interpretation. *Transactions of the Association for Computational Linguistics* 6:421–435.

Yan Shao, Christian Hardmeier, Jörg Tiedemann, and Joakim Nivre. 2017. Character-Based Joint Segmentation and POS Tagging for Chinese using Bidirectional RNN-CRF. In *The 8th International Joint Conference on Natural Language Processing*. pages 173–183.

Aaron Smith, Miryam de Lhoneux, Sara Stymne, and Joakim Nivre. 2018. An Investigation of the Interactions Between Pre-Trained Word Embeddings, Character Models and POS Tags in Dependency Parsing. In *Proceedings of the 2018 Conference on Empirical Methods in Natural Language Processing*.

Sara Stymne, Miryam de Lhoneux, Aaron Smith, and Joakim Nivre. 2018. Parser Training with Heterogeneous Treebanks. In *Proceedings of the 56th Annual Meeting of the ACL, Short papers*. pages 619–625.

Jörg Tiedemann. 2012. Parallel Data, Tools and Interfaces in OPUS. In Nicoletta Calzolari (Conference Chair), Khalid Choukri, Thierry Declerck, Mehmet Ugur Dogan, Bente Maegaard, Joseph Mariani, Jan Odijk, and Stelios Piperidis, editors, *Proceedings of the Eight International Conference on Language Resources and Evaluation (LREC'12)*. European Language Resources Association (ELRA).

Pak-Kwong Wong and Chorkin Chan. 1996. Chinese Word Segmentation Based on Maximum Matching and Word Binding Force. In *Proceedings of the 16th International Conference on Computational Linguistics*. pages 200–203.

Daniel Zeman, Jan Hajič, Martin Popel, Martin Potthast, Milan Straka, Filip Ginter, Joakim Nivre, and Slav Petrov. 2018. CoNLL 2018 Shared Task: Multilingual Parsing from Raw Text to Universal Dependencies. In *Proceedings of the CoNLL 2018 Shared Task: Multilingual Parsing from Raw Text to Universal Dependencies*.

Daniel Zeman, Martin Popel, Milan Straka, Jan Hajič, Joakim Nivre, Filip Ginter, Juhani Luotolahti, Sampo Pyysalo, Slav Petrov, Martin Potthast, Francis Tyers, Elena Badmaeva, Memduh Gökırmak, Anna Nedoluzhko, Silvie Cinková, Jan Hajič jr., Jaroslava Hlaváčová, Václava Kettnerová, Zdeňka Urešová, Jenna Kanerva, Stina Ojala, Anna Missilä, Christopher Manning, Sebastian Schuster, Siva Reddy, Dima Taji, Nizar Habash, Herman Leung, Marie-Catherine de Marneffe, Manuela Sanguinetti, Maria Simi, Hiroshi Kanayama, Valeria de Paiva, Kira Droganova, Héctor Martínez Alonso, Hans Uszkoreit, Vivien Macketanz, Aljoscha Burchardt, Kim Harris, Katrin Marheinecke, Georg Rehm, Tolga Kayadelen, Mohammed Attia, Ali Elkahky, Zhuoran Yu, Emily Pitler, Saran Lertpradit, Michael Mandl, Jesse Kirchner, Hector Fernandez Alcalde, Jana Strnadova, Esha Banerjee, Ruli Manurung, Antonio Stella, Atsuko Shimada, Sookyoung Kwak, Gustavo Mendonça, Tatiana Lando, Rattima Nitisaroj, and Josie Li. 2017. CoNLL 2017 Shared Task: Multilingual Parsing from Raw Text to Universal Dependencies. In *Proceedings of the CoNLL 2017 Shared Task: Multilingual Parsing from Raw Text to Universal Dependencies*.

Tree-stack LSTM in Transition Based Dependency Parsing

Ömer Kırnap   Erenay Dayanık   Deniz Yuret

Koç University
Artificial Intelligence Laboratory
İstanbul, Turkey
`okirnap,edayanik16,dyuret@ku.edu.tr`

Abstract

We introduce tree-stack LSTM to model state of a transition based parser with recurrent neural networks. Tree-stack LSTM does not use any parse tree based or hand-crafted features, yet performs better than models with these features. We also develop new set of embeddings from raw features to enhance the performance. There are 4 main components of this model: stack's σ-LSTM, buffer's β-LSTM, actions' LSTM and tree-RNN. All LSTMs use continuous dense feature vectors (embeddings) as an input. Tree-RNN updates these embeddings based on transitions. We show that our model improves performance with low resource languages compared with its predecessors. We participate in *CoNLL 2018 UD Shared Task* as the "KParse" team and ranked 16th in LAS, 15th in BLAS and BLEX metrics, of 27 participants parsing 82 test sets from 57 languages.

1 Introduction

Recent studies in neural dependency parsing creates an opportunity to learn feature conjunctions only from primitive features.(Chen and Manning, 2014) A designer only needs to extract primitive features which may be useful to take parsing actions. However, extracting primitive features from state of a parser still remains critical. On the other hand, representational power of recurrent neural networks should allow a model both to summarize every action taken from the beginning to the current state and tree-fragments obtained until a current state.

We propose a method to concretely summarize previous actions and tree fragments within current word embeddings. We employ word and context embeddings from (Kırnap et al., 2017) as an initial representer. Our model modifies these embeddings based on parsing actions. These embeddings are able to summarize, children-parent relationship. Finally, we test our system in *CoNLL 2018 Shared Task: Multilingual Parsing from Raw Text to Universal Dependencies*.

Rest of the paper is organized as follows: Section 2 summarizes related work done in neural transition based dependency parsing. Section 3 describes the models that we implement for tagging, lemmatization and dependency parsing. Section 4 discusses our results and section 5 presents our contributions.

2 Related Work

In this section we describe the related work done in neural transition based dependency parsing and morphological analysis.

2.1 Morphological Analysis and Tagging

Finite-state transducers (FST) have an important role in previous morphological analyzers. (Koskenniemi, 1983) Unlike modern neural systems, these type of analyzers are language dependent rule based systems. Morphological tagging, on the other hand, tries to solve tagging and analysis problem at the same stage. Koskenniemi proposed conditional random fields (CRFs) based model and Heigold et al. proposed neural network architectures to solve tagging and analysis problem immediately. Modern systems heavily based on word and context based features that we explain in the following paragraph.

2.2 Embedding Features

Chen and Manning, Kiperwasser and Goldberg, use pre-trained word and random part-of-speech (POS) embeddings. Ballesteros et al. use

Proceedings of the CoNLL 2018 Shared Task: Multilingual Parsing from Raw Text to Universal Dependencies, pages 124–132
Brussels, Belgium, October 31 – November 1, 2018. ©2018 Association for Computational Linguistics
https://doi.org/10.18653/v1/K18-2012

character-based word representation for the stack-LSTM parser. In Alberti et al., end-to-end approach is taken for both word and POS embeddings. In other words, one component of their model has responsibility to generate POS embeddings and the other to generate word embeddings.

2.3 Decision Module

We name a part of our model, which provides transitions from features, as decision module. Decision module is a neural architecture designed to find best feature conjunctions. Chen and Manning uses MLP, Dozat et al. applies BiLSTM stacked with MLP as a decision module. We inspire from Dyer et al.'s stack-LSTM which basically represents each component of a state (buffer, stack and actions) with an LSTM. We found new inputs to tree-RNN, and modify this model to obtain better results.

3 Model

In this section, we describe MorphNet (Dayanık et al., 2018) used for tagging and lemmatization; and Tree-stack LSTM used for dependency parsing. We train these models separately. MorphNet employs UDPipe (Straka et al., 2016) for tokenization to generate conll-u formatted file with missing head and dependency relation columns. Tree-stack LSTM takes that for dependency parsing. We detail these models in the remaining part of this section.

3.1 Lemmatization and Part of Speech Tagging

We implement MorphNet (Dayanık et al., 2018) for lemmatization and Part of Speech tagging. It is trained on (Nivre et al., 2018). MorphNet is a sequence-to-sequence recurrent neural network model used to produce a morphological analysis for each word in the input sentence. The model operates with a unidirectional Long Short Term Memory (LSTM) (Hochreiter and Schmidhuber, 1997) encoder to create a character-based word embeddings and a bidirectional LSTM encoder to obtain context embeddings. The decoder consists of two layers LSTM.

The input to the MorphNet consists of an N word sentence $S = [w_1, \ldots, w_N]$, where w_i is the i'th word in the sentence. Each word is input as a sequence of characters $w_i = [w_{i1}, \ldots, w_{iL_i}], w_{ij} \in \mathcal{A}$ where $\mathcal{A}$ is the set of alphanumeric characters and L_i is the number of characters in word w_i.

The output for each word consists of a stem, a part-of-speech tag and a set of morphological features, e.g. "earn+Upos=verb+Mood=indicative+Tense=past" for "earned". The stem is produced one character at a time, and the morphological information is produced one feature at a time. A sample output for a word looks like $[s_{i1}, \ldots, s_{iR_i}, f_{i1}, \ldots, f_{iM_i}]$ where $s_{ij} \in \mathcal{A}$ is an alphanumeric character in the stem, R_i is the length of the stem, M_i is the number of features, $f_{ij} \in \mathcal{T}$ is a morphological feature from a feature set such as $\mathcal{T} = \{\text{Verb},\text{Adjective},\text{Mood=Imperative},\text{Tense=Past}, \ldots\}$.

In Word Encoder we map each character w_{ij} to an A dimensional character embedding vector $a_{ij} \in \mathbb{R}^A$. The word encoder takes each word and processes the character embeddings from left to right producing hidden states $[h_{i1}, \ldots, h_{iL_i}]$ where $h_{ij} \in \mathbb{R}^H$. The final hidden state $e_i = h_{iL_i}$ is used as the word embedding for word w_i.

$$
\begin{aligned}
h_{ij} &= \text{LSTM}(a_{ij}, h_{ij-1}) & (1) \\
h_{i0} &= 0 & (2) \\
e_i &= h_{iL_i} & (3)
\end{aligned}
$$

We model context encoder by using a bidirectional LSTM. The inputs are the word embeddings $e_1, \cdots, e_N$ produced by the word encoder. The context encoder processes them in both directions and constructs a unique context embedding for each target word in the sentence. For a word w_i I define its corresponding context embedding $c_i \in \mathbb{R}^{2H}$ as the concatenation of the forward $\overrightarrow{c}_i \in \mathbb{R}^H$ and the backward $\overleftarrow{c}_i \in \mathbb{R}^H$ hidden states that are produced after the forward and backward LSTMs process the word embedding e_i. Figure illustrates the creation of the context vector for the target word earned.

$$
\begin{aligned}
\overrightarrow{c}_i &= \text{LSTM}_f(e_i, \overrightarrow{c}_{i-1}) & (4) \\
\overleftarrow{c}_i &= \text{LSTM}_b(e_i, \overleftarrow{c}_{i+1}) & (5) \\
\overrightarrow{c}_0 &= \overleftarrow{c}_{N+1} = 0 & (6) \\
c_i &= [\overrightarrow{c}_i; \overleftarrow{c}_i] & (7)
\end{aligned}
$$

The decoder is implemented as a 2-Layer LSTM network that outputs the correct tag for a single target word. By conditioning on the input embeddings and its own hidden state, the decoder learns to generate $y_i = [y_{i1}, \ldots, y_{iK_i}]$ where y_i is the correct tag of the target word w_i in sentence S, $y_{ij} \in \mathcal{A} \cup \mathcal{T}$ represents both stem characters and morphological feature tokens, and K_i is the total number of output tokens (stem + features) for word w_i. The first layer of the decoder is initialized with the context embedding c_i and the second layer is initialized with the word embedding e_i.

$$d_{i0}^1 = \text{relu}(W_d \times c_i \oplus W_{db}) \qquad (8)$$
$$d_{i0}^2 = e_i \qquad (9)$$
$$\qquad (10)$$

We parameterize the distribution over possible morphological features and characters at each time step as

$$p(y_{ij}|d_{ij}^2) = \text{softmax}(W_s \times d_{ij}^2 \oplus W_{sb}) \qquad (11)$$

where $W_s \in \mathbb{R}^{|\mathcal{Y}| \times H}$ and $W_{sb} \in \mathbb{R}^{|\mathcal{Y}|}$ where $\mathcal{Y} = \mathcal{A} \cup \mathcal{T}$ is the set of characters and morphological features in output vocabulary.

3.2 Word and Context Embeddings

We benefit pre-trained word embeddings from (Kırnap et al., 2017) in our parser. Both word and context embeddings are extracted from the language model described in section 3.1 of (Kırnap et al., 2017).

3.3 Features

We use limited number of continuous embeddings in parser model. These are POS, word, context, and morphological feature embeddings. Word and context embeddings are pre-trained and not fine-tuned during training. POS and morphological feature embeddings are randomly initialized and learned during training.

Abbrev	Feature
c	context embedding
v	word embedding
p	universal POS tag
f	morphological features

Table 1: Possible features for each word

3.4 Morphological Feature Embeddings

We introduce morphological feature embeddings, which differs from (Dyer et al., 2015), as an additional input to our model. Each feature is represented with 128 dimensional continuous vector.

We experiment that vector sizes lower than 128 reduces the performance of a parser, and higher than 128 does not bring further enhancements. We formulate morphological feature embeddings by adding feature vectors of a word. For example, suppose we are given a word *it* with following morphological features: Case=Nom and Gender=Neut and Number=Sing and Person=3 and PronType=Prs. We basically sum corresponding 5 unique vectors to provide morphological feature embedding. However, our experiments suggest that not all languages benefit from morphological feature embeddings. (See section 4 for details)

3.5 Dependency Label Embeddings

Each distinct dependency label defined in *CoNLL 2018 UD Shared Task* represented with a 128 dimensional continuous vector. These vectors combined to construct hidden states in tree-RNN part of our model. We randomly initialize these vectors and learned during training.

3.6 ArcHybrid Transition System

We implement the ArcHybrid Transition System which has three components, namely a stack of tree fragments σ, a buffer of unused words β and a set A of dependency arcs, $c = (\sigma, \beta, A)$. Stack is empty, there is no any arcs and, all the words of a sentence are in buffer initially. This system has 3 type of transitions:

- $\text{shift}(\sigma, b|\beta, A) = (\sigma|b, \beta, A)$

- $\text{left}_d(\sigma|s, b|\beta, A) = (\sigma, b|\beta, A \cup \{(b, d, s)\})$

- $\text{right}_d(\sigma|s|t, \beta, A) = (\sigma|s, \beta, A \cup \{(s, d, t)\})$

where $|$ denotes concatenation and (b, d, s) is a dependency arc between b (head) and s (modifier) with label d. The system terminates parsing when the buffer is empty and the stack has only one word assumed to be the root.

3.7 Tree-stack LSTM

Tree-stack LSTM has 4 main components: buffer's β-LSTM, stack's σ-LSTM, actions'-LSTM and tree's tree-RNN or t-RNN in short. We aim to represent each component of the transition system, $c = (\sigma, \beta, A)$, with a distinct LSTM similar to (Dyer et al., 2015). Initial inputs to these LSTMs are embeddings obtained by concatenating the features explained in section 3.3.

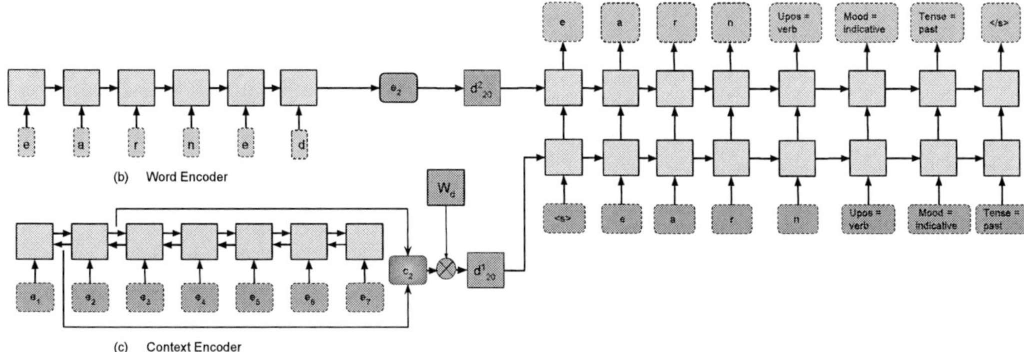

Figure 1: MorphNet illustration for the sentence *"Bush earned 340 points in 1969"* and target word ***"earned"***.

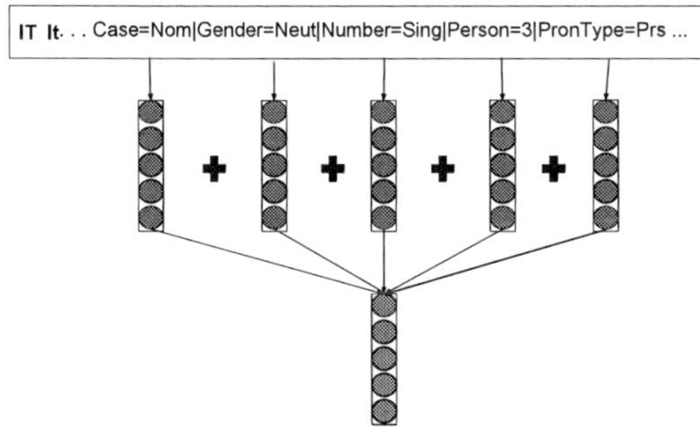

Figure 2: Morphological feature embeddings obtained by adding individual feature embeddings

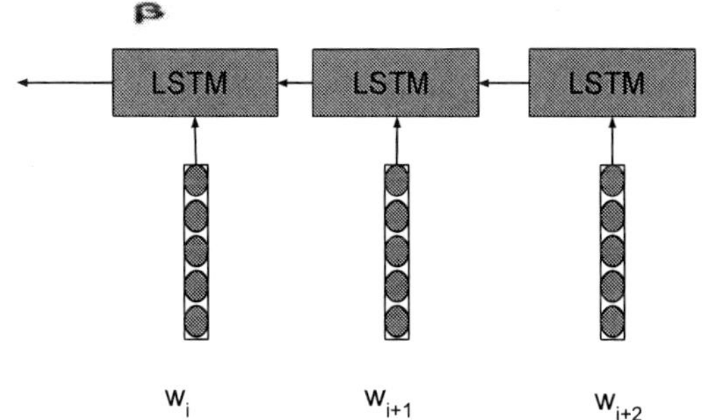

Figure 3: $\beta - LSTM$ processing a sentence. It starts to read from right to left. Each vector $((w_i)$ represents the concatenation of POS, language and morph-feat embeddings.

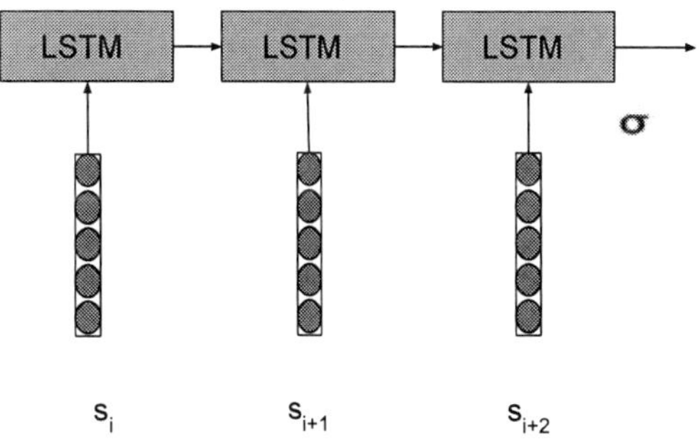

Figure 4: $\sigma - LSTM$ processing a sentence. It starts to read from left to right. Each input (s_i) is transformed version of initial feature vector. Transformations are based on local transitions see 3.6 for details.

Our model differs from (Dyer et al., 2015) by representing actions and dependency relations separately and including morphological feature embeddings. The transition system (see section 3.6 for details) is also different from theirs.

Buffer's β-LSTM is initialized with zero hidden state, and fed with input features from last word to the beginning. Similarly, stack's σ-LSTM is also initialized with zero hidden state and fed with input features from the beginning word to the last word of a stack. Actions' LSTM is also started with zero hidden state, and updated after each action. Inputs to σ-LSTM and β-LSTM are updated via tree-RNN.

We update either buffer's or stack's input embeddings based on parsing actions. For instance, suppose we are given β_i a top word in buffer and σ_i a final word in stack. The $left_d$ transition taken in current state. tree-RNN uses concatenation of previous embedding, σ_i, and dependency relation embedding (explained in 3.5) as a hidden h_{t-1}.Input of a tree-RNN is a previous word em-

bedding, β_i. Output h_t becomes a new word embedding for buffer's top word β_{i-new}. Figure 5 depicts this flow. Similarly to left transition, right transition updates the stack's second top word. Hidden state of an RNN is calculated by concatenating stack's top word and dependency relation.

There are 73 distinct actions for shift, labeled left and labeled right actions. We randomly initialize 128 dimensional vector for each labeled action and shift. These vectors become an input for action-LSTM shown in Figure 6.

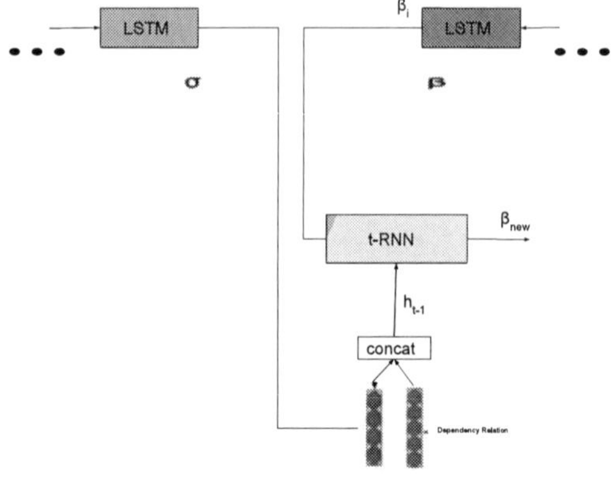

Figure 5: Buffer word's embedding update based on left move. Inputs are old embeddings obtained from Table 3.3

.

Concatenation of stack's LSTM, buffer's LSTM and actions' LSTM's final hidden layer becomes an input to MLP which outputs the probabilities for each transition in the next step.

3.8 Training

Our training strategy varies based on training data sizes. We divide datasets into 4 parts: 100k tokens or more, tokens in between 50k and 100k, and more than 20k less than 50k tokens.

For languages having more than 50k tokens in training data, we employ morphological feature-embeddings as an additional input dimension (see Figure 2). However, for languages having tokens less than 50k we do not use this feature dimension. Finally we realize that the languages with more than 100k tokens, using morphological feature embeddings does not improve parsing performance but we use that additional feature dimension.

We use 5-fold cross validation for languages without development data. We do not change the LSTMs' hidden dimensions, but record the number of epochs took for convergence. The average of these epochs is used to train a model with whole training set.

3.8.1 Optimization and Hyper-Parameters

We conduct experiments to find best set of hyper-parameters. We start with a dimension of 32 and increase the dimension by powers of two until 512 for LSTM hiddens, 1024 for LM matrix (explained in below). We report the best hyper-parameters in this paper. Although the performance does not decrease after the best setting, we choose the minimum-best size not to sacrifice from training speed.

All the LSTMs and tree-RNN have hidden dimension of 256. The vectors extracted from LM having dimension of 950, but we reduce that to 512 by a matrix-vector multiplication. This matrix is also learned. We use Adam optimizer with default parameters. (Kingma and Ba, 2014).Training is terminated if the performance does not improve for 9 epochs.

4 Results

In this section we inspect our best/worst results and the conclusions we obtain during *CoNLL 2018 UD Shared Task* experiments.

We submit our system to *CoNLL 2018 UD Shared Task* as "KParse" team. Our scoring is provided under the official *CoNLL 2018 UD Shared Task* website.[1] as well as in Table 4.1. All experiments are done with UD version 2.2 datasets (Nivre et al., 2018) and (Nivre et al., 2017) for training and testing respectively. The model improves performance by reducing hand-crafted feature selection. In order to analyze our tree-stack LSTM, we compare that model with Kırnap et al. sharing similar feature interests and transition system with our model. The difference between these two models is that Kırnap et al. based on hand-crafted feature selection from state, e.g. number of left children of buffer's first word. However, tree-stack LSTM only needs raw features and previous parsing actions.

Our model comparatively performs better with languages less than 50k training tokens, e.g. sv_lines and hu_szeged and tr_imst. However, when the number of training examples increases the performance improve slightly saturates, e.g. ar_padt, en_ewt. This may be due to convergence problems of our model. This conclusion

---

[1] http://universaldependencies.org/conll18/results.html

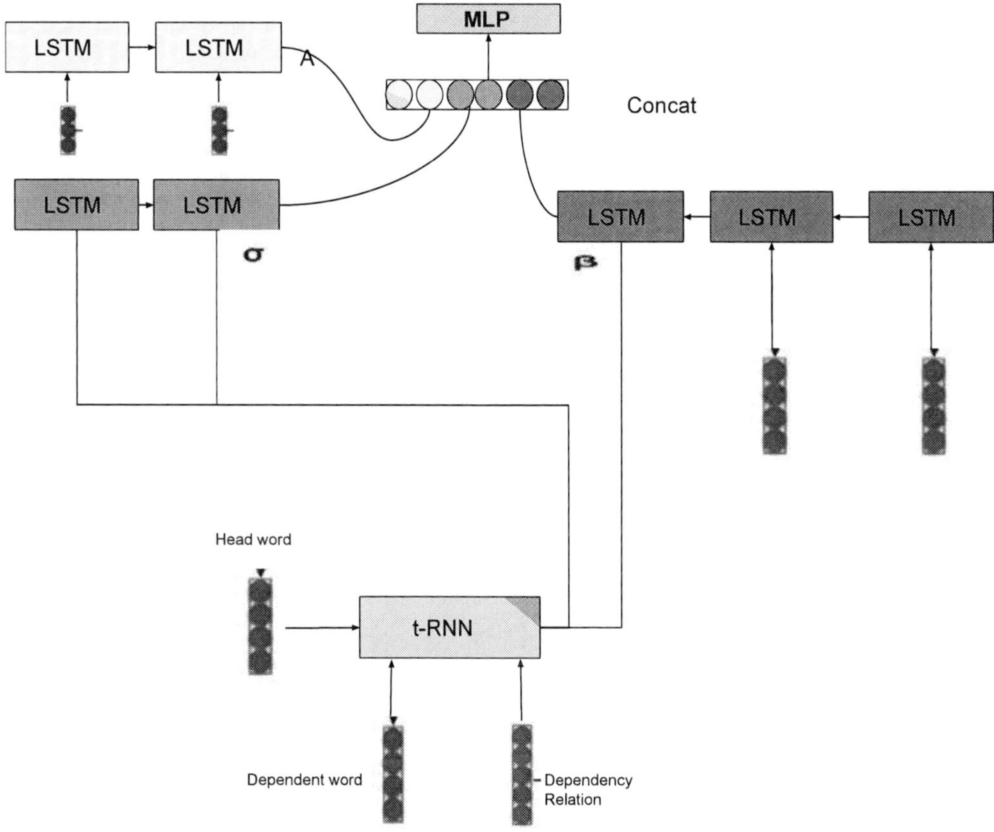

Figure 6: End-to-end tree-stack model composed of 4 main components, namely, β-LSTM, σ-LSTM and actions' LSTMs and the tree-RNN.

Lang code	Kırnap et al.	New Model
tr_imst	56.78	58.75
hu_szeged	66.21	68.18
en_ewt	74.87	75.77
ar_padt	67.83	68.02
cs_cac	83.39	83.57
sv_lines	71.12	74.81

Table 2: Comparison of two models

Lang code	Morp-Feats	no Morp-Feats
ko_gsd	73.74	72.54
got_proiel	54.33	53.24
id_gsd	75.76	73.97

Table 3: Morphological feature embeddings in some languages having tokens more than 50k and less than 100k in training data

is also agrees with our official ranking in *CoNLL 2018 UD Shared Task* because our ranking in low-resource languages is 10, but general ranking is 16.

We next analyze the performance gain by including morphological features with languages training token in between 50k and 100k. As we deduce from Table 3, tree-stack LSTM benefits from morphological information with mid-resource languages. However, we could not gain the similar performance enhancement with languages more than 100k training tokens.

4.1 Languages without Training Data

We have three criteria to choose a trained model for languages without training data. If there is a training corpus with the same language we use that as a parent. If there is no data from the same language, we pick a parent language from the same family. If there are more than one parent for a language, we select a parent with more training data.

We list our selections in Table 4.

Language	Parent Language
en_pud	en_ewt
ja_modern	ja_gsd
cs_pud	cs_pdt
sv_pud	sv_talbanken
fi_pud	fi_tdt
th_pud	id_gsd
pcm_nsc	en_ewt
br_keb	en_ewt

Table 4: Our parent choices in languages without train data

5 Discussion

We use tree-stack LSTM model in transition based dependency parsing framework. Our main motivation for this work is to reduce the human designed features extracted from state components. Our results prove that the model is able to learn better than its predecessors. Moreover, we examine that the model performs better in languages with low resources compared in *CoNLL 2018 UD Shared Task*. We also constitute morphological feature embeddings which become useful for dependency parsing. All of our work is done in transition based dependency parsing, which sacrifices performance due to locality and non projectiveness. This study opens a question on adapting the tree-stack LSTM in graph based dependency parsing. Our code is publicly available at `https://github.com/kirnap/ku-dependency-parser2`.

Acknowlegments

This work was supported by the Scientific and Technological Research Council of Turkey (TÜBİTAK) grants 114E628 and 215E201.

References

Chris Alberti, Daniel Andor, Ivan Bogatyy, Michael Collins, Dan Gillick, Lingpeng Kong, Terry Koo, Ji Ma, Mark Omernick, Slav Petrov, Chayut Thanapirom, Zora Tung, and David Weiss. 2017. Syntaxnet models for the conll 2017 shared task. *CoRR* abs/1703.04929. http://arxiv.org/abs/1703.04929.

Miguel Ballesteros, Chris Dyer, and Noah A Smith. 2015. Improved transition-based parsing by modeling characters instead of words with lstms. *arXiv preprint arXiv:1508.00657* .

Danqi Chen and Christopher D Manning. 2014. A fast and accurate dependency parser using neural networks. In *EMNLP*. pages 740–750.

Erenay Dayanık, Ekin Akyürek, and Deniz Yuret. 2018. Morphnet: A sequence-to-sequence model that combines morphological analysis and disambiguation. *arXiv preprint arXiv:1805.07946* .

Timothy Dozat, Peng Qi, and Christopher D Manning. 2017. Stanford's graph-based neural dependency parser at the conll 2017 shared task. *Proceedings of the CoNLL 2017 Shared Task: Multilingual Parsing from Raw Text to Universal Dependencies* pages 20–30.

Chris Dyer, Miguel Ballesteros, Wang Ling, Austin Matthews, and Noah A. Smith. 2015. Transition-based dependency parsing with stack long short-term memory. *CoRR* abs/1505.08075. http://arxiv.org/abs/1505.08075.

Georg Heigold, Guenter Neumann, and Josef van Genabith. 2017. An extensive empirical evaluation of character-based morphological tagging for 14 languages. In *Proceedings of the 15th Conference of the European Chapter of the Association for Computational Linguistics: Volume 1, Long Papers*. volume 1, pages 505–513.

Sepp Hochreiter and Jürgen Schmidhuber. 1997. Long short-term memory. *Neural Comput.* 9(8):1735–1780. https://doi.org/10.1162/neco.1997.9.8.1735.

Diederik Kingma and Jimmy Ba. 2014. Adam: A method for stochastic optimization. *arXiv preprint arXiv:1412.6980* .

Eliyahu Kiperwasser and Yoav Goldberg. 2016. Simple and accurate dependency parsing using bidirectional LSTM feature representations. *CoRR* abs/1603.04351. http://arxiv.org/abs/1603.04351.

Ömer Kırnap, Berkay Furkan Önder, and Deniz Yuret. 2017. Parsing with context embeddings. *Proceedings of the CoNLL 2017 Shared Task: Multilingual Parsing from Raw Text to Universal Dependencies* pages 80–87.

Kimmo Koskenniemi. 1983. Two-level model for morphological analysis. In *IJCAI*. volume 83, pages 683–685.

Joakim Nivre et al. 2017. Universal Dependencies 2.0 CoNLL 2017 shared task development and test data. LINDAT/CLARIN digital library at the Institute of Formal and Applied Linguistics, Charles University, Prague, http://hdl.handle.net/11234/1-2184. http://hdl.handle.net/11234/1-2184.

Joakim Nivre et al. 2018. Universal Dependencies 2.2. LINDAT/CLARIN digital library at the Institute of Formal and Applied Linguistics, Charles University, Prague, http://hdl.handle.net/11234/1-1983xxx. http://hdl.handle.net/11234/1-1983xxx.

Language	LAS	MLAS	BLEX	Ranks	Language	LAS	MLAS	BLEX	Ranks
af_afribooms	78.12	65.12	63.93	17-15-19	ar_padt	68.02	58.05	61.21	16-11-13
bg_btb	84.53	75.58	77.63	20-16-9	br_keb	8.91	0.35	1.77	19-15-19
bxr_bdt	9.93	0.49	0.69	18-22-23	ca_ancora	85.89	77.22	77.22	18-17-17
cs_cac	83.57	75.3	77.24	19-12-18	cs_fictree	82.67	71.93	75.31	18-15-16
cs_pdt	81.43	73.77	71.44	21-21-22	cs_pud	78.69	64.14	84.52	18-19-17
cu_proiel	59.42	46.96	81.55	23-22-21	da_ddt	76.4	67.05	63.09	17-15-19
en_ewt	75.77	66.78	68.76	20-20-18	en_gum	76.44	65.19	64.32	16-12-15
de_gsd	71.59	46.87	35.41	17-8-23	el_gdt	83.34	65.74	66.6	16-14-18
en_lines	73.96	64.91	62.76	17-15-19	en_pud	78.41	66.16	69.25	19-19-17
es_ancora	84.99	76.71	77.06	18-17-16	et_edt	74.52	65.7	63.5	20-19-17
eu_bdt	74.55	63.11	61.25	17-13-18	fa_seraji	81.18	74.84	71.65	17-16-14
fi_ftb	75.84	65.53	67.91	17-16-11	fi_pud	81.55	74.18	66.29	13-12-10
fi_tdt	78.42	70.4	65.89	16-15-12	fo_oft	22.5	0.29	5.44	20-19-20
fr_gsd	81.07	72.07	73.96	19-19-17	fr_sequoia	84.36	76.56	71.33	14-10-20
fr_spoken	57.32	15	57.76	10-10-10	fro_srcmf	76.92	67.85	71.35	20-19-20
ga_idt	63.13	34.36	40.76	13-19-16	gl_ctg	79.02	66.13	71.12	14-14-9
gl_treegal	70.45	52.15	56.38	10-9-9	got_proiel	54.33	40.58	40.51	24-24-22
grc_perseus	55.03	34.19	37.0	20-15-16	grc_proiel	62.11	43.92	37.00	22-21-20
he_htb	58.28	45.06	48.09	18-16-16	hi_hdtb	86.86	70.44	79.98	20-17-15
hr_set	81.6	65.23	68.74	17-8-18	hsb_ufal	30.81	6.22	15.39	8-9-7
hu_szeged	68.18	51.13	50.53	14-20-21	hy_armtdp	24.58	7.24	6.96	12-9-21
id_gsd	75.51	65.02	63.92	17-13-17	it_isdt	85.80	75.5	70.16	22-21-22
it_postwita	70.03	56.04	47.53	13-12-20	ja_gsd	73.30	59.46	59.89	14-14-20
ja_modern	23.35	8.94	10.13	5-4-5	kk_ktb	23.86	5.98	8.02	11-11-13
kmr_mg	23.39	3.97	7.56	15-15-16	ko_gsd	73.74	67.31	60.52	19-18-16
ko_kaist	78.81	71.49	65.29	19-19-16	la_ittb	75.79	71.49	71.66	20-19-19
la_perseus	51.6	33.65	38.04	11-8-8	la_proiel	59.35	46.36	51.13	20-19-19
lv_lvtb	72.33	57.08	60.54	16-13-14	nl_alpino	78.83	64.22	65.79	17-16-15
nl_lassysmall	76.70	63.97	64.58	16-15-15	no_bokmaal	82.32	37.93	73.52	20-19-18
no_nynorsk	80.57	70.78	72.27	20-19-17	no_nynorsklia	53.33	41.01	44.46	13-10-11
pcm_nsc	15.84	5.3	13.61	10-1-11	pl_lfg	86.12	71.96	76.71	21-21-20
pl_sz	82.83	63.76	73.05	16-17-14	pt_bosque	82.71	68.01	73.07	18-17-15
ro_rrt	80.90	72.39	72.59	17-14-14	ru_syntagrus	82.89	56.8	75.48	20-19-18
ru_taiga	60.55	39.41	44.05	11-9-9	sk_snk	75.75	53.49	61.0	20-20-16
sl_ssj	78.18	62.94	69.49	16-18-14	sl_sst	48.77	34.66	39.82	10-11-9
sme_giella	53.39	39.13	41.75	19-19-15	sr_set	80.85	67.46	72.09	20-19-16
sv_lines	74.81	59.72	67.35	17-15-15	sv_pud	70.77	43.04	54.67	16-12-15
sv_talbanken	77.91	69.25	69.87	17-16-17	th_pud	0.74	0.04	0.44	7-8-8
tr_imst	58.75	48.28	49.84	15-12-13	ug_udt	57.04	36.63	44.44	16-16-14
uk_iu	76.5	36.63	65.5	16-16-13	ur_udtb	78.12	51.25	64.66	17-15-15
vi_vtb	40.48	33.88	36.03	16-14-15	zh_gsd	59.76	50.87	53.11	19-15-18

Table 5: Our official results in *CoNLL 2018 UD Shared Task*, ranks are given in LAS-MLAS-BLEX order

Milan Straka, Jan Hajič, and Jana Straková. 2016. UD-Pipe: trainable pipeline for processing CoNLL-U files performing tokenization, morphological analysis, POS tagging and parsing. In *Proceedings of the 10th International Conference on Language Resources and Evaluation (LREC 2016)*. European Language Resources Association, Portoro, Slovenia.

Turku Neural Parser Pipeline: An End-to-End System for the CoNLL 2018 Shared Task

Jenna Kanerva[1,2] **Filip Ginter**[1] **Niko Miekka**[1] **Akseli Leino**[1] **Tapio Salakoski**[1]
[1]Turku NLP Group, Department of Future Technologies, University of Turku, Finland
[2]University of Turku Graduate School (UTUGS)
`firstname.lastname@utu.fi`

Abstract

In this paper we describe the TurkuNLP entry at the *CoNLL 2018 Shared Task on Multilingual Parsing from Raw Text to Universal Dependencies*. Compared to the last year, this year the shared task includes two new main metrics to measure the morphological tagging and lemmatization accuracies in addition to syntactic trees. Basing our motivation into these new metrics, we developed an end-to-end parsing pipeline especially focusing on developing a novel and state-of-the-art component for lemmatization. Our system reached the highest aggregate ranking on three main metrics out of 26 teams by achieving 1st place on metric involving lemmatization, and 2nd on both morphological tagging and parsing.

1 Introduction

The 2017 and 2018 CoNLL UD Shared tasks aim at an evaluation of end-to-end parsing systems on a large set of treebanks and languages. The 2017 task (Zeman et al., 2017) focused primarily on the evaluation of the syntactic trees produced by the participating systems, whereas the 2018 task (Zeman et al., 2018) adds further two metrics which also measure the accuracy of morphological tagging and lemmatization. In this paper, we present the TurkuNLP system submission to the *CoNLL 2018 UD Shared Task*. The system is an end-to-end parsing pipeline, with components for segmentation, morphological tagging, parsing, and lemmatization. The tagger and parser are based on the 2017 winning system by Dozat et al. (2017), while the lemmatizer is a novel approach utilizing the OpenNMT neural machine translation system for sequence-to-sequence learning. Our pipeline

ranked first on the evaluation metric related to lemmatization, and second on the metrics related to tagging and parsing.

2 Task overview

CoNLL 2018 UD Shared Task is a follow-up to the 2017 shared task of developing systems predicting syntactic dependencies on raw texts across a number of typologically different languages. In addition to the 82 UD treebanks for 57 languages, which formed the primary training data, the participating teams were allowed to use also additional resources such as Wikipedia dumps[1], raw web crawl data and word embeddings (Ginter et al., 2017), morphological transducers provided by Apertium[2] and Giellatekno[3], and the OPUS parallel corpus collection (Tiedemann, 2012). In addition to the 2017 primary metric (LAS), the systems were additionally evaluated also on metrics which include lemmatization and morphology prediction. In brief, the three primary metrics of the task are as follows (see Zeman et al. (2018) for detailed definitions):

LAS The proportion of words which have the correct head word with the correct dependency relation.

MLAS Similar to LAS, with the additional requirement that a subset of the morphology features is correctly predicted and the functional dependents of the word are correctly attached. MLAS is only calculated on content-bearing words, and strives to level the field w.r.t. morphological richness of languages.

---

[1]`https://dumps.wikimedia.org`
[2]`https://svn.code.sf.net/p/apertium/svn/languages`
[3]`https://victorio.uit.no/langtech/trunk/langs`

Proceedings of the CoNLL 2018 Shared Task: Multilingual Parsing from Raw Text to Universal Dependencies, pages 133–142
Brussels, Belgium, October 31 – November 1, 2018. ©2018 Association for Computational Linguistics
https://doi.org/10.18653/v1/K18-2013

BLEX The proportion of head-dependent content word pairs whose dependency relation and both lemmas are correct.

3   System overview and rationale

The design of the pipeline was dictated by the tight schedule and the limited manpower we were able to invest into its development. Our overall objective was to develop an easy-to-use parsing pipeline which carries out all the four tasks of segmentation, morphological tagging, parsing, and lemmatization, resulting in an end-to-end full parsing pipeline reusable in downstream applications. We also strove for the pipeline to perform well on all four tasks and all groups of treebanks, ranging from the large treebanks to the highly under-resourced ones. With this in mind, we decided to rely on openly available components when the acceptable performance is already met, and create our own components for those tasks we see clear room for improvement.

Therefore, for segmentation, tagging and parsing we leaned as much as possible on well-known components trained in the standard manner, and deviated from these only when necessary. Our approach to lemmatization, on the other hand, is original and previously unpublished. In summary, we rely for most but not all languages on the tokenization and sentence splitting provided by the UDPipe baseline (Straka et al., 2016). Tagging and parsing is carried out using the parser of Dozat et al. (2017), the winning entry of the 2017 shared task. Using a simple data manipulation technique, we also obtain the morphological feature predictions from the same tagger which was originally used to produce only universal part-of-speech (UPOS) and language-specific part-of-speech (XPOS) predictions. Finally, the lemmatization is carried out using the OpenNMT neural machine translation toolkit (Klein et al., 2017), casting lemmatization as a machine translation problem. All these components are wrapped into one parsing pipeline, making it possible to run all four steps with one simple command and gain state-of-the-art or very close to state-of-the-art results for each step. In the following, we describe each of these four steps in more detail, while more detailed description of the pipeline itself is given in Section 6.

3.1   Tokenization and sentence splitting

For all but three languages, we rely on the UD-Pipe baseline runs provided by the shared task organizers. The three languages where we decided to deviate from the baseline are Thai, Breton and Faroese. Especially for Thai we suspected the UD-Pipe baseline, trained without ever seeing a single character of the Thai alphabet, would perform poorly. For Breton, we were unsure about the way in which the baseline system tokenizes words with apostrophes like *arc'hant* (money), and without deeper knowledge of Breton language decided that it is better to explicitly keep all words with apostrophes unsegmented. We therefore developed a regular-expression based sentence splitter and tokenizer — admittedly under a very rushed schedule — which splits sentences and tokens on a handful of punctuation characters. While, after the fact, we can see that the UDPipe baseline performed well at 92.3%, our solution outperformed it by two percentage points, validating our choice. For Thai, we developed our own training corpus using machine translation (described later in the paper in Section 4.3), and trained UDPipe on this corpus, gaining a segmentation model at the same time. Indeed, the UDPipe baseline only reached 8.5% accuracy while our tokenizer performed at the much higher 43.2% (still far below the 70% achieved by the Uppsala team). Similarly, for Faroese we built training data by pooling the Danish-DDT, Swedish-Talbanken, and the three available Norwegian treebanks (Bokmaal, Nynorsk, NynorskLIA), and subsequntly trained the UDPipe tokenizer on this data. After the fact, we can see that essentially all systems performed in the 99–100% range on Faroese, and we could have relied on the UDPipe baseline.

On a side note, we did develop our own method for tokenization and sentence splitting but in the end, unsure about its stability and performance on small treebanks, we decided to "play it safe" and not include it in the final system. However, the newly developed tokenizer is part of our open-source pipeline release and trainable on new data.

3.2   Pre-trained embeddings

Where available, we used the pre-trained embeddings from the 2017 shared task (Ginter et al., 2017). Embeddings for Afrikaans, Breton, Buryat, Faroese, Gothic, Upper Sorbian, Armenian, Kurdish, Northern Sami, Serbian and Thai were ob-

134

tained from the embeddings published by Facebook[4] trained using the fastText method (Bojanowski et al., 2016), and finally for Old French (Old French-SRCMF) we took the embeddings trained using word2vec (Mikolov et al., 2013) on the treebank train section by the organizers in their baseline UDPipe model release. We did not pre-train any embeddings ourselves.

3.3 UPOS tagging

UPOS tagging for all languages is carried out using the system of Dozat et al. (2017) trained out-of-the-box with the default set of parameters from the CoNLL-17 shared task. The part-of-speech tagger is a time-distributed affine classifier over tokens in a sentence, where tokens are first embedded with a word encoder which sums together a learned token embedding, a pre-trained token embedding and a token embedding encoded from the sequence of its characters using unidirectional LSTM. After that bidirectional LSTM reads the sequence of embedded tokens in a sentence to create a context-aware token representations. These token representations are then transformed with ReLU layers separately for each affine tag classification layers (namely UPOS and XPOS). These two classification layers are trained jointly by summing their cross-entropy losses. For more detailed description, see Dozat and Manning (2016) and Dozat et al. (2017).

3.4 XPOS and FEATS tagging

As the tagger of Dozat et al. predicts the XPOS field, we used a simple trick of concatenating the `FEATS` field into `XPOS`, therefore manipulating the tagger into predicting the XPOS and morphological features as one long string. For example the original `XPOS` field value `N` and `FEATS` field value `Case=Nom|Number=Sing` in Finnish-TDT treebank gets concatenated into `XPOS=N|Case=Nom|Number=Sing` and this full string is predicted as one class by the tagger. After tagging and parsing, these values are again splitted into correct columns. This is a (embarrasingly) simple approach which leads to surprisingly good results, as our system ranks 3rd in morphological features with accuracy of 86.7% over all treebanks, 0.9pp below the Uppsala team which ranked 1st on this subtask.

We, in fact, did at first develop a comparatively complex morphological feature prediction component which outperformed the state-of-the-art on the 2017 shared task, but later we discovered that the simple technique described above somewhat surprisingly gives notably better results. We expected that the complex morphology of many languages leads to a large number of very rare morphological feature strings, a setting unsuitable for casting the problem as a single multi-class prediction task. Consequently, our original attempt at morphological tagging predicted value for each morphological category separately from a shared representation layer, rather than predicting the full feature string at once. To shed some light on the complexity of the problem in terms of the number of classes, and understand why a multi-class setting works well, we list in Table 1 the number of unique morphological feature strings needed to cover 80%, 90%, 95%, and 100% of the running words in the training data for each language. The number of unique feature combinations varies from 15 (Japanese-GSD, Vietnamese-VTB) to 2629 (Czech-PDT), and for languages with high number of unique combinations, we can clearly see that there is a large leap from covering 95% of running words to covering full 100%. For example in Czech-PDT, only 349 out of the 2629 feature combinations are needed to cover 95% of running words, and the rest 2280 (of which 588 are singletons) together accounts only 5% of running words. Based on these numbers our conclusions are that a focus on predicting the rare feature combinations correctly does not affect the accuracy much, and learning a reasonable number of common feature combinations well seems to be a good strategy in the end.

Interestingly, on our preliminary experiments with Finnish, we found that concatenating `FEATS` into `XPOS` improved also LAS by more than 0.5pp, since the parser takes the `XPOS` field as a feature and benefits from the additional morphological information present. To investigate this more closely and test whether the same improvement can be seen on other languages as well, we carry out an experiment where we train the tagger and parser without morphological information for Finnish and six more arbitrarily chosen treebanks. This new experiment then follows the original training setting used by the Stanford team on their CoNLL-17 submission, and by comparing this to

---

[4] `https://github.com/facebookresearch/fastText/blob/master/pretrained-vectors.md`

	80%	90%	95%	100%			80%	90%	95%	100%
Czech-PDT	96	194	349	2629		Arabic-PADT	22	35	53	322
Finnish-TDT	79	188	349	2052		Spanish-AnCora	28	48	71	295
Finnish-FTB	72	174	333	1762		Italian-ISDT	22	35	55	281
Czech-CAC	81	160	285	1745		Catalan-AnCora	28	47	68	267
Czech-FicTree	73	161	287	1464		French-GSD	19	31	46	225
Slovak-SNK	79	163	283	1199		Italian-PoSTWITA	23	39	56	224
Ukrainian-IU	91	186	322	1197		Galician-TreeGal	23	41	66	222
Polish-LFG	84	170	281	1171		Uyghur-UDT	21	40	63	214
Slovenian-SSJ	73	141	254	1101		Swedish-Talbanken	26	43	61	203
Croatian-SET	63	125	212	1099		Norwegian-Bokmaal	26	39	57	203
Latin-PROIEL	121	214	323	1031		French-Sequoia	25	43	62	200
Ancient Greek-PROIEL	114	203	308	1027		Indonesian-GSD	12	20	31	192
Urdu-UDTB	30	61	124	1001		Norwegian-Nynorsk	26	41	53	184
Polish-SZ	80	157	267	991		Swedish-LinES	25	43	61	173
Latin-ITTB	58	136	226	985		Persian-Seraji	11	19	31	162
Turkish-IMST	54	139	262	972		Danish-DDT	24	38	53	157
Hindi-HDTB	38	76	127	939		Armenian-ArmTDP	51	85	117	157
Estonian-EDT	43	89	151	918		English-EWT	19	32	45	150
German-GSD	58	96	141	909		Upper Sorbian-UFAL	48	88	111	134
Basque-BDT	51	100	169	884		English-LinES	18	29	43	104
Old Church Slavonic-PROIEL	78	168	276	859		English-GUM	16	27	40	104
Latvian-LVTB	57	119	218	828		Kazakh-KTB	29	49	71	98
Ancient Greek-Perseus	59	107	169	774		Norwegian-NynorskLIA	22	34	46	96
Russian-SynTagRus	67	124	176	734		Dutch-Alpino	16	24	31	63
Slovenian-SST	73	146	233	645		Afrikaans-AfriBooms	14	22	28	61
Gothic-PROIEL	75	138	214	623		Dutch-LassySmall	13	19	26	59
Hungarian-Szeged	40	90	166	581		Kurmanji-MG	24	35	46	58
Serbian-SET	48	85	131	539		Old French-SRCMF	11	15	19	57
Hebrew-HTB	19	45	85	521		Buryat-BDT	17	26	34	41
Romanian-RRT	34	58	97	451		Chinese-GSD	7	10	13	31
Bulgarian-BTB	33	63	107	432		Galician-CTG	7	9	11	27
Latin-Perseus	58	100	144	418		Korean-GSD	4	4	6	19
Portuguese-Bosque	20	35	60	396		Korean-Kaist	6	8	10	17
Russian-Taiga	66	126	182	376		French-Spoken	8	10	12	16
North Sami-Giella	39	78	127	369		Vietnamese-VTB	6	8	10	15
Irish-IDT	47	81	125	360		Japanese-GSD	5	7	9	15
Greek-GDT	57	90	123	348						

Table 1: The number of unique UPOS+morphlogical feature combinations needed to cover 80%, 90%, 95% and 100% of the running words in each treebank.

our main runs we can directly evaluate the effect of predicting additional morphological information. Three of the treebanks used in this experiment (Arabic-PADT, Czech-PDT and Swedish-Talbanken) seem to originally encode the full (or at least almost full) morphological information in the XPOS field in a language-specific manner (e.g. AAFS1----2A---- in Czech), whereas four treebanks seem to include only part-of-speech like information or nothing at all in the XPOS field (Estonian-EDT, Finnish-TDT, Irish-IDT and Russian-SynTagRus).

The results of this experiment are shown in Table 2. Four treebanks above the dashed line, those originally including only part-of-speech like information in the XPOS field, shows clear positive improvement in terms of LAS when the parser is able to see also morphological tags predicted together with the language-specific XPOS. The parser seeing the morphological tags (LAS_m column) shows improvements approx. from +0.3 to +0.9 for these four treebanks compared to the parser without morphological tags (LAS column). Three treebanks below the dashed line, those already including language-specific morphological information in the XPOS field, quite naturally does not benefit from additional morphology and shows mildly negative results in terms of LAS. However the difference in treebanks showing negative results is substantially smaller compared to those having positive effect (negative differences stay between -0.0 to -0.2), therefore based on these seven tree-

Treebank	LAS	LAS$_m$		UPOS	UPOS$_m$		XPOS	XPOS$_m$	
Estonian-EDT	83.40	**84.15**	(+0.75)	96.32	**96.45**	(+0.13)	97.81	**97.87**	(+0.06)
Finnish-TDT	85.74	**86.60**	(+0.86)	96.45	**96.66**	(+0.21)	97.48	**97.63**	(+0.15)
Irish-IDT	70.01	**70.88**	(+0.87)	91.87	**92.36**	(+0.49)	91.01	**91.05**	(+0.04)
Russian-SynT.	91.40	**91.72**	(+0.32)	**98.11**	98.03	(-0.08)	—	—	
Arabic-PADT	**72.67**	72.45	(-0.22)	90.39	**90.48**	(+0.19)	87.36	**87.39**	(+0.03)
Czech-PDT	**90.62**	90.57	(-0.05)	**98.76**	98.74	(-0.02)	**95.66**	95.44	(-0.22)
Swedish-Talb.	**85.87**	85.83	(-0.04)	97.40	**97.47**	(+0.07)	96.36	**96.41**	(+0.05)

Table 2: LAS, UPOS and XPOS scores for seven parsers trained with and without tagger predicting the additional morphological information. m after the score name stands for including the morphological information during training, i.e. the official result for our system. Note that when evaluating XPOS, the morphological information is already extracted from that field so the evaluation only includes prediction of original XPOS-tags, not morphological features.

banks the overall impact stays on positive side. Note that during parsing the parser only sees predicted morphological features, so this experiment confirms that predicting more complex information on lower-level can improve the parser.

Because of the fact that many treebanks include more than plain part-of-speech information in the language-specific XPOS field, likely more natural place for the morphological features would be the universal part-of-speech field UPOS which is guaranteed to include only universal part-of-speech information. However, with the limited time we had during the shared task period, we had no time to test whether adding morphological features harms the prediction of original part-of-speech tag, and we decided to use XPOS field as we thought it's least important of these two. Based on the results in the XPOS column of Table 2, we however see that additional information does not generally seem to harm the prediction of the original language-specific part-of-speech tags and hints towards the conclusion that likely the UPOS field could have been used with comparable performance.

3.5 Syntactic parsing

Syntactic parsing for all languages is carried out using the system of Dozat et al. trained out-of-the-box with the default set of parameters from the CoNLL-17 shared task. The parser architecture is quite similar as used in the tagger. Tokens are first embedded with a word encoder which sums together a learned token embedding, a pretrained token embedding and a token embedding encoded from the sequence of its characters using unidirectional LSTM. These embedded tokens are yet concatenated together with corresponding part-of-speech embeddings. After that bidirectional LSTM reads the sequence of embedded tokens in a sentence to create a context-aware token representations. These token representations are then transformed with four different ReLU layers separately for two different biaffine classifiers to score possible relations (HEAD) and their dependency types (DEPREL), and best predictions are later decoded to form a tree. These relation and type classifiers are again trained jointly by summing their cross-entropy losses. For more detailed description, see Dozat and Manning (2016) and Dozat et al. (2017).

3.6 Lemmatization

While in many real word industry applications especially for inflective languages the lemmatizer is actually the most needed component of the parsing pipeline, yet it's performance has been undesirable weak in previous state-of-the-art parsing pipelines for many inflectionally complex languages. For this reason we develop a novel and previously unpublished component for lemmatization.

We represent lemmatization as a sequence-to-sequence translation problem, where the input is a word represented as a sequence of characters concatenated with a sequence of its part-of-speech and morphological tags, while the desired output is the corresponding lemma represented as a sequence of characters. Therefore we are training the system to translate the word form characters + morphological tags into the lemma characters, where each word is processed independently from it's sentence context. For example, input and output sequences for the English word *circles* as a noun are:

```
INPUT: c i r c l e s UPOS=NOUN
       XPOS=NNS Number=Plur

OUTPUT: c i r c l e
```

As our approach can be seen similar to general machine translation problem, we are able to use any openly available machine translation toolkit and translation model implementations. Our current implementation is based on the Python version of the OpenNMT: Open-Source Toolkit for Neural Machine Translation (Klein et al., 2017). We use a deep attentional encoder-decoder network with 2 layered bidirectional LSTM encoder for reading the sequence of input characters + morphological tags and producing a sequence of encoded vectors. Our decoder is a 2 layered unidirectional LSTM with input feeding attention for generating the sequence of output characters based on the encoded representations. In input feeding attention (Luong et al., 2015) the previous attention weights are given as input in the next time step to inform the model about past alignment decisions and prevent the model to repeat the same output multiple times. We use beam search with beam size 5 during decoding.

As the lemmatizer does not see the actual sentence where a word appears, morphological tags are used in the input sequence to inform the system about the word's morpho-syntactic context. The tagger is naturally able to see the full sentence context and in most cases it should produce enough information for the lemmatizer to give it a possibility to lemmatize ambiguous words correctly based on the current context. During test time we run the lemmatizer as a final step in the parsing pipeline, i.e. after tagger and parser, so the lemmatizer runs on top of the predicted part-of-speech and morphological features. Adding the lemmatizer only after the tagger and parser (and not before like done in many pipelines) does not cause any degradation for the current pipeline as the tagger and parser by Dozat et al. (2017) do not use lemmas as features.

This method is inspired by the top systems from the CoNLL-SIGMORPHON 2017 Shared Task of Universal Morphological Reinflection (Cotterell et al., 2017), where the participants used encoder-decoder networks to generate inflected words from the lemma and given morphological tags (Kann and Schütze, 2017; Bergmanis et al., 2017). While the SIGMORPHON 2017 Shared Task was based on gold standard input features, to our knowledge we are the first ones to use similar techniques on reversed problem settings and to incorporate such lemmatizer into the full parsing pipeline to run on top of predicted morphological features.

4 Near-zero resource languages

There are nine very low resource languages: Breton, Faroese, Naija and Thai with no training data, and Armenian, Buryat, Kazakh, Kurmanji and Upper Sorbian with only a tiny training dataset. For the latter five treebanks with tiny training sample, we trained the tagger and parser in the standard manner, despite the tiny training set size. However, for four of these five languages (Armenian, Buryat, Kazakh and Kurmanji) we used Apertium morphological transducers (Tyers et al., 2010) to artificially extend the lemmatizer training data by including new words from the transducer not present in the original training data (methods are similar to those used with Breton and Faroese, for details see Section 4.1). Naija is parsed using the English-EWT models without any extra processing as it strongly resembles English language and at the same time lacks all resources. Breton, Faroese and Thai were each treated in a different manner described below.

4.1 Breton

Our approach to Breton was to first build a Breton POS and morphological tagger, and subsequently apply a delexicalized parser. To build the tagger, we selected 5000 random sentences from the Breton Wikipedia text dump and for each word looked up all applicable morphological analyzes in the Breton Apertium transducer converted into UD using a simple language-agnostic mapping from Apertium tags to UD tags. For words unknown to the transducer (59% of unique words), we assign all possible `UPOS+FEATS` strings produced by the transducer on the words it recognizes in the data. Then we decode the most likely sequence of morphological readings using a delexicalized 3-gram language model trained on the `UPOS+FEATS` sequences of English-EWT and French-GSD training data. Here we used the `lazy` decoder program[5] which is based on the KenLM language model estimation and querying system (Heafield, 2011). This procedure re-

---

[5] `https://github.com/kpu/lazy`

sults in 5000 sentences (96,304 tokens) of morphologically tagged Breton, which can be used to train the tagger in the usual manner. The syntactic parser was trained as delexicalized (FORM field replaced with underscore) on the English-EWT and French-GSD treebanks. The accuracy of UPOS and FEATS was 72% (3rd rank) and 56.6% (2nd rank) and LAS ranked 3rd with 31.8%. These ranks show our approach as competitive in the shared task, nevertheless the Uppsala team achieved some 14pp higher accuracies of UPOS and FEATS, clearly using a considerably better approach.

The Breton lemmatizer was trained using the same training data as used for the tagger, where for words recognized by the transducer the part-of-speech tag and morphological features are converted into UD with the language-agnostic mapping, and lemmas are used directly. Unknown words for transducer (i.e. those for which we are not able to get any lemma analysis) are simply skipped from the lemmatizer training. As the lemmatizer sees each word separately, skipping words and breaking the sentence context does not cause any problems. With this approach we achieved the 1st rank and accuracy of 77.6%, which is over 20pp better that the second best team.

To estimate the quality of our automatically produced training data for Breton tagging and lemmatization, we repeat the same procedure with the Breton test data[6], i.e. we use the combination of morphological transducer and language model as a direct tagger leaving out the part of training an actual tagger with the produced data as done in our original method. When evaluating these produced analyses against the gold standard, we get a direct measure of quality for this method. We measure three different scores: 1) Oracle full match of transducer readings converted to UD, where we measure how many tokens can receive a correct combination of UPOS and all morphological tags when taking into account all possible readings given by the transducer. For unknown words we include all combinations known from the transducer. This setting measures the best full match number achievable by the language model if it would predict everything perfectly. 2) Language model full match, i.e. how many tokens received a fully correct analysis when lan-

[6]Using development data in these experiments would be more desirable, but unfortunately we don't have any Breton development data available.

guage model was used to pick one of the possible analyses. 3) Random choice full match, i.e. how many tokens received a fully correct analysis when one of the possible analyses was picked randomly. On Breton test set our oracle full match is 55.5%, language model full match 51.0% and random full match 46.2%. We can see that using a language model to pick analyses shifts the performance more closer to oracle full match than random full match, showing somewhat positive results for the language model decoding. Unfortunately when we tried to replicate the same experiment for other low-resource languages, we did not see the same positive signal. However, the biggest weakness of this method seems to be in the oracle full match which is only 55.5%. This means that the correct analysis cannot be found from the converted transducer output for almost half of the tokens. A probable reason for this is the simple language-agnostic mapping from Apertium tags to UD tags which is originally developed for the lemmatizer training and strove for high precision rather than high recall. Our development hypothesis was that missing a tag in lemmatizer's input likely does not tremendously harm the lemmatizer, so when developing the mapping we rather left some tags out than caused a potential erroneous conversion. However, when the same mapping is used here, missing one common tag (for example VerbForm=Fin) can cause great losses in full match evaluation.

4.2 Faroese

For Faroese the starting situation was similar to Breton but as the coverage of the Faroese Apertium tranducer was weak, we decided to take an another approach. This is because we feared that the decoder input would have too many gaps to fill in and therefore the quality of produced data would decrease. For that reason the Faroese tagger and parser was trained in the usual manner using pooled training sets of related Nordic languages: Danish-DDT, Swedish-Talbanken, and the three available Norwegian treebanks (Bokmaal, Nynorsk, NynorskLIA). The pre-trained embeddings were Faroese from the Facebook's embeddings dataset, filtered to only contain words which Faroese has in common with one of the languages used in training. However, the Faroese lemmatizer is trained directly from the transducer output by analyzing vocabulary extracted from the

Faroese Wikipedia and turning Apertium analyses into UD using the same tag mapping table as in the Breton. On UPOS tagging our system ranks only 10th, whereas on both morphological feature prediction and lemmatization, we rank 1st.

4.3 Thai

As there is no training data and no Apertium morphological transducer for Thai, we machine translated the English-EWT treebank word-for-word into Thai, and used the result as training data for the Thai segmenter, tagger and parser. Here we utilized the Marian neural machine translation framework (Junczys-Dowmunt et al., 2018) trained on the 6.1 million parallel Thai-English sentences in OPUS (Tiedemann, 2012). Since we did not have access to a Thai tokenizer and Thai language does not separate words with spaces, we forced the NMT system into character-level mode by inserting a space between all characters in a sentence (both on the source and the target side) and again removing those after translation. After training the translation system, the English-EWT treebank is translated one word at a time, creating a token and sentence segmented Thai version of the treebank. Later all occurrences of English dots and commas were replaced with whitespaces in the raw input text (and accordingly absence of *SpaceAfter=No* tags in CoNNL-U) as Thai uses whitespace rather than punctuation as pause character, and rest of the words were merged together in raw text by including *SpaceAfter=No* feature for each word not followed by dot or comma. This word-by-word translation and Thai word merging technique gives us the possibility to train a somewhat decent sentence and word segmenter without any training data for a language which does not use whitespaces to separate words or even sentences. Furthermore, all *the* words were removed as they have no Thai counterpart, lemmas were dropped, all matching morphological features between English and Thai were copied, HEAD indices were updated because of removing before mentioned tokens, non-existent dependency relations in Thai were mapped to similar existent ones, and finally enhanced dependency graphs were dropped. The tagger and parser were then trained normally using this training data. Training a lemmatizer is not needed as the Thai treebank does not include lemma annotation.

Our Thai segmentation achieves 1st rank and accuracy of 12.4% on sentence segmentation and 5th rank and accuracy of 43.2% on tokenization. On UPOS prediction we have accuracy of 27.6% and 4th rank, and our LAS is 6.9% and we rank 2nd, while the best team on Thai LAS, CUNI x-ling, achieves 13.7%. English is not a particularly natural choice for the source language of a Thai parser, with Chinese likely being a better candidate. We still chose English because we were unable to train a good Chinese-Thai MT system on the data provided in OPUS and the time pressure of the shared task prevented us from exploring other possibilities. Clearly, bad segmentation scores significantly affect other scores as well, and when the parser and tagger are evaluated on top of gold segmentation, our UPOS accuracy is 49.8% and LAS 20.4%. These numbers are clearly better than with predicted segmentation but still far off from typical supervised numbers.

5 Results

The overall results of our system are summarized in Table 3, showing the absolute performance, rank, and difference to the best system / next best system for all metrics on several treebank groups — big, small, low-resource and parallel UD (PUD). With respect to the three main metrics of the task, we ranked 2nd on LAS, 2nd on MLAS and 1st on BLEX, and received the highest aggregate ranking out of 26 teams, of which 21 submitted non-zero runs for all treebanks. For LAS, our high rank is clearly due to balanced performance across all treebank groups, as our ranks in the individual groups are 3rd, 6th, 4th and 6th, still giving a 2nd overall rank. A similar pattern can also be observed for MLAS. Our 1st overall rank on the BLEX metric is undoubtedly due to the good performance in lemmatization, on which our system achieves the 1st rank overall as well as in all corpus groups except the low-resourced languages. Altogether, it can be seen in the results table that the two main strengths of the system is 1) lemmatization and 2) tagging of small treebanks, and on any metric, the system ranks between 1st and 5th place across all corpora (*all* column in Table 3).

6 Software release

The full parsing pipeline is available at
`https://turkunlp.github.com/`
`Turku-neural-parser-pipeline,`

	All	*Big*	*PUD*	*Small*	*Low*
LAS	73.28 (-2.56 / 2)	81.85 (-2.52 / 3)	71.78 (-2.42 / 6)	64.48 (-5.05 / 4)	22.91 (-4.98 / 6)
MLAS	60.99 (-0.26 / 2)	71.27 (-1.40 / 3)	57.54 (-1.21 / 5)	47.63 (-1.61 / 2)	3.59 (-2.54 / 5)
BLEX	**66.09 (+0.76 / 1)**	**75.83 (+0.37 / 1)**	**63.25 (+0.91 / 1)**	53.54 (-1.35 / 2)	11.40 (-2.58 / 2)
UAS	77.97 (-2.54 / 4)	85.32 (-2.29 / 5)	75.58 (-2.84 / 6)	71.50 (-4.44 / 5)	34.51 (-4.72 / 6)
CLAS	69.40 (-2.96 / 2)	78.26 (-3.03 / 4)	67.65 (-2.21 / 5)	59.28 (-5.57 / 4)	18.15 (-4.03 / 6)
UPOS tagging	89.81 (-1.10 / 4)	95.41 (-0.82 / 6)	85.59 (-1.92 / 9)	91.93 (-0.91 / 3)	52.53 (-8.54 / 4)
XPOS tagging	86.17 (-0.50 / 3)	94.47 (-0.69 / 4)	55.68 (-0.30 / 2)	**90.51 (+0.50 / 1)**	43.43 (-11.3 / 17)
Morph. features	86.70 (-0.89 / 3)	93.82 (-0.32 / 3)	85.24 (-1.81 / 5)	**85.63 (+0.58 / 1)**	40.04 (-8.91 / 4)
All morph. tags	79.83(-0.47 / 2)	91.08 (-0.42 / 3)	51.60 (-0.30 / 2)	**82.02 (+1.17 / 1)**	17.58 (-8.33 / 19)
Lemmatization	**91.24 (+1.92 / 1)**	**96.08 (+0.83 / 1)**	**85.76 (+0.07 / 1)**	**91.02 (+1.02 / 1)**	61.61 (-2.81 / 3)
Sentence segmt.	83.03 (-0.84 / 5)	86.09 (-3.43 / 7–21)	75.53 (-0.51 / 3–17)	83.33 (-0.12 / 2–20)	66.23 (-1.27 / 2)
Word segmt.	97.42 (-0.76 / 5)	98.81 (-0.40 / 8–21)	92.61 (-1.96 / 7–19)	99.43 (+0.20 / 1–19)	89.10 (-4.28 / 5)
Tokenization	97.83 (-0.59 / 4)	99.24 (-0.27 / 6–21)	92.61 (-1.96 / 7–19)	99.57 (+0.01 / 1–18)	89.85 (-3.49 / 5)

Table 3: Results in every treebank group, shown as "absolute score (difference / rank)". For first rank, the difference to the next best system is shown, for other ranks we show the difference to the best ranking system, shared ranks are shown as a range.

together with all the trained models. We have ported the parser of Dozat et al. into Python3, and included other modifications such as the ability to parse a stream of input data without reloading the model. The pipeline has a modular structure, which allowed us to easily reconfigure the components for languages which needed a non-standard treatment. The pipeline software is documented, and we expect it to be comparatively easy to extend it with own components.

7 Conclusions

In this paper we presented the TurkuNLP entry at the *CoNLL 2018 UD Shared Task*. This year we focused on building an end-to-end pipeline system for segmentation, morphological tagging, syntactic parsing and lemmatization based on well-known components, and including our novel lemmatization approach. On BLEX evaluation, a metric including lemmatization and syntactic tree, we rank 1st, reflecting the state-of-the-art performance on lemmatization. On MLAS and LAS, metrics including morphological tagging and syntactic tree, and plain syntactic tree, we rank 2nd on both. All these components are wrapped into one simple parsing pipeline that carries out all four tasks with one command, and the pipeline is available for everyone together with all trained models.

Acknowledgments

We would like to thank Tim Dozat and rest of the Stanford team for making their parser open-source, as well as Milan Straka and rest of the Prague team for making UDPipe software and models open-source. This work was supported by Academy of Finland, Nokia Foundation and Google Digital News Innovation Fund. Computational resources were provided by CSC – IT Center for Science, Finland.

References

Toms Bergmanis, Katharina Kann, Hinrich Schütze, and Sharon Goldwater. 2017. Training data augmentation for low-resource morphological inflection. In *Proceedings of the CoNLL SIGMORPHON 2017 Shared Task: Universal Morphological Reinflection*. Association for Computational Linguistics, Vancouver, pages 31–39. http://www.aclweb.org/anthology/K17-2002.

Piotr Bojanowski, Edouard Grave, Armand Joulin, and Tomas Mikolov. 2016. Enriching word vectors with subword information. *arXiv preprint arXiv:1607.04606* .

Ryan Cotterell, Christo Kirov, John Sylak-Glassman, Géraldine Walther, Ekaterina Vylomova, Patrick Xia, Manaal Faruqui, Sandra Kübler, David Yarowsky, Jason Eisner, and Mans Hulden. 2017. Conll-sigmorphon 2017 shared task: Universal morphological reinflection in 52 languages. In *Proceedings of the CoNLL SIGMORPHON 2017 Shared Task: Universal Morphological Reinflection*. Association for Computational Linguistics, Vancouver, pages 1–30. http://www.aclweb.org/anthology/K17-2001.

Timothy Dozat and Christopher D Manning. 2016. Deep biaffine attention for neural dependency parsing. *arXiv preprint arXiv:1611.01734* .

Timothy Dozat, Peng Qi, and Christopher D Manning. 2017. Stanford's graph-based neural dependency parser at the conll 2017 shared task. *Proceedings of the CoNLL 2017 Shared Task: Multilingual Parsing from Raw Text to Universal Dependencies* pages 20–30.

Filip Ginter, Jan Hajič, Juhani Luotolahti, Milan Straka, and Daniel Zeman. 2017. CoNLL 2017 shared task - automatically annotated raw texts and word embeddings. LINDAT/CLARIN digital library at the Institute of Formal and Applied Linguistics (
'UFAL), Faculty of Mathematics and Physics, Charles University. http://hdl.handle.net/11234/1-1989.

Kenneth Heafield. 2011. KenLM: faster and smaller language model queries. In *Proceedings of the EMNLP 2011 Sixth Workshop on Statistical Machine Translation*. Edinburgh, Scotland, United Kingdom, pages 187–197. https://kheafield.com/papers/avenue/kenlm.pdf.

Marcin Junczys-Dowmunt, Roman Grundkiewicz, Tomasz Dwojak, Hieu Hoang, Kenneth Heafield, Tom Neckermann, Frank Seide, Ulrich Germann, Alham Fikri Aji, Nikolay Bogoychev, André F. T. Martins, and Alexandra Birch. 2018. Marian: Fast neural machine translation in C++. In *Proceedings of ACL 2018, System Demonstrations*. Melbourne, Australia. https://arxiv.org/abs/1804.00344.

Katharina Kann and Hinrich Schütze. 2017. The lmu system for the conll-sigmorphon 2017 shared task on universal morphological reinflection. In *Proceedings of the CoNLL SIGMORPHON 2017 Shared Task: Universal Morphological Reinflection*. Association for Computational Linguistics, Vancouver, pages 40–48. http://www.aclweb.org/anthology/K17-2003.

Guillaume Klein, Yoon Kim, Yuntian Deng, Jean Senellart, and Alexander M. Rush. 2017. OpenNMT: Open-source toolkit for neural machine translation. In *Proceedings of the 55th annual meeting of the Association for Computational Linguistics (ACL'17)*.

Thang Luong, Hieu Pham, and Christopher D. Manning. 2015. Effective approaches to attention-based neural machine translation. In *Proceedings of the 2015 Conference on Empirical Methods in Natural Language Processing*. Association for Computational Linguistics, Lisbon, Portugal, pages 1412–1421. http://aclweb.org/anthology/D15-1166.

Tomas Mikolov, Ilya Sutskever, Kai Chen, Gregory S. Corrado, and Jeffrey Dean. 2013. Distributed representations of words and phrases and their compositionality. In *Advances in Neural Information Processing Systems 26: 27th Annual Conference on Neural Information Processing Systems 2013. Proceedings of a meeting held December 5-8, 2013, Lake Tahoe, Nevada, United States.*. pages 3111–3119. http://papers.nips.cc/paper/5021-distributed-representations-of-words-and-phrases-and-their-compositionality.

Milan Straka, Jan Hajič, and Jana Straková. 2016. UDPipe: trainable pipeline for processing CoNLL-U files performing tokenization, morphological analysis, POS tagging and parsing. In *Proceedings of the 10th International Conference on Language Resources and Evaluation (LREC 2016)*. European Language Resources Association, Portoro, Slovenia.

Jörg Tiedemann. 2012. Parallel data, tools and interfaces in opus. In Nicoletta Calzolari (Conference Chair), Khalid Choukri, Thierry Declerck, Mehmet Ugur Dogan, Bente Maegaard, Joseph Mariani, Jan Odijk, and Stelios Piperidis, editors, *Proceedings of the Eight International Conference on Language Resources and Evaluation (LREC'12)*. European Language Resources Association (ELRA), Istanbul, Turkey.

Francis Tyers, Felipe Sánchez-Martínez, Sergio Ortiz-Rojas, and Mikel Forcada. 2010. Free/open-source resources in the apertium platform for machine translation research and development. *The Prague Bulletin of Mathematical Linguistics* 93:67–76.

Daniel Zeman, Filip Ginter, Jan Hajič, Joakim Nivre, Martin Popel, Milan Straka, and et al. 2017. CoNLL 2017 Shared Task: Multilingual Parsing from Raw Text to Universal Dependencies. In *Proceedings of the CoNLL 2017 Shared Task: Multilingual Parsing from Raw Text to Universal Dependencies*. Association for Computational Linguistics, pages 1–20.

Daniel Zeman, Jan Hajič, Martin Popel, Martin Potthast, Milan Straka, Filip Ginter, Joakim Nivre, and Slav Petrov. 2018. CoNLL 2018 Shared Task: Multilingual Parsing from Raw Text to Universal Dependencies. In *Proceedings of the CoNLL 2018 Shared Task: Multilingual Parsing from Raw Text to Universal Dependencies*. Association for Computational Linguistics, Brussels, Belgium, pages 1–20.

SEx BiST: A Multi-Source Trainable Parser
with Deep Contextualized Lexical Representations

KyungTae Lim[*], Cheoneum Park[+], Changki Lee[+] and Thierry Poibeau[*]
[*]LATTICE (CNRS & ENS / PSL & Université Sorbonne nouvelle / USPC)
[+]Department of Computer Science, Kangwon National University
{kyungtae.lim, thierry.poibeau}@ens.fr,
{parkce, leeck}@kangwon.ac.kr

Abstract

We describe the SEx BiST parser (Semantically EXtended Bi-LSTM parser) developed at Lattice for the CoNLL 2018 Shared Task (*Multilingual Parsing from Raw Text to Universal Dependencies*). The main characteristic of our work is the encoding of three different modes of contextual information for parsing: (*i*) Treebank feature representations, (*ii*) Multilingual word representations, (*iii*) ELMo representations obtained via unsupervised learning from external resources. Our parser performed well in the official end-to-end evaluation (73.02 LAS – 4th/26 teams, and 78.72 UAS – 2nd/26); remarkably, we achieved the best UAS scores on all the English corpora by applying the three suggested feature representations. Finally, we were also ranked 1st at the optional event extraction task, part of the 2018 Extrinsic Parser Evaluation campaign.

1 Introduction

Feature representation methods are an essential element for neural dependency parsing. Methods such as Feed Forward Neural Network (FFN) (Chen and Manning, 2014) or LSTM-based word representations (Kiperwasser and Goldberg, 2016; Ballesteros et al., 2016) have been proposed to provide fine-grained token representations, and these methods provide state of the art performance. However, learning efficient feature representations is still challenging, especially for under-resourced languages.

One way to cope with the lack of training data is a multilingual approach, which makes it possible to use different corpora in different languages as training data. In most cases, for instance in the CoNLL 2017 shared task (Zeman et al., 2017), the teams that have adopted this approach used a multilingual delexicalized parser (i.e. a multi-source parser trained without taking into account lexical features). However, it is evident that delexicalized parsing cannot capture contextual features that depend on the meaning of words within the sentence.

Following previous proposals promoting a model-transfer approach with lexicalized feature representations (Guo et al., 2016; Ammar et al., 2016; Lim and Poibeau, 2017), we have developed the SEx BiST parser (Semantically EXtended Bi-LSTM parser), a multi-source trainable parser using three different contextualized lexical representations:

- *Corpus representation*: a vector representation of each training corpus.

- *Multilingual word representation*: a multilingual word representation obtained by the projection of several pre-trained monolingual embeddings into a unique semantic space (following a linear transformation of each embedding).

- *ELMo representation*: token-based representation integrating abundant contexts gathered from external resources (Peters et al., 2018).

In this paper, we extend the multilingual graph-based parser proposed by Lim and Poibeau (2017) with the three above representations. Our parser is open source and available at: `https://github.com/CoNLL-UD-2018/LATTICE/`.

Our parser performed well in the official end-to-end evaluation (73.02 LAS – 4th out of 26 teams, and 78.72 UAS – 2nd out of 26). We obtained very

Proceedings of the CoNLL 2018 Shared Task: Multilingual Parsing from Raw Text to Universal Dependencies, pages 143–152
Brussels, Belgium, October 31 – November 1, 2018. ©2018 Association for Computational Linguistics
https://doi.org/10.18653/v1/K18-2014

good results for French, English and Korean where we were able to extensively exploit the three above features (for these languages, we obtained the best UAS performance on all the treebanks, and among the best LAS performance as well). Unfortunately we were not able to exploit the same strategy for all the languages due to a lack of a GPU and, correspondingly, time for training, and also due a lack of training data for some languages.

The structure of the paper is as follows. We first describe the feature extraction and representation methods (Section 2 and 3) and then present our POS tagger and our parser based on multi-task learning (Section 4). We then give some details on our implementation (Section 5) and we finally provide an analysis of our official results (Section 6).

2 Deep Contextualized Token Representations

The architecture of our parser follows the multilingual LATTICE parser presented in Lim and Poibeau (2017), with the addition of the three feature representations presented in the introduction.

The basic token representations is as follows. Given a sentence of tokens $s=(t_1,t_2,..t_n)$, the ith token t_i can be represented by a vector x_i, which is the result of the concatenation ($\circ$) of a word vector w_i and a character-level vector c_i of t_i:

$$x_i = c_i \circ w_i$$
$$c_i = \text{Char}(t_i; \theta_c)$$
$$w_i = \text{Word}(t_i; \theta_w)$$

When the approach is monolingual, w_i corresponds to the external word embeddings provided by Facebook (Bojanowski et al., 2016). Otherwise we used our own multilingual strategy based on multilingual embeddings (see Section 3.2)

2.1 Character-Level Word Representation

Token t_i can be decomposed as a vector of characters $(ch_1, ch_2,.. ch_m)$ where ch_j is the jth character of t_i. The function Char (that generates the character-level word vector c_i) corresponds to a vector obtained from the hidden state representation h_j of the LSTM, with an initial state h_0 (m is the length of token t_i)[1]:

$$h_j = \text{LSTM}^{(ch)}(h_0, (ch_1,ch_2,..ch_m))_j$$
$$c_i = w_c h_m$$

For LSTM-based character-level representations, previous studies have shown that the last hidden layer h_m represents a summary of all the information based on the input character sequences (Shi et al., 2017). It is then possible to linearly transform this with a parameter w_c so as to get the desired dimensionality. Another representation method involves applying an attention-based linear transformation of the hidden layer matrix H_i, for which attention weights a_i are calculated as follows:

$$a_i = Softmax(w_{att} \, H_i^T)$$
$$c_i = a_i H_i$$

Since we apply the *Softmax* function, making weights sum up to 1 after a linear transformation of H_i with attention parameter w_{att}, the self-attention weight a_i intuitively corresponds to the most informational characters of token t_i for parsing. Finally, by summing up the hidden state H_i of each word according to its attention weights a_i, we obtain our character-level word representation vector for token t_i. Most recently, Dozat et al. (2017) suggested an enhanced character-level representation based on the concatenation of h_m and $a_i H_i$ so as to capture both the summary and context information in one go for parsing. This is an option that could be explored in the future.

After some empirical experiments, we chose bidirectional LSTM encoders rather than a single directional one and then introduced the hidden state H_i into the two-layered Multi-Layer Perceptron (MLP) without bias terms for computing the attention weight a_i:

$$a_i = Softmax(w_{att2} \, tanh(W_{att1} \, H_i^T))$$
$$c_i = a_i H_i$$

For training, we used the charter-level word representations for all the languages except Kazakh and Thai (see Section 5).

2.2 Corpus Representation

Following Lim and Poibeau (2017), we used a one-hot treebank representation strategy to encode

---

[1] Note that i refers to the ith token in the sentence and that j refers to the jth character of the ith token. Here, we use lowercase italics for vectors and uppercase italics for matrices. So a set of hidden state H_i is a matrix stacked on m characters. In this paper, all the letters w and W denote parameters that the system has to learn.

language-specific features. In other words, each language has its own set of specific lexical features.

For languages with several training corpora (e.g., French-GSD and French-Spoken), our parser computes an additional feature vector taking into account corpus specificities at word level. Following the recent work of Stymne et al. (2018), who proposed a similar approach for treebank representations, we chose to use a 12 dimensional vector for corpus representation. This representation tr_i is concatenated with the token representation x_i:

$$tr_i = \text{Treebank}(t_i; \theta_{\text{tr}})$$
$$x_i = c_i \circ w_i \circ tr_i$$

We used this approach (corpus representation) for 24 corpora, and its effectiveness will be discussed in Section 5.

2.3 Contextualized Representation

ELMo (Embedding from Language Model (Peters et al., 2018)) is a function that provides a representation based on the entire input sentence. ELMo contextualized embedding is a new technique for word representation that has achieved state-of-the-art performance across a wide range of language understanding tasks. This approach is able to capture both subword and contextual information. As stated in the original paper by Peters et al. (2018), the goal is to "learn a linear combination of the vectors stacked above each input word for each end task, which markedly improves performance over just using the top LSTM layer".

We trained our language model with bidirectional LSTM using ELMo as an intermediate layer in the bidirectional language model (biLM), and we used ELMo embeddings to improve again the performance of our model.

$$R_i = \{\mathbf{x}_i^{LM}, \overleftrightarrow{\mathbf{h}}_{i,j}^{LM} | = 1, ..., L\}$$
$$= \{\mathbf{h}_{i,j}^{LM} | = 0, ..., L\} \quad (1)$$

$$ELMo_i = E(R_i; \Theta) = \gamma \sum_{j=0}^{L} s_j \mathbf{h}_{i,j}^{LM} \quad (2)$$

In (1), $\mathbf{x}_i^{LM}$ and $\mathbf{h}_{i,0}^{LM}$ are word embedding vectors corresponding to the token layer. $\overleftrightarrow{\mathbf{h}}_{i,j}^{LM}$ is a hidden LSTM vector consisting of a multi-layer and a bidirectional LSTM layer. $\mathbf{h}_{i,j}^{LM}$ is a concatenated vector composed of $\mathbf{x}_i^{LM}$ and $\overleftrightarrow{\mathbf{h}}_{i,j}^{LM}$. We computed our model with all the biLM layers weighted. In (2), s_j is softmax weight that is trainable to normalize multi-layer LSTM layers. γ is the scalar parameter to efficiently train the model. We used a 1024 dimensions ELMo embedding.

3 Multilingual Feature Representations

The supervised, monolingual approach to parsing, based on syntactically annotated corpora, has long been the most common one. However, thanks to recent developments involving powerful word representation methods (a.k.a. word embeddings), it is now possible to develop accurate multilingual lexical models by mapping several monolingual embeddings into a single vector space. This multilingual approach to parsing has yielded encouraging results for both low- (Guo et al., 2015) and high-resource languages (Ammar et al., 2016). In this work, we extend the recent multilingual dependency parsing approach proposed by Lim and Poibeau (2017) that achieved state-of-the-art performance during the last CoNLL shared task by using multilingual embeddings mapped based on bilingual dictionaries.

3.1 Embedding Projection

There are different strategies to produce multilingual word embeddings (Ruder et al., 2018), but a very efficient one consists in simply projecting one word embedding on top of the other to make both representations share the same semantic space (Artetxe et al., 2016). The alternative involves directly generating bilingual word embeddings from bilingual corpora (Gouws et al., 2015; Gouws and Sgaard, 2015), but this requires a large amount of bilingual data aligned at sentence or document level. This kind of resource is not available for most language pairs, especially for under-resourced languages.

We thus chose to train independently monolingual word embeddings and then map these word embeddings one to another. This approach is powerful since monolingual word embeddings generally share a similar structure (especially if they have been trained on similar corpora) and so can be superimposed with little information loss.

To project embeddings, we applied the linear transformation method using bilingual dictionaries proposed by Artetxe et al. (2017). We took the bilingual dictionaries from OPUS[2] and Wikipedia.

The projection method can be described as follows. Let X and Y be the source and target word embedding matrix so that x_i refers to i^{th} word embedding of X and y_j refers to j^{th} word embedding of Y. And let D be a binary matrix where $D_{ij} = 1$, if x_i and y_j are aligned. Our goal is to find a transformation matrix W such that Wx approximates y. This is done by minimizing the sum of squared errors:

$$\arg\min_{W} \sum_{i=1}^{m} \sum_{j=1}^{n} D_{ij} \|x_i W - y_i\|^2$$

The method is relatively simple since converting a bilingual dictionary into D is quite straightforward. The size of the dictionary used for training is around 250 pairs, and the projected word embedding is around 1.8GB. The dictionaries and the projected word embeddings are publicly available on Github.[3]

3.2 Training with Multilingual Embedding

After having trained multilingual embeddings, we associate them with word representation w_i as follows:

$$w_i = \text{Word}(t_i; \theta_{\text{mw}})$$

We applied the multilingual embedding mostly to train the nine low-resource languages of the 2018 CoNLL evaluation, for which only a handful of annotated sentences were provided.

4 Multi-Task Learning for Tagging and Parsing

In this section, we describe our Part-Of-Speech (POS) tagger and dependency parser using the encoded token representation x_i based on Multi-Task Learning (MTL) (Zhang and Yang, 2017).

4.1 Part-Of-Speech Tagger

As presented in Section 2 and 3, our parser is based on models trained with a combination of features, encoding different contextual information. However, the attention mechanism for the character-level word vector c_i is focusing only on a limited number of features within the token, and

the word representation element w_i is thus needed to transform a bidirectional LSTM, as a way to capture the overall context of a sentence. Finally, a token is encoded as a vector g_i:

$$g_i = \text{BiLSTM}^{(\text{pos})}(g_0, (x_1, x_2, ...x_n))_i$$

We transform the token vector g_i to a vector of the desired dimensionality by two-layered MLP with a bias term to classify the best candidate of universal part-of-speech (UPOS):

$$p'_i = W_{pos2} \; leaky\_relu(W_{pos1} \; g_i^T) + b_{pos}$$

$$y'_i = \arg\max_{j} p'_{ij}$$

Finally, we randomly initialize the UPOS embedding as p_i and map the predicted UPOS y'_i as a POS vector:

$$p_i = \text{Pos}(y'_i; \theta_{\text{pos}})$$

4.2 Dependency Parser

To take into account the predicted POS vector on the main target task (i.e. parsing), we concatenate the predicted POS vector p_i with the word representation w_i and then we encode the resulting vector via BiLSTM. This enriches the syntactic representations of the token by back-propagation during training:

$$v_i = \text{BiLSTM}^{(\text{dep})}(v_0, (x_1, x_2, ...x_n))_i$$

Following Dozat and Manning (2016), we used a deep bi-affine classifier to score all the possible head and modifier pairs $Y = (h,m)$. We then selected the best dependency graph based on Eisner's algorithm (Eisner and Satta, 1999). This algorithm tries to find the maximum spanning tree among all the possible graphs:

$$\arg\max_{valid\ Y} \sum_{(h,m)\in Y} Score^{MST}(h, m)$$

With this algorithm, it has been observed that parsing results (for some sentences) can have multiple roots, which is not a desirable feature. We thus followed an empirical method that selects a unique root based on the word order of the sentence, as already proposed by Lim and Poibeau (2017) to ensure tree well-formedness. After the selection

---

[2] http://opus.nlpl.eu/
[3] https://github.com/jujbob/multilingual-models

of the best-scored tree, another bi-affine classifier is applied for the classification of relation labels, based on the predicted tree.

We trained our tagger and parser simultaneously using a single objective function with penalized terms:

$$loss = \alpha CrossEntropy(p', p^{(\text{gold})})$$
$$+ \beta CrossEntropy(arc', arc^{(\text{gold})})$$
$$+ \gamma CrossEntropy(dep', dep^{(\text{gold})})$$

where arc' and dep' refer to the predicted *arc (head)* and *dependency (modifier)* results.

Since UAS directly affects LAS, we assumed that UAS would be crucial for parsing unseen corpora such as *Finnish_PUD*, as well as other corpora from low-resource languages. Therefore, we gave more weight to the parameters predicting arc' than rel' and p', since arc' directly affects UAS. We set $\alpha = 0.1$, $\beta = 0.7$ and $\gamma = 0.2$. Unfortunately, during the testing phase, we did not adjust weight parameters that would have benefited LAS for the 61 big treebanks, and this made our results on big treebanks suffer a bit (7th) compared to those we obtained on Small and PUD treebanks (3rd) regarding LAS. This also explains the gap between the UAS and LAS scores in our overall results.

5 Implementation Details

In this section, we provide some details on our implementation for the CoNLL 2018 shared task (Zeman et al., 2018b).

5.1 Training

We have trained both monolingual and multilingual models for parsing. In the first case, we simply used the available Universal Dependency 2.2 corpora for training (Zeman et al., 2018a). In the second case, for the multilingual approach, as both multilingual word embeddings and corresponding training corpora (in the Universal Dependency 2.2 format) were required, we concatenated the corresponding available Universal Dependency 2.2 corpora to artificially create multilingual training corpora.

The number of epochs was set to 200, with one epoch processing the entire training corpus in each language and with a batch size of 32. We then picked the best five performing models to parse the test corpora on TIRA (Potthast et al., 2014).

The five models were used as an ensemble run (described in Section 5.2).

Hyperparameters. Each deep learning parser has a number of hyperparameters that can boost the overall performance of the system. In our implementation, most hyperparameter settings were identical to Dozat et al. (2017), except of course those concerning the additional features we have introduced before. We used 100 dimensional character-level word representations with a 200 dimensional MLP, as presented in Section 2, and for corpus representation, we used a 12 dimensional vector. We set the learning-rate to 0.002 with Adam optimization.

Multilingual Embeddings. As described in Section 3, we specifically trained multilingual embedding models for nine low-resource languages. Table 2 gives the list of languages for which we adopted this approach, along with the language used for knowledge transfer. We selected language pairs based on previous studies (Lim and Poibeau, 2017; Lim et al., 2018; Partanen et al., 2018) for *bxr, kk, kmr, sme,* and *hsb,* and the others where chosen based on the public availability of bilingual dictionaries (this explains why we chose to map several languages with English, even when there was no real linguistically motivated reason to do so). Since we could not find any pre-trained embeddings for *pcm_nsc*, we applied a delexicalized parsing approach based on an English monolingual model.

ELMo. We used ELMo weights to train specific models for five languages: Korean, French, English, Japanese and Chinese. ELMo weights were pre-trained using the CoNLL resources provided [4]. We used AllenNLP[5] for training, and used the default hyperparameters. We included ELMo only at the level of the input layer for both training and inference (we set up dropout to 0.5 and used 1024 dimensions for the ELMo embedding layer in our model). All the other hyper-parameters are the same as for our other models (without ELMo).

5.2 Testing

All the tests were done on the TIRA platform provided by the shared task organizers. During the test phase, we applied an ensemble mechanism using five models trained with two different "seeds". The seeds are integers randomly produced by the

---

[4] http://hdl.handle.net/11234/1-1989
[5] https://github.com/allenai/allennlp

Corpus	UAS	LAS	Rank(UAS)	Rank(LAS)	Baseline(LAS)
Overall (82)	**78.71**	**73.02**	**2**	**4**	65.80
Big treebanks only (61)	85.36	80.97	4	7	74.14
PUD treebanks only (5)	76.81	72.34	3	3	66.63
Small treebanks only (7)	75.67	68.12	2	3	55.01
Low-resource only (9)	37.03	23.39	4	5	17.17

Corpus	Method	UAS(Rank)	LAS(Rank)
af_afribooms		87.42 (7)	83.72 (8)
grc_perseus	*tr*	79.15 (4)	71.63 (8)
grc_proiel	*tr*	79.53 (5)	74.46 (8)
ar_padt		75.96 (8)	71.13 (10)
hy_armtdp	*tr, mu*	**53.56 (1)**	**37.01 (1)**
eu_bdt		85.72 (7)	81.13 (8)
br_keb	*tr, mu*	43.78 (3)	23.65 (5)
bg_btb		92.1 (9)	88.02 (11)
bxr_bdt	*tr, mu*	36.89 (3)	17.16 (4)
ca_ancora		92.83 (6)	89.56 (9)
hr_set		90.18 (8)	84.67 (9)
cs_cac	*tr*	93.43 (2)	91 (2)
cs_fictree	*tr*	**94.78 (1)**	91.62 (3)
cs_pdt	*tr*	92.73 (2)	90.13 (7)
cs_pud	*tr*	89.49 (7)	83.88 (9)
da_ddt		85.36 (8)	80.49 (11)
nl_alpino	*tr*	90.59 (2)	86.13 (5)
nl_lassysmall	*tr*	87.83 (2)	84.02 (4)
en_ewt	*tr, el*	**86.9 (1)**	84.02 (2)
en_gum	*tr, el*	**88.57 (1)**	**85.05 (1)**
en_lines	*tr, el*	**86.01 (1)**	81.44 (2)
en_pud	*tr, el*	**90.83 (1)**	**87.89 (1)**
et_edt		86.25 (7)	82.33 (7)
fo_oft	*tr, mu*	48.64 (9)	25.17 (17)
fi_ftb	*tr*	89.74 (4)	86.54 (6)
fi_pud	*tr*	90.91 (4)	88.12 (6)
fi_tdt	*tr*	88.39 (6)	85.42 (7)
fr_gsd	*tr, el*	**89.5 (1)**	86.17 (3)
fr_sequoia	*tr, el*	**91.81 (1)**	**89.89 (1)**
fr_spoken	*tr, el*	79.47 (2)	73.62 (3)
gl_ctg	*tr*	84.05 (7)	80.63 (10)
gl_treegal	*tr*	78.71 (2)	73.13 (3)
de_gsd		82.09 (8)	76.86 (11)
got_proiel		73 (6)	65.3 (8)
el_gdt		89.29 (8)	86.02 (11)
he_htb		66.54 (9)	62.29 (9)
hi_hdtb		94.44 (8)	90.4 (12)
hu_szeged		80.49 (8)	74.21 (10)
zh_gsd	*tr, el*	71.48 (5)	68.09 (5)
id_gsd		85.03 (3)	77.61 (10)
ga_idt		79.13 (2)	69.1 (4)

Corpus	Method	UAS(Rank)	LAS(Rank)
it_isdt	*tr*	92.41 (6)	89.96 (8)
it_postwita	*tr*	77.52 (6)	72.66 (7)
ja_gsd	*tr, el*	76.4 (6)	74.82 (6)
ja_modern		29.36 (8)	22.71 (8)
kk_ktb	*tr, mu*	39.24 (15)	23.97 (9)
ko_gsd	*tr, el*	88.03 (2)	84.31 (2)
ko_kaist	*tr, el*	**88.92 (1)**	86.32 (4)
kmr_mg	*tr, mu*	38.64 (3)	27.94 (4)
la_ittb	*tr*	87.88 (8)	84.72 (8)
la_perseus	*tr*	75.6 (3)	64.96 (3)
la_proiel	*tr*	73.97 (6)	67.73 (8)
lv_lvtb	*tr*	82.99 (8)	76.91 (11)
pcm_nsc	*tr, mu*	18.15 (21)	11.63 (18)
sme_giella	*tr, mu*	**76.66 (1)**	**69.87 (1)**
no_bokmaal		91.4 (5)	88.43 (11)
no_nynorsk	*tr*	90.78 (8)	87.8 (11)
no_nynorsklia	*tr*	76.17 (2)	68.71 (2)
cu_proiel		77.49 (6)	70.48 (8)
fro_srcmf		91.35 (5)	85.51 (7)
fa_seraji		89.1 (7)	84.8 (10)
pl_lfg	*tr*	95.69 (8)	92.86 (11)
pl_sz	*tr*	92.24 (9)	88.95 (10)
pt_bosque		89.77 (5)	86.84 (7)
ro_rrt		89.8 (8)	84.33 (10)
ru_syntagrus	*tr*	93.1 (4)	91.14 (6)
ru_taiga	*tr*	**79.77 (1)**	74 (2)
sr_set		90.48 (10)	85.74 (11)
sk_snk		86.81 (11)	82.4 (11)
sl_ssj	*tr*	87.18 (10)	84.68 (10)
sl_sst	*tr*	63.64 (3)	57.07 (3)
es_ancora		91.81 (6)	89.25 (7)
sv_lines	*tr*	85.65 (4)	80.88 (6)
sv_pud	*tr*	83.44 (3)	79.1 (4)
sv_talbanken	*tr*	89.02 (4)	85.24 (7)
th_pud	*tr, mu*	0.33 (21)	0.12 (21)
tr_imst		69.06 (7)	60.9 (11)
uk_iu		85.36 (10)	81.33 (9)
hsb_ufal	*tr, mu*	54.01 (2)	43.83 (2)
ur_udtb		87.4 (7)	80.74 (10)
ug_udt		75.11 (6)	62.25 (9)
vi_vtb		49.65 (6)	43.31 (8)

Table 1: Official experiment results for each corpus, where *tr (Treebank)*, *mu (Multilingual)* and *el (ELMo)* in the column Method denote the feature representation methods used (see Section 2 and 3).

Corpus	Projected languages	UAS	LAS
hy_armntdp	Greek	1	1
br_keb	English	3	5
bxr_bdt	Russian	3	4
fo_oft	English	9	17
kk_ktb	Turkish	15	9
kmr_mg	English	3	4
pcm_nsc	-	21	18
sme_giella	Finnish+Russian	1	1
th_giella	English	21	21
hsb_ufal	Polish	2	2

Table 2: Languages trained with multilingual word embeddings and their ranking.

Representation Methods	UAS	LAS
baseline	81.79	78.45
+em	83.39	80.15
+em, tr	83.67	80.64
+em, el	85.47	82.72
+em, tr, el	85.49	82.93

Table 3: Relative contribution of the different representation methods on the overall results.

Python *random* library and are used to initialize the two parameters W and w (see Section 2). Generally, an ensemble mechanism combines the best performing models obtained from different seeds, so as to ensure robustness and efficiency. In our case, due to a lack of a GPU, different models have been trained simply based on the use of two different seeds. Finally, the five best performing models produced by the two seeds were put together to form the ensemble model. This improved the performances by up to 0.6%, but other improvements could be expected by testing with a larger set of seeds.

5.3 Hardware Resources

The training process for all the language models with the ensemble and ELMo was done using 32 CPUs and 7 GPUs (Geforce 1080Ti) in approximately two weeks. The memory usage of each model depends on the size of external word embeddings (3GB RAM by default plus the amount needed for loading the external embeddings). In the testing phase on the TIRA platform, we submitted our models separately, since testing with a model trained with ELMo takes around three hours. Testing took 46.2 hours for the 82 corpora using 16 CPUs and 16GB RAM.

6 Results

In this section, we discuss the results of our system and the relative contributions of the different features to the global results.

Overall results. The official evaluation results are given in Table 1. Our system achieved 73.02 LAS (4th out of 26 teams) and 78.71 UAS (2nd out of 26).

The comparison of our results with those obtained by other teams shows that there is room for improvement regarding preprocessing. For example, our system is 0.86 points below HIT-SCIR (Harbin) for sentence segmentation and 1.03 for tokenization (HIT-SCIR obtained the best overall results). Those two preprocessing tasks (sentence segmentation and tokenization) affect tagging and parsing performance directly. As a result, our parser ranked second on small treebanks (LAS), where most teams used the default segmenter and tokenizer, avoiding the differences on this aspect. In contrast, we achieved 7th on the big treebanks, probably because there is a more significant gap (1.72) here at the tokenization level.

Corpus Representation. Results with corpus representation (corpora marked *tr* in column Method of Table 1) exhibit relatively better performance than those without it, since *tr* makes it possible to capture corpus-oriented features. Results were positive not only for small treebanks (e.g., *cs_fictree* and *ru_taiga*) but also for big treebanks (e.g., *cs_cac* and *ru_syntagrus*). Corpus representation with ELMo shows the best performance for parsing English and French.

Multilinguality. As described in Section 3, we applied the multilingual approach to most of the low-resource languages. The best result is obtained for *hy_armtdp*, while *sme_giella* and *hsb_ufal* also gave satisfactory results. We only applied the delexicalized approach to *pcm_nsc* since we could not find any pre-trained embeddings for this language. We got a relatively poor result for *pcm_nsc*, despite testing different strategies and different feature combinations (we assume that the English model is not fit for it).

Additionally, we found that character-level representation is not always helpful, even in the case of some low-resource languages. When we tested *kk_ktb* (Kazakh) trained with a Turkish corpus, with multilingual word embeddings and character-level representations, the performance dramatically decreased. We suspect this has to do with the writing systems (Arabic versus Latin), but this theory should be further investigated.

sme_giella is another exceptional case since we chose to use a multilingual model trained with three different languages. Although Russian and Finnish do not use the same writing system, applying character and corpus representation improve the results. This is because the size of the training corpus for *sme_giella* is around 900 sentences, which seems to be enough to capture its main characteristics.

Language Model (ELMo). We used ELMo embeddings for five languages: Korean, French, English, Japanese and Chinese (they are marked with *el* in the method column in Table 1). The experiments with ELMo models showed excellent overall performance. All the English corpora, *fr_gsd* and *fr_sequoia* in French, and Korean *ko_kaist* obtained the best UAS. We also obtained the best LAS for English *en_gum* and *en_pud*, and for *fr_sequoia* in French.

Contributions of the Different System Components to the General results. To analyze the

Task	Precision	Recall	F1(Rank)
Event Extraction	58.93	43.12	**49.80 (1)**
Negation Resolution	99.08	41.06	58.06 (12)
Opinion Analysis	63.91	56.88	60.19 (9)

Task	LAS	MLAS	BLEX
Intrinsic Evaluation	84.66 (1)	72.93 (3)	77.62 (1)

Table 4: Official evaluation results on three EPE task (see `https://goo.gl/3Fmjke`).

effect of the proposed representation methods on parsing, we evaluated four different models with different components. We set our baseline model with a token representation as $x_i = w_i \circ c_i \circ p_i$, where w_i is a randomly initialized word vector, c_i is a character-level word vector and p_i is a POS vector predicted by UDpipe1.1 (note that we did not apply our 2018 POS tagger here, since it is trained jointly with the parser and that affects the overall feature representation). We then initialized the word vector w_i with external word embeddings as provided by the CoNLL shared organizers. We also re-run the experiment by adding treebank and ELMo representations. The results are shown in Table 3 (*em* denotes the use of the external word embedding and *tr* and *el* denotes treebank and ELMo representations respectively.). We observe that each representation improves the overall results. This is especially true regarding LAS when using ELMo (*el*), which means this representation has a positive effect on relation labeling.

Extrinsic Parser Evaluation (EPE 2018). Participants in the CoNLL shared task were invited to also participate in the 2018 Extrinsic Parser Evaluation (EPE) campaign[6] (Fares et al., 2018), as a way to confirm the applicability of the developed methods on practical tasks. Three downstream tasks were proposed this year in the EPE: biomedical event extraction, negation resolution and opinion analysis (and each task was run independently from the others). For this evaluation, participants were only required to send a parsed version of the different corpora received as input back to the organizers using a UD-type format (the organizers then ran the different scripts related to the different tasks and computed the corresponding results). We trained one single English model for the three tasks using the three English corpora provided (*en_lines*, *en_ewt*, *en_gum*) without treebank embeddings (*tr*), since we did not know which corpus embedding would perform better. In addition,

we did not apply our ensemble process on TIRA since it would have been too time consuming.

Our results are listed in Table 4. They include an intrinsic evaluation (overall performance of the parser on the different corpora considered as a whole) (Nivre and Fang, 2017) and task-specific evaluations (i.e. results for the three different tasks). In the intrinsic evaluation, we obtained the best LAS among all the participating systems, which confirms the portability of our approach across different domains. As for the task-specific evaluations, we obtained the best result for event extraction, but our parser did not perform so well on negation resolution and opinion analysis. This means that specific developments would be required to properly address the two tasks under consideration, taking semantics into consideration.

7 Conclusion

In this paper, we described the SEx BiST parser (Semantically EXtended Bi-LSTM parser) developed at Lattice for the CoNLL 2018 Shared Task. Our system was an extention of our 2017 parser (Lim and Poibeau, 2017) with three deep contextual representations (multilingual word representation, corpus representations, ELMo representation). It also included a multi-task learning process able to simultaneously handle tagging and parsing. SEx BiST achieved 73.02 LAS (4th over 26 teams), and 78.72 UAS (2nd out of 26), over the 82 test corpora of the evaluation. In the future, we hope to improve our sentence segmenter and our tokenizer since this seems to be the most obvious target for improvements to our system. The generalization of ELMo representation to new languages (beyond what we could do for the 2018 evaluation) should also have a positive effect on the results.

Acknowledgments

KyungTae Lim is supported by the ANR ERA-NET ATLANTIS project. This work is also supported by the LAKME project funded by IDEX PSL (ANR-10-IDEX-0001-02). Lastly, we want to thank the National Science & Technology Information (NTIS) for providing computing resources and the Korean national R&D corpora.

---

[6]`http://epe.nlpl.eu/`

References

Waleed Ammar, George Mulcaire, Miguel Ballesteros, Chris Dyer, and Noah A. Smith. 2016. One parser, many languages. *CoRR* http://arxiv.org/abs/1602.01595.

Mikel Artetxe, Gorka Labaka, and Eneko Agirre. 2016. Learning principled bilingual mappings of word embeddings while preserving monolingual invariance. In *Proceedings of the 2016 Conference on Empirical Methods in Natural Language Processing (EMNLP), Austin, USA.* pages 2289–2294.

Mikel Artetxe, Gorka Labaka, and Eneko Agirre. 2017. Learning bilingual word embeddings with (almost) no bilingual data. In *Proceedings of the 55th Annual Meeting of the Association for Computational Linguistics (Volume 1: Long Papers).* pages 451–462. aclweb.org/anthology/P17-1042.

Miguel Ballesteros, Yoav Goldberg, Chris Dyer, and Noah A. Smith. 2016. Training with exploration improves a greedy stack lstm parser. In *Proceedings of the 2016 Conference on Empirical Methods in Natural Language Processing.* Association for Computational Linguistics, Austin, Texas, pages 2005–2010. https://aclweb.org/anthology/D16-1211.

Piotr Bojanowski, Edouard Grave, Armand Joulin, and Tomas Mikolov. 2016. Enriching word vectors with subword information. *arXiv preprint arXiv:1607.04606* .

Danqi Chen and Christopher D Manning. 2014. A fast and accurate dependency parser using neural networks. In *EMNLP.* pages 740–750.

Timothy Dozat and Christopher D. Manning. 2016. Deep biaffine attention for neural dependency parsing. *CoRR* abs/1611.01734. http://arxiv.org/abs/1611.01734.

Timothy Dozat, Peng Qi, and Christopher D. Manning. 2017. Stanford's graph-based neural dependency parser at the conll 2017 shared task. In *Proceedings of the CoNLL 2017 Shared Task: Multilingual Parsing from Raw Text to Universal Dependencies.* Association for Computational Linguistics, Vancouver, Canada, pages 20–30. http://www.aclweb.org/anthology/K/K17/K17-3002.pdf.

Jason Eisner and Giorgio Satta. 1999. Efficient parsing for bilexical context-free grammars and head automaton grammars. In *Proceedings of the 37th annual meeting of the Association for Computational Linguistics on Computational Linguistics.* Association for Computational Linguistics, pages 457–464.

Murhaf Fares, Stephan Oepen, Lilja vrelid, Jari Björne, and Richard Johansson. 2018. The 2018 Shared Task on Extrinsic Parser Evaluation. On the downstream utility of English Universal Dependency parsers. In *Proceedings of the 22nd Conference on Natural Language Learning.* Brussels, Belgia.

Stephan Gouws, Yoshua Bengio, and Greg Corrado. 2015. Bilbowa: Fast bilingual distributed representations without word alignments. In *Proceedings of the 32nd International Conference on Machine Learning.* Lille, France, volume 37 of *Proceedings of Machine Learning Research*, pages 748–756.

Stephan Gouws and Anders Sgaard. 2015. Simple task-specific bilingual word embeddings. In *HLT-NAACL.* The Association for Computational Linguistics, pages 1386–1390.

Jiang Guo, Wanxiang Che, David Yarowsky, Haifeng Wang, and Ting Liu. 2015. Cross-lingual dependency parsing based on distributed representations. In *Proceedings of ACL.*

Jiang Guo, Wanxiang Che, David Yarowsky, Haifeng Wang, and Ting Liu. 2016. A representation learning framework for multi-source transfer parsing. In *AAAI.* pages 2734–2740.

Eliyahu Kiperwasser and Yoav Goldberg. 2016. Simple and accurate dependency parsing using bidirectional LSTM feature representations. *Transactions of the Association for Computational Linguistics* 4:313–327. https://transacl.org/ojs/index.php/tacl/article/view/885.

KyungTae Lim, Niko Partanen, and Thierry Poibeau. 2018. Multilingual Dependency Parsing for Low-Resource Languages: Case Studies on North Saami and Komi-Zyrian. In *Proceedings of the Eleventh International Conference on Language Resources and Evaluation (LREC 2018).* Miyazaki, Japan.

KyungTae Lim and Thierry Poibeau. 2017. A system for multilingual dependency parsing based on bidirectional lstm feature representations. In *Proceedings of the CoNLL 2017 Shared Task: Multilingual Parsing from Raw Text to Universal Dependencies.* Association for Computational Linguistics, Vancouver, Canada, pages 63–70. http://www.aclweb.org/anthology/K/K17/K17-3006.pdf.

Joakim Nivre and Chiao-Ting Fang. 2017. Universal dependency evaluation. In *Proceedings of the NoDaLiDa 2017 Workshop on Universal Dependencies (UDW 2017).* pages 86–95.

Niko Partanen, KyungTae Lim, Michael Rießler, and Thierry Poibeau. 2018. Dependency parsing of code-switching data with cross-lingual feature representations. In *Proceedings of the Fourth International Workshop on Computatinal Linguistics of Uralic Languages.* pages 1–17.

Matthew E. Peters, Mark Neumann, Mohit Iyyer, Matt Gardner, Christopher Clark, Kenton Lee, and Luke Zettlemoyer. 2018. Deep contextualized word representations. *CoRR* abs/1802.05365. http://arxiv.org/abs/1802.05365.

Martin Potthast, Tim Gollub, Francisco Rangel, Paolo Rosso, Efstathios Stamatatos, and Benno Stein. 2014. Improving the reproducibility of PAN's shared tasks: Plagiarism detection, author identification, and author profiling. In Evangelos Kanoulas, Mihai Lupu, Paul Clough, Mark Sanderson, Mark Hall, Allan Hanbury, and Elaine Toms, editors, *Information Access Evaluation meets Multilinguality, Multimodality, and Visualization. 5th International Conference of the CLEF Initiative (CLEF 14)*. Springer, Berlin Heidelberg New York, pages 268–299. https://doi.org/10.1007/978-3-319-11382-1_22.

Sebastian Ruder, Ivan Vuli, and Anders Sgaard. 2018. A survey of cross-lingual word embedding models .

Tianze Shi, Felix G. Wu, Xilun Chen, and Yao Cheng. 2017. Combining global models for parsing universal dependencies. In *Proceedings of the CoNLL 2017 Shared Task: Multilingual Parsing from Raw Text to Universal Dependencies*. Association for Computational Linguistics, Vancouver, Canada, pages 31–39. http://www.aclweb.org/anthology/K/K17/K17-3003.pdf.

Sara Stymne, Miryam de Lhoneux, Aaron Smith, and Joakim Nivre. 2018. Parser training with heterogeneous treebanks. In *Proceedings of the 56th Annual Meeting of the Association for Computational Linguistics (Short Papers)*. Melbourne, Australia.

Dan Zeman et al. 2018a. Universal Dependencies 2.2 CoNLL 2018 shared task development and test data. LINDAT/CLARIN digital library at the Institute of Formal and Applied Linguistics, Charles University, Prague, `http://hdl.handle.net/11234/1-2184`. http://hdl.handle.net/11234/1-2184.

Daniel Zeman, Filip Ginter, Jan Hajič, Joakim Nivre, Martin Popel, Milan Straka, and et al. 2017. CoNLL 2017 Shared Task: Multilingual Parsing from Raw Text to Universal Dependencies. In *Proceedings of the CoNLL 2017 Shared Task: Multilingual Parsing from Raw Text to Universal Dependencies*. Association for Computational Linguistics, pages 1–20.

Daniel Zeman, Jan Hajič, Martin Popel, Martin Potthast, Milan Straka, Filip Ginter, Joakim Nivre, and Slav Petrov. 2018b. CoNLL 2018 Shared Task: Multilingual Parsing from Raw Text to Universal Dependencies. In *Proceedings of the CoNLL 2018 Shared Task: Multilingual Parsing from Raw Text to Universal Dependencies*. Association for Computational Linguistics, Brussels, Belgium, pages 1–20.

Yu Zhang and Qiang Yang. 2017. A survey on multitask learning. *arXiv preprint arXiv:1707.08114* .

The SLT-Interactions Parsing System at the CoNLL 2018 Shared Task

Riyaz Ahmad Bhat
Interactions LLC
Bengaluru, India
rbhat@interactions.com

Irshad Ahmad Bhat
LTRC, IIITH
Hyderabad, India
irshad.bhat@research.iiit.ac.in

Srinivas Bangalore
Interactions LLC
New Jersey, United States
sbangalore@interactions.com

Abstract

This paper describes our system (SLT-Interactions) for the CoNLL 2018 shared task: *Multilingual Parsing from Raw Text to Universal Dependencies*. Our system performs three main tasks: word segmentation (only for few treebanks), POS tagging and parsing. While segmentation is learned separately, we use neural stacking for joint learning of POS tagging and parsing tasks. For all the tasks, we employ simple neural network architectures that rely on long short-term memory (LSTM) networks for learning task-dependent features. At the basis of our parser, we use an arc-standard algorithm with Swap action for general non-projective parsing. Additionally, we use neural stacking as a knowledge transfer mechanism for cross-domain parsing of low resource domains. Our system shows substantial gains against the UDPipe baseline, with an average improvement of 4.18% in LAS across all languages. Overall, we are placed at the 12th position on the official test sets.

1 Introduction

Our system for the CoNLL 2018 shared task (Zeman et al., 2018) contains the following modules: word segmentation, part-of-speech (POS) tagging and dependency parsing. In some cases, we also use a transliteration module to transcribe data into Roman form for efficient processing.

- **Segmentation** We mainly use this module to identify word boundaries in certain languages such as Chinese where space is not used as a boundary marker.

- **POS tagging** For all the languages, we only focus on universal POS tags while ignoring language specific POS tags and morphological features.

- **Dependency parsing** We use an arc-standard transition system (Nivre, 2003) with an additional Swap action for unrestricted parsing (Nivre, 2009).

We rely on UDPipe 1.2 (Straka and Straková, 2017) for tokenization for almost all the treebanks except for Chinese and Japanese where we observed that the UDPipe segmentation had an adverse effect on parsing performance as opposed to gold segmentation on the development sets. Moreover, we also observed that training a separate POS tagger was also beneficial as the UDPipe POS tagger had slightly lower performance in some languages. However, other than tokenization, we ignored other morphological features predicted by UDPipe and didn't explore their effect on parsing.

Additionally, we use knowledge transfer approaches to enhance the performance of parsers trained on smaller treebanks. We leverage related treebanks (other treebanks of the same language) using neural stacking for learning better cross-domain parsers. We also trained a generic character-based parsing system for languages that have neither in-domain nor cross-domain training data.

Upon the official evaluation on 82 test sets, our system (SLT-Interactions) obtained the 12th position in the parsing task and achieved an average improvement of 4.18% in LAS over the UDPipe baseline.

153

Proceedings of the CoNLL 2018 Shared Task: Multilingual Parsing from Raw Text to Universal Dependencies, pages 153–159
Brussels, Belgium, October 31 – November 1, 2018. ©2018 Association for Computational Linguistics
https://doi.org/10.18653/v1/K18-2015

2 System Architecture

2.1 Text Processing

Given the nature of the shared task, sentence and word segmentation are the two major prerequisite tasks needed for parsing the evaluation data. For most of the languages, we rely on UDPipe for both sentence segmentation and word segmentation. However, in few languages such as Chinese and Japanese which do not use white space as explicit word boundary marker, we build our own word segmentation models. Our segmentation models use a simple neural network classifier that relies on character bidirectional LSTM (Bi-LSTM) representations of a focus character to produce a probabilistic distribution over two boundary markers: **B**egining of a word and **I**nside of a word. The segmentation network is shown in Figure 1. The models are trained on the respective training data sets by merging the word forms in each sentence into a sequence of characters. At inference, the segmentation model relies on sentence segmentation from UDPipe.

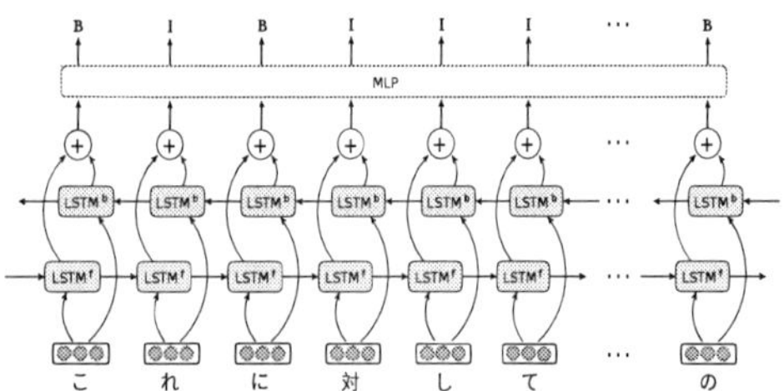

Figure 1: Word segmentation model based on character Bi-LSTM networks.

	ja_gsd			zh_gsd		
	Precision	Recall	F1-score	Precision	Recall	F1-score
B	97.43	97.26	97.35	96.50	96.48	96.49
I	96.35	96.58	96.46	93.94	93.96	93.95
avg	96.97	96.97	96.97	95.96	95.96	95.96

Table 1: Word segmentation results on Chinese and Japanese development sets. **B** and **I** mark the **B**egining and **I**nside of a word.

Other than word segmentation, we used Roman alphabet for Hindi. The goal is to normalize the spell variations in Hindi texts. We used an open source converter[1] that uses a deterministic mapping between Devanagari to Roman alphabet.

[1]https://github.com/ltrc/indic-wx-converter

2.2 Dependency Parsing

2.2.1 Parsing Algorithm

We employ an arc-standard transition system (Nivre, 2003) as our parsing algorithm. A typical transition-based parsing system uses the shift-reduce decoding algorithm to map a parse tree onto a sequence of transitions. Throughout the decoding process a stack and a queue data structures are maintained. The queue stores the sequence of raw input, while the stack stores the partially processed input which may be linked with the rest of the words in the queue. The parse tree is build by consuming the words in the queue from left to right by applying a set of transition actions. There are three kinds of transition actions that are performed in the parsing process: `Shift`, `Left-Arc`, `Right-Arc`. Additionally, we use a `Swap` action which reorders top node in the stack and the top node in the queue for parsing non-projective arcs (Nivre, 2009).

At training time, the transition actions are inferred from the gold parse trees and the mapping between the parser state and the transition action is learned using a simple LSTM-based neural networking architecture presented in Goldberg (2016). While training, we use the oracle presented in (Nivre et al., 2009) to restrict the number of `Swap` actions needed to parse non-projective arcs. Given that Bi-LSTMs capture global sentential context at any given time step, we use minimal set of features in our parsing model. At each parser state, we restrict our features to just two top nodes in the stack. Since `Swap` action distorts the linear order of word sequence, it renders the LSTM representations irrelevant in case of non-projective sentences. To capture this distortion, we also use the top most word in the queue as an additional feature.

2.3 Joint POS tagging and Parsing

Inspired by stack-propagation model of Zhang and Weiss (2016), we jointly model POS tagging and parsing using a stack of tagger and parser networks. The parameters of the tagger network are shared and act as a regularization on the parsing model. The overall model is trained by minimizing a joint negative log-likelihood loss for both tasks. Unlike Zhang and Weiss (2016), we compute the gradients of the log-loss function simultaneously for each training instance. While the parser network is updated given the parsing loss only, the tagger network is updated with respect to both tagging and parsing losses. Both tagger and parser networks comprise of an input layer, a feature layer, and an output layer as shown in Figure 2. Following Zhang and Weiss (2016), we refer to this model as stack-prop.

Tagger network: The input layer of the tagger encodes each input word in a sentence by concatenating a pre-trained word embedding with its character embedding given by a character Bi-LSTM. In the feature layer, the concatenated word and character representations are passed through two stacked Bi-LSTMs to generate a sequence of hidden representations which encode the contextual information spread across the sentence. The first Bi-LSTM is shared with the parser network while the other is specific to the tagger. Finally, output layer uses the feed-forward neural network with a softmax function for a probability distribution over the Universal POS tags. We only use the forward and backward hidden representations of the focus word for classification.

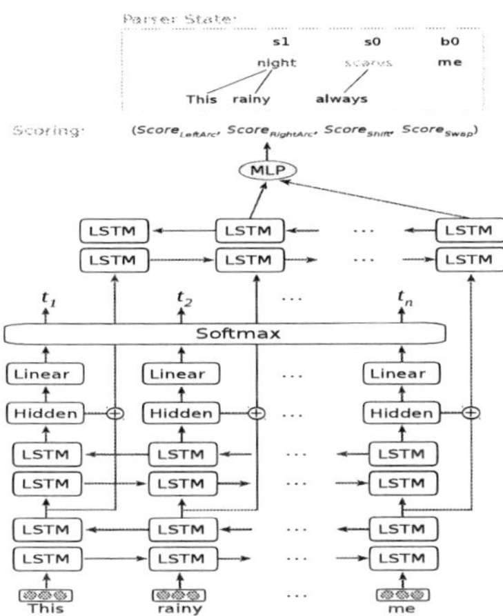

Figure 2: POS tagging and parsing network based on stack-propagation model proposed in (Zhang and Weiss, 2016).

Parser Network: Similar to the tagger network, the input layer encodes the input sentence using word and character embeddings which are then passed to the shared Bi-LSTM. The hidden representations from the shared Bi-LSTM are then concatenated with the dense representations from the feed-forward network of the tagger and passed through the Bi-LSTM specific to the parser. This ensures that the tagging network is penalized for the parsing error caused by error propagation by

back-propagating the gradients to the shared tagger parameters (Zhang and Weiss, 2016). Finally, we use a non-linear feed-forward network to predict the labeled transitions for the parser configurations. From each parser configuration, we extract the top node in the stack and the first node in the buffer and use their hidden representations from the parser specific Bi-LSTM for classification.

2.4 Cross-domain Transfer

Among 57 languages, 17 languages presented in the task have multiple treebanks from different domains. From among the 17 languages, almost 5 languages have at-least one treebank which is smaller in size than the rest containing no more than 2000 sentences for training. To boost the performance of parsers trained on these smaller treebanks (target), we leverage large cross-domain treebanks (source) in the same language using neural stacking as a knowledge transfer mechanism.

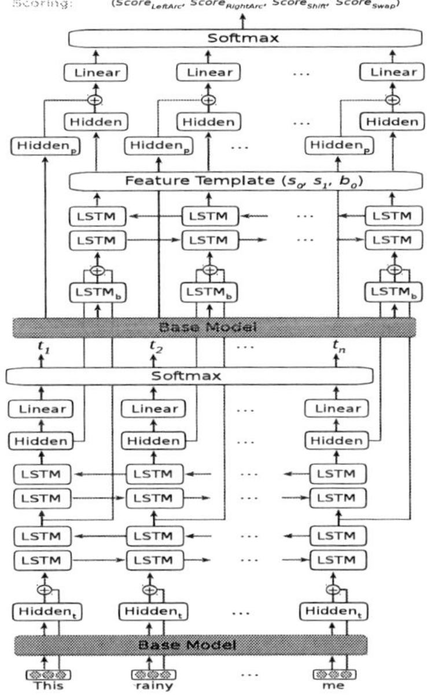

Figure 3: Knowledge transfer from resource-rich domains to resource-poor domains using neural stacking (Zhang and Weiss, 2016; Chen et al., 2016).

As we discussed above, we adapted feature-level neural stacking (Zhang and Weiss, 2016; Chen et al., 2016) for joint learning of POS tagging and parsing. Similarly, we also adapt this stacking approach for cross-domain knowledge transfer by incorporating the syntactic knowledge from resource-rich domain into resource-poor domain. Recently, Wang et al. (2017); Bhat et al. (2018) showed significant improvements in parsing social media texts by injecting syntactic knowledge from large cross-domain treebanks using neural stacking.

As shown in Figure 3, we transfer both POS tagging and parsing information from the source model. For tagging, we augment the input layer of the target tagger with the hidden layer of multi-layered perceptron (MLP) of the source tagger. For transferring parsing knowledge, hidden representations from the parser specific Bi-LSTM of the source parser are augmented with the input layer of the target parser which already includes the hidden layer of the target tagger, word and character embeddings. In addition, we also add the MLP layer of the source parser to the MLP layer of the target parser. The MLP layers of the source parser are generated using raw features from target parser configurations. Apart from the addition of these learned representations from the source model, the overall target model remains similar to the base model shown in Figure 2. The tagging and parsing losses are back-propagated by traversing back the forward paths to all trainable parameters in the entire network for training and the whole network is used collectively for inference.

3 Experiments

We train three kinds of parsing models based on the availability of training data: stack-prop models trained for languages having large treebanks, ii) stacking models for languages having smaller in-domain treebanks and large out-domain treebanks, and iii) backoff character models for those languages which have neither in-domain nor out-domain training data. We will first discuss the details about the experimental setup for all these models and subsequently, we will discuss the results.

3.1 Hyperparameters

Word Representations For the stack-prop and stacking models, we include lexical features in the input layer of the neural networks using 64-dimension pre-trained word embeddings concatenated with 64-dimension character-based embeddings obtained using a Bi-LSTM over the characters of a word. For each language, we include pre-trained embeddings only for 100K most frequent words in the raw corpora.

The distributed word representations for each language are learned separately from their monolingual corpora collected from Web to Corpus (W2C) (Majliš, 2011)[2] and latest wiki dumps[3]. The word representations are learned using Skip-gram model with negative sampling which is implemented in word2vec toolkit (Mikolov et al., 2013). For our backoff character model we only use 64-dimension character Bi-LSTM embeddings in the input layer of the network.

Hidden dimensions The word-level Bi-LSTMs have 128 cells while the character-level Bi-LSTMs have 64 cells. The POS tagger specific MLP has 64 hidden nodes while the parser MLP has 128 hidden nodes. We use hyperbolic tangent as an activation function in all tasks.

Learning We use momentum SGD for learning with a minibatch size of 1. The initial learning rate is set to 0.1 with a momentum of 0.9. The LSTM weights are initialized with random orthonormal matrices as described in (Saxe et al., 2013). We set the dropout rate to 30% for all the hidden states in the network. All the models are trained for up to 100 epochs, with early stopping based on the development set.

All of our neural network models are implemented in DyNet (Neubig et al., 2017).

4 Results

In Table 4, we present the results of our parsing models on all the official test sets, while in Table 5, we report the average results across evaluation sets. In both tables, we also provide comparison of results on all the evaluation matrices with the UDPipe baseline models. For 74 out of 82 treebanks, we have obtained an average improvement of 5.8% in LAS over the UDPipe baseline models. Although, we ranked 12th in the overall shared task, our rankings are particularly better for all those treebanks which were parsed using the stacking models or parsed after segmentation by our own segmentation models.

---

[2]As pointed out by one of the reviewers, W2C was not listed on the list of allowed resources. Using this data for training word embeddings might have a significant impact for resource-poor languages. Our results, therefore, might not be directly comparable with other participating teams and should be taken with a grain of salt!

[3]https://dumps.wikimedia.org

Our parsing system took around 1 hour 30 minutes to parse all the official test sets on TIRA virtual machine.

Impact of Word Segmentation   To evaluate the impact of our segmentation models, we conducted two parsing experiments; one using the segmentation from the UDPipe models, and the other using the segmentation from our own segmentation models. We compared the performance of both segmentations on Japanese and Chinese development sets. The results are shown in Table 2. As shown in the Table, we achieved an average improvement of 3% in LAS over the UDPipe baseline. By using our segmentation models, we have achieved better ranking for these two languages than our average ranking in the official evaluation.

	UDPipe			Our model		
	UPOS	**ULAS**	**LAS**	**UPOS**	**ULAS**	**LAS**
ja_gsd	89.14	78.73	77.47	90.92	82.57	81.30
zh_gsd	84.30	65.36	61.96	86.51	68.51	64.89

Table 2: Impact of our word segmentation models on Chinese and Japanese development sets.

Impact of Domain Adaptation   We also conducted experiments to evaluate the impact of neural stacking for knowledge transfer from resource-rich domains to resource-poor domains. In all the cases of neural stacking, we used the base models trained on those domains that have larger treebanks. We show the comparison of performance of stacking models with the base models trained on just the in-domain smaller treebanks. Results on development sets of multiple domains of English and French are shown in Table 3. For English domains, there is an improvement of 1% to 2% using `eng_ewt` as source domain for knowledge transfer, while for French improvements are quite high (2% to 5%) using `fr_gsd` as source domain. Similar to the impact of word segmentation, our ranking on treebanks that use neural stacking is better than our average.

	Base model			Stacking model		
	UPOS	**ULAS**	**LAS**	**UPOS**	**ULAS**	**LAS**
en_gum	96.29	86.96	83.53	96.68	88.51	85.47
en_lines	96.71	83.95	80.16	97.13	85.21	81.70
fr_sequoia	98.27	90.42	87.72	98.75	92.18	89.79
fr_spoken	95.91	82.40	74.96	97.25	86.01	79.82

Table 3: Impact of neural stacking on multiple domains of English and French.

5   Conclusion

In this paper, we have described our parsing models that we have submitted to CoNLL-2018 parsing shared task on Universal Dependencies. We have developed three types of models depending on the number of training samples. All of our models learn POS tag and parse tree information jointly using stack-propagation. For smaller treebanks, we have used neural stacking for knowledge transfer from large cross-domain treebanks. Moreover, we also developed our own segmentation models for Japanese and Chinese for improving the parsing results of these languages. We have significantly improved the baseline results from UDPipe for almost all the official test sets. Finally, we have achieved 12th rank in the shared task for average LAS.

References

Irshad Bhat, Riyaz A. Bhat, Manish Shrivastava, and Dipti Sharma. 2018. Universal dependency parsing for hindi-english code-switching. In *Proceedings of the 2018 Conference of the North American Chapter of the Association for Computational Linguistics: Human Language Technologies, Volume 1 (Long Papers)*. Association for Computational Linguistics, pages 987–998. http://aclweb.org/anthology/N18-1090.

Hongshen Chen, Yue Zhang, and Qun Liu. 2016. Neural network for heterogeneous annotations. In *Proceedings of the 2016 Conference on Empirical Methods in Natural Language Processing*. Association for Computational Linguistics, Austin, Texas, pages 731–741.

Eliyahu Kiperwasser and Yoav Goldberg. 2016. Simple and accurate dependency parsing using bidirectional lstm feature representations. *Transactions of the Association for Computational Linguistics* 4:313–327.

Martin Majliš. 2011. W2C web to corpus corpora. LINDAT/CLARIN digital library at the Institute of Formal and Applied Linguistics (ÚFAL), Faculty of Mathematics and Physics, Charles University. http://hdl.handle.net/11858/00-097C-0000-0022-6133-9.

Tomas Mikolov, Kai Chen, Greg Corrado, and Jeffrey Dean. 2013. Efficient estimation of word representations in vector space. *arXiv preprint arXiv:1301.3781* .

Graham Neubig, Chris Dyer, Yoav Goldberg, Austin Matthews, Waleed Ammar, Antonios Anastasopoulos, Miguel Ballesteros, David Chiang, Daniel Clothiaux, Trevor Cohn, et al. 2017. Dynet: The dynamic neural network toolkit. *arXiv preprint arXiv:1701.03980* .

	BASELINE UDPipe 1.2					SLT-Interactions				
	UPOS	**ULAS**	**LAS**	**MLAS**	**BLEX**	**UPOS**	**ULAS**	**LAS**	**MLAS**	**BLEX**
af_afribooms	95.12	82.02	77.88	64.48	66.60	97.42	86.05	83.07	68.66	72.89
ar_padt	89.34	71.44	66.41	55.01	57.60	90.34	75.38	71.52	58.00	63.20
bg_btb	97.72	88.88	84.91	75.30	73.78	98.54	91.84	88.64	78.63	78.00
br_keb	30.74	27.80	10.25	0.37	2.10	36.80	36.06	14.15	0.17	3.66
bxr_bdt	41.66	29.20	12.61	2.09	4.41	43.07	24.89	8.29	0.86	3.76
ca_ancora	98.00	88.66	85.61	76.74	77.27	98.66	91.77	89.42	80.79	82.21
cs_cac	98.32	87.11	83.72	70.89	77.65	99.00	91.37	89.14	74.27	83.37
cs_fictree	97.28	86.77	82.49	69.26	74.96	98.25	91.52	88.13	72.82	81.25
cs_pdt	98.21	86.88	83.94	74.32	79.39	98.70	90.74	88.44	77.07	84.14
cs_pud	96.57	85.29	80.08	66.53	73.79	96.85	88.63	83.76	68.39	77.33
cu_proiel	93.70	72.03	65.46	53.96	58.39	94.66	74.66	68.81	54.65	61.15
da_ddt	95.44	79.14	75.43	65.41	66.04	97.08	83.97	81.09	69.45	71.81
de_gsd	91.58	75.99	70.85	34.09	60.56	94.03	81.61	77.23	38.50	67.89
el_gdt	95.63	85.47	82.11	65.33	68.67	97.64	89.16	86.67	68.10	74.05
en_ewt	93.62	80.48	77.56	68.70	71.02	94.88	84.04	81.52	71.37	75.21
en_gum	93.24	78.48	74.20	62.66	62.14	95.99	85.47	82.42	67.95	70.41
en_lines	94.71	78.26	73.10	64.03	65.42	96.92	82.53	78.38	68.41	71.25
en_pud	94.15	83.05	79.56	67.59	71.14	95.66	87.36	84.64	71.41	76.89
es_ancora	98.14	87.42	84.43	76.01	76.43	98.74	90.90	88.68	80.77	81.93
et_edt	95.50	79.16	75.02	67.12	63.85	96.91	84.89	81.85	71.18	69.65
eu_bdt	92.34	75.00	70.13	57.65	63.50	95.72	83.08	79.57	63.57	72.15
fa_seraji	96.01	83.10	79.10	72.20	69.43	97.15	88.42	84.94	77.32	75.39
fi_ftb	92.28	79.86	75.64	65.22	61.76	95.02	86.90	83.64	70.66	68.89
fi_pud	95.84	83.33	80.15	73.16	65.46	86.74	65.44	54.12	48.74	50.14
fi_tdt	94.37	80.28	76.45	68.58	62.19	96.16	86.30	83.63	72.84	67.63
fo_oft	44.66	42.64	25.19	0.36	5.56	59.61	57.64	44.51	0.52	11.30
fr_gsd	95.75	84.17	81.05	72.16	74.22	96.12	87.56	84.74	75.31	78.44
fr_sequoia	95.84	83.85	81.12	71.34	74.41	97.83	89.66	88.11	77.90	82.62
fr_spoken	92.94	71.46	65.56	53.46	54.67	97.11	77.61	73.04	62.46	62.14
fro_srcmf	94.30	85.27	79.27	70.70	74.45	76.67	67.47	52.97	35.06	44.91
ga_idt	89.21	72.66	62.93	37.66	42.06	91.46	75.84	66.54	36.66	45.17
gl_ctg	96.26	79.15	76.10	62.11	65.29	96.92	82.93	80.46	67.90	70.93
gl_treegal	91.09	71.61	66.16	49.13	51.60	95.12	77.50	72.54	53.42	58.05
got_proiel	94.31	68.59	62.16	48.57	55.02	94.21	70.33	63.38	47.31	55.86
grc_perseus	82.37	64.40	57.75	31.05	38.74	90.45	71.11	65.00	39.96	43.70
grc_proiel	95.87	71.99	67.57	49.51	55.85	96.39	76.27	71.64	51.57	59.41
he_htb	80.87	62.18	57.86	44.09	46.51	82.60	65.68	62.13	47.57	51.89
hi_hdtb	95.75	91.41	87.15	69.09	79.93	97.48	94.22	91.08	72.79	63.66
hr_set	96.33	84.49	78.61	58.72	70.26	97.88	89.59	84.83	61.70	76.31
hsb_ufal	65.75	35.02	23.64	3.55	11.72	76.60	54.86	46.42	7.67	20.17
hu_szeged	90.59	72.55	66.76	52.82	56.92	95.14	79.93	74.80	58.08	64.77
hy_armtdp	65.40	36.81	21.79	6.84	11.94	43.41	33.17	11.61	1.13	5.36
id_gsd	92.99	80.63	74.37	63.42	62.50	93.79	83.98	77.66	65.76	65.99
it_isdt	97.05	88.91	86.26	77.06	77.12	97.93	91.22	89.14	79.79	81.00
it_postwita	93.94	72.34	66.81	53.64	53.99	95.43	77.21	72.54	57.89	59.96
ja_gsd	87.85	74.49	72.32	58.35	60.17	90.29	80.60	78.77	62.39	60.62
ja_modern	48.44	29.36	22.71	8.10	9.49	53.36	34.11	27.01	11.08	12.45
kk_ktb	48.94	39.45	24.21	7.62	9.79	40.98	21.92	7.10	0.95	2.65
kmr_mg	59.31	32.86	23.92	5.47	11.86	42.08	25.80	9.39	0.55	4.02
ko_gsd	93.44	69.21	61.40	54.10	50.50	95.56	85.21	81.82	76.51	68.66

Table 4: Accuracy of different parsing models on the evaluation set. POS tags are jointly predicted with parsing. LID = Language tag, TRN = Transliteration/normalization.

	BASELINE UDPipe 1.2					SLT-Interactions				
	UPOS	**ULAS**	**LAS**	**MLAS**	**BLEX**	**UPOS**	**ULAS**	**LAS**	**MLAS**	**BLEX**
All treebanks	87.32	71.64	65.80	52.42	55.80	88.12	75.46	69.98	54.52	59.68
Big treebanks	93.71	78.78	74.14	61.27	64.67	95.11	83.50	79.67	64.95	69.77
Parallel treebanks	85.23	71.22	66.63	51.75	54.87	85.07	70.96	64.73	48.47	54.90
Small treebanks	87.36	63.17	55.01	38.80	41.06	87.36	65.17	56.74	35.73	42.90
Low-resource treebanks	45.20	30.08	17.17	3.44	7.63	43.04	31.48	17.47	1.79	6.95

Table 5: POS tagging accuracies of different models on CS evaluation set. SP = stack-prop.

Joakim Nivre. 2003. An efficient algorithm for projective dependency parsing. In *Proceedings of the 8th International Workshop on Parsing Technologies (IWPT)*. Citeseer.

Joakim Nivre. 2009. Non-projective dependency parsing in expected linear time. In *Proceedings of the Joint Conference of the 47th Annual Meeting of the ACL and the 4th International Joint Conference on Natural Language Processing of the AFNLP: Volume 1-Volume 1*. Association for Computational Linguistics, pages 351–359.

Joakim Nivre, Marco Kuhlmann, and Johan Hall. 2009. An improved oracle for dependency parsing with online reordering. In *Proceedings of the 11th international conference on parsing technologies*. Association for Computational Linguistics, pages 73–76.

Andrew M Saxe, James L McClelland, and Surya Ganguli. 2013. Exact solutions to the nonlinear dynamics of learning in deep linear neural networks. *arXiv preprint arXiv:1312.6120*.

Milan Straka and Jana Straková. 2017. Tokenizing, pos tagging, lemmatizing and parsing ud 2.0 with udpipe. In *Proceedings of the CoNLL 2017 Shared Task: Multilingual Parsing from Raw Text to Universal Dependencies*. Association for Computational Linguistics, Vancouver, Canada, pages 88–99. http://www.aclweb.org/anthology/K/K17/K17-3009.pdf.

Hongmin Wang, Yue Zhang, GuangYong Leonard Chan, Jie Yang, and Hai Leong Chieu. 2017. Universal dependencies parsing for colloquial singaporean english. In *Proceedings of the 55th Annual Meeting of the Association for Computational Linguistics (Volume 1: Long Papers)*. Association for Computational Linguistics, Vancouver, Canada, pages 1732–1744.

Daniel Zeman, Jan Hajič, Martin Popel, Martin Potthast, Milan Straka, Filip Ginter, Joakim Nivre, and Slav Petrov. 2018. CoNLL 2018 Shared Task: Multilingual Parsing from Raw Text to Universal Dependencies. In *Proceedings of the CoNLL 2018 Shared Task: Multilingual Parsing from Raw Text to Universal Dependencies*. Association for Computational Linguistics, Brussels, Belgium, pages 1–20.

Yuan Zhang and David Weiss. 2016. Stack-propagation: Improved representation learning for syntax. In *Proceedings of the 54th Annual Meeting of the Association for Computational Linguistics (Volume 1: Long Papers)*. Association for Computational Linguistics, Berlin, Germany, pages 1557–1566.

Universal Dependency Parsing from Scratch

Peng Qi,* Timothy Dozat,* Yuhao Zhang,* Christopher D. Manning
Stanford University
Stanford, CA 94305
{pengqi, tdozat, yuhaozhang, manning}@stanford.edu

Abstract

This paper describes Stanford's system at the *CoNLL 2018 UD Shared Task*. We introduce a complete neural pipeline system that takes raw text as input, and performs all tasks required by the shared task, ranging from tokenization and sentence segmentation, to POS tagging and dependency parsing. Our single system submission achieved very competitive performance on big treebanks. Moreover, after fixing an unfortunate bug, our corrected system would have placed the 2nd, 1st, and 3rd on the official evaluation metrics LAS, MLAS, and BLEX, and would have outperformed all submission systems on low-resource treebank categories on all metrics by a large margin. We further show the effectiveness of different model components through extensive ablation studies.

1 Introduction

Dependency parsing is an important component in various natural langauge processing (NLP) systems for semantic role labeling (Marcheggiani and Titov, 2017), relation extraction (Zhang et al., 2018), and machine translation (Chen et al., 2017). However, most research has treated dependency parsing in isolation, and largely ignored upstream NLP components that prepare relevant data for the parser, *e.g.*, tokenizers and lemmatizers (Zeman et al., 2017). In reality, however, these upstream systems are still far from perfect.

To this end, in our submission to the *CoNLL 2018 UD Shared Task*, we built a raw-text-to-CoNLL-U pipeline system that performs all tasks required by the Shared Task (Zeman et al., 2018).[1] Harnessing the power of neural systems, this pipeline achieves competitive performance in each of the inter-linked stages: tokenization, sentence and word segmentation, part-of-speech (POS)/morphological features (UFeats) tagging, lemmatization, and finally, dependency parsing. Our main contributions include:

- New methods for combining symbolic statistical knowledge with flexible, powerful neural systems to improve robustness;
- A biaffine classifier for joint POS/UFeats prediction that improves prediction consistency;
- A lemmatizer enhanced with an *edit* classifier that improves the robustness of a sequence-to-sequence model on rare sequences; and
- Extensions to our parser from (Dozat et al., 2017) to model linearization.

Our system achieves competitive performance on big treebanks. After fixing an unfortunate bug, the corrected system would have placed the 2nd, 1st, and 3rd on the official evaluation metrics LAS, MLAS, and BLEX, and would have outperformed all submission systems on low-resource treebank categories on all metrics by a large margin. We perform extensive ablation studies to demonstrate the effectiveness of our novel methods, and highlight future directions to improve the system.[2]

2 System Description

In this section, we present detailed descriptions for each component of our neural pipeline system, namely the tokenizer, the POS/UFeats tagger, the lemmatizer, and finally the dependency parser.

---

*These authors contributed roughly equally.

[1]We chose to develop a pipeline system mainly because it allows easier parallel development and faster model tuning in a shared task context.

[2]To facilitate future research, we make our implementation public at: `https://github.com/stanfordnlp/UD-from-scratch`.

Proceedings of the CoNLL 2018 Shared Task: Multilingual Parsing from Raw Text to Universal Dependencies, pages 160–170
Brussels, Belgium, October 31 – November 1, 2018. ©2018 Association for Computational Linguistics
https://doi.org/10.18653/v1/K18-2016

2.1 Tokenizer

To prepare sentences in the form of a list of words for downstream processing, the tokenizer component reads raw text and outputs sentences in the CoNLL-U format. This is achieved with two subsystems: one for joint tokenization and sentence segmentation, and the other for splitting multiword tokens into syntactic words.

Tokenization and sentence segmentation. We treat joint tokenization and sentence segmentation as a unit-level sequence tagging problem. For most languages, a *unit* of text is a single character; however, in Vietnamese orthography, the most natural units of text are single *syllables*.[3] We assign one out of five tags to each of these units: end of token (EOT), end of sentence (EOS), multi-word token (MWT), multi-word end of sentence (MWS), and other (OTHER). We use bidirectional LSTMs (BiLSTMs) as the base model to make unit-level predictions. At each unit, the model predicts hierarchically: it first decides whether a given unit is at the end of a token with a score $s^{(\text{tok})}$, then classifies token endings into finer-grained categories with two independent binary classifiers: one for sentence ending $s^{(\text{sent})}$, and one for MWT $s^{(\text{MWT})}$.

Since sentence boundaries and MWTs usually require a larger context to determine (*e.g.*, periods following abbreviations or the ambiguous word "des" in French), we incorporate token-level information into a two-layer BiLSTM as follows (see also Figure 1). The first layer BiLSTM operates directly on raw units, and makes an initial prediction over the categories. To help capture local unit patterns more easily, we also combine the first-layer BiLSTM with 1-D convolutional networks, by using a one hidden layer convolutional network (CNN) with ReLU nolinearity at its first layer, giving an effect a little like a residual connection (He et al., 2016). The output of the CNN is simply added to the concatenated hidden states of the BiLSTM for downstream computation:

$$\mathbf{h}_1^{\text{RNN}} = [\overrightarrow{\mathbf{h}_1}, \overleftarrow{\mathbf{h}_1}] = \text{BiLSTM}_1(\mathbf{x}), \quad (1)$$

$$\mathbf{h}_1^{\text{CNN}} = \text{CNN}(\mathbf{x}), \quad (2)$$

$$\mathbf{h}_1 = \mathbf{h}_1^{\text{RNN}} + \mathbf{h}_1^{\text{CNN}}, \quad (3)$$

$$[\mathbf{s}_1^{(\text{tok})}, \mathbf{s}_1^{(\text{sent})}, \mathbf{s}_1^{(\text{MWT})}] = W_1 \mathbf{h}_1, \quad (4)$$

where $\mathbf{x}$ is the input character representations,

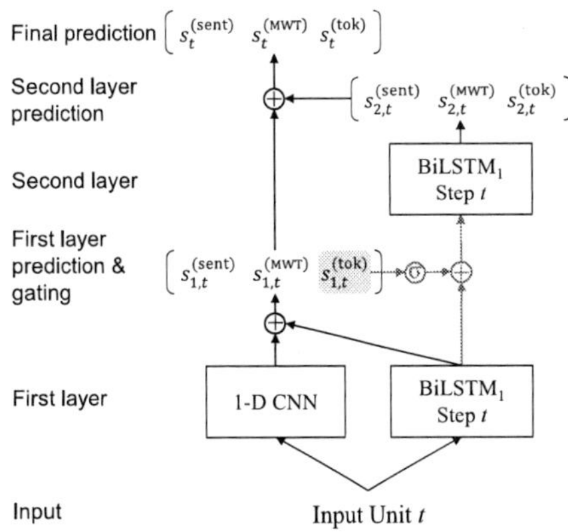

Figure 1: Illustration of the tokenizer/sentence segmenter model. Components in blue represent the gating mechanism between the two layers.

and W_1 contains the weights and biases for a linear classifier.[4] For each unit, we concatenate its trainable embedding with a four-dimensional binary feature vector as input, each dimension corresponding to one of the following feature functions: (1) does the unit start with whitespace; (2) does it start with a capitalized letter; (3) is the unit fully capitalized; and (4) is it purely numerical.

To incorporate token-level information at the second layer, we use a gating mechanism to suppress representations at non-token boundaries before propagating hidden states upward:

$$\mathbf{g}_1 = \mathbf{h}_1 \odot \sigma(\mathbf{s}_1^{(\text{tok})}) \quad (5)$$

$$\mathbf{h}_2 = [\overrightarrow{\mathbf{h}_2}, \overleftarrow{\mathbf{h}_2}] = \text{BiLSTM}_2(\mathbf{g}_1), \quad (6)$$

$$[\mathbf{s}_2^{(\text{tok})}, \mathbf{s}_2^{(\text{sent})}, \mathbf{s}_2^{(\text{MWT})}] = W_2 \mathbf{h}_2, \quad (7)$$

where $\odot$ is an element-wise product broadcast over all dimensions of $\mathbf{h}_1$ for each unit. This can be viewed as a simpler alternative to multi-resolution RNNs (Serban et al., 2017), where the first-layer BiLSTM operates at the unit level, and the second layer operates at the token level. Unlike multi-resolution RNNs, this formulation is end-to-end differentiable, and can more easily leverage efficient off-the-shelf RNN implementations.

To combine predictions from both layers of the BiLSTM, we simply sum the scores to obtain $\mathbf{s}^{(X)} = \mathbf{s}_1^{(X)} + \mathbf{s}_2^{(X)}$, where $X \in \{\text{tok, sent, MWT}\}$. The final probability over the tags is then

$$p_{\text{EOT}} = p_{+--} \qquad p_{\text{EOS}} = p_{++-}, \quad (8)$$

$$p_{\text{MWT}} = p_{+-+} \qquad p_{\text{MWS}} = p_{+++}, \quad (9)$$

where $p_{\pm\pm\pm} = \sigma(\pm s^{(\text{tok})})\sigma(\pm s^{(\text{sent})})\sigma(\pm s^{(\text{MWT})})$,

---

[3] In this case, we define a syllable as a consecutive run of alphabetic characters, numbers, or individual symbols, together with any leading white spaces before them.

[4] We will omit bias terms in affine transforms for clarity.

and $\sigma(\cdot)$ is the logistic sigmoid function. p_{OTHER} is simply $\sigma(-s^{(\text{tok})})$. The model is trained to minimize the standard cross entropy loss.

Multi-word Token Expansion. The tokenizer/sentence segmenter produces a collection of sentences, each being a list of tokens, some of which are labeled as multi-word tokens (MWTs). We must expand these MWTs into the underlying syntactic words they correspond to (*e.g.*, "im" to "in dem" in German), in order for downstream systems to process them properly. To achieve this, we take a hybrid approach to combine symbolic statistical knowledge with the power of neural systems.

The symbolic statistical side is a frequency lexicon. Many languages, like German, have only a handful of rules for expanding a few MWTs. We leverage this information by simply counting the number of times a MWT is expanded into different sequences of words in the training set, and retaining the most frequent expansion in a dictionary to use at test time. When building this dictionary, we lowercase all words in the expansions to improve robustness. However, this approach would fail for languages with rich clitics, a large set of unique MWTs, and/or complex rules for MWT expansion, such as Arabic and Hebrew. We capture this by introducing a powerful neural system.

Specifically, we train a sequence-to-sequence model using a BiLSTM encoder with an attention mechanism (Bahdanau et al., 2015) in the form of a multi-layer perceptron (MLP). Formally, the input multi-word token is represented by a sequence of characters $x_1, \ldots, x_I$, and the output syntactic words are represented similarly as a sequence of characters $y_1, \ldots, y_J$, where the words are separated by space characters. Inputs to the RNNs are encoded by a shared matrix of character embeddings E. Once the encoder hidden states $\mathbf{h}^{\text{enc}}$ are obtained with a single-layer BiLSTM, each decoder step is unrolled as follows:

$$\mathbf{h}_j^{\text{dec}} = \text{LSTM}_{\text{dec}}(E_{y_{j-1}}, \mathbf{h}_{j-1}^{\text{dec}}), \tag{10}$$

$$\alpha_{ij} \propto \exp(\mathbf{u}_\alpha^\top \tanh(W_\alpha[\mathbf{h}_j^{\text{dec}}, \mathbf{h}_i^{\text{enc}}])), \tag{11}$$

$$\mathbf{c}_j = \sum_i \alpha_{ij} \mathbf{h}_i^{\text{enc}}, \tag{12}$$

$$P(y_j = w | y_{<j}) \propto \mathbf{u}_w^\top \tanh(W[\mathbf{h}_j^{\text{dec}}, \mathbf{c}_j]). \tag{13}$$

Here, w is a character index in the output vocabulary, y_0 a special start-of-sequence symbol in the vocabulary, and $\mathbf{h}_0^{\text{dec}}$ the concatenation of the last hidden states of each direction of the encoder.

To bring the symbolic and neural systems together, we train them separately and use the following protocol during evaluation: for each MWT, we first look it up in the dictionary, and return the expansion recorded there if one can be found. If this fails, we retry by lowercasing the incoming token. If that fails again, we resort to the neural system to predict the final expansion. This allows us to not only account for languages with flexible MWTs patterns (Arabic and Hebrew), but also leverage the training set statistics to cover both languages with simpler MWT rules, and MWTs in the flexible languages seen in the training set without fail. This results in a high-performance, robust system for multi-word token expansion.

2.2 POS/UFeats Tagger

Our tagger follows closely that of (Dozat et al., 2017), with a few extensions. As in that work, the core of the tagger is a highway BiLSTM (Srivastava et al., 2015) with inputs coming from the concatenation of three sources: (1) a pretrained word embedding, from the word2vec embeddings provided with the task when available (Mikolov et al., 2013), and from fastText embeddings otherwise (Bojanowski et al., 2017); (2) a trainable frequent word embedding, for all words that occurred at least seven times in the training set; and (3) a character-level embedding, generated from a unidirectional LSTM over characters in each word. UPOS is predicted by first transforming each word's BiLSTM state with a fully-connected (FC) layer, then applying an affine classifier:

$$\mathbf{h}_i = \text{BiLSTM}_i^{(\text{tag})}(\mathbf{x}_1, \ldots, \mathbf{x}_n), \tag{14}$$

$$\mathbf{v}_i^{(\text{u})} = \text{FC}^{(\text{u})}(\mathbf{h}_i), \tag{15}$$

$$P(y_{ik}^{(\text{u})} | X) = \text{softmax}_k(W^{(\text{u})}\mathbf{v}_i^{(\text{u})}). \tag{16}$$

To predict XPOS, we similarly start with transforming the BiLSTM states with an FC layer. In order to further ensure consistency between the different tagsets (*e.g.*, to avoid a VERB UPOS with an NN XPOS), we use a *biaffine* classifier, conditioned on a word's XPOS state as well as an embedding for its gold (at training time) or predicted (at inference time) UPOS tag $y_{i*}^{(\text{u})}$:

$$\mathbf{v}_i^{(\text{x})} = \text{FC}^{(\text{x})}(\mathbf{h}_i), \tag{17}$$

$$\mathbf{s}_i^{(\text{x})} = [E_{y_{i*}^{(\text{u})}}^{(\text{u})}, 1]^\top \mathbf{U}^{(\text{x})}[\mathbf{v}_i^{(\text{x})}, 1], \tag{18}$$

$$P(y_{ik}^{(\text{x})} | y_{i*}^{(\text{u})}, X) = \text{softmax}_k(\mathbf{s}_i^{(\text{x})}). \tag{19}$$

UFeats is predicted analogously with separate parameters for each individual UFeat tag. The tagger is also trained to minimize the cross entropy loss.

Some languages have composite XPOS tags, yielding a very large XPOS tag space (*e.g.*, Arabic and Czech). For these languages, the biaffine classifier requires a prohibitively large weight tensor $\mathbf{U}^{(x)}$. For languages that use XPOS tagsets with a fixed number of characters, we classify each character of the XPOS tag in the same way we classify each UFeat. For the rest, instead of taking the biaffine approach, we simply share the FC layer between all three affine classifiers, hoping that the learned features for one will be used by another.

2.3 Lemmatizer

For the lemmatizer, we take a very similar approach to that of the multi-word token expansion component introduced in Section 2.1 with two key distinctions customized to lemmatization.

First, we build two dictionaries from the training set, one from a (word, UPOS) pair to the lemma, and the other from the word itself to the lemma. During evaluation, the predicted UPOS is used. When the UPOS-augmented dictionary fails, we fall back to the word-only dictionary before resorting to the neural system. In looking up both dictionaries, the word is never lowercased, because case information is more relevant in lemmatization than in MWT expansion.

Second, we enhance the neural system with an *edit* classifier that shortcuts the prediction process to accommodate rare, long words, on which the decoder is more likely to flounder. The concatenated encoder final states are put through an FC layer with ReLU nonlinearity and fed into a 3-way classifier, which predicts whether the lemma is (1) exactly identical to the word (*e.g.*, URLs and emails), (2) the lowercased version of the word (*e.g.*, capitalized rare words in English that are not proper nouns), or (3) in need of the sequence-to-sequence model to make more complex edits to the character sequence. During training time, we assign the labels to each word-lemma pair greedily in the order of identical, lowercase, and sequence decoder, and train the classifier jointly with the sequence-to-sequence lemmatizer. At evaluation time, predictions are made sequentially, *i.e.*, the classifier first determines whether any shortcut can be taken, before the sequence decoder model is used if needed.

2.4 Dependency Parser

The dependency parser also follows that of (Dozat et al., 2017) with a few augmentations. The highway BiLSTM takes as input pretrained word embeddings, frequent word and lemma embeddings, character-level word embeddings, summed XPOS and UPOS embeddings, and summed UFeats embeddings. In (Dozat et al., 2017), unlabeled attachments are predicted by scoring each word i and its potential heads with a biaffine transformation

$$\mathbf{h}_t = \text{BiLSTM}_t^{(\text{parse})}(\mathbf{x}_1, \ldots, \mathbf{x}_n), \quad (20)$$

$$\mathbf{v}_i^{(\text{ed})}, \mathbf{v}_j^{(\text{eh})} = \text{FC}^{(\text{ed})}(\mathbf{h}_i), \text{FC}^{(\text{eh})}(\mathbf{h}_j), \quad (21)$$

$$s_{ij}^{(e)} = [\mathbf{v}_j^{(\text{eh})}, 1]^\top U^{(e)}[\mathbf{v}_i^{(\text{ed})}, 1], \quad (22)$$

$$= \text{Deep-Biaff}^{(e)}(\mathbf{h}_i, \mathbf{h}_j), \quad (23)$$

$$P(y_{ij}^{(e)}|X) = \text{softmax}_j(\mathbf{s}_i^{(e)}), \quad (24)$$

where $\mathbf{v}_i^{(\text{ed})}$ is word i's *edge-dependent* representation and $\mathbf{v}_i^{(\text{eh})}$ its *edge-head* representation. This approach, however, does not explicitly take into consideration relative locations of heads and dependents during prediction; instead, such predictive location information must be implicitly learned by the BiLSTM. Ideally, we would like the model to explicitly condition on $(i - j)$, namely the dependent i and its potential head j's location relative to each other, in modeling $p(y_{ij})$.[5]

Here, we motivate one way to build this into the model. First we factorize the relative location of word i and head j into their *linear order* and the *distance* between them, *i.e.*, $P(y_{ij}|\text{sgn}(i - j), \text{abs}(i - j))$, where $\text{sgn}(\cdot)$ is the sign function. Applying Bayes' rule and assuming conditional independence, we arrive at the following

$$P(y_{ij}|\text{sgn}(i - j), \text{abs}(i - j)) \propto \quad (25)$$
$$P(y_{ij})P(\text{sgn}(i - j)|y_{ij})P(\text{abs}(i - j)|y_{ij}).$$

In a language where heads always follow their dependents, $P(\text{sgn}(i - j) = 1|y_{ij})$ would be extremely low, heavily penalizing rightward attachments. Similarly, in a language where dependencies are always short, $P(\text{abs}(i-j) \gg 0|y_{ij})$ would be extremely low, penalizing longer edges.

$P(y_{ij})$ can remain the same as computed in Eq. (24). $P(\text{sgn}(i - j)|y_{ij})$ can be computed similarly with a deep biaffine scorer (cf. Eqs. (20)–(23)) over the recurrent states. This results in the score of j preceding i; flipping the sign wherever i precedes j turns this into the log odds of the ob-

---

[5]Henceforth we omit the (e) superscript and X.

served linearization. Applying the sigmoid function then turns it into a probability:

$$s_{ij}^{(l)} = \text{Deep-Biaff}^{(l)}(\mathbf{h}_i, \mathbf{h}_j), \quad (26)$$

$$s_{ij}'^{(l)} = \text{sgn}(i - j)s_{ij}^{(l)}, \quad (27)$$

$$P(\text{sgn}(i - j)|y_{ij}) = \sigma(s_{ij}'^{(l)}). \quad (28)$$

This can be effortlessly incorporated into the edge score by adding in the log of this probability $-\log(1 + \exp(-s_{ij}'^{(l)}))$. Error is not backpropagated to this submodule through the final attachment loss; instead, it is trained with its own cross entropy, with error only computed on gold edges. This ensures that the model learns the conditional probability *given a true edge*, rather than just learning to predict the linear order of two words.

For $P(\text{abs}(i - j)|y_{ij})$, we use another deep biaffine scorer to generate a distance score. Distances are always no less than 1, so we apply $1 + \text{softplus}$ to predict the distance between i and j when there's an edge between them:

$$s_{ij}^{(d)} = \text{Deep-Biaff}^{(d)}(\mathbf{h}_i, \mathbf{h}_j), \quad (29)$$

$$s_{ij}'^{(d)} = 1 + \text{softplus}(s_{ij}^{(d)}). \quad (30)$$

where $\text{softplus}(x) = \log(1 + \exp(x))$. The distribution of edge lengths in the treebanks roughly follows a Zipfian distribution, to which the Cauchy distribution is closely related, only the latter is more stable for values at or near zero. Thus, rather than modeling the probability of an arc's length, we can use the Cauchy distribution to model the probability of an arc's *error* in predicted length, namely how likely it is for the predicted distance and the true distance to have a difference of $\delta_{ij}^{(d)}$:

$$\text{Zipf}(k; \alpha, \beta) \propto (k^\alpha / \beta)^{-1}, \quad (31)$$

$$\text{Cauchy}(x; \gamma) \propto (1 + x^2/\gamma)^{-1} \quad (32)$$

$$\delta_{ij}^{(d)} = \text{abs}(i - j) - s_{ij}'^{(d)}, \quad (33)$$

$$P(\text{abs}(i - j)|y_{ij}) \propto (1 + \delta_{ij}^{2(d)}/2)^{-1}. \quad (34)$$

When the difference $\delta_{ij}^{(d)}$ is small or zero, there will be effectively no penalty; but when the model expects a significantly longer or shorter arc than the observed distance between i and j, it is discouraged from assigning an edge between them. As with the linear order probability, the log of the distance probability is added to the edge score, and trained with its own cross-entropy on gold edges.[6]

At inference time, the Chu-Liu/Edmonds algorithm (Chu and Liu, 1965; Edmonds, 1967) is used to ensure a maximum spanning tree. Dependency relations are assigned to gold (at training time) or predicted (at inference time) edges $y_{i*}^{(e)}$ using another deep biaffine classifier, following (Dozat et al., 2017) with no augmentations:

$$\mathbf{s}_i^{(r)} = \text{Deep-Biaff}^{(r)}(\mathbf{h}_i, \mathbf{h}_{y_{i*}^{(e)}}), \quad (35)$$

$$P(y_{ik}^{(r)}|y_{i*}^{(e)}) = \text{softmax}_k(\mathbf{s}_i^{(r)}). \quad (36)$$

3 Training Details

Except where otherwise stated, our system is a pipeline: given a document of raw text, the tokenizer/sentence segmenter/MWT expander first splits it into sentences of syntactic words; the tagger then assigns UPOS, XPOS and UFeat tags to each word; the lemmatizer takes the predicted word and UPOS tag and outputs a lemma; finally, the parser takes all annotations as input and predicts the head and dependency label for each word.

All components are trained with early stopping on the dev set when applicable. When a dev set is unavailable, we split the training set into an approximately 7-to-1 split for training and development. All components (except the dependency parser) are trained and evaluated on the development set assuming all related components had oracle implementations. This means the tokenizer/sentence segmenter assumes all correctly predicted MWTs will be correctly expanded, the MWT expander assumes gold word segmentation, and all downstream tasks assume gold word segmentation, along with gold annotations of all prerequisite tasks. The dependency parser is trained with predicted tags and morphological features from the POS/UFeats tagger.

Treebanks without training data. For treebanks without training data, we adopt a heuristic approach for finding replacements. Where a larger treebank in the same language is available (*i.e.*, all PUD treebanks and Japanese-Modern), we used the models from the largest treebank available in that language. Where treebanks in related languages are available (as determined by language families from Wikipedia), we use models from the largest treebank in that related language. We

---

[6]Note that the penalty assigned to the edge score in this way is proportional to $\ln \delta_{ij}^{(d)}$ for high $\delta_{ij}^{(d)}$; using a Gamma or Poisson distribution to model the distance directly, or using a normal distribution instead of Cauchy, respectively, assigns penalties roughly proportional to $\delta_{ij}^{(d)}$, $\ln \Gamma(\delta_{ij}^{(d)})$, and $\delta_{ij}^{2(d)}$. Thus, the Cauchy is more numerically stable during training.

ended up choosing the models from English-EWT for Naija (an English-based pidgin), Irish-IDT for Breton (both are Celtic), and Norwegian-Nynorsk for Faroese (both are West Scandinavian). For Thai, since it uses a different script from all other languages, we use UDPipe 1.2 for all components.

Hyperparameters. The tokenizer/sentence segmenter uses BiLSTMs with 64d hidden states in each direction and takes 32d character embeddings as input. During training, we employ dropout to the input embeddings and hidden states at each layer with $p = .33$. We also randomly replace the input unit with a special <UNK> unit with $p = .33$, which would be used in place of any unseen input at test time. We add noise to the gating mechanism in Eq. (6) by randomly setting the gates to 1 with $p = .02$ and setting its temperature to 2 to make the model more robust to tokenization errors at test time. Optimization is performed with Adam (Kingma and Ba, 2015) with an initial learning rate of .002 for up to 20,000 steps, and whenever dev performance deteriorates, as is evaluated every 200 steps after the 2,000[th] step, the learning rate is multiplied by .999. For the convolutional component we use filter sizes of 1 and 9, and for each filter size we use 64 channels (same as one direction in the BiLSTM). The convolutional outputs are concatenated in the hidden layer, before an affine transform is applied to serve as a residual connection for the BiLSTM. For the MWT expander, we use BiLSTMs with 256d hidden states in each direction as the encoder, a 512d LSTM decoder, 64d character embeddings as input, and dropout rate $p = .5$ for the inputs and hidden states. Models are trained up to 100 epochs with the standard Adam hyperparameters, and the learning rate is annealed similarly every epoch after the 15th epoch by a factor of 0.9. Beam search of beam size 8 is employed in evaluation.

The lemmatizer uses BiLSTMs with 100d hidden states in each direction of the encoder, 50d character embeddings as input, and dropout rate $p = .5$ for the inputs and hidden states. The decoder is an LSTM with 200d hidden states. During training we jointly minimize (with equal weights) the cross-entropy loss of the edit classifier and the negative log-likelihood loss of the seq2seq lemmatizer. Models are trained up to 60 epochs with standard Adam hyperparameters.

The tagger and parser share most of their hyperparameters. We use 75d uncased frequent word and lemma embeddings, and 50d POS tag and UFeat embeddings. Pretrained embeddings and character-based word representations are both transformed to be 125d. During training, all embeddings are randomly replaced with a <drop> symbol with $p = .33$. We use 2-layer 200d BiLSTMs for the tagger and 3-layer 400d BiLSTMs for the parser. We employ dropout in all feedforward connections with $p = .5$ and all recurrent connections (Gal and Ghahramani, 2016) with $p = .25$ (except $p = .5$ in the tagger BiLSTM). All classifiers use 400d FC layers (except 100d for UFeats) with the ReLU nonlinearity. We train the systems with Adam ($\alpha = .003$, $\beta_1 = .9$, $\beta_2 = .95$) until dev accuracy decreases, at which point we switch to AMSGrad (Reddi et al., 2018) until 3,000 steps pass with no dev accuracy increases.

4 Results

The main results are shown in Table 1. As can be seen from the table, our system achieves competitive performance on nearly all of the metrics when macro-averaged over all treebanks. Moreover, it achieves the top performance on several metrics when evaluated only on big treebanks, showing that our systems can effectively leverage statistical patterns in the data. Where it is not the top performing system, our system also achieved competitive results on each of the metrics on these treebanks. This is encouraging considering that our system is comprised of single-system components, whereas some of the best performing teams used ensembles (*e.g.*, HIT-SCIR (Che et al., 2018)).

When taking a closer look, we find that our UFeats classifier is very accurate on these treebanks as well. Not only did it achieve the top performance on UFeats F_1, but also it helped the parser achieve top MLAS as well on big treebanks, even when the parser is not the best-performing as evaluated by other metrics. We also note the contribution from our consistency modeling in the POS tagger/UFeats classifier: in both settings the individual metrics (UPOS, XPOS, and UFeats) achieve a lower advantage margin over the reference systems when compared to the AllTags metric, showing that these reference systems, though sometimes more accurate on each individual task, are not as consistent as our system overall.

The biggest disparity between the all-treebanks and big-treebanks results comes from sentence

(a) Results on all treebanks

System	Tokens	Sent	Words	Lemmas	UPOS	XPOS	UFeats	AllTags	UAS	CLAS	LAS	MLAS	BLEX
Stanford	96.19	76.55	95.99	88.32	89.01	85.51	85.47	79.71	76.78	68.73	72.29	60.92	64.04
Reference	$98.42^{\dagger}$	$83.87^{\dagger}$	$98.18^{\ddagger}$	91.24^{*}	$90.91^{\ddagger}$	86.67^{*}	$87.59^{\ddagger}$	80.30^{*}	$80.51^{\dagger}$	$72.36^{\dagger}$	$75.84^{\dagger}$	61.25^{*}	66.09^{*}
Δ	−2.23	−7.32	−2.19	−2.92	−1.90	−1.16	−2.12	−0.59	−3.73	−3.63	−3.55	−0.33	−2.05
Stanford+	97.42	85.46	97.23	89.17	89.95	86.50	86.20	80.36	79.04	70.39	74.16	62.08	65.28
Δ	−1.00	**+1.59**	−0.95	−2.07	−0.96	−0.17	−1.39	**+0.06**	−1.47	−1.97	−1.68	**+0.83**	−0.81

(b) Results on big treebanks only

System	Tokens	Sent	Words	Lemmas	UPOS	XPOS	UFeats	AllTags	UAS	CLAS	LAS	MLAS	BLEX
Stanford	99.43	89.52	99.21	95.25	95.93	94.95	94.14	91.50	86.56	79.60	83.03	72.67	75.46
Reference	$99.51^{\dagger}$	$87.73^{\dagger}$	$99.16^{\dagger}$	96.08^{*}	$96.23^{\dagger}$	$95.16^{\dagger}$	94.11^{*}	91.45^{*}	$87.61^{\dagger}$	$81.29^{\dagger}$	$84.37^{\dagger}$	71.71^{*}	75.83^{*}
Δ	−0.08	**+1.79**	**+0.05**	−0.83	−0.30	−0.21	**+0.03**	**+0.05**	−1.05	−1.69	−1.34	**+0.96**	−0.37

Table 1: Evaluation results (F_1) on the test set, on all treebanks and big treebanks only. For each set of results on all metrics, we compare it against results from reference systems. A reference system is the top performing system on that metric if we are not top, or the second-best performing system on that metric. Reference systems are identified by superscripts (†: HIT-SCIR, ‡: Uppsala, ⋆: TurkuNLP, ∗: UDPipe Future). Shaded columns in the table indicate the three official evaluation metrics. "Stanford+" is our system after a bugfix evaluated unofficially; for more details please see the main text.

Treebanks	System	LAS	MLAS	BLEX
Small	Stanford+	**83.90**	**72.75**	**77.30**
	Reference	$69.53^{\dagger}$	$49.24^{\ddagger}$	$54.89^{\ddagger}$
Low-Res	Stanford+	**63.20**	**51.64**	**53.58**
	Reference	27.89^{*}	6.13^{*}	13.98^{*}
PUD	Stanford+	**82.25**	**74.20**	**74.37**
	Reference	$74.20^{\dagger}$	58.75^{*}	$63.25^{\bullet}$

Table 2: Evaluation results (F_1) on low-resource treebank test sets. Reference systems are identified by symbol superscripts (†: HIT-SCIR, ‡: ICS PAS, ⋆: CUNI x-ling, ∗: Stanford, •: TurkuNLP).

segmentation. After inspecting the results on smaller treebanks and double-checking our implementation, we noticed issues with how we processed data in the tokenizer that negatively impacted generalization on these treebanks.[7] This is devastating for these treebanks, as all downstream components process words at the sentence level.

We fixed this issue, and trained new tokenizers with all hyperparameters identical to our system at submission. We further built an unofficial evaluation pipeline, which we verified achieves the same evaluation results as the official system, and eval-

uated our entire pipeline by *only* replacing the tokenizer. As is shown in Table 1, the resulting system (Stanford+) is much more accurate overall, and we would have ranked 2nd, 1st, and 3rd on the official evaluation metrics LAS, MLAS, and BLEX, respectively.[8] On big treebanks, all metrics changed within only 0.02% F_1 and are thus not included. On small treebanks, however, this effect is more pronounced: as is shown in Table 2, our corrected system outperforms all submission systems on all official evaluation metrics on all low-resource treebanks by a large margin.

5 Analysis

In this section, we perform ablation studies on the new approaches we proposed for each component, and the contribution of each component to the final pipeline. For each component, we assume access to an oracle for all other components in the analysis, and show their efficacy on the dev sets.[9] For the ablations on the pipeline, we report macro-averaged F_1 on the test set.

---

[7]Specifically, our tokenizer was originally designed to be aware of newlines (\n) in double newline-separated paragraphs, but we accidentally prepared training and dev sets for low resource treebanks by putting each sentence on its own line in the text file. This resulted in the sentence segmenter overfitting to relying on newlines. In later experiments, we replaced all in-paragraph whitespaces with space characters.

[8]We note that the only system that is more accurate than ours on LAS is HIT's ensemble system, and we achieve very close performance to their system on MLAS (only 0.05% F_1 lower, which is likely within the statistical variation reported in the official evaluation).

[9]We perform treebank-level paired bootstrap tests for each ablated system against the top performing system in ablation with 10^5 bootstrap samples, and indicate statistical significance in tables with symbol superscripts (*:$p < 0.05$, **:$p < 0.01$, ***:$p < 0.001$).

System	Tokens	Sentences	Words
Stanford+	99.46	91.33	**99.27**
− gating	**99.47**	**91.34**	99.27
− conv	99.45	91.03	98.67
− seq2seq	–	–	98.97
− dropout	99.22*	88.78***	98.98*

Table 3: Ablation results for the tokenizer. All metrics in the table are macro-averaged dev F_1.

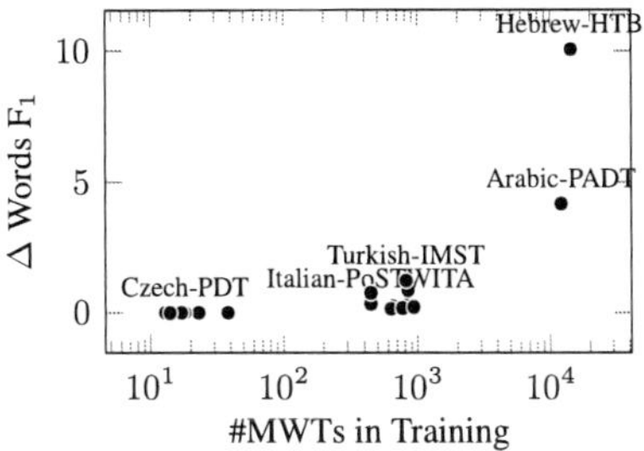

Figure 2: Effect of the seq2seq component for MWT expansion in the tokenizer.

Tokenizer. We perform ablation studies on the less standard components in the tokenizer, namely the gating mechanism in Eq. (6) (*gating*), the convolutional residual connections (*conv*), and the seq2seq model in the MWT expander (*seq2seq*), on all 61 big treebanks. As can be seen in Table 3, all but the gating mechanism make noticeable differences in macro F_1. When taking a closer look, we find that both *gating* and *conv* show a mixed contribution to each treebank, and we could have improved overall performance further through treebank-level component selection. One surprising discovery is that *conv* greatly helps identify MWTs in Hebrew (+34.89 Words F_1) and sentence breaks in Ancient Greek-PROIEL (+18.77 Sents F_1). In the case of *seq2seq*, although the overall macro difference is small, it helps with the word segmentation performance on all treebanks where it makes any meaningful difference, most notably +10.08 on Hebrew and +4.19 on Arabic in Words F_1 (see also Figure 2). Finally, we note that *dropout* plays an important role in safeguarding the tokenizer from overfitting.

POS/UFeats Tagger. The main novelty in our tagger is the explicit conditioning of XPOS and UFeats predictions on the UPOS prediction. We compare this against a tagger that simply shares the hidden features between the UPOS, XPOS, and UFeats classifiers. Since we used full-rank tensors in the biaffine classifier, treebanks with

System	UPOS	XPOS	UFeats	AllTags	PMI
Stanford	**96.50**	**95.87**	**95.01**	**92.52**	**.0514**
− biaff	96.47	95.71*	94.13***	91.32***	.0497*

Table 4: Ablation results for the tagger. All metrics are macro-averaged dev F_1, except PMI, which is explained in detail in the main text.

System	Big	Small	LowRes	All
Stanford	**96.56**	91.72*	**69.21**	**94.22**
− edit & seq2seq	89.97***	82.68***	63.50**	87.45***
− edit	96.48*	**91.80**	68.30	94.10
− dictionaries	95.37***	90.43***	66.02*	92.89***

Table 5: Ablation results for the lemmatizer, split by different groups of treebanks. All metrics in the table are macro-averaged dev F_1.

large, composite XPOS tagsets would incur prohibitive memory requirements. We therefore exclude treebanks that either have more than 250 XPOS tags or don't use them, leaving 36 treebanks for this analysis. We also measure consistency between tags by their pointwise mutual information

$$\text{PMI} = \log\left(\frac{p_c(\text{AllTags})}{p_c(\text{UPOS})p_c(\text{XPOS})p_c(\text{UFeats})}\right),$$

where $p_c(X)$ is the accuracy of X. This quantifies (in nats) how much more likely it is to get all tags right than we would expect given their individual accuracies, if they were independent. As can be seen in Table 4, the added parameters do not affect UPOS performance significantly, but do help improve XPOS and UFeats prediction. Moreover, the biaffine classifier is markedly more consistent than the affine one with shared representations.

Lemmatizer. We perform ablation studies on three individual components in our lemmatizer: the edit classifier (*edit*), the sequence-to-sequence module (*seq2seq*) and the dictionaries (*dictionaries*). As shown in Table 5, we find that our lemmatizer with all components achieves the best overall performance. Specifically, adding the neural components (i.e., *edit & seq2seq*) drastically improves overall lemmatization performance over a simple dictionary-based approach (+6.77 F_1), and the gains are consistent over different treebank groups. While adding the edit classifier slightly decreases the F_1 score on small treebanks, it improves the performance on low-resource languages substantially (+0.91 F_1), and therefore leads to an overall gain of 0.11 F_1. Tree-

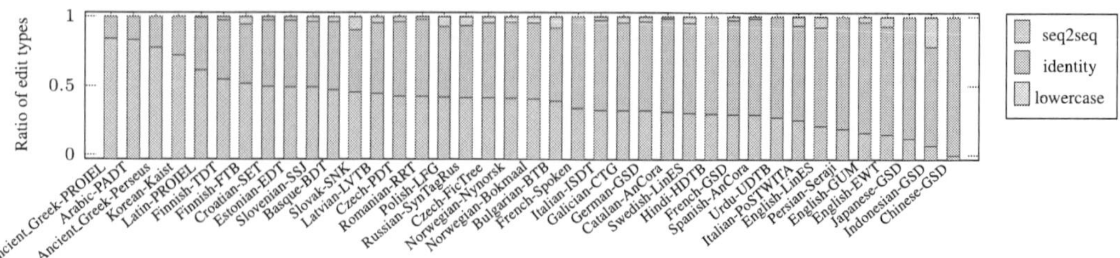

Figure 3: Edit operation types as output by the *edit* classifier on the official dev set. Due to space limit only treebanks containing over 120k dev words are shown and sorted by the ratio of *seq2seq* operation.

System	LAS	CLAS
Stanford	**87.60**	**84.68**
− *linearization*	87.55*	84.62*
− *distance*	87.43***	84.48***

Table 6: Ablation results for the parser. All metrics in the table are macro-averaged dev F_1.

banks where the largest gains are observed include Upper_Sorbian-UFAL (+4.55 F_1), Kurmanji-MG (+2.27 F_1) and English-LinES (+2.16 F_1). Finally, combining the neural lemmatizer with dictionaries helps capture common lemmatization patterns seen during training, leading to substantial improvements on all treebank groups.

To further understand the behavior of the edit classifier, for each treebank we present the ratio of all predicted edit types on dev set words in Figure 3. We find that the behavior of the edit classifier aligns well with linguistic knowledge. For example, while Ancient Greek, Arabic and Korean require a lot of complex edits in lemmatization, the vast majority of operations in Chinese and Japanese are simple identity mappings.

Dependency Parser. The main innovation for the parsing module is terms that model locations of a dependent word relative to possible head words in the sentence. Here we examine the impact of these terms, namely linearization (Eq. (28)) and distance (Eq. (34)). For this analysis, we exclude six treebanks with very small dev sets. As can be seen in Table 6, both terms contribute significantly to the final parser performance, with the distance term contributing slightly more.

Pipeline Ablation. We analyze the contribution of each pipeline component by incrementally replacing them with gold annotations and observing performance change. As shown in Figure 4, most downstream systems benefit moderately from gold sentence and word segmentation, while the parser

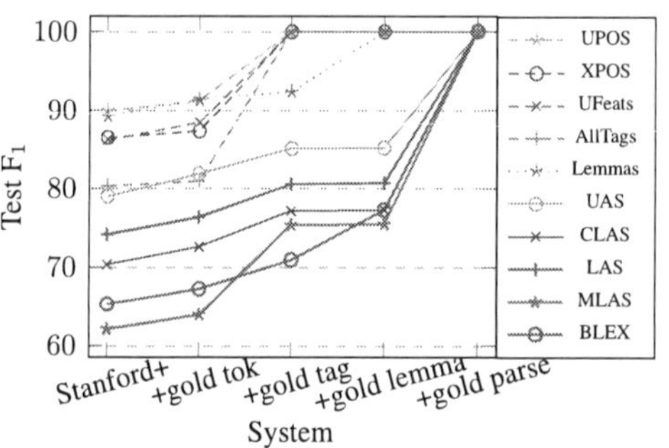

Figure 4: Pipeline ablation results. Dashed, dotted, and solid lines represent tagger, lemmatizer, and parser metrics, respectively. Official evaluation metrics are highlighted with thickened lines.

largely only benefits from improved POS/UFeats tagger performance (aside from BLEX, which is directly related to lemmatization performance and benefits notably). Finally, we note that the parser still is far from perfect even given gold annotations from all upstream tasks, but our components in the pipeline are very effective at closing the gap between predicted and gold annotations.

6 Conclusion & Future Directions

In this paper, we presented Stanford's submission to the *CoNLL 2018 UD Shared Task*. Our submission consists of neural components for each stage of a pipeline from raw text to dependency parses. The final system was very competitive on big treebanks; after fixing our preprocessing bug, it would have outperformed all official systems on all metrics for low-resource treebank categories.

One of the greatest opportunities for further gains is through the use of context-sensitive word embeddings, such as ELMo (Peters et al., 2018) and ULMfit (Howard and Ruder, 2018). Although this requires a large resource investment, HIT-SCIR (Che et al., 2018) has shown solid improvements from incorporating these embeddings.

References

Dzmitry Bahdanau, Kyunghyun Cho, and Yoshua Bengio. 2015. Neural machine translation by jointly learning to align and translate. *ICLR* .

Piotr Bojanowski, Edouard Grave, Armand Joulin, and Tomas Mikolov. 2017. Enriching word vectors with subword information. *Transactions of the Association for Computational Linguistics* 5:135–146. http://aclweb.org/anthology/Q17-1010.

Wanxiang Che, Yijia Liu, Yuxuan Zheng Bo Wang, and Ting Liu. 2018. Towards better UD parsing: Deep contextualized word embeddings, ensemble, and treebank concatenation. In *Proceedings of the CoNLL 2018 Shared Task: Multilingual Parsing from Raw Text to Universal Dependencies*.

Huadong Chen, Shujian Huang, David Chiang, and Jiajun Chen. 2017. Improved neural machine translation with a syntax-aware encoder and decoder. In *Proceedings of the 55th Annual Meeting of the Association for Computational Linguistics*.

Yoeng-Jin Chu and Tseng-Hong Liu. 1965. On the shortest arborescence of a directed graph. *Scientia Sinica* 14:1396–1400.

Timothy Dozat, Peng Qi, and Christopher D. Manning. 2017. Stanford's graph-based neural dependency parser at the CoNLL 2017 Shared Task. In *Proceedings of the CoNLL 2017 Shared Task: Multilingual Parsing from Raw Text to Universal Dependencies*. pages 20–30. http://www.aclweb.org/anthology/K/K17/K17-3002.pdf.

Jack Edmonds. 1967. Optimum branchings. *Journal of Research of the National Bureau of Standards* 71:233–240.

Yarin Gal and Zoubin Ghahramani. 2016. Dropout as a Bayesian approximation: Representing model uncertainty in deep learning. In *International Conference on Machine Learning*. pages 1050–1059.

Kaiming He, Xiangyu Zhang, Shaoqing Ren, and Jian Sun. 2016. Deep residual learning for image recognition. In *CVPR*.

Jeremy Howard and Sebastian Ruder. 2018. Universal language model fine-tuning for text classification. In *Proceedings of the 56th Annual Meeting of the Association for Computational Linguistics*.

Diederik P Kingma and Jimmy Ba. 2015. Adam: A method for stochastic optimization. *ICLR* .

Diego Marcheggiani and Ivan Titov. 2017. Encoding sentences with graph convolutional networks for semantic role labeling. In *Proceedings of the Conference on Empirical Methods for Natural Language Processing*.

Tomas Mikolov, Ilya Sutskever, Kai Chen, Greg S Corrado, and Jeff Dean. 2013. Distributed representations of words and phrases and their compositionality. In *Advances in Neural Information Processing Systems*. pages 3111–3119.

Matthew E Peters, Mark Neumann, Mohit Iyyer, Matt Gardner, Christopher Clark, Kenton Lee, and Luke Zettlemoyer. 2018. Deep contextualized word representations.

Sashank J Reddi, Satyen Kale, and Sanjiv Kumar. 2018. On the convergence of Adam and beyond. *ICLR* .

Iulian Vlad Serban, Tim Klinger, Gerald Tesauro, Kartik Talamadupula, Bowen Zhou, Yoshua Bengio, and Aaron C Courville. 2017. Multiresolution recurrent neural networks: An application to dialogue response generation. In *AAAI*. pages 3288–3294.

Rupesh Kumar Srivastava, Klaus Greff, and Jürgen Schmidhuber. 2015. Highway networks. In *Proceedings of the Deep Learning Workshop at the International Conference on Machine Learning*.

Daniel Zeman, Jan Hajič, Martin Popel, Martin Potthast, Milan Straka, Filip Ginter, Joakim Nivre, and Slav Petrov. 2018. CoNLL 2018 Shared Task: Multilingual Parsing from Raw Text to Universal Dependencies. In *Proceedings of the CoNLL 2018 Shared Task: Multilingual Parsing from Raw Text to Universal Dependencies*. Association for Computational Linguistics, Brussels, Belgium, pages 1–20.

Daniel Zeman, Martin Popel, Milan Straka, Jan Hajic, Joakim Nivre, Filip Ginter, Juhani Luotolahti, Sampo Pyysalo, Slav Petrov, Martin Potthast, Francis Tyers, Elena Badmaeva, Memduh Gokirmak, Anna Nedoluzhko, Silvie Cinkova, Jan Hajic jr., Jaroslava Hlavacova, Václava Kettnerová, Zdenka Uresova, Jenna Kanerva, Stina Ojala, Anna Missilä, Christopher D. Manning, Sebastian Schuster, Siva Reddy, Dima Taji, Nizar Habash, Herman Leung, Marie-Catherine de Marneffe, Manuela Sanguinetti, Maria Simi, Hiroshi Kanayama, Valeria dePaiva, Kira Droganova, Héctor Martínez Alonso, Çağr Çöltekin, Umut Sulubacak, Hans Uszkoreit, Vivien Macketanz, Aljoscha Burchardt, Kim Harris, Katrin Marheinecke, Georg Rehm, Tolga Kayadelen, Mohammed Attia, Ali Elkahky, Zhuoran Yu, Emily Pitler, Saran Lertpradit, Michael Mandl, Jesse Kirchner, Hector Fernandez Alcalde, Jana Strnadová, Esha Banerjee, Ruli Manurung, Antonio Stella, Atsuko Shimada, Sookyoung Kwak, Gustavo Mendonca, Tatiana Lando, Rattima Nitisaroj, and Josie Li. 2017. CoNLL 2017 Shared Task: Multilingual Parsing from Raw Text to Universal Dependencies. In *Proceedings of the CoNLL 2017 Shared Task: Multilingual Parsing from Raw Text to Universal Dependencies*. Association for Computational Linguistics, pages 1–19.

Yuhao Zhang, Peng Qi, and Christopher D. Manning. 2018. Graph convolution over pruned dependency trees improves relation extraction. In *Proceedings of the Conference on Empirical Methods for Natural Language Processing*.

NLP-Cube: End-to-end raw text processing with neural networks

Tiberiu Boros
Adobe Systems
Romania
boros@adobe.com

Stefan Daniel Dumitrescu
RACAI
Romania
sdumitrescu@racai.ro

Ruxandra Burtica
Adobe Systems
Romania
burtica@adobe.com

Abstract

We introduce NLP-Cube: an end-to-end Natural Language Processing framework, evaluated in CoNLL's "Multilingual Parsing from Raw Text to Universal Dependencies 2018" Shared Task. It performs sentence splitting, tokenization, compound word expansion, lemmatization, tagging and parsing. Based entirely on recurrent neural networks, written in Python, this ready-to-use open source system is freely available on GitHub[1]. For each task we describe and discuss its specific network architecture, closing with an overview on the results obtained in the competition.

1 Introduction and Shared task description

NLP-Cube is a freely available Natural Language Processing (NLP) system that performs: **sentence splitting**, **tokenization**, **lemmatization**, **tagging** and **parsing**. The system takes raw-text as input and annotates it, generating a CoNLL-U[2] format file. Written in Python, it is based entirely on recurrent neural networks built in DyNET (Neubig et al., 2017). The paper focuses on each NLP task, its architecture, motivating our choice and comparing it to the current state-of-the-art[3]

The "Multilingual Parsing from Raw Text to Universal Dependencies" 2018 Shared Task (Zeman et al., 2018) targets primarily learning to generate syntactic dependency trees and secondarily the end-to-end text preprocessing pipeline (from raw text segmentation up to parsing), all in a multilingual setting. The task is open to anybody, and participants can choose whether to focus on parsing or attacking the end-to-end problem. The task itself is not simple, having to handle typologically different languages, some of them having little or even no training data. Based on the Universal Dependencies (UD) Corpus[4] (Nivre et al., 2016, 2018), participants have to target 82 languages, with datasets annotated in the CoNLL-U format. Their systems, given raw text as input, have to correctly: segment a text into sentences (marked as SS in the results table, or Sentence Splitting), segment sentences into words (marked as Tok, from Tokenization), expand single tokens/words into compound words (marked as Word), and, for each word, predict its universal part-of-speech (UPOS), language-dependent part-of-speech (XPOS), morphological attributes (Morpho), and dependency link to another word and its label, evaluated as 5 different metrics named CLAS, BLEX, MLAS, UAS, and LAS. Each of these metrics is well described in the Shared Task; for brevity, in this paper we will focus mostly on UAS - Unlabeled Attachment Score measuring only the linking to the correct word, and LAS - Labeled Attachment Score, measuring both linking to another word and correctly predicting the link's label. Section 4 presents NLP-Cube's results for all these metrics for all languages in the Shared Task.

The paper is organized as follows: in section 2 we first discuss generics, then move to each particular task. We further present some training as-

---

[1] https://github.com/adobe/NLP-Cube

[2] The CoNLL-U format is well described in the official Universal Dependencies (UD) website and in (Nivre et al., 2018) and is the standard format of the UD Corpus.

[3] We must note that in the official runs our system was affected by a bug which had a negative impact on the quality of the lexicalized features (See section 2.1 for details). Due to the fact that were unable to retrain the models to meet the Shared Task's deadline (at the time of submitting this article we are still retraining them), we are reposting all new results on the GitHub project page.

[4] http://universaldependencies.org/

Proceedings of the CoNLL 2018 Shared Task: Multilingual Parsing from Raw Text to Universal Dependencies, pages 171–179
Brussels, Belgium, October 31 – November 1, 2018. ©2018 Association for Computational Linguistics
https://doi.org/10.18653/v1/K18-2017

pects of our system in section 3, followed by results in section 4, closing with section 6 on conclusions.

2 Processing pipeline

The end-to-end system is a standard processing pipeline having the following components: a sentence splitter, tokenizer, compound word expander (specific to the UD format), lemmatizer, tagger and a parser.

2.1 Input features

Our system is able to work with both lexicalized (word embeddings and character embeddings) and delexicalized, morphological features (UPOS, XPOS and ATTRs). However, we observed that when using morphological features as input (for example using POS tags as input for parsing), the performance of the end-to-end system generally degrades. This is mainly because while training is done using gold-standard morphological features (e.g. the parser is trained on gold POS tags), at runtime these features are predicted at an earlier step and then used as "gold" input (e.g. the parser would be given tagger-predicted POS tags as input). There are several ways in which this effect can be mitigated with varying degrees of success; in our approach we preferred to use only lexicalized features as input for all our modules, with the exception of the lemmatizer which is heavily dependent on morphological information.

In what follows, when we refer to **lexicalized features**, we mean a concatenation of the following:

1. **external word embeddings**: 300-dimensional standard word embeddings using Facebook's FastText (Bojanowski et al., 2016) vectors[5] projected to a 100-dimensional space using a linear transformation); to these we included a trainable <UNK> token;

2. **holistic word embeddings**: these represent all words in the trainset which have a frequency of at least 2. They are 100-dimensional trainable embeddings, also including a <UNK> token for unseen tokens in the testset;

3. **character word embeddings**: 100-dimensional word representation generated

---

[5]Available on github.com/facebookresearch/fastText

by applying a network over the word's symbols.

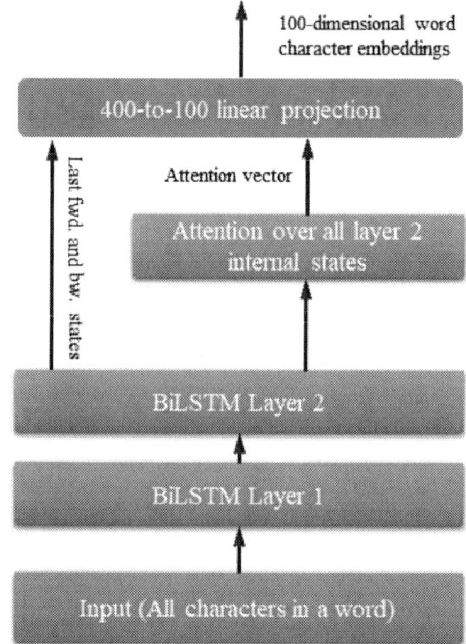

Figure 1: Word Character network for computing character-level features

The character word embeddings are obtained by applying a two-layer bidirectional LSTM network (size 200, using 0.33 dropout only on the recurrent connections) on a word's characters/symbols (see Figure 1). We then concatenate the final outputs from the second layer (top) forward and backward LSTM with an attention vector (totaling 400 values: 100 from last fwd. state, 100 from last bw. state and 200 from the attention). The attention is computed over all the network *states*, using the final *internal states* of the top forward and backward layers for conditioning. Let $f_{k,(1,n)}$ be the forward states of the top layer (k-th) in the character network and $b_{k,(1,n)}$ be its backward counterpart. If $f_{k,n}$ is the forward state corresponding to the last character of a word and $b_{k,1}$ is the backward state of the first letter of that word, then the character-level embeddings (E_c) are computed as in Equations 1, 2 and 3.

$$s_i = V \cdot \tanh(W^1 \cdot (f_{k,i} \oplus b_{k,i}) + W^2 \cdot (f_{k,n}^* \oplus b_{k,1}^*)) \tag{1}$$

$$\alpha_i = \frac{\exp(s_i)}{\sum_{k=1}^n \exp(s_k)} \tag{2}$$

172

$$E_c = \sum_{i=1}^{n} \alpha_i \cdot \left(f_{k,i}^* \oplus b_{k,i}^* \right) \qquad (3)$$

Finally, we linearly project E_c to an 100-dimensional vector. Note, that we use f^* and b^* for the *internal states* of the LSTM cells and that the missing superscript means the variables refer to the output of the LSTM cells.

The **morphological features** are computed by adding three distinct (trainable) embeddings of size 100: one for UPOS, one for XPOS and one for ATTRS.

2.2 Tokenization and sentence splitting

For most languages in the Shared Task our system uses raw text as input. Exceptions apply to the low-resourced languages for which we had little or no training data. In these cases we use the input provided by the UDPipe baseline system (Straka et al., 2016) which is already in CoNLL-U format.

For tokenization and sentence splitting we use the same network architecture (see Figure 2) and labeling strategy for all languages. The process is sequential: first we run sentence splitting and then we perform tokenization on the segmented sentences. In both steps, we use identical networks; arguably we could achieve both tasks in a single pass over the input data (the same architecture could perform both sentence splitting and tokenization). However, the best performing network parameters for sentence splitting are not identical to the best performing network parameters for tokenization. With this in mind, we trained two separate models for the two tasks.

For every symbol (s_i) in the input text, the decision for tokenization or sentence splitting (after s_i) is generated using a softmax layer that takes as input 4 distinct vectors (final output states) of:

1. **Forward Network**: A unidirectional LSTM that sees the input symbol by symbol in natural order;

2. **Peek Network**: A unidirectional LSTM , that peeks at a limited window of symbols[6] in front of the current symbol - the input is fed to the network in reverse order;

3. **Language Model (LM) Network**: A unidirectional LSTM that takes as input external word embeddings for previously genera-

---

[6]We set the value to 5 based on empirical observations

ted words; it updates only when a new word is predicted by the network;

4. **Partial Word Embeddings (PWE) Network**: It is often the case that we are able to generate valid (known) words made up of symbols from the previously tokenized word up to the current symbol. If the joined symbols form a word that exists in the embeddings, we use these embeddings. Otherwise we use the unknown word embedding. We project the embedding using the same 300-to-100 linear transformation.

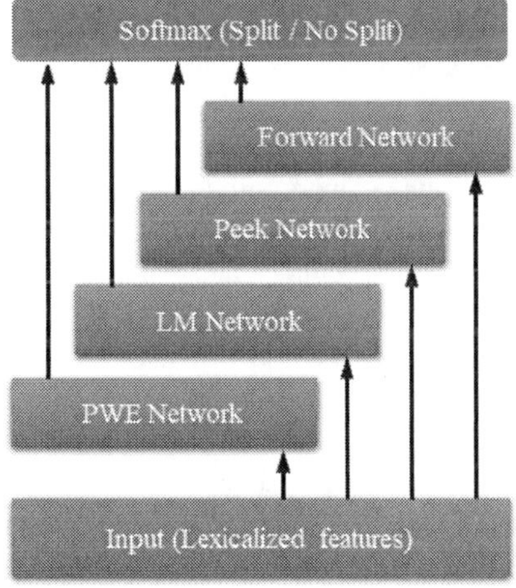

Figure 2: Tokenization and Sentence Splitting

For regularization, we observed that adding two auxiliary softmax layers (with same labels as final layer) for the Forward Network and the Peek Network slightly reduces overfitting. Intuitively, the Forward Network should be able to tokenize/sentence split based only on the previous characters and the Peek Network should also share this trait.

Moreover, the LM Network combined with the PWE Network should be able to "determine" if it makes sense (from the Language Modeling point-of-view) to generate another word, based on the previous words. This is highly important for languages that don't use spaces to delimit words inside an utterance (e.g. Chinese, Japanese etc.).

For the large treebanks in the UD corpus our tokenization method placed second, with an overall token-level score of 99.46%, the highest score being 99.51%. On the same treebanks, for sentence splitting we placed 5th, with an overall F-score of 86.83% (highest was 89.52%).

2.3 Lemmatization and compound word expansion

Lemmatization (automatically inferring a word's canonical form) and compound word expansion (automatically expanding collapsed tokens into their constituents) are similar in the sense that both start from a sequence of symbols and have the task of generating another sequence of symbols. One difference is that lemmatization is also dependent on the input word's morphological attributes and part-of-speech, whereas compound word expansion doesn't have such data available (at least not for the UD corpus and consequently not for our system).

At first glance the two tasks can easily be solved using sequence to sequence models. It is important to mention that by analyzing some input examples, one can easily see that input-output sequences have monotonic alignments. This implies that the standard encoder-decoder with attention model is too complex and resource consuming for these two tasks.

We propose a method that uses an **attention-free encoder-decoder model**, which is less computationally expensive and, surprisingly, provides a 3-5% absolute increase in accuracy (at word level) as opposed to its attention-based counterpart.

The model is composed of a bidirectional LSTM encoder and an unidirectional LSTM decoder. Similarly to a Finite State Transducer (FST) we train a model to output any symbol from the alphabet and three additional special symbols: <COPY>, <INC> and <EOS>. During training, we use a dynamic algorithm to monotonically align the input symbols to the output symbols. Based on these alignments, we create the "gold-standard" decoder output, which aims at copying as many input characters to the output as possible, while incrementing the input cursor and emitting new symbols only as a last resort.

Trying to find a comprehensive example for English proves difficult (most lemmas are obtained by simply copying a portion of the input word) and we prefer to address lemmatization for a Romanian example because it allows a better exploration of the output sequence of symbols. A good example is the lemmatization process for the word "fetelor" (en.: girls), which has the canonical form "fată" (en.: girl). The alignment process will generate the following source-destination pairs of indexes: 1-1, 3-3. The pairs map only symbols that are identical in the input and output sequence. The output symbol list for the decoder to learn is: <COPY>a<INC><INC><COPY>a<EOS>[7].

Let $E_{(\overline{1,n})}$ be the output of the encoder for a sequence of n input symbols and i be an internal index which takes values from 1 to n. The algorithm we use in the decoding process is:

```
E <- encoder(word)
out <- ''
i <- 1
do {
    inp=f(E[i], word)
    c_out = decoder(inp)
    if c_out == '<COPY>'
        out <- out + word[i]
    else if c_out == '<INC>'
        i <- i + 1
    else if c_out != '<EOS>'
        out <- out + c_out
} while (c_out != '<EOS>')
```

In the code above $f(E[i], word)$ is generically defined for both lemmatization and compound word expansion. The function uses the output of the encoder for position i and, for lemmatization, it concatenates this vector with morphological features (see Section 2.1 for details). The compound word expander directly uses E[i] as input for the decoder.

To our knowledge, the attention-free encoder decoder provides state-of-the-art results[8], our results being up-to-par with the highest ranking system in the UD Shared Task. The results are reported without using any lexicon for known words, and by employing the heuristic of leaving numbers and proper nouns unchanged.

2.4 Tagging

Tagging is achieved using a two-layer bidirectional LSTM (same size for all languages). The input of the network is composed only of lexicalized features (see Section 2.1) and the output contains three softmax layers that independently predict UPOS, XPOS and ATTRS. Though the ATTRS label is composed by multiple key-value pairs for each morphological attribute of the word (e.g.

---

[7] As a reviewer kindly noted, a <COPY> might not always be followed by an <INC>; We cannot exclude the possibility that a word in a certain language might have a single letter that has to be copied twice in the lemma. We thank the reviewer for pointing this out.

[8] The results from the official UD Shared Tasks are affected by the aforementioned bug in our system, which degraded our accuracy with 5% on average

gender, case, number etc.), we treat the concatenated strings as a single value.

We performed a number of experiments trying to predict individual morphological attributes, but the overall accuracy degraded and we preferred this naive approach to other tagging strategies.

For regularization, we use an auxiliary layer of softmax functions (Szegedy et al., 2015), located after the first bidirectional LSTM layer. The objective function is also designed to maximize the prediction probabilities for the same labels as the main softmax functions.

Note: The tagger is completely independent from the parser and we don't use any morphological information for parsing.

2.5 Parsing

Our parser is inspired by Kiperwasser and Goldberg (2016) and Dozat et al. (2017), in the sense that we use multiple stacked bidirectional LSTM layers and project 4 specialized representations for each word in a sentence, which are later aggregated in a multilayer perceptron in order to produce arc and label probabilities.

We observed that training the parser on both morphological and lexical features biases the model into relying on correct previously-predicted tags. This does not hold for end-to-end parsing, which implies that we use predicted (thus imperfect) morphology. Also, in this Shared Task we can only train a tagger using the provided corpora, which means that it has access to the same features and training examples as the parser itself.

Taking all this into account, an interesting question arises: *"Why would tagging followed by parsing (learned on an identical training dataset) be better than multi-task learning and joint prediction of arcs, labels and POS tags?"*. The answer that we came to is .. that it is not. Actually, we observed that jointly training a parser to also output morphological features increases the absolute UAS and LAS scores by up to 1.5% (at least for our own models).

Our parser architecture (Figure 3) is composed of 5 layers of bidirectional LSTMs (sized 300, 300, 200, 200, 200). After the first two layers we introduce an auxiliary loss using three softmax layers for the three independent morphological labels: UPOS, XPOS and ATTRS. After the final stacked layer we project 4 specialized representation which are used in a bi-affine attention for predicting arcs between words and a softmax layer for predicting the label itself (after we decode the graph into a parsing tree).

There are several interesting observations which apply to this approach (but they could be generally true):

Observation 1: If we compute the accuracy of the auxiliary predicted tags and compare it to that of the independent tagger, we get an slight increased accuracy for the UPOS labels and decreased figures for XPOS and ATTRS. This could mean that the contribution to parsing of the UPOS labels is higher than that of XPOS labels and morphological attributes. Of course, we are also using lexicalized features, so this conclusion might be false. Note: In the end-to-end system we use the tagger to predict POS tags for UPOS, XPOS and ATTRS; the slight gain in accuracy of using UPOS tags predicted by the parser are offset by the complexity of picking labels from separate modules and more parameter logic for the end-user of our system (for example, if a user requests only POS tags he would then need to run the parser just for UPOSes).

Observation 2: In theory, the parsing tree should be computed as the minimum or maximum spanning tree (MST) from the complete graph that we create using the network. A standard way to do this is to use Chu–Liu/Edmonds' algorithm. However, in our initial experiments we used a greedy method, which almost never generated MSTs. The algorithm worked by sorting all possible arcs, based on the probabilities from highest to lowest. Then we would start from the most probable arc and iteratively add arcs if they would not introduce cycles. While this is similar to Kruskal's algorithm, it never holds for directed graphs. When we switched to the MST algorithm we obtained lower UAS and LAS scores for the parser. We checked the validity of the results and, indeed, the score of MST trees is higher than that of greedy trees. Also, we tried multiple MST implementation including our own, which reduces any chance of coding errors. The conclusion is that in order to obtain good UAS/LAS scores, one should always favor strong arc scores over lower-confidence relations between words. The MST algorithm removes high confidence relations and replaces them with subsets of lower scoring relationships that provide a "global-optimum". Our intuition is that if one wants to use a MST tree algorithm to produce a parsing tree, this algorithm should be inte-

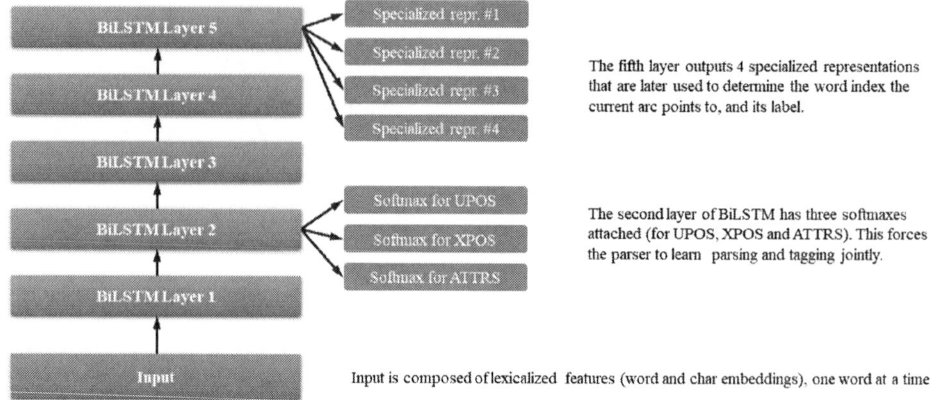

Figure 3: Parser architecture

grated at training time and not just employed over an already trained network. However, the high computational complexity of this algorithm has a strong negative impact on the training time making it very hard to validate this theory.

3 Training details

Regarding drop-out, for all tasks we use a consistent strategy: similar to the methodology of Dozat et al. (2017) we randomly drop each representation[9] independently and we scale the others to cope with the missing input. The default parameters used in our process are also close to those proposed in the aforementioned paper, with the exception that we found a batch-size of 1000 to provide better results. The batch size refers to the number of tokens included in one training iteration. Our models are implemented using DyNET (Neubig et al., 2017), which is a framework for neural networks with dynamic computation graph. This implies that we don't require bucketing and padding in our approach. Instead, when we compute a batch we add sentences until the total number of tokens reaches the batch threshold (1000). Often, we overflow the input size, because rarely the number of tokens sum up to exactly 1000.

The global early-stopping condition is that the task-specific metric over the development set doesn't improve over 20 consecutive training epochs.

All models that use auxiliary softmax functions, weight the auxiliary loss by an empirically selected value of 0.2. Whenever more than one aux

softmax layers are used, the weighed value is equally divided between the losses (i.e. if we use two auxiliary loss layers, each will infer a loss that is scaled with the value 0.1, not 0.2).

At runtime the end-to-end system performs the following operations sequentially: (a) it segments the input raw text using the best accuracy sentence splitter model, it then (b) tokenizes the sentences using the best accuracy tokenizer network model, (c) it generates compound words with the best accuracy compound word expander model over the tokens, (d) it predicts POS tags using each of the best performing network model for UPOS, XPOS and ATTRS respectively, (e) generates parse links and labels using the best UAS model (and not the LAS one, though we save this one as well), finally (f) filling in the lemma with the best accuracy lemmatizer model.

We used the same hyperparameters for all languages. They were chosen based on a few languages that we initially tested on, and used these values for all other languages. However, each task has its own set of hyperparameters that can be tuned individually. Except the input sizes (like the 300-to-100 linear transform in the tokenizer), all other LSTM sizes are configurable through the automatically generated config file for each task.

4 Results

We summarized our results in table 1 showing NLP-Cube's individual task scores for each language, and two tables comparing our ranking by task: table 2 with the score average over all treebanks and table 3 concerning only the large treebanks. Complete scores are available on the offi-

---

[9]For the tokenizer we even drop entire LSTM-outputs that represent the input of the final Softmax layer - but we still infer loss via the auxiliary softmaxes

Language	Tok	SS	Word	Lemma	UPOS	XPOS	Morpho	CLAS	BLEX	MLAS	UAS	LAS
af_afribooms	99.97	99.65	99.97	94.35	97.54	93.40	96.46	78.02	70.30	71.47	87.89	84.33
ar_padt	99.98	77.35	91.10	48.65	87.71	84.37	84.58	64.96	33.12	58.13	71.53	67.61
bg_btb	99.93	92.95	99.93	88.60	98.53	95.75	96.36	85.09	69.37	79.67	92.47	88.93
br_keb	92.26	91.97	91.71	44.26	30.74	0.00	29.57	7.26	1.93	0.34	26.95	9.90
bxr_bdt	83.26	31.52	83.26	16.05	34.99	83.26	37.95	1.01	0.03	0.06	6.32	2.42
ca_ancora	99.98	99.27	99.94	97.49	98.45	98.51	97.94	86.24	83.57	82.54	92.91	90.49
cs_cac	99.99	99.76	99.91	95.03	98.96	94.37	93.69	88.80	82.64	80.71	92.90	90.72
cs_fictree	99.99	98.60	99.90	94.92	98.00	93.43	94.49	86.89	80.13	78.23	93.01	89.68
cs_pdt	99.99	91.01	99.85	94.75	98.76	95.65	95.22	87.81	81.69	81.73	91.63	89.45
cs_pud	99.55	91.70	99.40	92.22	97.17	92.93	92.04	81.96	75.30	72.76	89.60	84.82
cu_proiel	100.00	37.28	100.00	80.96	93.23	93.52	85.27	65.68	54.38	53.66	74.60	67.70
da_ddt	99.85	91.79	99.85	93.15	96.93	99.85	96.15	79.90	71.67	72.62	85.91	83.03
de_gsd	99.70	81.19	99.62	76.71	93.83	96.78	88.54	72.96	42.49	54.79	82.09	77.24
el_gdt	99.88	89.61	99.24	88.86	96.95	96.65	92.52	81.62	66.38	71.28	89.12	86.19
en_ewt	99.26	76.32	99.26	94.51	95.25	94.83	96.03	79.31	73.77	73.75	85.49	82.79
en_gum	99.65	82.13	99.65	91.70	94.71	94.42	95.64	75.01	65.38	67.42	84.10	80.59
en_lines	99.91	87.80	99.91	93.89	96.38	95.01	96.46	75.40	67.82	69.28	82.58	78.03
en_pud	99.74	95.70	99.74	94.32	95.14	93.88	94.99	82.36	76.12	72.76	88.27	85.31
es_ancora	99.98	98.32	99.75	97.73	98.33	98.34	97.90	84.66	82.02	81.05	91.36	89.06
et_edt	99.90	91.86	99.90	87.67	96.13	97.28	93.47	80.04	67.33	71.94	86.09	82.30
eu_bdt	99.97	99.83	99.97	85.34	95.09	99.97	89.97	79.57	63.94	67.31	85.63	81.53
fa_seraji	100.00	99.50	99.08	87.51	96.43	96.18	96.35	81.75	69.77	78.42	88.45	85.21
fi_ftb	100.00	86.01	99.95	83.35	94.21	91.97	93.54	79.83	63.16	71.89	87.56	83.74
fi_pud	99.67	93.29	99.67	76.66	96.59	0.03	94.56	85.14	58.90	78.41	90.05	87.28
fi_tdt	99.70	88.73	99.70	77.92	95.52	96.52	92.41	81.74	58.42	73.04	87.06	83.74
fo_oft	99.51	93.04	97.41	46.83	44.66	0.00	24.06	18.93	5.87	0.33	39.92	24.72
fr_gsd	99.68	94.20	97.82	94.53	95.16	97.82	94.78	82.01	78.11	73.86	87.89	84.66
fr_sequoia	99.86	89.86	97.77	93.35	96.08	97.77	95.19	81.91	76.06	75.50	87.83	85.27
fr_spoken	100.00	21.63	100.00	90.62	95.22	97.45	100.00	57.63	52.78	53.41	72.76	65.81
fro_srcmf	100.00	74.19	100.00	100.00	94.54	94.42	96.50	72.36	72.36	66.90	84.88	77.39
ga_idt	99.56	95.38	99.56	84.98	91.01	90.40	79.78	53.98	41.89	35.54	76.80	65.37
gl_ctg	99.84	96.59	99.17	94.93	96.86	96.30	99.04	75.10	69.73	68.20	83.90	81.07
gl_treegal	99.50	84.99	95.06	84.67	90.25	86.75	88.27	57.80	46.62	47.68	71.13	64.90
got_proiel	100.00	28.03	100.00	80.85	93.45	94.17	84.42	59.23	46.76	46.32	70.22	62.83
grc_perseus	99.97	98.81	99.97	71.09	87.82	76.11	83.81	58.83	35.14	39.00	73.11	66.17
grc_proiel	100.00	44.57	100.00	83.17	95.52	95.68	88.23	67.08	54.13	53.38	77.76	73.04
he_htb	99.98	100.00	85.16	81.33	82.48	82.45	80.71	55.64	51.70	49.77	67.53	63.32
hi_hdtb	99.98	98.84	99.98	96.71	97.16	96.49	93.25	87.30	84.70	76.01	94.65	91.27
hr_set	99.92	95.56	99.92	89.95	97.72	99.92	90.52	82.77	71.56	69.81	90.64	85.81
hsb_ufal	98.60	74.51	98.60	63.76	65.75	98.60	49.80	24.85	17.36	8.13	42.58	31.02
hu_szeged	99.80	94.18	99.80	83.14	94.97	99.80	89.37	74.17	56.22	59.93	81.52	75.85
hy_armtdp	97.21	92.41	96.47	70.79	65.40	96.47	57.07	23.40	17.36	10.44	44.53	29.63
id_gsd	99.95	93.59	99.95	80.99	93.09	94.24	95.44	75.86	53.26	66.00	85.00	78.14
it_isdt	99.75	96.81	99.68	96.88	97.79	97.63	97.54	85.53	81.42	81.57	92.49	90.21
it_postwita	99.73	21.80	99.45	85.10	95.47	95.35	95.74	60.47	49.49	55.41	73.34	69.18
ja_gsd	93.14	94.92	93.14	91.97	90.57	93.14	93.13	68.05	67.33	64.81	81.29	78.79
ja_modern	65.98	0.00	65.98	54.14	47.71	0.00	64.15	4.42	4.07	2.76	16.67	13.60
kk_ktb	92.26	75.57	92.89	23.49	57.84	56.04	38.32	13.15	0.76	2.69	39.48	19.64
kmr_mg	94.33	69.14	94.01	64.64	59.31	58.77	48.39	17.91	11.69	5.87	34.86	24.18
ko_gsd	99.87	93.90	99.87	38.39	95.27	88.24	99.70	79.75	21.93	76.44	86.10	82.09
ko_kaist	100.00	100.00	100.00	30.05	95.12	84.14	100.00	83.63	15.26	79.50	88.13	86.00
la_ittb	99.97	92.50	99.97	96.17	97.93	93.75	95.31	83.99	79.82	76.98	89.20	86.34
la_perseus	100.00	98.67	100.00	67.55	85.69	68.29	72.63	45.39	28.48	29.01	63.46	51.92
la_proiel	99.99	35.16	99.99	87.92	94.62	94.76	86.50	64.23	56.27	52.18	72.74	67.36
lv_lvtb	99.68	98.05	99.68	86.24	93.73	83.09	88.44	74.87	61.18	61.31	83.41	78.18
nl_alpino	99.89	90.75	99.89	92.76	95.68	93.80	96.07	80.42	71.95	72.73	89.32	85.95
nl_lassysmall	99.84	77.48	99.84	92.47	95.83	94.12	95.45	75.26	66.41	69.25	85.37	81.75
no_bokmaal	99.87	96.64	99.87	84.13	97.70	99.87	95.83	85.90	80.26	79.28	90.83	88.55
no_nynorsk	99.96	94.28	99.96	82.42	97.42	99.96	95.41	85.90	76.43	78.33	90.83	88.53
no_nynorsklia	99.99	99.86	99.99	75.80	85.36	99.99	81.19	48.26	40.44	35.31	64.43	52.94
pcm_nsc	91.20	0.00	87.97	75.25	44.44	87.97	42.47	9.89	8.16	2.67	22.39	9.62
pl_lfg	99.94	99.91	99.94	92.20	98.31	92.47	93.53	91.76	81.68	82.67	95.77	93.73
pl_sz	99.98	99.14	99.33	88.71	97.13	89.58	89.88	85.90	72.76	74.06	91.00	88.01
pt_bosque	99.69	87.88	97.59	94.65	94.46	97.59	93.71	81.23	77.56	70.62	86.80	84.36
ro_rrt	99.74	95.62	99.74	94.79	97.46	96.73	96.83	80.68	74.65	76.26	90.44	85.25
ru_syntagrus	99.71	98.79	99.71	92.28	98.41	99.71	96.20	89.14	79.49	84.09	92.69	90.94
ru_taiga	97.36	70.37	97.36	76.11	90.31	97.34	80.62	53.82	37.50	39.17	66.39	58.18
sk_snk	99.97	86.00	99.97	84.26	95.92	82.53	87.01	83.20	65.14	66.99	88.87	85.77
sl_ssj	99.91	97.51	99.91	91.93	97.85	92.52	92.79	86.56	75.56	76.83	91.49	89.39
sl_sst	100.00	24.43	100.00	86.50	91.92	83.70	83.79	41.82	35.69	33.27	54.04	46.77
sme_giella	99.75	98.79	99.75	74.28	87.36	88.68	80.64	53.20	37.51	39.90	66.82	57.40
sr_set	99.97	92.61	99.97	89.36	97.62	99.97	92.58	83.87	71.08	73.71	90.84	86.96
sv_lines	99.96	87.44	99.96	91.40	95.99	93.65	88.92	79.24	69.08	64.33	85.04	80.80
sv_pud	98.57	91.23	98.57	80.71	93.20	90.80	77.28	75.40	56.38	48.35	82.40	78.16
sv_talbanken	99.95	93.60	99.95	92.92	97.25	95.41	95.63	82.33	73.42	75.03	88.32	85.00
th_pud	8.56	0.39	8.56	8.56	5.86	0.02	5.67	0.31	0.31	0.00	0.58	0.53
tr_imst	99.86	97.09	97.92	82.94	92.52	91.87	87.81	58.14	47.63	48.76	68.78	61.53
ug_udt	99.91	83.83	99.91	87.60	88.42	91.47	84.23	53.52	45.02	38.48	74.56	60.98
uk_iu	99.65	95.43	99.65	86.06	96.50	88.46	88.60	79.61	64.21	66.86	86.44	83.24
ur_udtb	100.00	98.60	100.00	96.57	93.60	91.82	83.10	76.08	72.90	55.29	87.92	81.97
vi_vtb	87.20	92.88	87.20	81.37	78.28	76.55	86.95	41.95	37.93	37.10	51.83	45.64
zh_gsd	93.14	98.80	93.14	92.38	88.58	88.41	92.21	65.39	64.52	59.22	73.44	69.60

Table 1: End-to-end parsing results obtained in the CoNLL official evaluation campaign

	Score	Rank	Range	Average	Median
SS	82.55	21	83.87 - 13.33	79.35	83.01
Token	97.36	19	98.42 - 78.45	95.90	97.39
Word	96.8	21	98.18 - 78.11	95.55	96.97
Lemma	81.21	20	91.24 - 57.1	82.85	87.77
UPOS	88.5	10	90.91 - 71.38	86.96	87.9
XPOS	86.46	2	86.67 - 4.88	75.53	84.83
Morpho	85.08	7	87.59 - 59.1	82.25	83.74
UAS	76.16	10	80.51 - 50.86	72.83	74.72
LAS	70.82	10	75.84 - 47.02	67.26	69.11

Table 2: Overall Results

	Score	Rank	Range	Average	Median
SS	86.83	5	89.52 - 15.44	83.01	86.09
Tok	99.46	2	99.51 - 84.57	98.32	99.24
Word	98.87	5	99.21 - 84.14	97.94	98.81
Lemma	86.85	21	96.08 - 58.14	88.18	93.34
UPOS	95.02	10	96.23 - 79.83	93.56	94.06
XPOS	93.71	5	95.16 - 6.46	82.31	91.81
Morpho	92.68	7	94.14 - 65.42	89.76	90.85
UAS	84.55	8	87.61 - 62.07	80.59	82.27
LAS	80.48	8	84.37 - 58.14	76.220	77.98

Table 3: Results for Big Treebanks

cial website[10] and due to space restrictions the description of each individual score is available online[11] as well. For example, for sentence splitting (SS) and tokenization (Token), the figures reported are F1 scores. For tables 2 and 3 we did not include in the max-min/average/median calculation the lowest performing system as it had a very low score and would skew the overall ranking. For the Rank value in the tables please note that there were 25 systems participating (excluding the lowest competitor), so rank 10 means 10th position out of 25.

Overall, NLP-Cube performed above average for most tasks and treebanks, and, even better if we consider only the large treebanks. Due to the hidden bug we discovered very late in the TIRA testing period (mentioned in the introduction) we can see consistently bad performance for the tasks of compound word expansion and lemmatization where the character network has a large influence. Considering that for most languages we performed end-to-end processing, a low performance in the early processing chain compounded the error and led to lower scores.

5 Use-cases

We've built NLP-Cube with the vision that it would help in higher-level NLP tasks like Machine Translation, Named Entity Recognition or Question Answering, to name a few.

Part of NLP-Cube, we have a Named Entity Recognition (NER) system[12] that employs Graph-Based-Decoding (GBD) over a hybrid network architecture composed of bidirectional LSTMs for word-level encoding, which had great results[13].

We're currently working on integrating Universal Morphological Reinflection and also Machine Translation tasks in NLP-cube. We welcome feedback and contributions to the project, as well as new ideas and areas we could cover.

6 Conclusions

This paper introduces NLP-Cube: an end-to-end system that performs text segmentation, lemmatization, part-of-speech tagging and parsing. It allows training of any model given datasets in the CoNLL-U format. Written in Python, it is open-source, easily usable ("pip install nlpcube") and provides models for the large treebanks in the Universal Dependency Corpus.

We presented and discussed each NLP task. Results place NLP-Cube in the upper half of the best performing end-to-end text preprocessing systems. As we retrain our models, new scores will be continuously updated online[14].

Finally, we highlight a few ideas:

1. We presented a lemmatizer / compound word expander that uses a Finite State Transducer-style algorithm that is faster and has better results than the classic attention-based encoder-decoder model (with the mention that it requires monotonic alignments between symbols) (see section 2.3);

2. We obtained better results for Morphological Attributes when using each example as a single class instead of splitting and predicting their presence or not at every instance (see section 2.4);

3. Parsing based on lexicalized features only, and at the same time, performing UPOS, XPOS and ATTRS prediction jointly with arc index and labeling led to a higher performance than parsing based on previously predicted morphological features generated by a tagger (see section 2.5).

---

[10]http://universaldependencies.org/conll18/results.html

[11]http://universaldependencies.org/conll18/evaluation.html

[12]https://github.com/adobe/NLP-Cube/tree/dev.gbd-ner

[13]http://opensource.adobe.com/NLP-Cube/blog/posts/1-gbd/results.html

[14]https://github.com/adobe/NLP-Cube

References

Piotr Bojanowski, Edouard Grave, Armand Joulin, and Tomas Mikolov. 2016. Enriching word vectors with subword information. *arXiv preprint arXiv:1607.04606* .

Timothy Dozat, Peng Qi, and Christopher D Manning. 2017. Stanford's graph-based neural dependency parser at the conll 2017 shared task. *Proceedings of the CoNLL 2017 Shared Task: Multilingual Parsing from Raw Text to Universal Dependencies* pages 20–30.

Eliyahu Kiperwasser and Yoav Goldberg. 2016. Simple and accurate dependency parsing using bidirectional lstm feature representations. *arXiv preprint arXiv:1603.04351* .

Graham Neubig, Chris Dyer, Yoav Goldberg, Austin Matthews, Waleed Ammar, Antonios Anastasopoulos, Miguel Ballesteros, David Chiang, Daniel Clothiaux, Trevor Cohn, et al. 2017. Dynet: The dynamic neural network toolkit. *arXiv preprint arXiv:1701.03980* .

Joakim Nivre, Marie-Catherine de Marneffe, Filip Ginter, Yoav Goldberg, Jan Hajič, Christopher Manning, Ryan McDonald, Slav Petrov, Sampo Pyysalo, Natalia Silveira, Reut Tsarfaty, and Daniel Zeman. 2016. Universal Dependencies v1: A multilingual treebank collection. In *Proceedings of the 10th International Conference on Language Resources and Evaluation (LREC 2016)*. European Language Resources Association, Portorož, Slovenia, pages 1659–1666.

Joakim Nivre et al. 2018. Universal Dependencies 2.2. LINDAT/CLARIN digital library at the Institute of Formal and Applied Linguistics, Charles University, Prague, `http://hdl.handle.net/11234/1-1983xxx`. http://hdl.handle.net/11234/1-1983xxx.

Milan Straka, Jan Hajič, and Jana Straková. 2016. UDPipe: trainable pipeline for processing CoNLL-U files performing tokenization, morphological analysis, POS tagging and parsing. In *Proceedings of the 10th International Conference on Language Resources and Evaluation (LREC 2016)*. European Language Resources Association, Portorož, Slovenia.

Christian Szegedy, Wei Liu, Yangqing Jia, Pierre Sermanet, Scott Reed, Dragomir Anguelov, Dumitru Erhan, Vincent Vanhoucke, and Andrew Rabinovich. 2015. Going deeper with convolutions. In *Proceedings of the IEEE conference on computer vision and pattern recognition*. pages 1–9.

Daniel Zeman, Jan Hajič, Martin Popel, Martin Potthast, Milan Straka, Filip Ginter, Joakim Nivre, and Slav Petrov. 2018. CoNLL 2018 Shared Task: Multilingual Parsing from Raw Text to Universal Dependencies. In *Proceedings of the CoNLL 2018 Shared Task: Multilingual Parsing from Raw Text to Universal Dependencies*. Association for Computational Linguistics, Brussels, Belgium, pages 1–20.

Towards JointUD: Part-of-speech Tagging and Lemmatization using Recurrent Neural Networks

Gor Arakelyan, Karen Hambardzumyan, Hrant Khachatrian
YerevaNN / 9, Charents str., apt. 38, Yerevan, Armenia
Yerevan State University / 1, Alex Manoogian str., Yerevan, Armenia
`{gor.arakelyan,mahnerak,hrant}@yerevann.com`

Abstract

This paper describes our submission to *CoNLL 2018 UD Shared Task*. We have extended an LSTM-based neural network designed for sequence tagging to additionally generate character-level sequences. The network was jointly trained to produce lemmas, part-of-speech tags and morphological features. Sentence segmentation, tokenization and dependency parsing were handled by UDPipe 1.2 baseline. The results demonstrate the viability of the proposed multitask architecture, although its performance still remains far from state-of-the-art.

1 Introduction

The Universal Dependencies project (Nivre et al., 2016) aims to collect consistently annotated treebanks for many languages. Its current version (2.2) (Nivre et al., 2018) includes publicly available treebanks for 71 languages in CoNLL-U format. The treebanks contain lemmas, part-of-speech tags, morphological features and dependency relations for every word.

Neural networks have been successfully applied to most of these tasks and produced state-of-the-art results for part-of-speech tagging and dependency parsing. Part-of-speech tagging is usually defined as a sequence tagging problem and is solved with recurrent or convolutional neural networks using word-level softmax outputs or conditional random fields (Lample et al., 2016; Strubell et al., 2017; Chiu and Nichols, 2016). Reimers and Gurevych (2017) have studied these architectures in depth and demonstrated the effect of network hyperparameters and even random seeds on the performance of the networks.

Neural networks have been applied to dependency parsing since 2014 (Chen and Manning, 2014). The state-of-the-art in dependency parsing is a network with deep biaffine attention module, which won *CoNLL 2017 UD Shared Task* (Dozat et al., 2017).

Nguyen et al. (2017) used a neural network to jointly learn POS tagging and dependency parsing. To the best of our knowledge, lemma generation and POS tagging have never been trained jointly using a single multitask architecture.

This paper describes our submission to *CoNLL 2018 UD Shared Task*. We have designed a neural network that jointly learns to predict part-of-speech tags, morphological features and lemmas for the given sequence of words. This is the first step towards *JointUD*, a multitask neural network that will learn to output all labels included in UD treebanks given a tokenized text. Our system used UDPipe 1.2 (Straka et al., 2016) for sentence segmentation, tokenization and dependency parsing.

Our main contribution is the extension of a sequence tagging network by Reimers and Gurevych (2017) to support character-level sequence outputs for lemma generation. The proposed architecture was validated on nine UD v2.2 treebanks. The results are generally not better than the UDPipe baseline, but we did not extensively tune the network to squeeze most out of it. Hyperparameter search and improved network design are left for the future work.

2 System Architecture

Our system used in *CoNLL 2018 UD Shared Task* consists of two parts. First, it takes the raw input and produces CoNLL-U file using UDPipe 1.2. Then, if the corresponding neural model exists, the columns corresponding to lemma, part-of-speech and morphological features are replaced by the

180

Proceedings of the CoNLL 2018 Shared Task: Multilingual Parsing from Raw Text to Universal Dependencies, pages 180–186
Brussels, Belgium, October 31 – November 1, 2018. ©2018 Association for Computational Linguistics
https://doi.org/10.18653/v1/K18-2018

predictions of the neural model. Note that UDPipe 1.2 did not use the POS tags and lemmas produced by our neural model. We did not train neural models for all treebanks, so most of our submissions are just the output of UDPipe.

The codename of our system in the Shared Task was *ArmParser*. The code is available on GitHub[1].

3 Neural model

In this section we describe the neural architecture that takes a sequence of words and outputs lemmas, part-of-speech tags, and 21 morphological features. POS tag and morphological feature prediction is done using a sequence tagging network from (Reimers and Gurevych, 2017). To generate lemmas, we extend the network with multiple decoders similar to the ones used in sequence-to-sequence architectures.

Suppose the sentence is given as a sequence of words $w_1, \ldots, w_n$. Each word consists of characters $w_i = c_i^1 \ldots c_i^{n_i}$. For each w_i, we are given its lemma as a sequence of characters: $l_i = l_i^1 \ldots l_i^{m_i}$, POS tag $p_i \in P$, and 21 features $f_i^1 \in F^1, \ldots, f_i^{21} \in F^{21}$. The sets $P, F^1, \ldots, F^{21}$ contain the possible values for POS tags and morphological features and are language-dependent: the sets are constructed based on the training data of each language. Table 1 shows the possible values for POS tags and morphological features for *English - EWT* treebank.

The network consists of three parts: embedding layers, feature extraction layers and output layers.

3.1 Embedding layers

By $\text{Emb}^d(a)$ we denote a d-dimensional embedding of the integer a. Usually, a is an index of a word in a dictionary or an index of a character in an alphabet.

Each word w_i is represented by a concatenation of three vectors: $e(w_i) = (e_{word}(w_i), e_{casing}(e), e_{char}(w))$. The first vector, $e_{word}(w_i)$ is a 300-dimensional pretrained word vector. In our experiments we used FastText vectors (Bojanowski et al., 2017) released by Facebook[2]. The second vector, $e_{casing}(w_i)$, is a one-hot representation of eight casing features, described in Table 2.

The third vector, $e_{char}(w_i)$ is a character-level representation of the word. We map each character to a randomly initialized 30-dimensional vector $\widetilde{c}_i^j = Emb^{30}(c_i^j)$, and apply a bi-directional LSTM on these embeddings. $e_{char}(w_i)$ is the concatenation of the 25-dimensional final states of two LSTMs.

The resulting $e(w_i)$ is a 358-dimensional vector.

3.2 Feature extraction layers

We denote a recurrent layer with inputs $x_1, \ldots, x_n$ and hidden states $h_1, \ldots, h_n$ by $h_i = RNN(x_i, h_{i-1})$. We use two types of recurrent cells: LSTM (Hochreiter and Schmidhuber, 1997) and GRU (Cho et al., 2014).

We apply three layers of LSTM with 150-dimensional hidden states on the embedding vectors:

$$h_i^j = LSTM\left(h_i^{j-1}, h_{i-1}^{j-1}\right) \quad j = 1, 2, 3$$

where $h_i^0 = e(w_i)$. We also apply 50% dropout before each LSTM layer.

The obtained 150-dimensional vectors represent the words with their contexts, and are expected to contain necessary information about the lemma, POS tag and morphological features.

3.3 Output layers

3.3.1 POS tags and features

Part-of-speech tagging and morphological feature prediction are word-level classification tasks. For each of these tasks we apply a linear layer with softmax activation.

$$\widetilde{p}_i = softmax(W_p h_i^3 + b_p)$$
$$\widetilde{f}_i^k = softmax\left(W_{f^k} h_i^3 + b_{f^k}\right) \quad k = 1, \ldots, 21$$

The dimensions of the matrices W_p, W_{f^k} and vectors b_p, b_{f^k} depend on the training set for the given language: $W_p \in \mathbb{R}^{|P| \times 150}$, $W_{f^k} \in \mathbb{R}^{|F^k| \times 150}$, $k = 1, \ldots, 21$. So we end up with 22 cross-entropy loss functions:

$$L_p = \frac{1}{n} \sum_{i=1}^{n} ce(\widetilde{p}_i, p_i)$$

$$L_{f^k} = \frac{1}{n} \sum_{i=1}^{n} ce\left(\widetilde{f}_i^k, f_i^k\right) \quad k = 1, \ldots, 21$$

Tag	Values
POS	PROPN (6.328%), PUNCT (11.574%), ADJ (6.102%), NOUN (16.997%), VERB (11.254%), DET (7.961%), ADP (8.614%), AUX (6.052%), PRON (9.081%), PART (2.721%), SCONJ (1.881%), NUM (1.954%), ADV (5.158%), CCONJ (3.279%), X (0.414%), INTJ (0.336%), SYM (0.295%)
Number	Sing (27.357%), Plur (6.16%), None (66.483%)
Degree	Pos (5.861%), Cmp (0.308%), Sup (0.226%), None (93.605%)
Mood	Ind (7.5%), Imp (0.588%), None (91.912%)
Tense	Past (4.575%), Pres (5.316%), None (90.109%)
VerbForm	Fin (9.698%), Inf (4.042%), Ger (1.173%), Part (2.391%), None (82.696%)
Definite	Def (4.43%), Ind (2.07%), None (93.5%)
Case	Acc (1.284%), Nom (4.62%), None (94.096%)
Person	1 (3.255%), 3 (5.691%), 2 (1.396%), None (89.658%)
PronType	Art (6.5%), Dem (1.258%), Prs (7.394%), Rel (0.569%), Int (0.684%), None (83.595%)
NumType	Card (1.954%), Ord (0.095%), Mult (0.033%), None (97.918%)
Voice	Pass (0.589%), None (99.411%)
Gender	Masc (0.743%), Neut (0.988%), Fem (0.24%), None (98.029%)
Poss	Yes (1.48%), None (98.52%)
Reflex	Yes (0.049%), None (99.951%)
Foreign	Yes (0.009%), None (99.991%)
Abbr	Yes (0.04%), None (99.96%)
Typo	Yes (0.052%), None (99.948%)

Table 1: The values for part-of-speech and morphological features for *English - EWT* treebank.

numeric	All characters are numeric
mainly numeric	More than 50% of characters are numeric
all lower	All characters are lower cased
all upper	All characters are upper cased
initial upper	The first character is upper cased
contains digit	At least one of the characters is digit
other	None of the above rules applies
padding	This is used for the padding placeholders for short sequences

Table 2: Casing features used in the embedding layer.

3.3.2 Lemma generation

This subsection describes our main contribution. In order to generate the lemmas for all words, we add one GRU-based decoder per each word. These decoders share the weights and work in parallel. The i-th decoder outputs $\widetilde{l}_i^1, \ldots, \widetilde{l}_i^{m_i}$, the predicted characters of the lemma of the i-th word. We denote the inputs to the i-th decoder by $x_i^1, \ldots, x_i^{m_i}$. Each of x_i^j is a concatenation of four vectors:

$$x_i^j = \left(h_i^3, \widehat{c}_i^j, \pi_i^j, \widehat{l}_i^{j-1} \right).$$

1. h_i^3 is the representation of the i-th word after feature extractor LSTMs. This is the only part of x_i^j vector that does not depend on j. This trick is important to make sure that word-level information is always available in the decoder.

2. $\widehat{c}_i^j = Emb^{30}(c_i^j)$ is the same embedding of the j-th character of the word used in the character-level BiLSTM described in Section 3.1.

3. π_i^j is some form of positional encoding. It indicates the number of characters remaining till the end of the input word: $\pi_i^j = Emb^5(n_i - j + 1)$. Positional encodings were introduced in (Sukhbaatar et al., 2015) and were successfully applied in neural machine translation (Gehring et al., 2017; Vaswani et al., 2017).

4. $\widehat{l}_i^{j-1}$ is the indicator of the previous character of the lemma. During training it is the one-hot vector of the ground-truth: $\widehat{l}_i^{j-1} = onehot(l_i^{j-1})$. During inference it is the output of the GRU in the previous timestep $\widehat{l}_i^{j-1} = \widetilde{l}_i^{j-1}$.

These inputs are passed to a single layer of GRU network. The output of the decoder is formed by applying another dense layer on the GRU state:

$$s_i^j = GRU(x_i^j, s_i^{j-1})$$
$$\widetilde{l}_i^j = W_o s_i^j + b_o$$

Here, $s_i^j \in \mathbb{R}^{150}$, $W_o \in \mathbb{R}^{|C| \times 150}$, where $|C|$ is the number of characters in the alphabet. The initial state of the GRU is the output of the feature extractor LSTM: $s_i^0 = h_i^3$. All GRUs share the weights.

The loss function for lemma output is:

$$L_l = \frac{1}{n} \sum_{i=1}^{n} \frac{1}{n_i} \sum_{j=1}^{n_i} ce\left(\widetilde{l}_i^j, l_i^j\right)$$

3.4 Multitask loss function

The combined loss function is a weighted average of the loss functions described above:

$$L = \lambda_l L_l + \lambda_p L_p + \sum_{k=1}^{21} \lambda_{f^k} L_{f^k} \qquad (1)$$

The final version of our system used $\lambda_p = 0.2$ and $\lambda_l = \lambda_{f^k} = 1$ for every k.

4 Experiments

We have implemented the architecture defined in the previous section using Keras framework. Our implementation is based on the codebase for (Reimers and Gurevych, 2017)[3]. The new part of the architecture (lemma generation) is quite slow. The overall training speed is decreased by more than three times when it is enabled. We have left speed improvements for future work.

To train the model we used RMSProp optimizer with early stopping. The initial learning rate was 0.001, and it was decreased to 0.0005 since the seventh epoch. The training was stopped when the loss function was not improved on the development set for five consecutive epochs.

Due to time constraints, we have trained our neural architecture on just nine treebanks. These include three English and two French treebanks.

Our system was evaluated on Ubuntu virtual machines in TIRA platform (Potthast et al., 2014) and on our local machines using the test sets available on UD GitHub repository (Zeman et al., 2018a).

The version we ran on TIRA had a bug in the preprocessing pipeline and was doubling new line symbols in the input text. Raw texts in UD v2.2 occasionally contain new line symbols inside the sentences. These symbols were duplicated due to the bug, and the sentence segmentation part of UDPipe treated them as two different sentences. The evaluation scripts used in *CoNLL 2018 UD Shared Task* obviously penalized these errors. After the deadline of the Shared Task, we ran the same models (without retraining) on the test sets on our local machines without new line symbols.

Additionally, we locally trained models for two more non-Indo-European treebanks: Arabic PADT and Korean GSD.

4.1 Results

Table 3 shows the main metrics of *CoNLL 2018 UD Shared Task* on the nine treebanks that we used for training our models. For each of the metrics we report five scores, two scores on our local machine (our model and UDPipe 1.2), and three scores from the official leaderboard[4] (our model, UDPipe baseline, the best score for that particular treebank). LAS metric evaluates sentence segmentation, tokenization and dependency parsing, so the numbers for our models should be identical to UDPipe 1.2. MLAS metric additionally takes into account POS tags and morphological features, but not the lemmas. BLEX metric evaluates dependency parsing and lemmatization. The full description of these metrics are available in (Zeman et al., 2018b) and in *CoNLL 2018 UD Shared Task* website[5]. Table 4 compares the same models using another set of metrics that measure the performance of POS tagging, morphological feature extraction and lemmatization.

---

[3]https://github.com/UKPLab/
emnlp2017-bilstm-cnn-crf

[4]http://universaldependencies.org/
conll18/results.html
[5]http://universaldependencies.org/
conll18/evaluation.html

| Metric | LAS | | | | | MLAS | | | | | BLEX | | | | |
| Environment | Local | | TIRA | | | Local | | TIRA | | | Local | | TIRA | | |
Model	Our	UDPipe	Our	UDPipe	Winner	Our	UDPipe	Our	UDPipe	Winner	Our	UDPipe	Our	UDPipe	Winner
English EWT	77.12	77.12	65.69	77.56	84.57	62.12	68.27	57.73	68.70	76.33	66.35	70.53	60.73	71.02	78.44
English GUM	74.21	74.21	60.89	74.20	85.05	56.43	62.66	44.73	62.66	73.24	58.75	62.14	48.54	62.14	73.57
English LinES	73.08	73.08	60.52	73.10	81.97	55.25	64.00	44.89	64.03	72.25	57.91	65.39	47.24	65.42	75.29
French Spoken	65.56	65.56	58.94	65.56	75.78	51.50	53.46	47.08	53.46	64.67	50.07	54.67	48.77	54.67	65.63
French Sequoia	81.12	81.12	66.14	81.12	89.89	64.56	71.34	55.68	71.34	82.55	62.50	74.41	58.99	74.41	84.67
Finnish TDT	76.45	76.45	58.65	76.45	88.73	62.52	68.58	48.24	68.58	80.84	38.56	62.19	28.87	62.19	81.24
Finnish FTB	75.64	75.64	65.48	75.64	88.53	54.06	65.22	44.15	65.22	79.65	46.57	61.76	38.95	61.76	82.44
Swedish LinES	74.06	74.06	60.21	74.06	84.08	50.16	58.62	40.10	58.62	66.58	55.58	66.39	44.80	66.39	77.01
Swedish Talbanken	77.72	77.72	62.70	77.91	88.63	58.49	69.06	46.89	69.22	79.32	59.64	69.89	48.41	70.01	81.44
Arabic PADT	65.06	65.06	N/A	66.41	77.06	51.79	53.81	N/A	55.01	68.54	2.89	56.34	N/A	57.60	70.06
Korean GSD	61.40	61.40	N/A	61.40	85.14	47.73	54.10	N/A	54.10	80.75	0.30	50.50	N/A	50.50	76.31

Table 3: Performance of our model compared to UDPipe 1.2 baseline and the winner models of *CoNLL 2018 UD Shared Task*.

| Metric | POS | | | | | UFeat | | | | | Lemma | | | | |
| Environment | Local | | TIRA | | | Local | | TIRA | | | Local | | TIRA | | |
Model	Our	UDPipe	Our	UDPipe	Winner	Our	UDPipe	Our	UDPipe	Winner	Our	UDPipe	Our	UDPipe	Winner
English EWT	90.47	93.61	92.96	93.62	95.94	93.95	94.60	93.87	94.60	96.03	91.51	95.92	95.77	95.88	97.23
English GUM	91.00	93.23	89.94	93.24	96.44	93.70	93.89	91.61	93.90	96.68	89.26	94.36	88.66	94.36	96.18
English LinES	88.93	94.71	87.99	94.71	97.06	92.81	94.97	91.05	94.97	97.08	86.84	95.84	85.37	95.84	96.56
French Spoken	92.67	92.94	92.18	92.94	97.17	99.97	100.00	100.00	100.00	100.00	86.28	95.84	95.39	95.84	97.50
French Sequoia	92.81	95.84	95.11	95.84	98.15	93.77	94.97	94.36	94.97	97.50	79.41	97.03	96.56	97.03	97.99
Finnish TDT	92.72	94.37	92.35	94.37	97.30	89.10	92.06	88.49	92.06	95.58	62.25	86.49	59.50	86.49	95.32
Finnish FTB	86.77	92.28	86.44	92.28	96.70	89.40	92.74	88.82	92.74	96.89	73.06	88.70	72.35	88.70	97.02
Swedish LinES	90.02	93.97	89.74	93.97	97.37	83.65	87.23	82.75	87.23	89.61	82.15	94.58	80.59	94.58	96.90
Swedish Talbanken	91.30	95.35	91.07	95.36	97.90	89.23	94.34	87.93	94.36	96.82	82.99	95.30	81.71	95.28	97.82
Arabic PADT	88.50	89.35	N/A	89.34	93.63	83.07	83.39	N/A	83.42	90.96	7.42	87.42	N/A	87.41	91.61
Korean GSD	85.34	93.44	N/A	93.44	96.33	99.49	99.51	N/A	99.51	99.70	12.87	87.03	N/A	87.03	94.02

Table 4: Additional metrics describing the performance of our model, UDPipe 1.2 baseline, and the winner models of *CoNLL 2018 UD Shared Task*.

5 Discussion

5.1 Input vectors for lemma generation

The initial versions of the lemma decoder did not get the state of the LSTM below h_i^3 and positional embedding π_i^j as inputs. The network learned to produce lemmas with some accuracy but with many trivial errors. In particular, after training on *English - EWT* treebank, the network learned to remove s from the end of the plural nouns. But it also started to produce ¡end-of-the-word¿ symbol even if s was in the middle of the word. We believe the reason was that there was almost no information available that would allow the decoder to distinguish between plural suffix and a simple s inside the word. One could argue that the initial state of the GRU (h_i^3) could contain such information, but it could have been lost in the GRU.

To remedy this we decided to pass h_i^3 as an input at every step of the decoder. This idea is known to work well in image caption generation. The earliest usage of this trick we know is in (Donahue et al., 2015).

Additionally, we have added explicit information about the *position* in the word. Unlike (Vaswani et al., 2017), we encode the number of characters left before the end of the word. This choice might be biased towards languages where the ending of the word is the most critical in lemmatization.

By combining these two ideas we got significant improvement in lemma generation for English. We did not do ablation experiments to determine the effect of each of these additions.

The additional experiments showed that this architecture of the lemmatizer does not generalize to Arabic and Korean. We will investigate this problem in the future work.

5.2 Balancing different tasks

Multitask learning in neural networks is usually complicated because of varying difficulty of individual tasks. The λ coefficients in (1) can be used to find optimal balance between the tasks. Our initial experiments with all λ coefficients equal to 1 showed that the loss term for POS tagging (L_p) had much higher values than the rest. We decided to set $\lambda_p = 0.2$ to give more weight to the other tasks and noticed some improvements in lemma generation.

We believe that more extensive search for better coefficients might help to significantly improve the overall performance of the system.

5.3 Fighting against overfitting

The main challenge in training these networks is to overcome overfitting. The only trick we used was to apply dropout layers before feature extractor LSTMs. We did not apply recurrent dropout (Gal and Ghahramani, 2016) or other noise injection techniques, although recent work in language modeling demonstrated the importance of such tricks for obtaining high performance models (Merity et al., 2018).

6 Conclusion

In this paper we have described our submission to *CoNLL 2018 UD Shared Task*. Our neural network was learned to jointly produce lemmas, part-of-speech tags and morphological features. It is the first step towards a fully multitask neural architecture that will also produce dependency relations. Future work will include more extensive hyperparameter tuning and experiments with more languages.

Acknowledgments

We would like to thank Tigran Galstyan for helpful discussions on neural architecture. We would also like to thank anonymous reviewers for their comments. Additionally, we would like to thank Marat Yavrumyan and Anna Danielyan. Their efforts on bringing Armenian into UD family motivated us to work on sentence parsing.

References

Piotr Bojanowski, Edouard Grave, Armand Joulin, and Tomas Mikolov. 2017. Enriching word vectors with subword information. *Transactions of the Association for Computational Linguistics* 5:135–146.

Danqi Chen and Christopher Manning. 2014. A fast and accurate dependency parser using neural networks. In *Proceedings of the 2014 conference on empirical methods in natural language processing (EMNLP)*. pages 740–750.

Jason P.C. Chiu and Eric Nichols. 2016. Named entity recognition with bidirectional lstm-cnns. *Transactions of the Association for Computational Linguistics* 4:357–370. https://transacl.org/ojs/index.php/tacl/article/view/792.

Kyunghyun Cho, Bart van Merrienboer, Caglar Gulcehre, Dzmitry Bahdanau, Fethi Bougares, Holger Schwenk, and Yoshua Bengio. 2014. Learning phrase representations using rnn encoder–decoder for statistical machine translation. In *Proceedings of the 2014 Conference on Empirical Methods in Natural Language Processing (EMNLP)*. Association for Computational Linguistics, pages 1724–1734. https://doi.org/10.3115/v1/D14-1179.

Jeffrey Donahue, Lisa Anne Hendricks, Sergio Guadarrama, Marcus Rohrbach, Subhashini Venugopalan, Kate Saenko, and Trevor Darrell. 2015. Long-term recurrent convolutional networks for visual recognition and description. In *Proceedings of the IEEE conference on computer vision and pattern recognition*. pages 2625–2634.

Timothy Dozat, Peng Qi, and Christopher D. Manning. 2017. Stanford's graph-based neural dependency parser at the conll 2017 shared task. In *Proceedings of the CoNLL 2017 Shared Task: Multilingual Parsing from Raw Text to Universal Dependencies*. Association for Computational Linguistics, pages 20–30. https://doi.org/10.18653/v1/K17-3002.

Yarin Gal and Zoubin Ghahramani. 2016. A theoretically grounded application of dropout in recurrent neural networks. In *Advances in neural information processing systems*. pages 1019–1027.

Jonas Gehring, Michael Auli, David Grangier, Denis Yarats, and Yann N Dauphin. 2017. Convolutional Sequence to Sequence Learning. *ArXiv e-prints* .

Sepp Hochreiter and Jürgen Schmidhuber. 1997. Long short-term memory. *Neural computation* 9(8):1735–1780.

Guillaume Lample, Miguel Ballesteros, Kazuya Kawakami, Sandeep Subramanian, and Chris Dyer. 2016. Neural architectures for named entity recognition. In *Proc. NAACL-HLT*.

Stephen Merity, Nitish Shirish Keskar, and Richard Socher. 2018. Regularizing and optimizing LSTM language models. In *International Conference on Learning Representations*. https://openreview.net/forum?id=SyyGPP0TZ.

Dat Quoc Nguyen, Mark Dras, and Mark Johnson. 2017. A novel neural network model for joint pos tagging and graph-based dependency parsing. In *Proceedings of the CoNLL 2017 Shared Task: Multilingual Parsing from Raw Text to Universal Dependencies*. Association for Computational Linguistics, Vancouver, Canada, pages 134–142. http://www.aclweb.org/anthology/K17-3014.

Joakim Nivre, Marie-Catherine de Marneffe, Filip Ginter, Yoav Goldberg, Jan Hajič, Christopher Manning, Ryan McDonald, Slav Petrov, Sampo Pyysalo, Natalia Silveira, Reut Tsarfaty, and Daniel Zeman. 2016. Universal Dependencies v1: A multilingual treebank collection. In *Proceedings of the 10th International Conference on Language Resources and Evaluation (LREC 2016)*. European Language Resources Association, Portoro, Slovenia, pages 1659–1666.

Joakim Nivre et al. 2018. Universal Dependencies 2.2. LINDAT/CLARIN digital library at the Institute of Formal and Applied Linguistics, Charles University, Prague, `http://hdl.handle.net/11234/1-1983xxx`. http://hdl.handle.net/11234/1-1983xxx.

Martin Potthast, Tim Gollub, Francisco Rangel, Paolo Rosso, Efstathios Stamatatos, and Benno Stein. 2014. Improving the reproducibility of PAN's shared tasks: Plagiarism detection, author identification, and author profiling. In Evangelos Kanoulas, Mihai Lupu, Paul Clough, Mark Sanderson, Mark Hall, Allan Hanbury, and Elaine Toms, editors, *Information Access Evaluation meets Multilinguality, Multimodality, and Visualization. 5th International Conference of the CLEF Initiative (CLEF 14)*. Springer, Berlin Heidelberg New York, pages 268–299. https://doi.org/10.1007/978-3-319-11382-1_22.

Nils Reimers and Iryna Gurevych. 2017. Reporting Score Distributions Makes a Difference: Performance Study of LSTM-networks for Sequence Tagging. In *Proceedings of the 2017 Conference on Empirical Methods in Natural Language Processing (EMNLP)*. Copenhagen, Denmark, pages 338–348. http://aclweb.org/anthology/D17-1035.

Milan Straka, Jan Hajič, and Jana Straková. 2016. UD-Pipe: trainable pipeline for processing CoNLL-U files performing tokenization, morphological analysis, POS tagging and parsing. In *Proceedings of the 10th International Conference on Language Resources and Evaluation (LREC 2016)*. European Language Resources Association, Portoro, Slovenia.

Emma Strubell, Patrick Verga, David Belanger, and Andrew McCallum. 2017. Fast and accurate entity recognition with iterated dilated convolutions. In *Proceedings of the 2017 Conference on Empirical Methods in Natural Language Processing*. pages 2670–2680.

Sainbayar Sukhbaatar, Jason Weston, Rob Fergus, et al. 2015. End-to-end memory networks. In *Advances in neural information processing systems*. pages 2440–2448.

Ashish Vaswani, Noam Shazeer, Niki Parmar, Jakob Uszkoreit, Llion Jones, Aidan N Gomez, Łukasz Kaiser, and Illia Polosukhin. 2017. Attention is all you need. In *Advances in Neural Information Processing Systems*. pages 5998–6008.

Dan Zeman et al. 2018a. Universal Dependencies 2.2 CoNLL 2018 shared task development and test data. LINDAT/CLARIN digital library at the Institute of Formal and Applied Linguistics, Charles University, Prague, `http://hdl.handle.net/11234/1-2184`. http://hdl.handle.net/11234/1-2184.

Daniel Zeman, Jan Hajič, Martin Popel, Martin Potthast, Milan Straka, Filip Ginter, Joakim Nivre, and

Slav Petrov. 2018b. CoNLL 2018 Shared Task: Multilingual Parsing from Raw Text to Universal Dependencies. In *Proceedings of the CoNLL 2018 Shared Task: Multilingual Parsing from Raw Text to Universal Dependencies*. Association for Computational Linguistics, Brussels, Belgium, pages 1–20.

CUNI x-ling: Parsing under-resourced languages in CoNLL 2018 UD Shared Task

Rudolf Rosa and **David Mareček**

Charles University, Faculty of Mathematics and Physics
Institute of Formal and Applied Linguistics
Malostranské náměstí 25, 118 00 Praha, Czechia
{rosa,marecek}@ufal.mff.cuni.cz

Abstract

This is a system description paper for the *CUNI x-ling* submission to the *CoNLL 2018 UD Shared Task*. We focused on parsing under-resourced languages, with no or little training data available. We employed a wide range of approaches, including simple word-based treebank translation, combination of delexicalized parsers, and exploitation of available morphological dictionaries, with a dedicated setup tailored to each of the languages. In the official evaluation, our submission was identified as the clear winner of the Low-resource languages category.

1 Introduction

This paper describes our submission to the CoNLL 2018 shared task on Multilingual Parsing from Raw Text to Universal Dependencies (Zeman et al., 2018; Nivre et al., 2016).

Our primary focus was on the 4 languages with no annotated training data (treebanks) available, as we have significant experience with such a setting (Mareček, 2016; Rosa et al., 2017; Rosa, 2018a); in the shared task, these are Naija, Faroese, Thai, and Breton. Apart from Naija, there are at least some non-treebank resources available for each of the languages, such as parallel data, monolingual data, or morphological dictionaries.[1] Furthermore, we also employ treebanks for other languages together with several cross-lingual parsing methods; in our work, we will refer to the language being parsed as the *target language*, and the other languages that we exploit when parsing it as

Language	Sentences	Tokens
Buryat	19	153
Kurmanji	20	242
Upper Sorbian	23	460
Kazakh	31	529
Armenian	50	804

Table 1: Sizes of available training data.

the *source languages*. We used a different setup for each of the languages, based on its characteristics and on the available resources.

Our secondary focus was on the 5 languages with only tiny training data available – see Table 1. However, as we had no previous experience with this particular setup, we tried to build upon our successful approaches for languages with no training data, combining the resources available for the target language with treebanks for different (but preferably close) source languages.

In the official evaluation of the shared task, our submission achieved the highest average scores in all of the main evaluation metrics when averaged over the 9 low-resource languages. We scored particularly well for the languages with no training data available, winning for 3 of them. For the languages with small training data available, our submission was usually not the highest scoring one, but still performed very competitively.

2 Approach

Our baseline approach for parsing a target language is to train the UDPipe tokenizer, tagger and parser (Straka et al., 2016) on UD 2.2 training data for the target language (Nivre et al., 2018), using the default settings. For target languages with no treebank, we need to use training data for another language and cross-lingual techniques. For target languages with small training data, we also use

---

[1] Parallel data actually exist for all of the languages, at least in the form of the New Testament part of the Bible and the Universal Declaration of Human Rights; however, using these datasets was not allowed in the shared task.

Proceedings of the CoNLL 2018 Shared Task: Multilingual Parsing from Raw Text to Universal Dependencies, pages 187–196
Brussels, Belgium, October 31 – November 1, 2018. ©2018 Association for Computational Linguistics
https://doi.org/10.18653/v1/K18-2019

cross-lingual techniques, as an enrichment of the baseline approach to achieve better performance.

In this section, we introduce several approaches that we apply to many or most of the target languages; the specific setups used for each of the target languages are described in later sections.

2.1 Treebank translation using parallel data

Tiedemann (2014) introduced the approach of automatically translating the word forms in a source treebank into the target language, and then training a pseudo-target parser (and/or a tagger) on the resulting pseudo-target treebank.

This approach was further investigated by Rosa et al. (2017), Rosa and Žabokrtský (2017) and Rosa (2018a), finding that the sophistication of the Machine Translation (MT) system plays a rather minor role in cross-lingual parsing, while there is a significant benefit in using word-based translation – this forces the translations to be more literal, and enables a trivial approach to annotation transfer.

In this work, we use probably the simplest possible approach, based on extracting a dictionary from word-aligned data, and translating each source word into the target word most frequently aligned to it, ignoring any context or other information. While we had found that using state-of-the-art statistical MT tools leads to slightly better results, it is also much more computationally demanding, which may be a bottleneck when one needs to process a lot of language pairs in a short time.

Our treebank translation pipeline is:

1. obtain *OpenSubtitles2018*[2] (Lison and Tiedemann, 2016) sentence-aligned source-target parallel data from Opus[3] (Tiedemann, 2012)

2. tokenize the parallel data with source and target UDPipe tokenizers

3. obtain intersection word-alignment with FastAlign[4] (Dyer et al., 2013)

4. extract the translation table: for each source word, take the target word most frequently aligned to it, and store it as its translation

5. translate the source training treebank into the target language, replacing each word form

and each lemma[5] by its translation from the translation table (keep the word untranslated if it does not appear in the translation table)

6. now UDPipe can be trained in a standard way on the resulting pseudo-target treebank and applied to target texts

2.2 UniMorph morphology post-corrections

One of the available resources is UniMorph (Sylak-Glassman, 2016),[6] a project on universal morphology annotation that covers a majority of the low-resource languages in this shared task. It provides a list of words associated with lemmas and morphological features. The annotation of features is unfortunately different from that used in Universal Dependencies, however, almost all the features can be mapped to them. The data available for low-resource languages is as follows:

- large data (10,000 words): Armenian, Breton, Faroese, and Kurmanji

- small data (257 words): Kazakh

- no data: Buryat, Naija, Thai, and Upper Sorbian; for Upper Sorbian, we use the large data for the similar Lower Sorbian

The POS tag of the word can be found also among the features, however, sometimes it does not match the UPOS; e.g. the copula verbs are *AUX* in UD but *V* (verb) in UniMorph.

We use the UniMorph lexicon for correcting the morphological features, lemmas, and tags. If a token is found in the lexicon, we change its tag (unless it is *AUX*), lemma, and morphological features according to the lexicon. Each feature that was mapped from UniMorph style to UD style is added to the features obtained by the tagger. In case it was there but with a different value, the value is changed.

We chose to post-correct the morphological annotation only after parsing. This way, the parser cannot benefit from the potentially better morphological annotation; however, the target parser seems to benefit from being applied to an annotation more similar to what it was trained on.[7]

[2]http://www.opensubtitles.org/
[3]http://opus.nlpl.eu/
[4]https://github.com/clab/fast_align

[5]We translate *lemmas* using the dictionary extracted on *forms*, as we typically do not have another choice anyway. We assume that the lemma is a prominent word form and is thus likely to be translated correctly even in this way.
[6]https://unimorph.github.io/
[7]We have not evaluated the influence on delexicalized

2.3 Combining multiple parsers

For cross-lingual parsing of target languages without any training data, McDonald et al. (2013) showed that combining syntactic information from multiple source languages can lead to a more accurate parsing than when using only one source language. Moreover, this idea can be easily extended to target languages with small training data, combining the target language resources with larger resources for other close languages (Zhang and Barzilay, 2015).

To combine the multilingual resources, we use the weighted parse tree combination method of Rosa and Žabokrtský (2015), which is based on the work of Sagae and Lavie (2006). It consists of training separate parsers on the source language treebanks (and also the target language treebank if it is available), applying them independently to the input sentence, and then combining the resulting dependency trees into a directed graph, with each edge weighted by a sum of weights of the parsers which produced this edge. The final parse tree is then obtained by applying the directed maximum spanning tree algorithm of Chu and Liu (1965) and Edmonds (1967) to the weighted graph.

To make the source parser applicable to the target language sentences, we either use a translation approach (translating the source training treebank into the target language, or translating the target input data into the source language), or we train a delexicalized parser, which only uses the part-of-speech as its input, disregarding the word forms.

The parsers need to be weighted according to their expected performance on the target language data. Moreover, for efficiency reasons, we want to only select a few most promising source languages to use; we usually combine only 3 sources.[8] For target languages with small training data available, we simply evaluate the source parsers on the target treebank, select the ones that perform best, and weight them according to their LAS;[9] the target parser is weighted by a hand-crafted weight slightly above the highest-scoring source parser.[10]

For languages with no treebank data available, we used the typological similarity score of Agić (2017) computed on the WALS dataset (Dryer and Haspelmath, 2013).

We use a similar approach to combine multiple predictors for the dependency relation label, part of speech tag, morphological features, and morphological lemma. However, as opposed to dependency trees, there are no strict structural constraints, which means that instead of the spanning tree algorithm, we can use a simple weighted voting.

2.4 Using pre-trained word embeddings

The UDPipe parser uses vector representations of input word forms, which it by default trains jointly with training the parser, i.e. using only the words that appear in the training treebank. However, the parsing accuracy can typically be improved by pre-training the word embeddings on larger monolingual data, and using these fixed embeddings in the parser instead.[11] For low-resource languages, this becomes even more promising, as the training treebanks are tiny or non-existent, and pre-training the word embeddings on much larger data can both improve performance on words unseen in the training data (which are most words) as well as indirectly provide the parser with some more knowledge of the structure of the target language (Rosa et al., 2017). This is especially useful when using translation approaches, where the parser is not actually exposed to genuine target texts during training; in such cases, the word embeddings bring in such exposure at least indirectly.

We use the word embeddings of Bojanowski et al. (2016) pre-trained on Wikipedia texts, which are available online[12] for nearly all of our focus languages (with the only exception of Naija).

3 Languages with low training data

For all the languages with some small training data available, we use this data for training a base UDPipe model, and combine it with additional models trained on data for other close source languages.

---

source parsers. However, the delexicalized parsers do not use morphological features, and UniMorph-based postprocessing does not seem to change the UPOS tags very often, so we do not expect a strong influence.

[8] Note that combining only two parsers does not make much sense due to the combination/voting mechanism.

[9] Labelled Attachment Score; see Section 5.

[10] We want to enable combining the information from the parsers, but we also want to give most power to the target parser. Therefore, we manually choose a target weight higher

than the highest source weight, but lower than the sum of the two lowest source weights.

[11] https://ufal.mff.cuni.cz/udpipe/ users-manual#udpipe_training_parser_ embeddings

[12] https://github.com/facebookresearch/ fastText/blob/master/pretrained-vectors. md

Target weight	Additional sources' weights	
0.57 Armenian	0.56 Latvian	0.51 Estonian
0.45 Buryat	0.41 Hindi	0.38 Uyghur
0.44 Kazakh	0.33 Turkish	0.29 Uyghur
0.52 Kurmanji	0.47 Latin	0.45 Greek

Table 2: Weights of the target parser and additional delexicalized source parsers used in parser combination. Weights are based on LAS achieved by the parsers on the target training treebank.

3.1 Armenian, Buryat, Kazakh, Kurmanji

Our setup is identical for four of the target languages – we train UDPipe on the target training data, and combine it with delexicalized parsers for two close source languages, selected and weighted based on the LAS they achieve on the target training treebank:

1. train a UDPipe tokenizer, tagger and parser on the small target training data; use the pre-trained word embeddings for the parser

2. train delexicalized parsers for two other close source languages

3. tokenize and tag the input with the target model

4. parse it with the target parser and the delexicalized source language parsers

5. do a weighted combination of the parse trees, using LAS on target treebank as weights

6. post-fix the morphology using data from Uni-Morph, rewriting UPOS and lemmas and merging morphological features (except for Buryat for which UniMorph is not available)

In Table 2, we list the additional source languages and the weights used for the parser combination.

3.2 Upper Sorbian

For Upper Sorbian, our setup is a bit more complex, combining the target model with source models both for tagging and parsing:

1. apply Polish tokenizer

2. combine Upper Sorbian tagger with Polish tagger and pseudo-Upper Sorbian tagger trained on MonoTranslated Czech treebank

Predicting lemmas:

0.40 U.Sorb.	0.60 Polish	0.51 Czech

Predicting UPOS tags:

1.00 U.Sorb.	0.69 Polish	0.65 Czech

Predicting morphological features:

0.30 U.Sorb.	0.10 Polish	0.24 Czech

Parsing:

0.53 U.Sorb.	0.70 Croatian	0.73 Czech
	0.66 Russian	0.69 Slovak
	0.68 Slovene	

Table 3: Weights used for combining the individual UDPipe predictors for the Upper Sorbian target and for the additional source languages.

3. apply UniMorph morphology post-correction based on Lower Sorbian UniMorph data

4. combine Upper Sorbian parser with delexicalized Czech, Croatian, Russian, Slovak and Slovene parsers

The combination weights are listed in Table 3.

Upper Sorbian is very similar to Czech and Polish, even lexically, which we tried to exploit by using Czech and Polish treebanks also to train taggers for Upper Sorbian.

We found the similarity with Polish to be sufficient for the Polish tagger to be directly applicable to Upper Sorbian texts without any translation.

For Czech, we decided to try to translate the Czech treebank into a pseudo-Upper Sorbian treebank, as the orthographic variance is higher for this language pair. However, as there are no parallel data available, we resorted to an approximate translation approach. First, we preprocessed the Czech treebank by changing '-v-' to '-w-' and 'o-' to 'wo-', as this seems to be a regular difference between Czech and Upper Sorbian. We then applied the MonoTrans system (Rosa, 2017), which tries to map the source words onto similar target words; the similarity is computed based on an edit distance of the word forms, and on their frequencies in monolingual corpora.[13]

Moreover, evaluation of the Upper Sorbian tools on the Upper Sorbian training data indicated a very low performance of the tools (even without cross-validation); therefore, we often give more power to the cross-lingual tools than to the Upper Sorbian

---

[13] We used the Czech treebank and the Upper Sorbian texts from Wikipedia (Rosa, 2018b) as monolingual corpora.

tools in the combinations. The weights we use are the accuracies of the tools on the Upper Sorbian training data (LAS for parsing, UPOS accuracy for UPOS, etc.); this time, the target weights are obtained in the same way as the source weights, i.e. they are not hand-crafted.

4 Languages with no training data

We list the processing pipeline for each of the languages, together with detailed descriptions of processing steps specific for the language.

4.1 Naija

1. apply English tokenizer

2. "translate" words to English

3. apply English tagger and parser

4. copy lowercased form to lemma, remove final '-s' if there is one

For Naija (Nigerian Pidgin) we have no data available at all. Some basic information about this language can be found on Wikipedia,[14] where there are also links to other resources. A couple of sentences can be found also on the web of Jehovah Witnesses[15] and we also looked into the translation of the Declaration of Human Rights.[16] Based on these resources, we conclude that Naija is very similar to English, but differs mainly in the most common words and function words. We also learned that its written form is not standardized, since different resources showed different level of similarity with English spelling. While the texts of Jehovah Witnesses were almost English (*We come from different different place and we dey speak different different language.*), the example from the web of the University of Hawai[17] shows more differences:
Naija: *A bai shu giv mai broda.*
English: *I bought shoes that I gave to my brother.*

Since we did not know what spelling is used in the testing treebank, we decided to use the tools trained on English, applied to Naija inputs processed with a couple of translation rules which we devised based on the Naija texts which we read.

First, some Naija words are directly translated into English using the following small dictionary:

sey	→ that	de	→	is
na	→ is	don	→	has
wey	→ which	am	→	him
im	→ his	go	→	will
wetin	→ what	no	→	not
dey	→ is	di	→	the
deh	→ is	pikin	→	small
foh	→ in	sebi	→	right
e	→ he	abi	→	right
dem	→ they	nna	→	man
dis	→ this	sabi	→	know

It seems that Naija language is very simple and many words are homonymous when translating into English. It is of course possible that not all translations are correct, since the dictionary was developed mainly by choosing the most probable English word based on the example context.

Second, we used a couple of regular expressions to translate remaining non-English words.[18]

$$
\begin{array}{llll}
i & \to y & k & \to c \\
d & \to th & \char94 & \to h \\
t & \to th & \$ & \to t \\
a\$ & \to er & o & \to ou
\end{array}
$$

We perform the above substitutions on each unknown Naija word one after another, until it becomes a known English word. If no English word is reached after all the substitutions are done, the original word is used.

It is evident that any information found about such a highly low-resource language is crucial. We read a couple of web pages with examples of Naija, and based on that we built the small dictionary. If we were limited to read only the English Wikipedia article about the Naija language, the dictionary would be of course smaller and the results would be worse. In Table 4, we show the results when no translation rules are used and Naija is parsed by English parser, and the results when only the information from the Wikipedia article about Naija is used.

4.2 Thai

1. obtain a Thai tokenizer

2. translate Indonesian, Chinese and Vietnamese treebanks into Thai, using *OpenSub-*

---

[14] https://en.wikipedia.org/wiki/Nigerian_Pidgin
[15] https://www.jw.org/pcm/
[16] https://unicode.org/udhr/translations.html
[17] http://www.hawaii.edu/satocenter/langnet/definitions/naija.html

[18] For this purposes, we define that a word is English if it has more than five occurrences in the first 3 million words of the English Wikipedia dump.

Naija	LAS	MLAS	BLEX
no translation	16.1	2.7	14.9
using Wikipedia	22.3	2.6	19.4
using all sources	30.1	4.6	26.0

Table 4: Comparison of Naija results with no translation, only with Wikipedia examples, and the full setup which also uses information we learned from other websites.

titles2018 parallel data;[19]

3. train pseudo-Thai taggers and parsers on the translated treebanks; use pre-trained Thai word embeddings for the parsers

4. combine the taggers and parsers (with weights 0.75, 0.55, 0.40 based on LAS of the source parsers on source development data)

The crucial part of Thai analysis is tokenization, since there are no tokenized texts available; however, we need tokenization both in the main processing pipeline, as well as to tokenize the parallel data for the translation step. The only data comprising separated Thai tokens are the word vectors trained on Wikipedia[20] (Bojanowski et al., 2016). The tokens are ordered according to their frequency and are associated with the vectors.

We used a very simple approach. We generated a synthetic Thai text by sampling Thai tokens from the list of tokens available. Since we do not know the token distribution, we decided that the probability $Prob(t)$ of a token is inversely proportional to the square root of its order $Ord(t)$:

$$Prob(t) \propto \frac{1}{\sqrt{Ord(t)}}$$

The lexicon itself contains a lot of foreign words (English, Japanese, Chinese), which caused that approximately every third generated word was not Thai. We therefore filtered out all the tokens containing English, Japanese, or Chinese characters.[21] After a token is sampled, the end of sentence is generated with a probability of 5%.

By this procedure, we generated a text of one million tokens in total. We generated two variants, one with tokens separated by spaces and one without spaces. Using these two files, we trained the UDPipe tokenizer for Thai.[22] We assume that since the tokens were sampled randomly, the only information the tokenizer can learn are the tokens itself and therefore the tokenization of real Thai texts should be reasonable.

The parameters of the sampling procedure could be tuned if we had even a tiny example of tokenized text in Thai.

4.3 Faroese

1. train devowelled Nynorsk tagger and parser

2. apply Nynorsk tokenizer

3. apply devowelled Nynorsk tagger and parser

4. copy lowercased form to lemma

5. apply UniMorph morphology post-correction

Faroese is quite close to the Nynorsk variant of Norwegian; even applying the Nynorsk models directly to Faroese texts yields competitive results. Unfortunately, there is no parallel data available to perform standard treebank translation.

However, as shown by Rosa et al. (2017), lexically similar languages can be brought even closer by *devowelling* the words, i.e. by removing all vowels, which acts as a sort of a poor man's translation into an intermediary pivot language. We thus devowel the Nynorsk treebank to obtain a devowelled Nynorsk tagger and parser, and apply it to devowelled Faroese texts.

4.4 Breton

1. translate French treebank into Breton, using *OpenSubtitles2018* parallel data

2. train pseudo-Breton tagger and parser on the translated treebank (by mistake, we did not use pre-trained Breton word embeddings)

3. apply French tokenizer

4. apply pseudo-Breton tagger and parser

5. apply UniMorph morphology post-correction

---

[19] Vietnamese uses a lot of tokens with internal spaces; for the translation, we replaced the spaces with underscores.

[20] `https://github.com/facebookresearch/fastText/blob/master/pretrained-vectors.md`

[21] For filtering, we used the regular expression `[a-z A-Z \u4E00-\u9FFF \u3040-\u309F \u30A0-\u30FF \u4e00-\u9fff]`

[22] As recommended by the UDPipe manual, we use the `dimension=64` setting.

Submission	LAS	MLAS	BLEX	UPOS
CUNI xling	**27.9**	**6.1**	**14.0**	<u>57.6</u>
Uppsala	<u>25.9</u>	<u>5.2</u>	9.0	**61.1**
TurkuNLP	22.9	3.6	<u>11.4</u>	52.5
Baseline	17.2	3.4	7.6	45.2

Table 5: Macro-average LAS, MLAS, BLEX and UPOS on the 9 low-resource languages. Best result in bold, second-best result underlined.

Breton is a Celtic language; however, we do not have much treebank or parallel data for Celtic languages. Therefore, we decided to only use French as a single source, since due to the long-term contact, Breton is similar to French in some aspects, and there is at least some parallel data available.

5 Evaluation

The evaluation of the submissions to the shared task was performed by the organizers via the TIRA evaluation platform (Potthast et al., 2014), running the submitted systems on secret test data and reporting their performance in LAS (labeled attachment score), MLAS (morphology-aware labeled attachment score), and BLEX (bi-lexical dependency score). For a full description of the metrics, see (Zeman et al., 2018) or the shared task website;[23] here, we only note that while LAS only evaluates parsing accuracy, MLAS also includes evaluation of tagging (UPOS and morphological features), while BLEX also includes lemmatization. We also list UPOS tagging accuracies.

Table 5 shows the average scores over the 9 low-resource languages. Our submission achieved the best average result in all the 3 main scoring metrics; for comparison, we also list the submissions that scored second-best in the metrics, and the baseline setup.

Table 6 reports the results individually for each low-resource language, together with the ranking of our submission among all of the 26 participants.

All scores are adapted from official results.[24]

5.1 Languages with no training data

For the languages with no training data, which were our primary focus, our submission typically scores best in all of the metrics, with the exception of Breton. Our results are particularly strong for Thai, 2x-3x higher than the second best system.

By analyzing our setup for Breton and comparing it to the setups used by other participants of the shared task, we found that we had unfortunately taken several clearly suboptimal steps:

- We overlooked the availability of *Ofis Publik ar Brezhoneg*,[25] a Breton-French parallel corpus of 60,000 sentences, considerably larger and probably cleaner than the 17,000 *OpenSubtitles2018* sentences we used.

- We failed to note the peculiar Breton spelling with a lot of intra-word apostrophes, which calls for an adaptation of the tokenizer.

- We forgot to use the available pre-trained word embeddings.

Another case where our solution performs poorly is MLAS score for Naija, which does not even surpass the baseline. We made the mistake of keeping the morphological features predicted by the English tagger, even though the pidgin language exhibits little or no inflection, and a better approach would thus be not to predict any morphological features at all (i.e. to always return '_'). Indeed, in the now-released test data, no morphological features are annotated in the Naija treebank.

We also did not do well in UPOS tagging for Faroese, probably because of the devowelling.

5.2 Languages with low training data

For the languages with some small training data available, we score a bit worse. Our submission is usually among the top 5 submissions and always above the baseline, but it is rarely the best. Nevertheless, as this setting was only our secondary focus and as we had no prior experience with it, we are still happy about our results.

In general, our submission performs particularly well in MLAS, which is probably thanks to our exploitation of the UniMorph dictionary. For Armenian and Kazakh, we managed to win in MLAS and BLEX, although we are not sure why, as our setup was similar for all of the languages. We note, however, that the available training data are largest for these two languages; as we train UDPipe on the target data with the default settings, not adapted to the small size of the training data in any way, our approach is probably better suited for

---

[23] http://universaldependencies.org/conll18/evaluation.html

[24] http://universaldependencies.org/conll18/results.html

[25] http://opus.nlpl.eu/OfisPublik.php

Target	LAS				MLAS				BLEX				UPOS			
language	ours		comp.		ours		comp.		ours		comp.		ours		comp.	
Breton	26.9	4	38.6	1	3.0	4	13.9	1	11.4	4	20.7	1	52.7	4	85.0	1
Faroese	**49.4**	**1**	47.2	2	**1.1**	**1**	0.8	2	**14.4**	**1**	14.4	2	58.7	6	65.5	1
Naija	**30.1**	**1**	24.5	2	4.6	6	5.3	1	**26.0**	**1**	22.9	2	**67.9**	**1**	57.2	2
Thai	**13.7**	**1**	6.9	2	**6.3**	**1**	2.2	2	**10.8**	**1**	3.5	2	**39.4**	**1**	33.8	2
Buryat	17.1	5	19.5	1	2.5	2	3.0	1	5.6	4	6.7	1	42.3	7	50.8	1
U.Sorb.	33.4	5	46.4	1	8.5	2	9.1	1	14.6	10	21.1	1	69.9	4	79.5	1
Armen.	30.1	4	37.0	1	**13.4**	**1**	10.4	2	**19.0**	**1**	18.3	2	71.4	2	75.4	1
Kazakh	26.3	2	31.9	1	**8.9**	**1**	8.6	2	**11.3**	**1**	10.2	2	54.6	5	61.7	1
Kurm.	24.0	8	30.4	1	6.9	3	8.0	1	12.6	3	13.7	1	**61.5**	**1**	61.3	2

Table 6: LAS, MLAS, BLEX and UPOS of our submission (*ours*), as well as the best result achieved among the other participants (*comp.*). The ranks are also listed.

Submission	LAS	MLAS	BLEX	UPOS
Best	75.8	61.3	66.1	90.9
Baseline	65.8	52.4	55.8	87.3
CUNI xling	64.9	50.4	54.1	88.7

Table 7: Macro-average LAS, MLAS, BLEX and UPOS on all 82 test sets for 57 languages.

languages with somewhat larger training data. We hypothesize that the training procedure should be modified when the training data are small, e.g. by lowering the number of training iterations over the data, or by reducing the complexity of the model; however, we have not performed any experiments in this direction.

5.3 All languages

For completeness, we also include the macro-average evaluation of our submission on all 82 test sets in Table 7; for all but the 9 low-resourced ones, we simply submitted a standard UDPipe system trained with default parameters.

We usually rank slightly below the official baseline (typically around the 20th position), with a huge loss to the winner. This shows that the parser we use is not very strong in itself, in contrast with most of our competitors' parsers. Nevertheless, by applying various specialized cross-lingual techniques, we managed to surpass even the stronger parsers on the low-resource languages.

6 Conclusion

In this paper, we described our submission to the *CoNLL 2018 UD Shared Task*, in which we focused on under-resourced languages.

We have devised a separate processing pipeline tailored to each low-resource language, based on what resources are available for it and how similar to other resource-rich languages it is. Our approach mostly revolves around simple dictionary-based machine translation, employment of pre-trained word embeddings, combination of delexicalized parsers for close languages, and exploitation of a morphological dictionary.

Our submission achieved the best average result in all the three main evaluation metrics on the low-resource languages. For the languages with no training data, our submission usually outperformed all other submissions. For the languages with small training data, our submission was usually among the top 5 out of all the 26 submissions.

Our approach demonstrates that even quite simple methods can work well, as in the context-independent word-based dictionary-lookup translation. On the other hand, we did not surpass a LAS of 50 for any of the under-resourced languages, only reaching 28 on average. This shows that, even though the various techniques we used can bring huge improvements over the baselines, the resulting parsing accuracies are probably still too low for most practical purposes.

Acknowledgments

This work was supported by the grant 18-02196S of the Grant Agency of the Czech Republic and the grant CZ.02.1.01/0.0/0.0/16_013/0001781 of the Ministry of Education, Youth and Sports of the Czech Republic. This work has been using language resources and tools developed, stored and distributed by the LINDAT/CLARIN project of the Ministry of Education, Youth and Sports of the Czech Republic (project LM2015071).

References

Željko Agić. 2017. Cross-lingual parser selection for low-resource languages. In *Proceedings of the NoDaLiDa 2017 Workshop on Universal Dependencies (UDW 2017)*. Association for Computational Linguistics, Gothenburg, Sweden, pages 1–10. http://www.aclweb.org/anthology/W17-0401.

Piotr Bojanowski, Edouard Grave, Armand Joulin, and Tomas Mikolov. 2016. Enriching word vectors with subword information. *CoRR* abs/1607.04606. http://arxiv.org/abs/1607.04606.

Yoeng-Jin Chu and Tseng-Hong Liu. 1965. On shortest arborescence of a directed graph. *Scientia Sinica* 14(10):1396.

Matthew S. Dryer and Martin Haspelmath, editors. 2013. *WALS Online*. Max Planck Institute for Evolutionary Anthropology, Leipzig. http://wals.info/.

Chris Dyer, Victor Chahuneau, and Noah A. Smith. 2013. A simple, fast, and effective reparameterization of IBM model 2. In *Proceedings of the 2013 Conference of the North American Chapter of the Association for Computational Linguistics: Human Language Technologies*. Association for Computational Linguistics, Atlanta, Georgia, pages 644–648. http://www.aclweb.org/anthology/N13-1073.

Jack Edmonds. 1967. Optimum branchings. *Journal of Research of the National Bureau of Standards B* 71(4):233–240.

Pierre Lison and Jörg Tiedemann. 2016. Opensubtitles2016: Extracting large parallel corpora from movie and TV subtitles. In *Proceedings of the 10th International Conference on Language Resources and Evaluation (LREC 2016)*. European Language Resources Association.

David Mareček. 2016. Twelve years of unsupervised dependency parsing. In Broňa Brejová, editor, *Proceedings of the 16th ITAT: Slovenskočeský NLP workshop (SloNLP 2016)*. Comenius University in Bratislava, Faculty of Mathematics, Physics and Informatics, CreateSpace Independent Publishing Platform, Bratislava, Slovakia, volume 1649 of *CEUR Workshop Proceedings*, pages 56–62.

Ryan McDonald, Joakim Nivre, Yvonne Quirmbach-Brundage, Yoav Goldberg, Dipanjan Das, Kuzman Ganchev, Keith Hall, Slav Petrov, Hao Zhang, Oscar Täckström, Claudia Bedini, Núria Bertomeu Castelló, and Jungmee Lee. 2013. Universal dependency annotation for multilingual parsing. In *Proceedings of the 51st Annual Meeting of the Association for Computational Linguistics*. pages 92–97.

Joakim Nivre, Marie-Catherine de Marneffe, Filip Ginter, Yoav Goldberg, Jan Hajič, Christopher Manning, Ryan McDonald, Slav Petrov, Sampo Pyysalo, Natalia Silveira, Reut Tsarfaty, and Daniel Zeman. 2016. Universal Dependencies v1: A multilingual treebank collection. In *Proceedings of the 10th International Conference on Language Resources and Evaluation (LREC 2016)*. European Language Resources Association, Portorož, Slovenia, pages 1659–1666.

Joakim Nivre et al. 2018. Universal Dependencies 2.2. LINDAT/CLARIN digital library at the Institute of Formal and Applied Linguistics, Charles University, Prague, `http://hdl.handle.net/11234/1-1983xxx`. http://hdl.handle.net/11234/1-1983xxx.

Martin Potthast, Tim Gollub, Francisco Rangel, Paolo Rosso, Efstathios Stamatatos, and Benno Stein. 2014. Improving the reproducibility of PAN's shared tasks: Plagiarism detection, author identification, and author profiling. In Evangelos Kanoulas, Mihai Lupu, Paul Clough, Mark Sanderson, Mark Hall, Allan Hanbury, and Elaine Toms, editors, *Information Access Evaluation meets Multilinguality, Multimodality, and Visualization. 5th International Conference of the CLEF Initiative (CLEF 14)*. Springer, Berlin Heidelberg New York, pages 268–299. https://doi.org/10.1007/978-3-319-11382-1_22.

Rudolf Rosa. 2017. Monotrans: Statistical machine translation from monolingual data. In Jaroslava Hlaváčová, editor, *Proceedings of the 17th conference ITAT 2017: Slovenskočeský NLP workshop (SloNLP 2017)*. ÚFAL MFF UK, CreateSpace Independent Publishing Platform, Praha, Czechia, volume 1885 of *CEUR Workshop Proceedings*, pages 201–208.

Rudolf Rosa. 2018a. *Discovering the structure of natural language sentences by semi-supervised methods*. Ph.D. thesis, Charles University, Faculty of Mathematics and Physics, Praha, Czechia.

Rudolf Rosa. 2018b. Plaintext Wikipedia dump 2018. LINDAT/CLARIN digital library at the Institute of Formal and Applied Linguistics (ÚFAL), Faculty of Mathematics and Physics, Charles University. http://hdl.handle.net/11234/1-2735.

Rudolf Rosa and Zdeněk Žabokrtský. 2015. KL_{cpos^3} – a language similarity measure for delexicalized parser transfer. In *Proceedings of the 51st Annual Meeting of the Association for Computational Linguistics and the 7th International Joint Conference on Natural Language Processing of the Asian Federation of Natural Language Processing, Short Papers*. Association for Computational Linguistics, Stroudsburg, PA, USA.

Rudolf Rosa and Zdeněk Žabokrtský. 2017. Error analysis of cross-lingual tagging and parsing. In Jan Hajič, editor, *Proceedings of the 16th International Workshop on Treebanks and Linguistic Theories*. Univerzita Karlova, Univerzita Karlova, Praha, Czechia, pages 106–118.

Rudolf Rosa, Daniel Zeman, David Mareček, and Zdeněk Žabokrtský. 2017. Slavic forest, Norwegian wood. In Preslav Nakov, Marcos Zampieri,

Nikola Ljubešić, Jörg Tiedemann, Shervin Malmasi, and Ahmed Ali, editors, *Proceedings of the Fourth Workshop on NLP for Similar Languages, Varieties and Dialects (VarDial4)*. Association for Computational Linguistics, Association for Computational Linguistics, Stroudsburg, PA, USA, pages 210–219.

Kenji Sagae and Alon Lavie. 2006. Parser combination by reparsing. In *Proceedings of HLT-NAACL*. ACL, pages 129–132.

Milan Straka, Jan Hajič, and Jana Straková. 2016. UD-Pipe: trainable pipeline for processing CoNLL-U files performing tokenization, morphological analysis, POS tagging and parsing. In *Proceedings of the 10th International Conference on Language Resources and Evaluation (LREC 2016)*. European Language Resources Association, Portorož, Slovenia.

John Sylak-Glassman. 2016. The composition and use of the universal morphological feature schema (unimorph schema). Technical report, Technical report, Department of Computer Science, Johns Hopkins University.

Jörg Tiedemann. 2012. Parallel data, tools and interfaces in OPUS. In *LREC*. volume 2012, pages 2214–2218.

Jörg Tiedemann. 2014. Rediscovering annotation projection for cross-lingual parser induction. In *Proceedings of COLING 2014, the 25th International Conference on Computational Linguistics: Technical Papers*. pages 1854–1864.

Daniel Zeman, Jan Hajič, Martin Popel, Martin Potthast, Milan Straka, Filip Ginter, Joakim Nivre, and Slav Petrov. 2018. CoNLL 2018 Shared Task: Multilingual Parsing from Raw Text to Universal Dependencies. In *Proceedings of the CoNLL 2018 Shared Task: Multilingual Parsing from Raw Text to Universal Dependencies*. Association for Computational Linguistics, Brussels, Belgium, pages 1–20.

Yuan Zhang and Regina Barzilay. 2015. Hierarchical low-rank tensors for multilingual transfer parsing. Association for Computational Linguistics.

UDPipe 2.0 Prototype at CoNLL 2018 UD Shared Task

Milan Straka
Charles University
Faculty of Mathematics and Physics
Institute of Formal and Applied Linguistics
straka@ufal.mff.cuni.cz

Abstract

UDPipe is a trainable pipeline which performs sentence segmentation, tokenization, POS tagging, lemmatization and dependency parsing (Straka et al., 2016). We present a prototype for UDPipe 2.0 and evaluate it in the *CoNLL 2018 UD Shared Task: Multilingual Parsing from Raw Text to Universal Dependencies*, which employs three metrics for submission ranking. Out of 26 participants, the prototype placed first in the MLAS ranking, third in the LAS ranking and third in the BLEX ranking. In extrinsic parser evaluation EPE 2018, the system ranked first in the overall score.

The prototype utilizes an artificial neural network with a single joint model for POS tagging, lemmatization and dependency parsing, and is trained only using the CoNLL-U training data and pretrained word embeddings, contrary to both systems surpassing the prototype in the LAS and BLEX ranking in the shared task.

The open-source code of the prototype is available at http://github.com/CoNLL-UD-2018/UDPipe-Future.

After the shared task, we slightly refined the model architecture, resulting in better performance both in the intrinsic evaluation (corresponding to first, second and second rank in MLAS, LAS and BLEX shared task metrics) and the extrinsic evaluation. The improved models will be available shortly in UDPipe at http://ufal.mff.cuni.cz/udpipe.

1 Introduction

The Universal Dependencies project (Nivre et al., 2016) seeks to develop cross-linguistically consistent treebank annotation of morphology and syntax for many languages. The latest version of UD 2.2 (Nivre et al., 2018) consists of 122 dependency treebanks in 71 languages. As such, the UD project represents an excellent data source for developing multi-lingual NLP tools which perform sentence segmentation, tokenization, POS tagging, lemmatization and dependency tree parsing.

The goal of the *CoNLL 2018 Shared Tasks: Multilingual Parsing from Raw Text to Universal Dependencies* (*CoNLL 2018 UD Shared Task*) is to stimulate research in multi-lingual dependency parsers which process raw text only. The overview of the task and the results are presented in Zeman et al. (2018). The current shared task is a reiteration of previous year's *CoNLL 2017 UD Shared Task* (Zeman et al., 2017).

This paper describes our contribution to *CoNLL 2018 UD Shared Task*, a prototype of UDPipe 2.0. UDPipe (Straka et al., 2016)[1] is an open-source tool which automatically generates sentence segmentation, tokenization, POS tagging, lemmatization and dependency trees, using UD treebanks as training data. The current version UDPipe 1.2 (Straka and Straková, 2017) is used as a baseline in *CoNLL 2018 UD Shared Task*. UDPipe 1.2 achieves low running times and moderately sized models, however, its performance is behind the current state-of-the-art, placing 13th, 17th and 18th in the three metrics (MLAS, LAS and BLEX, respectively). As a participation system in the shared task, we therefore propose a prototype for UDPipe 2.0, with the goal of reaching state-of-the-art performance.

---

[1] http://ufal.mff.cuni.cz/udpipe

Proceedings of the CoNLL 2018 Shared Task: Multilingual Parsing from Raw Text to Universal Dependencies, pages 197–207
Brussels, Belgium, October 31 – November 1, 2018. ©2018 Association for Computational Linguistics
https://doi.org/10.18653/v1/K18-2020

The contributions of this paper are:

- Description of UDPipe 2.0 prototype, which placed 1st in MLAS, 3rd in LAS and 3rd in BLEX, the three metrics of *CoNLL 2018 UD Shared Task*. In extrinsic parser evaluation EPE 2018, the prototype ranked first in overall score.

  The prototype employs an artificial neural network with a single joint model for POS tagging, lemmatization, and parsing. It utilizes solely CoNLL-U training data and word embeddings, and does not require treebank-specific hyperparameter tuning.

- Runtime performance measurements of the prototype, using both CPU-only and GPU environments.

- Ablation experiments showing the effect of word embeddings, regularization techniques and various joint model architectures.

- Post-shared-task model refinement, improving both the intrinsic evaluation (corresponding to 1st, 2nd and 2nd rank in MLAS, LAS and BLEX shared task metrics) and the extrinsic evaluation. The improved models will be available soon in UDPipe.[2]

2   Related Work

Deep neural networks have recently achieved remarkable results in many areas of machine learning. In NLP, end-to-end approaches were initially explored by Collobert et al. (2011). With a practical method for pretraining word embeddings (Mikolov et al., 2013) and routine utilization of recurrent neural networks (Hochreiter and Schmidhuber, 1997; Cho et al., 2014), deep neural networks achieved state-of-the-art results in many NLP areas like POS tagging (Ling et al., 2015), named entity recognition (Yang et al., 2016) or machine translation (Vaswani et al., 2017).

The wave of neural network parsers was started recently by Chen and Manning (2014) who presented fast and accurate transition-based parser. Many other parser models followed, employing various techniques like stack LSTM (Dyer et al., 2015), global normalization (Andor et al., 2016), biaffine attention (Dozat and Manning, 2016) or recurrent neural network grammars (Kuncoro et al., 2016), improving LAS score in English and Chinese dependency parsing by more than 2 points

in 2016. The neural graph-based parser of Dozat et al. (2017) won the last year's *CoNLL 2017 UD Shared Task* by a wide margin.

3   Model Overview

The objective of the shared task is to parse raw texts. In accordance with the CoNLL-U format, the participant systems are required to:

- tokenize the given text and segment it into sentences;
- split multi-word tokens into individual words (CoNLL-U format distinguishes between the surface tokens, e.g., `won't`, and words, e.g., `will` and `not`);
- perform POS tagging, producing UPOS (universal POS) tags, XPOS (language-specific POS) tags and UFeats (universal morphological features);
- perform lemmatization;
- finally perform dependency parsing, including universal dependency relation labels.

We decided to reuse the tokenization, sentence segmentation and multi-word token splitting available in UDPipe 1.2, i.e., the baseline solution, and focus on POS tagging, lemmatization, and parsing, utilizing a deep neural network architecture.

For practical reasons, we decided to devise a joint model for POS tagging, lemmatization, and parsing, with the goal of sharing at least the trained word embeddings, which are usually the largest part of a trained neural network model.

For POS tagging, we applied a straightforward model in the lines of Ling et al. (2015) – first representing each word with its embedding, contextualizing them with bidirectional RNNs (Graves and Schmidhuber, 2005), and finally using a softmax classifier to predict the tags. To predict all three kinds of tags (UPOS, XPOS and UFeats), we reuse the embeddings and the RNNs, and only employ three different classifiers, each for one kind of the tags.

To accomplish lemmatization, we convert each lemma to a rule generating it from the word form, and then classify each input word into one of such rules. Assuming that lemmatization and POS tagging could benefit one another, we reuse the contextualized embeddings of the tagger, and lemmatize through the means of a fourth classifier (in addition to the three classifiers producing UPOS, XPOS and UFeats tags).

---

[2]http://ufal.mff.cuni.cz/udpipe

Regarding the dependency parsing, we reimplemented a biaffine attention parser of (Dozat et al., 2017), which won the previous year's shared task. The parser also processes contextualized embeddings, followed by additional attention and classification layers. We considered two levels of sharing:

- *loosely joint model*, where only the word embeddings are shared;
- *tightly joint model*, where the contextualized embeddings are shared by the tagger and the parser.

4 Model Implementation

We now describe each model component in a greater detail.

4.1 Tokenization and Sentence Segmentation

We perform tokenization, sentence segmentation and multi-word token splitting with the baseline UDPipe 1.2 approach. In a nutshell, input characters are first embedded using trained embeddings, then fixed size input segments (of 50 characters) are processed by a bidirectional GRU (Cho et al., 2014), and each character is classified into three classes – a) there is a sentence break after this character, b) there is a token break after this character, and c) there is no break after this character. For detailed description, see Straka and Straková (2017).

We only slightly modified the baseline models in the following way: in addition to the segments of size 50 we also consider longer segments of 200 characters during training (and choose the best model for each language according to the development set performance). Longer segments improve sentence segmentation performance for treebanks with nontrivial sentence breaks – such sentence breaks are caused either by the fact that a treebank does not contain punctuation, or that semantic sentence breaks (e.g., end of heading and start of a text paragraph) are not annotated in the treebank. The evaluation of longer segments models is presented later in Section 6.1.

4.2 Embedding Input Words

We represent each input word using three kinds of embeddings, as illustrated in Figure 1.

- *pretrained word embeddings*: pretrained word embeddings are computed using large plain texts and are constant throughout the

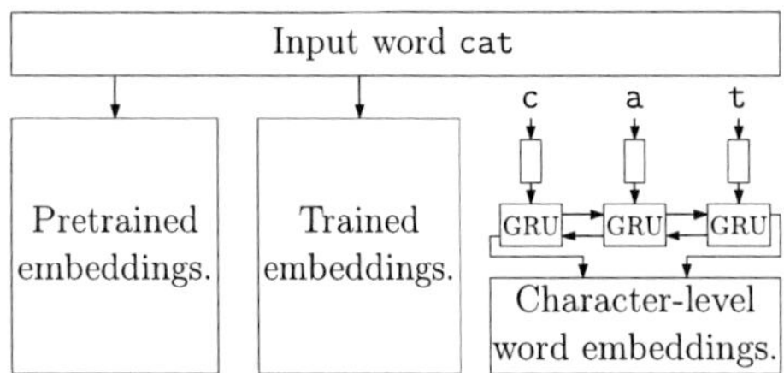

Figure 1: Word embeddings used in the model.

training. We utilize either word embeddings provided by the *CoNLL 2017 UD Shared Task* organizers (of dimension 100), Wikipedia fastText embeddings[3] (of dimension 300), or no pretrained word embeddings, choosing the alternative resulting in highest development accuracy. To limit the size of the pretrained embeddings, we keep at most 1M most frequent words of fastText embeddings, or at most 3M most frequent words of the shared task embeddings.

- *trained word embeddings*: trained word embeddings are created for every training word, initialized randomly, and trained with the rest of the network.
- *character-level word embeddings*: character-level word embeddings are computed similarly as in Ling et al. (2015), utilizing a bidirectional GRU.

4.3 POS Tagging

We process the embedded words through a multi-layer bidirectional LSTM (Hochreiter and Schmidhuber, 1997) to obtain contextualized embeddings. In case multiple RNN layers are employed, we utilize residual connections on all but the first layer (Wu et al., 2016).

For each of the three kinds of tags (UPOS, XPOS and UFeats), we construct a dictionary containing all unique tags from the training data. Then, we employ a softmax classifier for each tag kind processing contextualized embeddings and generating a class from the corresponding tag dictionary.

However, a single-layer softmax classifier has only a limited capacity. To allow more non-linear processing for each tag kind, we prepend a dense layer with tanh non-linearity and a residual connection before each softmax classifier.

---

[3] http://github.com/facebookresearch/fastText/ blob/master/pretrained-vectors.md

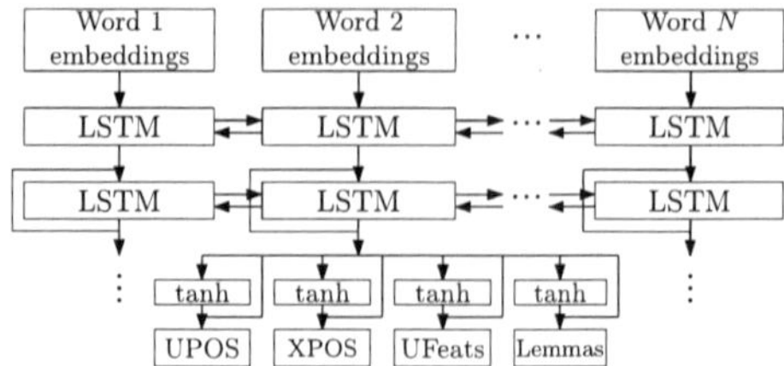

Figure 2: Tagger and lemmatizer model.

The illustration of the tagger and the lemmatizer is illustrated in Figure 2.

4.4 Lemmatization

We lemmatize input words by classifying them into lemma generation rules. We consider these rules as a fourth tag kind (in addition to UPOS, XPOS and UFeats) and use analogous architecture.

To construct the lemma generation rule from a given form and lemma, we proceed as follows:

- We start by finding the longest continuous substring of the form and the lemma. If it is empty, we use the lemma itself as the class.

- If there is a common substring of the form and the lemma, we compute the shortest edit script converting the prefix of the form into the prefix of the lemma, and the shortest edit script converting the suffix of the form to the suffix of the lemma.

  We consider two variants of the edit scripts. The first one permits only character operations `delete_current_char` and `insert_char(c)`. The second variant additionally allows `copy_current_char` operation. For each treebank, we choose the variant producing less unique classes for all training data.

- All above operations are performed case insensitively. To indicate correct casing of the lemma, we consider the lemma to be a concatenation of segments, where each segment is composed of either a sequence of lowercase characters, or a sequence of uppercase characters. We represent the lemma casing by encoding the beginning of every such segment, where the offsets in the first half of the lemma are computed relatively to the start of the lemma, and the offsets in the second half of the lemma are computed relatively to the end of the lemma.

	Lemma generation rules
Minimum	6
Q1	199
Median	490
Mean	877
Q3	831
Maximum	8475

Table 1: Statistics of number of lemma generation rules for 73 treebank training sets of the *CoNLL 2018 UD Shared Task*.

Considering all 73 treebank training sets of the *CoNLL 2018 UD Shared Task*, the number of created lemma generation rules according to the above procedure is detailed in Table 1.

4.5 Dependency Parsing

We base our parsing model on a graph-based biaffine attention parser architecture of the last year's shared task winner (Dozat et al., 2017).

The model starts again with contextualized embeddings produced by bidirectional RNNs, with an artificial ROOT word prepended before the beginning of the sentence. The contextualized embeddings are non-linearly mapped into arc-head and arc-dep representation, which are combined using biaffine attention to produce for each word a distribution indicating the probability of all other words being its dependency head. Finally, we produce an arborescence (i.e., directed spanning tree) with maximum probability by utilizing the Chu-Liu/Edmonds algorithm (Chu and Liu, 1965; Edmonds, 1967).

To generate labels for dependency arcs, we proceed analogously – we non-linearly map the contextualized embeddings into rel-head and rel-dep and combine them using biaffine attention, producing for every possible dependency edge a probability distribution over dependency labels.

4.6 Joint Model Variants

We consider two variants of a joint tagging and parsing model, illustrated in Figure 3.

- The *tightly joint model* shares the contextualized embeddings between the tagger and the parser. Notably, the shared contextualized embeddings are computed using 2 layers of bidirectional LSTM. Then, both the tagger and the parser employ an additional layer of bidirectional LSTM, resulting in 4 bidirectional RNN layers.

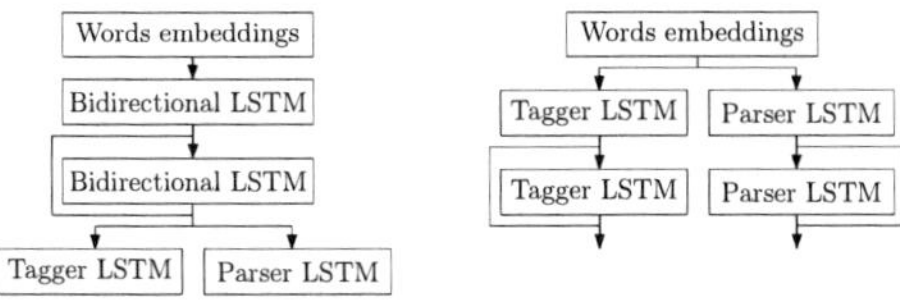

Figure 3: The tightly joint model (on the left) and the loosely joint model (on the right).

- The *loosely joint model* shares only the word embeddings between the tagger and the parser, which both compute contextualized embeddings using 2 layers of bidirectional LSTM, resulting again in 4 RNN layers.

There is one additional difference between the tightly and loosely joint model. While in the tightly joint model the generated POS tags influence the parser model only independently through the shared contextualized embeddings (i.e., the POS tags can be considered regularization of the parser model), the loosely joint model extends the parser word embeddings by the embeddings of the predicted UPOS, XPOS and UFeats tags. Note that we utilize the predicted tags even during training (instead of the gold ones).

4.7 Model Hyperparameters

Considering the 73 treebank training sets of the *CoNLL 2018 UD Shared Task*, we do not employ any treebank-specific hyperparameter search. Most of the hyperparameters were set according to a single Czech-PDT treebank (the largest one), and no effort has been made to adjust them to the other treebanks.

To compute the character-level word embeddings, we utilize character embeddings and GRUs with dimension of 256. The trained word embeddings and the sentence-level LSTMs have a dimension of 512. The UPOS, XPOS and UFeats embeddings, if used, have a dimension of 128. The parser arc-head, arc-dep, rel-head and rel-dep representations have dimensions of 512, 512, 128 and 128, respectively.

4.8 Neural Network Training

For each of the 73 treebanks with a training set we train one model, utilizing only the training treebank and pretrained word embeddings. Each model was trained using the Adam algorithm (Kingma and Ba, 2014) on a GeForce GTX 1080 GPU with a batch size of 32 randomly chosen sentences (for batch size of 64 sentences train-

ing ended with out-of-memory error for some treebanks). The training consists of 60 epochs, with the learning rate being 0.001 for the first 40 epochs and 0.0001 for the last 20 epochs. To sufficiently train smaller treebanks, each epoch consists of one pass over the training data or 300 batches, whatever is larger.

Following Dozat and Manning (2016); Vaswani et al. (2017), we modify the default value of β_2 hyperparameter of Adam, but to a different value than both of the above papers – to 0.99, which resulted in best performance on the largest treebank. We also make sure Adam algorithm does not update first and second moment estimates for embeddings not present in a batch.

We regularize the training by several ways:

- We employ dropout with dropout probability 50% on all embeddings and hidden layers, with the exception of RNN states and residual connections.
- We utilize label smoothing of 0.03 in all softmax classifications.
- With a probability of 20%, we replace trained word embedding by an embedding of an unknown word.

With the described training method and regularization techniques, the model does not seem to overfit at all, or very little. Consequently, we do not perform early stopping and always utilize the model after full 60 epochs of training.

The training took 2-4 hours for most of the treebanks, with the two largest Russian-SynTagRus and Czech-PDT taking 15 and 20 hours, respectively.

5 CoNLL 2018 UD Shared Task

The official *CoNLL 2018 UD Shared Task* evaluation was performed using a TIRA platform (Potthast et al., 2014), which provided virtual machines for every participants' systems. During test data evaluation, the machines were disconnected from the internet, and reset after the evaluation finished – this way, the entire test sets were kept private even during the evaluation.

The shared task contains test sets of three kinds:

- For most treebanks large training and development sets were available, in which case we trained the model on the training set and choose among the pretrained word embeddings and tightly or loosely joint model according to performance on the development set.

- For several treebanks very small training sets and no development sets were available. In these cases we manually split 10% of the training set to act as a development set and proceed as in the above case.
- Nine test treebanks contained no training data at all. For these treebanks we adopted the baseline model strategy:

  For Czech-PUD, English-PUD, Finnish-PUD, Japanese-Modern, and Swedish-PUD there were other treebank variants of the same language available in the training set. Consequently, we processed these treebanks using models trained for Czech PDT, English EWT, Finnish TDT, Japanese GSD, and Swedish Talbanken, respectively.

  For Breton-KEB, Faroese-OFT, Naija-NSC, and Thai-PUD, we trained a universal mixed model, by using first 200 sentences of each training set (or less in case of very small treebanks) as training data and first 20 sentences of each development treebank as development data.

5.1 Shared Task Evaluation

The official *CoNLL 2018 UD Shared Task* results are presented in Table 4. In addition to F1 scores, we also include rank of our submission (out of the 26 participant systems).

In the three official metrics (LAS, MLAS and BLEX) our system reached third, first and third average performance. Additionally, our system achieved best average performance in XPOS and AllTags metrics. Furthermore, the lemmatization F1 score was the second best.

Interestingly, although our system achieves highest average score in MLAS (which is a combination of dependency parsing and morphological features), it reaches only third best average LAS and fourth best average UFeats. Furthermore, the `TurkuNLP` participation system surpasses our system in both LAS and UFeats. We hypothesise that the high performance of our system in MLAS metric is caused by the fact that the tagger and parser models are joined, thus producing consistent annotations.

Finally, we note that the segmentation improvements outlined in Section 4.1 resulted in third average F1 score of our system.

Event Extraction	Negation Resolution	Opinion Analysis	Overall Score
49.66 3	58.45 3	60.46 7	**56.19 1**

Table 2: UDPipe 2.0 prototype results in EPE 2018. For each metric we present F1 score percentage and also rank.

	Model size
Average	**139.2MB**
Minimum	90.5MB
Q1	110.0MB
Median	132.0MB
Q3	145.1MB
Maximum	347.1MB
UDPipe 1.2	*13.2MB*

Table 3: Statistics of the model sizes.

5.2 Extrinsic Parser Evaluation

Following the First Shared Task on Extrinsic Parser Evaluation (Oepen et al., 2017), the 2018 edition of Extrinsic Parser Evaluation Initiative (EPE 2018) ran in collaboration with the *CoNLL 2018 UD Shared Task*. The initiative allowed to evaluate the English systems submitted to the CoNLL shared task against three EPE downstream systems – biological event extraction, negation resolution, and fine-grained opinion analysis.

The results of our system are displayed in Table 2. Even though our system ranked only 3rd, 3rd, and 7th in the downstream task F1 scores, it was the best system in the overall score (and average of the three F1 scores).

5.3 Model Size

The statistics of the model sizes is listed in Table 3. Average model size is approximately 140MB, which is more than 10 times larger than baseline UDPipe 1.2 models. Note however that we do not perform any model quantization (which should result in almost four times smaller models, following for example approach of Wu et al. (2016)), and we did not consider the model size during hyperparameter selection. Taking into account that the largest part of the models are the trained word embeddings, the model size could be reduced substantially by reducing trained word embeddings dimension.

5.4 Runtime Performance

The runtime performance of our system is presented in Table 6. Compared to the baseline UDPipe 1.2, tagging and parsing on a single CPU

202

Language	Tokens	Words	Sentences	UPOS	XPOS	UFeats	AllTags	Lemmas	UAS	LAS	MLAS	BLEX
Afrikaans-AfriBooms	99.75 4	99.75 4	98.25 4	**97.82** 1	**94.23** 1	**97.45** 1	94.08 2	97.11 2	87.74 6	84.99 4	**75.67** 1	75.74 3
Ancient Greek-PROIEL	**100.00** 1	**100.00** 1	49.15 4	97.34 3	97.74 2	**91.98** 1	**90.53** 1	91.08 19	79.50 6	75.78 5	59.82 5	62.62 7
Ancient Greek-Perseus	99.96 4	99.96 4	98.73 3	92.10 4	84.27 2	90.30 2	83.18 2	81.78 20	77.94 7	72.49 6	51.55 6	49.46 7
Arabic-PADT	**99.98** 1	93.71 4	**80.89** 1	90.64 3	87.81 3	88.05 3	87.38 2	88.94 3	76.30 7	72.34 6	63.77 2	65.66 3
Armenian-ArmTDP	97.21 3	96.47 3	92.41 2	65.29 21	—	40.09 23	33.14 21	57.46 20	49.60 3	36.42 2	4.14 20	13.03 8
Basque-BDT	99.97 3	99.97 3	99.83 3	96.08 2	—	92.21 2	**90.13** 1	95.19 4	86.03 5	82.65 5	**71.73** 1	77.25 3
Breton-KEB	91.03 22	90.62 20	90.36 20	36.58 7	**0.01** 1	36.84 4	**0.00** 1	54.99 4	36.54 7	13.87 7	1.24 5	5.78 6
Bulgarian-BTB	99.91 25	99.91 25	95.56 3	98.83 3	**97.01** 1	**97.69** 1	**96.37** 1	97.41 3	92.82 4	89.70 3	**83.12** 1	83.17 2
Buryat-BDT	97.07 3	97.07 3	90.90 3	41.66 8	—	38.34 3	30.00 2	56.83 2	29.20 11	12.61 10	2.09 4	4.41 6
Catalan-AnCora	**99.98** 1	**99.98** 1	**99.68** 1	**98.85** 1	**98.85** 1	**98.36** 1	**97.81** 1	**98.90** 1	92.97 3	90.79 3	**84.07** 1	**85.47** 1
Chinese-GSD	90.04 6	90.04 6	96.25 24	85.83 7	85.64 4	89.13 5	84.61 5	90.01 6	68.73 9	65.67 8	55.97 7	61.38 7
Croatian-SET	**99.93** 1	**99.93** 1	94.64 24	98.02 3	—	92.12 1	**91.44** 1	96.69 2	90.33 7	85.93 6	72.85 2	79.84 2
Czech-CAC	**100.00** 1	**99.99** 1	**100.00** 1	99.33 2	**96.36** 1	**96.08** 1	**95.66** 1	98.14 3	92.62 6	90.32 7	**83.42** 1	86.24 4
Czech-FicTree	**100.00** 1	**100.00** 1	98.84 2	98.49 4	94.94 3	95.74 3	94.53 2	97.80 3	93.05 8	90.06 8	81.11 5	84.76 6
Czech-PDT	99.93 4	99.93 3	93.41 2	99.01 3	96.93 2	96.85 2	**96.38** 1	**98.71** 1	92.32 6	90.32 5	**85.10** 1	87.47 3
Czech-PUD	99.25 22	99.25 22	94.95 22	96.84 6	93.64 2	93.55 2	**92.09** 1	**96.44** 1	89.66 5	84.86 4	**75.81** 1	80.32 2
Danish-DDT	**99.90** 1	**99.90** 1	91.41 4	97.72 2	—	97.09 2	96.03 2	96.66 3	85.67 6	83.33 5	75.29 3	76.83 4
Dutch-Alpino	99.93 2	99.93 2	**90.97** 1	**96.90** 1	**94.93** 1	96.51 1	**94.36** 1	**96.76** 1	90.11 5	87.09 4	76.09 2	77.76 2
Dutch-LassySmall	99.83 5	99.83 5	76.54 4	95.98 5	94.51 3	95.65 4	93.58 3	95.78 4	86.80 5	83.15 5	72.10 4	72.63 6
English-EWT	99.02 24	99.02 24	77.05 2	95.43 4	95.05 3	95.99 3	93.68 2	**97.23** 1	85.01 8	82.51 7	74.71 3	77.64 4
English-GUM	99.75 2	99.75 2	78.79 4	95.55 5	95.42 2	96.39 3	94.26 2	**96.18** 1	84.60 8	81.35 7	70.74 4	71.67 5
English-LinES	99.93 23	99.93 23	87.21 24	96.77 4	95.72 2	96.67 3	93.26 2	96.44 2	82.73 9	78.26 10	70.66 6	71.73 7
English-PUD	99.67 21	99.67 21	96.19 4	95.68 3	94.59 2	95.32 2	**91.78** 1	95.87 2	87.80 7	85.02 7	74.45 5	78.20 5
Estonian-EDT	99.93 3	99.93 3	91.55 5	97.31 2	98.08 2	**95.81** 1	**94.47** 1	94.88 2	86.29 6	83.26 6	76.62 2	76.29 2
Faroese-OFT	99.50 15	97.40 23	**96.25** 1	62.00 3	**4.23** 1	32.19 7	**1.04** 1	51.31 6	54.95 5	41.99 5	0.74 3	13.49 3
Finnish-FTB	**100.00** 1	**99.99** 1	87.83 3	96.38 3	**95.27** 1	**96.89** 1	93.95 2	94.74 3	88.77 7	86.13 7	78.77 3	78.46 4
Finnish-PUD	99.63 3	99.63 3	90.70 23	97.61 2	—	**96.87** 1	0.00 4	90.64 3	89.69 8	87.69 7	82.17 5	76.00 3
Finnish-TDT	99.68 23	99.68 23	90.32 4	96.75 5	97.52 4	95.43 3	94.17 2	90.18 3	88.10 7	85.72 6	79.25 3	73.99 3
French-GSD	99.69 3	98.81 4	94.29 3	96.32 5	—	96.07 3	95.13 2	96.75 3	88.74 4	85.74 4	77.29 3	79.88 4
French-Sequoia	99.85 2	99.14 4	86.99 4	97.56 6	—	97.00 4	96.25 3	97.36 3	90.07 5	88.04 6	81.45 3	83.04 5
French-Spoken	**100.00** 1	**100.00** 1	21.63 3	95.47 8	97.37 3	—	93.00 2	95.98 3	76.20 7	71.16 7	60.17 6	60.87 6
Galician-CTG	99.89 2	99.21 2	97.23 2	96.98 3	96.62 3	99.05 2	96.24 3	97.53 4	84.42 3	81.88 3	69.75 3	74.46 3
Galician-TreeGal	**99.69** 1	98.73 1	83.90 2	94.44 2	**91.64** 1	**93.08** 1	**90.49** 1	95.05 2	78.66 3	**74.25** 1	**60.63** 1	**64.29** 1
German-GSD	99.60 2	99.61 2	82.32 2	94.04 2	96.93 2	89.96 2	84.47 2	96.14 2	82.76 4	78.17 5	56.84 3	69.79 4
Gothic-PROIEL	**100.00** 1	**100.00** 1	29.88 4	95.75 2	96.38 2	**90.05** 1	**87.64** 1	92.39 18	74.92 3	69.39 2	**56.45** 1	61.92 3
Greek-GDT	99.87 2	99.86 3	90.71 4	97.73 3	97.71 3	94.27 3	93.45 2	94.74 4	91.27 3	89.05 3	77.43 2	77.18 5
Hebrew-HTB	99.96 24	85.15 25	99.69 24	82.53 6	82.54 4	81.29 2	80.36 2	82.88 3	67.22 8	63.65 7	51.36 4	54.13 4
Hindi-HDTB	**100.00** 1	**100.00** 1	98.63 24	97.56 2	97.09 2	**94.10** 1	**92.06** 1	98.45 3	94.85 3	91.75 2	**78.30** 1	86.42 3
Hungarian-Szeged	99.79 24	99.79 24	96.12 2	95.48 2	—	92.41 3	91.28 2	92.99 3	83.08 4	78.51 4	**67.13** 1	70.39 4
Indonesian-GSD	**100.00** 1	**100.00** 1	93.53 3	93.55 6	94.45 4	95.77 3	88.78 2	99.60 3	84.91 8	78.58 4	67.58 4	75.94 2
Irish-IDT	99.30 4	99.30 4	92.60 3	91.58 2	90.41 2	82.40 2	78.46 2	87.52 2	78.50 4	70.22 2	45.53 2	51.29 2
Italian-ISDT	99.79 3	99.71 2	**99.38** 1	98.09 2	97.94 2	**97.83** 1	**97.16** 1	**98.21** 1	92.66 4	90.75 4	83.46 3	84.48 3
Italian-PoSTWITA	99.75 2	**99.47** 1	28.95 5	95.29 7	95.77 2	94.48 2	94.48 2	94.91 4	77.34 7	73.23 6	61.29 4	61.71 5
Japanese-GSD	90.46 6	90.46 6	**95.01** 1	88.88 7	—	90.45 6	88.88 6	90.01 4	76.13 11	74.54 9	61.99 6	63.48 5
Japanese-Modern	65.98 5	65.98 5	0.00 2	48.51 7	**0.00** 1	64.14 7	**0.00** 1	54.76 6	28.41 16	22.39 15	7.33 15	9.06 15
Kazakh-KTB	93.11 5	92.74 6	81.56 2	48.94 11	49.16 5	46.86 4	38.92 2	57.36 4	39.45 10	24.21 3	7.62 4	9.79 3
Korean-GSD	99.86 4	99.86 4	93.26 3	96.13 3	89.81 4	99.63 3	87.44 4	91.37 3	86.58 6	83.12 6	78.56 6	73.85 3
Korean-Kaist	**100.00** 1	**100.00** 1	**100.00** 1	95.65 2	86.73 3	—	86.62 3	93.53 2	88.13 6	86.16 6	80.46 4	78.15 2
Kurmanji-MG	94.33 3	94.01 3	69.14 3	52.50 22	50.21 20	41.05 21	28.34 18	52.44 21	37.29 5	29.09 3	2.40 19	9.51 12
Latin-ITTB	99.94 4	99.94 4	82.49 3	98.28 5	**95.29** 1	96.36 2	**94.30** 1	98.56 3	88.00 6	85.22 6	79.73 2	82.86 5
Latin-PROIEL	**100.00** 1	**100.00** 1	35.36 5	96.75 2	**96.93** 1	91.26 2	**90.06** 1	95.54 4	73.96 7	69.79 6	58.03 4	64.54 5
Latin-Perseus	99.99 22	99.99 22	**99.15** 1	87.64 7	73.25 2	78.02 4	71.22 2	75.44 20	70.33 6	60.08 7	40.75 4	39.86 7
Latvian-LVTB	99.37 24	99.37 24	**98.66** 1	94.63 6	**87.10** 1	91.48 2	**85.67** 1	93.33 3	83.52 6	79.32 6	67.24 3	70.92 4
Naija-NSC	96.63 7	93.27 6	0.00 4	41.52 21	—	—	5.83 17	89.72 6	26.89 11	12.60 13	3.72 11	11.06 14
North Sami-Giella	99.84 2	99.84 2	98.33 2	90.65 4	91.95 3	86.82 2	81.88 2	78.43 20	74.40 4	68.95 4	54.07 2	48.25 5
Norwegian-Bokmaal	99.81 4	99.81 4	97.13 2	98.14 2	—	96.95 2	**96.20** 1	**98.20** 1	91.81 3	89.98 3	**83.68** 1	**85.82** 1
Norwegian-Nynorsk	99.92 23	99.92 23	93.49 3	97.88 2	—	96.85 2	95.98 1	**97.80** 1	91.12 4	88.97 4	**81.86** 1	84.05 3
Norwegian-NynorskLIA	**99.99** 1	**99.99** 1	**99.86** 1	89.74 7	—	89.52 3	84.32 2	92.65 18	67.49 6	59.35 7	46.57 6	49.97 6
Old Church Slavonic-PROIEL	**100.00** 1	**100.00** 1	40.54 4	96.34 2	96.62 2	93.69 3	**88.12** 1	88.93 20	79.06 3	74.84 2	62.60 2	65.71 5
Old French-SRCMF	**100.00** 1	**100.00** 1	**100.00** 1	96.22 1	96.15 1	97.79 1	95.52 1	—	**91.72** 1	**87.12** 1	**80.28** 1	**84.11** 1
Persian-Seraji	**100.00** 1	99.65 2	98.75 4	97.32 2	97.33 2	**97.45** 1	96.90 1	97.05 2	89.48 4	86.14 3	**80.83** 1	80.28 3
Polish-LFG	99.90 4	99.90 4	99.65 24	98.56 3	**94.18** 1	95.28 1	93.23 1	96.73 3	96.21 6	94.53 5	**86.93** 1	89.07 3
Polish-SZ	99.99 2	99.88 3	**98.20** 1	92.55 2	92.40 4	**91.36** 1	95.31 3	92.78 6	90.59 6	79.76 5	82.89 3	
Portuguese-Bosque	99.64 23	99.51 21	88.47 23	96.37 5	—	95.77 3	93.43 3	97.38 3	89.48 7	87.04 6	74.16 5	80.01 4
Romanian-RRT	99.64 24	99.64 24	95.57 4	97.56 3	96.92 4	97.14 4	96.69 3	97.61 3	90.16 7	85.65 5	77.94 3	79.35 4
Russian-SynTagRus	99.63 3	99.63 3	98.64 4	**98.71** 1	—	97.17 1	96.90 1	97.94 2	92.96 5	91.46 4	**86.76** 1	87.90 2
Russian-Taiga	98.14 1	98.14 1	87.38 1	90.42 5	**98.12** 1	80.89 4	78.02 4	83.55 4	70.54 8	63.80 8	44.93 5	48.51 6
Serbian-SET	**99.97** 1	**99.97** 1	93.26 2	**98.18** 1	—	94.26 1	**93.77** 1	96.56 2	91.68 5	88.15 4	**77.73** 1	81.75 2
Slovak-SNK	**100.00** 1	**100.00** 1	84.96 4	96.65 3	85.98 2	90.33 3	84.60 2	95.66 2	87.96 7	85.06 7	72.08 3	78.44 2
Slovenian-SSJ	98.26 24	98.26 24	76.74 5	96.83 6	93.26 3	93.48 3	92.67 2	96.22 2	87.43 8	85.59 8	77.95 3	81.22 4
Slovenian-SST	**100.00** 1	**100.00** 1	22.90 3	92.58 8	84.68 3	84.65 5	81.57 3	92.56 3	58.32 8	52.84 8	40.24 5	44.57 6
Spanish-AnCora	99.96 24	99.94 22	**98.96** 1	98.80 3	**98.80** 1	98.43 1	**97.82** 1	**99.02** 1	91.64 7	89.55 6	83.16 3	84.44 3
Swedish-LinES	99.96 2	99.96 2	85.25 3	96.66 4	94.60 4	89.42 4	86.39 3	96.61 2	84.82 8	80.68 8	65.77 6	75.67 4
Swedish-PUD	98.26 24	98.26 24	88.89 23	93.31 6	91.66 3	77.80 5	75.61 3	86.23 6	81.62 8	77.90 8	49.90 4	64.04 4
Swedish-Talbanken	99.88 5	99.88 5	95.79 3	97.79 2	96.43 3	96.59 4	95.43 2	97.08 3	89.32 3	86.36 3	79.08 2	80.73 4
Thai-PUD	8.53 20	8.53 20	0.20 21	5.67 18	0.12 6	6.59 6	0.12 2	—	0.88 9	0.65 13	0.04 7	0.23 17
Turkish-IMST	99.86 2	**97.92** 1	97.09 2	93.58 4	92.82 3	91.25 3	89.00 3	92.74 4	69.34 6	63.07 6	54.02 4	56.69 5
Ukrainian-IU	99.76 2	99.76 2	96.86 2	97.17 3	**91.52** 1	**91.45** 1	90.12 1	95.94 3	87.11 5	84.06 5	**72.27** 1	77.11 4
Upper Sorbian-UFAL	**98.64** 1	**98.64** 1	67.24 22	65.51 21	—	49.63 18	43.46 15	63.54 17	35.72 15	24.29 15	3.41 19	11.88 12
Urdu-UDTB	**100.00** 1	**100.00** 1	98.59 24	93.69 6	91.50 6	81.97 6	77.27 4	97.33 2	87.17 8	81.32 7	54.72 6	72.87 4
Uyghur-UDT	99.58 5	99.58 5	82.82 4	88.92 6	91.47 4	86.80 4	78.33 3	92.86 4	76.61 2	65.23 2	**45.78** 1	54.17 2
Vietnamese-VTB	85.05 5	85.05 5	93.31 2	77.61 5	75.91 4	84.83 5	75.80 4	84.76 2	50.98 5	46.45 3	40.26 3	42.88 2
Total	97.46 7	97.04 7	83.64 3	89.37 6	**86.67** 1	86.67 4	80.30 1	89.32 2	77.90 5	73.11 3	**61.25** 1	64.49 3

Table 4: Official *CoNLL 2018 UD Shared Task* results of the UDPipe 2.0 prototype. For each metric we present F1 score percentage and also rank (out of the 26 participant systems).

Experiment	UPOS	XPOS	UFeats	AllTags	Lemmas	UAS	LAS	MLAS	BLEX
Shared task submission	95.73	94.79	94.11	91.45	95.12	85.28	81.83	71.71	74.67
Baseline tokenization&segmentation	95.69	94.75	94.07	91.41	95.09	85.10	81.65	71.53	74.48
No precomputed word embeddings	95.23	94.19	93.45	90.52	94.82	84.52	80.88	69.98	73.30
Best model on development set	95.74	94.80	94.12	91.47	95.16	85.28	81.83	71.76	74.69
Checkpoint average of 5 last epochs	95.74	94.81	94.12	91.48	95.14	85.30	81.84	71.80	74.69
No label smoothing	95.66	94.70	94.01	91.26	94.98	85.16	81.68	71.31	74.32
Loosely joint model for all treebanks	95.71	94.82	94.13	91.49	95.29	85.14	81.68	71.71	74.72
Tightly joint model for all treebanks	95.75	94.76	94.06	91.40	94.79	85.34	81.88	71.61	74.33
Tagging each class independently	95.56	94.71	94.04	—	95.47	—	—	—	—
Adding connection between character-level embeddings and the lemma classifier.									
Loosely joint model for all treebanks	95.74	94.85	94.21	91.60	95.86	85.17	81.73	71.89	75.37
Tightly joint model for all treebanks	95.80	94.83	94.17	91.57	95.80	85.44	81.99	71.90	75.54
Best joint model for all treebanks	95.78	94.83	94.19	91.57	95.83	85.38	81.95	71.94	75.55

Table 5: Average score of different variants of our system.

Configuration	Tagging&parsing speed	Speedup to 1 thread CPU
PyPI Tensorflow 1.5.1, CPU version		
1 thread	111 w/s	1
2 threads	191 w/s	1.7
4 threads	326 w/s	2.9
8 threads	517 w/s	4.7
16 threads	624 w/s	5.6
PyPI Tensorflow 1.5.1, GPU version *GeForce GTX 1080*		
1 thread	2320 w/s	20.9
2 threads	2522 w/s	22.7
4 threads	2790 w/s	25.1
UDPipe 1.2, no parallelism available		
1 thread	*1907 w/s*	*17.2*

Table 6: Average runtime performance of our system.

thread is more than 17 times slower. Utilizing 8 CPU threads speeds up the performance of the prototype by a factor of 4.7, which is still more than 3 times slower than the baseline models. Nevertheless, when GPU is employed during tagging and parsing, the runtime speed of our system surpasses baseline models.

We note that runtime performance has not been a priority during hyperparameter model selection. There are many possible trade-offs which would make inference faster, and some of them will presumably decrease the system performance only slightly.

6 Ablation Experiments

All ablation experiment results in this section are performed using test sets of 61 so called "big treebanks", which are treebanks with provided development data, disregarding small treebanks and test treebanks without training data.

6.1 Baseline Sentence Segmentation

The performance of our system using baseline tokenization and segmentation models (cf. Section 4.1) is displayed in Table 5. The effect of achieving better sentence segmentation influences parsing more than tagging, which can handle wrong sentence segmentation more gracefully.

6.2 Pretrained Word Embeddings

Considering that pretrained word embeddings have demonstrated effective similarity extraction from large plain text (Mikolov et al., 2013), they have a potential of substantially increasing tagging and parsing performance. To quantify their effect, we have evaluated models trained without pretrained embeddings, presenting results in Table 5. Depending on the metric, the pretrained word embeddings improve performance by 0.3-1.7 F1 points.

6.3 Regularization Methods

The effect of early stopping, checkpoint averaging of last 5 epochs and label smoothing is shown also in Table 5. While early stopping and checkpoint averaging have little effect on performance, early stopping demonstrate slight improvement of 0.1-0.4 F1 points.

6.4 Tightly vs Loosely Joint Model

The last model variants presented in Table 5 show the effect of always using either the tightly or loosely joint model for all treebanks. In present implementation, loosely joint model accomplishes better tagging accuracy, while deteriorating parsing slightly. The tightly joint model performs slightly worse during tagging and most notably

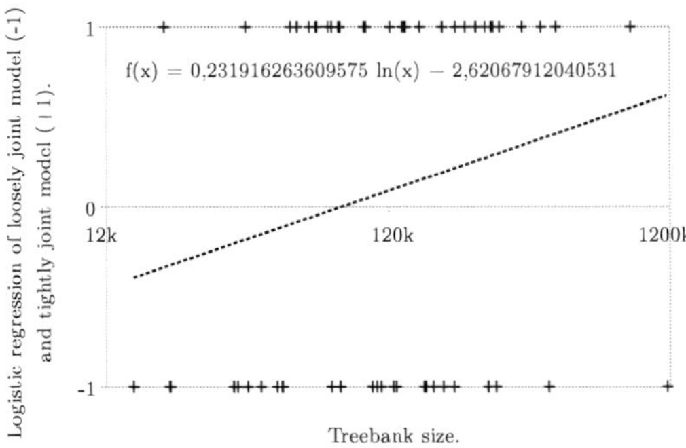

Figure 4: Logarithmic regression of using tightly joint models (+1) and loosely joint models (-1) depending on treebank size in words.

during lemmatization, while improving dependency parsing.

Finally, Figure 4 shows result of logarithmic regression of using tightly or loosely joint model, depending on treebank size in words. Accordingly, the loosely joint model seems to be more suited for smaller treebanks, while the tightly joint model appear to be more suited for larger treebanks.

7   Post-competition Improved Models

Motivated by the decrease in lemmatization performance of the tightly joint model architecture, we refined the architecture of the models by *adding a direct connection from character-level word embeddings to the lemma classifier*. Our hope was to improve lemmatization performance in the tightly joint architecture by providing the lemma classifier a direct access to the embeddings of exact word composition.

As seen in Table 5, the improved models perform considerably better, and with only minor differences between the tighty and loosely joint architectures. We therefore consider only the tightly joint improved models, removing a hyperparameter choice (which joint architecture to use).

The improved models show a considerable increase of 0.68 percentage points in lemmatization performance and minor increase in other tagging scores. The parsing performance also improves by 0.87, 0.19, and 0.16 points in BLEX, MLAS and LAS F1 scores in the ablation experiments.

Encouraged by the results, we performed an evaluation of the improved models in TIRA, achieving 73.28, 61.25, and 65.53 F1 scores in LAS, MLAS and BLEX metrics, which corresponds to increases of 0.17, 0.00 and 1.04 percentage points. Such scores would rank 2nd, 1st, and 2nd in the shared task evaluation. We also submitted the improved models to extrinsic evaluation EPE 2018, improving the F1 scores of the three downstream tasks listed in Table 2 by 0.87, 0.00, and 0.27 percentage points, corresponding to 1st, 3rd, and 4th rank. The overall score of the original models, already the best achieved in EPE 2018, further increased by 0.38 points with the improved models.

8   Conclusions and Future Work

We described a prototype for UDPipe 2.0 and its performance in the *CoNLL 2018 UD Shared Task*, where it achieved 1st, 3rd and 3rd in the three official metrics, MLAS, LAS and BLEX, respectively. The source code of the prototype is available at `http://github.com/CoNLL-UD-2018/UDPipe-Future`.

We also described a minor modification of the prototype architecture, which improves both the intrinsic and the extrinsic evaluation. These improved models will be released shortly in UDPipe at `http://ufal.mff.cuni.cz/udpipe`, utilizing quantization to decrease model size.

Acknowledgments

The work described herein has been supported by the City of Prague under the "OP PPR" program, project No. CZ.07.1.02/0.0/0.0/16_023/0000108, grant GAUK 578218/2018 of Charles University, and it has been using language resources developed by the LINDAT/CLARIN project of the Ministry of Education, Youth and Sports of the Czech Republic (project LM2015071).

I would like to thank Jana Straková for considerably improving the quality of the paper.

References

Daniel Andor, Chris Alberti, David Weiss, Aliaksei Severyn, Alessandro Presta, Kuzman Ganchev, Slav Petrov, and Michael Collins. 2016. Globaly normalized transition-based neural networks. In *Association for Computational Linguistic*. http://arxiv.org/abs/1603.06042.

Danqi Chen and Christopher Manning. 2014. A fast and accurate dependency parser using neural networks. In *Proceedings of the 2014 Conference on Empirical Methods in Natural Language*

Processing (EMNLP). Association for Computational Linguistics, Doha, Qatar, pages 740–750. http://www.aclweb.org/anthology/D14-1082.

KyungHyun Cho, Bart van Merrienboer, Dzmitry Bahdanau, and Yoshua Bengio. 2014. On the properties of neural machine translation: Encoder-decoder approaches. CoRR abs/1409.1259. http://arxiv.org/abs/1409.1259.

Y. J. Chu and T. H. Liu. 1965. On the shortest arborescence of a directed graph. Science Sinica 14.

Ronan Collobert, Jason Weston, Léon Bottou, Michael Karlen, Koray Kavukcuoglu, and Pavel Kuksa. 2011. Natural language processing (almost) from scratch. The Journal of Machine Learning Research 12:2493–2537.

Timothy Dozat and Christopher D. Manning. 2016. Deep Biaffine Attention for Neural Dependency Parsing. CoRR abs/1611.01734. http://arxiv.org/abs/1611.01734.

Timothy Dozat, Peng Qi, and Christopher D. Manning. 2017. Stanford's Graph-based Neural Dependency Parser at the CoNLL 2017 Shared Task. In Proceedings of the CoNLL 2017 Shared Task: Multilingual Parsing from Raw Text to Universal Dependencies. Association for Computational Linguistics, Vancouver, Canada, pages 20–30. http://www.aclweb.org/anthology/K17-3002.

Chris Dyer, Miguel Ballesteros, Wang Ling, Austin Matthews, and Noah A. Smith. 2015. Transition-based dependency parsing with stack long short-term memory. In Proceedings of the 53rd Annual Meeting of the Association for Computational Linguistics and the 7th International Joint Conference on Natural Language Processing (Volume 1: Long Papers). Association for Computational Linguistics, Beijing, China, pages 334–343. http://www.aclweb.org/anthology/P15-1033.

Jack Edmonds. 1967. Optimum branchings. Journal of Research of the National Bureau of Standards, B 71:233–240.

Alex Graves and Jürgen Schmidhuber. 2005. Framewise phoneme classification with bidirectional lstm and other neural network architectures. Neural Networks pages 5–6.

Sepp Hochreiter and Jürgen Schmidhuber. 1997. Long short-term memory. Neural Comput. 9(8):1735–1780. https://doi.org/10.1162/neco.1997.9.8.1735.

Diederik P. Kingma and Jimmy Ba. 2014. Adam: A method for stochastic optimization. CoRR abs/1412.6980. http://arxiv.org/abs/1412.6980.

Adhiguna Kuncoro, Miguel Ballesteros, Lingpeng Kong, Chris Dyer, Graham Neubig, and Noah A. Smith. 2016. What do recurrent neural network grammars learn about syntax? CoRR abs/1611.05774. http://arxiv.org/abs/1611.05774.

Wang Ling, Tiago Luís, Luís Marujo, Ramón Fernandez Astudillo, Silvio Amir, Chris Dyer, Alan W. Black, and Isabel Trancoso. 2015. Finding function in form: Compositional character models for open vocabulary word representation. CoRR abs/1508.02096. http://arxiv.org/abs/1508.02096.

Tomas Mikolov, Ilya Sutskever, Kai Chen, Gregory S. Corrado, and Jeffrey Dean. 2013. Distributed representations of words and phrases and their compositionality. In Advances in Neural Information Processing Systems 26: 27th Annual Conference on Neural Information Processing Systems 2013. Proceedings of a meeting held December 5-8, 2013, Lake Tahoe, Nevada, United States.. pages 3111–3119. http://papers.nips.cc/paper/5021-distributed-representations-of-words-and-phrases-and-their-compositionality.

Joakim Nivre, Marie-Catherine de Marneffe, Filip Ginter, Yoav Goldberg, Jan Hajič, Christopher Manning, Ryan McDonald, Slav Petrov, Sampo Pyysalo, Natalia Silveira, Reut Tsarfaty, and Daniel Zeman. 2016. Universal Dependencies v1: A multilingual treebank collection. In Proceedings of the 10th International Conference on Language Resources and Evaluation (LREC 2016). European Language Resources Association, Portorož, Slovenia, pages 1659–1666.

Joakim Nivre et al. 2018. Universal dependencies 2.2. LINDAT/CLARIN digital library at the Institute of Formal and Applied Linguistics (ÚFAL), Faculty of Mathematics and Physics, Charles University. http://hdl.handle.net/11234/1-2837.

Stephan Oepen, Lilja Øvrelid, Jari Björne, Richard Johansson, Emanuele Lapponi, Filip Ginter, and Erik Velldal. 2017. The 2017 Shared Task on Extrinsic Parser Evaluation. Towards a reusable community infrastructure. In Proceedings of the 2017 Shared Task on Extrinsic Parser Evaluation at the Fourth International Conference on Dependency Linguistics and the 15th International Conference on Parsing Technologies. Pisa, Italy, pages 1 – 16.

Martin Potthast, Tim Gollub, Francisco Rangel, Paolo Rosso, Efstathios Stamatatos, and Benno Stein. 2014. Improving the reproducibility of PAN's shared tasks: Plagiarism detection, author identification, and author profiling. In Evangelos Kanoulas, Mihai Lupu, Paul Clough, Mark Sanderson, Mark Hall, Allan Hanbury, and Elaine Toms, editors, Information Access Evaluation meets Multilinguality, Multimodality, and Visualization. 5th International Conference of the CLEF Initiative (CLEF 14). Springer, Berlin Heidelberg New York, pages 268–299. https://doi.org/10.1007/978-3-319-11382-1_22.

Milan Straka, Jan Hajič, and Jana Straková. 2016. UD-Pipe: trainable pipeline for processing CoNLL-U files performing tokenization, morphological analysis, POS tagging and parsing. In Proceedings of the 10th International Conference on Language

Resources and Evaluation (LREC 2016). European Language Resources Association, Portorož, Slovenia.

Milan Straka and Jana Straková. 2017. Tokenizing, POS Tagging, Lemmatizing and Parsing UD 2.0 with UDPipe. In *Proceedings of the CoNLL 2017 Shared Task: Multilingual Parsing from Raw Text to Universal Dependencies*. Association for Computational Linguistics, Vancouver, Canada, pages 88–99. http://www.aclweb.org/anthology/K/K17/K17-3009.pdf.

Ashish Vaswani, Noam Shazeer, Niki Parmar, Jakob Uszkoreit, Llion Jones, Aidan N. Gomez, Lukasz Kaiser, and Illia Polosukhin. 2017. Attention is all you need. *CoRR* abs/1706.03762. http://arxiv.org/abs/1706.03762.

Yonghui Wu, Mike Schuster, Zhifeng Chen, Quoc V Le, Mohammad Norouzi, Wolfgang Macherey, Maxim Krikun, Yuan Cao, Qin Gao, Klaus Macherey, et al. 2016. Google's neural machine translation system: Bridging the gap between human and machine translation. *arXiv preprint arXiv:1609.08144* .

Zhilin Yang, Ruslan Salakhutdinov, and William W. Cohen. 2016. Multi-task cross-lingual sequence tagging from scratch. *CoRR* abs/1603.06270. http://arxiv.org/abs/1603.06270.

Daniel Zeman, Jan Hajič, Martin Popel, Martin Potthast, Milan Straka, Filip Ginter, Joakim Nivre, and Slav Petrov. 2018. CoNLL 2018 Shared Task: Multilingual Parsing from Raw Text to Universal Dependencies. In *Proceedings of the CoNLL 2018 Shared Task: Multilingual Parsing from Raw Text to Universal Dependencies*. Association for Computational Linguistics, Brussels, Belgium, pages 1–20.

Daniel Zeman, Martin Popel, Milan Straka, Jan Hajič, Joakim Nivre, Filip Ginter, Juhani Luotolahti, Sampo Pyysalo, Slav Petrov, Martin Potthast, Francis Tyers, Elena Badmaeva, Memduh Gökırmak, Anna Nedoluzhko, Silvie Cinková, Jan Hajič jr., Jaroslava Hlaváčová, Václava Kettnerová, Zdeňka Urešová, Jenna Kanerva, Stina Ojala, Anna Missilä, Christopher Manning, Sebastian Schuster, Siva Reddy, Dima Taji, Nizar Habash, Herman Leung, Marie-Catherine de Marneffe, Manuela Sanguinetti, Maria Simi, Hiroshi Kanayama, Valeria de Paiva, Kira Droganova, Héctor Martínez Alonso, Çağrı Çöltekin, Umut Sulubacak, Hans Uszkoreit, Vivien Macketanz, Aljoscha Burchardt, Kim Harris, Katrin Marheinecke, Georg Rehm, Tolga Kayadelen, Mohammed Attia, Ali Elkahky, Zhuoran Yu, Emily Pitler, Saran Lertpradit, Michael Mandl, Jesse Kirchner, Hector Fernandez Alcalde, Jana Strnadova, Esha Banerjee, Ruli Manurung, Antonio Stella, Atsuko Shimada, Sookyoung Kwak, Gustavo Mendonça, Tatiana Lando, Rattima Nitisaroj, and Josie Li. 2017. CoNLL 2017 Shared Task: Multilingual Parsing from Raw Text to Universal Dependencies. In *Proceedings of the CoNLL 2017 Shared Task: Multilingual Parsing from Raw Text to Universal Dependencies*. Association for Computational Linguistics, Vancouver, Canada, pages 1–19.

Universal Morpho-syntactic Parsing and the Contribution of Lexica:
Analyzing the ONLP Lab Submission to the CoNLL 2018 Shared Task

Amit Seker
Open University of Israel
amitse@openu.ac.il

Amir More
Open University of Israel
habeanf@gmail.com

Reut Tsarfaty
Open University of Israel
reutts@openu.ac.il

Abstract

We present the contribution of the ONLP lab at the Open University of Israel to the CoNLL 2018 UD SHARED TASK on MULTILINGUAL PARSING FROM RAW TEXT TO UNIVERSAL DEPENDENCIES. Our contribution is based on a transition-based parser called *yap: yet another parser* which includes a standalone morphological model, a standalone dependency model, and a joint morphosyntactic model. In the task we used *yap*'s standalone dependency parser to parse input morphologically disambiguated by UD-Pipe, and obtained the official score of 58.35 LAS. In a follow up investigation we use *yap* to show how the incorporation of morphological and lexical resources may improve the performance of end-to-end raw-to-dependencies parsing in the case of a *morphologically-rich* and *low-resource* language, Modern Hebrew. Our results on Hebrew underscore the importance of CoNLL-UL, a UD-compatible standard for accessing external lexical resources, for enhancing end-to-end UD parsing, in particular for morphologically rich and low-resource languages. We thus encourage the community to create, convert, or make available more such lexica.

1 Introduction

The Universal Dependencies (UD) initiative[1] is an international, cross-linguistic and cross-cultural initiative aimed at providing morpho-syntactically annotated data sets for the world's languages under a unified, harmonized, annotation scheme.

The UD scheme (Nivre et al., 2016) adheres to two main principles: (i) there is a single set of POS tags, morphological properties, and dependency labels for all treebanks, and their annotation obeys a single set of annotation principles, and (ii) the text is represented in a two-level representation, clearly mapping the written space-delimited source tokens to the (morpho)syntactic words which participate in the dependency tree.

The CoNLL 2018 UD SHARED TASK is a multilingual parsing evaluation campaign wherein, contrary to previous shared tasks such as CoNLL-06/07 (Buchholz and Marsi, 2006; Nivre et al., 2007) corpora are provided with raw text, and the end goal is to provide a complete morpho-syntactic representation, including automatically resolving all of the token-word discrepancies. Contrary to the previous SPMRL shared tasks (Seddah et al., 2013, 2014), the output of all systems obeys a single annotation scheme, allowing for reliable cross-system and cross-language evaluation.

This paper presents the system submitted by the ONLP lab to the shared task, including the dependency models trained on the train sets, assuming morphologically disambiguated input tokens by UDpipe (Straka et al., 2016). We successfully parsed 81 test treebanks of UDv2 set (Nivre et al., 2017) participating in the CoNLL 2018 UD SHARED TASK (Zeman et al., 2018), obtaining the official score of LAS 58.35 average on all treebanks. We then present an analysis of case of Modern Hebrew, a low-resource morphologically rich language (MRL), which is known to be notoriously hard to parse, due to its high morphological word ambiguity and the small size of the treebank. We investigate the contribution of an external lexicon and a standalone morphological component, and show that inclusion of such lexica can lead to above 10% LAS improvement on this MRL.

---

[1] universaldependencies.org

Proceedings of the CoNLL 2018 Shared Task: Multilingual Parsing from Raw Text to Universal Dependencies, pages 208–215
Brussels, Belgium, October 31 – November 1, 2018. ©2018 Association for Computational Linguistics
https://doi.org/10.18653/v1/K18-2021

Our investigation demonstrates the importance of sharing not only syntactic treebanks but also lexical resources among the UD community, and we propose the UD-compatible CoNLL-UL standard for external lexica(More et al., 2018) for sharing broad-coverage lexical resources in the next UD shared tasks, and in general.

The remainder of this document is organized as follows: In Section 2, we present our parser's formal system and statistical models. In Section 3 we present technical issues relevant to the official run for the shared task followed by our results on all languages. In Section 4 we proceed with an analysis of the performance on Modern Hebrew in the task, compared against its performance augmented with a lexicon-backed morphological analyzer. We finally discuss in Section 5 directions for future work and conclude by embracing the CoNLL-UL standard (More et al., 2018) for UD-anchored lexical resource as means to facilitate and improve raw-to-dependencies UD parsing.

2   Our Framework

The parsing system presented by the ONLP Lab for this task is based on *yap — yet another parser*, a transition-based parsing system that relies on the formal framework of Zhang and Clark (2011), an efficient computational framework designed for structure prediction and based on the generalized perceptron for learning and beam search for decoding. This section briefly describes the formal settings and specific models available via *yap*.[2]

2.1   Formal Settings

Formally, a transition system is a quadruple (C, T, c_s, C_t) where C is a set of configurations, T a set of transitions between the elements of C, c_s an initialization function, and $C_t \subset C$ a set of terminal configurations. A transition sequence $y = t_n(t_{n-1}(...t_1(c_s(x))))$ for an input x starts with an initial configuration $c_s(x)$ and results in a terminal configuration $c_n \in C_t$. In order to determine *which* transition $t \in T$ to apply given a configuration $c \in C$, we define a model that learns to predict the transition that would be chosen by an oracle function $O : C \to T$, which has access to the gold output. We employ an objective function

$$F(x) = argmax_{y \in GEN(x)} Score(y)$$

<hr>

[2] https://github.com/habeanf/yap

which scores output candidates (transition sequence in $GEN(x)$) such that the most plausible sequence of transitions is the one that most closely resembles the one generated by an oracle.

To compute $Score(y)$, y is mapped to a global feature vector $\Phi(y) = \{\phi_i(y)\}$ where each feature $\phi_i(y)$ is a count of occurrences of a pattern defined by a feature function. Given this vector, $Score(y)$ is calculated as the dot product of $\Phi(y)$ and a weights vector $\vec{\omega}$:

$$Score(y) = \Phi(y) \cdot \vec{\omega} = \sum_{c_j \in y} \sum_i \omega_i \phi_i(c_j)$$

Following Zhang and Clark (2011), we learn the weights vector $\vec{\omega}$ via the *generalized perceptron*, using the *early-update* averaged variant of Collins and Roark (2004). For decoding, the framework uses the *beam search* algorithm, which helps mitigate otherwise irrecoverable errors in the transition sequence.

2.2   Morphological Analysis

The input to the morphological disambiguation (MD) component in particular and to the *yap* parsing system in general is a lattice L representing all of the morphological analysis alternatives of k surface tokens of the input stream $x = x_1, ..., x_k$, such that each $L_i = MA(x_i)$ is generated by a *morphological analysis* (MA) component, the lattice concatenate the lattices for the whole input sentence x. Each *lattice-arc* in L has a *morpho-syntactic representation* (MSR) defined as $m = (b, e, f, t, g)$, with b and e marking the start and end nodes of m in L, f a form, t a universal part-of-speech tag, and g a set of attribute=value universal features. These *lattice-arc* correspond to potential nodes in the intended dependency tree.

2.3   Morphological Disambiguation

The *morphological disambiguation* (MD) component of our parser is based on More and Tsarfaty (2016), modified to accommodate UD POS tags and morphological features. We provide here a brief exposition of the transition system, as shall be needed for our later analysis, and refer the reader to the original paper for an in-depth discussion (More and Tsarfaty, 2016).

A configuration for morphological disambiguation $C_{MD} = (L, n, i, M)$ consists of a lattice L, an index n representing a node in L, an index i s.t. $0 \leq i < k$ representing a specific token's lattice, and a set of disambiguated morphemes M.

The initial configuration function is defined to be $c_s(x) = (L, bottom(L), 0, \emptyset)$, where $L = MA(x_1) \circ ... \circ MA(x_k)$, and $n = bottom(L)$, the bottom of the lattice. A configuration is terminal when $n = top(L)$ *and* $i = k$. To traverse the lattice and disambiguate the input, we define an open set of transitions using the MD_s transition template:

$$MD_s : (L, p, i, M) \rightarrow (L, q, i, M \cup \{m\})$$

Where $p = b$, $q = e$, and s relates the transition to the disambiguated morpheme m using a parameterized delexicalization $s = DLEX_{oc}(m)$:

$$DLEX_{OC}(m) = \begin{cases} (\text{-}, \text{-}, \text{-}, t, g) & \text{if } t \in OC \\ (\text{-}, \text{-}, f, t, g) & \text{otherwise} \end{cases}$$

In words, $DLEX$ projects a morpheme either with or without its form depending on whether or not the POS tag is an open-class with respect to the form. For UD, we define:

$$OC = \left\{ \begin{matrix} ADJ, AUX, ADV, PUNCT, NUM, \\ INTJ, NOUN, PROPN, VERB \end{matrix} \right\}$$

We use the parametric model of More and Tsarfaty (2016) to score the transitions at each step. Since lattices may have paths of different length and we use beam search for decoding, the problem of variable-length transition sequences arises. We follow More and Tsarfaty (2016), using the $ENDTOKEN$ transition to mitigate the biases induced by variable-length sequences.

2.4 Syntactic Disambiguation

A syntactic configuration is a triplet $C_{DEP} = (\sigma, \beta, A)$ where σ is a stack, β is a buffer, and A a set of labeled arcs. For dependency parsing, we use a specific variant of Arc Eager that was first presented by (Zhang and Nivre, 2011). The differences between plain arc-eager and the arc-zeager variant are detailed in Figure 1.

The features defined for the parametric model also follows the definition of non-local features by Zhang and Nivre (2011), with one difference: we created one version of each feature with a morphological signature (all feature values of the relevant node) and one without. this allows to capture phenomena like agreement.

2.5 Joint Morpho-Syntactic Processing

Given the standalone morphological and syntactic disambiguation it is possible to embed the two into a single joint morpho-syntactic transition system with a "router" that decides which of the transition systems to apply in a given configuration, and train the morphosyntactic model to maximize a single objective function. We implement such joint parser in yap but we have not used it in the task, and we thus leave its description out of this exposition. For further discussion and experiments with the syntactic and joint morpho-syntactic variants in yap we refer the reader to (More et al., In Press).

3 Shared Task Implementation

For sentence segmentation and tokenization up to and including full morphological disambiguation for all languages, we rely on the UDPipe (Straka et al., 2016). Our parsing system implementation is *yap – yet another parser*, an open-source natural language processor written in Go[3]. Once compiled, the processor is a self-contained binary, without any dependencies on external libraries.

For the shared task the processor was compiled with Go version 1.10.3. During the test phase we wrapped the processor with a bash script that invoked yap serially on all the treebanks. Additionally, in order to train on all treebanks we limited the size of all training sets to the first 50,000 sentences for the parser.

Finally, our training algorithm iterates until convergence, where performance is measured by F_1 for *labeled attachment score* when evaluated on languages' respective development sets. We define convergence as two consecutive iterations resulting in a monotonic decrease in F_1 for LAS, and used the best performing model up to that point. For some languages we observed the F_1 never monotonically decreased twice, so after 20 iterations we manually stopped training and used the best performing model.

For some treebanks (cs_cac, fr_sequoia, ru_syntagrus) the serialization code, which relies on Go's built-in encoder package, failed to serialize the in-memory model because it is larger than 2^{30} bytes. To overcome the limitation we downloaded the go source code, manually changed the const field holding this limit and compiled the go source code.

Our strategy for parsing low resource languages was to use another treebank in the same language when such existed for the following:

---

[3]`https://golang.org`

Arc Eager:	Conf.	$c = (\sigma, \beta, A)$		$\sigma_h = A$ *second, 'head' stack*
	Initial	$c_s(x = x_1, ..., x_n) = ([0], [1, ..., n], \emptyset)$		
	Terminal	$C_t = \{c \in C | c = ([0], [], A)\}$		
	Transitions	$(\sigma, [i|\beta], A) \rightarrow ([\sigma|i], \beta, A)$	(SHIFT)	
		$([\sigma|i], [j|\beta], A) \rightarrow ([\sigma|i|j], \beta, A \cup \{(i, l, j)\})$	(ArcRight$_l$)	
		if $(k, l', i) \notin A$ *and* $i \neq 0$ *then*		
		$([\sigma|i], [j|\beta], A) \rightarrow ([\sigma], [j|\beta], A \cup \{(j, l, i)\})$	(ArcLeft$_l$)	
		if $(k, l', i) \in A$ *then*		
		$([\sigma|i], \beta, A) \rightarrow (\sigma, \beta, A \cup \{(i, l, j)\})$	(REDUCE)	

Arc ZEager:	Conf.	$c = (\sigma, \sigma_h, \beta, A)$		$\sigma_h = A$ *second, 'head' stack*
	Initial	$c_s(x = x_1, ..., x_n) = ([]_\sigma, []_h, [1, ..., n], \emptyset)$		Note: no root
	Terminal	$C_t = \{c \in C | c = ([]_\sigma, \sigma_h, [], A)\}$		For any σ_h, A
	Transitions	$([i]_\sigma, \sigma_h, []_\beta, A) \rightarrow ([]_\sigma, \sigma_h, []_\beta, A)$	(POPROOT)	
		$([\sigma|i], \sigma_h, []_\beta, A) \rightarrow (\sigma, \sigma_h, []_\beta, A)$	(REDUCE$_2$)	
		if $T_L! =$**REDUCE** *then*		$T_L = $ Last Transition
		$(\sigma, \sigma_h, [i|\beta], A) \rightarrow ([\sigma|i], [\sigma_h|i], \beta, A)$	(SHIFT)	
		if $|\beta| > 0$ *and* $(|\sigma| > 1$ *and* $(|\beta| > 1$ *or* $|\sigma_h| = 1))$ *then*		
		$([\sigma|i], \sigma_h, [j|\beta], A) \rightarrow ([\sigma|i|j], \sigma_h, \beta, A \cup \{(i, l, j)\})$	(ArcRight$_l$)	
		if $|\beta| > 0$ *and* $|\sigma| > 0$ *then*		
		$([\sigma|i], \sigma_h, \beta, A) \rightarrow ([\sigma], \sigma_h, \beta, A \cup \{(i, l, j)\})$	(REDUCE$_1$)	
		if $|\beta| > 0$ *and* $|\sigma| > 0$ *and* $(k, l', i) \notin A$ *and* $i = k$ *then*		
		$([\sigma|i], [\sigma_h|k], [j|\beta], A) \rightarrow ([\sigma], [\sigma_h], [j|\beta], A \cup \{(j, l, i)\})$	(ArcLeft$_l$)	

Figure 1: Arc-Eager (Kübler et al., 2009, Chapter 3) and Arc-ZEager (Zhang and Nivre, 2011) Systems.

- cs_pud: cs_pdt

- en_pud:en_lines

- fi_pud: fi_ftb

- sv_pud: sv_lines

- ja_modern: ja_gsd

For treebanks where no resource in the same language is available we used the parsing model trained for English:

- br_keb: en_ewt

- fo_oft: en_ewt

- pcm_nsc: en_ewt

- th_pud: en_ewt

Tables 2 and 3 present our official results for all languages. Our system is ranked 22 with an average LAS score of 58.35. Our highest performing languages are Italian and Hindi — interestingly, both of which are considered morphologically rich, and both with LAS around 82. Our lowest performing languages (with up to 20 LAS) are the low-resource languages listed above, with Thai (0 LAS) as an outlier.

4 The Case of MRLs: A Detailed Analysis for Modern Hebrew

As is well known, and as observed in this particular task, *morphologically rich languages* are most challenging to parse in the raw-to-dependencies parsing scenarios. This is because the initial automatic segmentation and morphological disambiguation may contain irrecoverable errors which will undermine parsing performance.

In order to investigate the errors of our parser we took a particular MRL that is known to be hard to parse (Modern Hebrew, ranked 58 in the LAS ranking, with basline 58.73 accuracy) and contrasted the Baseline UDPipe results with the results of our parser, with and without the use of external lexical and morphological resources. Table 1 lists the results of the different parsing models on our dev set. In all of the parsing scenarios, we used UDPipe's built in sentence segmentation, to make sure we parse the exact same sentences. We then contrasted UDPipe's full pipeline with the *yap* output for different morphological settings. We used the Hebrew UD train set for training and the Hebrew UD for analyzing the empirical results.

Initially, we parsed the dev set with the same system we used for the shared task, namely, *yap* dependency parser which parses the morphologically diambiguated output by UDPipe (yap DEP). Here we see that yap DEP results (59.19) are lower than the full UDPipe pipeline (61.95).

Model	Lexicon	Sentence Segmentation	Morphological Disambiguation	Parser	Results on dev LAS / MLAS / BLEX
UDPipe full	–	UDPipe	UDPipe	UDPipe	61.95 / 49.28 / 51.45
yap DEP	–	UDPipe	UDPipe	*yap*	59.19 / 49.19 / 33.75
yap full	Basline	UDPipe	*yap*	*yap*	52.25 / 37.85 / 29.59
	HebLex				60.94 / 39.49 / 33.85
	HebLex-Infused				71.39 / 61.42 / 41.86
yap GOLD	–	Gold	Gold	*yap*	79.33 / 72.56 / 47.62

Table 1: The Contribution of Lexical Resources: Analysis of the Case for Modern Hebrew

We then moved on to experiment with yap's complete pipeline, including a data-driven morphological analyzer (MA) to produce input lattices, transition-based morphological disambiguation and transition-based parsing. The results now dropped relative to the UDPipe baseline and relative to our own yap DEP system, from 59.19 to 52.25 LAS. Now, interestingly, when we replace the baseline data-driven MA learned from the treebank alone with an MA backed with an external broad-coverage lexicon called HebLex (adapted from (Adler and Elhadad, 2006)), the LAS results arrive at 60.94 LAS, outperforming the results obtained by yap DEP (UDPipe morphology with yap dependencies) and close much of the gap with the UDPipe full model. This suggests that much of the parser error stems from missing lexical knowledge concerning the morphologically rich and ambiguous word forms, rather than parser errors.

Finally, we simulated an ideal morphological lattices, by artificially infusing the path that indicates the correct disambiguation into the HebLex lattices in case it has been missing. Note that we still provide an ambiguous input signal, with many possible morphological analyses, only now we guarantee that the correct analysis exists in the lattice. For this setting, we see a significant improvement in LAS, obtaining 71.39 (much beyond the baseline) without changing any of the parsing algorithms involved. So, for morphologically rich and ambiguous languages it appears that lexical coverage is a major factor affecting task performance, especially in the resource scarce case.

Note that the upper-bound of our parser, when given a completely disambiguated morphological input stream, provides LAS of 79.33, which is a few points above the best system (Stanford) in the raw-to-dependencies scenario.

5 Discussion and Conclusion

This paper presents our submission to the CoNLL 2018 UD Shared Task. Our submitted system assumed UDpipe up to and including morphological disambiguation, and employed a state-of-the-art transition-based parsing model to successfully parse 81 languages in the UDv2 set, with the average LAS of 58.35, ranked 22 among the shared task participants.

A detailed post-task investigation of the performance that we conducted on Modern Hebrew, including the shared task and a number of variants, has shown that for the MRL case much of the parser errors may be attributed to incomplete morphological analyses or a complete lack thereof for the source tokens in the input stream.

In the future we intend to investigate sophisticated ways for incorporating additional external lexical and morphological knowledge, explicitely by means of broad-coverage lexica obeying the CoNLL-UL format (More et al., 2018), or implicitly by means of pre-trained word embeddings on large volumes of data. Note, however, that the utility of word-embedding themselves present an open questions in the case of morphologically rich and ambigous source token, where each token may be equivalent to multiple syntactic words in a language like English.

We additionally intend to replace the handcrafted feature model with neural-network based feature extraction mechanisms, and we aim to explore universal morphosyntactic parsing via *joint* morphosyntactic modeling, as previously advocated in different settings (Tsarfaty and Goldberg, 2008; Bohnet and Nivre, 2012; Andor et al., 2016; Bohnet et al., 2013; Li et al., 2011; Bohnet and Nivre, 2012; Li et al., 2014; Zhang et al., 2014)..

Treebank	UAS	LAS	MLAS	CLAS	BLEX
af_afribooms	79.83	73.01	60.73	64.99	41.46
ar_padt	71.62	64.87	53.54	60.69	5.13
bg_btb	87.94	77.81	69.16	73.11	25.18
br_keb	26.46	7.01	0.42	3.06	1.98
bxr_bdt	30.52	11.14	1.65	4.71	2.52
ca_ancora	86.94	80.49	70.37	72.92	53.34
cs_cac	85.41	76.25	64.77	73.22	24.89
cs_fictree	84.33	72.63	59.28	68.01	29.12
cs_pdt	83.09	74.6	65.51	72.12	29.79
cs_pud	74.26	49.25	31.59	35.74	15.69
cu_proiel	69.22	55.34	46.96	54.08	16.22
da_ddt	77.18	69.43	60.7	65.25	39.45
de_gsd	74.93	65.44	30.98	59.06	37.04
el_gdt	83.9	77.37	60.25	70.09	25.2
en_ewt	79.69	71	63.06	66.87	51.34
en_gum	78.24	69.91	58.8	62.85	46.55
en_lines	77.58	68.11	60.28	64.23	44.05
en_pud	72.12	63.73	53.73	58.79	43.33
es_ancora	87.61	81.55	73.01	75.48	52.31
et_edt	76.5	64.52	56.69	61.37	21.73
eu_bdt	69.27	55.21	43.35	50.71	21.14
fa_seraji	83.41	76.32	70.75	72.56	57.72
fi_ftb	75.5	59.82	48.98	52.84	16.82
fi_pud	56.32	38.3	40.59	44.04	15.81
fi_tdt	75.29	63.58	56.5	60.84	19.59
fo_oft	41.41	18.92	0.36	11.98	5.07
fr_gsd	84.89	78.15	69.18	72.91	50.51
fr_sequoia	83.7	77.93	69.18	72.92	49.55
fr_spoken	69.94	61.29	51.17	52.69	41.01
fro_srcmf	84.56	68.55	62.02	64.67	64.67
ga_idt	72.64	59.62	34.63	47.71	25.64
gl_ctg	80.39	75.59	63.47	68.3	40.79
gl_treegal	71.88	64.13	47.71	54.36	34.4
got_proiel	66.12	53.17	42.68	50.49	16.86
grc_perseus	46.75	35.21	17.91	28.08	5.24
grc_proiel	64.75	55.52	38.44	46.53	7.58
he_htb	63.19	55.94	43.12	46.99	31.79
hi_hdtb	91.1	82.35	65.28	77.12	59.25
hr_set	83.32	73.71	54.4	70.23	22.76
hsb_ufal	38.15	26.84	4.73	19.27	3.98
hu_szeged	68.53	54.32	41	48.46	30.73

Table 2: Official Shared-Task Results

Treebank	UAS	LAS	MLAS	CLAS	BLEX
hy_armtdp	40.83	25.04	8.42	17.09	6.96
id_gsd	82.19	72.23	61.93	70.05	41.53
it_isdt	89.25	82.22	72.45	75.06	52.7
it_postwita	73.97	66.35	53.96	56.95	41.03
ja_gsd	74.21	68.45	52.96	54.81	50.63
ja_modern	29.3	22.68	8.29	10.6	9.42
kk_ktb	37.92	17.34	4.33	9.25	2.89
kmr_mg	35.77	25.1	7.77	19.95	6.53
ko_gsd	69.4	55.13	49.99	51.85	17.26
ko_kaist	74.3	59.36	52.62	54.96	12.26
la_ittb	72.77	63.19	54.81	60.29	21.93
la_perseus	43.97	28.12	16.31	23.67	7.46
la_proiel	59.01	48.13	36.96	43.96	14.95
lv_lvtb	73.29	59.67	46.27	54.42	20.58
nl_alpino	79.22	70.95	56.57	62.7	42.48
nl_lassysmall	80.03	70.54	58.26	62.3	43.05
no_bokmaal	86.01	77.43	69.77	74.18	43.89
no_nynorsk	84.25	75.89	67.57	71.83	40.5
no_nynorsklia	58.15	42.21	32.58	36.57	30.99
pcm_nsc	26.11	12.4	4.57	14.68	14.68
pl_lfg	90.22	73.65	60.48	70.55	29.06
pl_sz	85.38	71.87	54.81	68.9	22.67
pt_bosque	84.35	77.46	62.64	69.99	52.06
ro_rrt	82.35	73.01	63.78	66.46	29.07
ru_syntagrus	82.93	74.39	66.49	71.54	23.83
ru_taiga	61.97	48.86	31.77	42.96	18.03
sk_snk	77.99	66.71	48.45	63.6	18.27
sl_ssj	78.61	71.24	57.51	67.57	23.79
sl_sst	51.43	40.88	28.96	35.62	22.96
sme_giella	64.09	48.62	37.23	44.08	17.25
sr_set	85.41	76.78	64.7	73.57	24.1
sv_lines	78.84	68.77	54.28	66.28	37.24
sv_pud	70.7	42.7	16.79	30.36	16.14
sv_talbanken	82.12	73.24	65.84	70.02	36
th_pud	0	0	0	0	0
tr_imst	60.24	43.95	34.37	39.01	15.95
ug_udt	67.47	45.67	28.89	35.67	24.12
uk_iu	78.45	69.36	51.42	64.69	21.97
ur_udtb	84.45	74.5	48.8	66.66	53.69
vi_vtb	45.43	37.05	32.18	33.78	33.78
zh_gsd	62.77	55.97	46.88	51.02	50.74

Table 3: Official Shared-Task Results

Acknowledgements

We thank the CoNLL Shared Task Organizing Committee for their hard work and their timely support. We also thank the TIRA platform team (Potthast et al., 2014) for providing a system that facilitates competition and reproducible research. The research towards this shared task submission has been supported by the European Research Council, ERC-StG-2015 Grant 677352, and by an Israel Science Foundation (ISF) Grant 1739/26, for which we are grateful.

References

Meni Adler and Michael Elhadad. 2006. An unsupervised morpheme-based hmm for hebrew morphological disambiguation. In *Proceedings of the 21st International Conference on Computational Linguistics and the 44th Annual Meeting of the Association for Computational Linguistics*. Association for Computational Linguistics, Stroudsburg, PA, USA, ACL-44, pages 665–672. https://doi.org/10.3115/1220175.1220259.

Daniel Andor, Chris Alberti, David Weiss, Aliaksei Severyn, Alessandro Presta, Kuzman Ganchev, Slav Petrov, and Michael Collins. 2016. Globally normalized transition-based neural networks. In *Proceedings of the 54th Annual Meeting of the Association for Computational Linguistics, ACL 2016, August 7-12, 2016, Berlin, Germany, Volume 1: Long*

Papers. http://aclweb.org/anthology/P/P16-1231.pdf.

Bernd Bohnet and Joakim Nivre. 2012. A transition-based system for joint part-of-speech tagging and labeled non-projective dependency parsing. In *Proceedings of the 2012 Joint Conference on Empirical Methods in Natural Language Processing and Computational Natural Language Learning*. Association for Computational Linguistics, Stroudsburg, PA, USA, EMNLP-CoNLL '12, pages 1455–1465. http://dl.acm.org/citation.cfm?id=2390948.2391114.

Bernd Bohnet, Joakim Nivre, Igor Boguslavsky, Richárd Farkas, Filip Ginter, and Jan Hajic. 2013. Joint morphological and syntactic analysis for richly inflected languages. *TACL* 1:415–428. http://dblp.uni-trier.de/db/journals/tacl/tacl1.html.

Sabine Buchholz and Erwin Marsi. 2006. CoNLL-X shared task on multilingual dependency parsing. In *Proceedings of CoNLL-X*. pages 149–164.

Michael Collins and Brian Roark. 2004. Incremental parsing with the perceptron algorithm. In *Proceedings of the 42Nd Annual Meeting on Association for Computational Linguistics*. Association for Computational Linguistics, Stroudsburg, PA, USA, ACL '04. https://doi.org/10.3115/1218955.1218970.

Sandra Kübler, Ryan McDonald, and Joakim Nivre. 2009. *Dependency Parsing*. Number 2 in Synthesis Lectures on Human Language Technologies. Morgan & Claypool Publishers.

Zhenghua Li, Min Zhang, Wanxiang Che, Ting Liu, and Wenliang Chen. 2014. Joint optimization for chinese POS tagging and dependency parsing. *IEEE/ACM Trans. Audio, Speech & Language Processing* 22(1):274–286. https://doi.org/10.1109/TASLP.2013.2288081.

Zhenghua Li, Min Zhang, Wanxiang Che, Ting Liu, Wenliang Chen, and Haizhou Li. 2011. Joint models for chinese pos tagging and dependency parsing. In *Proceedings of the Conference on Empirical Methods in Natural Language Processing*. Association for Computational Linguistics, Stroudsburg, PA, USA, EMNLP '11, pages 1180–1191. http://dl.acm.org/citation.cfm?id=2145432.2145557.

Amir More, Özlem Çetinoglu, Çagri Çöltekin, Nizar Habash, Benoît Sagot, Djamé Seddah, Dima Taji, and Reut Tsarfaty. 2018. Conll-ul: Universal morphological lattices for universal dependency parsing. In *Proceedings of the Eleventh International Conference on Language Resources and Evaluation, LREC 2018, Miyazaki, Japan, May 7-12, 2018.*.

Amir More, Amit Seker, Victoria Basmova, and Reut Tsarfaty. In Press. Joint transition-based models for morpho-syntactic parsing: Parsing strategies for mrls and a case study from modern hebrew. In *Transactions of ACL*.

Amir More and Reut Tsarfaty. 2016. Data-driven morphological analysis and disambiguation for morphologically rich languages and universal dependencies. In *Proceedings of COLING 2016, the 26th International Conference on Computational Linguistics: Technical Papers*. The COLING 2016 Organizing Committee, Osaka, Japan, pages 337–348. http://aclweb.org/anthology/C16-1033.

Joakim Nivre, Željko Agić, Lars Ahrenberg, et al. 2017. Universal dependencies 2.0 CoNLL 2017 shared task development and test data. LINDAT/CLARIN digital library at the Institute of Formal and Applied Linguistics, Charles University. http://hdl.handle.net/11234/1-2184.

Joakim Nivre, Marie-Catherine de Marneffe, Filip Ginter, Yoav Goldberg, Jan Hajič, Christopher Manning, Ryan McDonald, Slav Petrov, Sampo Pyysalo, Natalia Silveira, Reut Tsarfaty, and Daniel Zeman. 2016. Universal Dependencies v1: A multilingual treebank collection. In *Proceedings of the 10th International Conference on Language Resources and Evaluation (LREC 2016)*. European Language Resources Association, Portoro, Slovenia, pages 1659–1666.

Joakim Nivre, Johan Hall, Sandra Kübler, Ryan McDonald, Jens Nilsson, Sebastian Riedel, and Deniz Yuret. 2007. The CoNLL 2007 shared task on dependency parsing. In *Proceedings of the CoNLL Shared Task Session of EMNLP-CoNLL 2007*. pages 915–932.

Martin Potthast, Tim Gollub, Francisco Rangel, Paolo Rosso, Efstathios Stamatatos, and Benno Stein. 2014. Improving the reproducibility of PAN's shared tasks: Plagiarism detection, author identification, and author profiling. In Evangelos Kanoulas, Mihai Lupu, Paul Clough, Mark Sanderson, Mark Hall, Allan Hanbury, and Elaine Toms, editors, *Information Access Evaluation meets Multilinguality, Multimodality, and Visualization. 5th International Conference of the CLEF Initiative (CLEF 14)*. Springer, Berlin Heidelberg New York, pages 268–299. https://doi.org/10.1007/978-3-319-11382-1_22.

Djamé Seddah, Sandra Kübler, and Reut Tsarfaty. 2014. Introducing the spmrl 2014 shared task on parsing morphologically-rich languages. pages 103–109.

Djame Seddah, Reut Tsarfaty, Sandra Kübler, Marie Candito, D. Jinho Choi, Richárd Farkas, Jennifer Foster, Iakes Goenaga, Koldo Gojenola Galletebeitia, Yoav Goldberg, Spence Green, Nizar Habash, Marco Kuhlmann, Wolfgang Maier, Joakim Nivre, Adam Przepiórkowski, Ryan Roth, Wolfgang Seeker, Yannick Versley, Veronika Vincze, Marcin Woliński, Alina Wróblewska, and Villemonte Eric de la Clergerie. 2013. Proceedings of the fourth workshop on statistical parsing of morphologically-rich languages. Association for Computational Linguistics, pages 146–182. http://aclweb.org/anthology/W13-4917.

Milan Straka, Jan Hajič, and Jana Straková. 2016. UD-Pipe: trainable pipeline for processing CoNLL-U files performing tokenization, morphological analysis, POS tagging and parsing. In *Proceedings of the 10th International Conference on Language Resources and Evaluation (LREC 2016)*. European Language Resources Association, Portoro, Slovenia.

Reut Tsarfaty and Yoav Goldberg. 2008. Word-based or morpheme-based? annotation strategies for modern Hebrew clitics. In *Proceedings of LREC*.

Daniel Zeman, Jan Hajič, Martin Popel, Martin Potthast, Milan Straka, Filip Ginter, Joakim Nivre, and Slav Petrov. 2018. CoNLL 2018 Shared Task: Multilingual Parsing from Raw Text to Universal Dependencies. In *Proceedings of the CoNLL 2018 Shared Task: Multilingual Parsing from Raw Text to Universal Dependencies*. Association for Computational Linguistics, Brussels, Belgium, pages 1–20.

Meishan Zhang, Yue Zhang, Wanxiang Che, and Ting Liu. 2014. Character-level chinese dependency parsing. In *In Proceedings of the ACL*.

Yue Zhang and Stephen Clark. 2011. Syntactic processing using the generalized perceptron and beam search. *Computational Linguistics* 37(1):105–151. https://doi.org/10.1162/coli_a_00037.

Yue Zhang and Joakim Nivre. 2011. Transition-based dependency parsing with rich non-local features. In *Proceedings of the 49th Annual Meeting of the Association for Computational Linguistics: Human Language Technologies: Short Papers - Volume 2*. Association for Computational Linguistics, Stroudsburg, PA, USA, HLT '11, pages 188–193. http://dl.acm.org/citation.cfm?id=2002736.2002777.

SParse: Koç University Graph-Based Parsing System for the CoNLL 2018 Shared Task

Berkay Furkan Önder   **Can Gümeli**   **Deniz Yuret**

Koç University
Artificial Intelligence Laboratory
İstanbul, Turkey
`bonder17,cgumeli,dyuret@ku.edu.tr`

Abstract

We present SParse, our Graph-Based Parsing model submitted for the CoNLL 2018 Shared Task: Multilingual Parsing from Raw Text to Universal Dependencies (Zeman et al., 2018). Our model extends the state-of-the-art biaffine parser (Dozat and Manning, 2016) with a structural meta-learning module, SMeta, that combines local and global label predictions. Our parser has been trained and run on Universal Dependencies datasets (Nivre et al., 2016, 2018) and has 87.48% LAS, 78.63% MLAS, 78.69% BLEX and 81.76% CLAS (Nivre and Fang, 2017) score on the Italian-ISDT dataset and has 72.78% LAS, 59.10% MLAS, 61.38% BLEX and 61.72% CLAS score on the Japanese-GSD dataset in our official submission. All other corpora are evaluated after the submission deadline, for whom we present our unofficial test results.

1 Introduction

End-to-end learning with neural networks has proven to be effective in parsing natural language (Kiperwasser and Goldberg, 2016). Graph-based dependency parsers (McDonald et al., 2005) represent dependency scores between words as a matrix representing a weighted fully connected graph, from which a spanning tree algorithm extracts the best parse tree. This setting is very compatible with neural network models that are good at producing matrices of continuous numbers.

Compared to transition-based parsing (Kırnap et al., 2017; Kiperwasser and Goldberg, 2016), which was the basis of our university's last year entry, graph-based parsers have the disadvantage of producing n^2 entries for parsing an n-word sentence. Furthermore, algorithms used to parse these entries can be even more complex than $O(n^2)$. However, graph-based parsers allow easy-to-parallelize static architectures rather than sequential decision mechanisms and are able to parse non-projective sentences. Non-projective graph-based parsing is the core of last year's winning entry (Dozat et al., 2017).

Neural graph-based parsers can be divided into two components: encoder and decoder. The encoder is responsible for representing the sentence as a sequence of continuous feature vectors. The decoder receives this sequence and produces the parse tree, by first creating a graph representation and then extracting the maximum spanning tree (MST).

We use a bidirectional RNN (bi-RNN) to produce a contextual vector for each word in a sentence. Use of bi-RNNs is the defacto standard in dependency parsing, as it allows representing each word conditioned on the whole sentence. Our main contribution in the encoder part is to the word embeddings feeding the bi-RNN. We use word vectors coming from a language model pretrained on very large language corpora, similar to Kırnap et al. (2017). We extend word embeddings with learnable embeddings for UPOS tags, XPOS tags and FEATs where applicable.

Our decoder can be viewed as a more structured version of the state-of-the-art biaffine decoder of Dozat et al. (2017), where we attempt to condition the label-seeking units to a parse-tree instead of simple local predictions. We propose a meta-learning module that allows structured and unstructured predictions to be combined as a weighted sum. This additional computational complexity is paid off by our simple word-level model in the encoder part. We call it that we call structured meta-biaffine decoder or shortly SMeta.

We implemented our model using Knet deep

216

Proceedings of the CoNLL 2018 Shared Task: Multilingual Parsing from Raw Text to Universal Dependencies, pages 216–222
Brussels, Belgium, October 31 – November 1, 2018. ©2018 Association for Computational Linguistics
https://doi.org/10.18653/v1/K18-2022

learning framework (Yuret, 2016) in Julia language (Bezanson et al., 2017). Our code will be made available publicly.

We could only get official results for two corpora due to an unexpected software bug. Therefore, we present unofficial results obtained after the submission deadline as well.

2   Related work

Kiperwasser and Goldberg (2016) use trainable BiLSTMs to represent features of each word, instead of defining the features manually. They formulated the structured prediction using hinge loss based on the gold parse tree and parsed scores.

Dozat and Manning (2016) propose deep biaffine attention combined with the parsing model of Kiperwasser and Goldberg (2016), which simplifies the architecture by allowing implementation with a single layer instead of two linear layers.

Stanford's Graph-based Neural Dependency Parser (Dozat et al., 2017) at the CoNLL 2017 Shared Task (Zeman et al., 2017) is implemented with four ReLU layers, two layers for finding heads and dependents of each word, and two layers for finding the dependency relations for each head-dependent pair. The outputs are then fed into two biaffine layers, one for determining the head of the word, and another for determining the dependency relation of head-dependent pair.

We propose a dependency parsing model based on the graph-based parser by Dozat and Manning (2016). We are adding a meta-biaffine decoder layer, similar to the tagging model proposed by Bohnet et al. (2018), for computing the arc labels based on the full tree constructed from the unlabeled arc scores instead of computing them independently.

Our parsing model uses pretrained word embeddings from Kırnap et al. (2017). Our parser uses the same language model with Kırnap et al. (2017), in which graph based-parsing algorithms are applied. However, a transition-based parsing model is given in Kırnap et al. (2017). Therefore, some adaptations are made on the features proposed by Kırnap et al. (2017) in order to use them in a graph based parsing model. We did not use contextual features coming from the language model or features related to words in stack and buffer. Instead, we trained a three-layer BiLSTM from scratch to encode contextual features.

3   Model

In this section, we depict important aspects of our architecture which is shown in Figure 1. We discuss encoder and decoder separately and then give the model hyper-parameters used.

3.1   Encoder

Word Model

We used four main features to represent each word in a sentence: a pre-trained word embedding, UPOS tag embedding, XPOS tag embedding and FEAT embedding.

Pre-trained words come from the language model in Kırnap et al. (2017). This model represents each word using a character-level LSTM, which is a suitable setting for morphologically rich languages, as shown in Dozat et al. (2017). We use the word vectors without further training.

UPOS and XPOS tag embeddings are represented by vectors randomly initialized using unit Gaussian distribution.

Morphological features, also called FEATs, are different in the sense that there are zero or more FEATs for each word. We follow a simple strategy: we represent each FEAT using a randomly initialized vector and add all FEAT embeddings for each word. We simply used zero for word vectors without any morphological features.

For practical reasons, we also needed to represent ROOT word of a sentence. We do so by randomly initializing a word embedding and setting all other embeddings to zero.

At test time, we used tags and morphological features produced by MorphNet (Dayanık et al., 2018). For languages where this model is not available, we directly used UDPipe results (Straka et al., 2016).

Sentence Model

We used a three-layer bidirectional LSTM to represent a sentence. We used the hidden size of 200 for both forward and backward LSTMs. Dropout (Srivastava et al., 2014) is performed at the input of each LSTM layer, including the first layer. Our LSTM simply use nth hidden state for nth word, different from the language model in Kırnap et al. (2017).

The language model discussed in the previous section also provides context embeddings. We performed experiments for combining our own contextual representation with this representation

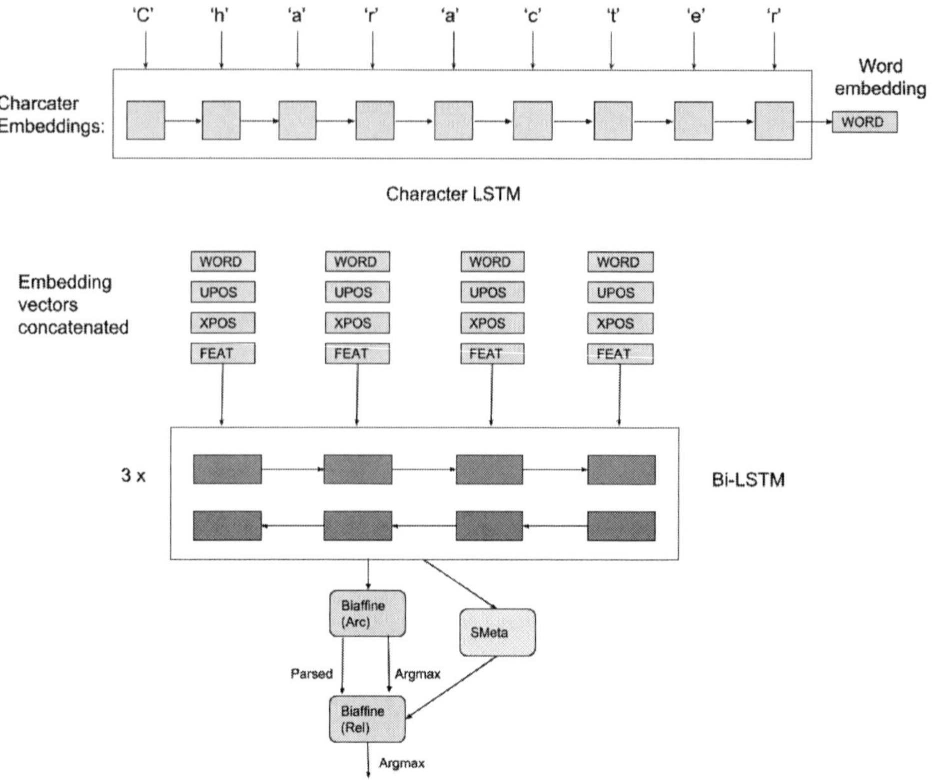

Figure 1: Overall model architecture.

using various concatenation and addition strategies, but we observed poorer performance in terms of generalization. Also, using the language model directly as a feature extractor led to unsatisfactory performance, different from last years' transition-based entry of our institution (Kırnap et al., 2017).

3.2 Decoder

Structured Meta-Biaffine Decoder (SMeta)

Deep biaffine decoder (Dozat and Manning, 2016) is the core of last year's winning entry (Dozat et al., 2017), so we used this module as our starting point. Biaffine architecture is computationally efficient and can be used with easy-to-train softmax objective, different from harder-to-optimize hinge loss objectives as in Kiperwasser and Goldberg (2016).

Similar to (Dozat et al., 2017), we produce four different hidden vectors, two for arcs and two for relations (or labels). Formally

$$\mathbf{h}_i^{(arc-dep)} = \mathbf{MLP}^{(arc-dep)}(\mathbf{h}_i) \qquad (1)$$

$$\mathbf{h}_i^{(arc-head)} = \mathbf{MLP}^{(arc-head)}(\mathbf{h}_i) \qquad (2)$$

$$\mathbf{h}_i^{(rel-dep)} = \mathbf{MLP}^{(rel-dep)}(\mathbf{h}_i) \qquad (3)$$

$$\mathbf{h}_i^{(rel-head)} = \mathbf{MLP}^{(rel-head)}(\mathbf{h}_i) \qquad (4)$$

where $\mathbf{h}_i$ represents ith hidden state of the bi-LSTM embedding. The vectors correspond to arcs seeking their dependents, arcs seeking their heads, and corresponding relations. **MLP** can be any neural network module. Here, we simply use dense layers followed by ReLU activations, as in (Dozat et al., 2017).

Now, we perform the biaffine transformation to compute the score matrix representing the graph,

$$\begin{aligned} \mathbf{s}_i^{(arc)} &= H^{(arc-head)} W^{(arc)} \mathbf{h}_i \\ &+ H^{(arc-head)} \mathbf{b}^{\mathbf{T}(arc)} \end{aligned} \qquad (5)$$

where $H^{(arc-head)}$ represents matrix of $\mathbf{h}_i^{(arc-head)}$ vectors, $W^{(arc)}$ and $\mathbf{b}^{(arc)}$ are learnable weights.

Up to this point, our decoder is identical to the one in (Dozat et al., 2017). The difference is in the computation of predicted arcs. We compute two different predictions:

$$y_i^{'l(arc)} = \arg\max_j s_{ij}^{(arc)} \qquad (6)$$

$$\mathbf{p} = parse(S^{(arc)}) \qquad (7)$$

$$y_i^{'s(arc)} = p_i \qquad (8)$$

Here $S^{(arc)}$ is the matrix of arc scores and $parse$ is a spanning tree algorithm that computes the indices of the predicted arcs. Now, we compute label scores using these two predictions. First, we compute coefficient vector $\mathbf{k}$ using the bi-RNN encodings,

$$\mathbf{h}' = \frac{\sum_{i=1}^{n} \mathbf{h}_i}{n} \qquad (9)$$

$$\mathbf{k} = W^{(meta)}\mathbf{h}' + \mathbf{b}^{(meta)} \qquad (10)$$

where n is the number of words in the sentence, W and $\mathbf{b}$ are learned parameters. Averaging over time is inspired by the global average pooling operator in the vision literature (Lin et al., 2013), transforming temporal representation to a global one.

We now compute the weighted sum of label predictions using coefficient vector $\mathbf{k}$.

$$\begin{aligned}
s_i^{l(rel)} = \; & \mathbf{h}_{y_i^{'l(arc)}}^{T(rel-head)} \mathbf{U}^{(rel)} \mathbf{h}_i^{(rel-dep)} \\
& + W^{(rel)} cat(\mathbf{h}_i^{(rel-dep)}, \mathbf{h}_{y_i^{'l(arc)}}^{(rel-head)}) \\
& + \mathbf{b}^{(rel)}
\end{aligned} \qquad (11)$$

$$\begin{aligned}
s_i^{s(rel)} = \; & \mathbf{h}_{y_i^{'s(arc)}}^{T(rel-head)} \mathbf{U}^{(rel)} \mathbf{h}_i^{(rel-dep)} \\
& + W^{(rel)} cat(\mathbf{h}_i^{(rel-dep)}, \mathbf{h}_{y_i^{'s(arc)}}^{(rel-head)}) \\
& + \mathbf{b}^{(rel)}
\end{aligned} \qquad (12)$$

$$s_i^{(rel)} = k_1 s_i^{l(rel)} + k_2 s_i^{s(rel)} \qquad (13)$$

$$y_i^{'(rel)} = \arg\max_j s_{ij}^{(rel)} \qquad (14)$$

where $\mathbf{U}^{(rel)}$, $W^{(rel)}$ and $\mathbf{b}^{(rel)}$ are learned parameters.

Our model is trained using sum of softmax losses similar to (Dozat et al., 2017).

Parsing algorithms

In our parsing model, Chu-Liu-Edmonds algorithm (Chu, 1965; Edmonds, 1967) and Eisner (1996)'s algorithm are used interchangeably, during both the training of parser models and parsing phase of test datasets. On the languages whose training dataset consists of more than 250,000 words, Chu-Liu-Edmonds algorithm is used for parsing since it has a complexity of $O(n^2)$, where n is the number of words.

This approach allows us to train our models on relatively larger datasets in less amount of time, compared to the Eisner's algorithm whose time complexity is $O(n^3)$.

On training datasets having at most 250,000 words, Eisner's algorithm is used during both training and parsing phase. Eisners algorithm produces only projective trees and Chu-Liu-Edmonds algorithm produces both projective and non-projective trees. This means the number of possible trees Eisner's algorithm can generate is fewer compared to Chu-Liu-Edmonds algorithm, so even though Eisner's algorithm has higher time complexity than Chu-Liu-Edmonds algorithm, parsing models are trained faster when Eisner's algorithm is used.

3.3 Hyperparameters

We used a 150-dimensional tag and feature embeddings and 350-dimensional word embeddings for the word model. Bi-RNN sentence model has the hidden size of 200 for both forward and backward RNNs, producing 400-dimensional feature context vectors. We used the hidden size of 400 for arc MLPs and 100 for relation MLPs.

4   Training

We used Adam optimizer (Kingma and Ba, 2014) with its standard parameters. Based on dataset size, we trained the model for 25 to 100 epochs and selected the model based on its validation labeled attachment accuracy.

We sampled sentences with identical number of words in a minibatch. In training corpora that are sufficiently large, we sampled minibatches so that approximately 500 tokens exist in a single minibatch. We reduced this size to 250 for relatively small corpora. For very small corpora, we simply sample a constant number of sentences as a minibatch.

Dataset	LAS	MLAS	BLEX	Dataset	LAS	MLAS	BLEX
ar_padt	67.57%	56.22%	58.84%	hu_szeged	73.84%	56.03%	63.31%
bg_btb	85.85%	76.28%	74.73%	id_gsd	76.88%	65.34%	64.89%
ca_ancora	87.60%	79.05%	79.49%	it_isdt	87.51%	78.81%	78.75%
cs_cac	86.05%	73.54%	80.14%	it_postwita	69.48%	56.20%	56.73%
cs_fictree	84.21%	71%	76.86%	ja_modern	22.91%	8.47%	9.73%
cs_pdt	86.07%	76.54%	81.39%	ko_gsd	75.52%	69.15%	63.18%
cs_pud	81.80%	68.19%	75.10%	ko_kaist	81.64%	74.46%	68.86%
cu_proiel	67.80%	56.51%	60.93%	la_ittb	77.66%	68.09%	73.91%
da_ddt	77.90%	68.14%	68.64%	la_perseus	47.45%	29.99%	32.47%
de_gsd	70.65%	34.50%	60.40%	la_proiel	64.29%	51.80%	58.05%
el_gdt	83.65%	66.76%	70.14%	lv_lvtb	71.52%	57.26%	60.20%
en_ewt	77.87%	68.57%	70.83%	nl_alpino	78.28%	63.38%	66.08%
en_gum	75.51%	63.95%	63.52%	nl_lassysmall	78.10%	65.73%	66.77%
en_lines	73.97%	65.15%	66.06%	pl_lfg	88.21%	75.40%	79.25%
en_pud	81.31%	69.85%	73.18%	pl_sz	83.01%	65.10%	73.34%
es_ancora	86.94%	79.14%	79.58%	pt_bosque	84.32%	70.27%	75.29%
et_edt	77.45%	69.58%	66.05%	ro_rrt	82.74%	74.19%	74.60%
eu_bdt	73.84%	60.49%	66.38%	ru_syntagrus	88.22%	80.16%	81.05%
fa_seraji	81.74%	75.15%	71.93%	ru_taiga	40.01%	23.92%	25.44%
fi_ftb	76.62%	66.28%	62.88%	sk_snk	77.81%	56.11%	62.23%
fi_tdt	79.30%	71.07%	64.37%	sl_ssj	78.46%	64.93%	70.50%
fr_gsd	82.32%	72.91%	74.97%	sl_sst	43.63%	31.14%	35.41%
fr_sequoia	82.60%	73.07%	76.07%	sv_lines	74.87%	59.32%	67.25%
fr_spoken	64.62%	53.15%	54.18%	sv_pud	71.66%	43.65%	55.60%
ga_idt	35.84%	13.07%	16.77%	sv_talbanken	79.06%	70.55%	71.16%
gl_ctg	80.31%	67.77%	70.72%	tr_imst	60.19%	49.57%	51.02%
got_proiel	62.40%	49.19%	55.15%	ug_udt	58.48%	38.18%	45.94%
grc_perseus	61.82%	34.17%	41.16%	uk_iu	75.93%	57.81%	64.84%
grc_proiel	68.03%	49.40%	55.62%	ur_udtb	78.41%	51.28%	64.94%
he_htb	60.09%	46.32%	49.19%	vi_vtb	41.27%	34.73%	36.95%
hi_hdtb	87.66%	70%	80.47%	zh_gsd	59.51%	49.33%	54.33%
hr_set	80.86%	60.65%	72.36%				

Table 1: Our unofficial F1 scores. Tests are done in TIRA (Potthast et al., 2014) machine allocated for the task.

We saved best models with corresponding configurations, scores and optimization states during training for recovery. We then re-create the model files for the best models of each corpus by removing the optimization states.

MorphNet is the morphological analysis and disambiguation tool proposed by Dayanık et al. (2018), which we used while training our parsing model. During training of the parser, CoNLL-U formatted training dataset files, which are produced by UDPipe (Straka et al., 2016), are given to MorphNet as input. Then, MorphNet applies its own morphological analysis and disambiguation, and new CoNLL-U formatted files produced by MorphNet are used by our parser.

Even though we used lemmatized and tagged outputs generated by MorphNet while training our parser, we run our parser on outputs generated by UDPipe, due to time constrains during parsing.

5   Results and Discussion

Short after the testing period ended, our parser obtained results on 64 treebank test sets out of 82, which are shown in Table 1. According to the results announced including the unofficial runs, we had an average LAS score of 57% on the 64 test sets on which our model is run and ranked 24th among the best runs of 27 teams. The MLAS score of our model is 46.40% and our model is ranked 22nd out of the submissions of 27 models. And, the BLEX score of our model is 49.17% and our model is ranked 21st out of the best BLEX results of all 27 models including unofficial runs.[1]

According to the results, our model performs better at datasets with comparably larger training data. For instance, our model has around 90% LAS score on Catalan, Indian, Italian, Polish and Russian languages which have higher number of tokens in training data. Furthermore, our model performs relatively well in some low-resource languages like Turkish and Hungarian. However, on the datasets with very small or no training data, such as Japanese Modern, Russian Taiga and Irish IDT, we get lower scores. Hence, our model benefits from large amount of data during training process, but prediction with low resources remains as an issue for our model.

---

[1] Best results of each team including unofficial runs are announced in `http://universaldependencies.org/conll18/results-best-all.html` Our results and rankings announced in the paper are taken from the CoNLL 2018 best results webpage in September 2, 2018 and may change with the inclusion of new results of participated teams later.

6   Contributions

In this work, we proposed a new decoding mechanism, called SMeta, for graph-based neural dependency parsing. This architecture attempts to combine structured and unstructured prediction methods using meta-learning. We coupled this architecture with custom training methods and algorithms to evaluate its performance.

Acknowledgments

This work was supported by the Scientific and Technological Research Council of Turkey (TÜBİTAK) grants 114E628 and 215E201. Special thanks to Ömer Kırnap and Erenay Dayanık for sharing their experiences with us.

References

Jeff Bezanson, Alan Edelman, Stefan Karpinski, and Viral B Shah. 2017. Julia: A fresh approach to numerical computing. *SIAM review* 59(1):65–98.

Bernd Bohnet, Ryan McDonald, Goncalo Simoes, Daniel Andor, Emily Pitler, and Joshua Maynez. 2018. Morphosyntactic tagging with a meta-bilstm model over context sensitive token encodings. *arXiv preprint arXiv:1805.08237* .

Yoeng-Jin Chu. 1965. On the shortest arborescence of a directed graph. *Scientia Sinica* 14:1396–1400.

Erenay Dayanık, Ekin Akyürek, and Deniz Yuret. 2018. Morphnet: A sequence-to-sequence model that combines morphological analysis and disambiguation. *arXiv preprint arXiv:1805.07946* .

Timothy Dozat and Christopher D Manning. 2016. Deep biaffine attention for neural dependency parsing. *arXiv preprint arXiv:1611.01734* .

Timothy Dozat, Peng Qi, and Christopher D Manning. 2017. Stanford's graph-based neural dependency parser at the conll 2017 shared task. *Proceedings of the CoNLL 2017 Shared Task: Multilingual Parsing from Raw Text to Universal Dependencies* pages 20–30.

Jack Edmonds. 1967. Optimum branchings. *Journal of Research of the national Bureau of Standards B* 71(4):233–240.

Jason M Eisner. 1996. Three new probabilistic models for dependency parsing: An exploration. In *Proceedings of the 16th conference on Computational linguistics-Volume 1*. Association for Computational Linguistics, pages 340–345.

Diederik Kingma and Jimmy Ba. 2014. Adam: A method for stochastic optimization. *arXiv preprint arXiv:1412.6980* .

Eliyahu Kiperwasser and Yoav Goldberg. 2016. Simple and accurate dependency parsing using bidirectional LSTM feature representations. *CoRR* abs/1603.04351. http://arxiv.org/abs/1603.04351.

Ömer Kırnap, Berkay Furkan Önder, and Deniz Yuret. 2017. Parsing with context embeddings. *Proceedings of the CoNLL 2017 Shared Task: Multilingual Parsing from Raw Text to Universal Dependencies* pages 80–87.

Min Lin, Qiang Chen, and Shuicheng Yan. 2013. Network in network. *arXiv preprint arXiv:1312.4400* .

Ryan McDonald, Fernando Pereira, Kiril Ribarov, and Jan Hajič. 2005. Non-projective dependency parsing using spanning tree algorithms. In *Proceedings of the conference on Human Language Technology and Empirical Methods in Natural Language Processing*. Association for Computational Linguistics, pages 523–530.

Joakim Nivre, Marie-Catherine de Marneffe, Filip Ginter, Yoav Goldberg, Jan Hajič, Christopher Manning, Ryan McDonald, Slav Petrov, Sampo Pyysalo, Natalia Silveira, Reut Tsarfaty, and Daniel Zeman. 2016. Universal Dependencies v1: A multilingual treebank collection. In *Proceedings of the 10th International Conference on Language Resources and Evaluation (LREC 2016)*. European Language Resources Association, Portoro, Slovenia, pages 1659–1666.

Joakim Nivre and Chiao-Ting Fang. 2017. Universal dependency evaluation. In *Proceedings of the NoDaLiDa 2017 Workshop on Universal Dependencies (UDW 2017)*. pages 86–95.

Joakim Nivre et al. 2018. Universal Dependencies 2.2. LINDAT/CLARIN digital library at the Institute of Formal and Applied Linguistics, Charles University, Prague, `http://hdl.handle.net/11234/SUPPLYTHENEWPERMANENTIDHERE!`

Martin Potthast, Tim Gollub, Francisco Rangel, Paolo Rosso, Efstathios Stamatatos, and Benno Stein. 2014. Improving the reproducibility of PAN's shared tasks: Plagiarism detection, author identification, and author profiling. In Evangelos Kanoulas, Mihai Lupu, Paul Clough, Mark Sanderson, Mark Hall, Allan Hanbury, and Elaine Toms, editors, *Information Access Evaluation meets Multilinguality, Multimodality, and Visualization. 5th International Conference of the CLEF Initiative (CLEF 14)*. Springer, Berlin Heidelberg New York, pages 268–299. https://doi.org/10.1007/978-3-319-11382-1_22.

Nitish Srivastava, Geoffrey Hinton, Alex Krizhevsky, Ilya Sutskever, and Ruslan Salakhutdinov. 2014. Dropout: a simple way to prevent neural networks from overfitting. *The Journal of Machine Learning Research* 15(1):1929–1958.

Milan Straka, Jan Hajič, and Jana Straková. 2016. UDPipe: trainable pipeline for processing CoNLL-U files performing tokenization, morphological analysis, POS tagging and parsing. In *Proceedings of the 10th International Conference on Language Resources and Evaluation (LREC 2016)*. European Language Resources Association, Portoro, Slovenia.

Deniz Yuret. 2016. Knet: beginning deep learning with 100 lines of julia. In *Machine Learning Systems Workshop at NIPS 2016*.

Daniel Zeman, Jan Hajič, Martin Popel, Martin Potthast, Milan Straka, Filip Ginter, Joakim Nivre, and Slav Petrov. 2018. CoNLL 2018 Shared Task: Multilingual Parsing from Raw Text to Universal Dependencies. In *Proceedings of the CoNLL 2018 Shared Task: Multilingual Parsing from Raw Text to Universal Dependencies*. Association for Computational Linguistics, Brussels, Belgium, pages 1–20.

Daniel Zeman, Martin Popel, Milan Straka, Jan Hajič, Joakim Nivre, Filip Ginter, Juhani Luotolahti, Sampo Pyysalo, Slav Petrov, Martin Potthast, Francis Tyers, Elena Badmaeva, Memduh Gökırmak, Anna Nedoluzhko, Silvie Cinková, Jan Hajič jr., Jaroslava Hlaváčová, Václava Kettnerová, Zdeňka Urešová, Jenna Kanerva, Stina Ojala, Anna Missilä, Christopher Manning, Sebastian Schuster, Siva Reddy, Dima Taji, Nizar Habash, Herman Leung, Marie-Catherine de Marneffe, Manuela Sanguinetti, Maria Simi, Hiroshi Kanayama, Valeria de Paiva, Kira Droganova, Héctor Martínez Alonso, Çağrı Çöltekin, Umut Sulubacak, Hans Uszkoreit, Vivien Macketanz, Aljoscha Burchardt, Kim Harris, Katrin Marheinecke, Georg Rehm, Tolga Kayadelen, Mohammed Attia, Ali Elkahky, Zhuoran Yu, Emily Pitler, Saran Lertpradit, Michael Mandl, Jesse Kirchner, Hector Fernandez Alcalde, Jana Strnadova, Esha Banerjee, Ruli Manurung, Antonio Stella, Atsuko Shimada, Sookyoung Kwak, Gustavo Mendonça, Tatiana Lando, Rattima Nitisaroj, and Josie Li. 2017. CoNLL 2017 Shared Task: Multilingual Parsing from Raw Text to Universal Dependencies. In *Proceedings of the CoNLL 2017 Shared Task: Multilingual Parsing from Raw Text to Universal Dependencies*. Association for Computational Linguistics, Vancouver, Canada, pages 1–19.

ELMoLex: Connecting ELMo and Lexicon features
for Dependency Parsing

Ganesh Jawahar   **Benjamin Muller**   **Amal Fethi**   **Louis Martin**
Éric de La Clergerie   **Benoît Sagot**   **Djamé Seddah**
Inria
{firstname.lastname}@inria.fr

Abstract

In this paper, we present the details of
the neural dependency parser and the neural tagger submitted by our team 'ParisNLP'
to the CoNLL 2018 Shared Task on parsing from raw text to Universal Dependencies. We augment the deep Biaffine (BiAF)
parser (Dozat and Manning, 2016) with novel
features to perform competitively: we utilize
an indomain version of ELMo features (Peters et al., 2018) which provide context-
dependent word representations; we utilize
disambiguated, embedded, morphosyntactic
features from lexicons (Sagot, 2018), which
complements the existing feature set. Henceforth, we call our system 'ELMoLex'. In
addition to incorporating character embeddings, ELMoLex leverage pre-trained word
vectors, ELMo and morphosyntactic features
(whenever available) to correctly handle rare
or unknown words which are prevalent in
languages with complex morphology. EL-
MoLex[1] ranked 11th by Labeled Attachment
Score metric (70.64%), Morphology-aware
LAS metric (55.74%) and ranked 9th by
Bilexical dependency metric (60.70%). In an
extrinsic evaluation setup, ELMoLex ranked
7th for Event Extraction, Negation Resolution
tasks and 11th for Opinion Analysis task by F1
score.

1   Introduction

The goal of this paper is to describe ELMoLex, the
parsing system submitted by our team 'ParisNLP' to
the CoNLL 2018 Shared Task on parsing from raw

---

text to Universal Dependencies (Zeman et al., 2018).
The backbone of ELMoLex is the BiAF parser (Dozat
and Manning, 2016) consisting of a large, well-tuned
network that generates word representations, which
are then fed to an effective, biaffine classifier to predict the head of each modifier token and the class of
the edge connecting these tokens. In their follow-up
work (Dozat et al., 2017), the authors further enrich
the parser by utilizing character embeddings for generating word representations which could help in gen-
eralizing to rare and unknown words (also called Out
Of Vocabulary (OOV) words). They also train their
own taggers using a similar architecture and use the
resulting Part of Speech (PoS) tags for training the
parser in an effort to leverage the potential benefits
in PoS quality over off-the-shelf taggers.

We identify two potential shortcomings of the BiAF
parser. The first problem is the *context independence*
of the word embedding layer of the parser: the meaning of a word varies across linguistic contexts, which
could be hard to infer automatically for smaller treebanks (especially) due to lack of data. To handle this
bottleneck, we propose to use Embeddings from Language Model (ELMo) features (Peters et al., 2018)
which are context dependent (function of the entire
input sentence) and obtained from the linear combination of several layers of a pre-trained BiLSTM-
LM[2]. The second problem is the *linguistic naivety*[3]
of the character embeddings: they can generalize
over relevant sub-parts of each word such as prefixes

---

[1] Code to reproduce our tagging and parsing experiments is publicly accessible at `https://github.com/`
`BenjaminMullerGit/NeuroTaggerLex` and `https:`
`//github.com/ganeshjawahar/ELMoLex` respectively.

[2] Due to lack of time, we could train BiLSTM-LMs on the treebank data only (indomain version). We leave it for future work to
train the model on large raw corpora from each language, which
we believe could further strengthen our parser.

[3] The term *linguistic naivety* was introduced by Matthews et al.
(2018) to refer to the fact that character-based embeddings for
a sentence must discover that words exist and are delimited by
spaces (basic linguistic facts that are built in to the structure of
word-based models). In our context, we use a different meaning
of this term as the term corresponds to the word-level character-
based embeddings.

Proceedings of the CoNLL 2018 Shared Task: Multilingual Parsing from Raw Text to Universal Dependencies, pages 223–237
Brussels, Belgium, October 31 – November 1, 2018. ©2018 Association for Computational Linguistics
https://doi.org/10.18653/v1/K18-2023

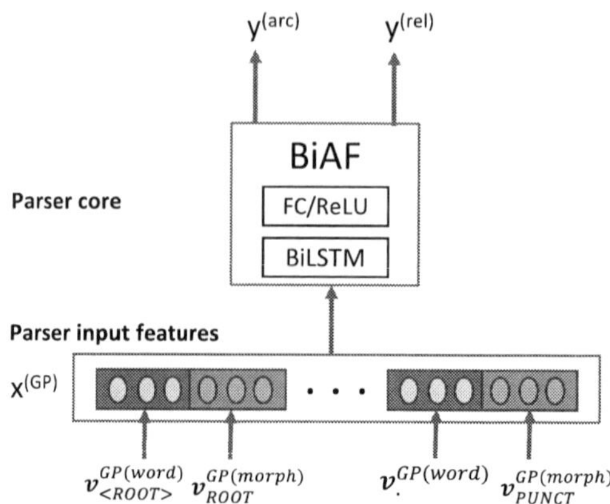

Figure 1: Architecture of ELMoLex which uses BiAF parser as its backbone. Arrows indicate structural dependence, but not necessarily trainable parameters.

or suffixes, which can be problematic for unknown words which do not always follow such generalizations (Sagot and Martínez Alonso, 2017). We attempt to lift this burden by resorting to external lexicons[4], which provides information for both word with an irregular morphology and word not present in the training data, without any quantitative distinction between relevant and less relevant information. To tap the information from the morphological features (such as gender, tense, mood, etc.) for each word present in the lexicon efficiently, we propose to embed the features and disambiguate them contextually with the help of attention (Bahdanau et al., 2014), before combining them for the focal word.

We showcase the potential of ELMoLex in parsing 82 treebanks provided by the shared task. ELMoLex ranked 11th by Labeled Attachment Score (LAS) metric (70.64%), Morphology-aware LAS (MLAS) metric (55.74%) and ranked 9th by BiLEXical dependency (BLEX) metric (60.70%). We perform ablation and training time studies to have a deeper understanding of ELMoLex. In an extrinsic evaluation setup (Fares et al., 2018), ELMoLex ranked 7th for Event Extraction, Negation Resolution tasks and 11th for Opinion Analysis task by F1 score. On an average, ELMoLex ranked 8th with a F1 score of 55.48%.

2 ELMoLex

The model architecture of ELMoLex, which uses BiAF parser (Dozat and Manning, 2016) (which in turn is based on Kiperwasser and Goldberg (2016)) as its backbone, is displayed in Figure 1. For our

shared task submission, we assume tokenization and segmentation is already done[5]; we henceforth train ELMoLex on gold tokens and PoS tags provided by UDPipe (Straka et al., 2016). We evaluate our model using the segmentation and PoS tags provided by UDPipe, except for certain languages where we use the tokens and PoS tag predicted by our own tokenizer and taggers (as respectively explained in Section 2.6 and 2.7)[6] respectively.

2.1 Backbone parser

ELMoLex uses the BiAF parser (Dozat and Manning, 2016), a state-of-the-art graph-based parser, as its backbone. BiAF parser consumes a sequence of tokens and their PoS tags, which is fed through a multilayer BiLSTM network. The output state of the final LSTM layer is then fed through four separate ReLU layers, producing four specialized vector representations: first for the word as a modifier seeking its head; second for the word as a head seeking all its modifiers; third for the word as a modifier deciding on its label; and lastly for the word as head deciding on the labels of its modifiers. These vectors become the input to two biaffine classifiers: one computes a score for each token pair, with the highest score for a given token indicating that token's most probable head; the other computes a score for each label for a given token/head pair, with the highest score representing the most probable label for the arc from the head to the

---

[4]We use lexicon information for treebanks from 43 languages provided by UDLexicons (Sagot, 2018).

[5]We explored a wide variety of tokenization and segmentation techniques in our last year submission (de La Clergerie et al., 2017). Our primary focus for this year is to explore novel neural network layers for both tagging and parsing.

[6]Due to lack of time, we could not train the taggers effectively for all the languages and use the predicted PoS from UDPipe for training our parser.

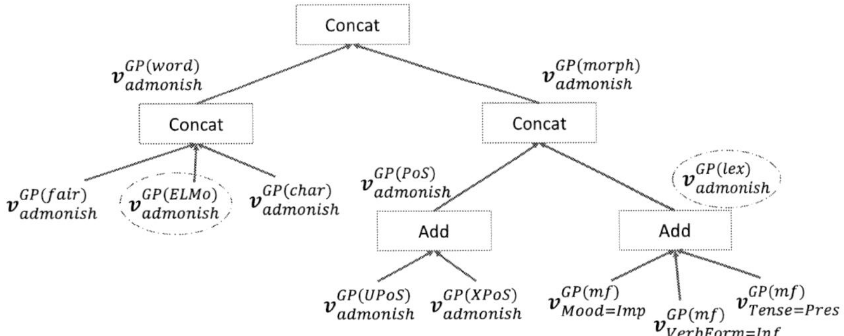

Figure 2: Architecture of embedding model used by ELMoLex for the word 'admonish'. $\mathbf{v}^{GP(ELMo)}$ and $\mathbf{v}^{GP(lex)}$ (red ellipses) are our major contributions. Arrows indicate structural dependence, but not necessarily trainable parameters.

modifier. We refer the readers to Dozat and Manning (2016) for further details.

Formally, the BiAF parser consumes a sequence of n word embeddings $(\mathbf{v}_1^{GP(word)}, \ldots, \mathbf{v}_n^{GP(word)})$ and n tag embeddings $(\mathbf{v}_1^{GP(tag)}, \ldots, \mathbf{v}_n^{GP(tag)})$ as input, which can be written as:

$$
\begin{aligned}
\mathbf{x}_i^{GP} &= \mathbf{v}_i^{GP(word)} \oplus \mathbf{v}_i^{GP(tag)}, \\
\mathbf{v}_i^{GP(word)} &= \mathbf{v}_i^{GP(token)} + \mathbf{v}_i^{GP(w2v)} + \mathbf{v}_i^{GP(char)}, \quad (1) \\
\mathbf{v}_i^{GP(tag)} &= \mathbf{v}_i^{GP(UPoS)} + \mathbf{v}_i^{GP(XPoS)}.
\end{aligned}
$$

In the equation 1, $\mathbf{v}_i^{GP(token)}$, $\mathbf{v}_i^{GP(w2v)}$, $\mathbf{v}_i^{GP(char)}$ represent the holistic frequent word embedding, pre-trained word embedding (fixed) and LSTM based character-level embeddings respectively, whereas the Universal PoS (UPoS) and language-specific (XPoS) tag embeddings are represented by $\mathbf{v}_i^{GP(UPoS)}$ and $\mathbf{v}_i^{GP(XPoS)}$ respectively. Note that '+' denotes element-wise addition operator, while '$\oplus$' denotes concatenation operator.

ELMoLex reformulates the input embedding layer of BiAF parser in a few ways (as illustrated in Figure 2): we utilize an indomain version of ELMo features ($\mathbf{v}_i^{GP(ELMo)}$) which provide context-dependent word representation (as discussed in Section 2.2); we utilize disambiguated, embedded, morphosyntactic features from lexicons ($\mathbf{v}_i^{GP(lex)}$), which provide information that is especially relevant for word with an irregular morphology (Sagot and Martínez Alonso, 2017), thereby complementing the existing feature set (as discussed in Section 2.3). Incorporating them, equation 1 now becomes:

$$
\begin{aligned}
\mathbf{x}_i^{GP} &= \mathbf{v}_i^{GP(word)} \oplus \mathbf{v}_i^{GP(morph)}, \\
\mathbf{v}_i^{GP(word)} &= \mathbf{v}_i^{GP(fair)} \oplus \mathbf{v}_i^{GP(char)} \oplus \mathbf{v}_i^{GP(ELMo)}, \\
\mathbf{v}_i^{GP(morph)} &= \mathbf{v}_i^{GP(PoS)} \oplus \mathbf{v}_i^{GP(lex)}, \quad (2) \\
\mathbf{v}_i^{GP(PoS)} &= \mathbf{v}_i^{GP(UPoS)} + \mathbf{v}_i^{GP(XPoS)}.
\end{aligned}
$$

In the equation 2, $\mathbf{v}_i^{GP(fair)}$ and $\mathbf{v}_i^{GP(char)}$ represent the learnable embeddings that are associated with frequent words in the vocabulary (pre-initialized from FAIR word vectors (Bojanowski et al., 2017)) and convolution-based character-level embeddings (Ma et al., 2018)[7] respectively. Apart from these changes in the embedding layer, we replace the decoding strategy (tree construction from the predicted graph) of our parser from greedy decoding (used by BiAF parser) to Chu-Liu-Edmonds algorithm (Chu and Liu, 1967), which further improves performance during evaluation.

2.2 ELMo features

In natural language, the meaning of a word changes when the underlying linguistic context changes. This fact is not captured by static word embeddings due to their *context independence*. Employing a deep, contextualized word representation, ELMo (Peters et al., 2018), which is a function of the entire sentence, yields promising result for several downstream tasks such as Question Answering, Textual Entailment and Sentiment Analysis. We attempt to test whether this hypothesis holds for dependency parsing. This is an interesting experiment as the authors of ELMo obtain larger improvements for tasks with small train set (sample efficient), indicating that smaller treebanks deprived of useful information could potentially enjoy good improvements.[8]

The backbone of ELMo is a BiLSTM-based neural Language Model (BiLSTM-LM), which is trained

---

[7] For obtaining character emebddings, we prefer convolution operation (introduced in dos Santos and Zadrozny (2014)) over LSTM (used by BiAF and introduced in Ballesteros et al. (2015)) as the former is parallelizable and efficient especially for large treebanks.

[8] ELMoLex rank 8th overall for small treebanks by LAS metric.

on a large raw corpus. We attempt to explore in this work whether we can train an indomain version of a BiLSTM-LM effectively using the available training data. The main challenge to accomplish this task is to learn transferable features in the absence of abundant raw data. Inspired by the authors of BiAF who use a large, well-tuned network to create a high performing graph parser, we implement a large BiLSTM-LM network (independent of the ELMoLex parser) which is highly regularized to prevent data overfitting and able to learn useful features. Our BiLSTM-LM consumes both the word and tag embedding as input, which can be formally written as:

$$
\begin{aligned}
\mathbf{x}_i^{LM} &= \mathbf{v}_i^{LM(word)} \oplus \mathbf{v}_i^{LM(UPoS)}, \\
\mathbf{v}_i^{LM(word)} &= \mathbf{v}_i^{LM(fair)} \oplus \mathbf{v}_i^{LM(char)}.
\end{aligned}
\tag{3}
$$

In equation 3, the notations $\mathbf{v}_i^{LM(fair)}$, $\mathbf{v}_i^{LM(char)}$ and $\mathbf{v}_i^{LM(UPoS)}$ are the counterparts of $\mathbf{v}_i^{GP(fair)}$, $\mathbf{v}_i^{GP(char)}$ and $\mathbf{v}_i^{GP(UPoS)}$ respectively.

Note that ELMo, as proposed in Peters et al. (2018), builds only on character embeddings, automatically inferring the PoS information in the lower layers of the LSTM network. Since we have less training data to work with, we feed the PoS information explicitly which helps in easening the optimization process of our BiLSTM-LM network. Given a sequence of n words, $x_1^{LM}, \ldots, x_n^{LM}$, BiLSTM-LM learns by maximizing the log likelihood of forward LSTM and backward LSTM directions, which can be defined as:

$$
\begin{aligned}
&\sum_{i=1}^{n} (log \Pr(x_i^{LM} | x_1^{LM}, \ldots, x_{i-1}^{LM}; \Theta_x; \overrightarrow{\Theta}_{LSTM}, \overrightarrow{\Theta}_s)) \\
&+ (log \Pr(x_i^{LM} | x_{i+1}^{LM}, \ldots, x_n^{LM}; \Theta_x; \overleftarrow{\Theta}_{LSTM}, \overleftarrow{\Theta}_s)).
\end{aligned}
\tag{4}
$$

We share the word embedding layer (Θ_x) of both LSTMs and learn the rest of the parameters independently. Unlike Peters et al. (2018), we do not tie the Softmax layer (Θ_s) in both the LSTM directions. Essentially, ELMo features are computed by a task-specific linear combination of the BiLSTM-LM's intermediate layer representations. If L represents the number of layers in BiLSTM-LM, ELMo computes a set of $2L + 1$ representations:

$$
\begin{aligned}
R_k &= \{\mathbf{x}_k^{LM}, \overleftarrow{\mathbf{h}}_{k,j}^{LM}, \overrightarrow{\mathbf{h}}_{k,j}^{LM} | j = 1, \ldots, L\} \\
&= \{\mathbf{h}_{k,j}^{LM} | j = 1, \ldots, L\},
\end{aligned}
\tag{5}
$$

where $\mathbf{h}_{k,0}^{LM}$ is the word embedding layer (Equation 3) and $\mathbf{h}_{k,j}^{LM} = \overleftarrow{\mathbf{h}}_{k,j}^{LM} \oplus \overrightarrow{\mathbf{h}}_{k,j}^{LM}$, for each BiLSTM layer.

The authors of ELMo (Peters et al., 2018) show that different layers of BiLSTM-LM carry different types of information: lower-level LSTM states capture syntactic aspects (e.g., they can be used for PoS tagging); higher-level LSTM states model context-dependent aspects of word meaning (e.g., they can be used for word sense disambiguation); This observation is exploited by ELMoLex which can smartly select among all of these signals the useful information for dependency parsing. Thus, ELMo features for a word are computed by attending (softly) to the informative layers in R, as follows:

$$
\mathbf{v}_i^{GP(ELMo)} = \mathbb{E}(R_k; \Theta^{elmo}) = \gamma^{elmo} \sum_{j=0}^{L} s_j^{elmo} \mathbf{h}_{k,j}^{LM}.
\tag{6}
$$

In equation 6, s^{elmo} corresponds to the softmax-normalized weights, while γ^{elmo} lets ELMoLex to scale the entire ELMo vector.

2.3 Lexicon features

Character-level models depend on the internal character-level make-up of a word. They exploit the relevant sub-parts of a word such as suffixes or prefixes to generate word representations. They can generalize to unknown words if these unknown words follow such generalizations. Otherwise, they fail to add any improvement (Sagot and Martínez Alonso, 2017) and we may need to look for other sources to complement the information provided by character-level embeddings. We term this problem as *linguistic naivety*.

ELMoLex taps into the large inventory of morphological features (gender, number, case, tense, mood, person, etc.) provided by external resources, namely the UDLexicons (Sagot, 2018) lexicon collection, which cover words with an irregular morphology as well as words not present in the training data. Essentially, these lexicons consist of ⟨word, UPoS, morphological features⟩ triplets, which we query using ⟨word, UPoS⟩ pair resulting in one or more hits. When we attempt to integrate the information from these hits, we face the challenge of disambiguation as not all the morphological features returned by the query are relevant to the focal ⟨word, UPoS⟩ pair. ELMoLex relies on attention mechanism (Bahdanau et al., 2014) to select the relevant morphological features, thereby having the capability to handle noisy or irrelevant features by paying no attention.

Put formally, given a sequence of m morphological feature embeddings $(\mathbf{v}_{mf_1}^{GP(mf)}, \ldots, \mathbf{v}_{mf_m}^{GP(mf)})$ for a word i, the lexicon-based embedding for the word

Target	Source(s)
hy_armtdp	grc_perseus, grc_proiel
kk_ktb	tr_imst, ug_udt
hsb_ufal	*mixed*
kmr_mg	fa_seraji
bxr_bdt	tr_imst, ug_udt, ko_gsd, ko_kaist, ja_gsd
pcm_nsc	*mixed*
en_pud	en_ewt
th_pud	*mixed*
ja_modern	ja_gsd
br_keb	*mixed*
fo_oft	da_ddt, sv_talbanken, sv_lines, no_nynorsklia, no_bokmaal, no_nynorsk
fi_pud	fi_tdt
sv_pud	sv_talbanken
cs_pud	cs_pdt

Table 1: Treebanks to source the training data for Delexicalized Parsing of a given target treebank.

$(\mathbf{v}_i^{GP(lex)})$ can be computed as follows:[9]

$$\mathbf{v}_i^{GP(lex)} = \sum_{j=1}^{m} s_{mf_j}^{lex} \mathbf{v}_{mf_j}^{GP(mf)}. \tag{7}$$

In equation 7, $s_{mf_j}^{lex}$ corresponds to the softmax-normalized weight which is a learnable parameter for each available morphological feature (in this case, it is mf_j). The general idea to perform a weighted sum to extract relevant features has been previously studied in the context of sequence labeling (Rei et al., 2016) for integrating word and character level features. Combining the distributional knowledge of words along with the semantic lexicons has been extensively studied for estimating high quality word vectors, also referred to as 'retrofitting' in literature (Faruqui et al., 2015).

2.4 Delexicalized Parsing

We perform delexicalized "language family" parsing for treebanks with less than 50 or no train sentences (as shown in Table 1). The delexicalized version of ELMoLex throws away word-level information such as $\mathbf{v}^{GP(word)}$ and $\mathbf{v}^{GP(char)}$ and works with the rest. The source treebanks are concatenated to form one large treebank, which is then used to train the delexicalized parser for the corresponding target treebank. In case of "mixed model", we concatenate at most 300 sentences from each treebank to create the training data.

2.5 Handling OOV words

Out Of Vocabulary (OOV) word problem is prevalent in languages with rich morphology and an accurate parser should come up with smart techniques to perform better than substituting a learned unknown vocabulary token ('UNK') during evaluation. To circumvent this problem, ELMoLex relies on four signals from the proposed embedding layer:

- $\mathbf{v}^{GP(fair)}$: If an OOV word is present in the FAIR word vectors, ELMoLex directly substitute the word embedding without any transformation.[10] If OOV word is absent, we resort to using 'UNK' token.

- $\mathbf{v}^{GP(ELMo)}$: For an OOV word, the ELMo layer of ELMoLex computes the context-dependent word representation based on the other vocabulary words present in the focal sentence.

- $\mathbf{v}^{GP(char)}$: Character-level embedding layer of ELMoLex computes the representation based on the known characters extracted from the OOV word naturally.

- $\mathbf{v}^{GP(lex)}$: If an OOV word is present in the external lexicon, ELMoLex queries with the ⟨word, PoS⟩ pair and computes the representation based on the known set of morphological features.

2.6 Neural Tagger with embedded lexicon

As described in Dozat et al. (2017), the BiAF model benefits from Part-of-Speech (PoS) inputs only if their accuracy is high enough. Our idea was therefore to design an accurate tagger in order to improve the performance of the parser.

Moreover, the shared task allows the use of external resources such as lexicons. A lexicon is simply a collection of possibilities in terms of PoS and morphological features usually provided for a large amount of words. In the context of neural taggers, an external lexicon can be seen as an external memory that can be useful in two ways:

- *For making training faster.* At initialization, for a given token, all possible PoS tags are equiprobable of being predicted by the network. The model only learns from the example it sees. By providing the model with a constrained set of

---

[9] We experienced inferior results with other lexicon-based representations such as n-hot vector (having active value corresponding to the each of the morphological feature), unweighted average of morphological feature embeddings and morphological feature group based embedded attention.

[10] Inspired by Mikolov et al. (2013), we experimented with a linear transformation of the FAIR word vectors to the trained word embedding space, which resulted in poor performance. This confirms the intuition that the learned word embedding space is a non-linear transformation of the pre-trained word vectors.

possible tags as input features we can expect the training process to be faster.

- *For helping the model with OOV tokens.* Indeed, the lexicon provides information - potentially complementary to the character based representation - on OOV tokens that could be useful at inference.

Generally speaking, this experience is interesting because it challenges the idea that neural models, if deep enough and trained on enough data, don't require external resources and can learn everything in an end-to-end manner. As we will see for tagging, external pre-computed resources such as lexicons are of a great help.

The tagger we design is based on the neural tagging model with lexicon described in Sagot and Martínez Alonso (2017) and adapted using architectural insights from Dozat and Manning (2016). In short, words are represented in three ways. The first part is a trainable word vector (initialized with the FAIR vectors described in Bojanowski et al. (2017)). The second part is a character-based representation either computed using 1-dimensional convolution or a recurrent LSTM cell. The third component is an n-hot encoded vector of the tags that appear in an external lexicon, possibly embedded in a continuous space. These three components are summed, providing a *morphologically and lexically-enriched word representation*. This vector is then fed to a two layer BiLSTM that encodes the sentence level context, followed by two heads, one for predicting UPoS and the other for predicting morphological features. Each head is composed of a dense layer followed by a softmax layer.

2.7 Specific Tokenization post-processing for Arabic

To improve the Arabic tokenizer, we noticed that tokenization is very error-prone wherein most of the errors come from wrong analysis of the letter 'و'. Indeed, in Arabic, this letter (which is a coordinate conjunction, "and") is usually concatenated to the next word (e.g 'وقطر', "and Qata") but is sometimes just a part of the word (e.g 'وافق', "he agrees"). This ambiguity confuses the UDPipe tokenizer. Our fix consists in splitting that letter from its word whenever UDPipe was unable to provide a proper UPoS tag. This simple fix led to a 0.7% improvement in word segmentation compared to the UDPipe baseline and led us to rank 4th on Arabic in the final LAS metric.

Treebank	Neural Tagger	UDPipe
af_afribooms	95.33	**95.53**
da_dadt	**95.54**	95.18
el_gdt	**95.48**	94.80
fr_sequoia	**96.13**	95.78
fr_spoken	**95.71**	93.70
hu_szeged	**93.07**	92.56
sv_lines	**95.27**	94.37
tr_imst	**91.08**	91.02
vi_vtb	77.10	**77.80**
zh_gsd	**84.26**	83.24

Table 2: UPoS F1 on Dev. datasets (used as test)

3 Results

The implementation of ELMoLex as well as the neural tagger are based on the publicly available BiAF parser code provided by CMU (Ma et al., 2018). Similar to Dozat et al. (2017), we use mostly the same set of hyper-parameters (as displayed in Appendix A), which makes ELMoLex robust across a wide variety of treebanks present in the shared task (Zeman et al., 2018). For treebanks with no development data, we perform a 5-fold cross validation to identify the average number of epochs taken to train each fold. By setting the maximum number of epochs to this average number, we then train ELMoLex on 90% of the training data and use the rest of the training data for selecting our best model. When we do not find external lexicon in UDLexicons (Sagot, 2018) for a given language, we skip the lexicon based features ($\mathbf{v}^{GP(lex)}$) and work with the rest. ELMoLex ran for $\sim$26 hours on the TIRA virtual machine (Potthast et al., 2014) sequentially, which can be trivially parallelized to run within two hours. Our shared task results are displayed in Appendix B.

3.1 Performance Analysis of the Tagger

Given the general architecture we presented in Section 2.6, we are able to test a few key questions: Is recurrent cell better suited at encoding word morphology compared to 1-D convolution layer ? Is embedding the lexical information into a continuous space useful for improving the performance ? And finally, is using an external lexicon always useful for better UPoS tagging ? We summarize our results as follows:

- Convolution layer works better than recurrent cell for languages such as Vietnamese and Chinese.

- Leveraging an external lexicon helps the tagger for most of the languages, specifically for languages such as French (tested on *fr_sequoia*

Treebank	Vanilla		NLM Init.		ELMo		Lex		ELMoLex	
nl_lassysmall	73.57	(230)	74.08	(751)	74.10	(779)	**74.23**	(979)	74.05	(500)
fr_spoken	61.83	(94)	61.97	(141)	62.07	(175)	62.28	(275)	**62.49**	(383)
el_gdt	81.43	(148)	82.06	(687)	82.09	(764)	**82.48**	(1358)	**82.48**	(2028)
it_postwita	64.95	(369)	66.35	(225)	65.27	(266)	**65.67**	(600)	65.63	(518)
ro_rrt	81.21	(430)	81.08	(1139)	81.39	(1325)	**81.60**	(1694)	81.47	(890)
tr_imst	53.72	(249)	53.67	(624)	54.00	(735)	**54.16**	(670)	53.97	(1559)
uk_iu	78.62	(316)	78.73	(271)	**79.21**	(330)	79.14	(731)	78.87	(1891)

Table 3: Ablation study of ELMoLex. LAS dev. score along with training time (with 90% of the training data with the rest used for selecting the best model) in minutes is reported for selected treebanks. For NLM Init. and ELMoLex models, we report the time taken to train the parser (excluding the time taken to train the underlying BiLSTM-LM). All the reported models uses Chu-Liu-Edmonds algorithm (Chu and Liu, 1967) for constructing the final parse tree.

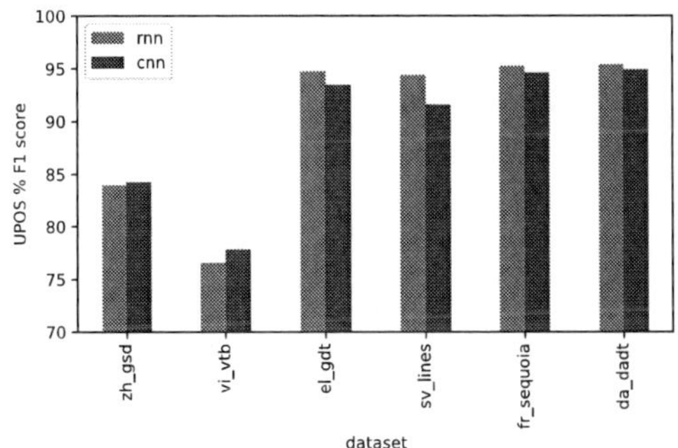

Figure 3: Comparing morphological embedding technique: RNN vs CNN

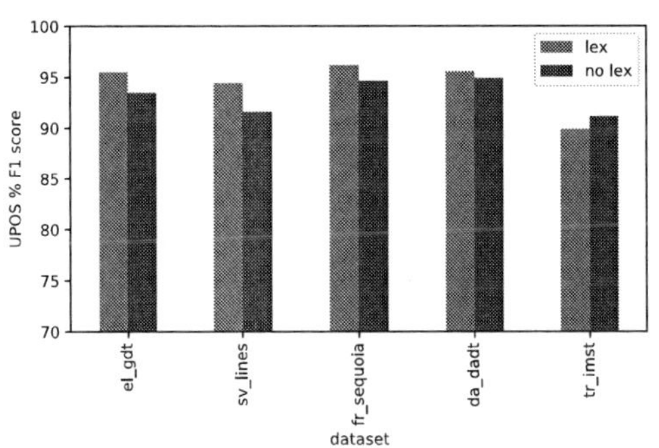

Figure 4: Impact of external lexicons

and *fr_spoken*), Greek, Danish, Hungarian and Swedish. The only language for which the lexicon did not help is Turkish.

- Using a continuous embedding layer for lexicon features always leads to better performance compare to straight n-hot encoding.

We now present in more details the performance of our model regarding these three dimensions. The results are reported on development datasets treated as a strict test set.

As we notice in Figure 3, using a convolution layer as a morphological embedding technique provides poorer results compared to a recurrent cell except for two cases: Chinese and Vietnamese. This suggests that the different morphology and tokenization complexity that we find for Europeans languages compared to Chinese and Vietnamese might well require different kind of embedding architectures. Intuitively, we could say that the character-wise sequential structure of the Europeans languages is better modeled by a recurrent cell, while a language like Chinese with overlaying phenomenons is better modeled by a convolution layer.

We now describe the impact of an external lexicon for UPoS tagging (Figure. 4). We present the results only for the datasets for which the RNN cell was providing the best results. We compare two architectures: the neural tagger using a recurrent cell for morphology with an external lexicon (embedded in a continuous space) and the same architecture without external lexicons. For all the treebanks (except Turkish), the lexicon helps the UPoS tagging performance.

The last component of the neural tagger we analyze is the input technique of the lexical information. We compare two techniques. The first one is the architecture described in Sagot and Martínez Alonso (2017) for which the lexical information is feeded using a n-hot encoded vector which is then concatenated with the other word representation vectors. The second one embeds in a continuous space the lexicon tags before averaging them providing a single vector that summarizes the lexical information of a given word. As we see in Figure 5, in all languages we experimented with, the embedding layers provides better results than a simple n-hot encoded representation.

For most of the treebanks, we performed significantly above the UDPipe baseline for UPoS tagging. Our results are summarized in Table 2. Unfortunately, we reached these results too late before the deadline, and we did not get the time to retrain our parser on our

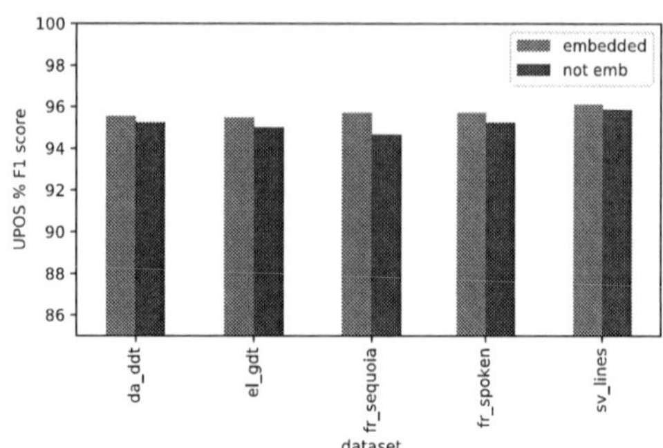

Figure 5: Impact of lexicon embedding technique

Treebank	ParisNLP-2017	ParisNLP-2018
el_edt	82.25	86.83 (+4.58)
hu_szeged	66.82	74.36 (+7.54)
sv_lines	76.61	79.92 (+3.31)
tr_imst	56.03	61.27 (+5.24)

Table 4: Comparing LAS scores for 2017 and 2018 participation of ParisNLP. The increase in the absolute LAS points are enclosed in the ellipses.

own, predicted PoS tags. Therefore, at test time, we only used the predicted tags for treebanks for which we were confident that our predicted tags would help the parser. It resulted in using our system for four treebanks: *el_gdt*, *hu_szeged*, *sv_lines* and *tr_imst*. In Appendix C,you will find the performance of our Neural tagger and our ELMoLex parser trained on our predicted tags for which we were able to retrain the models after the system submission deadline.

3.2 Ablation Study of the Parser

To unpack the benefits obtained from each of our contributions, we perform ablation studies with the following variants of ELMoLex: ELMoLex without ELMo and lexicon features, which is effectively the *vanilla* BiAF model (Ma et al., 2018); initializing the BiLSTM layer of the vanilla model with that of a pre-trained BiLSTM-LM (*NLM Init.*)[11]; ELMoLex with the ELMo features only (ELMo); ELMoLex with the lexicon features only (Lex); ELMoLex with both ELMo and Lexicon features (full version); The models used in the ablation study are trained on 90% of the training data, tuned on the remaining 10% and tested on the development set provided by the organizers.

The results are displayed in Table 3[12]. We make the following important observations: (1) Utilizing either ELMo or Lexicon or both always outperform the BiAF model; (2) External lexicons brings in valuable information about OOV words and words with irregular morphology, thereby outperforming BiAF (which relies for those cases on character embeddings only) by a large margin; (3) ELMo entails high train time due to the additional LSTM operation over the entire

sentence, but exhibits strong performance over BiAF model which naturally leads us to combine it along with the lexicon information to create ELMoLex (our final submission system).

In summary, in contrast with our participation to the shared task last year (de La Clergerie et al. (2017)[13], we decided to focus on neural models wherein we explored many architectures and ideas both for tagging and parsing. As a result we reached superior performance in the final LAS score compared to our last year submission. To illustrate this, we compare the results of our current submission with that of the last year for four treebanks (Table 4) and observe significant improvements in the LAS score.

3.3 Extrinsic Evaluation of the Parser

A "good" parser should not only perform well in the intrinsic metrics such as LAS, BLAS and BLEX, but should strengthen a real world NLP system by providing relevant syntactic features. To understand the impact of ELMoLex in a downstream NLP application, we participiated in the shared task on Extrinsic Parser Evaluation (Fares et al., 2018). The goal of this task is to evaluate the parse trees predicted by ELMoLex on three downstream applications: biological event extraction, fine-grained opinion analysis, and negation resolution, for its usefulness. Since all the tasks are based on English language, we train ELMoLex on *en_ewt* treebank (which is the largest English treebank provided by the organizers (Zeman et al., 2018)) without changing the hyper-parameters (as disclosed in Appendix A). We refer the readers to Fares et al. (2018) for details about each of the downstream task and the accompanying system (which takes the features dervied from ELMoLex) used to solve the task. Our extrinsic evaluation results[14] are displayed in Table 5. ELMoLex ranked 7th for Event Extraction, Negation Resolution tasks and 11th for Opinion Analysis task by F1 score. On an average, ELMoLex

---

[11] Our final submission to the shared task did not have the NLM pre-initialization feature.

[12] The training time reported in the table is an over-estimate, as it is captured when several parsers (at most four of them) are running together in a single GTX 1070 GPU.

[13] Our team 'ParisNLP' ranked 6th in the unofficial ranking.

[14] In our last year joint submission with Stanford (Schuster et al., 2017), we evaluated different semantic dependencies representations and also compared different parsing strategies.

Downstream Task	Precision	Recall	F1 Score
Event Extraction	55.66 (-3.6)	43.56 (-9.87)	48.87 (-4.72)
Negation Resolution	100 (0)	40.68 (-2.07)	57.83 (-1.91)
Opinion Analysis	63.01 (-3.66)	56.78 (-6.1)	59.73 (-4.99)

Table 5: Results on the downstream tasks for our ELMoLex system trained on the en_ewt treebank with the corresponding difference from the best system enclosed in ellipses.

ranked 8th with a F1 score of 55.48%.

4   Conclusion

We presented our parsing system, ELMoLex, which successfully integrates context-dependent ELMo and lexicon-based representations to overcome the context independency and linguistic naivety problem in the embedding layer of the BiAF model respectively. We showed the analysis of our neural tagger, whose competitive performance in PoS estimation is capitalized by ELMoLex to achieve strong gains in parsing quality for four treebanks. We also performed an ablation study to understand the source of gains brought by ELMoLex. We evaluated ELMoLex on three downstream applications to understand its usefulness.

In the next step of our work, we plan to: (1) compare the performance in utilizing recurrent layer over the convolution layer for character embeddings (similar to our neural tagger experiment) which underlies our parser; (2) pursue the NLM initialization feature further to inspect if using it can enrich ELMoLex; (3) observe the performance when we augment the in-domain train data for our BiLSTM-LM with massive raw data (such as Wikipedia); (4) train our parser and tagger jointly with the gold PoS tags; and (5) exploit lattice information (More et al., 2018; Buckman and Neubig, 2018) which captures rich linguistic knowledge.

Acknowledgments

We thank the organizers and the data providers who made this shared task possible within the core Universal Dependencies framework (Nivre et al., 2016), namely the authors of the UD version 2.0 datasets (Nivre et al., 2018), the baseline UDPipe models (Straka et al., 2016), and the team behind the TIRA evaluation platform (Potthast et al., 2014) to whom we owe a lot. We also thank José Carlos Rosales Núñez for useful discussions. This work was funded by the ANR projects ParSiTi (ANR-16-CE33-0021) and SoSweet (ANR15-CE38-0011-01).

References

Dzmitry Bahdanau, Kyunghyun Cho, and Yoshua Bengio. 2014. Neural machine translation by jointly learning to align and translate. *CoRR* abs/1409.0473. http://arxiv.org/abs/1409.0473.

Miguel Ballesteros, Chris Dyer, and Noah A. Smith. 2015. Improved transition-based parsing by modeling characters instead of words with lstms. In *Proceedings of the 2015 Conference on Empirical Methods in Natural Language Processing, EMNLP 2015, Lisbon, Portugal, September 17-21, 2015*. pages 349–359. http://aclweb.org/anthology/D/D15/D15-1041.pdf.

Piotr Bojanowski, Édouard Grave, Armand Joulin, and Tomas Mikolov. 2017. Enriching word vectors with subword information. *TACL* 5:135–146. https://transacl.org/ojs/index.php/tacl/article/view/999.

Jacob Buckman and Graham Neubig. 2018. Neural lattice language models. *CoRR* abs/1803.05071. http://arxiv.org/abs/1803.05071.

Yoeng-Jin Chu and Tseng-Hong Liu. 1967. On the shortest arborescence of a directed graph. In *Science Sinica*. pages 1396–1400.

Éric Vilemonte de La Clergerie, Benoît Sagot, and Djamé Seddah. 2017. The ParisNLP entry at the CoNLL UD Shared Task 2017: A Tale of a # ParsingTragedy. In *Conference on Computational Natural Language Learning*. pages 243–252.

Cícero Nogueira dos Santos and Bianca Zadrozny. 2014. Learning character-level representations for part-of-speech tagging. In *Proceedings of the 31th International Conference on Machine Learning, ICML 2014, Beijing, China, 21-26 June 2014*. pages 1818–1826. http://jmlr.org/proceedings/papers/v32/santos14.html.

Timothy Dozat and Christopher D. Manning. 2016. Deep Biaffine Attention for Neural Dependency Parsing. *CoRR* abs/1611.01734. http://arxiv.org/abs/1611.01734.

Timothy Dozat, Peng Qi, and Christopher D Manning. 2017. Stanford's Graph-based Neural Dependency Parser at the CoNLL 2017 Shared Task. *Proceedings of the CoNLL 2017 Shared Task: Multilingual Parsing from Raw Text to Universal Dependencies* pages 20–30.

Murhaf Fares, Stephan Oepen, Lilja Øvrelid, Jari Björne, and Richard Johansson. 2018. The 2018 Shared Task on Extrinsic Parser Evaluation. On the downstream utility of English Universal Dependency parsers. In *Proceedings of the 22nd Conference on Natural Language Learning*. Brussels, Belgia.

Manaal Faruqui, Jesse Dodge, Sujay Kumar Jauhar, Chris Dyer, Eduard H. Hovy, and Noah A. Smith. 2015. Retrofitting word vectors to semantic lexicons. In *NAACL HLT 2015, The 2015 Conference of the North American Chapter of the Association for Computational Linguistics: Human Language Technologies, Denver, Colorado, USA, May 31 - June 5, 2015*. pages 1606–1615. http://aclweb.org/anthology/N/N15/N15-1184.pdf.

Eliyahu Kiperwasser and Yoav Goldberg. 2016. Simple and accurate dependency parsing using bidirectional LSTM feature representations. *Transactions of the Association for Computational Linguistics (TACL)* 4:313–327. https://transacl.org/ojs/index.php/tacl/article/view/885.

Xuezhe Ma, Zecong Hu, Jingzhou Liu, Nanyun Peng, Graham Neubig, and Eduard H. Hovy. 2018. Stack-pointer networks for dependency parsing. *CoRR* abs/1805.01087. http://arxiv.org/abs/1805.01087.

Austin Matthews, Graham Neubig, and Chris Dyer. 2018. Using Morphological Knowledge in Open-Vocabulary Neural Language Models. In *Proceedings of the 2018 Conference of the North American Chapter of the Association for Computational Linguistics: Human Language Technologies, NAACL-HLT 2018*. New Orleans, Louisiana, USA, pages 1435–1445. https://aclanthology.info/papers/N18-1130/n18-1130.

Tomas Mikolov, Quoc V. Le, and Ilya Sutskever. 2013. Exploiting similarities among languages for machine translation. *CoRR* abs/1309.4168. http://arxiv.org/abs/1309.4168.

Amir More, Özlem Çetinoglu, Çagri Çöltekin, Nizar Habash, Benoît Sagot, Djamé Seddah, Dima Taji, and Reut Tsarfaty. 2018. Conll-ul: Universal morphological lattices for universal dependency parsing. In *Proceedings of the Eleventh International Conference on Language Resources and Evaluation, LREC 2018*. Miyazaki, Japan.

Joakim Nivre, Mitchell Abrams, Željko Agić, Lars Ahrenberg, Lene Antonsen, Maria Jesus Aranzabe, Gashaw Arutie, Masayuki Asahara, Luma Ateyah, Mohammed Attia, Aitziber Atutxa, Liesbeth Augustinus, Elena Badmaeva, Miguel Ballesteros, Esha Banerjee, Sebastian Bank, Verginica Barbu Mititelu, John Bauer, Sandra Bellato, Kepa Bengoetxea, Riyaz Ahmad Bhat, Erica Biagetti, Eckhard Bick, Rogier Blokland, Victoria Bobicev, Carl Börstell, Cristina Bosco, Gosse Bouma, Sam Bowman, Adriane Boyd, Aljoscha Burchardt, Marie Candito, Bernard Caron, Gauthier Caron, Gülşen Cebiroğlu Eryiğit, Giuseppe G. A. Celano, Savas Cetin, Fabricio Chalub, Jinho Choi, Yongseok Cho, Jayeol Chun, Silvie Cinková, Aurélie Collomb, Çağrı Çöltekin, Miriam Connor, Marine Courtin, Elizabeth Davidson, Marie-Catherine de Marneffe, Valeria de Paiva, Arantza Diaz de Ilarraza, Carly Dickerson, Peter Dirix, Kaja Dobrovoljc, Timothy Dozat, Kira Droganova, Puneet Dwivedi, Marhaba Eli, Ali Elkahky, Binyam Ephrem, Tomaž Erjavec, Aline Etienne, Richárd Farkas, Hector Fernandez Alcalde, Jennifer Foster, Cláudia Freitas, Katarína Gajdošová, Daniel Galbraith, Marcos Garcia, Moa Gärdenfors, Kim Gerdes, Filip Ginter, Iakes Goenaga, Koldo Gojenola, Memduh Gökırmak, Yoav Goldberg, Xavier Gómez Guinovart, Berta Gonzáles Saavedra, Matias Grioni, Normunds Grūzītis, Bruno Guillaume, Céline Guillot-Barbance, Nizar Habash, Jan Hajič, Jan Hajič jr., Linh Hà Mỹ, Na-Rae Han, Kim Harris, Dag Haug, Barbora Hladká, Jaroslava Hlaváčová, Florinel Hociung, Petter Hohle, Jena Hwang, Radu Ion, Elena Irimia, Tomáš Jelínek, Anders Johannsen, Fredrik Jørgensen, Hüner Kaşıkara, Sylvain Kahane, Hiroshi Kanayama, Jenna Kanerva, Tolga Kayadelen, Václava Kettnerová, Jesse Kirchner, Natalia Kotsyba, Simon Krek, Sookyoung Kwak, Veronika Laippala, Lorenzo Lambertino, Tatiana Lando, Septina Dian Larasati, Alexei Lavrentiev, John Lee, Phương Lê Hồng, Alessandro Lenci, Saran Lertpradit, Herman Leung, Cheuk Ying Li, Josie Li, Keying Li, KyungTae Lim, Nikola Ljubešić, Olga Loginova, Olga Lyashevskaya, Teresa Lynn, Vivien

Macketanz, Aibek Makazhanov, Michael Mandl, Christopher Manning, Ruli Manurung, Cătălina Mărănduc, David Mareček, Katrin Marheinecke, Héctor Martínez Alonso, André Martins, Jan Mašek, Yuji Matsumoto, Ryan McDonald, Gustavo Mendonça, Niko Miekka, Anna Missilä, Cătălin Mititelu, Yusuke Miyao, Simonetta Montemagni, Amir More, Laura Moreno Romero, Shinsuke Mori, Bjartur Mortensen, Bohdan Moskalevskyi, Kadri Muischnek, Yugo Murawaki, Kaili Müürisep, Pinkey Nainwani, Juan Ignacio Navarro Horñiacek, Anna Nedoluzhko, Gunta Nešpore-Bērzkalne, Lương Nguyễn Thị, Huyền Nguyễn Thị Minh, Vitaly Nikolaev, Rattima Nitisaroj, Hanna Nurmi, Stina Ojala, Adédayọstling Robert Olúòkun, Lilja Øvrelid, Niko Partanen, Elena Pascual, Marco Passarotti, Agnieszka Patejuk, Siyao Peng, Cenel-Augusto Perez, Guy Perrier, Slav Petrov, Jussi Piitulainen, Emily Pitler, Barbara Plank, Thierry Poibeau, Martin Popel, Lauma Pretkalniņa, Sophie Prévost, Prokopis Prokopidis, Adam Przepiórkowski, Tiina Puolakainen, Sampo Pyysalo, Andriela Rääbis, Alexandre Rademaker, Loganathan Ramasamy, Taraka Rama, Carlos Ramisch, Vinit Ravishankar, Livy Real, Siva Reddy, Georg Rehm, Michael Rießler, Larissa Rinaldi, Laura Rituma, Luisa Rocha, Mykhailo Romanenko, Rudolf Rosa, Davide Rovati, Valentin Roșca, Olga Rudina, Shoval Sadde, Shadi Saleh, Tanja Samardžić, Stephanie Samson, Manuela Sanguinetti, Baiba Saulīte, Yanin Sawanakunanon, Nathan Schneider, Sebastian Schuster, Djamé Seddah, Wolfgang Seeker, Mojgan Seraji, Mo Shen, Atsuko Shimada, Muh Shohibussirri, Dmitry Sichinava, Natalia Silveira, Maria Simi, Radu Simionescu, Katalin Simkó, Mária Šimková, Kiril Simov, Aaron Smith, Isabela Soares-Bastos, Antonio Stella, Milan Straka, Jana Strnadová, Alane Suhr, Umut Sulubacak, Zsolt Szántó, Dima Taji, Yuta Takahashi, Takaaki Tanaka, Isabelle Tellier, Trond Trosterud, Anna Trukhina, Reut Tsarfaty, Francis Tyers, Sumire Uematsu, Zdeňka Urešová, Larraitz Uria, Hans Uszkoreit, Sowmya Vajjala, Daniel van Niekerk, Gertjan van Noord, Viktor Varga, Veronika Vincze, Lars Wallin, Jonathan North Washington, Seyi Williams, Mats Wirén, Tsegay Woldemariam, Taksum Wong, Chunxiao Yan, Marat M. Yavrumyan, Zhuoran Yu, Zdeněk Žabokrtský, Amir Zeldes, Daniel Zeman, Manying Zhang, and Hanzhi Zhu. 2018. Universal dependencies 2.2. LINDAT/CLARIN digital library at the Institute of Formal and Applied Linguistics (ÚFAL), Faculty of Mathematics and Physics, Charles University. http://hdl.handle.net/11234/1-2837.

Joakim Nivre, Marie-Catherine de Marneffe, Filip Ginter, Yoav Goldberg, Jan Hajič, Christopher Manning, Ryan McDonald, Slav Petrov, Sampo Pyysalo, Natalia Silveira, Reut Tsarfaty, and Daniel Zeman. 2016. Universal Dependencies v1: A multilingual treebank collection. In *Proceedings of the 10th International Conference on Language Resources and Evaluation (LREC 2016)*. European Language Resources Association, Portorož, Slovenia, pages 1659–1666.

Matthew E. Peters, Mark Neumann, Mohit Iyyer, Matt Gardner, Christopher Clark, Kenton Lee, and Luke Zettlemoyer. 2018. Deep contextualized word representations. In *Proceedings of the 2018 Conference of the North American Chapter of the Association for Computational Linguistics: Human Language Technologies, NAACL-HLT 2018, New Orleans, Louisiana, USA, June 1-6, 2018, Volume 1 (Long Papers)*. pages 2227–2237. https://aclanthology.info/papers/N18-1202/n18-1202.

Martin Potthast, Tim Gollub, Francisco Rangel, Paolo Rosso, Efstathios Stamatatos, and Benno Stein. 2014. Improving the reproducibility of PAN's shared tasks: Plagiarism detection, author identification, and author profiling. In Evangelos Kanoulas, Mihai Lupu, Paul Clough, Mark Sanderson, Mark Hall, Allan Hanbury, and Elaine Toms, editors, *Information Access Evaluation meets Multilinguality, Multimodality, and Visualization. 5th International Conference of the CLEF Initiative (CLEF 14)*. Springer, Berlin Heidelberg New York, pages 268–299. https://doi.org/10.1007/978-3-319-11382-1_22.

Marek Rei, Gamal K. O. Crichton, and Sampo Pyysalo. 2016. Attending to characters in neural sequence labeling models. In *COLING 2016, 26th International Conference on Computational Linguistics, Proceedings of the Conference: Technical Papers, December 11-16, 2016, Osaka, Japan*. pages 309–318. http://aclweb.org/anthology/C/C16/C16-1030.pdf.

Benoît Sagot. 2018. A multilingual collection of conll-u-compatible morphological lexicons. In

Proceedings of the Eleventh International Conference on Language Resources and Evaluation, LREC 2018. Miyazaki, Japan.

Benoît Sagot and Héctor Martínez Alonso. 2017. Improving neural tagging with lexical information. In *Proceedings of the 15th International Conference on Parsing Technologies, IWPT 2017*. Pisa, Italy, pages 25–31. https://aclanthology.info/papers/W17-6304/w17-6304.

Sebastian Schuster, Éric De La Clergerie, Marie Candito, Benoît Sagot, Christopher D. Manning, and Djamé Seddah. 2017. Paris and Stanford at EPE 2017: Downstream evaluation of graph-based dependency representations. In *Proceedings of the 2017 Shared Task on Extrinsic Parser Evaluation at the Fourth International Conference on Dependency Linguistics and the 15th International Conference on Parsing Technologies*. Pisa, Italy, page 47–59.

Milan Straka, Jan Hajič, and Jana Straková. 2016. UDPipe: trainable pipeline for processing CoNLL-U files performing tokenization, morphological analysis, POS tagging and parsing. In *Proceedings of the 10th International Conference on Language Resources and Evaluation (LREC 2016)*. European Language Resources Association, Portorož, Slovenia.

Daniel Zeman, Jan Hajič, Martin Popel, Martin Potthast, Milan Straka, Filip Ginter, Joakim Nivre, and Slav Petrov. 2018. CoNLL 2018 Shared Task: Multilingual Parsing from Raw Text to Universal Dependencies. In *Proceedings of the CoNLL 2018 Shared Task: Multilingual Parsing from Raw Text to Universal Dependencies*. Association for Computational Linguistics, Brussels, Belgium, pages 1–20.

Appendix A: Hyper-parameters Used

	Hyper-parameter	ELMoLex Value	BiLSTM-LM Value	Neural Tagger Value
Embed	CNN window	3	3	3
	char-LSTM	-	-	300
	CNN filters	100	100	300
	character embed. size	100	100	100
	word embed. size	300	300	300
	PoS embed. size	100	100	-
	lexicon based embed. size	100	-	300
LSTM	layers	3	3	2
	hidden state	512	150	400
	arc MLP size	512	-	-
	label MLP size	128	-	400
	BPTT	10	-	-
Dropout	embeddings	0.33	0.33	0.33
	LSTM hidden states	0.33	0.33	0.5
	LSTM layers	0.33	0.33	0.33
Optimization	optimizer	Adam	Adam	Adam
	init learning rate	0.001	0.001	0.001
	(β_1, β_2)	(0.9, 0.9)	(0.9, 0.9)	(0.9, 0.9)
	decay rate	0.75	0.75	0.75
	gradient clipping	5.0	5.0	5.0
	schedule	10	10	10
	maximum epochs	1000	variable [15]	1000
	batch size	variable[16]	variable[16]	12

Table 6: Hyper-parameters for all the models used in the experiments.

Appendix B: CoNLL Final Results

Treebank	LAS	MLAS	BLEX	Treebank	LAS	MLAS	BLEX
af_afribooms	82.97 (-2.50)	69.59 (-6.08)	72.57 (-3.87)	hy_armtdp	12.49 (-24.52)	1.98 (-11.38)	6.24 (-12.80)
ar_padt	72.77 (-4.29)	58.95 (-9.59)	63.62 (-6.44)	id_gsd	77.44 (-2.61)	65.06 (-3.30)	65.58 (-10.98)
bg_btb	88.85 (-2.37)	79.07 (-4.05)	77.92 (-6.39)	it_isdt	89.51 (-2.49)	80.43 (-3.46)	81.33 (-3.43)
br_keb	10.53 (-28.11)	0.34 (-13.57)	2.23 (-18.47)	it_postwita	69.73 (-9.66)	55.95 (-12.55)	57.63 (-11.71)
bxr_bdt	15.06 (-4.47)	1.78 (-1.20)	3.61 (-3.04)	ja_gsd	74.44 (-8.67)	60.38 (-12.24)	63.05 (-10.74)
ca_ancora	89.96 (-1.65)	81.63 (-2.44)	83.03 (-2.44)	ja_modern	13.63 (-14.70)	3.06 (-8.76)	4.49 (-9.30)
cs_cac	90.31 (-1.30)	75.72 (-7.70)	84.87 (-1.92)	kk_ktb	23.50 (-8.43)	5.88 (-3.05)	8.62 (-2.71)
cs_fictree	89.39 (-2.63)	74.18 (-10.05)	82.86 (-4.95)	kmr_mg	17.93 (-12.48)	4.09 (-3.89)	7.99 (-5.67)
cs_pdt	90.27 (-1.41)	79.13 (-5.97)	86.31 (-1.60)	ko_gsd	82.22 (-2.92)	75.17 (-5.68)	69.25 (-7.06)
cs_pud	82.68 (-3.45)	67.87 (-7.94)	76.23 (-4.30)	ko_kaist	85.49 (-1.42)	77.49 (-3.80)	72.29 (-7.26)
cu_proiel	70.54 (-5.19)	57.01 (-6.30)	63.56 (-7.75)	la_ittb	84.64 (-2.44)	74.66 (-5.18)	81.33 (-3.04)
da_ddt	81.22 (-5.06)	70.47 (-6.84)	71.74 (-6.33)	la_perseus	55.02 (-17.61)	32.08 (-17.69)	37.15 (-15.60)
de_gsd	77.64 (-2.72)	36.95 (-21.09)	67.94 (-3.46)	la_proiel	67.90 (-5.71)	53.02 (-6.34)	61.85 (-5.75)
el_gdt	86.83 (-2.82)	67.92 (-10.74)	74.12 (-5.97)	lv_lvtb	78.16 (-5.81)	60.19 (-7.70)	66.52 (-5.88)
en_ewt	81.42 (-3.15)	71.53 (-4.80)	74.97 (-3.47)	nl_alpino	85.17 (-4.39)	69.52 (-7.00)	74.06 (-5.09)
en_gum	78.43 (-6.62)	65.12 (-8.12)	66.25 (-7.32)	nl_lassysmall	80.79 (-6.05)	67.44 (-6.67)	69.79 (-6.75)
en_lines	76.64 (-5.33)	66.73 (-5.52)	68.95 (-6.34)	no_bokmaal	88.90 (-2.33)	79.58 (-4.10)	82.26 (-3.56)
en_pud	80.75 (-7.14)	67.89 (-6.97)	72.19 (-8.34)	no_nynorsk	88.67 (-2.32)	78.08 (-3.78)	81.57 (-2.87)
es_ancora	89.13 (-1.80)	81.18 (-2.75)	82.59 (-2.33)	no_nynorsklia	54.39 (-15.95)	39.68 (-17.83)	45.47 (-15.51)
et_edt	81.78 (-3.57)	71.59 (-5.38)	69.82 (-9.55)	pcm_nsc	11.32 (-18.75)	3.49 (-1.81)	9.80 (-16.24)
eu_bdt	80.45 (-3.77)	63.40 (-8.33)	72.50 (-5.65)	pl_lfg	92.96 (-1.90)	76.96 (-9.97)	84.14 (-6.28)
fa_seraji	85.14 (-2.97)	77.73 (-3.10)	75.48 (-4.96)	pl_sz	89.03 (-3.20)	67.31 (-13.46)	78.85 (-7.44)
fi_ftb	83.73 (-4.80)	71.43 (-8.22)	69.33 (-13.11)	pt_bosque	86.53 (-1.28)	71.73 (-4.21)	78.02 (-2.60)
fi_pud	71.64 (-18.59)	62.46 (-21.32)	57.40 (-25.04)	ro_rrt	84.75 (-2.12)	76.02 (-2.66)	77.28 (-3.69)
fi_tdt	83.06 (-5.67)	73.16 (-7.68)	67.47 (-13.77)	ru_syntagrus	91.41 (-1.07)	81.74 (-5.02)	84.65 (-4.00)
fo_oft	29.48 (-19.95)	0.34 (-0.73)	7.16 (-7.24)	ru_taiga	62.15 (-12.09)	38.46 (-23.13)	45.77 (-18.59)
fr_gsd	85.00 (-1.89)	75.38 (-3.06)	78.51 (-2.67)	sk_snk	84.22 (-4.63)	58.52 (-16.49)	67.08 (-13.66)
fr_sequoia	85.32 (-4.57)	74.70 (-7.85)	79.13 (-5.54)	sl_ssj	84.48 (-6.99)	67.85 (-14.53)	76.57 (-6.66)
fr_spoken	66.41 (-9.37)	53.30 (-11.37)	55.96 (-9.67)	sl_sst	50.62 (-10.77)	35.21 (-10.72)	41.82 (-9.12)
fro_srcmf	85.53 (-1.59)	76.96 (-3.32)	82.14 (-1.97)	sme_giella	65.95 (-3.92)	48.73 (-8.74)	49.28 (-10.82)
ga_idt	67.24 (-3.64)	39.68 (-6.11)	46.29 (-8.89)	sr_set	87.02 (-1.64)	72.20 (-5.53)	78.10 (-5.18)
gl_ctg	81.25 (-1.51)	68.48 (-2.44)	71.77 (-3.37)	sv_lines	79.92 (-4.16)	61.59 (-4.99)	72.27 (-4.74)
gl_treegal	70.48 (-3.77)	51.10 (-9.53)	56.75 (-7.54)	sv_pud	71.77 (-8.58)	42.69 (-9.05)	55.48 (-10.64)
got_proiel	66.37 (-3.18)	51.20 (-5.25)	59.18 (-4.80)	sv_talbanken	84.27 (-4.36)	73.98 (-5.34)	76.49 (-4.95)
grc_perseus	71.76 (-7.63)	39.22 (-15.76)	49.39 (-9.29)	th_pud	0.23 (-13.47)	0.00 (-6.29)	0.01 (-10.76)
grc_proiel	74.51 (-4.74)	54.87 (-5.40)	62.83 (-6.20)	tr_imst	61.71 (-4.73)	48.32 (-7.41)	52.34 (-7.79)
he_htb	62.17 (-13.92)	47.82 (-15.56)	51.52 (-13.52)	ug_udt	61.27 (-5.78)	40.73 (-5.05)	49.48 (-5.94)
hi_hdtb	90.98 (-1.43)	72.25 (-6.05)	84.80 (-1.94)	uk_iu	81.33 (-7.10)	59.99 (-12.28)	70.06 (-8.32)
hr_set	84.53 (-2.83)	61.82 (-11.62)	75.94 (-4.56)	ur_udtb	81.10 (-2.29)	52.34 (-5.64)	68.57 (-5.22)
hsb_ufal	28.15 (-18.27)	4.88 (-4.21)	15.06 (-6.03)	vi_vtb	43.04 (-12.18)	35.45 (-12.16)	38.89 (-5.13)
hu_szeged	74.36 (-8.30)	55.98 (-11.15)	63.76 (-9.41)	zh_gsd	62.80 (-13.97)	52.47 (-14.15)	58.01 (-14.96)

	LAS	MLAS	BLEX
All treebanks	70.64 (-5.20)	55.74 (-5.51)	60.70 (-5.39)
Big treebanks only	80.29 (-4.08)	65.88 (-6.79)	70.95 (-4.88)
PUD treebanks only	64.09 (-10.11)	48.79 (-9.96)	53.16 (-10.09)
Small treebanks only	60.84 (-8.69)	40.71 (-8.53)	46.08 (-8.81)
Low-resource languages only	16.52 (-11.37)	2.53 (-3.60)	6.75 (-7.23)

Table 7: Results on each treebank in the shared task along with the macro average over all of them (with the corresponding difference from the best system enclosed in ellipses).

Appendix C: Performance of ELMoLex trained and tested using the NeuroTagger tags

Treebank	UPOS	LAS	MLAS	BLEX
da_ddt	95.53 (+0.09)	81.69(+0.47)	69.19 (-1.28)	72.57(+0.83)
de_gsd	91.97 (+0.39)	77.09(-0.55)	37.24(+0.29)	67.71(-0.23)
eu_bdt	92.74 (+0.4)	79.94(-0.51)	61.84(-1.56)	72.02(-0.48)
el_gdt**	96.35 (-)	87.31(+0.48)	68.68(+0.76)	75.07(+0.95)
fr_sequoia	96.66 (+0.82)	87.31 (+1.99)	76.11(+1.41)	81.43(+2.3)
fr_spoken	94.63 (+1.69)	66.98(+0.57)	54.1(+0.8)	56.6(+0.64)
hr_set	96.96 (+0.63)	84.56 (+0.03)	61.88 (+0.06)	75.98(+0.06)
hu_szeged**	91.82 (-)	73.86(-0.5)	55.59 (-0.39)	63.38 (-0.38)
sv_lines**	95.28 (-)	79.57 (-0.35)	61.35(-0.24)	72.2(-0.07)
zh_gsd**	83.59 (+0.12)	64.56 (+1.76)	52.85(+0.38)	60.24(+2.23)

	UPOS	LAS	MLAS	BLEX
Average gain	+0.59	+0.34	0.02	+0.58

Table 8: Performance of ELMOLEX trained and tested using tags from the neural tagger (with the corresponding absolute difference from our submission final results) and average absolute gain of using the neural tagger compared to tags used at the submissions **indicates datasets for which tags from the neural tagger where used at test time for the submission

A Morphology-based Representation Model for LSTM-based Dependency Parsing of Agglutinative Languages

Şaziye Betül Özateş[*], Arzucan Özgür[*], Tunga Güngör[*], Balkız Öztürk[‡]
[*]Department of Computer Engineering
[‡]Department of Linguistics
Boğaziçi University
Bebek, 34342 İstanbul, Turkey
`saziye.bilgin,arzucan.ozgur,gungort,balkiz.ozturk@boun.edu.tr`

Abstract

We propose two word representation models for agglutinative languages that better capture the similarities between words which have similar tasks in sentences. Our models highlight the morphological features in words and embed morphological information into their dense representations. We have tested our models on an LSTM-based dependency parser with character-based word embeddings proposed by Ballesteros et al. (2015). We participated in the CoNLL 2018 Shared Task on multilingual parsing from raw text to universal dependencies as the BOUN team. We show that our morphology-based embedding models improve the parsing performance for most of the agglutinative languages.

1 Introduction

This paper describes our submission to the CoNLL 2018 Shared Task (Zeman et al., 2018b) on parsing of Universal Dependencies (UD) (Nivre et al., 2016). We propose morphologically enhanced character-based word embeddings to improve the parsing performance especially for agglutinative languages. We apply our approach to a transition-based dependency parser by Ballesteros et al. (2015) that uses stack Long Short Term Memory structures (LSTMs) to predict the parser state. This parser uses character-level word representation, which has been shown to perform better for languages with rich morphology (Ballesteros et al., 2015; Dozat et al., 2017). From our experiment results performed on UD version 2.2 data sets (Nivre et al., 2018; Zeman et al., 2018a) we observe that including morphological information to a character-based word embedding model yields

a better learning of relationships between words and increases the parsing performance for most of the agglutinative languages with rich morphology.

The rest of the paper is organized as follows: Section 2 provides a brief description of the LSTM-based dependency parser used in this study and introduces our embedding models. Section 3 gives the implementation details of our system and describes the training strategies we apply to different languages. Section 4 discusses our results on the shared task as well as the post-evaluation experiments and Section 5 concludes the paper.

2 Parsing Model

We use the LSTM-based parser by Ballesteros et al. (2015). It is an improved version of a state-of-the-art transition-based dependency parser proposed by Dyer et al. (2015) and uses stack LSTM structures with push and pop operations to learn representations of the parser state. Instead of lookup-based word representations, bidirectional LSTM modules are used to create character-based encodings of words. With this character-based modelling, the authors obtain improvements on the dependency parsing of many morphologically rich languages.

2.1 Character Embeddings of Words

The character-based word embedding model using bi-LSTMs in (Ballesteros et al., 2015) is depicted in Figure 1. The authors compute character-based vector representations of words using bi-LSTMs. Their embedding system reads each word character by character from the beginning to the end and computes an embedding vector of the character sequence, which is denoted as $\vec{w}$ in Figure 1. The system also reads the word character by character from the end to the beginning and the produced embedding is denoted as $\overleftarrow{w}$. These two embedding vectors and the learned representation of the

Proceedings of the CoNLL 2018 Shared Task: Multilingual Parsing from Raw Text to Universal Dependencies, pages 238–247
Brussels, Belgium, October 31 – November 1, 2018. ©2018 Association for Computational Linguistics
https://doi.org/10.18653/v1/K18-2024

POS-tag of the word t are concatenated to produce the vector representation of the word. A linear mapping of POS-tag words to integers is used to create a representation of the POS tags as in (Ballesteros et al., 2015).

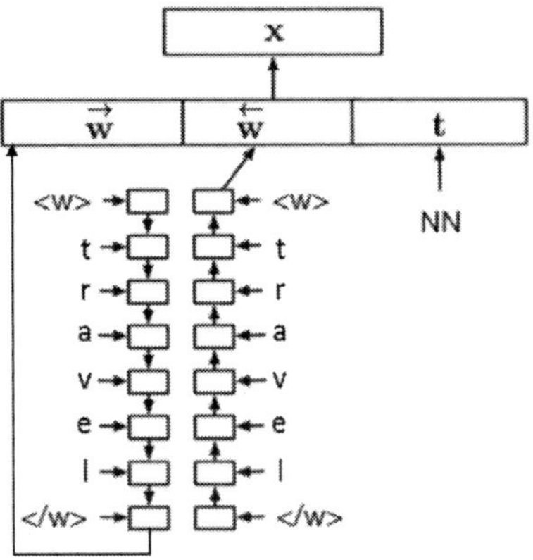

Figure 1: Vector represetntation of the word *travel* with the character-based embedding model in (Ballesteros et al., 2015).

2.2 Morphology-based Character Embeddings

To improve the parsing performance of the LSTM parser with character-based word embeddings mentioned in Section 2.1, we include the morphological information of words to the embedding model. In agglutinative languages like Turkish, a stem usually takes different suffixes and by this way, different meanings are created using a single root-word. Words that share the same suffixes tend to have similar roles in a sentence. For instance, gerunds in Turkish are a kind of derivational suffixes. Verbs that take the same gerund as a suffix have usually the same role in sentences. Table 1 shows some statistics of verbs with gerunds in the development data set of Turkish-IMST treebank for demonstration purposes. The first column shows some example suffixes that attach to verbs and turn them to adverbs. The second column shows the number of verbs with the corresponding suffix in the development set. The third column shows the statistics of the dependency labels of these verbs. As it can be seen from the table, these suffixes help determining the role of the word they attach to. Therefore, representing each word using its corresponding lemma and suffixes separately and utilizing the morphological infor-

mation of words can improve the parsing performance in agglutinative languages.

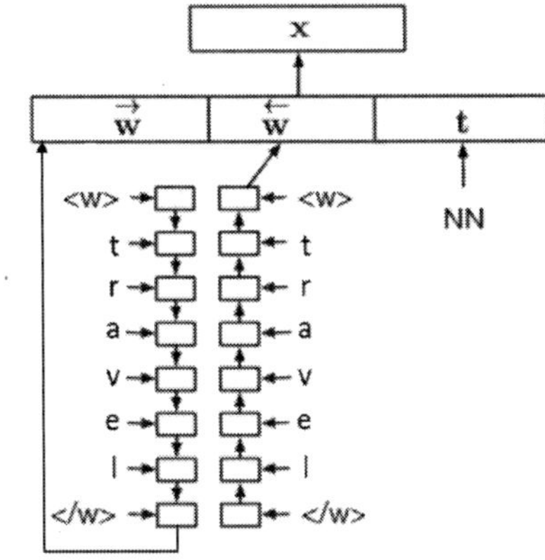

Figure 2: Vector representation of the word *travel* with the character-based embedding model in (Ballesteros et al., 2015).

Lemma-Suffix Model

For agglutinative languages where the stem of a word does not change in different word forms, we created a model that uses lemma and suffix information of words in character-based embeddings. In this model, each word is separated to its lemma and suffixes. Then, the embedding system first reads the lemma of the word character by character from the beginning to the end and computes an embedding vector of the character sequence of the lemma which is denoted as $\vec{r}$. Secondly, the system reads the lemma character by character from the end to the beginning and the produced embedding is denoted as $\overleftarrow{r}$. A similar process is performed for the suffixes of the word and the produced vectors are denoted as $\vec{s}$ and $\overleftarrow{s}$. These four embedding vectors and the vector representation of the POS-tag of the word t are then concatenated to produce the vector representation of the word. POS-tag representations are created by linearly mapping the POS-tag words to integers as in (Ballesteros et al., 2015). Vector representation of an example word using this model is depicted in Figure 3.

Morphological Features Model

The lemma-suffix model is suitable only for agglutinative languages which make use of suffixes to create different word forms. For languages that do not have this type of grammar, we created another model where the specific morphological fea-

Suffix	Number of Occurrences	Dependency Label				
-Ip	41	23 nmod	8 compound	5 conj	4 obj	1 root
-ArAk	32	26 nmod	3 conj	2 compound	1 root	
-ken	20	18 nmod	1 conj	1 acl		
-IncA	8	7 nmod	1 compound			
-mAdAn	7	4 nmod	2 compound	1 obj		
-DIkçA	3	3 nmod				

Table 1: Number of occurrences of some example suffixes and the corresponding dependency labels of verbs with these suffixes in the development data of *Turkish-IMST* treebank.

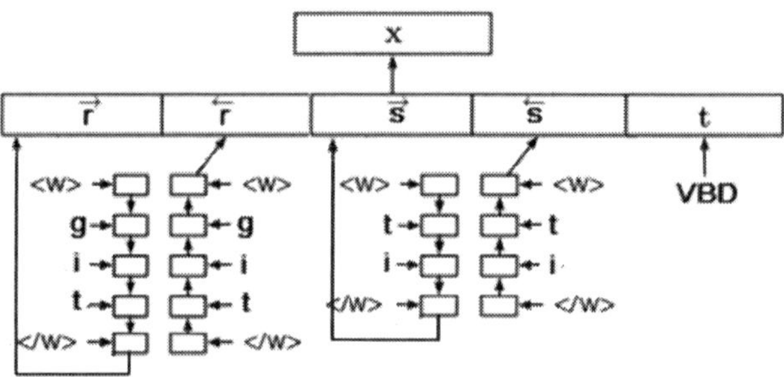

Figure 3: Character-based word embedding of a Turkish word *gitti* (*"it went"* in English) using lemma-suffix embedding model.

tures of each word are embedded to the dense representations of the words. The reason behind this choice is that some morphological features have a direct impact in identifying the dependency labels of words. For instance, if a word has a *case* feature and its value is *accusative*, then it is usually an object of the sentence. By extracting and utilizing such morphological features, we can improve the parsing accuracy for languages that suit this model.

In this model, the embedding of a word is created character by character as in Section 2.1. Then, the embedding vector of each of its selected morphological features are created by reading the feature value character by character from the beginning to the end. Finally, these embedding vectors and the vector representation of the POS-tag of the word are concatenated to produce the vector representation of the word.

The vector representation of an example word using its morphological features is shown in Figure 4.

3 Implementation

The systems participating in the CoNLL 2018 Shared Task on UD Parsing are expected to parse raw text without any gold-standard pre-processing operations such as tokenization, lemmatization,

and morphological analysis. However, the baseline pre-processed versions of the raw text by the UDPipe system (Straka et al., 2016) are available for the participants who want to focus only on the dependency parsing task. We used the automatically annotated version of the corpora provided by UDPipe, since our primary aim is to observe the effect of our embedding models on the dependency parsing of agglutinative languages.

	No morp.parser		With morp.parser	
Word	*Lemma*	*Suffix*	*Lemma*	*Suffix*
Her	her	-	her	-
şeyden	şey	den	şey	DAn
önce	önce	-	önce	-
sanatçıydı	sanat	çıydı	sanat	CHY DH

Table 2: Lemma and suffix separation example without using morphological analyzer and disambiguator and with using morphological analyzer and disambiguator on the Turkish sentence *"Her şeyden önce sanatçıydı."* (English meaning: *"She was an artist before anything else."*)

In the implementation of the lemma-suffix embedding model, we did not utilize any morphological analyzer and disambiguator tools to find the lemmas and the suffixes of the words. Instead, for each word in the treebank we extracted its corresponding *lemma* information from the conll-u ver-

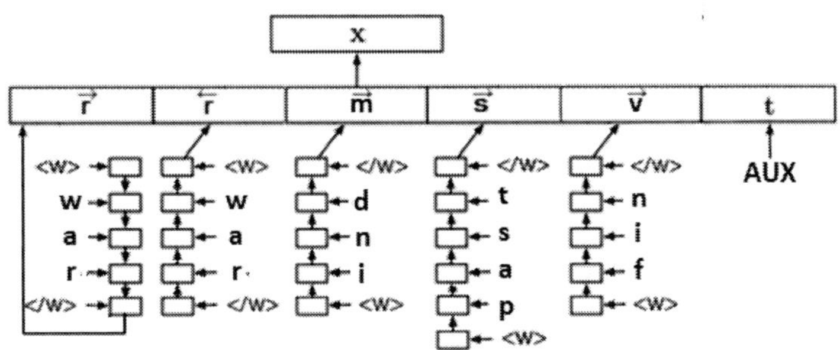

Figure 4: Character-based word embedding of a German word *war* (*"was"* in English) with its morphological features being $Mood = Ind|Number = Sing|Person = 3|Tense = Past|VerbForm = Fin$ using morphological features embedding model. The selected features for German are *Case, Mood, Tense,* and *VerbForm*. Since there is no *Case* feature in the morphological features of *war*, the *Case* feature is represented with an empty string in the word vector of *war*.

sion of the treebank data and subtracted the lemma from the word to find the suffix information. We compared these two approaches on the Turkish-IMST treebank. For this purpose, we utilized the Turkish morphological parser and disambiguator by (Sak et al., 2008). A comparison between the two approaches is shown on an example sentence in Table 2. We observed that finding the suffixes by subtracting the lemmas from the words gives the same parsing performance as using a morphological analyzer tool to find the lemma and suffixes of a word. So, we opted not to use a morphological analyzer and disambiguator for the languages with the lemma-suffix embedding model due to the additional costs of these tools.

3.1 Embedding Model Selection for Different Languages

We applied the lemma-suffix model in 2.2 to Buryat, Hungarian, Kazakh, Turkish, and Uyghur languages because these languages have agglutinative morphology, take suffixes, and the stem of a word usually does not change in different word forms. We also applied this model to Danish to observe the effect in parsing performance of a language with little inflectional morphology.

For the languages that do not follow this scheme, we applied the morphological features embedding model in 2.2. Table 3 shows the morphological features selected for these languages in the shared task. We selected four morphological features from the input conll-u files for most of the languages. For French, Indonesian, and Old French, we used less than four features because

there are less than four common morphological features in the conll-u files of these languages.

For Persian, Japanese, Korean, Vietnamese, and Chinese, we used the baseline embedding model due to the lack of representative morphological features in their corresponding conll-u files.

Languages without Training Data

We trained a mixed language parser model with morphological features embedding model for the languages with no training data. For training this parser model, we used the mixed language training data supplied by the organizers of the shared task. This data is created by including the first 200 sentences of each treebank.

In the shared task, this model is applied to the *Buryat-KEB, Czech-PUD, English-PUD, Faroese-OFT, Japanese-Modern, Naija-NSC, Swedish-PUD,* and *Thai-PUD* treebanks.

We trained parser models for the *Upper Sorbian-UFAL* and *Galician-TreeGal* treebanks using the morphological features embedding model and for the *Buryat-BDT* treebank using the lemma-suffix embedding model. However, we used the mixed language parser model for these treebanks in the shared task due to some software issues.

3.2 Training Specifications

Our model mostly uses the same hyper-parameter configuration with the original settings of the parser in (Ballesteros et al., 2015) with a few exceptions. We used stochastic gradient descent trainer with a learning rate of 0.13. We replaced

Language	Morphological Features			
Afrikaans	Aspect	Case	Tense	VerbForm
Ancient Greek	Aspect	Case	Tense	VerbForm
Arabic	Aspect	Case	Mood	VerbForm
Armenian	Aspect	Case	Tense	VerbForm
Basque	Aspect	Case	Tense	VerbForm
Bulgarian	Aspect	Case	Tense	VerbForm
Catalan	AdpType	Mood	Tense	VerbForm
Croatian	Case	Mood	Tense	VerbForm
Czech	Aspect	Case	Tense	VerbForm
Dutch	Degree	Case	Tense	VerbForm
English	Case	Mood	Tense	VerbForm
Estonian	Case	Mood	Tense	VerbForm
French	Mood	Tense	VerbForm	
Finnish	Case	Mood	Tense	VerbForm
Galician	Case	Mood	Tense	VerbForm
German	Case	Mood	Tense	VerbForm
Gothic	Case	Mood	Tense	VerbForm
Greek	Aspect	Case	Tense	VerbForm
Hebrew	HebBinyan	HebSource	Tense	VerbForm
Hindi	Aspect	Case	Tense	VerbForm
Indonesian	PronType	Degree		
Irish	Case	Mood	Tense	VerbForm
Italian	PronType	Mood	Tense	VerbForm
Kurmanji	Case	Mood	Tense	VerbForm
Latin	Case	Mood	Tense	VerbForm
Latvian	Aspect	Case	Tense	VerbForm
North Sami	Case	Mood	Tense	VerbForm
Norwegian	Case	Mood	Tense	VerbForm
Old Church Slavonic	Case	Mood	Tense	VerbForm
Old French	Tense	VerbForm		
Polish	Aspect	Case	Tense	VerbForm
Portuguese	PronType	Mood	Tense	VerbForm
Romanian	Case	Mood	Tense	VerbForm
Russian	Aspect	Case	Tense	VerbForm
Serbian	PronType	Mood	Tense	VerbForm
Slovak	Aspect	Case	Tense	VerbForm
Slovenian	Aspect	Case	Tense	VerbForm
Spanish	Case	Mood	Tense	VerbForm
Swedish	Case	Mood	Tense	VerbForm
Ukrainian	Aspect	Case	Tense	VerbForm
Upper Sorbian	Case	Mood	Tense	VerbForm
Mixed Language	Case	Mood	Tense	VerbForm

Table 3: List of morphological features used for the languages with the morphological features embedding model.

the original character-based embedding model with our embedding models. In the lemma-suffix model, the forward word vector and the backward word vector of the lemma of a word both have 50 dimensions. The forward and backward word vectors of the suffix of a word also have 50 dimensions each. In the morphological features model, each of the forward and backward word vectors of a word have 50 dimensions. Each of the four morphological feature vectors have 25 dimensions. If a morphological feature is absent in a word, an embedding vector of an empty string is created for that feature. So, we increased the dimension of the character-based representations to 200 in total.

The original parser is not compatible with UD parsing. We adapted it to be able to take input and produce output in conll-u format. The source code of our modified version of the LSTM-based parser by Ballesteros et al. (2015) can be found at `https://github.com/CoNLL-UD-2018/BOUN`.

A full run over the 82 test sets takes about 3 hours when no pre-trained embeddings are used, and 20 hours when the CoNLL-17 pre-trained word embeddings from (Ginter et al., 2017) are used on the TIRA virtual machine (Potthast et al., 2014). The largest of the test sets needs 4 GB memory without pre-trained word vectors. When the CoNLL-17 pre-trained vectors are used, memory usage can reach to 32 GB depending on the pre-trained vector sizes.

4 Results

This section presents the parsing performance of our parser models on the CoNLL-18 Shared Task as well as the post-evaluation scores of our models.

4.1 Shared Task

Table 4 shows our official LAS, MLAS, and BLEX results in the CoNLL-18 Shared Task. The models that use the CoNLL-17 pre-trained word embeddings from (Ginter et al., 2017) are indicated in *pre-trained vectors* column. We also trained parser models using pre-trained word embeddings for *Czech-PDT, German-GSD, English-EWT, English-GUM, English-LinES, Spanish-AnCora, Indonesian-GSD, Latvian-LVTB, Swedish-LinES, Swedish-Talbanken,* and *Turkish-IMST*. However, we could not run these models with their corresponding embedding files

inside the TIRA virtual machine due to some unknown memory and disk issues.

Although the parser we used does not obtain competitive performance when compared with the best performing systems in the shared task, it achieves better performance on the treebanks with no training data when compared to its performance on treebanks with training data. We exclude the parallel UD treebanks from this judgment because one can get better performance on parallel UD treebanks by training the parser using the training data of the treebanks that have the same language with the parallel UD treebanks (e.g., the training data of *English-EWT* for *English-PUD*, *Czech-PDT* for *Czech-PUD* etc.). Due to time-constraints, we did not focus on the parallel UD treebanks and treated them as unknown languages.

4.2 Post-Evaluation

We performed another set of experiments using our models on the test data of UD version 2.2 data sets. The purpose of these experiments is to investigate the effect of our embedding models on parsing performance. Here we used the gold-standard conll-u files instead of the automatically annotated corpora by UDPipe, since our aim in these experiments is to observe the performance difference between our embedding models and the baseline embedding model.

In Table 5, we compare our models with the baseline model proposed in (Ballesteros et al., 2015). Due to time constraints, we trained all models without pre-trained word embeddings.

From the comparative results shown in Table 5, we observe that on the languages that have rich inflectional and derivational processes mostly by adding suffixes to words, our morphological features model outperforms the baseline model in terms of parsing scores. This is the case for the Bulgarian, Croatian, Czech, Basque, Gothic, Latin, Polish, Russian, Slovak, Slovene, North Sami, and Ukrainian languages.

The morphological features model is not suitable for the grammatical structure of Arabic, which has derivational morphology and it also fails to outperform the baseline in Romanic languages like French, Spanish, Catalan, Galician, and Portuguese. The possible reason behind this failure might be the analytic structure of the grammar of these languages where every morpheme is

Treebank	LAS Rank	LAS	MLAS	BLEX	Pre-trained vectors
af-afribooms	23	72.09	58.08	59.42	-
ar-padt	19	66.84	55.68	58.22	ar.vec
bg-btb	21	82.74	72.76	71.14	-
br-keb	10	10.59	0.43	2.21	-
bxr-bdt	19	9.12	1.01	2.46	-
ca-ancora	21	85.03	75.73	76.15	ca.vec
cs-cac	21	83.22	70.50	76.98	cs.vec
cs-fictree	20	82.00	68.75	74.49	cs.vec
cs-pdt	20	83.24	74.04	78.45	-
cs-pud	21	69.60	56.86	63.13	-
cu-proiel	22	60.39	47.99	52.96	cu.vec
da-ddt	21	73.03	63.21	63.69	da.vec
de-gsd	24	56.85	27.51	45.83	-
el-gdt	20	82.11	65.23	68.59	el.vec
en-ewt	22	73.61	64.00	66.11	-
en-gum	22	72.07	60.46	59.93	-
en-lines	22	68.92	59.03	59.74	-
en-pud	23	69.28	56.99	60.04	-
es-ancora	21	83.02	73.95	74.40	-
et-edt	17	75.47	67.74	64.42	et.vec
eu-bdt	19	70.41	57.83	63.36	eu.vec
fa-seraji	19	79.62	73.09	69.84	fa.vec
fi-ftb	20	75.34	65.24	61.69	fi.vec
fi-pud	20	60.07	53.14	48.14	-
fi-tdt	20	75.68	67.56	61.21	fi.vec
fo-oft	19	23.73	0.34	5.81	-
fr-gsd	21	80.07	71.01	72.70	fr.vec
fr-sequoia	21	80.03	70.04	73.03	fr.vec
fr-spoken	25	58.88	45.56	46.02	-
fro-srcmf	22	76.56	68.00	71.17	-
ga-idt	21	55.57	28.92	34.56	-
gl-ctg	18	76.36	62.94	66.00	-
gl-treegal	21	63.43	46.11	48.83	-
got-proiel	21	58.18	44.69	50.63	-
grc-perseus	21	54.57	28.46	35.31	grc.vec
grc-proiel	20	64.77	46.68	52.86	grc.vec
he-htb	21	57.28	43.42	45.94	he.vec
hi-hdtb	21	85.88	67.93	78.21	-
hr-set	22	75.91	56.67	67.43	hr.vec
hsb-ufal	10	29.04	7.18	15.67	-
hu-szeged	22	63.47	50.91	54.57	hu.vec

Treebank	LAS Rank	LAS	MLAS	BLEX	Pre-trained vectors
hy-armtdp	18	21.22	5.66	11.03	-
id-gsd	21	74.01	63.22	62.50	-
it-isdt	23	84.96	75.13	75.21	-
it-postwita	17	67.94	54.15	54.81	it.vec
ja-gsd	21	72.21	58.04	59.78	-
ja-modern	19	18.82	5.02	6.27	-
kk-ktb	21	12.88	2.22	3.95	kk.vec
kmr-mg	21	14.12	2.59	6.65	-
ko-gsd	17	74.99	69.00	62.99	ko.vec
ko-kaist	17	81.45	74.22	68.61	ko.vec
la-ittb	18	76.32	67.78	72.02	la.vec
la-perseus	21	41.94	26.20	28.93	la.vec
la-proiel	21	58.20	45.91	52.11	la.vec
lv-lvtb	20	68.47	54.24	57.43	-
nl-alpino	21	75.94	60.99	63.59	nl.vec
nl-lassysmall	22	74.48	61.40	62.77	nl.vec
no-bokmaal	21	81.47	72.64	73.73	-
no-nynorsk	22	78.48	68.49	69.75	-
no-nynorsklia	21	46.98	35.58	38.54	-
pcm-nsc	19	11.60	3.84	9.60	-
pl-lfg	22	85.11	71.71	75.43	-
pl-sz	22	79.71	61.89	69.76	-
pt-bosque	19	82.62	67.97	72.83	pt.vec
ro-rrt	20	80.18	71.00	71.44	ro.vec
ru-syntagrus	17	84.69	76.43	77.43	ru.vec
ru-taiga	24	45.93	29.00	31.09	-
sk-snk	21	74.37	53.95	59.97	sk.vec
sl-ssj	20	76.78	62.89	68.32	sl.vec
sl-sst	20	44.43	32.07	36.20	sl.vec
sme-giella	20	52.97	42.13	39.10	-
sr-set	23	75.79	62.84	66.68	-
sv-lines	22	72.04	57.75	64.68	-
sv-pud	22	64.55	37.53	48.00	-
sv-talbanken	21	76.93	67.83	68.50	-
th-pud	7	0.70	0.04	0.52	-
tr-imst	22	50.33	40.54	42.00	-
ug-udt	19	55.61	35.98	43.63	ug.vec
uk-iu	20	74.34	56.38	63.46	uk.vec
ur-udtb	21	77.04	50.47	63.40	ur.vec
vi-vtb	20	39.06	25.90	27.61	vi.vec
zh-gsd	22	56.43	46.55	51.20	zh.vec

Table 4: Our official results in the CoNLL-18 Shared Task.

Treebank	Embedding model	LAS		MLAS		BLEX	
		Baseline	Our model	Baseline	Our model	Baseline	Our model
af-afribooms	MF	82.16	**82.80**	73.17	**74.35**	75.48	**76.37**
ar-padt	MF	**78.80**	78.60	**73.59**	73.33	**74.66**	74.39
bg-btb	MF	86.52	**87.41**	80.88	**82.00**	81.33	**82.38**
ca-ancora	MF	**87.21**	87.03	**80.56**	80.23	**81.07**	80.79
cs-cac	MF	87.37	**87.85**	84.12	**84.94**	84.78	**85.49**
cs-fictree	MF	83.49	**86.03**	77.80	**81.64**	78.58	**82.34**
cs-pdt	MF	86.66	**88.47**	83.39	**85.89**	83.91	**86.38**
cu-proiel	MF	**75.73**	75.59	**69.85**	69.62	**72.09**	71.97
da-ddt	LS	77.34	**78.04**	71.45	**71.48**	72.97	**73.33**
de-gsd	MF	77.45	**77.79**	69.79	**70.26**	72.40	**73.24**
el-gdt	MF	83.22	**83.98**	74.83	**76.69**	75.57	**77.53**
en-ewt	MF	**83.88**	83.58	**79.44**	78.95	**79.96**	79.51
en-gum	MF	80.34	**81.46**	73.30	**74.34**	73.87	**75.03**
en-lines	MF	**75.89**	73.83	**71.06**	67.75	**72.53**	69.28
es-ancora	MF	**86.71**	85.55	**80.65**	78.97	**81.17**	79.61
et-edt	MF	80.25	**81.49**	76.59	**78.28**	77.40	**78.98**
eu-bdt	MF	74.07	**74.65**	69.97	**71.21**	71.69	**72.74**
fi-ftb	MF	82.76	**83.88**	77.86	**79.02**	78.54	**79.89**
fi-tdt	MF	80.39	**80.46**	76.33	**76.60**	76.96	**77.31**
fr-gsd	MF	**84.69**	83.77	**78.56**	77.59	**79.13**	78.39
fr-sequoia	MF	**83.16**	82.49	**76.75**	75.96	**77.38**	76.40
fr-spoken	MF	67.99	**68.70**	57.82	**58.19**	58.68	**59.04**
fro-srcmf	MF	**83.01**	82.54	**76.90**	76.44	**77.78**	77.43
ga-idt	MF	61.02	**63.23**	45.21	**47.98**	48.68	**51.90**
gl-ctg	MF	**81.56**	80.70	**70.76**	69.41	**75.38**	74.25
got-proiel	MF	71.88	**74.95**	64.13	**67.99**	66.78	**70.78**
grc-perseus	MF	**61.22**	60.10	**50.75**	49.95	**53.92**	52.79
grc-proiel	MF	79.26	**79.28**	64.54	64.12	67.09	**67.16**
he-htb	MF	**80.06**	79.80	**71.56**	70.97	**72.02**	71.52
hi-hdtb	MF	**92.11**	91.51	**87.64**	86.72	**88.38**	87.46
hr-set	MF	80.12	**81.36**	74.75	**76.45**	76.22	**77.90**
hu-szeged	LS	64.00	**68.33**	56.44	**62.55**	59.75	**66.11**
hy-armtdp	MF	**29.60**	28.56	21.65	**25.14**	24.04	**28.56**
it-isdt	MF	88.91	**89.23**	82.77	**83.34**	83.20	**83.79**
it-postwita	MF	**79.19**	79.10	**72.30**	72.26	72.84	**72.91**
kk-ktb	LS	**35.92**	35.34	**25.89**	25.19	30.09	**30.18**
la-ittb	MF	83.86	**85.37**	79.06	**80.93**	80.02	**82.10**
la-perseus	MF	47.48	**51.82**	41.00	**46.56**	44.56	**51.79**
la-proiel	MF	68.81	**70.95**	62.15	**64.66**	64.95	**67.11**
lv-lvtb	MF	73.48	**75.43**	66.19	**68.67**	67.37	**69.66**
nl-alpino	MF	**80.60**	79.11	**72.53**	70.60	**73.25**	71.44
nl-lassysmall	MF	**81.15**	79.19	**74.84**	72.37	**75.52**	73.26
no-bokmaal	MF	**88.53**	88.22	**84.48**	83.87	**84.96**	84.46
no-nynorsk	MF	**86.64**	85.42	**82.00**	80.39	**82.94**	81.21
no-nynorsklia	MF	**66.27**	64.76	**58.40**	56.92	**60.12**	58.55
pl-lfg	MF	92.02	**92.68**	88.93	**89.80**	89.16	**90.01**
pl-sz	MF	85.86	**89.56**	81.34	**86.50**	82.02	**87.17**
pt-bosque	MF	**83.28**	83.20	**75.64**	74.85	**76.95**	76.28
ro-rrt	MF	**81.22**	80.84	**74.26**	74.03	**75.55**	75.36
ru-syntagrus	MF	88.01	**88.14**	84.35	**84.86**	84.72	**85.24**
ru-taiga	MF	48.95	**56.57**	40.82	**50.74**	42.74	**52.33**
sk-snk	MF	78.49	**82.66**	73.94	**79.61**	74.58	**80.46**
sl-ssj	MF	86.23	**88.82**	81.84	**85.33**	82.23	**85.80**
sl-sst	MF	64.47	**65.41**	57.67	**59.38**	59.31	**61.22**
sme-giella	MF	66.21	**71.55**	58.73	**66.87**	61.22	**69.03**
sr-set	MF	**80.71**	80.36	**75.36**	74.84	**76.74**	76.38
sv-lines	MF	76.86	**77.43**	72.98	**73.75**	74.13	**74.72**
sv-talbanken	MF	**83.03**	82.39	**78.36**	77.68	**79.27**	78.58
tr-imst	LS	55.45	**56.74**	49.29	**50.42**	50.45	**51.97**
ug-udt	LS	**58.02**	56.97	**47.47**	45.52	**50.18**	47.86
uk-iu	MF	76.10	**78.87**	70.57	**74.66**	70.77	**74.95**
ur-udtb	MF	**86.07**	86.04	79.43	**79.77**	80.75	**81.02**

Table 5: Comparison of our embedding models with the baseline char-based word embedding model explained in Section 2.1. MF stands for the morphological features embedding model and LS stands for the lemma-suffix embedding model.

	Singular	Plural	Singular	Plural
Nominative	*ember*	*ember-ek*	*adam*	*adam-lar*
Accusative	*ember-et*	*ember-ek-et*	*adam-ı*	*adam-lar-ı*
Dative	*ember-nek*	*ember-ek-nek*	*adam-a*	*adam-lar-a*
Locative	*ember-ben*	*ember-ek-ben*	*adam-da*	*adam-lar-da*

Table 6: Word-morpheme structure on the Hungarian word *ember* and the Turkish word *adam* (English meaning: *man*).

Treebank	Number of words	Embedding dimension	LAS	MLAS	BLEX
tr-imst without pre-trained embeddings	-	-	56.74	50.42	51.97
tr-imst with CoNLL-17 ud-word-embeddings	3,633,786	100	59.11	53.02	54.51
tr-imst with Facebook word-embeddings	416,051	300	59.69	53.56	54.98

Table 7: The effect of using pre-trained word embeddings on parsing performance on Turkish-IMST test data set.

an independent word. English, Hebrew, Hindi and Urdu languages are also categorized as mostly analytic languages which do not use inflections and have a low morpheme-per-word ratio (Moravcsik, 2013). Dutch, Norwegian, and Swedish languages have a very simplified inflectional grammar. So, these languages are not represented well using our morphology-based embedding models. Besides, our model is not the best choice for the languages that have high ratio of morphophonological modifications to the root word like Old Church Slavonic.

The lemma-suffix embedding model is applied to the Danish, Hungarian, Kazakh, Turkish, and Uyghur languages. The best performance is reached in the Hungarian language with more than 4% increase in LAS score. Our model outperforms the baseline in Turkish too. These languages are highly agglutinative languages where words may consist of several morphemes and the boundaries between morphemes are clearcut. In this type of languages, there is a one-to-one form-meaning correspondence and shape of a morpheme is invariant (Moravcsik, 2013). An example word-morpheme relationship in Hungarian and Turkish languages is shown in Table 6. As it can be seen from the table, this structure is very suitable to the lemma-suffix embedding model.

However, the lemma-suffix model fails to reach better performance than the baseline system on the Kazakh and Uyghur treebanks. A possible reason might be that our embedding model increases the complexity of the system unnecessarily for these languages with very little training data. Although Danish can be considered as an analytic language with a simplified inflectional grammar, the lemma-suffix model outperforms the baseline for this language.

Table 7 shows the parsing scores of the parser with lemma-suffix embedding model on the test data of *Turkish-IMST* treebank version 2.2. We compared the parsing performances when the parser does not use pre-trained word embeddings, when it uses pre-trained embeddings from CoNLL-17 UD word embeddings, and when it uses pre-trained embeddings from word vectors trained on Wikipedia by Facebook (Bojanowski et al., 2017). From the results, we observe that the usage of pre-trained word vectors increases the parsing performance by great extent for Turkish. We also observe that Facebook word vectors outperform the CoNLL-17 UD word vectors, although the number of words in the Facebook vectors data set is much smaller than the number of words in the CoNLL-17 UD word vectors data set.

5 Conclusion

We introduced two morphology-based adaptations of the character-based word embedding model in (Ballesteros et al., 2015) and experimented with these models on the UD version 2.2 data set. The experiment results suggest that our models utilizing morphological information of words increases the parsing performance in agglutinative languages.

Acknowledgments

This work was supported by the Scientific and Technological Research Council of Turkey (TÜBİTAK) under grant number 117E971 and as a graduate scholarship.

References

Miguel Ballesteros, Chris Dyer, and Noah A. Smith. 2015. Improved transition-based parsing by modeling characters instead of words with lstms. In *Proceedings of the 2015 Conference on Empirical Methods in Natural Language Processing*. Association for Computational Linguistics, pages 349–359. https://doi.org/10.18653/v1/D15-1041.

Piotr Bojanowski, Edouard Grave, Armand Joulin, and Tomas Mikolov. 2017. Enriching word vectors with subword information. *Transactions of the Association for Computational Linguistics* 5:135–146. http://aclweb.org/anthology/Q17-1010.

Timothy Dozat, Peng Qi, and Christopher D. Manning. 2017. Stanford's graph-based neural dependency parser at the conll 2017 shared task. In *Proceedings of the CoNLL 2017 Shared Task: Multilingual Parsing from Raw Text to Universal Dependencies*. Association for Computational Linguistics, pages 20–30. https://doi.org/10.18653/v1/K17-3002.

Chris Dyer, Miguel Ballesteros, Wang Ling, Austin Matthews, and Noah A. Smith. 2015. Transition-based dependency parsing with stack long short-term memory. In *Proceedings of the 53rd Annual Meeting of the Association for Computational Linguistics and the 7th International Joint Conference on Natural Language Processing (Volume 1: Long Papers)*. Association for Computational Linguistics, pages 334–343. https://doi.org/10.3115/v1/P15-1033.

Filip Ginter, Jan Hajič, Juhani Luotolahti, Milan Straka, and Daniel Zeman. 2017. CoNLL 2017 shared task - automatically annotated raw texts and word embeddings. LINDAT/CLARIN digital library at the Institute of Formal and Applied Linguistics (ÚFAL), Faculty of Mathematics and Physics, Charles University. http://hdl.handle.net/11234/1-1989.

E.A. Moravcsik. 2013. *Introducing Language Typology*. Cambridge introductions to language and linguistics. Cambridge University Press. https://books.google.com.tr/books?id=9sdanQAACAAJ.

Joakim Nivre, Marie-Catherine de Marneffe, Filip Ginter, Yoav Goldberg, Jan Hajič, Christopher Manning, Ryan McDonald, Slav Petrov, Sampo Pyysalo, Natalia Silveira, Reut Tsarfaty, and Daniel Zeman. 2016. Universal Dependencies v1: A multilingual treebank collection. In *Proceedings of the 10th International Conference on Language Resources and Evaluation (LREC 2016)*. European Language Resources Association, Portoro, Slovenia, pages 1659–1666.

Joakim Nivre et al. 2018. Universal Dependencies 2.2. LINDAT/CLARIN digital library at the Institute of Formal and Applied Linguistics, Charles University, Prague, http://hdl.handle.net/11234/1-1983xxx. http://hdl.handle.net/11234/1-1983xxx.

Martin Potthast, Tim Gollub, Francisco Rangel, Paolo Rosso, Efstathios Stamatatos, and Benno Stein. 2014. Improving the reproducibility of PAN's shared tasks: Plagiarism detection, author identification, and author profiling. In Evangelos Kanoulas, Mihai Lupu, Paul Clough, Mark Sanderson, Mark Hall, Allan Hanbury, and Elaine Toms, editors, *Information Access Evaluation meets Multilinguality, Multimodality, and Visualization. 5th International Conference of the CLEF Initiative (CLEF 14)*. Springer, Berlin Heidelberg New York, pages 268–299. https://doi.org/10.1007/978-3-319-11382-1_22.

Haşim Sak, Tunga Güngör, and Murat Saraçlar. 2008. Turkish language resources: Morphological parser, morphological disambiguator and web corpus. In *Advances in natural language processing*, Springer, pages 417–427.

Milan Straka, Jan Hajič, and Jana Straková. 2016. UDPipe: trainable pipeline for processing CoNLL-U files performing tokenization, morphological analysis, POS tagging and parsing. In *Proceedings of the 10th International Conference on Language Resources and Evaluation (LREC 2016)*. European Language Resources Association, Portoro, Slovenia.

Dan Zeman et al. 2018a. Universal Dependencies 2.2 CoNLL 2018 shared task development and test data. LINDAT/CLARIN digital library at the Institute of Formal and Applied Linguistics, Charles University, Prague, http://hdl.handle.net/11234/1-2184. http://hdl.handle.net/11234/1-2184.

Daniel Zeman, Jan Hajič, Martin Popel, Martin Potthast, Milan Straka, Filip Ginter, Joakim Nivre, and Slav Petrov. 2018b. CoNLL 2018 Shared Task: Multilingual Parsing from Raw Text to Universal Dependencies. In *Proceedings of the CoNLL 2018 Shared Task: Multilingual Parsing from Raw Text to Universal Dependencies*. Association for Computational Linguistics, Brussels, Belgium, pages 1–20.

AntNLP at CoNLL 2018 Shared Task:
A Graph-based Parser for Universal Dependency Parsing

Tao Ji, Yufang Liu, Yijun Wang, Yuanbin Wu, Man Lan
[1]Department of Computer Science and Technology
[2]East China Normal University
{taoji, yfliu, yjwang}.antnlp@gmail.com
{ybwu, mlan}@cs.ecnu.edu.cn

Abstract

We describe the graph-based dependency parser in our system (AntNLP) submitted to the *CoNLL 2018 UD Shared Task*. We use bidirectional lstm to get the word representation, then a bi-affine pointer networks to compute scores of candidate dependency edges and the MST algorithm to get the final dependency tree.

From the official testing results, our system gets 70.90 LAS F1 score (rank 9/26), 55.92 MLAS (10/26) and 60.91 BLEX (8/26).

1 Introduction

The focus of the *CoNLL 2018 UD Shared Task* is learning syntactic dependency parsers that can work over many typologically different languages, even low-resource languages for which there is little or no training data. The Universal Dependencies (Nivre et al., 2017a,b) treebank collection has 82 treebanks over 57 kinds of languages.

In this paper we describe our system (AntNLP) submitted to the *CoNLL 2018 UD Shared Task*. Our system is based on the deep biaffine neural dependency parser (Dozat and Manning, 2016). The system contains a BiLSTM feature extractor for getting context-aware word representation and two biaffine classifiers to predict the head token of each word and the label between a head and its dependent.

There are three main metrics for this task, LAS (labeled attachment score), MLAS (morphology-aware labeled attachment score) and BLEX (bi-lexical dependency score). From the official testing results, our system gets 70.90 LAS F1 score (rank 9/26), 55.92 MLAS (10/26) and 60.91 BLEX (8/26). In a word, Our system is ranked top 10 according to the three metrics described above.

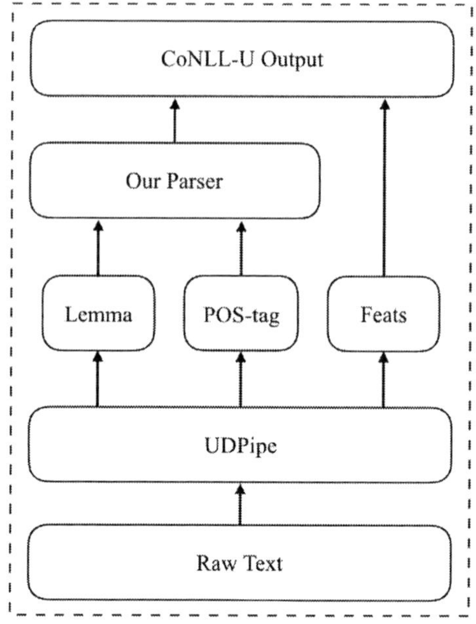

Figure 1: The structure of the entire system.

Additionally, in the categories of small treebanks, our system obtains the sixth place with a MLAS score of 63.73. Besides that, our system ranked tenth in the EPE 2018 campaign with a 55.71 F1 score.

The rest of this paper is organized as follows. Section 2 gives a brief description of our overall system, including the system framework and parser architecture. In Section 3, 4 we describe our monolingual model and multilingual model. In Section 5, we briefly list our experimental results.

2 System Overview

The *CoNLL 2018 UD Shared Task* aims to construct dependency trees based on raw texts, which means that the participants should not only build

Proceedings of the CoNLL 2018 Shared Task: Multilingual Parsing from Raw Text to Universal Dependencies, pages 248–255
Brussels, Belgium, October 31 – November 1, 2018. ©2018 Association for Computational Linguistics
https://doi.org/10.18653/v1/K18-2025

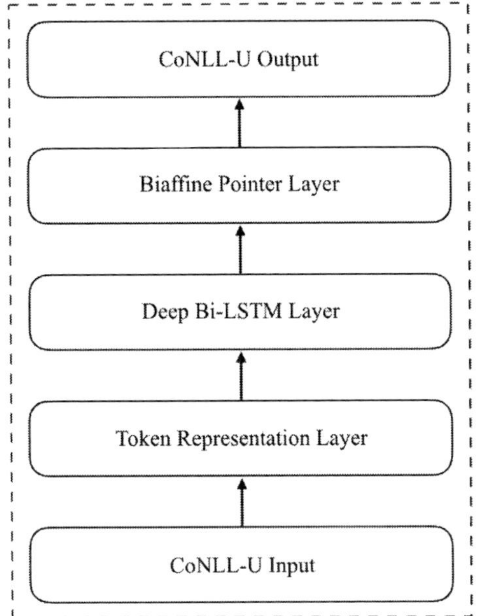

Figure 2: The architecture of our parser system.

the parsing model, but also preprocess systems of the sentence segmentation, tokenization, POS-tagging and morphological analysis. We use pre-processors from the official UDPipe tool in our submission. The structure of the entire system is shown in Figure 1. Our main focus is on building a graph-based parser.

We implement a graph-based bi-affine parser following Dozat and Manning (2016). The parser architecture is shown in Figure 2, which consists of the following components:

- **Token representation**, which produces the context independent representation of each token in the sentence.

- **Deep Bi-LSTM Encoder**, which produces the context-aware representation of each token in the sentence based on context.

- **Bi-affine Pointer Networks**, which assign probabilities to all possible candidate edges.

We describe the three sub-modules in the following sections in detail.

2.1 Token representation

Recent studies on dependency parsing show that densely embedded word representation could help to improve empirical parser performance. For example: Chen and Manning (2014) map words and

POS tags to a d-dimensional vector space. Dozat and Manning (2016) use the pre-trained GloVe embeddings as an extra representation of the word. Ma et al. (2018) use Convolutional Neural Networks (CNNs) to encode character-level information of a word.

The token representation module of our parser also uses dense embedding representations. Details on token embeddings are given in the following.

- **Word** $\mathrm{e_i^w}$: The word embedding is randomly initialized from the normal distribution $\mathcal{N}(0, 1)$ ($e_i^w \in \mathbb{R}^{100}$).

- **Lemma** $\mathrm{e_i^l}$: The lemma embedding is randomly initialized from the normal distribution $\mathcal{N}(0, 1)$ ($e_i^l \in \mathbb{R}^{100}$).

- **Pre-trained Word** $\mathrm{e_i^{pw}}$: The FastText pre-trained word embedding ($e_i^{pw} \in \mathbb{R}^{300}$). We will not update e_i^{pw} during the training process.

- **UPOS** $\mathrm{e_i^u}$: The UPOS-tag embedding is randomly initialized from the normal distribution $\mathcal{N}(0, 1)$ ($e_i^u \in \mathbb{R}^{100}$).

- **XPOS** $\mathrm{e_i^x}$: The XPOS-tag embedding is randomly initialized from the normal distribution $\mathcal{N}(0, 1)$ ($e_i^x \in \mathbb{R}^{100}$).

- **Char** $\mathrm{e_i^c}$: The character-level embedding is obtained by the character-level CNNs ($e_i^c \in \mathbb{R}^{64}$).

Our parser uses two kinds of token representations, one is a lexicalized representation of the monolingual model, another one is the delexicalized representation of the multilingual model.

The lexicalized representation x_i^l of token w_i is defined as:

$$x_i^l = [\underbrace{e_i^w + e_i^l}_{word};\ \underbrace{e_i^u + e_i^x}_{POS};\ e_i^{pw};\ e_i^c] \qquad (1)$$

and the delexicalized representation x_i^d of token w_i is defined as:

$$x_i^d = [e_i^u;\ e_i^x;\ e_i^c] \qquad (2)$$

In the following sections, we uses x_i to represent x_i^l or x_i^d when the context is clear.

2.2 Deep Bi-LSTM Encoder

Generally, the token embeddings defined above are context independent, which means that the sentence-level information is ignored. In recent years, some work shows that the deep BiLSTM can effectively capture the contextual information of words (Dyer et al., 2015; Kiperwasser and Goldberg, 2016; Dozat and Manning, 2016; Ma et al., 2018).

In order to encode context features, we use a 3-layer sentence level BiLSTM on top of $x_{1:n}$:

$$\vec{h}_t = \text{LSTM}(\vec{h}_{t-1}, x_i, \vec{\theta})$$
$$\overleftarrow{h}_t = \text{LSTM}(\overleftarrow{h}_{t+1}, x_i, \overleftarrow{\theta})$$
$$v_i = \vec{h}_i \circ \overleftarrow{h}_i$$

$\vec{\theta}$ are the model parameters of the forward hidden sequence $\vec{h}$. $\overleftarrow{\theta}$ are the model parameters of the backward hidden sequence $\overleftarrow{h}$. The vector v_i is our final vector representation of ith token in s, which takes into account both the entire history $\vec{h}_i$ and the entire future $\overleftarrow{h}_i$ by concatenating $\vec{h}_i$ and $\overleftarrow{h}_i$.

2.3 Biaffine Pointer Networks

How to determine the probability of each dependency edge is an important part of the graph-based parser. The work of Dozat and Manning (2016) shows that the biaffine pointer (attention) networks can calculate the probability of each dependency edge well. Here we used a similar biaffine pointer network structure.

In order to better represent the direction of the dependency edges, we use multi-layer perceptron (MLP) networks to learn each word as the representation of head and dependent words, rather than simply exchanging feature vectors. And we also separate the predictions of dependent edges and their labels. First, for each v_i, we use two MLPs to define two pointers h_i^{arc} and s_i^{arc}, which is the representation of v_i with respect to whether it is seen as a head or a modifier of an candidate edge.

$$h_i^{arc} = \text{MLP}_{head}^{(arc)}(v_i)$$
$$s_i^{arc} = \text{MLP}_{dep}^{(arc)}(v_i)$$

Similarly, we use h_i^{rel} and s^{rel} to describe x_i when determine the relation label of a candidate edge.

$$h_i^{rel} = \text{MLP}_{head}^{(rel)}(v_i)$$
$$s_i^{rel} = \text{MLP}_{dep}^{(rel)}(v_i)$$

We first use the arc-biaffine pointer networks to predict the probability of a dependency edge between any two words. For any two words w_i and w_j in a sentence, the probability $p_{i\to j}^{(arc)}$ that they form a dependency edge $w_i \to w_j$ is as follows:

$$a_{i\to j}^{(arc)} = h_i^{arc} \cdot \text{W}^{(arc)} \cdot s_j^{arc} + u^{(arc)} \cdot s_j^{arc}$$
$$p_{i\to j}^{(arc)} = \text{softmax}(a_{i\to *}^{(arc)})[j]$$

where $\theta^{arc} = \{\text{W}^{(arc)}, u^{(arc)}\}$ are the model parameters, $a_{i\to j}^{(arc)}$ is the computed score of the dependency edge. $a_{i\to *}^{(arc)}$ is a vector, and the kth dimension is the score of the dependency edge $a_{i\to k}^{(arc)}$. $p_{i\to j}^{(arc)}$ is the jth dimension of normalization of the vector $a_{i\to *}^{(arc)}$, meaning the probability of dependency edge $w_i \to w_j$.

We obtain a dependency tree representation T of a complete graph $p_{*\to *}^{(arc)}$ using the maximum spanning tree (MST) algorithm. The probability $p_{i\xrightarrow{r}j}^{(rel)}$ of the relation r of each dependency edge $w_i \to w_j \in T$ is then computed. The definition of $p_{i\xrightarrow{r}j}^{(rel)}$ is as follows:

$$a_{i\xrightarrow{*}j}^{(rel)} = h_i^{rel} \cdot \text{W}^{(rel)} \cdot s_j^{rel}$$
$$+ \text{V}^{(rel)} \cdot h_i^{rel} + \text{U}^{(rel)} \cdot s_j^{rel}$$
$$p_{i\xrightarrow{r}j}^{(rel)} = \text{softmax}(a_{i\xrightarrow{*}j}^{(rel)})[r]$$

where $\theta^{rel} = \{\text{W}^{(rel)}, \text{V}^{(rel)}, \text{U}^{(rel)}\}$ are the model parameters, $\text{W}^{(rel)}$ is a 3-dimensional tensor. $a_{i\xrightarrow{*}j}^{(rel)}$ is a vector, and the kth dimension is the score of the dependency edge $w_i \xrightarrow{k} w_j$.

2.4 Training Details

We train our model by minimizing the negative log likelihood of the gold standard $(w_i \xrightarrow{r(w_i)} w_{h(w_i)})$ arcs in all training sentences:

$$J^{(arc)} = -\frac{1}{|\tau|} \sum_{S\in\tau} \sum_{i=1}^{N_S} \log p_{i\to h(w_i)}^{(arc)}$$

$$J^{(rel)} = -\frac{1}{|\tau|} \sum_{S\in\tau} \sum_{i=1}^{N_S} \log p_{i\xrightarrow{r(w_i)}h(w_i)}^{(rel)}$$

$$J = J^{(arc)} + J^{(rel)}$$

where τ is the training set, $h(w_i)$ and $r(w_i)$ is w_i's gold standard head and relation within sentence S, and N_s is the number of words in S.

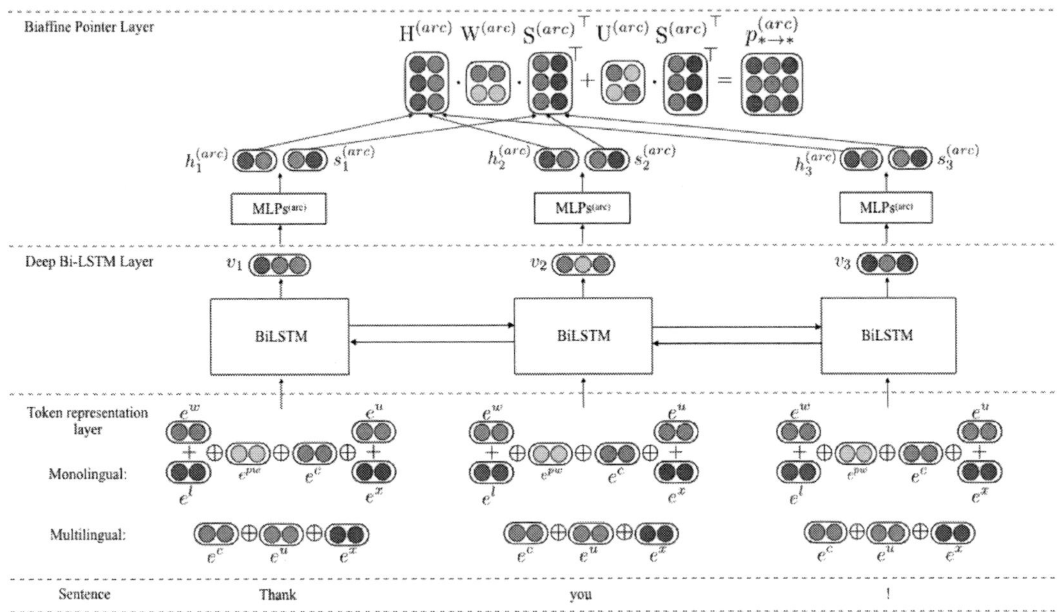

Figure 3: The architecture of our parser system.

3 Monolingual Model

There are 82 treebanks in the *CoNLL 2018 UD Shared Task*, including 61 big treebanks, 5 PUD treebanks (additional parallel test sets), 7 small treebanks and 9 low-resource language treebanks. There are several languages in which there are many treebanks, such as *en_ewt*, *en_gum* and *en_lines* in English. We combine training sets and development sets for multiple treebanks of the same language. And then just train a model for the language and make predictions on its different treebanks.

For each language of UD version 2.2 sets (Nivre et al., 2018; Zeman et al., 2018) with both a training set and a development set, we train a parser using lexicalized token representation and only using its monolingual training set (no cross-lingual features)[1] . The architecture of the monolingual model is shown in Figure 3.

4 Multilingual Model

For 7 languages without a development set, we divide them into two classes based on the size of their training set, which can be fine-tuned (*ga*, *sme*) and can not be fine-tuned (*bxr*, *hsb*, *hy*, *kk*, *kmr*).

For each language of UD version 2.2 sets (Nivre

et al., 2018; Zeman et al., 2018) with both a training set and a development set, we train a parser using delexicalized token representation as a cross-language model. The architecture of the multilingual model is shown in Figure 3. The training set of these 5 languages are then used as a development set to validate the performance of each cross-language model (see Table 1). We select the best performance model as a cross-language model for the corresponding language. For both *ga* and *sme*, we manually divide the development set from the training set and fine-tune the cross-language model. Prediction and fine-tuning results are shown in the Table 2.

5 Experimental Results

We trained our system based on a Nvidia GeForce GTX Titan X. We used the official TIRA (Potthast et al., 2014) to evaluate the system.

We used Dynet neural network library to build our system (Neubig et al., 2017). The hyper-parameters of the final system used for all the reported experiments are detailed in Table 5.

5.1 Overall Results

The main official evaluation results are given in Table 4. And the Table 6 shows the per-treebank LAS F1 results. Our system achieved 70.90 F1 (LAS) on the overall 82 tree banks, ranked 9th out

---

[1] In total, we trained 46 monolingual models.

Language	#Train	Cross language	LAS
Buryat (bxr)	19	Uyghur (ug)	27.45
Upper_Sorbian (hsb)	23	Croatian (hr)	39.35
Armenian (hy)	50	Latvian (lv)	29.35
Kazakh (kk)	9	Turkish (tr)	23.44
Kurmanji (kmr)	19	Persian (fa)	26.03

Table 1: Corpus listed above are languages that don't have development set and the training set size is too small to be fine-tuned. "#Train" means the number of sentences. "Cross Language" means the language with the highest LAS score for corresponding origin language in our delexicalized cross-language model.

Corpus	#Total	#Train	#Dev	Cross language	LAS	Fine-tune
Irish (ga)	566	476	90	Hebrew (he)	36.13	68.49
North_Sami (sme)	2464	1948	516	Swedish (sv)	36.13	63.00

Table 2: Corpus listed above are languages that don't have development set. Because the training set size is much bigger, we decide to divide the training set into two parts, one for training set and the other for development set.

Origin language	language family	Cross Language	Language family
Buryat (bxr)	Mongolic	Uyghur (ug)	Turkic_Southeastern
Upper_Sorbian (hsb)	IE_Slavic	Croatian (hr)	IE_Slavic
Armenian (hy)	IE_Armenian	Latvian (lv)	IE_Baltic
Kazakh (kk)	Turkic_Northwestern	Turkish (tr)	Turkic_Southwestern
Kurmanji (kmr)	IE_Iranian	Persian (fa)	IE_Iranian
Irish (ga)	IE_Celtic	Hebrew (he)	Afro-Asiatic_Semitic
North_Sami (sme)	Uralic_Sami	Swedish (sv)	IE_Germanic

Table 3: language families and genera for origin language and cross language (IE = Indo-European).[2]

Corpus	FLAS	Baseline	Rank	MLAS	Baseline	Rank	BLEX	Baseline	Rank
All treebanks(82)	70.90	65.80	9	55.92	52.42	10	60.91	55.80	8
Big treebanks(61)	79.61	74.14	12	65.43	61.27	11	70.34	64.67	9
PUD treebanks(5)	68.87	66.63	11	53.47	51.75	10	57.71	54.87	8
Small treebanks(7)	63.73	55.01	6	42.24	38.80	7	48.31	41.06	6
Low resource(9)	18.59	17.17	10	3.43	2.82	9	8.61	7.63	8

Table 4: Official experiment results with rank. (number): number of corpora. FLAS means F1 score of LAS.

word/lemma dropout	0.33
upos/xpos tag dropout	0.33
char-CNN dropout	0.33
BiLSTM layers	3
BiLSTM hidden layer dimensions	400
Hidden units in $MLP^{(arc)}$	500
Hidden units in $MLP^{(rel)}$	100
Learning rate	0.002
Optimization algorithm	Adam

Table 5: Hyper-parameter values used in shared task.

of 26 teams. Compared to the baseline obtained with UDPipe1.2 (Straka et al., 2016), our system gained 5.10 LAS improvement on average. Our system shows better results on 7 small treebanks. Performance improvement are more obvious when considering only small treebanks(for example, our system ranked fourth best on *ru_taiga* and *sl_sst*). Besides that, our system ranked tenth in the EPE[3] 2018 campaign with a 55.71 F1 score.

5.2 Discussion on Multilingual Model

As described in section 4, we trained 46 cross-language models and selected the corresponding cross-language model for 7 languages that did not have a development set. Generally, cross-language models are trained in the language of the same family. However, apart from grammatical similarity, the language family division also considers the linguistic history, geographical location and other factors. We want to select a language's cross-language model to consider only grammatical similarity. So we use a cross-language model to predict the results in this language as a basis for selection.

In table 3, the experimental results show that the Cross-language model with the best performance in *hsb*, *hy*, *kk*, and *kmr* languages comes from the same language family, while the Cross-language model with the best performance in *bxr*, *ga*, and *sme* is not from the same language family. Therefore, constructing a cross-language model according to the language of the same family is only applicable to some languages, not all of them. We've only chosen the best performing cross-language model at the moment. In the future, we will try to select the top-k cross-language model.

[2]Information from http://universaldependencies.org.
[3]http://epe.nlpl.eu

6 Conclusions

In this paper, we present a graph-based dependency parsing system for the *CoNLL 2018 UD Shared Task*, which composed of a BiLSTMs feature extractor and a bi-affine pointer networks. The results suggests that a deep BiLSTM extractor and a bi-affine pointer networks is a way to achieve competitive parsing performances. We will continue to improve our system in our future work.

Acknowledgments

References

Danqi Chen and Christopher D Manning. 2014. A fast and accurate dependency parser using neural networks. In *Empirical Methods in Natural Language Processing (EMNLP)*.

Timothy Dozat and Christopher D. Manning. 2016. Deep biaffine attention for neural dependency parsing. *CoRR* abs/1611.01734. http://arxiv.org/abs/1611.01734.

Chris Dyer, Miguel Ballesteros, Wang Ling, Austin Matthews, and Noah A. Smith. 2015. Transition-based dependency parsing with stack long short-term memory. In *Proceedings of the 53rd Annual Meeting of the Association for Computational Linguistics and the 7th International Joint Conference on Natural Language Processing of the Asian Federation of Natural Language Processing, ACL 2015, July 26-31, 2015, Beijing, China, Volume 1: Long Papers*. pages 334–343. http://aclweb.org/anthology/P/P15/P15-1033.pdf.

Eliyahu Kiperwasser and Yoav Goldberg. 2016. Simple and accurate dependency parsing using bidirectional LSTM feature representations. *TACL* 4:313–327. https://transacl.org/ojs/index.php/tacl/article/view/885.

Xuezhe Ma, Zecong Hu, Jingzhou Liu, Nanyun Peng, Graham Neubig, and Eduard H. Hovy. 2018. Stack-pointer networks for dependency parsing. *CoRR* abs/1805.01087. http://arxiv.org/abs/1805.01087.

Graham Neubig, Chris Dyer, Yoav Goldberg, Austin Matthews, Waleed Ammar, Antonios Anastasopoulos, Miguel Ballesteros, David Chiang, Daniel Clothiaux, Trevor Cohn, Kevin Duh, Manaal Faruqui, Cynthia Gan, Dan Garrette, Yangfeng Ji, Lingpeng Kong, Adhiguna Kuncoro, Gaurav Kumar, Chaitanya Malaviya, Paul Michel, Yusuke Oda, Matthew Richardson, Naomi Saphra, Swabha Swayamdipta, and Pengcheng Yin. 2017. Dynet: The dynamic neural network toolkit. *arXiv preprint arXiv:1701.03980* .

Corpus	AntNLP	Rank	Best	Baseline
af_afr*	82.63	11	85.47	77.88
ar_pad*	70.75	12	77.06	66.41
bg_btb	87.24	13	91.22	84.91
br_keb	10.06	16	38.64	10.25
bxr_bdt	19.53	1	1	12.61
ca_anc*	89.28	13	91.61	85.61
cs_cac	90.47	6	91.61	83.72
cs_fic*	90.14	7	92.02	82.49
cs_pdt	89.41	9	91.68	83.94
cs_pud	84.76	6	86.13	80.08
cu_pro*	68.23	13	75.73	65.46
da_ddt	80.56	10	86.28	75.43
de_gsd	76.88	10	80.36	70.85
el_gdt	85.76	12	89.65	82.11
en_ewt	80.74	12	84.57	77.56
en_gum	79.70	11	85.05	74.20
en_lin*	79.25	5	81.97	73.10
en_pud	84.60	9	87.89	79.56
es_anc*	88.84	11	90.93	84.43
et_edt	81.37	11	85.35	75.02
eu_bdt	79.01	11	84.22	70.13
fa_ser*	83.98	11	88.11	79.10
fi_ftb	83.72	11	88.53	75.64
fi_pud	85.50	10	90.23	80.15
fi_tdt	83.18	11	88.73	76.45
fo_oft	20.13	21	49.43	25.19
fr_gsd	84.84	10	86.89	81.05
fr_seq*	85.32	10	89.89	81.12
fr_spo*	70.96	8	75.78	65.56
fro_src*	83.13	12	87.12	79.27
ga_idt	64.38	11	70.88	62.93
gl_ctg	81.12	8	82.76	76.10
gl_tre*	72.03	8	74.25	66.16
got_pro*	62.97	14	69.55	62.16
grc_per*	70.76	9	79.39	57.75
grc_pro*	73.82	9	79.25	67.57
he_htb	61.43	12	76.09	57.86
hi_hdt*	90.44	11	92.41	87.15
hr_set	83.48	12	87.36	78.61
hsb_ufa*	31.36	6	46.42	23.64
hu_sze*	73.19	12	82.66	66.76
hy_arm*	25.09	10	37.01	21.79
id_gsd	76.86	16	80.05	74.37
it_isd*	89.14	12	92.00	86.26
it_pos*	72.30	9	79.39	66.81
ja_gsd	72.82	17	83.11	72.32
ja_mod*	12.94	22	28.33	22.71
kk_ktb	19.26	18	31.93	24.21
kmr_mg	23.20	16	30.41	23.92
ko_gsd	80.15	12	85.14	61.40
ko_kai*	85.01	11	86.91	70.25
la_itt*	83.14	12	87.08	75.95
la_per*	60.99	5	72.63	47.61
la_pro*	66.24	12	73.61	59.66
lv_lvt*	75.56	12	83.97	69.43
nl_alp*	84.69	11	89.56	77.60
nl_las*	82.04	8	86.84	74.56
no_bok*	89.19	7	91.23	83.47
no_nyn*	88.26	9	90.99	82.13
no_nyn*	66.26	4	70.34	48.95
pcm_nsc	18.30	6	30.07	12.18
pl_lfg	91.16	13	94.86	87.53
pl_sz	85.03	14	92.23	81.90
pt_bos*	86.71	8	87.81	82.07
ro_rrt	84.92	8	86.87	80.27
ru_syn*	90.20	10	92.48	84.59
ru_tai*	68.99	4	74.24	55.51
sk_snk	81.14	12	88.85	75.41
sl_ssj	83.26	12	91.47	77.33
sl_sst	56.30	4	61.39	46.95
sme_gie*	57.15	13	69.87	56.98
sr_set	85.77	10	88.66	82.07
sv_lin*	80.01	10	84.08	74.06
sv_pud	76.54	10	80.35	70.63
sv_tal*	83.41	12	88.63	77.91
th_pud	0.36	18	13.70	0.70
tr_ims*	59.68	12	66.44	54.04
ug_udt	61.42	10	67.05	56.26
uk_iu	79.91	12	88.43	74.91
ur_udt*	79.85	14	83.39	77.29
vi_vtb	42.65	11	55.22	39.63
zh_gsd	62.83	13	76.77	57.91

Table 6: Official experiment results on each treebank. The results in table are F1(LAS). *: some corpus' name too long to display completely, using * to indicate omission.

Joakim Nivre et al. 2017a. Universal Dependencies 2.0. LINDAT/CLARIN digital library at the Institute of Formal and Applied Linguistics, Charles University, Prague, http://hdl.handle.net/11234/1-1983. http://hdl.handle.net/11234/1-1983.

Joakim Nivre et al. 2017b. Universal Dependencies 2.0 CoNLL 2017 shared task development and test data. LINDAT/CLARIN digital library at the Institute of Formal and Applied Linguistics, Charles University, Prague, http://hdl.handle.net/11234/1-2184. http://hdl.handle.net/11234/1-2184.

Joakim Nivre et al. 2018. Universal Dependencies 2.2. LINDAT/CLARIN digital library at the Institute of Formal and Applied Linguistics, Charles University, Prague, http://hdl.handle.net/11234/1-1983xxx. http://hdl.handle.net/11234/1-1983xxx.

Martin Potthast, Tim Gollub, Francisco Rangel, Paolo Rosso, Efstathios Stamatatos, and Benno Stein. 2014. Improving the reproducibility of PAN's shared tasks: Plagiarism detection, author identification, and author profiling. In Evangelos Kanoulas, Mihai Lupu, Paul Clough, Mark Sanderson, Mark Hall, Allan Hanbury, and Elaine Toms, editors, *Information Access Evaluation meets Multilinguality, Multimodality, and Visualization. 5th International Conference of the CLEF Initiative (CLEF 14)*. Springer, Berlin Heidelberg New York, pages 268–299. https://doi.org/10.1007/978-3-319-11382-1_22.

Milan Straka, Jan Hajič, and Jana Straková. 2016. UDPipe: trainable pipeline for processing CoNLL-U files performing tokenization, morphological analysis, POS tagging and parsing. In *Proceedings of the 10th International Conference on Language Resources and Evaluation (LREC 2016)*. European Language Resources Association, Portoro, Slovenia.

Dan Zeman et al. 2018. Universal Dependencies 2.2 CoNLL 2018 shared task development and test data. LINDAT/CLARIN digital library at the Institute of Formal and Applied Linguistics, Charles University, Prague, http://hdl.handle.net/11234/1-2184. http://hdl.handle.net/11234/1-2184.

A Simple yet Effective Joint Training Method for
Cross-Lingual Universal Dependency Parsing

Danlu Chen*[1], Mengxiao Lin*[12], Zhifeng Hu*[1], Xipeng Qiu[1]
[1]Fudan University
[2]Megvii Inc
danluchen@fb.com, linmengxiao@megvii.com, {zfhu16,xipeng}@fudan.edu.cn

Abstract

This paper describes Fudan's submission to CoNLL 2018's shared task Universal Dependency Parsing. We jointly train models when two languages are similar according to linguistic typology and then do an ensemble of the models using a simple re-parse algorithm. Our system outperforms the baseline method by 4.4% and 2.1% on the development and test set of *CoNLL 2018 UD Shared Task*, separately.[1]. Our code is available on https://github.com/taineleau/FudanParser.

1 Introduction

Dependency Parsing has been a fundamental task in Natural Language Processing (NLP). Recently, universal dependency parsing (Zeman et al., 2018a,b; Nivre et al., 2018) has unified the annotations of different languages and thus made transfer learning among languages possible. Several works using cross-lingual embedding (Duong et al., 2015; Guo et al., 2015) have successfully increased the accuracy of cross-lingual parsing. Beyond embedding-based methods, a natural question is whether we can use a simple way to utilize the universal information. Some previous research either regarded the universal information as extra training signals (e.g., delexicalized embedding (Dehouck and Denis, 2017)), or implicitly trained a network with all features (e.g., adversarial training for parsing in Sato et al. (2017)). In our system, we manually and explicitly share the universal annotations via a shared LSTM component.

Similar to Vania et al. (2017), different languages are first grouped based on typology, as shown in table 1. Then, we train a shared model for each pair of languages within the same group, and apply a simple ensemble method over all trained models. Note that our method is orthogonal to other cross-lingual approaches for universal parsing such as cross-lingual embedding.

In the following parts, we first describe the baseline method (Section 2) and our system (Section 3). We show the result on both development set and test set in Section 4 and provide some analysis of the model in Section 5.

2 Baseline

In this section, we briefly introduce the baseline system, UDPipe 1.2 (Straka and Straková, 2017), which is an improved version of original UDPipe (Straka et al., 2016). The tokenizing, POS tagging and lemma outputs of UDPipe are utilized by FudanParser.

UDPipe employs a GRU network during the inference of segmentation and tokenization. The tagger uses characters features to predict the POS and lemma tags. Finally, a transition-based neural dependency parser with one hidden layer predicts the transition actions. The parser also makes use of the information from lemmas, POS taggings and dependency relationships through a group of embeddings precomputed by word2vec.

In the later discussion, we take the baseline performance result from the web page of the shared task [2] for comparison.

3 System Description

In this submission, we only consider parsing in an end-to-end manner and handle each treebank sep-

---

* Authors contributed equally.

[1]Unfortunately, we did not finish the run before the deadline. As a result, the official accuracy gain for test set is only 0.54% and we ranks 17th out of 27 teams.

[2]http://universaldependencies.org/conll18/baseline.html

Proceedings of the CoNLL 2018 Shared Task: Multilingual Parsing from Raw Text to Universal Dependencies, pages 256–263
Brussels, Belgium, October 31 – November 1, 2018. ©2018 Association for Computational Linguistics
https://doi.org/10.18653/v1/K18-2026

Group	Datasets
germanic	Afrikaans-AfriBooms Danish-DDT Dutch-Alpino Dutch-LassySmall English-EWT English-GUM English-LinES German-GSD Gothic-PROIEL Norwegian-Bokmaal Norwegian-Nynorsk Swedish-LinES Swedish-Talbanken
indo-iranian	Hindi-HDTB Persian-Seraji Urdu-UDTB
latin	Latin-ITTB Latin-PROIEL Latvian-LVTB
romance	Catalan-AnCora French-GSD French-Sequoia French-Spoken Galician-CTG Italian-ISDT Italian-PoSTWITA Old_French-SRCMF Portuguese-Bosque Romanian-RRT Spanish-AnCora
semitic	Arabic-PADT Hebrew-HTB
slavic	Bulgarian-BTB Croatian-SET Czech-CAC Czech-FicTree Czech-PDT Old_Church_Slavonic-PROIEL Polish-LFG Polish-SZ Russian-SynTagRus Serbian-SET Slovak-SNK Slovenian-SSJ
turkish	Turkish-IMST Ukrainian-IU Uyghur-UDT
uralic	Estonian-EDT Finnish-FTB Finnish-TDT

Table 1: Grouping languages according to typology.

arately. We first train a monotonic model for all "big" treebanks. Besides, for each language, there are $N-1$ models fine-tuned from joint-trained (see Figure 2), where N is the number of languages in the same language group.

For small treebanks where training set is less than 50 sentences, we use the delexicalized method the same as Shi et al. (2017)'s approach for the surprise languages. Shi et al. (2017) took delexicalized features (morphology and POS tag) as input and apply 50% dropout rate to the input. In practice, we found that the baseline method performs much better than ours on"fi_pud", "br_keb" "ja_modern" and "th_pud", so we use the baseline method instead for these languages.

Our whole system needs about 90 hours to do the inference of all models on TIRA and requires no more than 560M main memory.

3.1 Architecture

Features We use words, characters as the lexical information, and use morphological features[3] and POS tags as the delexicalized information. We also tried subword embeddings, but it mostly did not help. More precisely, the character-level features are treated as bag-of-characters. Similarly, we use bag-of-morphology for morphological features (one can see **number=single** as a character). We first assign the embedding vectors for characters and morphological features, and then for each word, we apply a Convolutional Network (CNN) to encode variable length embeddings into one fixed length feature.

Biaffine BiLSTM. Similar to Shi et al. (2017); Sato et al. (2017); Vania et al. (2017), we use last year's first-place model (Dozat et al., 2017), the graph-based biaffine bizLSTM model as our backbone. Given a sentence of N words, the input is first fed to a bi-directional LSTM and obtain the feature of each word w_i. A head MLP and a dependent MLP are used to translate the features, which is then fed into a hidden layer to calculate the biaffine attention. Finally, we are able to compute the score of arcs and labels in following way:

---

[3]we take the *features* column of the UD data as the morphological features, which includes case, number, tense, mood and so on. See `http://universaldependencies.org/u/feat/index.html` for detailed information.

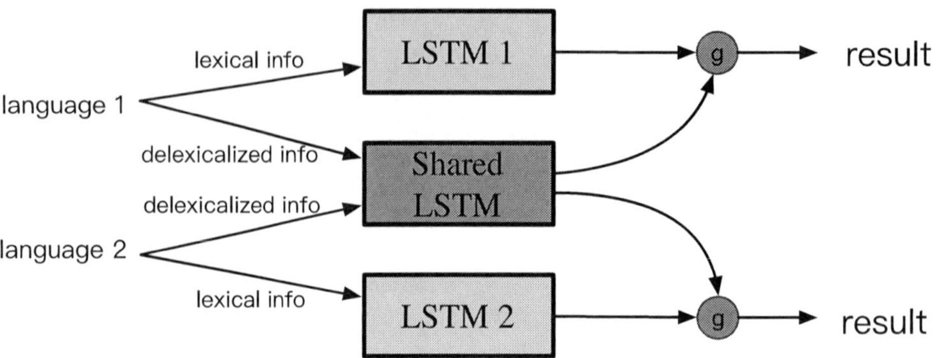

Figure 1: An illustration of the joint training framework for two languages.

$$h_i^h = \mathrm{MLP}_{head}(w_i)$$
$$h_i^d = \mathrm{MLP}_{dep}(w_i)$$
$$s_i = H^h U_1 h_i^d + H^h u_2$$

where $U_1 \in \mathbb{R}^{d \times d}$ and $u_2 \in \mathbb{R}^d$ are trainable parameters.

3.2 Joint Training

For a joint training model of N languages, we have $N+1$ Biaffne Bi-LSTMs (called LSTMs), see Figure 1. For each language, we have a language-specific LSTM to process the lexical information such as word- or character- level embedding, and the output is $w_{i,j}^l$. For all languages we have a shared LSTM which takes delexicalized information such as morphology and POS tags as input and the output is $w_{i,j}^d$. Inspired by Sato et al. (2017), we use a gating mechanism to combine these two set of features. Formally,

$$x = [w_{i,j}^l; w_{i,j}^d],$$

$$g = G(x), y = x \odot g,$$

where w^l indicates lexical feature, w^d indicates delexicalized feature, and $\odot$ is element-wise multiplication.

The difference between Sato et al. (2017) and ours is that we remove the adversarial training loss, which is because we have already use the universal information in the shared network.

3.3 Fine-tuning

We fine-tunning each joint-training model for 100 steps (see Figure 2).

3.4 Tree Ensemble

We follow the re-parsing method proposed in Sagae and Lavie (2006) to perform model ensemble. Suppose k parsing trees have been obtained, denoted by $T_1, T_2, ...T_k$, a new graph is constructed by setting the score of each edge to

$$S[u \to v] = \sum_{i=1}^{k} [u \to v] \in T_k$$

This graph is feed to a MST algorithm to get the ensemble parsing tree T_e. Then the relation label of edge $[u \to v]$ in T_e is voted by all inputs T_i that contains edge $[u \to v]$.

3.5 Hyper-parameters

We followed the hyper-parameter settings in (Dozat et al., 2017). We train $30,000$ steps for each model and then fine-tune (onot necessary) for 100 steps for the given language. For all the input features, the dimension is 100. For LSTM, we use hidden size equals to 400 and the number of layers is 3. 0.33% dropout rate is applied to the input and LSTM hidden layer. We use Bayesian dropout (Gal and Ghahramani, 2016) in the LSTM layers. We also use word dropout (dropping the whole word with a probability) in the input layer.

4 Results

The results of the test and development set are shown in Table 5 and Table 6, respectively. The first three columns are the baseline results and the second three columns are the results of our submission. Also, we list the performance improvement of Fudan Parser compared to the baseline system in the last three columns.

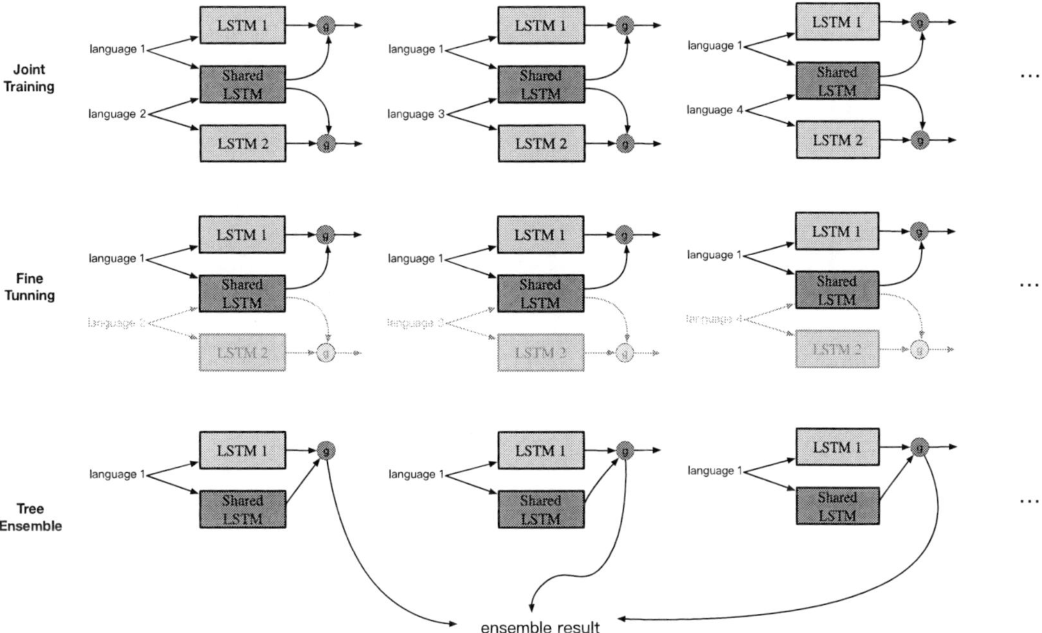

Figure 2: Take four languages as an example. We aim at testing sentence in language 1. We first jointly train languages 1 and other three languages in three separate network. And then we only keep LSTM 1 and the shared LSTM part to fine tune the models for language 1. Finally we re-parse it as an ensemble to obtain the final parsing tree for a given sentence in language 1.

As shown in both Table 6 and 6, we find that our system achieves higher improvements on the datasets with large size of training data. It is reasonable since our model contains enormous parameters, which is easy to get overfitting if the training set is too small. More analysis are included in Section 5.

5 Analysis

5.1 Language similarity

The accuracy of the joint training model actually reveals the syntactic similarity between two languages. The accuracy of three language groups, Slavic (Table 2), Romance (Table 3) and Germanic (Table 4). A number in row i, column j means the accuracy of language i testing on the model jointly training on language i and language j. The **bold** font indicates it is the best model for language i. We can see that for every language, jointly trained models consistently beat single models (the number on the diagonal) which shows the efficacy of the proposed approach.

5.2 Morphology

Morphology is extremely helpful when predicting the dependency between words, especially for those morphology rich languages. However, the UD Parsing task is not done in an end-to-end fashion (i.e. the input morphological features are not the ground-true labels) and thus the morphology information is noisy. The performance is hurt greatly because of the noisy predicted morphology features. A significant accuracy gain should be obtained if a better morphology prediction model is used.

6 Conclusion

Our system provided a simple yet effective method –sharing the universal features to the same part of neural network– to boost the accuracy of syntactic parsing. We also demonstrated that morphological feature plays an important role in syntactic parsing, which is a promising direction to work on.

In the future, we can investigate a better way to do the ensemble or apply a multi-model compression method (e.g. knowledge distillation) to reduce the computational cost. Also, we can explore

Table 2: Slavic languages joint training result.

Acc.(%)	bg	hr	cs	pl	ru	sk	sl	max improvement
bg	92.6	92.5	**92.8**	92.7	92.7	92.3	92.4	0.2
hr	85.7	86	**86.1**	85.2	85.5	85.8	85.5	0.1
cs	91.2	91.2	91.2	91.1	**91.3**	91.3	91.2	0.1
pl	**90.4**	89.8	90.2	90.1	90.2	90.4	90.8	0.3
ru	84.4	84.7	**85.2**	84.4	83.8	84.1	84.6	1.4
sk	86.4	86.2	**87.8**	85.9	86.4	86.7	86.1	1.1
sl	91.4	**91.8**	91.7	91.4	91.4	91	91.2	0.6
Avg.								0.54
# samples	8908	7690	68496	6101	3851	8484	6479	

Table 3: Romance languages joint training result.

Acc. (%)	ca	fr	gl	it	pt	ro	es	max improvement
ca	92.6	92.4	92.6	**92.7**	92.6	92.4	92.5	0.1
fr	93.1	92.9	93	**93.4**	93.2	93.1	93.2	0.5
gl	**86.9**	86.3	86.1	86.7	86.4	86.3	86.4	0.8
it	93	92.6	92.7	92.3	93	92.8	**93.1**	0.8
pt	**93**	92.8	92.7	92.8	92.6	92.9	92.8	0.4
ro	88.8	88.9	88.9	**89**	88.7	88.4	88.7	0.6
es	90.9	90.8	90.5	**91.1**	91	90.6	90.7	0.4
Avg.								0.56
# samples	13124	14554	2277	12839	8332	8044	14188	

Table 4: Germanic languages joint training result.

Acc. (%)	da	nl	en	de	sv	max improvement
da	85	85.1	85	85.2	**85.6**	0.6
nl	89	88.8	88.7	**89.3**	88.6	0.5
en	**89.4**	89.1	88.9	88.9	89.1	0.5
de	88.5	**88.9**	88.7	88.6	88.5	0.3
sv	85.7	85	**86.5**	85.9	85	1.5
Avg.						0.68
# samples	4384	12331	12544	14119	4303	

a more sophisticated model (e.g., Neural Architecture Search (Zoph and Le, 2016)) for joint training on multiple languages.

	Baseline			Fudan			Improvement		
Language code	LAS	MLAS	BLEX	LAS	MLAS	BLEX	LAS	MLAS	BLEX
af_afribooms	77.88%	64.48%	66.60%	80.02%	67.34%	66.04%	2.14%	2.86%	-0.56%
grc_perseus	57.75%	31.05%	38.74%	63.31%	34.58%	38.22%	5.56%	3.53%	-0.52%
grc_proiel	67.57%	49.51%	55.85%	69.54%	51.35%	53.03%	1.97%	1.84%	-2.82%
ar_padt	66.41%	55.01%	57.60%	67.33%	55.88%	58.63%	0.92%	0.87%	1.03%
hy_armtdp	21.79%	5.00%	11.94%	26.24%	10.00%	13.85%	4.45%	5.00%	1.91%
eu_bdt	70.13%	57.65%	63.50%	72.74%	58.98%	57.41%	2.61%	1.33%	-6.09%
br_keb	10.25%	0.00%	0.00%	10.25%	0.00%	0.00%	0.00%	0.00%	0.00%
bg_btb	84.91%	75.30%	73.78%	86.47%	77.04%	77.70%	1.56%	1.74%	3.92%
bxr_bdt	12.61%	0.00%	5.00%	12.61%	0.00%	5.00%	0.00%	0.00%	0.00%
ca_ancora	85.61%	76.74%	77.27%	88.37%	80.17%	66.01%	2.76%	3.43%	-11.26%
hr_set	78.61%	58.72%	70.26%	81.01%	60.92%	66.61%	2.40%	2.20%	-3.65%
cs_cac	83.72%	70.89%	77.65%	86.28%	73.90%	79.54%	2.56%	3.01%	1.89%
cs_fictree	82.49%	69.26%	74.96%	85.22%	72.01%	77.18%	2.73%	2.75%	2.22%
cs_pdt	83.94%	74.32%	79.39%	85.35%	75.89%	74.68%	1.41%	1.57%	-4.71%
cs_pud	80.08%	66.53%	73.79%	81.05%	67.97%	68.99%	0.97%	1.44%	-4.80%
da_ddt	75.43%	65.41%	66.04%	78.38%	68.20%	62.51%	2.95%	2.79%	-3.53%
nl_alpino	77.60%	61.55%	64.76%	79.02%	63.89%	60.53%	1.42%	2.34%	-4.23%
nl_lassysmall	74.56%	61.85%	63.14%	77.41%	64.64%	49.81%	2.85%	2.79%	-13.33%
en_ewt	77.56%	68.70%	71.02%	78.44%	68.99%	62.92%	0.88%	0.29%	-8.10%
en_gum	74.20%	62.66%	62.14%	75.29%	63.36%	57.45%	1.09%	0.70%	-4.69%
en_lines	73.10%	64.03%	65.42%	74.83%	65.78%	62.80%	1.73%	1.75%	-2.62%
en_pud	79.56%	67.59%	71.14%	78.80%	67.20%	64.26%	-0.76%	-0.39%	-6.88%
et_edt	75.02%	67.12%	63.85%	77.80%	69.82%	61.53%	2.78%	2.70%	-2.32%
fo_oft	25.19%	0.00%	5.00%	26.95%	0.00%	5.00%	1.76%	0.00%	0.00%
fi_ftb	75.64%	65.22%	61.76%	78.27%	68.03%	66.99%	2.63%	2.81%	5.23%
fi_pud	80.15%	73.16%	65.46%	80.15%	73.16%	65.46%	0.00%	0.00%	0.00%
fi_tdt	76.45%	68.58%	62.19%	79.18%	70.74%	59.79%	2.73%	2.16%	-2.40%
fr_gsd	81.05%	72.16%	74.22%	83.19%	74.01%	68.58%	2.14%	1.85%	-5.64%
fr_sequoia	81.12%	71.34%	74.41%	83.39%	73.59%	69.28%	2.27%	2.25%	-5.13%
fr_spoken	65.56%	53.46%	54.67%	65.63%	52.96%	52.82%	0.07%	-0.50%	-1.85%
gl_ctg	76.10%	62.11%	65.29%	80.38%	67.42%	71.64%	4.28%	5.31%	6.35%
gl_treegal	66.16%	49.13%	51.60%	68.08%	50.06%	52.80%	1.92%	0.93%	1.20%
de_gsd	70.85%	34.09%	60.56%	71.88%	35.12%	34.30%	1.03%	1.03%	-26.26%
got_proiel	62.16%	48.57%	55.02%	65.49%	51.72%	54.63%	3.33%	3.15%	-0.39%
el_gdt	82.11%	65.33%	68.67%	82.56%	65.58%	64.68%	0.45%	0.25%	-3.99%
he_htb	57.86%	44.09%	46.51%	58.87%	44.89%	47.37%	1.01%	0.80%	0.86%
hi_hdtb	87.15%	69.09%	79.93%	88.43%	70.48%	81.52%	1.28%	1.39%	1.59%
hu_szeged	66.76%	52.82%	56.92%	68.74%	54.66%	53.52%	1.98%	1.84%	-3.40%
zh_gsd	57.91%	48.49%	52.92%	60.13%	49.17%	54.29%	2.22%	0.68%	1.37%
id_gsd	74.37%	63.42%	62.50%	75.51%	63.54%	71.50%	1.14%	0.12%	9.00%
ga_idt	62.93%	37.66%	42.06%	64.87%	39.22%	42.44%	1.94%	1.56%	0.38%
it_isdt	86.26%	77.06%	77.12%	88.28%	79.48%	72.47%	2.02%	2.42%	-4.65%
it_postwita	66.81%	53.64%	53.99%	67.58%	53.93%	44.53%	0.77%	0.29%	-9.46%
ja_gsd	72.32%	58.35%	60.17%	73.16%	59.39%	60.92%	0.84%	1.04%	0.75%
ja_modern	22.71%	10.00%	10.00%	22.71%	10.00%	10.00%	0.00%	0.00%	0.00%
kk_ktb	24.21%	10.00%	10.00%	24.21%	10.00%	10.00%	0.00%	0.00%	0.00%
ko_gsd	61.40%	54.10%	50.50%	74.94%	68.34%	62.21%	13.54%	14.24%	11.71%
ko_kaist	70.25%	61.49%	57.68%	82.74%	75.55%	69.47%	12.49%	14.06%	11.79%
kmr_mg	23.92%	5.00%	11.86%	23.92%	5.00%	11.86%	0.00%	0.00%	0.00%
la_ittb	75.95%	66.08%	71.87%	80.07%	71.95%	76.29%	4.12%	5.87%	4.42%
la_perseus	47.61%	30.16%	32.19%	49.99%	31.35%	33.75%	2.38%	1.19%	1.56%
la_proiel	59.66%	47.05%	53.65%	63.93%	51.19%	54.64%	4.27%	4.14%	0.99%
lv_lvtb	69.43%	54.96%	58.25%	70.89%	56.14%	57.30%	1.46%	1.18%	-0.95%
pcm_nsc	12.18%	5.00%	10.87%	10.00%	5.00%	5.00%	-2.18%	0.00%	-5.87%
sme_giella	56.98%	46.05%	42.35%	61.58%	49.88%	44.19%	4.60%	3.83%	1.84%
no_bokmaal	83.47%	74.65%	76.32%	85.29%	76.97%	70.82%	1.82%	2.32%	-5.50%
no_nynorsk	82.13%	72.40%	74.22%	84.09%	74.71%	69.97%	1.96%	2.31%	-4.25%
no_nynorsklia	48.95%	37.60%	40.69%	52.84%	40.67%	43.70%	3.89%	3.07%	3.01%
fro_srcmf	79.27%	70.70%	74.45%	82.70%	75.06%	78.96%	3.43%	4.36%	4.51%
cu_proiel	65.46%	53.96%	58.39%	70.03%	58.51%	63.28%	4.57%	4.55%	4.89%
fa_seraji	79.10%	72.20%	69.43%	79.57%	71.96%	69.42%	0.47%	-0.24%	-0.01%
pl_lfg	87.53%	74.54%	78.58%	88.78%	75.92%	77.55%	1.25%	1.38%	-1.03%
pl_sz	81.90%	63.84%	71.98%	83.54%	65.25%	72.25%	1.64%	1.41%	0.27%
pt_bosque	82.07%	67.40%	72.04%	84.59%	70.21%	62.91%	2.52%	2.81%	-9.13%
ro_rrt	80.27%	71.48%	71.87%	82.67%	74.11%	71.11%	2.40%	2.63%	-0.76%
ru_syntagrus	84.59%	76.87%	78.01%	87.70%	79.58%	82.35%	3.11%	2.71%	4.34%
ru_taiga	55.51%	36.79%	39.79%	57.94%	38.59%	42.12%	2.43%	1.80%	2.33%
sr_set	82.07%	70.04%	74.12%	83.54%	70.86%	66.69%	1.47%	0.82%	-7.43%
sk_snk	75.41%	54.38%	60.35%	78.45%	56.57%	67.75%	3.04%	2.19%	7.40%
sl_ssj	77.33%	63.47%	68.93%	79.15%	65.05%	69.10%	1.82%	1.58%	0.17%
sl_sst	46.95%	34.19%	38.73%	46.19%	33.61%	38.00%	-0.76%	-0.58%	-0.73%
es_ancora	84.43%	76.01%	76.43%	87.66%	80.08%	68.03%	3.23%	4.07%	-8.40%
sv_lines	74.06%	58.62%	66.39%	75.87%	59.96%	64.81%	1.81%	1.34%	-1.58%
sv_pud	70.63%	43.38%	54.47%	72.26%	44.27%	52.52%	1.63%	0.89%	-1.95%
sv_talbanken	77.91%	69.22%	70.01%	80.00%	70.66%	71.49%	2.09%	1.44%	1.48%
th_pud	0.70%	0.03%	0.42%	0.70%	0.03%	0.42%	0.00%	0.00%	0.00%
tr_imst	54.04%	44.50%	45.91%	57.57%	46.59%	46.27%	3.53%	2.09%	0.36%
uk_iu	74.91%	56.78%	63.72%	76.27%	57.66%	63.11%	1.36%	0.88%	-0.61%
hsb_ufal	23.64%	5.00%	11.72%	29.92%	10.00%	15.16%	6.28%	5.00%	3.44%
ur_udtb	77.29%	50.31%	63.74%	77.91%	50.78%	64.30%	0.62%	0.47%	0.56%
ug_udt	56.26%	36.82%	43.53%	55.88%	35.84%	43.16%	-0.38%	-0.98%	-0.37%
vi_vtb	39.63%	33.49%	35.72%	39.53%	32.33%	32.07%	-0.10%	-1.16%	-3.65%

Table 5: All results on test set.

	Baseline			Fudan			Improvement		
Language code	LAS	MLAS	BLEX	LAS	MLAS	BLEX	LAS	MLAS	BLEX
el_gdt	81.37%	63.92%	65.21%	82.31%	64.62%	61.66%	0.94%	0.70%	-3.55%
tr_imst	54.83%	44.25%	45.81%	58.65%	46.16%	45.81%	3.82%	1.91%	0.00%
id_gsd	74.40%	63.51%	63.29%	74.82%	63.16%	71.21%	0.42%	-0.35%	7.92%
da_ddt	75.16%	65.29%	66.07%	78.20%	68.34%	63.80%	3.04%	3.05%	-2.27%
et_edt	76.50%	68.27%	64.17%	79.86%	71.38%	62.30%	3.36%	3.11%	-1.87%
got_proiel	62.03%	48.16%	54.39%	75.09%	61.20%	63.54%	13.06%	13.04%	9.15%
sl_ssj	77.72%	63.96%	68.97%	83.77%	69.66%	72.37%	6.05%	5.70%	3.40%
en_gum	76.63%	65.57%	67.20%	78.81%	67.61%	62.09%	2.18%	2.04%	-5.11%
cu_proiel	66.12%	54.48%	59.16%	79.39%	67.52%	70.80%	13.27%	13.04%	11.64%
ur_udtb	77.44%	49.91%	63.55%	77.92%	50.79%	64.01%	0.48%	0.88%	0.46%
fro_srcmf	79.15%	70.43%	74.27%	81.90%	74.01%	77.87%	2.75%	3.58%	3.60%
hi_hdtb	87.26%	69.78%	80.59%	88.55%	71.17%	82.16%	1.29%	1.39%	1.57%
ko_gsd	57.25%	49.06%	44.24%	72.41%	65.18%	57.04%	15.16%	16.12%	12.80%
cs_fictree	83.16%	70.72%	75.80%	85.99%	73.49%	77.82%	2.83%	2.77%	2.02%
gl_ctg	76.32%	62.58%	65.57%	81.75%	68.93%	73.42%	5.43%	6.35%	7.85%
lv_lvtb	70.67%	57.79%	60.96%	0.00%	0.00%	0.00%	0.00%	0.00%	0.00%
fr_gsd	85.81%	77.80%	79.16%	88.83%	81.24%	70.55%	3.02%	3.44%	-8.61%
ru_syntagrus	83.87%	75.78%	77.27%	0.00%	0.00%	0.00%	0.00%	0.00%	0.00%
hu_szeged	68.41%	56.47%	60.17%	70.67%	58.33%	57.56%	2.26%	1.86%	-2.61%
sv_lines	76.23%	62.16%	67.63%	77.91%	63.39%	65.60%	1.68%	1.23%	-2.03%
no_bokmaal	84.56%	75.95%	78.04%	86.54%	78.64%	72.31%	1.98%	2.69%	-5.73%
sv_talbanken	75.39%	66.87%	68.25%	0.00%	0.00%	0.00%	0.00%	0.00%	0.00%
es_ancora	85.08%	76.81%	77.48%	88.21%	80.75%	68.74%	3.13%	3.94%	-8.74%
he_htb	61.95%	49.28%	51.45%	79.89%	65.68%	67.50%	17.94%	16.40%	16.05%
uk_iu	77.94%	59.66%	68.07%	78.75%	60.11%	66.23%	0.81%	0.45%	-1.84%
grc_proiel	69.13%	52.42%	57.92%	77.67%	61.50%	59.95%	8.54%	9.08%	2.03%
eu_bdt	70.06%	57.46%	63.39%	72.94%	59.11%	56.95%	2.88%	1.65%	-6.44%
fi_ftb	75.76%	65.72%	62.68%	79.90%	70.61%	69.82%	4.14%	4.89%	7.14%
cs_pdt	84.85%	75.35%	80.55%	86.83%	77.45%	75.86%	1.98%	2.10%	-4.69%
sk_snk	75.73%	54.34%	59.71%	80.35%	57.64%	69.80%	4.62%	3.30%	10.09%
hr_set	77.84%	59.60%	69.99%	80.63%	61.89%	66.75%	2.79%	2.29%	-3.24%
no_nynorsk	82.75%	73.88%	75.76%	85.07%	76.64%	72.06%	2.32%	2.76%	-3.70%
grc_perseus	57.89%	30.80%	40.49%	63.21%	34.03%	39.99%	5.32%	3.23%	-0.50%
fr_spoken	65.09%	54.00%	55.42%	73.46%	64.24%	63.19%	8.37%	10.24%	7.77%
pl_sz	82.65%	63.92%	72.59%	84.02%	65.11%	73.04%	1.37%	1.19%	0.45%
fi_tdt	76.39%	68.60%	62.33%	0.00%	0.00%	0.00%	0.00%	0.00%	0.00%
ca_ancora	85.63%	77.04%	77.56%	88.30%	80.31%	67.64%	2.67%	3.27%	-9.92%
ar_padt	66.81%	55.67%	57.90%	76.11%	63.98%	65.94%	9.30%	8.31%	8.04%
sr_set	82.12%	69.12%	73.06%	84.49%	70.73%	67.66%	2.37%	1.61%	-5.40%
bg_btb	84.67%	74.54%	73.78%	86.73%	76.96%	78.24%	2.06%	2.42%	4.46%
vi_vtb	43.65%	37.39%	39.18%	57.34%	49.57%	47.08%	13.69%	12.18%	7.90%
de_gsd	75.55%	38.52%	65.39%	77.00%	39.91%	40.77%	1.45%	1.39%	-24.62%
fr_seguoia	82.72%	74.13%	76.34%	85.71%	76.53%	71.16%	2.99%	2.40%	-5.18%
cs_cac	84.42%	72.17%	78.29%	86.46%	74.65%	77.70%	2.04%	2.48%	-0.59%
pl_lfg	88.79%	75.15%	79.18%	89.98%	76.88%	79.01%	1.19%	1.73%	-0.17%
en_lines	75.78%	66.29%	68.57%	78.17%	67.59%	67.22%	2.39%	1.30%	-1.35%
zh_gsd	57.39%	48.19%	52.84%	70.09%	58.37%	64.74%	12.70%	10.18%	11.90%
it_postwita	65.85%	52.14%	52.90%	77.23%	66.00%	53.42%	11.38%	13.86%	0.52%
la_proiel	61.33%	48.40%	55.10%	74.41%	61.54%	64.39%	13.08%	13.14%	9.29%
fa_seraji	79.78%	73.03%	73.35%	80.41%	72.61%	73.63%	0.63%	-0.42%	0.28%
af_afribooms	80.19%	65.98%	70.40%	80.95%	67.26%	68.10%	0.76%	1.28%	-2.30%
ko_kaist	71.00%	63.32%	59.19%	83.17%	77.37%	71.51%	12.17%	14.05%	12.32%
la_ittb	73.23%	59.94%	67.43%	78.06%	66.21%	72.02%	4.83%	6.27%	4.59%
en_ewt	77.62%	68.58%	70.98%	0.00%	0.00%	0.00%	0.00%	0.00%	0.00%
ug_udt	56.88%	37.43%	43.34%	57.78%	37.54%	44.08%	0.90%	0.11%	0.74%
pt_bosque	84.93%	73.22%	76.02%	88.19%	76.65%	66.58%	3.26%	3.43%	-9.44%
ro_rrt	80.32%	71.21%	71.82%	83.42%	74.27%	71.73%	3.10%	3.06%	-0.09%
nl_lassysmall	73.61%	59.99%	61.71%	77.63%	64.44%	52.55%	4.02%	4.45%	-9.16%
it_isdt	85.95%	77.20%	77.37%	87.81%	79.30%	71.82%	1.86%	2.10%	-5.55%
nl_alpino	80.21%	67.14%	69.77%	81.66%	69.04%	58.68%	1.45%	1.90%	-11.09%
ja_gsd	75.48%	62.39%	64.58%	92.51%	83.13%	85.11%	17.03%	20.74%	20.53%

Table 6: All results on development set.

References

Mathieu Dehouck and Pascal Denis. 2017. Delexicalized word embeddings for cross-lingual dependency parsing. In *EACL*. hal.inria.fr, volume 1, pages 241–250.

Timothy Dozat, Peng Qi, and Christopher D Manning. 2017. Stanford's graph-based neural dependency parser at the conll 2017 shared task. *Proceedings of the CoNLL 2017 Shared Task: Multilingual Parsing from Raw Text to Universal Dependencies* pages 20–30.

Long Duong, Trevor Cohn, Steven Bird, and Paul Cook. 2015. Low resource dependency parsing: Cross-lingual parameter sharing in a neural network parser. In *Proceedings of the 53rd Annual Meeting of the Association for Computational Linguistics and the 7th International Joint Conference on Natural Language Processing (Volume 2: Short Papers)*. volume 2, pages 845–850.

Yarin Gal and Zoubin Ghahramani. 2016. A theoretically grounded application of dropout in recurrent neural networks. In *Advances in neural information processing systems*. pages 1019–1027.

Jiang Guo, Wanxiang Che, David Yarowsky, Haifeng Wang, and Ting Liu. 2015. Cross-lingual dependency parsing based on distributed representations. In *Proceedings of the 53rd Annual Meeting of the Association for Computational Linguistics and the 7th International Joint Conference on Natural Language Processing (Volume 1: Long Papers)*. volume 1, pages 1234–1244.

Joakim Nivre et al. 2018. Universal Dependencies 2.2. LINDAT/CLARIN digital library at the Institute of Formal and Applied Linguistics, Charles University, Prague, `http://hdl.handle.net/11234/1-1983xxx`. http://hdl.handle.net/11234/1-1983xxx.

Kenji Sagae and Alon Lavie. 2006. Parser combination by reparsing. In *Proceedings of the Human Language Technology Conference of the NAACL, Companion Volume: Short Papers*. Association for Computational Linguistics, pages 129–132.

Motoki Sato, Hitoshi Manabe, Hiroshi Noji, and Yuji Matsumoto. 2017. Adversarial training for cross-domain universal dependency parsing. In *Proceedings of the CoNLL 2017 Shared Task: Multilingual Parsing from Raw Text to Universal Dependencies*. Association for Computational Linguistics, pages 71–79. https://doi.org/10.18653/v1/K17-3007.

Tianze Shi, Felix G. Wu, Xilun Chen, and Yao Cheng. 2017. Combining global models for parsing universal dependencies. In *Proceedings of the CoNLL 2017 Shared Task: Multilingual Parsing from Raw Text to Universal Dependencies*. Association for Computational Linguistics, pages 31–39. https://doi.org/10.18653/v1/K17-3003.

Milan Straka, Jan Hajič, and Jana Straková. 2016. UD-Pipe: trainable pipeline for processing CoNLL-U files performing tokenization, morphological analysis, POS tagging and parsing. In *Proceedings of the 10th International Conference on Language Resources and Evaluation (LREC 2016)*. European Language Resources Association, Portoro, Slovenia.

Milan Straka and Jana Straková. 2017. Tokenizing, pos tagging, lemmatizing and parsing ud 2.0 with udpipe. In *Proceedings of the CoNLL 2017 Shared Task: Multilingual Parsing from Raw Text to Universal Dependencies*. Association for Computational Linguistics, Vancouver, Canada, pages 88–99. http://www.aclweb.org/anthology/K/K17/K17-3009.pdf.

Clara Vania, Xingxing Zhang, and Adam Lopez. 2017. Uparse: the edinburgh system for the conll 2017 ud shared task. In *Proceedings of the CoNLL 2017 Shared Task: Multilingual Parsing from Raw Text to Universal Dependencies*. Association for Computational Linguistics, pages 100–110. https://doi.org/10.18653/v1/K17-3010.

Dan Zeman et al. 2018a. Universal Dependencies 2.2 CoNLL 2018 shared task development and test data. LINDAT/CLARIN digital library at the Institute of Formal and Applied Linguistics, Charles University, Prague, `http://hdl.handle.net/11234/1-2184`. http://hdl.handle.net/11234/1-2184.

Daniel Zeman, Filip Ginter, Jan Hajič, Joakim Nivre, Martin Popel, Milan Straka, and et al. 2018b. CoNLL 2018 Shared Task: Multilingual Parsing from Raw Text to Universal Dependencies. In *Proceedings of the CoNLL 2018 Shared Task: Multilingual Parsing from Raw Text to Universal Dependencies*. Association for Computational Linguistics, pages 1–20.

Barret Zoph and Quoc V Le. 2016. Neural architecture search with reinforcement learning. *arXiv preprint arXiv:1611.01578* .

Author Index